D0081296

The Phenomenology
of Aesthetic Experience

Mikel Dufrenne

Translated by

The Phenomenology of Aesthetic Experience

EDWARD S. CASEY

ALBERT A. ANDERSON

WILLIS DOMINGO

LEON JACOBSON

NORTHWESTERN UNIVERSITY PRESS

EVANSTON 1973

BH
301
.E8
D8313

111.85 D85

Dufrenne, Mikel.

The phenomenology of
aesthetic
experience.

Copyright © 1973 by Northwestern University Press
All rights reserved
Library of Congress Catalog Card Number: 73–76806
ISBN 0–8101–0426–1
Printed in the United States of America

Originally published in French under the title
Phénoménologie de l'expérience esthétique, by
Mikel Dufrenne, © 1953, by Presses Universitaires de France.

Edward S. Casey is Associate Professor of Philosophy at Yale University.

Albert A. Anderson is Associate Professor of
Philosophy at Clark University.

Willis Domingo is a Ph.D. candidate in History
of Art at Princeton University and presently
a Fulbright Fellow in Paris.

Leon Jacobson has taught History of Art at
several universities and is presently associated
with Americana Prints.

Dabney Lancaster Library
Longwood College
Farmville, Virginia

Northwestern University

STUDIES IN *Phenomenology &*

Existential Philosophy

GENERAL EDITOR

James M. Edie

CONSULTING EDITORS

Hubert L. Dreyfus

William Earle

J. N. Findlay

Dagfinn Føllesdal

Marjorie Grene

Aron Gurwitsch

Emmanuel Levinas

Alphonso Lingis

Maurice Natanson

Paul Ricoeur

George Schrader

Calvin O. Schrag

Herbert Spiegelberg

Charles Taylor

To My Friends

74-00917

Contents

Translator's Foreword

I

The Phenomenology of Aesthetic Experience capped one of the most remarkable decades in the history of modern philosophy. Its publication exactly twenty years ago in 1953 marked the end of ten years of intensive and unusually productive philosophical activity in France. These years opened with the appearance of Jean-Paul Sartre's *Being and Nothingness* in 1943, and they witnessed, in rapid succession, Raymond Polin's *The Creation of Values* (1944), Maurice Merleau-Ponty's *Phenomenology of Perception* (1945), *Humanism and Terror* (1947), and *Sense and Nonsense* (1948), Paul Ricoeur's *Freedom and Nature* (1950), Gabriel Marcel's *Mystery of Being* (1951), and Sartre's *Saint Genêt* (1952). This is an imposing list of achievements for such a short period of time, a period which began under the difficult circumstances of German occupation. But even more significant than the creation of such a series of masterworks was the fact that in this decade France—and more particularly Paris—became the new center for the burgeoning phenomenological movement. With the death in 1938 of Edmund Husserl, the movement's founder and patriarch, and with the isolation of Martin Heidegger in Germany throughout the war, the decade in question can be considered not only as the consolidation of the French phase of phenomenology but as its Golden Age: the years in which phenomenology assumed, irrevocably, a different direction and allure than it had possessed in its inaugural German phase.[1]

1. The terms "French phase" and "German phase" are those of Herbert Spiegelberg, in *The Phenomenological Movement: A Historical Introduction,* 2d ed., 2 vols. (The Hague: Nijhoff, 1965). The reader is referred to Spiegelberg's detailed account of the French phase, *ibid.,* II, 395 ff.

[xv]

This critical transition was effected by directing an almost exclusive attention onto concrete and corporeal strata of experience, as typified in Sartre's trenchant analyses of "concrete relations with others" (e.g., the look) or in Merleau-Ponty's profoundly evocative descriptions of the lived body. Dufrenne was no exception to this trend toward the concrete. He followed suit, portraying aesthetic experience primarily in its lived and felt aspects. In this respect, it is by no means accidental that his *Phenomenology* brings the decade in question to a close. For it represents a return to that fundamental and most concrete level of human experience which the Greeks had called *aisthēsis:* "sense experience." After Baumgarten and Kant, aesthetic experience had become increasingly divorced from sensory experience: the "aesthetic" came, by the end of the nineteenth century, to connote what is elevated, elitist, and exclusive. In opposition to such aestheticism, Dufrenne attempted to restore a measure of the Greek meaning of *aisthēsis* by providing a basis for aesthetic experience in the open availability of feeling and perception. Thus he approached aesthetic experience in much the same manner in which his compatriots were treating other regions of human experience, such as the body or volition. For all of these loosely affiliated thinkers, "phenomenology" meant not so much a common method of research and analysis (in fact, there was no such common method) as a common conviction that the primary task of philosophy is to describe various regions of human experience in the most nuanced manner possible. Dufrenne's book carries out this task by turning to the largely unexplored region of aesthetic experience. It is a striking fact that, with the sole exception of Sartre's *Saint Genêt* (itself largely an exercise in existential psychoanalysis), phenomenology in its French phase had not taken up the phenomenon of art with the attentiveness it deserved—especially in Paris, where so much of modern art had been born! By thus filling a major gap, *The Phenomenology of Aesthetic Experience* completes a decade of extraordinary philosophical ferment.[2]

2. It is worth observing that Sartre, Dufrenne's senior classmate at the Ecole Normale Supérieure, not only opened the decade in question with the publication of *Being and Nothingness* but also in effect closed it. For it was in 1954 that, by Sartre's own account, he began the conversion to a committed Marxism which led to the repudiation of his early work and to the writing of such manifestly nonphenomenological works as *Critique de la raison dialectique, Les Mots,* and most recently *L'Idiot de la famille.* If there are existential and phenomenological strains remaining in these later works, they are distinctly subordinated to Sartre's overriding historical,

Dufrenne's treatise, which was originally submitted as his principal thesis at the Sorbonne, represents a culmination in a second major sense. It not only marks the concluding point of a golden period in French philosophy but forms the apex of forty years of effort in the specific field of phenomenological aesthetics. During these years, activity in this area was mostly intermittent and tentative. Such a relative lack of achievement is surprising in view of the considerable promise which phenomenology holds for the investigation of art. Husserl himself, who was as culpable as anyone else in neglecting aesthetic phenomena and whose demand for rigor could easily be mistaken as an anti-art stance, nevertheless claimed that in achieving *Wesensschau* or eidetic insight "one can draw numerous examples from history and, even more fruitfully, from art and particularly poetry." [3] More important for our purposes, however, is the way in which phenomenological reduction as outlined and prescribed by Husserl represents an apt analogue to a central feature of aesthetic experience. The analogy consists in the following parallelism. On the one hand, the phenomenological reduction involves the mental operation of placing transcendent, transphenomenal aspects of experience—especially the ontic trait of empirical reality or existence—in "brackets," thereby suspending the efficacy of these aspects as determinative of the course and content of conscious experience.[4] On the other hand, in experiencing works of art, particularly those of a dramatic character, the spectator spontaneously withholds credence in the content of this experience as actually present or

---

social, and political concerns. For Dufrenne's account of Sartre's *Critique*, see "La Critique de la raison dialectique" in *Esprit* (April, 1961), reprinted in *Jalons* (The Hague: Nijhoff, 1966).

3. Edmund Husserl, *Ideen I* (The Hague: Nijhoff, 1950), § 70; English translation by W. R. Boyce Gibson, *Ideas* (New York: Humanities Press, 1931). Husserl continues: "Of course, [such examples] are fictions; but the originality in the invention of forms, the richness of details . . . elevate them very high above the creations of our own imagination. . . . 'Fiction' constitutes the vital element of phenomenology as of all eidetic sciences" (*ibid.*, translation modified). Moreover, Husserl occasionally analyzes works of art in his own writings (see *ibid.*, § 111; and *Formal and Transcendental Logic*, trans. D. Cairns [The Hague: Nijhoff, 1969], § 2, p. 21). Even these exceptions, however, function only as passing illustrations in Husserl's investigations and not as possessing intrinsic interest in themselves or as suggesting the basis for an aesthetics.

4. For Husserl's own description of phenomenological reduction, see *Ideas*, §§ 27–32; and *Cartesian Meditations*, trans. D. Cairns (The Hague: Nijhoff, 1960), § 11. See also Spiegelberg, *Phenomenological Movement*, II, 690–94.

taking place—in brief, there is (in Coleridge's phrase) a "willing suspension of disbelief." The experience of art, then, can be likened to a spontaneous reduction.[5]

Now, the very existence of this parallelism—which may be, in the end, more than mere parallelism—makes it all the more puzzling that phenomenologists from Husserl onward have been so noticeably remiss when it comes to the consideration of aesthetic experience. On the basis of the striking affinity between one of the principal procedures of phenomenological method and one of the primary features of aesthetic experience, one would have expected the opposite, namely, that phenomenologists would be both eager and successful in applying their method to aesthetic phenomena. Instead, we are presented with a discouraging picture of largely desultory attempts to probe these phenomena. Perhaps phenomenology was felt, paradoxically, to be *too* suitable for such an enterprise, making aesthetic experience all too easily accessible to description. Or perhaps it was merely a case of philosophically benign neglect, motivated by a belief that other concerns were more pressing.[6]

Nevertheless, there have been two significant exceptions to this pattern of neglect. They merit mention here, for Dufrenne's *Phenomenology* is culminating more with respect to them than with regard to the nontradition in phenomenological aesthetics to which I have just been pointing.

5. The fact that Sartre and Merleau-Ponty disagree with Husserl as to the nature of phenomenological reduction offers, contrary to first impressions, only further confirmation of the parallelism in question, for both consider reduction to be a spontaneous affair and not the result of laborious mental exertion. "The most important lesson which the reduction teaches us," writes Merleau-Ponty, "is the impossibility of a complete reduction" (*Phenomenology of Perception,* trans. C. Smith [New York: Humanities Press, 1962], p. xiv). In other words, the reduction is continually being performed, at least in part, by a body or a consciousness in living contact with its surrounding world. Sartre goes even further and makes the spontaneity of reduction an ingredient in the spontaneity of consciousness itself. (See Sartre, *The Transcendence of the Ego,* trans. F. Williams and R. Kirkpatrick [Ann Arbor: University of Michigan Press, 1957], *passim.*)

6. This latter explanation appears to obtain in the case of such figures as Husserl himself (who was above all concerned with establishing phenomenology as an objective and fundamental "science of sciences"), Max Scheler (whose overriding interest in ethical and social problems makes his essay "On the Tragic" [trans. B. Stambler in *Cross Currents,* IV (1954), 178–91] all the more poignant as an exception), Fritz Kaufmann (whose *Das Reich des Schönen* [Stuttgart: Kohlhammer, 1960] was left unfinished at the author's death), and even the early Sartre (who devotes only several cramped pages to analyzing art in the conclusion to *L'Imaginaire* [Paris: Gallimard, 1940]).

(1) *Moritz Geiger*

Geiger published his "Contributions to the Phenomenology of Aesthetic Enjoyment" in the first volume of Husserl's *Yearbook for Philosophy and Phenomenological Research* in 1913, precisely forty years before the publication of *The Phenomenology of Aesthetic Experience*.[7] Although Geiger sets out to discern the "common characteristics of all aesthetic enjoyment," and although he carries out his analyses with considerable skill, he ends by providing more of an account of enjoyment in general than of enjoyment which is specifically aesthetic. The essay is highly suggestive but fragmentary; and the same can be said of Geiger's later collection, *Zügange zur Ästhetik*.[8] Geiger's other interests—which included experimental psychology, relativity physics, and the axiomatic bases of geometry—inevitably restricted his stake in aesthetics, with the consequence that no unified system, not even a general description, of aesthetic experience is to be found in his work. We are left with a torso of scintillating but largely unconnected insights into this experience.

(2) *Roman Ingarden*

No such critique can be made of Ingarden's seminal writings in aesthetics, which exhibit an admirable rigor and unity. Ingarden, more than anyone else, first established systematically and in depth the possibility of a genuinely phenomenological aesthetics. At the same time, he gave concrete examples of his conception of such an aesthetics in a series of books and essays which date from the publication of *Das literarische Kunstwerk* in 1931 until his recent death. In effect, it was Ingarden who showed phenomenological aesthetics to be a viable and valuable

7. See *Jahrbuch für Philosophie und phänomenologische Forschung*, I, pt. 2. For Dufrenne's own assessment of the state of aesthetics in 1913, see his recent article, "L'Esthétique en 1913," in L. Brion-Guerry, ed., *L'Année 1913* (Paris: Klincksieck, 1971).

8. Moritz Geiger, *Zügange zur Ästhetik* (Leipzig: Der neue Geist, 1928). Geiger was engaged in writing a more systematic work at his death. It is a curious fact that Dufrenne does not refer to any of Geiger's writings, despite the affinity between the two philosophers' conceptions of "depth" in aesthetic experience. For a comment on this, see Spiegelberg, *Phenomenological Movement*, II, 585. It appears that Geiger's work was almost completely unknown in France—the fate of a number of the lesser figures of the German phase of the phenomenological movement.

enterprise. This achievement should not be underestimated. Ingarden's succinct and lucid formal analyses of the literary work of art—conceived as a "multiply stratified creation"—have left their mark not only on Dufrenne's thinking but also on the theoretical foundations of formalist literary criticism, especially as embodied in the "New Criticism." [9]

Nevertheless, two reservations need to be made with regard to Ingarden's unquestionable and irreplaceable contribution to phenomenological aesthetics. First, he conceives the work of art in a severely constricted manner, insofar as it is considered to be a "purely intentional object" and thus as heteronomous, depending on consciousness for its animation and concretion. [10] Dufrenne will effectively criticize this position for not according sufficient credit to the autonomy of the work of art. Second—and more crucially—Ingarden's work in aesthetics is seen by Ingarden himself as only preliminary to other epistemological and (above all) ontological concerns, particularly the issue of realism vs. idealism. Thus he has written that all of his work in aesthetics was "from the very beginning considered as a preparation for the solution to the problem of reality." [11] As a consequence, Ingarden's aesthetic investigations are accorded a secondary status which is not overcome by the recognition of "metaphysical qualities" and of "value qualities" within the work of art. [12] The virtue of these investigations lies in their perspicuous and consistent character. Their corresponding defect, however, is found in the absence of a comprehensive theory specifying what an aesthetic object is and how it is to be distinguished from other kinds of objects. The highly concentrated character of Ingarden's analyses—which focus on one art at a time—does not allow for the explicit emergence of this sort of general theory.

9. In this regard, see René Wellek and Austin Warren, *Theory of Literature* (New York: Harcourt, Brace, 1942). This extremely influential book is more indebted to Ingarden than its authors care to admit. Compare Ingarden's own comments in *Das literarische Kunstwerk,* 3d ed., Tübingen: Niemeyer, 1965), pp. xix–xxiv (English translation by George G. Grabowicz, *The Literary Work of Art* [Evanston, Ill.: Northwestern University Press, 1973], pp. lxxviii–lxxix).

10. See *Literary Work of Art,* § 68. It should be added that I have here considerably simplified the complexity of Ingarden's position.

11. Roman Ingarden, *Untersuchungen zur Ontologie der Kunst* (Tübingen: Niemeyer, 1962), p. viii (English translation, *Investigations into the Ontology of Art,* forthcoming from Northwestern University Press). Even Ingarden's later explorations into the role of values in art can be seen in the same ontological context. See in this regard Ingarden's *Erlebnis, Kunstwerk, und Wert* (Tübingen: Niemeyer, 1969), pp. 23, 260.

12. See *Literary Work of Art,* §§ 49–53, 68.

It is precisely such a theory that Dufrenne's *Phenomenology of Aesthetic Experience* may be said to propose. Following a discussion of the aesthetic object that is not restricted in its import to any single art, the longest and most detailed chapter in Dufrenne's book (Chapter 4) seeks to differentiate aesthetic objects from other kinds of objects with regard to differences in basic structure. Hence, from the start, Dufrenne's project establishes itself as more encompassing than Ingarden's. This encompassing character is only reinforced as the book continues, successively exploring a broad range of the problems raised by the experience of art. The specific problem of the aesthetic object's mode of being—whose determination had been Ingarden's primary preoccupation—is given its place but is not allowed to dominate the book's other ambitious aims.

In respect to comprehensiveness, then, Dufrenne's *Phenomenology* culminates the more detailed and more delimited efforts of his predecessors to provide a distinctively phenomenological treatment of art. This monumental essay is at once the fruition and the extension of earlier explorations in phenomenological aesthetics, and it crowns Geiger's and Ingarden's pioneering work.[13] *The Phenomenology of Aesthetic Experience* is, in sum, the single most comprehensive and accomplished book in phenomenological aesthetics to have appeared. Thus we may agree with the leading historian of phenomenology when he writes that this book "is not only the most voluminous but easily the most impressive achievement of the phenomenological movement in aesthetics so far." [14]

13. For Ingarden's acknowledgment of *The Phenomenology of Aesthetic Experience* as proceeding in the same direction as his own work, see *Untersuchungen zur Ontologie*, p. ix. But Ingarden cites in the same breath the work of Brelet, Langer, Gilson, and Pepper, apparently without realizing the special significance of Dufrenne's book as a continuation of his own work.

14. Spiegelberg, *Phenomenological Movement*, II, 597. Spiegelberg also comments that the *Phenomenology* "stands out by its systematic structure as well as by the richness of its concrete insights" (*ibid.*, p. 580). Praise for Dufrenne's book comes not only from phenomenologists. Monroe Beardsley, the eminent American aesthetician, claims that the book is written with "considerable clarity, insight, and originality" and that it is "[one of the] two outstanding works in phenomenological aesthetics [that] have appeared." (These statements are from, respectively, Monroe C. Beardsley, *Aesthetics from Classical Greece to the Present* [New York: Macmillan, 1966], p. 371; and his article, "History of Aesthetics," *The Encyclopedia of Philosophy*, ed. Paul Edwards [New York: Macmillan & Free Press, 1967], I, 33. The other "outstanding work" is Ingarden's *Literary Work of Art*.) Harold Osborne, the dean of British aestheticians, has written recently that Dufrenne's account is "the most readable and rewarding work

II

BUT THE PRESENT BOOK *is* voluminous, and it may be helpful for the sake of preliminary orientation to sketch an overview of it as a whole. To this end, it should first of all be remarked that in both its French editions *La Phénoménologie de l'expérience esthétique* appeared in two separate volumes.[15] The first volume, *The Aesthetic Object,* is nearly twice as long as the second, *Aesthetic Perception.* Each volume is in turn subdivided into two parts, thereby producing the four major parts of the translation below. It is important to keep this schematic structure of the work in mind, for the necessity of publishing the present translation in a single volume tends to weaken the force of the fundamental dichotomy between "aesthetic object" and "aesthetic perception." This dichotomy not only gives an exoskeletal shape to the entire project but furnishes the two primary terms—perception and object—for Dufrenne's dialectically interwoven analyses. These terms also serve to define the main movement of the book—a movement proceeding from a consideration of the aesthetic object to a theory concerning the perception of this object. But two warnings must be issued here. First, aesthetic object and aesthetic perception are, strictly speaking, inseparable. As we shall see, one calls for the other and each depends on the other. Second, the book ends with a set of reflections which are transcendental and ontological in character and which attempt to break free from the subject-object dialectic which is so central to the rest of the book. This suggests that the inner structure of the work is tripartite and not quadripartite as the division into four parts implies. Such will be the hypothesis guiding the following exposition, which will accordingly be divided into three sections: the aesthetic object, the perceiving subject, and the reconciliation of subject and object.

(1) *The aesthetic object*

As there has already been occasion to remark, the aesthetic object is treated first, and it is treated at greater length than

---

from this [phenomenological] school" to be written in French. (See Harold Osborne, ed., *Aesthetics* [Oxford: Oxford University Press, 1972], p. 1.)

15. The first edition dates from 1953; the second, unchanged edition was published in 1967.

any other single topic in the book. There are at least three reasons for Dufrenne's decision to dwell on the aesthetic object in this determined manner. First, the aesthetic object is *prima facie* more accessible than aesthetic experience as such. It presents itself to perception as a closed whole and thus lends itself to precise descriptions. Second, phenomenological method is better equipped to deal with the object or content of experience than with experience qua act. As "intentional analysis," it tends naturally to begin with noematic analysis, leaving noetic analysis (its necessary correlate) for a later stage.[16] Third and more important, Dufrenne takes the spectator's point of view in this book. And *what* the spectator experiences is precisely the aesthetic object, toward which his "outer concentration" (to use a term of Geiger's) is primarily directed. Had Dufrenne chosen to write from the artist's standpoint, the result would have been an emphasis on the *act* of creation, not on its product. The danger in adopting an approach which stresses the artist's activity lies in its temptation to psychologism, that is, the attempt to define the aesthetic object in terms of the psychological states or processes discoverable in the artist. Harking back to Husserl's original attack on psychologism, Dufrenne refuses this temptation.[17]

How, then, is the aesthetic object to be defined? One way is in terms of its difference from the work of art. For the aesthetic object and the work of art should not be confused with one another. The work of art is the perduring structural foundation for the aesthetic object. It has a constant being which is not dependent on being experienced, while the aesthetic object exists only as appearance, that is, only as experienced by the spectator. In its essential thinghood, the work of art can be used for alien purposes—as portraits are sometimes used for the purpose of identifying their subjects as historical personages. As aesthetically perceived, however, the work of art *becomes* an aesthetic

16. For Husserl's conception of intentional analysis and for the implicit priority of the noematic over the noetic within this analysis, see *Cartesian Meditations*, §§ 17, 20–21. The intentional object is taken as a "transcendental clue" and thus is a privileged point of departure.

17. See Edmund Husserl, *Logical Investigations*, trans. J. N. Findlay (New York: Humanities Press, 1970), I, chaps. 3–10. An opposition to psychologism in all spheres of human experience is one of the basic convictions which unites the most diverse phenomenologists and thus justifies the general appellation "phenomenological movement." For a further attempt to support the choice of the spectator's standpoint, see the account of Dufrenne's thesis defense in *Revue de métaphysique et de morale*, LVIII (1953), 432–36.

object. It gains a strictly aesthetic, or felt, dimension which it lacked as a work of art. This metamorphosis is contingent in the sense that it depends on a specific act of perception to effect it, but it is noncontingent insofar as the *telos,* truth, and vocation of the work of art are found in the aesthetic object.[18] Unlike Ingarden, who makes a closely related distinction between work of art and aesthetic object, Dufrenne does not conceive the aesthetic object as the "concretion" of the work of art. The aesthetic object is simply the work of art as perceived—and perceived for its own sake. In brief, Dufrenne holds that "aesthetic object and work of art are distinct in that aesthetic perception must be joined to the work of art in order for the aesthetic object to appear." [19]

The critical nature of the transition from the work of art to the aesthetic object becomes most evident when we consider the work's material character. Every work of art requires a material basis, a substratum of specific materials such as paints, sounds, or stone. The materials of a work together compose its "matter," on whose basis it endures and is subject to the ravages of time. But in experiencing the work, we are not concerned with this matter as such. Instead, we direct our attention to the work's matter insofar as it has been transformed into particular forms constituted by colors, notes, or sculpted stone. In short, in perceiving the work aesthetically we are no longer concerned with its matter per se, but with what Dufrenne calls "the sensuous" [*le sensible*]. The sensuous, a key term, is precisely what the work's matter becomes when perceived aesthetically. As such, it serves to constitute the aesthetic object—an object which can now be defined as "a coalescence of sensuous elements" (p. 13). More exactly, the aesthetic object is constituted by the extension and exaltation of the sensuous. Thus the aesthetic object is said

18. Among representative statements are the following. "Thus the work has its *telos* in the aesthetic object and is understood through it" (p. 17). "If the [aesthetic object] draws its being from the work and is clarified by reference to it, then, conversely, the work has its truth in the aesthetic object" (pp. 232–33; see also p. 117). "[The work's] vocation is to transcend itself toward the aesthetic object, in which alone it attains, along with its public sanction, the fullness of its being" (p. 5). Unless otherwise indicated, all page numbers given hereafter will be those of the translation below, which will sometimes be referred to as "the *Phenomenology.*"

19. P. lxv. Related statements are that "the aesthetic object *is* the work insofar as it is perceived" (p. 232) and that "the aesthetic object is nothing else but the work of art perceived for its own sake" (p. 16). For Ingarden's notion of *Konkretisation,* see *Literary Work of Art,* §§ 61–64.

to be "the apotheosis of the sensuous" (p. 11) and "the sensuous appearing in its glory" (p. 86).

As a consequence, we must distinguish between the "brute sensuousness" which we encounter in ordinary perception and the "aesthetic sensuousness" which is unique to aesthetic objects.[20] It is this latter sensuousness which serves to distinguish the aesthetic object from other kinds of objects whose sensuous character is reducible to unexpressive sensory constituents. Aesthetic sensuousness is not, however, merely the result of refining such constituents through the attainment of formal perfection. It possesses a forceful and even demanding character of its own, asking that the spectator pay homage to its "irresistible and magnificent presence" (p. 86). Confronted with the "sovereign imperialism" of the aesthetic object as constituted by the sensuous, both spectator and performer are expected to be submissive and to realize that their task is to do justice to the aesthetic object, not to dominate it.[21] From the spectator's and performer's standpoints, the aesthetic object seems to take the initiative, prescribing its own norm and asserting its own autonomy. It is as if the aesthetic object willed *itself* into existence and were intent on retaining the upper hand. It is at this point that the object-pole of aesthetic experience is most emphatically in evidence.[22]

The sensuous, then, is indispensable for the aesthetic object, that is, for the *appearing* of the work of art. "The being of the work of art yields itself only through its sensuous presence, which allows us to apprehend it as an aesthetic object" (p. 44). Nevertheless, although responsible for the aesthetic object's peculiar plenitude (its "intuitive abundance," in Geiger's phrase) and for its uniquely imposing mode of presence, the sensuous is not the *only* component of the aesthetic object. Another crucial constituent is its meaning or sense [*le sens*]. Even if an aesthetic object is not to be confused with a merely signifying object, it is nonetheless not a meaningless object. It is fully meaningful— indeed, it is saturated with meaning. In the context of action or

20. "Art can express only by virtue of the sensuous and according to an operation which transforms brute sensuousness into aesthetic sensuousness" (pp. 137–38).

21. For the notion of submissiveness, see pp. 27, 45; the aesthetic object's "sovereign imperialism" is mentioned on p. 155; and the idea of doing justice to the aesthetic object is found on pp. liii, lxiv, 63, 72.

22. On the aesthetic object as taking the initiative, see pp. 59, 231; on its being its own norm, see pp. lxii, 66; on its autonomy, p. 199; and on willing itself, p. 33.

knowledge, meaning tends to function as an objective signification, surpassing the immediate confines of the experience in
question. In aesthetic experience, however, it plays a quite different role. Instead of leading us beyond what is sensuously
given—as it does in the case of action or knowledge—it rivets
us to the sensuous itself, exhibiting its internal structure. Meaning in art is therefore neither nonexistent nor transcendent. It is
"immanent in the sensuous, being its very organization" (p. 12).
Moreover, it is not translatable into the crisp clarity of prose, for
it is inexhaustible, always existing in surplus. Even as inexhaustible, though, it remains wholly immanent in the sensuous.
For *all* the aesthetic object's meaning is given in the sensuous;
none of it exists outside of or beyond the perimeter of the sensuous. Thus, while acknowledging a distinctly nonsensuous element in art, Dufrenne anchors this element securely in the sensuous, which remains the necessary (but not sufficient) basis for
the constitution of the aesthetic object.

Meaning organizes the sensuous by means of spatial and
temporal "schemata"—the term is designedly Kantian—which
differ in complexity and configuration from art to art. But every
art occupies space in some specific way, just as every art is also
always inherently temporal. In Chapters 8 and 9 below, Dufrenne
analyzes music and painting in terms of various formal schemata. His aim, however, is not to provide a comparative aesthetics of these arts.[23] Rather, he seeks to show that the traditional
distinction between "temporal arts" and "spatial arts" is quite
misleading. In all the arts, both temporal and spatial factors are
present. Time and space become correlative and even continuous,
so that the space of every aesthetic object is temporalized and its
time spatialized. The direct consequence of this spatializing of
time and temporalizing of space is to turn the aesthetic object
into a "quasi subject," that is, a being capable of harboring internal spatiotemporal relationships within itself. These relationships constitute in turn the "world" of the aesthetic object—a
world which is more like an atmosphere than an objective cosmos
filled with discrete entities and events. Dufrenne here takes Ingarden's notion of a "world of the work"—which Ingarden had
restricted, in literature, to represented objects and states of af-

23. Examples of comparative aesthetics are Etienne Souriau's *La Cor-
respondance des arts* (Paris: Flammarion, 1947) and Thomas Munro's
The Arts and Their Interrelations (New York: Liberal Arts Press, 1949).
Dufrenne draws on both these works, while rejecting their general aims.

fairs—a step further and posits an "expressed world." [24] This expressed world, whose description in Chapter 5 constitutes one of Dufrenne's most original contributions, is characterized less by its specific contents than by the singular affective quality which permeates it. This affective quality makes the world of the aesthetic object expressive and endows the aesthetic object with the inner complexity and coherence of a quasi subject. In sum, then, space and time "are internal to the aesthetic object and are assumed by it. It is they that make it a quasi subject capable of a world which it expresses" (p. 248).

As a quasi subject, the aesthetic object can be considered as being in its own unique way what Sartre had called a *for-itself*. Within its expressed world, the aesthetic object opens up a spatio-temporal field which is ceaselessly filled and then emptied in the unfolding of aesthetic experience. Hence temporal and spatial schemata, creating an expressed (and expressive) world, secure for the aesthetic object the status of a self-transcending for-itself. At the same time, however, these schemata remain the forms *of* the sensuous and operate only *within* it. In other words, the sensuous constitutes the *in-itself* character of the aesthetic object —the basis for the imperious presence of this object. It is through the sensuous that the aesthetic object is akin to nature, the ultimate in-itself within human experience. Since the aesthetic object thus includes both a sensuous base and an inherent world, it embodies that very combination of the in-itself with the for-itself which Sartre had declared to be impossible in *Being and Nothingness*.[25]

(2) *The perceiving subject*

But the aesthetic object is not only an in-itself-for-itself. It is an in-itself-for-itself-*for-us*. It exists in order to be perceived— and perceived by *us* as its spectators.[26] Thus the mode of being of

24. For Ingarden's notion of the represented world within art, see *Literary Work of Art*, §§ 31–37.

25. See Jean-Paul Sartre, *Being and Nothingness*, trans. Hazel Barnes (New York: Philosophical Library, 1956), pp. 617–25. On the notion of the aesthetic object as an in-itself-for-itself, see below, pp. 224 ff., 328–29.

26. It is also, of course, perceived by performers, critics, and the artist himself. However, none of these normally accords to the aesthetic object that special perception which it solicits from the spectator: "perception *par excellence*, pure perception, which has no aim other than its own object and which does not try to resolve itself in action" (p. lxiv).

the aesthetic object is neither that of an ideal signification nor that of a purely intentional object. It is, rather, "the being of a sensuous thing which is realized only in perception" (p. 218). Accordingly, the aesthetic object exists for us not because it is designed to please us but because it needs us to perceive it. We as its spectators are its essential witnesses, called upon to confirm it in its autonomy. More important still, we are needed to *complete* it, since "the aesthetic object is completed only in the consciousness of the spectator." [27] In order to complete the aesthetic object, we cannot remain passive: art is not pure contemplation. We must become actively engaged in the object itself, even to the point of becoming lost or alienated in it. [28]

The form this involvement takes, however, is none other than that of perception: "the aesthetic object moves me to do nothing but perceive" (p. 86). For aesthetic experience remains always and only a form of perceptual experience. Consequently, Dufrenne is driven to present (in Part 3) a general theory of perception. In this theory, perception is seen as proceeding through three stages: (*a*) At the level of *presence*, perception occurs very much as Merleau-Ponty had described it: as global, prereflective, and at one with the body. [29] It is here that we experience the irrecusable force of the sensuous and submit ourselves to this force through the agency of the body. (*b*) At the next level, that of *representation* and *imagination*, perception tends to objectify, shaping the inchoate contents of perceived presence into dis-

---

27. P. 204. Other related statements are to be found at pp. 47, 71, 218, 223.

28. "We must speak of an alienation of the subject in the object and perhaps even of a bewitchment by it. . . . In short, the witness is not a pure spectator but an involved one" (p. 56; see also pp. 231–32). The spectator's involvement stops short, however, of his becoming the creator of the aesthetic object or of his being led to concrete action outside aesthetic experience proper. Thus Dufrenne's position is to be distinguished both from theories that base themselves on the creative activity of the artist and from those that view art as merely an occasion for social or political action. But this is not to claim that Dufrenne's position excludes the possibility of concrete action on the part of the spectator. Such action, if it occurs, is simply not part of aesthetic experience as such.

29. The impact of Merleau-Ponty's *Phenomenology of Perception* on Dufrenne was profound. One may even venture to say that *The Phenomenology of Aesthetic Experience* represents the extension of Merleau-Ponty's thesis concerning the "primacy of perception" to the domain of aesthetic experience. Dufrenne himself writes that "if the ordinary [perceived] object undermines Merleau-Ponty's thesis to a certain extent—or, more precisely, obliges it to account for the possibility of the movement from what is perceived to what is thought—the aesthetic object confirms it" (p. 223). But it confirms it only at the level of presence, not at the next two levels.

tinguishable entities and events. Imagination in its transcendental function sweeps out a spatiotemporal field in which particular objects and states of affairs may appear as represented in given acts of empirical imagining. Important as its activity is, imagination does not, for Dufrenne, play a central role in aesthetic experience. The aesthetic object's appearance is already fully articulate and fully eloquent. It already says so much that it does not need further elaboration. Thus "the genuine work of art spares us the expense of an exuberant imagination." [30] (c) The last stage in the full development of perception is one of *reflection* and *feeling*. When perception follows its normal course, it tends to flow into understanding and knowledge by becoming a form of objective reflection. But perception can also veer toward a different sort of reflection which is "sym-pathetic" rather than objectifying and is more closely related to feeling than to understanding. Such reflection clarifies and supports feeling, entering into a dialectical relationship with it.[31] In the process, perception becomes properly aesthetic, for it is above all through feeling that the aesthetic object becomes accessible. How so? Feeling, which stems from the depth of the perceiving subject, allows the spectator to respond to the depth of the aesthetic object, that is, to its expressed world. This response is not merely an emotional one but consists in the apprehension or "reading" of the singular affective quality characterizing the expressed world. Through feeling, then, we connect with the aesthetic object's inherent expressiveness. Dufrenne concludes that "the very height of aesthetic perception is found in the feeling which reveals the expressiveness of the work." [32]

30. P. 366. Dufrenne even goes so far as to suggest that imagination must be *restrained* in aesthetic experience: "the aesthetic object takes us back to innocence by repressing emotions and imagination, which exasperate themselves over the nothingness of the imaginary" (p. 340; see also pp. 129, 325, 543). This conspicuous demotion of the place of imagination in aesthetic experience is an aspect of Dufrenne's antagonism to Romantic and idealist theories of art where imagination is given a characteristically elevated and inflated role. Even if imagination is essential to artistic creation, the relation of this act of creation to the spectator's grasp of the aesthetic object is tenuous, and, in any case, no comparable exertion of imagination is called for on the part of the spectator.

31. For the development of this notion, see pp. 422 ff.

32. P. 49. It is noteworthy that Susanne Langer's major work in aesthetics, *Feeling and Form*, which also appeared in 1953, similarly argues for the central role of feeling in aesthetic experience as well as for its close connection with expressive form. Langer would concur with Dufrenne's assertion that expression is "the ultimate form of the aesthetic object" (p. 142), since for Langer expression is "a presentation of a highly articulated form wherein the beholder recognizes . . . the forms of human feeling"

With the notion of feeling, we reach the *terminus ad quem* of the movement toward the subject-pole. It is a terminal point which corresponds to the extreme point of the object-pole, that is, to expression, the ultimate form of the aesthetic object. For feeling, as we have just seen, consists precisely in reading the aesthetic object's expression and in resonating with this expression. In this capacity, feeling is the final phase in the spectator's completion of the aesthetic object: "aesthetic experience culminates in feeling as the reading of expression" (p. 437). Accordingly, it is at this same point that the autonomy of the aesthetic object is at its lowest. For this object is dependent on the spectator not just for being observed—i.e., for being ratified in its objective being—but for being founded in its very expressiveness. The aesthetic "object is not valid for itself alone; it elicits and embodies a feeling which simultaneously grounds the object and surpasses it" (p. 521). This feeling is always *someone's* feeling; it is not disembodied or impersonal, but the expression of the depth of a human subject. Consequently, it is through feeling, and through feeling alone, that the human subject becomes present in the aesthetic object. This peculiar type of presence occurs in two ways. First, the *artist* is present in the object he creates—not in person but in terms of the expressed world which he brings into being. "The aesthetic object contains the subjectivity of the subject who has created it, who expresses himself in it, and whom in turn it manifests."[33] Second, the *spectator* becomes present in the aesthetic object as well. Through the reading of expression, and by drawing on the resources of his own feeling, he engages himself in the expressed world. *His*

(Susanne K. Langer, *Feeling and Form* [London: Routledge & Kegan Paul, 1953], p. 82; see also pp. 369–91). Like Dufrenne, she rejects the reduction of feeling in art to the evocation of emotion, and she even speaks in this regard of a "phenomenology of feeling" (*ibid.*, pp. 52–57). The primary difference between the two positions lies in Dufrenne's appeal to the depth dimension of the perceiving subject and in the correlation of this dimension with the depth of the expressed world. A third major work in aesthetics to appear in 1953, Nicolai Hartmann's *Ästhetik* (Berlin: De Gruyter, 1953), also argues for the objectivity of expressive form in art, but in terms of a theory of "levels" in the work of art which is reminiscent of Ingarden. (See Ingarden's comments on Hartmann in *Untersuchungen zur Ontologie*, pp. 33–35.)

33. P. 196. It should be added that what is thus manifested is not the artist as a historical or psychological being but the artist only insofar as he is responsible for a particular work. The artist is thus expressed in the aesthetic object—but only indirectly and as an animating force, not as its empirical creator.

depth meets and matches the object's depth, and he can no longer pretend to be an impassive onlooker.[34]

(3) *Reconciliation of subject and object*

The subjective and objective poles bifurcating most of Dufrenne's analysis are not wholly discontinuous. This is evident in the claim that the sensuous element in art is something shared by the spectator and by the aesthetic object: "the sensuous is an act common both to the person who feels and to what is felt" (p. 48; repeated at p. 225). We are now in a position to understand the basis for this claim. The sensuous serves as a *tertium quid* for the two principal kinds of aesthetic depth—the depth of the expressed world and the depth of the beholder of this world. Both these depths involve feeling, which is definable only in terms of their interaction. If feeling can therefore be defined as "the reciprocity of two depths" (p. 483), it can be seen as the means by which the perceiving subject and the aesthetic object are capable of reconciliation. Feeling is not only the culmination of aesthetic perception but the nodal point at which subject and object merge in aesthetic experience, realizing a unique sort of "communion" there.[35]

The reconciliation of subject and object in aesthetic experience—their fundamental reciprocity—is revealed in still another way: in terms of the "transcendental" or *a priori* dimension of this experience. This dimension, which is described in

34. It is in this manner that Dufrenne seeks to combat the endemic danger of all spectator-based aesthetic theories. As opposed to those aesthetic theories which model themselves on the creative process and which situate the human subject (the person of the artist) *too close* to the aesthetic object, spectator-oriented theories tend to place the human subject (in the person of the observer) *too far* from the object. To avoid this mistake, Dufrenne gives the spectator entry into the world of the aesthetic object. But like the artist, the spectator is present there only indirectly, not in person but by the proxy of feeling.

35. P. 228. In many respects, this communion between spectator and object forms the central problematic of Dufrenne's entire essay. The question constantly being posed, at least implicitly, is: how do the aesthetic object and the perceiving spectator come together in aesthetic experience? In his thesis defense, Dufrenne asserted that "the idea of the reciprocity of subject and object serves as the guiding thread" (in *Révue de métaphysique et de morale*, p. 432). This reciprocity is evident in Dufrenne's characteristic assertion that the aesthetic object's "perfection as an object is to be a quasi subject, but it attains this expressive subjectivity only by the rigor and certainty of its objective being" (p. 425).

Part 4, is present insofar as the aesthetic object's affective quality not only characterizes but *constitutes* its expressed world, serving as its guiding principle. To be constitutive in this manner is to possess the status of an *a priori*, a "cosmological" *a priori* serving to order an expressed world.[36] Now, the perceiving subject also exhibits an *a priori* aspect. This subject could not apprehend or comprehend the *a priori* structure of the expressed world—its constitutive atmosphere or affective quality—unless the same subject already possessed certain affective categories which allowed him to recognize the affective quality as a certain *kind* of quality—as "tragic," "sublime," or whatever. Our knowledge of such categories is itself *a priori* in character; it is antecedently possessed and thus "virtual," yet lucidly certain once awakened. Dufrenne considers this virtual knowledge to be an important aspect of the subject's total being—of his "existential" *a priori*. But since virtual knowledge is in turn knowledge of the *a priori* in its objective, cosmological embodiments, there is an inner link between the subject and the content of his experience: "the existential and the cosmological are one" (p. 555). Therefore, at the level of the *a priori*—which is traditionally misinterpreted as either exclusively subject-centered or exclusively object-centered—subject and object realize a profound reconciliation.[37]

But beyond reconciliation is unity, and Dufrenne's final suggestion is that the existential and the cosmological—man and world—may both belong to a larger unity. This unity is that of being, the ultimate ontological term. Such an interpretation follows from reflection on the *a priori* itself: "to be at once a determination of subject and object, the *a priori* must be a characteristic of being, which is anterior to subject and object and which makes their affinity possible."[38] This shift to the ontological

36. "An affective quality is an *a priori* when, expressed by the work, it is constitutive of the world of the aesthetic object" (p. 446). See also pp. 437 ff. for the development of this theme.

37. For a further, and much more deeply ramified, development of this theme, see Mikel Dufrenne, *The Notion of the A Priori*, trans. Edward S. Casey (Evanston, Ill.: Northwestern University Press, 1966), Pt. 3. It is suggested in this later work that the reconciliation in question takes place within a much broader spectrum of human experience than can be found in aesthetic experience alone.

38. Pp. 455–56. Compare also Dufrenne's statement at his thesis defense: "the *a priori* is the expression of a meaning which belongs to being" (*Révue de métaphysique et de morale*, p. 432).

dimension underlies Dufrenne's theory of truth in art. Art can be true—can bear on the real—because both art and reality are themselves only aspects of an all-encompassing being. "Art bespeaks the real because both art and reality are subordinate to being" (p. 539). Instead of being a flight from the real—as it becomes when it is conceived as strictly imaginary in character —art illuminates the real.[39] But it does so only through feeling, which delivers the real's "affective essence."[40] Thus art attains truth not through representation or imitation of the real, but by eliciting and expressing the real's affective essence *within* itself and in its own terms: "it is through its intrinsic quality and from within itself that the aesthetic object relates to the real and displays its truth there" (pp. 527–28).

But *where* exactly is this truth displayed? *In the sensuous.* In Dufrenne's claim for art's truthfulness, a truthfulness which is conveyed by affective quality, the sensuous has not been left behind. On the contrary, it remains potently present. For the function of affective quality, like the meaning of which it is the expressive counterpart, is precisely to organize the sensuous. Hence affective quality is immanent in the sensuous and inseparable from it in aesthetic experience. In art, then, the affective and the sensuous—feeling and perceiving—adumbrate each other:

> By allowing us to perceive an exemplary object whose whole reality consists in being sensuous, art invites us and trains us to read expression and to discover the atmosphere which is revealed only to feeling. Art makes us undergo *the absolute experience of the affective.* [p. 542; my italics]

"Absolute experience" hints at being, but such experience discloses being not in its totality—not as designated by metaphysical concepts—but only in part and in the immanence of affectivity. This affectivity, constituted and structured by its own intrinsic "affective" *a priori*, belongs equally to the aesthetic object and to the perceiving subject. Although this object and this subject,

39. "The aesthetic object takes on the original function of truth, which is to precede the real in order to illuminate it, not to repeat it" (p. 528). See also p. 539.

40. For the notion of "affective essence," see pp. 520 f. and especially the statement on p. 525: "It is through feeling that one rejoins the real . . . since feeling delivers an affective essence with which the real is in accord."

which we have seen to require each other in the essential reciprocity of aesthetic experience, may both finally be mere aspects of being, we cannot *know* that they are. In the absence of any such definitive knowledge, we can affirm with assurance only that the aesthetic and the ontological, art and being, are continuous and not dirempt elements in human experience.

If *The Phenomenology of Aesthetic Experience* thus leads us from the phenomenological to the ontological via the transcendental or *a priori,* it does not end by turning its back on either phenomenology or aesthetic experience. Not only does ontology continually return us to man, the subject of aesthetic experience, but an ontological interpretation of art is itself aided by a prior phenomenology of aesthetic experience: "an ontology of aesthetic experience finds that it can be explicated in terms of the essential themes treated by its phenomenology." [41] Phenomenology, though initially forced to acknowledge and to describe the subject-object dichotomy entailed by its method and its implicit metaphysics, is nevertheless able to rise above its own presuppositions and to envision the possibility of overcoming this dichotomy. And in aesthetic experience, the dichotomy *must* be overcome, at least temporarily, if it is indeed the case that "it is in me that the aesthetic object is constituted as other than me" (p. 232). But whether the dichotomy is finally overcome or not—and whether being is ever actually attained or not—its polar terms come to communicate with each other in the vital interaction called forth by aesthetic experience. Through art, I regain contact with the real as illuminated by the possible—and, beyond the real, I may gain a presentiment of being. In the concluding chapters of *The Phenomenology of Aesthetic Experience,* art and phenomenology are seen to join forces within the larger perspective afforded by ontology. Aesthetic experience and phenomenological method are shown to contribute to a correlative vision, while each embodies a similar destiny in subtly different ways. Thus is made good, within the bounds of a single work, the tacit promise of mutual illumination which had been present from the beginning of the phenomenological movement but which had remained, before Dufrenne's achievement, conspicuously unfulfilled.

51. P. 556. Note also the question posed by Dufrenne: "Does not the ontological lead us back to the anthropological?" (*ibid.*). The clear implication is that it does and that there is no way of definitively transcending the human factor in experience.

III

FOR ALL ITS COMPREHENSIVENESS, *The Phenomenology of Aesthetic Experience* is a book that leaves as many questions unresolved as it answers. One unresolved question, for example, is whether or not a "pure aesthetics," that is, a complete system of aesthetic categories, can be constructed. Although Dufrenne clearly considers this to be a legitimate possibility insofar as it is based on a recognition of the affective *a priori*, he does not take a definite stand on the issue, adopting instead a position midway between belief in the reality of fixed aesthetic categories and commitment to art's "unforeseeable" character.[42] Thus Dufrenne seeks to maintain both that there can be genuine novelty in the successive forms which art assumes—i.e., that the history of art, art's *a posteriori* dimension, can be quite contingent—and that the appearance of new forms awakens a latent or virtual *a priori* knowledge in the perceiving subject. In other words, Dufrenne wants it both ways, espousing a deliberately ambiguous position which he sums up in the statement that "the *a priori* is revealed only in the *a posteriori*." [43]

If the *Phenomenology* thus does not resolve questions such as that of a pure aesthetics, nevertheless this early work does contain a stock of seminal insights on which Dufrenne will repeatedly draw in his later writings. In this respect, it can justifiably be regarded as Dufrenne's *chef-d'oeuvre*, his "chief work," a work that contains much that will be followed up only subsequently. It is not the first book in Dufrenne's prolific writing career. Nor is it his last book in aesthetics. And it is perhaps not even his most pivotal work.[44] But *The Phenomenology of Aesthetic*

42. See pp. 485–500, esp, pp. 491–92.
43. P. 492. Other formulations of the same position include the following: "The *a priori* is contemporaneous with the *a posteriori*" (p. 471); "the *a priori* is actualized only through the *a posteriori*" (p. 496). Articulated here is a basic stance which distinguishes Dufrenne's conception of phenomenology from Husserl's. Where Husserl sought a nonempirical intuition of essences, Dufrenne believes that essences—which include meanings and the *a priori* itself—are revealed only within the empirical realm. Thus Dufrenne characterizes his own understanding of phenomenology as "a description which aims at an essence, itself defined as a meaning immanent in the phenomenon and given with it" (p. xlviii n.).
44. Dufrenne's first book, written in collaboration with Paul Ricoeur, was *Karl Jaspers et la philosophie de l'existence* (Paris: Editions du Seuil, 1947). Besides the *Phenomenology,* he has published two books specifically in aesthetics: *Le Poétique* (Paris: Presses Universitaires de France, 1963)

Experience is uncontestably Dufrenne's *basic* book, the book which forms the basis for all subsequent works, their philosophical *fons et origo*. And one reason for its ability to play this foundational role lies precisely in the fact that it leaves so many problems unresolved and so many directions still to be explored.

Take, for instance, the statement cited just above: "the *a priori* is revealed only in the *a posteriori*." This may seem self-evident, but in fact it raises a host of difficult questions. *How* is the *a priori* thus revealed? *Who* or *what* does the revealing, and who or what is revealed? In what exact sense can the *a priori* be said to be *in* [*dans*]—or *on* [*sur*], as Dufrenne sometimes says—the *a posteriori*? Is it there as a phenomenal feature, as a metaphysical constituent, or as an epistemological structure? Dufrenne's response to such troubling questions—which in the *Phenomenology* are mostly left dangling—was to think out and write another book in which the *a priori* is systematically investigated in terms of its major types and its primary modes of appearance. This book, *The Notion of the A Priori*, at once builds on the preliminary foundations laid down in Part 4 of the *Phenomenology* and expands the horizons within which the earlier project was conceived. In the new book, published in 1959, we have not only a more adequate classification of the *a priori* but a radical rethinking of the entire problematic posed by the notion of the *a priori*.[45] Nevertheless, even if Dufrenne comes to disagree with himself on certain points—e.g., on the role of the human subject in relation to the *a priori*—*The Phenomenology of Aesthetic Experience* remains the indisputable source for *The Notion of the A Priori*. For the latter can be viewed as a detailed development of the basic theme that the *a priori* is revealed only in the *a posteriori*—a development which ends in what Dufrenne will call an "empiricism of the transcendental."[46] In the course of this development, Dufrenne situates the human subject squarely in nature and history and places him on an even level with the world. Moreover, this latter idea—the equality or affinity of man and world—is itself modeled on the way in which the aesthetic

and *Esthétique et philosophie* (Paris: Klincksieck, 1967). It can be argued that Dufrenne's pivotal or central book—the work that forms the crucial point of transition to his later writings—is *The Notion of the A Priori*. For a defense of this interpretation, see the present writer's Introduction to that volume.

45. The change in classification can be gauged by comparing Chapter 16, esp. p. 461 n., of the *Phenomenology* with pts. 1 and 2 of *The Notion of the A Priori*.

46. See *The Notion of the A Priori*, pp. 7, 173.

object and the perceiving subject were reconciled at the end of the *Phenomenology*. Thus the tantalizing but incomplete suggestions concerning the nature and role of the *a priori* which we find in the earlier work motivate and fructify the much more thorough discussions to be found in the work that immediately succeeds it. Indeed, the two works form companion pieces and together constitute the essential documents of the period during which Dufrenne accomplished his most fertile and original philosophical thinking.

The continuing influence of *The Phenomenology of Aesthetic Experience* did not, however, cease with the appearance of *The Notion of the A Priori* at the end of the 1950s. There is also a close kinship between the *Phenomenology* and the five books which Dufrenne published in the next decade. Let us in closing take a brief look at these works in the light of their relationship with the book which is translated below.

In *Le Poétique*, perhaps the most significant of the books in question, Dufrenne discusses not so much poetry per se as the "poetic state" that poetry induces. This state, representing the acme of aesthetic experience, is one in which we experience not only the aesthetic object and its world but, beyond and through these, Nature. Conceived as an overwhelming but ultimately benevolent "power of powers," Nature by itself is mute. Yet in seeking to express itself, it speaks to us first through primordial images, such as water and sky, darkness and light.[47] These primordial images, which have archetypal status, become embodied in art, which thus becomes expressive of Nature: "all art is expressive like Nature; but it expresses Nature, while Nature expresses itself."[48] In this regard, all art imitates Nature, but not in the sense of reproducing it. Rather, art transforms Nature into world and thus into that which is coeval with man. But if man and world form a "fundament" [*fondement*] through their affinity for each other, they are both rooted in Nature as their "ground" or "source" [*fond*]: "Nature, the source which produces a consciousness capable of illuminating itself, represents the *a priori* of the *a priori* linking man to the world at the level of the fundament."[49]

47. On the notion of these "great images," see *Le Poétique*, pp. 173 ff. See also the discussion of "pre-images" in Dufrenne's *Language and Philosophy*, trans. H. B. Veatch (Bloomington: Indiana University Press, 1963), pp. 92–96.
48. *Le Poétique*, p. 180. For related claims, see pp. 4, 164, 166.
49. *Ibid.*, p. 181. Thus Nature is seen by Dufrenne as the ontological origin of all the *a priori* factors in experience. See *ibid.*, p. 4.

This bold attempt at a speculative philosophy of Nature in the tradition of Schelling, Spinoza, and the later Merleau-Ponty presents at first glance a striking contrast with *The Phenomenology of Aesthetic Experience*. No longer is the aesthetic object the ultimate term of the objective pole of the analysis. It has been replaced, or rather surpassed, by Nature:

> It is true that aesthetic perception places us in the presence of objects which are usually constructed by men: works of art. But these objects possess an aura of nature, and we shall try to show that in them, and through the artist as intermediary, it is Nature which delivers itself and speaks.[50]

This statement seems to undermine the effort of the *Phenomenology* to restrict itself to the spectator's experience of self-enclosed aesthetic objects. Nevertheless, nothing that is claimed in *Le Poétique* contradicts *The Phenomenology of Aesthetic Experience,* and the two works are closely connected with one another in two significant ways. On the one hand, *Le Poétique* complements the *Phenomenology* by stressing certain phenomena which were given short shrift in the latter. The artist is one of these phenomena, and Dufrenne accordingly devotes an entire section of *Le Poétique* to the role of the poet and to the nature of poetic inspiration and imagination. More crucial, however, is the fact that nature is finally given its due, being in effect the primary subject of *Le Poétique*. In the *Phenomenology*, the problems posed by the natural object as aesthetically perceived had been brushed aside by the decision to confine consideration to the man-created work of art. As in the case of the *a priori*, Dufrenne promised to treat such problems in another work.[51] *Le Poétique* fulfills

---

50. *Ibid.*, p. 4.

51. "The aestheticization of nature raises psychological and cosmological problems which tend to go beyond the confines of a phenomenology of aesthetic experience. That is why we are saving their study for a later work" (*Phenomenology*, p. li; see also pp. lxvii, 502, 551 n. The promissory note for a study of the *a priori* is found at p. 461 n.). It should be mentioned that Dufrenne wrote an article entitled "The Aesthetic Experience of Nature" two years afterward (*Revue internationale de philosophie*, Vol. XXXI [1955], reprinted in *Esthétique et philosophie*, pp. 38–61), in which nature, aesthetically perceived, is said to be shown in its essential "necessity." But this article only hints at the ideas to be explored in *Le Poétique*. It is also to be noted that in his thesis defense Dufrenne was taken to task by Etienne Souriau for having neglected the role of nature in aesthetic experience and thus for having "deprived himself of the principal force from the contemplative point of view" (*Revue de métaphysique et de morale*, p. 433). It is precisely the conception of Nature as a primordial force which Dufrenne seeks to establish in *Le Poétique*, which also explicitly admits the possibility of an aesthetic experience of Nature: "the

this promise, restoring to Nature the central position in aesthetic experience which had been denied it in *The Phenomenology of Aesthetic Experience.*

On the other hand, *Le Poétique* continues several themes which had existed only in germinal form in the *Phenomenology*. As we have seen, the aesthetic object, despite its pronounced differences from the natural object, had been described in the *Phenomenology* by such adjectives as "inexhaustible," "overflowing," and "imperious"—all of which are now used to characterize Nature itself. Further, the aesthetic object, considered as an in-itself because of its "elementary power" (p. 225) and "independent character" (p. 230), was earlier explicitly likened to nature: "the sensuous as fixed, given form and life, finally becomes an [aesthetic] object, constituting a nature which has the anonymous, blind force of Nature." [52] In this premonitory statement, Dufrenne anticipates his later distinction between "nature" (i.e., the totality of organic and inorganic phenomena) and "Nature" (the ultimate generative force underlying nature and man). Even more important, *Le Poétique* carries out and completes the very course of development which had given to the *Phenomenology* its distinctive structure. In the Introduction to the latter, Dufrenne wrote that "we shall pass from the phenomenological to the transcendental, and the transcendental will itself flow into the metaphysical" (p. lxvi). In the Foreword to *Le Poétique*, Dufrenne announces, with a touch of triumph, that "we have made the leap from the transcendental to the ontological, a leap which had previously tempted us without our having completed it." [53] The leap in question is from the fundament—from the equilibrium of man and world, made possible by the bivalent, transcendental character of the *a priori*—to the source or ground of the fundament itself. Consequently, what remained a conjecture at the close of *The Phenomenology of Aesthetic Experience*—namely, that beyond the concordance of subject and object there may be a more fundamental unity—becomes an actual claim in *Le Poétique*: Nature *is* the unfathomable source of man and world alike and hence also of art. But Nature, despite its ontological priority, *needs* art, just as the aesthetic object needs

aesthetic experience of a landscape makes us experience our connaturality with Nature" (*Le Poétique,* p. 148).

52. *Phenomenology*, p. 91. At several points Dufrenne even says explicitly that "the aesthetic object *is* nature" (pp. 85, 88, 91, 230).

53. *Le Poétique,* p. 4. It should be noted that, unlike Heidegger, Dufrenne does not make an essential distinction between metaphysics and ontology.

the spectator; and in both cases the aim is the same: "the glory of appearing." [54]

The four other books which appeared in the 1960s cannot be said to be as complementary to, or as continuous with, the *Phenomenology* as *Le Poétique*. Nor do they fulfill explicit promissory notes issued in the earlier work. But they do develop certain of its submerged themes. Perhaps the most important of these themes is that of man. In the *Phenomenology* itself, Dufrenne adopts a position which is again characteristically ambiguous. On the one hand, man is admitted to be essential to the creation and enjoyment of aesthetic objects which are "made by man for man" (p. 457). The sensuous, the very basis of aesthetic objects, is said to "pass through man" (p. 36). On the strength of these observations and others (including the view that the aesthetic object is historical), Dufrenne concludes that "an aesthetic humanism is possible, indeed inevitable" (p. 158; see also pp. 65–71). On the other hand, we know that he regards being as more ultimate than man, who is presented as only one aspect of (or perspective on) being. [55] Doubtless aware of the ambivalence of this early position, Dufrenne comes to insist increasingly on the critical role of man—not just in art but within Nature as well. In *Le Poétique*, not only is man depicted as "consubstantial" with Nature, but Nature itself is claimed to be "anthropocentric" insofar as it appears "only with man and to man, producing man [precisely] in order to appear itself." [56] In *Jalons*, a collection of essays published in 1966, Dufrenne asserts that "the philosopher seeks only to become aware of man in the world." [57] Finally, in *Pour l'homme*, his most recent book, Dufrenne explicitly and somewhat polemically defends the nature and dignity of man against recent French critics of humanism. Heidegger, Lévi-Strauss, Foucault, Althusser, Lacan, and others are upbraided for their failure to give full credit to man as "an exceptional and irreducible being." [58] Yet even at this late point in his career Dufrenne is again answering a question first raised in *The Phenomenology of Aesthetic Experience:* "can one give man his

54. This phrase occurs in *Le Poétique* on p. 172. It echoes similar phrases in the *Phenomenology*, e.g., on pp. 86, 223.

55. See pp. 538 ff. for the theme of "the subordination of man to being" (p. 552).

56. *Le Poétique*, p. 164. See also pp. 158, 185.

57. *Jalons*, p. 5.

58. *Pour l'homme* (Paris: Editions du Seuil, 1968), p. 223. Dufrenne specifically denies that "man" is a mere concept. See pp. 145 ff.

due?"[59] Dufrenne does not deliver this due for years to come, but a testimony to man as a creative and active being is present, explicitly or implicitly, in all his later writings.

In *Language and Philosophy,* Dufrenne explores still another submerged theme from the *Phenomenology*—the character and function of language, especially metaphoric and poetic language. This intense interest in language—which is evident in Sartre and in Merleau-Ponty and even more so in such recent figures as Jacques Derrida and Gilles Deleuze—is not found in such concerted fashion in the parent work. But there is a remarkable section on "Expression in Language" (Part 1, Chapter 4) which delineates Dufrenne's later concern with the expressive potentiality of both verbal and nonverbal language. In this section, he writes that "while expression is a limit of language, it is also [its] foundation" (p. 134). The expressiveness of language, first manifested in human gestures, forms a paradigm for the expressiveness of the aesthetic object itself, for in both language and object "expression presents its meaning directly to us without orienting us (in the manner of naming) toward the universe of reason" (p. 133). In *Lauguage and Philosophy,* as well as in the first few chapters of *Le Poétique,* Dufrenne presents an account of language which renders these earlier formulations more precise. Three levels of language are distinguished: information, signification, and expression. It is at the last level, in which meaning is immanent in the sign, that poetry becomes possible and that we can speak of a language of Nature.[60]

If Dufrenne's later considerations of language thus take us back to the domain of art, his *Esthétique et philosophie* places us directly within this domain, thereby bringing us full cycle from *The Phenomenology of Aesthetic Experience. Esthétique et philosophie* is a collection of essays in aesthetics whose original publication dates extend from the year following the appearance of the *Phenomenology* to the late 1960s. Ranging in subject matter from the question of aesthetic values to the death of art, these

59. *Phenomenology,* p. 555. This question could be said to contain, though only implicitly, a third promissory note, this time calling for a more complete study of man. This study was initiated in Dufrenne's secondary thesis, *La Personnalité de base* (Paris: Presses Universitaires de France, 1953; 2d ed., 1966) and could be said to culminate in *Pour l'homme,* pt. 2.

60. See also in this connection Dufrenne's important article, "L'Art est-il langage?" (*Revue d'esthétique,* Vol. XIX [1966], reprinted in *Esthétique et philosophie,* pp. 73–112). This article contains Dufrenne's most comprehensive critique of a structuralist interpretation of art.

essays exhibit the unusual scope of Dufrenne's interests and proficiencies within aesthetics, a scope whose capacious character undermines any claim to the effect that a phenomenologically oriented aesthetics must be parochial or limiting. What strikes the reader of this collection are the versatility of Dufrenne's talents, the depth of his insight, and the amplitude of his outlook. But *Esthétique et philosophie* also serves to remind us that Dufrenne's central concern in philosophy has been directed, throughout his writing career, toward the arena of art. It has been aesthetics that has been the guiding passion of this career and its primary inspiration. And Dufrenne's most enduring achievement in aesthetics—the single work for which he will be longest remembered—is *The Phenomenology of Aesthetic Experience*.

THE PRESENT TRANSLATION, the first into any foreign language, is based on the unabridged French text as it appears in its two original editions. The formidable length of this text has called for collaboration, and I wish to thank my fellow translators for having persisted in the face of the constant, and sometimes caustic, criticism which I offered at various stages of their efforts. Acting as general editor, I have sought consistency of terminology and continuity of style wherever possible. In addition, this volume has profited enormously from the expert editorial advice of Shelley Abelson, Ralph Carlson, and Joy Neuman of the Northwestern University Press. My wife, Brenda Casey, has assisted at a number of critical points. Mikel Dufrenne was consulted on a series of perplexing problems, and his translators are indebted to him for his genial and unfailing encouragement.

EDWARD S. CASEY

Oxford
June, 1973

The Phenomenology
of Aesthetic Experience

Introduction:
Aesthetic Experience
and Aesthetic Object

To UNDERTAKE an inquiry into aesthetic experience may appear ambitious. Let us therefore state our aim precisely and indicate its limits. The aesthetic experience which we wish to describe, in order to engage afterward in its transcendental analysis and bring out its metaphysical meaning, is the experience of the spectator and not that of the artist himself. To be sure, there is an aesthetic experience of the artist; and an investigation of the creative process in the artist is often the royal road of aesthetics. Many theories of art, and the classification of the arts which they sometimes propose, are based upon a psychology of creation. One example is Alain's theory, in which the spectator plays the part, if not of creator, then at least of actor—as in the case of ceremony, the earliest of the arts and one that pervades all the other arts to some degree—and in which the catharsis at work in the spectator (even in the solitary spectator) is modeled on a catharsis in the creator resulting from the act of creation.[1] More generally, when "operational" theories of art, which have today supplanted "psychologistic" ones, consider the work, they emphasize the result of the creative process and are wary of an analysis of feeling which is always on the verge of slipping into psychologism and subordinating the *esse* of the work to its *percipi*. Certainly, the study of the creative process does lead us

---

1. The aesthetics implicit in Alain's *Les Dieux* is perhaps different in that it deals more with the meaning of works (and, through them, of religions). It is less concerned with showing how the imaginary is harnessed in the creative act than with seeking out the true within the imaginary as it reveals itself to the spectator in great works. [See Alain, *Les Dieux* (Paris: Gallimard, 1947).—Trans.]

[xlv]

quite readily to aesthetics. It gives full due to the work in its actuality, directly raising important questions concerning the relations between art and technique. It is not, however, any the less risky. In fact, on the one hand, it offers no complete guarantee against the snare of psychologism and may go astray in evoking the historical background or psychological circumstances of creation. On the other hand, by restricting aesthetic experience to that of the artist, the study of the creative process tends to emphasize certain features of this experience—exalting, for instance, a sort of will to power at the expense of the receptive meditation which aesthetic contemplation calls forth.

It is not because of these pitfalls that we have chosen to study the experience of the spectator. Our proposal has its own dangers, as we shall see. Moreover, we believe that an exhaustive study of aesthetic experience would in any case have to unite the two approaches, since, while it is true that art presupposes the initiative of an artist, it is also true that it awaits consecration by a public. And, at a deeper level, the experiences of creator and spectator are not unconnected; for the artist becomes the spectator of his own work as he creates it, and the spectator associates himself with the artist, whose act he recognizes in the work. That is why, although limiting ourselves to the experience of the spectator, we shall all the same need to evoke the creator. But the creator then in question is the one whom the work reveals, not the one who historically created the work. The creative act is not necessarily the same for the creator who originally performs it as for the spectator who imagines it through the work. Furthermore, if one must be something of a poet or painter in order to appreciate poetry or understand painting, it is not after the fashion of real poets and painters. To create and to appreciate the creation remain two very different modes of behavior which perhaps occur seldom in the same individual. To penetrate into the artist's depths through his work is not the same as to be an artist. Certainly, if "the aesthetic," viewed as parallel to "the religious" or "the philosophic" (i.e., as Hegelian category of Absolute Spirit), becomes incarnate, if an "aesthetic life" is realized, this seems to happen among certain outstanding artists rather than among individuals who are part of an anonymous public. How can we equate the intense, ongoing emotion of the creator with the pleased glance which alights for a moment upon his work? If art has a metaphysical meaning, Promethean or not, is it not because of the obscure and triumphant will of the one who invents a world? Undoubtedly. But, in the first place, there is no assurance that the true poet has a poetic soul radiating, as it were, from him into his reader. An aesthetic of creation would have to explain why genius sometimes dwells in personalities whom psychology considers mediocre, and it would have to account for the spirit's strange vicissitudes. A spectator aesthetic at least spares us the disappointment of learning that Gauguin was a drunkard, that Schumann died mad, that Rimbaud gave up poetry for money-making, and that Claudel no longer understands his own work. Second, if we pay homage to the act of the genius, finding in it a model value and sometimes a metaphysical meaning, we do so only by inferring the life from the work and, consequently, only on condition that the work be recognized first of all; the assent and enthusiasm of the public save Van Gogh from being merely a schizophrenic, Verlaine a drunkard, Proust an invert, and Genêt a petty thief. Third, even if the spectator's experience is less spectacular than the creator's, it is not less individual and decisive. We may say, paradoxically, that the spectator, who has the responsibility of granting recognition to the work and, through it, of rescuing its creator's truth, is under greater necessity to make himself equal to the work than was the artist in creating it. To arise in the world of men, the "aesthetic" must enlist the aesthetic life of the creator as well as the aesthetic experience of the spectator.

We therefore do not dream of discrediting the study of the former; but it cannot be confused with the study of the latter. Whatever the interest in comparing them, the subjects of these two studies are different; and this is the case even though these subjects do imply one another, in that the artist calls to the spectator through his work, while the spectator communes with the creator and in some sense participates in his act. This is why we feel justified in choosing to study the spectator's experience to the exclusion of the artist's. An inquiry into art, as either a sociological or an anthropological fact, or even as a Hegelian category of Spirit, would undoubtedly have to be oriented toward creative activity. On the other hand, an inquiry into aesthetic experience is directed toward the spectator's contemplation of the aesthetic object. Accordingly, we shall henceforth apply the term "aesthetic experience" to the spectator's experience—again without implying that it is the only kind.

But this choice leads to a peculiar difficulty. It is obviously necessary to define aesthetic experience by reference to the object being experienced, which we shall call the "aesthetic object." But, to locate this object in turn, we cannot have recourse to the work of art insofar as it is identifiable only through the activity of the artist; the aesthetic object can itself be defined only as the correlate of aesthetic experience. Are we not therefore caught in a circle? We must define the aesthetic object by reference to aesthetic experience and aesthetic experience by reference to the aesthetic object. It is within this circle that the whole problem of the subject-object relationship is found. The same circle is found in phenomenology, which makes use of it in defining intentionality and in describing the interdependence of noesis and noema.[2] The circle also has an anthropological meaning which we shall continually rediscover when evoking aesthetic perception. For it attests that the sensuous or perceptible element [le sensible][3] exalted by this perception is, to use an old formula, an act common to perceiver and perceived—in other words, between the thing and the one who perceives it there is an understanding anterior to any logos. But perhaps the problem of circularity can be adequately dealt with only in an ontology such as Hegel's, in which Kant's transcendental philosophy is reinterpreted and reshaped. According to Hegel, the consciousness which is directed toward the object is constitutive, yet only on condition that the object lend itself to the constituting. But this subsumption is possible only if we presuppose a self-constitution of the object which in some way embraces the subject, since subject and object compose a moment of the Absolute to whose finality they bear witness; the subject-object pair has itself been constituted in the interests of the self-realizing Absolute. The

2. It will be seen that we are not striving to follow Husserl to the letter. We understand phenomenology in the sense in which Sartre and Merleau-Ponty have acclimated this term in France: a description which aims at an essence, itself defined as a meaning immanent in the phenomenon and given with it. The essence is something to be discovered, but by way of an unveiling, not a leap from the known to the unknown. Phenomenology applies primarily to the human, because consciousness is consciousness of self; in this, we have the model of the phenomenon: appearing as the appearing of meaning to itself. Not until the end of this work shall we consider the use of the term in Hegelian metaphysics, in which the phenomenon is an adventure of being reflecting upon itself whereby essence is surpassed in the concept.

3. The term le sensible is a central one throughout the present work. For Dufrenne, it has Kantian overtones because of its derivation from sensibilité (Sinnlichkeit in German), which Kant opposes to "understanding." At the same time, Dufrenne wants to stress the strongly perceptual character of aesthetic experience, in a sense of perception that is close to the English word "sensuous." Since sensible has misleading connotations in English, we have decided to use "sensuous," and occasionally "perceptible," as the adjectival forms, and "the sensuous" and (less frequently) "the sensuous element" as the noun forms, for this difficult term.—Trans.

subject-object affinity exhibits a unity similar to Spinoza's Substance as set in motion, the being-at-the-end-of-oppositions in which idea and thing, subject and object, noesis and noema, are dialectically united. But all interpretation aside, this circle henceforth presents us with a twofold difficulty, of doctrine and of method.

With regard to doctrine, we shall always have to ask ourselves whether the aesthetic object, being tied to the perception in which it appears, reduces to this appearing or instead constitutes an in-itself [*en-soi*]. We shall always have to pull away from either an idealism or a psychologism by recalling that perception, aesthetic or nonaesthetic, does not create a new object, and that the object as aesthetically perceived is no different from the thing objectively known or created that solicits this perception (in this case, the perception of the work of art). Within the aesthetic experience which unites them, we can therefore distinguish the object from its perception in order to study each separately. This distinction seems legitimate when we realize that the unity of subject and object is not like a compound whose nature is violated by analysis and, more precisely, that the intentionality which expresses their unity does not exclude realism. Perhaps there is a plane where this dissociation is no longer possible, where phenomenological reflection flows into Hegelian reflection upon the Absolute, where one presumes the identity of consciousness and its object (consciousness and object being two moments in the dialectic of being, inseparable and ultimately identical). But there is also a plane on which consciousness—as a subject's individual consciousness, capable of attention, knowledge, and various attitudes—arises in the world, borne by an individuality, and confronts its object. Here the transcendental shades into the anthropological, and phenomenology becomes a psychology without psychologism. The subject can then be considered as separate and consciousness as subjective, a mode of that subject's being; and the object of consciousness can itself be treated as separate. For the same reflection which discovers the relation between noesis and noema also discovers that this relation has already been effected prior to consciousness, which is as much founded as foundational and is the giver of meaning on condition that there is a given. We are in the world. This means that consciousness is the principle of a world and that every object is revealed and articulated in accordance with the attitude which consciousness adopts toward it and in terms of consciousness's experience of it. But it also means that this consciousness awakens in a world already organized, where it finds itself the heir to a tradition and the beneficiary of a history, and where it initiates a new history itself.

Consciousness, then, can be treated by an anthropology which shows how consciousness adjusts itself to a natural or cultural given, even though this given has transcendental meaning only by reference to consciousness. Here constitutive consciousness is also a natural consciousness. That is why we can (1) describe consciousness in its advent and genesis, and (2) presuppose its object and deal with the object prior to consciousness, even though there is no object except *for* a consciousness. We are also justified in this endeavor by the fact of the intersubjectivity which is at the root of history and which has its anthropological equivalent in what Comte called "humanity": there is always someone for whom the object exists as object. I can refer to an object which is present for someone else because it already exists for me, and vice versa. From this standpoint, if the object is presupposed and is always already given, consciousness too is presupposed, being always already present. Thus the object is always relative to consciousness, to *a* consciousness, but only because consciousness is always relative to the object, coming into the world with a history in which it is multiple, in which one consciousness crosses another as it encounters the object. We may therefore distinguish aesthetic object from aesthetic perception. But how are we then to define the aesthetic object, and what order are we to institute between the two stages of its study?

This question raises a methodological problem. If we start with aesthetic perception, we are tempted to subordinate the aesthetic object to that perception. We then end by conferring a broad meaning upon the aesthetic object: any object which has been aestheticized by any kind of aesthetic experience would be considered aesthetic. For example, the title of aesthetic object could be conferred upon the image (if any) which the artist forms of his work before undertaking it, simply by calling it an imaginary aesthetic object. We could likewise extend the application of the term to objects in the natural world: the harmony of a pine and a maple which Claudel encounters on a Japanese road, a silhouette momentarily glimpsed, and the countryside viewed at the end of a climb are aesthetic objects as rightfully as a monument or a sonata. But the definition of aesthetic experience then becomes a loose one, because we do not introduce enough precision into the definition of the aesthetic object. And how shall we introduce it?—by subordinating the experience to the object instead of the object to the experience, and by defining the object itself through the work of art.

This is the path we shall follow, and its advantage is immediately apparent. As no one doubts the presence of works of art and the genuineness of the finest works, the aesthetic object, if we define it in relation to them, can be easily located. And, at the same time, the aesthetic experience to be described will be an exemplary one, free of the impurities sometimes imported into the perception of an aesthetic object stemming from the world of nature, as when the contemplation of an alpine landscape is blended with the pleasant feelings awakened by the fresh air or the scent of hay, by the pleasure of solitude, the joy of climbing, or the heightened feeling of freedom. But one may also regret that the investigation of the natural aesthetic object is then deferred. However, we think our method is the right one, because aesthetic experience derived directly from the work of art is surely the purest and perhaps also the first historically; in other words, the aestheticization of nature raises psychological and cosmological problems which tend to go beyond the confines of a phenomenology of aesthetic experience. We are thus saving their study for a later work.[4]

We shall therefore start from the aesthetic object, defining it initially on the basis of the work of art. Doctrinally, we are justified in this by what we have just said: the correlation of the object with the act which grasps it does not subordinate the object to that act. We can thus locate the aesthetic object by examining the work of art as a thing in the world, independently of the act which aims at it. Does this mean that we must consider the aesthetic object as identical with the work of art? Not exactly. First, for a factual reason: the work of art does not fill the entire field of aesthetic objects: it occupies only a limited, though privileged, sector of it. But also for a logical reason: the aesthetic object can be defined only by an at least implicit reference to aesthetic experience, while the work of art is defined outside that experience as that which induces it. The two are identical to the extent that aesthetic experience aims at and unerringly reaches the object which induces it. We must not, in any case, interpose between them the difference between an ideal and a real thing,

4. Dufrenne, *Le Poétique* (Paris: Presses Universitaires de France, 1963), as well as "L'Expérience esthétique de la nature," *Revue internationale de philosophie*, IX (1955), 98–115.—Trans.

or we shall be returning to the psychologism rejected by the theory of intentionality. For the aesthetic object is within consciousness without being of it; and, conversely, the work of art is outside consciousness, a thing among things, yet it exists only as referred to a consciousness. But a nuance nevertheless separates aesthetic object and work of art, a nuance which our study will have to respect (one which, we may add, will become apparent in those arts in which creation calls for performance). Both are noemata having the same content but differing in that the noesis is different: the work of art, as present in the world, may be grasped in a perception which neglects its aesthetic quality—as when I am inattentive at the theater—or which seeks to understand and justify it instead of experiencing it, as the critic may do. The aesthetic object, on the other hand, is the object aesthetically perceived, that is, perceived as aesthetic. And that gives the measure of the difference. The aesthetic object is the work of art perceived *as* a work of art, that is, the work of art which gets the perception it solicits and deserves and which is fulfilled in the spectator's docile consciousness. More succinctly, the aesthetic object is the work of art as perceived. And this provides the key for defining its ontological status. Aesthetic perception founds the aesthetic object, yet only by giving it its due, that is, by submitting to it. Aesthetic perception completes but does not create the aesthetic object. To perceive aesthetically is to perceive faithfully; perception is a task, for there are inept perceptions which fall short of the aesthetic object and only an adequate perception realizes its aesthetic quality. We shall thus presuppose a perspicuous perception when we analyze aesthetic experience: its phenomenology will be implicitly a deontology. But we are also presupposing the existence of the work which requires this lucid perception. In this way, we are able to get out of the circle within which the correlation of the aesthetic object with aesthetic experience encloses us. But we emerge from the circle only on condition of not forgetting it, that is, by first defining the object as an object for perception, and perception as the perception of that object (which, moreover, will force us into repetitions and into a particularly detailed development of the first two parts of this work, which deal with the aesthetic object and the work of art).

Another question is about to claim our attention. But first, the difficulty which has given us pause may be expressed in another way. In deciding to break out of the circle within which the correlation of the aesthetic object with aesthetic perception

encloses us and to take the work of art as the point of departure
for our reflections—in order to rediscover, on its basis, the
aesthetic object and then aesthetic perception—we are resorting
to the empirical and the historical. Is this not a *saltus mortalis*
for an analysis which aspires to be eidetic? We do not think so.
Max Scheler teaches us that moral essences reveal themselves
historically without, however, being entirely relative to history.
Does this not also hold for the essence of aesthetic experience?
Phenomenology certainly cannot object to an anthropology
which demonstrates the advent of aesthetic consciousness in the
cultural world. In fact, phenomenology supports such an anthropology, by demonstrating that the subject is bound to the
object not only in order to constitute it but also to become constituted itself. Aesthetic experience occurs in a cultural world
where works of art offer themselves and where we are taught to
recognize and appreciate them. We know that certain objects
commend themselves to us and expect us to do them justice. It
is not possible to ignore the empirical conditions of aesthetic
experience any more than we can ignore the conditions to which
the development of logical thinking in science and philosophy
has had to submit. We must therefore return to the empirical in
order to learn how aesthetic experience is realized in actual fact.
For humanity, history is that "already there" which runs back
into prehistory, just as the individual turns back toward the
shadowy pit of birth which attests that we are in the world because we have *come* into it. It is in this way that the work of art
is already there to solicit our experience of the aesthetic object
and, as such, offers us a starting point for our inquiry. But the
historicity of artistic production, the diversity of art forms and of
judgments of taste, no more imply a relativism destructive of
an eidetic of art than the historicity of the ethos implies a similar
relativism in Scheler's eidetic of moral values. The fact that
art assumes many guises bears witness to a certain power in it,
a will to self-realization. This ought to sharpen rather than blunt
our comprehension of art. We realize this today, when the
museum welcomes and enshrines all styles and contemporary
art is in quest of its most extreme possibilities.

It would seem, in fact, that aesthetic reflection finds itself
presently at a privileged moment in history, a moment when art
is blossoming. The death of art proclaimed by Hegel—an event
which, for him, derives from the death of God and the coming
of absolute knowledge—perhaps means the resurrection of an
authentic art which no longer has anything but itself to declare.

It may even be that aesthetic experience, as we shall attempt to describe it, is a recent discovery. We may recall Malraux's well-known espousal of the idea that the aesthetic object—insofar as it is bound up with aesthetic experience and however old the work—is a new star in the universe of art. Today our finally liberated gaze is capable of rendering past works the homage which their contemporaries were perhaps unable to accord them and of converting them into aesthetic objects. We can neither ignore this idea nor refuse to use it. After all, what we have to say about aesthetic experience in an age which has discovered primitive art styles and passed through surrealism, abstract painting, and atonal music is perhaps of greater value than what Baudelaire could say in the era of Baudry and Meissonier (although Baudelaire was by no means fooled by them, knowing enough to praise Delacroix and Daumier and not to become the dupe of Ingres and the Pre-Raphaelites). And, in any case, we are destined to play the role which history assigns us and to share in the aesthetic consciousness of our time. Just as *Homo estheticus* exists in history, where he finds himself in the presence of works of art, so our thinking is also situated in history, where it is confronted with a particular theory and practice of art. Now, it will probably be maintained that thinking which is thus influenced by history must bear the mark of relativism. However, even if aesthetic experience is a recent invention, a certain essence tends to be manifested within it, and we must sift it out. What we discover in history, and even thanks to it, is not altogether historical. We are persuaded of this by art itself, which is perhaps a more universal language than rational discourse and does its best to deny the kind of time in which civilizations perish. In the name of an eidetic elucidation—and even if this is possible only through history—we can judge history, or at least relax its grip and show how the phenomenon of art has manifested itself outside the historical limits within which we first confine it in order to describe it, limits which we must draw in the light of a particular historical state of thought. Perhaps we shall then see that aesthetic experience is not entirely an invention of the twentieth century, any more than love is, in a famous phrase, an invention of the twelfth century. Aesthetic experience may be induced through the ages by markedly differing works of art, but it always tends to realize a certain exemplary form.

Our study would thus seem to lead to an ontology of art, one which we shall restrict ourselves to evoking only at the end. And that is where any inquiry into history leads when we grant that essences are unveiled in it. For if history is the place where they first appear, is it not also the locus of their full realization? Consequently, instead of being the source of relativism, is not history the handmaiden of an absolute? Is it not the agency by which we realize the truth of art and of aesthetic experience, which in itself is not historical? And must we not speak of art as an absolute which simultaneously gives rise to artists and their public, to the works as well as to the perceptions which do them justice? Is not aesthetic experience—through which we hope to discover art—the action of art within us, the result of an inspiration parallel to that which grips the artist?

But our purpose is more modest. In referring to the empirical, we are seeking above all to find in it a point of departure for a phenomenological study, since it is advisable to distinguish between what belongs to the object and what is part of the subject. Therefore, we start with the facts that, on the one hand, there are works of art, and that, on the other, there are attitudes toward these works. Yet a difficulty, to which history is again no stranger, stops us at once: how do we choose from the multiplicity open to us? A crucial problem is raised by the diversity of the arts. Must we not pause at least to set them in order? The classification of the arts is indeed one of the tasks usually claimed by the aesthetician. We shall not undertake it, however, because our aim is to define aesthetic experience and, consequently, to dwell on what every art has in common. It could be objected that the differences among the arts are such that we cannot disregard them without losing ourselves in meaningless generalities. And we shall certainly have to take these differences into account when analyzing a particular aesthetic object or aesthetic experience and, therefore, when starting from a given work of art. Admittedly, an inquiry centered on art cannot go far without introducing a certain classification of the arts. But an inquiry into aesthetic experience, even if it starts from the empirical reality of works of art, may gain from not dwelling upon their diversity, so that it can better bring out what is essential in this experience. Only when we have some idea of this essentiality can we indicate the main lines of an inquiry into the structures common to works in the different arts (an inquiry which could ultimately turn back into an examination of their differences). If there is a unity among the arts, and if art can be regarded sociologically as an autonomous institution—one which, in the very heart of the social *consensus*, obeys a dynamism of its own—is this not because there is a unity in aesthetic experience?

This experience, we repeat, may take different forms in the course of history, according to the art or mode of taste which is dominant. But Kant thought it possible to define the moral law even if no moral act had ever been performed. Similarly, we can define aesthetic experience, despite our having to seek illustrations of it in history. In trying to grasp it in its specificity as beyond differences between the arts, we shall remain in line with an eidetic approach.

However, another problem, one which cannot be dismissed, immediately arises: which of the countless works brought forth by the various arts must we regard as authentic and choose for reference? In fact, there are, in the cultural world to which we lay claim and which is the daily bread of all our experiences, objects in which aesthetic quality does not always clearly prevail. Is an armchair a fully aesthetic object? And what of the Limoges service on which I dine? Are there degrees of aesthetic quality, as suggested by the traditional distinction between minor and major arts? Etienne Souriau has given the problem an ingenious solution, which consists of measuring not the aesthetic quality of a given object but the quantity of "art work" [*travail d'art*] expended in its production. When art is defined by its "skeuo-poetic function"—as an "activity aiming to create things" [5]—it is possible to distinguish between creation and mere production in a given process of manufacture and "to establish *quantitatively* and *accurately* the percentage of art work in the total work." [6] But this solution involves an analysis of artistic creation, and we doubt whether we could perform such an analysis effectively from our proposed spectator's viewpoint. From this viewpoint, an answer to the problem may be provided by a sociological investigation which would establish the criteria used in each society and epoch for discerning what is considered authentic art—that is, the work of an artist and not the product of an artisan or a collector's curio.[7]

We cannot seriously consider undertaking such a study. It is

5. Etienne Souriau, *L'Avenir de l'esthétique* (Paris: Alcan, 1929), p. 133.

6. *Ibid.*, p. 148.

7. The problem of the discrimination of the work of art can be raised in a very concrete way. Thomas Munro supplies us with an interesting example of this in recalling a lawsuit whose verdict made legal history in the United States. The question arose as to whether or not an abstract sculpture by Brancusi deserved to be called art. Only this classification finally allowed its owner to get it into the United States without paying duty. (See Munro, *The Arts and Their Interrelations* [New York: Liberal Arts Press, 1949], pp. 7 f.)

not without interest, but it would mean accepting historical relativism without reservation and risk discouraging an eidetic inquiry. Children's drawings or Sunday painters' canvases tell us about painting only after we have first been told about their creators; and the information which these works provide concerns the psychology of the painter much more than the essence of painting.[8] We, on the other hand, believe—without trying to prove it in the present work—that only in the light of a particular idea of authentic art can questions be asked about its limiting cases. To solve the problems raised by the "primitive arts," as well as by the minor arts or by such by-products of art as military bands, amateurish poetry, Hollywood westerns, or cheap novels, we must know what aesthetic experience is and why works on the borderline of art cannot awaken aesthetic experience and be converted into aesthetic objects. We subscribe to Malraux's dictum: "Any analysis of our relation to art is useless if it applies equally to two paintings, one of which is a work of art and the other not."[9]

But then, once more, how can we determine which is the work of art, worthy of becoming an aesthetic object for us? We shall push empiricism to its limit—as Aristotle does in his definition of the virtues—and subscribe to the opinion of the best, which is also ultimately the general opinion, the opinion of all those having an opinion. The work of art is whatever is recognized and held up as such for our approval. Empiricism furnishes us with the means for not remaining in the empirical. By accepting the judgments and preferences of our culture, we waste no time in trying to discover what each separate culture prefers or sanctions; we do not allow ourselves to be seduced by aesthetic relativism; we are free to discover what the work of art is, and how it evokes aesthetic experience, without deliberating endlessly over the choice of these works. We need only place all the odds of a venerable tradition on our side. Unanimously ac-

---

8. Even here, there are reservations to be made. The true painter is neither a child nor an amateur, as Malraux has clearly shown. He is a man for whom painting exists first and foremost, and it is in his work that we recognize him. We can no more derive him from the child than, elsewhere, the normal from the pathological. The psychology which focuses upon the creator assumes that his creation reflects his personality. This psychology ought perhaps to be given second place if, as we believe, the creator's truth is more in his work than in his empirical individuality. Perhaps psychology meets its limits here.

9. From André Malraux, *The Voices of Silence,* trans. Stuart Gilbert (Garden City, N.Y.: Doubleday, 1953), p. 611.

cepted works of art will be our most reliable guides to the aesthetic object and to aesthetic experience.

At this point, we would like to make an important aside. Rather than falling back on opinion at the outset, why not try to discover a criterion intrinsic to authentic works: could the *quid proprium* of aesthetic objects be beauty? Does not the characteristic of beauty or the claim to beauty delimit the domain of aesthetic objects? However, we shall avoid invoking the concept of the beautiful, because it is a notion which, depending on the extension we give it, seems either useless for our purposes or dangerous. Even if we define the beautiful as *the* specific aesthetic quality and give this quality an axiological accent, as is often done, we do not escape the relativism which we hoped to avoid. Subjectivism besets every value judgment, including judgments of taste pronounced on beauty, with the result that the sought-for objective criterion suddenly appears unreliable. It therefore seems better to deny any axiological accent to aesthetic quality and to look elsewhere for the essence of the aesthetic object by defining this object through its structure, whether in terms of how it is brought forth (as in an aesthetics of creation) or in terms of how it appears (as in an aesthetics of aesthetic experience). This is all the more advisable when we examine the aesthetic experience in which the subject becomes aware of the aesthetic object and see that the feeling of beauty is quite subdued there. If we describe it as a certain feeling of pleasure, there is no assurance that this feeling is always experienced or even that a judgment of taste is always pronounced; and, if it is pronounced, it is often at the edge of our contact with the work of art and pronounced only in order to express preferences which, to be honest, we know are subjective and which decide nothing whatever about the being of the work. Can we not construct an aesthetics which lays aside value judgments and accords to those valuations which are immanent in the spectator's experience only the limited importance they deserve?

But we can also define the beautiful in such a way that we can undertake an objective aesthetics which need not debate the beautiful endlessly in order to justify our value judgments. In this case, the beautiful designates a value which is in the object and attests to its being. Thus we lend the beautiful an ontic meaning by considering it as one among other aesthetic categories, e.g., the pretty, the sublime, or the graceful. These latter categories allude less to the impression produced by the object than to its very structure, inviting us to account for the impression by this structure. Yet it appears that the beautiful cannot give rise to an analysis so precise as that which can be made of the sublime or of the graceful, of which Bayer has given such a remarkable description.[10] Indeed, all the definitions of the beautiful offered by dogmatic aesthetic theories seem inadequate. Nevertheless, a certain kind of art, which one may call "classical" and whose traditions are still alive, has striven to turn the beautiful into a definite and even a paramount and exclusive aesthetic category by stressing certain dominant qualities, like harmony, purity, nobility, and serenity—of which a Raphael *Madonna*, a Bossuet *Sermon*, a Mansart building, and a *sonata da chiesa* ("church sonata") give us a clear enough idea. And the prestige of admittedly beautiful works which are inspired by this conception has long inclined aesthetic inquiry toward the theme of the beautiful. However, this inquiry has not sufficiently considered the possibility that the beautiful, thus positively defined by a particular content, may be a special aesthetic category, or else a combination of several categories proper to certain works only, rather than being the property of every aesthetic object. The beautiful as a symbol of perfection has been confused with the beautiful as a special characteristic. Because of this confusion, a particular aesthetic theory and practice have been absolutized. To dispel the confusion, it is enough to observe, as Malraux does, that among the many forms of art which come before us, now that the aesthetic world is round at last, very few have evidenced the concern for beauty found in classical art.[11] And, more to the point, classical art itself was overcome for a time by other art forms, such as the baroque at the beginning of the seventeenth century—forms which have scarcely stopped haunting it and to which it has at times given way, for example, in various kinds of mannerism. Must we believe that all the works in which the grotesque, the tragic, the sinister, and the sublime hold sway are not beautiful? Must we, like Voltaire, reproach Shakespeare for the joking of his gravedigger or, like Boileau, criticize Molière for his Scapin? We see at once that too narrow an understanding of the term "beautiful" is dangerous: it leads to an arbitrary and sterilizing dogmatism.

10. See Raymond Bayer, *L'Esthétique de la grâce*, 2 vols. (Paris: Alcan, 1934).—Trans.

11. Here Dufrenne refers to Malraux's notion that photography and perfected processes of reproduction have introduced a universally accessible "museum without walls." See Malraux, *Voices*, pt. 1.—Trans.

It is far better, on the one hand, to refuse the monopoly of beauty to works considered classical—i.e., to refuse to employ the word "beautiful" to designate a particular category or style which we can easily define in another way and which we must so define as soon as we are to aim at some precision—and, on the other hand, to reserve this term for the designation of a quality which may be common to every aesthetic object. For nonclassical works are beautiful too and are so intended, but in a sense which overflows every aesthetic category and particular content.

But we see then that this understanding of the beautiful can be extended to objects entirely foreign to the realm of the aesthetic object: A moral act, a logical argument, or, for that matter, ordinary objects in whose manufacture no aesthetic concern has intervened can be called beautiful without there being any ground for doubting the seriousness with which the word is used each time. Does this mean that in being thus extended the concept of beauty becomes useless? Not exactly, for we would be unable to banish all reference to beauty without some degree of bad faith. When we speak of aesthetic objects, is it not with the understanding that they are beautiful? And if we deliberately center our attention on works qualified and recommended by a long tradition, is it not because we know them to be beautiful? At the same time, we are spared the trouble of solving the problem of degrees of aesthetic quality. For, after all, if we preselect our examples, if we call upon Balzac rather than Ohnet, Valéry rather than François Coppée, Wagner rather than Adam, it is because we are really introducing a scale of values surreptitiously and assuming that the beautiful is like an appanage of the aesthetic object as well as the guarantee of its authenticity. An aesthetics which would pretend to regard all aesthetic objects as equal would be slighting the most favorable cases, the most characteristic objects in which the essence of aesthetic being is most clearly evident. In this sense, the beautiful is implied in all aesthetic reflection. But what does the beautiful mean here other than what we have called the authenticity of the work of art? The notion of beauty ceases to be dangerous only to become useless again: it names rather than solves the problem. For now it does not designate a definite kind of object but the manner in which each object measures up to its own type and, so to speak, fulfills its calling while reaching the fullness of its being. We say an object is beautiful in the same way that we say it is true when we judge, in the sense emphasized by Hegel, that a storm is a true storm, or that Socrates is a true philoso-

pher. The difference betwen the two terms, which orients the
beautiful toward its aesthetic usage and justifies the priority
which the aesthetic sometimes claims, is that the beautiful
designates the truth of the object when this truth is immediately
sensuous and recognized, when the object imperiously announces
the ontic perfection it enjoys. The beautiful is the true made
visible, it sanctions what is felicitous [*heureux*] before reflection
does.[12] A locomotive is true for the engineer when it runs well,
but it is beautiful for me when it expresses speed and power immediately and as if triumphantly. Because it expresses in this
way, it is aestheticized. It is when the object is beautiful that it
becomes an aesthetic object, because it then solicits the aesthetic
attitude from us. A beautiful line of reasoning is one which I can
momentarily follow like a melody, since I master it with pleasure. Likewise, when a beautiful landscape is before me, it is
as if I were in a museum before a painting: I listen to the
object, which tells me above all of its perfection.

These remarks suffice to illuminate the judgment of aesthetic
value: a chromo lacks beauty because it is not a true painting,
carnival music because it is not true music, trashy verses because they do not constitute a true poem.[13] The opposite of the
beautiful is not the ugly, as we have known since Romanticism.
The opposite of the beautiful is the abortive, in the case of the
work which claims to be an aesthetic object, and the indifferent,
in the case of the object which makes no such claim. This implies that the aesthetic object can be imperfect: who will dispute
it? But we cannot measure the aesthetic object's imperfection
by some external standard. It is imperfect because it does not
succeed in being what it claims to be, because it does not realize
its essence; and it is in terms of what it aspires to be that it
must be judged and that it judges itself. If Picasso's harlequins

12. This definition of the beautiful does not, moreover, exclude a definition which refers to the subject and to the use of his faculties, as in Kant's
philosophy. For the aesthetic quality which the object eminently possesses
lies, as one already suspects, in offering itself completely to perception by
delivering its whole meaning to the senses, with the result that, if the subject reflects upon himself, he feels fulfilled. He understands in perceiving
and can truly say that the beautiful is that which produces in him a
harmony of imagination and understanding.

13. Let us note, however, that, in the atmosphere of a fair, with its
noisy, gaping crowds and jumble of booths, carnival music can be beautiful. It realizes its being, which is no longer that of an aesthetic object. But
if it is transposed into true music, as Stravinsky has done in *Petrouchka*, it
is obliged to undergo a transmutation in order to correspond to the aesthetic
being to which it has been promoted.

sought to be Watteau's figures, they would be failures—as would Byzantine frescoes if they aimed at being Greek paintings, and modal music if it aspired to be tonal. But if an object makes no claim to being aesthetic, it has not failed. It can even be beautiful in its own sphere, as a tool or a tree is beautiful. But it is essential to the aesthetic object that *it* be aesthetic: it makes promises that it must keep. In other words, it is essential to an aesthetic object that it embody its own norm—not a norm which our thinking or taste imposes on it, but one which it imposes on itself or which its creator has imposed on it. And perhaps we must even say that it is a norm which it imposes on its creator, for it requires him to be authentic. We cannot say here what this norm of the aesthetic object is—especially since it is invented afresh by each such object, and each has no other law than the one it makes for itself. But we can at least say that, whatever the means of a work may be, the aim it sets itself in order to be a masterpiece is fullness of sensuous being and of the meaning immanent in the sensuous. Now, the work is truly meaningful in its unique way only if the artist is authentic: it says something only if he has something to say, if he truly wants to say something. Malraux, placing the accent on the conquering aspect of creation which results from an incessant rivalry with Creation, expresses himself as follows: "Every masterpiece, implicitly or openly, tells of a human victory over the blind force of destiny." [14] This victory is conveyed to us only through the authenticity of the artist—that is, through the authenticity of the aesthetic object itself. The norm of the aesthetic object is its will to the absolute. And to the extent that the aesthetic object proclaims and attains this norm, the object itself becomes in turn a norm for aesthetic perception. Thus the aesthetic object assigns to aesthetic perception the task of approaching the work of art without any prejudice, of giving it as much credit as possible, of placing it in a position to furnish the proof of its being.

Basically, it is not we who decide what is beautiful. The object itself decides, and it does so by manifesting itself. The aesthetic judgment is passed from within the object rather than within us. We do not define the beautiful, we ascertain what the object is. And, in probing the aesthetic object in general, we must no longer look for its specific difference in a definition of the beautiful. Not that we refuse all use of the idea of beauty or challenge the judgment of taste; in deciding to refer to uni-

14. Malraux, *Voices*, p. 630.—Trans.

versally admired works, we are tacitly subscribing to this judgment. But what we ask of it is not to supply the criterion of the aesthetic object but to recommend the works which will most reliably manifest this criterion—i.e., works which are aesthetic objects to the fullest extent. Thus an aesthetics is possible which does not reject aesthetic valuation yet is not subservient to it. It is an aesthetics which recognizes beauty without creating a theory of beauty, because basically there is no theory to create: there is the stating of what aesthetic objects are, and to the degree that they truly *are* they are beautiful.

This remark ends our digression on the beautiful. For it is by recognizing what beauty means that we can understand what the model aesthetic perception is which we have both to invoke (in order to define the aesthetic object) and to describe (in order to define aesthetic experience). This perception—or, differently expressed, the judgment of taste constitutive of aesthetic experience—must at once be distinguished from judgments, sometimes vociferously maintained, which express our special tastes, that is, affirm our preferences. The latter raise the vexing question of the relativity of the beautiful, for they make it appear that the aesthetic sensibility is limited, and at least partly determined, by the nature of the individual and his culture. These determinations bear primarily on our preferences, and our preferences are not constitutive of aesthetic experience but only add a personal note to it. Quite possibly they also dictate our breadth of vision, our errors or failures of appreciation: thus the neoclassical observer failed to "see" Gothic cathedrals. But these value judgments, which can so bias and becloud perception, are foreign to it in principle, because their goal is not, as in the case of perception, the apprehension of the reality of the aesthetic object. Taste is not the organ of aesthetic perception, it can at best either sharpen or dull it. We can perceive and acknowledge a work of art without appreciating it, and we can appreciate a work without giving it its due, like someone enraptured by a melody because of the memories it awakens. Nevertheless, when the judgment of taste does not merely specify our preferences but registers the beautiful—that is, when it is hardly a judgment at all—it is, even if limited in its application, universal in its validity, and precisely because it lets the object speak. The historicity of diverse tastes is no argument against the validity of *taste*, and, of course, it counts even less as an objection to the project of describing the aesthetic object.

But this description must also distinguish between aesthetic perception and still other judgments by means of which we institute a hierarchy among works—just as we rank human beings by judging, for example, that a hero is greater than an average man. Thus we say that the religious music of a Bach is greater than the court music of a Lully, or that Hugo's epics are greater than his elegies; thus does Boileau condemn *Les Fourberies de Scapin* in the name of *Le Misanthrope*. And Boileau was doubtless wrong if he ruled out farce as an aesthetic object capable of beauty, that is, if he believed farce to be merely abortive comedy. Such judgments can be pronounced only if everything else is equal and with respect to works of equal beauty. In such instances, the value judgment is legitimate but it bears less on the beauty of the work than on its sublimity or, rather, its depth —that is, on dimensions which must be called existential, and all the more so because, as we shall see, we are prone to assimilate the depth of the work to the human quality of its creator. In this case, we are no longer concerned with aesthetic quality: it is a matter of what the object is expressing, not of the way the object is expressing it. This revelation is certainly essential and lies at the heart of aesthetic experience; but while it justifies an existential axiology, it by no means determines a judgment of taste. The work may indeed possess content and depth only if it is beautiful, but this content is, in itself, incommensurable with beauty; the judgment to which it gives rise is not one of taste, and the hierarchy of works which it suggests is not an aesthetic hierarchy.

Above all, the work requires of us a perception which gives it full credit. Now, it is clear that no matter what our judgment of taste may be about a given work, it is possible to have imperfect, maladroit, or incomplete perceptions of it, whether through the fault of performance, as when an orchestra is bad, or the fault of circumstance, as when a painting is poorly illuminated, or the fault of the spectator, as when he is inattentive or, for lack of training, simply not qualified. These failed perceptions have no ill consequences in the sphere of action, but they do prevent the aesthetic object from appearing. It is therefore of interest to examine them in order to realize that the aim of aesthetic perception is nothing other than the unveiling constitutive of its object. But if we wish to describe this aesthetic object, we must presuppose a model perception which makes it appear. Nor is it arbitrary to announce the criterion of this perception. It is perception *par excellence*, pure perception, which has no aim other than its own object and does not try to resolve itself in action. This perception is called forth by the work of art itself just as it stands and as it can be objectively described. And in the event that we had any doubt about this criterion, we could still have recourse to the empirical and fall back upon the judgment of the best.

Thus we rediscover everywhere the correlation of aesthetic object and aesthetic perception. This correlation lies at the center of our work, whose main lines we can now announce, also indicating that with which we shall not deal. We shall start with the work of art, but without restricting ourselves to it alone; our task will not be one of criticism, except indirectly. The work of art will then lead us to the aesthetic object. It is to the latter that we shall devote most of our time, because it presents the most difficult problems. We know by now to what extent we can identify the aesthetic object with the work of art, at least when we invoke it in the work—while acknowledging that the natural world can also harbor or give rise to such objects. Aesthetic object and work of art are distinct in that aesthetic perception must be joined to the work of art in order for the aesthetic object to appear. However, this does not mean that the work of art is real and the aesthetic object ideal, as if the former existed as a thing in the world and the latter as a representation or signification in consciousness. Moreover, there is no reason to attribute a monopoly of such nonindependent existence to the aesthetic object. Every object, including natural objects and works of art considered as things given in the cultural world, is an object for consciousness. Nothing enjoys an existence which would free it from the obligation to be present to a consciousness (even if only a virtual one) in order to be recognized as a thing. In other words, the ontological problem which the aesthetic object raises is one which is posed by any perceived thing; and if we agree to call "object" the thing as perceived (or offered to a possible perception, for example, to others' perceptions), we must say that everything is an object. The difference between work of art and aesthetic object arises from the fact that the work of art can be considered as an ordinary thing, that is, as the object of a perception and a thought which distinguish it from other things without according it special treatment. But the work of art can, in addition, be the object of an aesthetic perception, the only kind of perception which does it justice. The painting on my wall is a thing for the mover but an aesthetic object for the art lover; it is both, but alternately, for the expert who cleans it. Likewise, the tree is a thing for the woodcutter and yet may be an aesthetic object for the stroller. Does this mean that ordinary perception is false and only aesthetic perception true? Not exactly, for the work of art is also a thing, and we shall see that nonaesthetic perception may serve to take note of its aesthetic being without, however, truly apprehending it. Going deeper, we shall see that the aesthetic object retains its thinglike characteristics while still being more than a thing.

Consequently, everything we shall say about the work of art will hold true for the aesthetic object, and the two terms may appear to merge. But it is nevertheless important to separate them: (1) when we come to describe aesthetic perception as such, because its correlate is then the aesthetic object alone; (2) when we examine the objective structures of the work of art, because reflection on these structures clearly implies that we are substituting reflection for perception, that we are ceasing to perceive the object in order to study it as an occasion for perceiving—thereby revealing within the object itself a demand for aesthetic perception.

After addressing these problems, we shall outline an objective analysis of the work. This analysis will confirm what the description of the aesthetic object will have suggested to us. Then we shall describe aesthetic perception itself by contrasting it with ordinary perception, which will be seen in its dialectical movement, just as the aesthetic object is to be contrasted with the perceived thing in general. We shall thus have grasped aesthetic experience (that of the spectator) while proceeding in terms of a practically unavoidable dichotomy—a dichotomy which must be surmounted, even if this results in certain repetitions in our analysis. So far as we can, we shall atone for these repetitions by making Part III briefer than Parts I and II. In Part IV, finally, we shall ask what aesthetic experience signifies and under what conditions it is possible. We shall pass from the phenomenological to the transcendental, and the transcendental will itself flow into the metaphysical. For, in asking how aesthetic experience is possible, we shall be led to ask whether and how it can be true. And we shall then be concerned with knowing to what extent the revelation which the work of art provides—the world to which it introduces us—is due solely to the initiative of the artist whose subjectivity is expressed in the work (thus investing it with subjectivity), or whether being itself is revealed, with the artist as the occasion or instrument of this revelation. Must we choose between an anthropological and an ontological exegesis of aesthetic experience? Perhaps the problem would present itself differently were we to examine the aesthetic object which arises in nature; but we shall merely allude to this object, since we have decided to confine ourselves to the aesthetic experience aroused by art. Moreover, it is pointless to anticipate further the problems which aesthetic experience raises. These problems will take on their full meaning only after our description of aesthetic experience itself—a description to which we shall devote the major portion of this work.

PART I
Phenomenology of the
Aesthetic Object

1 / Aesthetic Object
and Work of Art

WE ARE GOING TO ATTEMPT to describe the aesthetic object, first basing our analyses on an example. This object is primarily, although not exclusively, the work of art as grasped in aesthetic experience. But how is the aesthetic object to be distinguished from the work of art? And what is a work of art in the first place? We have already decided to rely on cultural tradition, but this recourse leaves certain questions in abeyance. Offhand, however, it does not seem difficult to pick out the work of art and to say what it is, especially if we agree not to worry about borderline cases—i.e., not to ask ourselves whether a piece of furniture which is a work of art when it is signed by Boulle remains one when it is manufactured by Lévitan,[1] or whether the vase in which I set my flowers is as rightfully a work of art as a Louvre amphora. But two notions overlap here: the choice and the being of the genuine work of art. As to choice, we can indeed fall back upon the sociological criterion of tradition. But what about being? Tradition and the experts who simultaneously promote and serve this tradition may tell us that the canvases of this painter or the symphonies of that composer do indeed possess the quality of a work of art. But our reflective powers are then immediately engaged by the problem of the being of the work thus selected and held up as an example, in order that

---

1. The two best-known members of this historic French family of cabinetmakers were Pierre Boulle (1580–1635) and his grandson, André Charles Boulle (1642–1732). Lévitan is a manufacturer of contemporary furniture and has three retail outlets on the Champs Elysées in Paris.—Trans.

reflection may find in this being, if not the reason for the choice (assuming that the beautiful is not an objectively definable and universally valid criterion), at least its confirmation. Such reflection does not altogether escape the aporia to which we have already referred. To elucidate the nature of the work, we presuppose an object whose quality as a work has already been recognized and we justify a choice made before reflection. However, if we cannot avoid presuppositions, we need not therefore avoid the ontic problem.

Does this problem actually arise? At first glance, nothing is simpler than to say what the work of art is: it is this statue, picture, or opera . . . But just a moment! Can we point to an opera by Wagner as we point to a statue by Rodin, that is, locate it somewhere in the realm of things and thus assign it an undeniable reality? We may say that it was created not to be seen but to be heard, whereby we imply that the aim of a work is aesthetic perception. But, having been created, it surely has the being of a thing. And what was created? Wagner wrote a libretto and a score. Is the work reducible to certain signs on paper that the printer reproduces? Yes and no. When Wagner set down the last chord in his manuscript, he could say that his work was completed. But when the composer's job is done, the performer's begins. The work has been finished, but it has not yet been made manifest and present. I may even possess the score of *Tristan and Isolde*, but am I then in the presence of the work? Certainly not, if I do not know how to read music. I am faced by a veritable mist of signs on paper and am as far removed from the work—I dare not say farther, because there are no degrees in the infinite distance between presence and absence—as if I were faced with a summary of the libretto or a commentary on the work. If, on the other hand, these signs do have a meaning for me—a musical meaning, of course—then they usher me into the presence of the work, and I can study it as does, for example, the critic who analyzes it or the orchestra leader who prepares to conduct it. But how do these signs acquire a meaning, if not by evoking (in a way we shall explore later) the music itself, that is, a virtual performance, past or future? Consequently, the musical work is itself only when performed: thus is it present. Nevertheless it already existed, and in more than outline form, the moment Wagner laid down his pen. The performance adds nothing. And yet it adds everything: the possibility of being heard, that is, of being present in its own way to a consciousness and becoming an aesthetic object for that consciousness.

That is, the work is locatable by reference to the aesthetic object. And this is true in the plastic arts as well. That statue in the park, this picture on the wall, are undeniably there. It seems pointless to ask about their being as works—or rather, any such questioning will immediately find its answer, since the work is there, lending itself to analysis, to the study of its creation, structure, or meaning. However, just as the score is studied with a future listening in mind, so is the plastic work analyzed with reference to the aesthetic perception it is meant to invite. We select it as a work of art from among indifferent things only because we know that it invites this perception—while, say, a scribble on a wall or a snowman in the back yard neither deserves nor gets it. And that is how, relying upon a particular tradition, we judge those works of art to be genuine which we know to exist fully only when perceived and appreciated for themselves. Thus the work of art, however undeniable the reality which the creative act confers upon it, has an equivocal existence, because its vocation is to transcend itself toward the aesthetic object in which alone it attains, along with its public sanction, the fullness of its being. In pondering the work of art, we discover the aesthetic object, and it is in terms of this object that we shall have to speak of the work.

Let us then cease to wonder where the musical work proper resides, so that we may witness the emergence of the aesthetic object; for if I am to know the work, it must be present before me as an aesthetic object. Suppose, for example, that I am watching a performance of *Tristan and Isolde*. This performance has a date, it is an event, perhaps a world event, even a historic one. It is something which happens to people, possibly affecting their futures through the emotions they experience, the decisions they make, or simply the other people they meet. And is it also an event for the work itself? Yes and no. It can be an event to the extent to which the work has been affected and transformed by the performance, that is, through the interpretations given it by the singers, musicians, or stage designers. A new production may be an event for the work, just as much as the views of the critic who will on the morrow suggest a new interpretation of the music or of the philosopher who will invite us to understand the night, day, or love-death themes in some novel way. As a result of this event, something in the interpretation of the work may be modified either on the performer's or on the spectator's part. But will the being itself of the work be affected? No, if we grant that the performance is subservient to the work and that the work, itself independent of the performance, cannot be compromised by it. For the work, the performance is only an occasion for manifesting itself, an occasion whose advantage is better appreciated when it is compared for a moment with "bargain" performances. One such "performance," for example, may be reading the libretto in an edition where it is presented without the music. I am then in the presence of a different kind of aesthetic object, one which is a dramatic poem, not the aesthetic object known as an opera. There is a being of the literary object, even if it has not been expressly intended by Wagner, because it has a poetic quality which enables it to exist aesthetically after it has been separated from the music, just as the text of *Pelléas et Mélisande* can exist independently (though in this case it preexisted the music). I read the libretto as a poem in order to experience its charm, not just to learn about the action or to find a piece of objective information. In the same way, ballet music can be played for its own sake, but it then seems to lack something, like a movie shown with its sound track off. (One could not read a Mozart libretto that way, since it is only a pretext for the music in which it is swallowed up. The Mozart libretto, separated from the score, has no aesthetic value and cannot, on the basis of its explicit meaning alone, retain the being of an aesthetic object.) On the other hand, I can also, if trained, read the score of *Tristan and Isolde*. Am I then in the presence of the opera itself? Not exactly. I am merely faced with signs which allow and regulate its performance, and these signs take on their full meaning for me only if I know how to read them correctly, that is, if I can evoke, with all their properties, the sounds which the signs invite us to produce. It will nonetheless be claimed that these signs constitute the work itself: are they not what Wagner set down? But Wagner did not set down these signs the way an artist paints a picture. The signs are there only as strict directions to the performer, who must convert them into sounds, and to the listener, who must hear them as sounds and not read them as signs. The listener may take the score to the concert and read it while listening. He is then, in fact, learning to listen while reading, and it is always the listening which remains the aim of this exercise (moreover, as we shall see, the recognition of sounds may aid perception, concentrating and orienting it). Thus listening has the last word, and its occasional evocation by reading is, at best, an ersatz listening or else a preparation for listening.

What, then, is the being of this operatic work which is pres-

ent before me in this way? What happens to it when its performance ends? The first question leads us back to our starting
point. In the reality of the event which is the performance, what
rightfully belongs to the aesthetic object? What is it at which I
aim as aesthetic object? One could, if need be, annex to this
object all aspects of the production which contribute to its
epiphany: the entire opera house, including the stage with its
actors, the maids in the dressing rooms, the stagehands in the
wings, and finally the auditorium itself with its crowd of spectators. But here a distinction already asserts itself between that
which brings about the production and that which is an integral
part of it. The electrician who controls the lights, the dressmaker
who has designed the costumes, even the director do not take part
in the production. They remain in the wings, absent from the
spectacle. We see even now that perception rules here, that it is
perception which decides what is part of the production. The
hall, for example, is a part, for it is not irrelevant that the performance unfolds in this sumptuous place where marble, gold,
and velvet look down upon the solemnity of the production,
drown out daily care, and, by an effect akin to that of incense,
prepare us for the magic of art. The spectators too are part of
the production, for it is no more irrelevant that thousands of
gazes converge and that a human intercommunication is knit
in silence. All this is as rightfully a part of the production as the
conductor's baton seen rising from the pit, for it is in the background of the perceptions directed toward the stage. However,
let us not go too far. We cannot identify the production with the
aesthetic object—or everything that may help to present the
opera and to create a favorable climate for its perception with the
opera itself. And it is perception, again, which will enable us to
discern the specifically aesthetic object. For what is marginal
does not detain it. Attention turns away from the marginal so
as not to take it too seriously. I accord it only a potential rather
than an actual existence, a neutral one in any case, unless an
incident such as a loud-talking neighbor or a power failure leads
me back into what Husserl calls a positing attitude. I did not
come to the opera house as Balzac's heroes came to the Théâtre
des Italiens; I came to hear *Tristan and Isolde*.

My eye travels to the stage where this opera is being performed. I see the performers acting and singing. But they do
not yet constitute the aesthetic object. Kirsten Flagstad, who has
such a splendid air of health, is not Isolde, the frail Isolde who
is dying of love. Small matter, for what counts is her voice, which

must be and is the voice of Isolde.[2] But how can I say that it "is" the voice of Isolde? Because there is an Isolde whom the text imposes and whom we discover through the performer's acting and singing, which inform us about this text in case we are not already familiar with it, so that the singer herself furnishes the norm for judging her: she indicates the true Isolde who is her model and judge. Moreover, in the usual aesthetic attitude, I am not concerned to judge the singers. I do not even perceive them *as* singers unless some incident—as earlier the power failure, but here awkwardness, a sour note, or nervousness, interrupting or distorting their roles—leads me to recognize and judge them as singers and to accuse them of betraying the role which they are assuming and to which I was relating through them. Ordinarily, I do not say, "Lorentz is pretending to die," but rather, "Tristan is dying." The opera singer is neutralized, perceived only in his role, not as himself. He is to the opera somewhat as a blank canvas is to a finished painting. The canvas can detract from or enhance the painting, depending on whether, for example, the sizing has been well or poorly prepared; but the canvas is still not the painting.

But then again what are Tristan and Isolde for me, and what is the status of their story, the subject of the opera? Here we must introduce a distinction: if we are talking about the story as outlined in the program, this is certainly not yet the aesthetic object either. I knew the story before watching the performance, and still everything remained to be known. The story may, moreover, have intrinsic qualities through which it more or less lends itself to an artistic treatment. In the story of *Tristan and Isolde* there are a certain aura of legend, a Homeric simplicity of narration, and a violent purity of passions that confer on the subject a dramatic and poetic character suitable for bringing out Wagner's genius. But these aesthetic properties are still only virtual in the subject of the story, and it is in the completed work that

2. It would be different in the theater, where acting is more closely connected with the voice. There the word is no longer borne by the song (in which, moreover, it is lost) but reigns supreme; the work of mimicry is devoted to bringing the word to its highest peak of presence and expression, while emphasizing all its shades of meaning. Also, the actor has to resemble the character he is embodying. But if resemblance and acting are less necessary and sometimes impossible in an opera (an aria cannot be sung if one is acting; and how can one act out an aria?), they are not any the less welcome and may help to explicate the music. The success of such a collaboration was revealed to many Parisians a few years ago by the Vienna Opera Company's performance of Mozart's *Abduction from the Seraglio.*

they are actualized. Without this actualization, the story would be merely an indifferent tale. It is therefore only the story as presented before me—and if I am careful not to lose my way in it—which can deliver to me the aesthetic object and which I follow with all my attention. And how? I indeed relate to Tristan and Isolde through the singers, but not as a dupe. I do not call a doctor when I see Tristan stretched out on his couch, and I am fully aware that he is a legendary being who is as mythical as a centaur. Besides, marginal perceptions keep reminding me that I am at the theater as a spectator. Thus Tristan and Isolde are, as Husserl says of the Knight and Death in Dürer's engraving, "merely depicted," constituting "a mere portrait." [3] That is why I accept without difficulty such unlikely things as, for example, that the dying Tristan has so much voice left for singing, that the shepherd is such a good musician, and that the actors wear costumes and indulge in conventional gestures. The meaning of the work is not affected by all this. Likewise, I readily accept a libretto's modifications of a legend if the latter is already codified, like Corneille's taking liberties with history. In short, I do not adopt the attitude of children, who want not a single word changed in the stories reread to them because they have not yet adopted the aesthetic attitude and are more interested in what is said, of which they want to lose nothing, than in the way it is said.

There is indeed a truth of the opera; it resides not in the story but in the poem and music in which the opera comes to fruition. If Isolde were not true, it would be with respect not to the story but to a truth of her own, which it is the work's mission to disclose and crystallize and which the work can state only through the music: it is against the music that Wagner would be sinning. Thus, I am a dupe neither of the real—e.g., the actors, the sets, the hall itself—nor even of the unreal—i.e., the represented object. For the represented object too is neutralized, since we do not actually posit it as unreal. [4] We could almost

3. See Edmund Husserl, *Ideen I*, § 111; English translation by W. R. Boyce Gibson, *Ideas* (New York: Humanities Press, 1931), pp. 309 ff.—Trans.

4. It is here that we part company with Sartre, whose theory we shall bring up later, and with Husserl as well. Husserl's doctrine is rather confused on this point, because, on the one hand, the unreal, which is "portraitlike," merges with the imaginary (image and portrait being reunited in the term *Bild*), and, on the other hand, the imaginary is the result of neutralization. Now it appears—and this would, moreover, accord with Husserl's general theory, which subordinates all positing modifications of belief to the more basic modification of neutrality, and which

say of this unreal, as we could say of a dream, that it is an unreality which is not completely unreal. And that is why imagination can also be participation. Although I am not led to the point of calling a doctor to attend Tristan, I am led far enough to be moved, to fear, to hope, to live with him in some sense. However, my feelings are no longer quite real, because they remain Platonic, inactive; I experience them as if I were not involved in them, and as if it were somehow not I experiencing them but, in my place, a delegate of humanity, an impersonal "I" entrusted with pale copies of emotions whose eddies fade out quickly without leaving a trace (the feelings which I experience more deeply come, as we shall see, from somewhere else, deeper within the object). Nearly everything happens as if, during the play, the real and the unreal were balancing one another, as if the neutralization were proceeding not from me but from the objects themselves. What occurs on the stage invites me to neutralize what happens in the hall and vice versa. Furthermore, even on the stage, the story as it unfolds invites me to neutralize the actors and vice versa. In brief, I do not posit the real as real, because there is also the unreal which this real designates; I do not posit the unreal as unreal, because there is also the real which promotes and supports this unreal.

We have thus sorted out the real from the unreal, but we have not yet located the aesthetic object. The latter is not the real or the unreal, because neither is self-sufficient—each refers to the other which denies it—and because both, having been in some manner disqualified through neutralization, are not grasped in themselves. Let us then return to what is happening on the stage. What I hear are neither singers nor Tristan and Isolde singing, but songs: songs and not voices, songs which music, not the orchestra, accompanies. It is this verbal and musical ensemble which I came to hear, this is what is real for me, this is what constitutes the aesthetic object. The real and the unreal between which we drew a distinction are only alternative means in the service of this object. The singer lends his voice and therewith his whole body, for the voice must be carried by the body, just as the singing is sustained and underlined by the acting, and the body in turn must be prolonged and framed by

---

consequently invites differentiating this latter modification from imagination—that, in the present instance, the unreal is given first and then undergoes neutralization, or at least that the unreal qua unreal is already neutralized without needing a neutrality-modification to become so. [See Husserl, *Ideas*, §§ 109-12, pp. 306 ff.—Trans.]

the stage set. Everything happens in accordance with the singing and conspires to exalt our hearing. Yet the actor's voice and gestures, as well as the setting in which he moves, do belong in a sense to the aesthetic object, since they too can be foreseen and regulated by the composer. But they do not belong to the aesthetic object as if they were things in the real world, as if the voice were that of Lorentz, the lighting an electrical effect, and the forest in the second act a forest of canvas and cardboard. Even if all this human or physical material has been perceived, it is immediately neutralized and excluded from the aesthetic object. This also happens in the case of the unreal: I do indeed grasp this voice as that of Isolde herself, this forest as the forest of the Cornwall ruled by King Mark, this cup as filled with a love potion. There, if you please, is the primary sense of the scene, but that is not, in fact, what interests me, what is actually communicated to me. What interests me is the *way* Isolde, love potion, and forest are communicated to me, the effects which can be drawn from that other material, the subject, what songs Isolde's story gives rise to, what cries are wrung forth by the love potion, what color harmonies make up the forest. The subject as unreal is still a means in the service of the work, this time no longer to manifest it but to give rise to it in the first place.

Therefore, what is irreplaceable, the very substance of the work, is the sensuous or perceptible element [*le sensible*] which is communicated only in its presence; it is that fullness of the music into which I strive to be absorbed, that conjunction of color, song, and orchestral accompaniment whose every nuance I strive to grasp and whose every development I strive to follow. That is why I am at the opera tonight, unlike the usherettes seating the audience, the business manager estimating the crowd and counting the receipts, the director arranging the actors and spotting their mistakes and disobediences, and the radio technician broadcasting the sound as noise. I came to open myself to the work, to be present at this sonorous unfolding supported by plastic, pictorial, and almost choreographic elements—in short, to experience an apotheosis of the sensuous. My eyes and ears have been invited to this feast, although all of me is, of course, present: my consciousness which gives and demands meaning could not be left in the theater cloakroom, and it takes part in the production. But it does so on one main condition, namely, that it employ itself from the start in preserving the purity and wholeness of the sensuous—and precisely by neutralizing things that could change it and divert it from appearing, such as the head-shakings of our neighbor, the clumsiness of an extra on the stage, or the weaving about of the conductor. The sensuous, maintained as such at the price of this vigilance, then takes on a meaning or sense [*sens*] with which consciousness can be satisfied. It is a necessary meaning, for the sensuous could not be grasped if it were pure disorder, if sounds were only noise, words only cries, actors and sets only shadows and unrecognizable blots. And this sense is immanent in the sensuous, being its very organization. The sensuous is given first and sense is regulated by it. When I read the program earlier, it was to its sense or meaning that I paid attention, especially because my reading had been guided by questions. Who was taking the part of Tristan, who designed the sets, what was the structure of the work?[5] Yet when the curtain goes up and the prelude begins, I no longer ask questions but wait: if I listen and watch, meaning will be given to me as well. Meaning disengages itself from the perceived as that through which the perceived is perceived.

What, in fact, is the meaning? It is simultaneously single and multiple. First, it is the unity of the musical phrase, leitmotiv, or variation, e.g., an oboe solo ringing out against a silent orchestra, or an ensemble of sounds as in the prelude. The appreciation of these unities, which are articulated and composed to form the totality of the work, enables me to understand the music. I no longer understand the music when I lose all sense of form and the sounds reach me in an order which is scattered into a sort of blinding dust. But the meaning of the opera is also an intelligible meaning: the unity of the set representing the action and finally, above all, the unity of the verbal phrases signifying the drama, ordering and supporting that whole which is the story of Tristan and Isolde as performed. I say "as performed" advisedly, because it is the performance [*représentation*]—the deployment of the words, of the gestures which vivify them, and of the surroundings in which they are uttered—which conveys to me what is represented [*représenté*] in the work. It is the whole train of words which gradually composes the drama, rather than the drama which chooses the words. In this sense, the represented object ceases to be unreal. It is in-

5. It is not irrelevant, in fact, that I prepared myself to perceive not only by learning about the subject and reading the libretto if need be but even by learning about the structure of the opera, for example, about the musical function and metaphysical significance of Wagner's leitmotivs. This preliminary research has no other purpose than to clear the way for my perception of the aesthetic object. We shall return to this point when describing aesthetic perception.

deed unreal with respect to the real, everyday world around me, but, insofar as it is the life of the poem, the meaning which gives unity to the words, it is not unreal. Yet it becomes once again unreal with respect to a higher form of meaning, one which unifies the previous meanings. For there is a deeper unity in the work as a whole, in which are gathered together the different facets of the sensuous being which offers itself to me—a unity in which an alliance is sealed among this phrase in the poem, that flight of song, this choreographic movement of the actors, that play of light over the color scheme of the set. Of this alliance I must be the witness, and it is not always easy to apportion my attention equally among all the solicitations of the sensuous without privileging one of its aspects or one of its meanings, neglecting the music to become interested in the story or neglecting the words to follow the orchestrally accompanied singing. Nevertheless, practically equal attention is always possible, because the object itself invites this and, more precisely, because the different aspects, poetical, musical, or plastic, have still another meaning, an expressive one which goes beyond what is purely intelligible and comes to convergence in a coalescence of sensuous elements. It is out of the affinity of these different expressions that the total expression of the work, which is its highest meaning, is constituted, and it is again perception which delivers this meaning to me.[6] For such meaning is the very face of the sensuous as turned toward me: it is present only by virtue of the sensuous, which in turn finds in this meaning its *raison d'être*. When Isolde dies with a cry of love to which the music lends preterhuman accents, when her gestures, her singing, the light, and the music which bathe her all conspire to express the exaltation of ardor and the unfathomable victory of love, when the sensuous, unleashed and yet controlled, gives vent to something which it alone has the power to say, then I directly encounter the work and I understand it. But what have I understood? Here an endless questioning concerning meaning can begin. What is the meaning of what the work has told me, not

6. This unity of expressions is doubtless possible only because there exists among the different arts, considered as means to expression, an at least possible unity whose path has been clearly pointed out by Hegel, as follows. The pictorial which issues from the sculptural by way of the bas-relief calls to music as the result of the progressive disappearance of the sculptural element in it, and the musical in turn calls to the poetic. It is through this dialectic that the undertaking of a total art, like that of Wagner, is objectively possible. But it is in the convergence of expressions and ultimately in the ruling unity of a common affective theme that we must look for the sensuous and lived unity of the work.

only more or less rationally through its words but also insistently through its music—the explosion of that miraculous passion, the exaltation of the night, the strange love-death theme? I shall refer to them during the opera's intermission or after leaving, when reflection has succeeded contemplation. But the substance of this reflection was given to me in and with the aesthetic object, yet without my becoming fully conscious of it—as if the music were transmitting to me a message to which reflection will never be equal. For what the aesthetic object tells me, it tells through its presence in the very bosom of what is perceived.

Thus I am in the presence of the aesthetic object as soon as I belong to it. I have become indifferent to the outside world, which I perceive only marginally and which I give up considering so as to experience the truth of what has been presented to me. What has been presented is the sensuous in its glory, not a sensuousness that is unorganized and meaningless but one which says itself, so to speak, through the strict logic of its development and also says something else (it does the latter both through what it represents—to the extent that it is regulated by a representation—and through what it expresses in saying itself).

We shall have to test and adjust these preliminary points by examining other aesthetic objects. To the degree that we must have recourse to the empirical, the eidetic cannot exclude all induction. But we can even now measure the distance between aesthetic object and work of art. The work of art is what is left of the aesthetic object when it is not perceived—the aesthetic object in the state of the possible, awaiting its epiphany. This may be the place to rehabilitate the empiricist formula that the work lives as a permanent possibility of sensation. However, one can just as truly say that, because the sensuous whole is organized in terms of an idea, it lives as an idea which has not been thought through and is set forth in signs, while waiting for a consciousness to come and animate it. Nevertheless, we do not have the right to speak of the work's existence as timeless. Even if its idea can claim such an existence in an intelligible heaven (because it proceeds from a rational necessity which gives it access to the eternal, as in the Spinozist philosophy), the idea immanent in the work is so deeply enmeshed in the sensuous of which it is only the armature (as the Hegelian idea is enmeshed in the world and in the history whose living logic it is) that it cannot exist independently of an exhibition of the sensuous. The idea which outlives the manifestation of the work of art, the idea which reflection is able to isolate and consign to an intelligible heaven, is no longer the idea of the work but an idea about or for the work. Such is the idea of Tristan which I am able to entertain as I write these lines. Let us say, therefore, that the work has only a virtual or abstract existence, the existence of a system of signs which are pregnant with the sensuous and make possible the impending performance. It exists on paper and on call, as it were: virtual, like the Bergsonian past, it exists in the memory of the performers who preserve the recollection of previous performances. Is that not how a ballet is perpetuated insofar as it has not yet found a way of being written down? And is it not through oral tradition that the earliest poems have been handed down? But these signs are not just ordinary ones. They are the promise of the aesthetic object, and the work does not reduce precisely to them. The work is truly communicated only when the score is performed, when the performer joins the creator. This is why the score is already as much a work of art as the libretto or any poem on paper, providing we can read, that is, hear, at least virtually, the music it calls for. That is also the way in which the plastic work exists. The painting and the statue are still only signs waiting to blossom into a performance, the performance which the spectator himself will give by lending this object his attention, by allowing it to manifest the sensuous which slumbers within it as long as no look or gaze [*regard*] comes to awaken it. What the artist has created is not yet completely the aesthetic object but only the means for that object to exist whenever the sensuous is recognized as such by the proper gaze. The object lives its own life only with the spectator's collaboration, and even the artist must turn spectator to complete his work. To someone who expressed surprise at his always sculpting in a kind of frenzy, Michelangelo replied, "I hate the stone because it comes between me and my statue." But the stone continues to keep away the statue only as long as no gaze comes to release the statue, to find it in the very contemplation of the stone.

Thus, we have set out from the work of art, which we assumed to be immediately given and identifiable, in order to rejoin the aesthetic object. Yet it is the aesthetic object which we most easily locate (although we must still clear up a number of problems, especially that of its being), while the work of art as an empirical reality in the cultural world seems to elude us the moment we question ourselves about its being. This means that work of art and aesthetic object reflect and are understood through one another. For the performance, which is the presentation of the work, is at the same time the means by which it becomes an aesthetic object; and the moment it becomes an aesthetic object, the work of art is truly a work of art. But there is another condition, independent of performance, for the advent of the aesthetic object, namely, the perception that recognizes it as such. One can fall short of the aesthetic object. I would be doing this at the opera if I paid attention only to the way the work was performed or composed, or if I were so sensitive to the charms of my female neighbor or to my own reveries that the opera became for me nothing more than a background sound, even an unwelcome gift. I am still in the presence of the work, but it would be absurd to consider the work as the correlate of an inattentive or inept perception, for, as a matter of fact, the work loses its meaning as a work as soon as we neglect or ignore the aesthetic object which it can be. If the work is to be distinguished from the aesthetic object without being disqualified, it is only in the case of an intelligent and attentive meditation of the kind which, more than merely enjoying the work, inquires into its nature. The work is then described less in terms of the spectator's contemplation than of the artist's activity and the critic's learning, i.e., as a product or as a problem. It is linked to reflection, that of the artist who judges it as he creates it and that of the spectator who wants to know whence it came, how it was created, and what effect it produces. But it is only when the spectator decides to exist wholly for the work, in accordance with a perception which is resolved to remain nothing but perception, that the object appears before him as an aesthetic object.[7] For the aesthetic object is nothing else but the work of art perceived for its own sake. The problem it raises, psychologically, is that of a faithful perception and, ontologically, that of the status of any perceived object, particularly one which asks only to be perceived. The distinction between work of art and aesthetic object could be tightly drawn only by a psychology which radically subordinates the being of the object to consciousness, making the aesthetic object a mere mental representation and the work, by contrast, a thing. But aesthetic experience, which is a form of perceptual experience, furnishes evidence that the per-

7. That which aesthetic experience brings about on the plane of perception is what would be considered absolute knowledge on the plane of logic, a knowledge which ceases to be knowledge in order to let meaning appear. But this meaning remains to be stated, whereas, on the plane of perception, meaning has already been stated by the work itself in an irreproachable and definitive manner. Perhaps there is no contemplation other than aesthetic.

ceived is not just the mentally represented, that the object is always already constituted, and, consequently, that the aesthetic object refers to the work and is inseparable from it. That is why the descriptions which follow concern the work of art and the aesthetic object at one and the same time. They bear upon the work insofar as it has its *telos* in the aesthetic object and is understood through it.[8]

We are first, however, going to inquire somewhat more closely into the two conditions which permit the aesthetic object to appear: on the one hand, the work must be fully present, implying that it needs to be performed, particularly in the case of certain arts and in a sense for all; on the other, a spectator or, better, a public must be present before it.[9]

8. The distinction which we have just drawn between work of art and aesthetic object, although governed by the phenomenological analysis of its relation to the subject and his intention, blends in many respects with the distinction which Etienne Souriau makes in his penetrating "existential analysis of the work of art" between "physical existence," in which the work has a body, and "phenomenal existence," in which it appears to the senses (*La Correspondance des arts* [Paris: Flammarion, 1947], pp. 45–72). The other two modes of existence which Souriau then discerns, "reic existence," which is that of "the world of beings and things which art sets up through the sole means of play in harmonizing sensuous qualia," and "transcendental existence," which is that of the "inexpressible content" of the work, seem to be linked with phenomenal existence, and in such a way that the study of the aesthetic object proper must proceed in terms of the three degrees of phenomenal, reic, and transcendental existence. It is precisely this road that we shall follow in studying the sensuous, the represented object, and expression—three aspects of the aesthetic object, if not three planes of existence. We shall make every effort to show that analysis must separate them but that aesthetic perception unites them in grasping "form." We can find no better recommendation for the phenomenology of the aesthetic object than this confluence with Souriau's existential analysis. And we shall have further occasion to take advantage of the latter. For the present, we acknowledge our debt to a line of thinking with which our agreement is not, one suspects, accidental.

9. "Performance," "perform," and "performer" will be used, for the most part, to translate respectively *exécution, exécuter,* and *exécutant.* While "execution," "execute," and "executant" would be literal equivalents of the French terms, we have opted for "performance" and its derivatives because of Dufrenne's stress on the perceived and presented character of the aesthetic object. As essentially perceived, the aesthetic object is destined to be presented, and thus to be "performed," before a public. While this is clearly the case in the instance of the musical and theatrical arts—which Dufrenne here tends to take as paradigmatic—it also holds true in the plastic arts, which, in being perceived aesthetically, give "performances" in the sense of offering sensuous presentations to the spectator. All aesthetic objects attain their most complete form—they are "per-formed"—in being sensuously presented to perception. Execution—i.e., production, technical making, or rendering—is a necessary but not a sufficient condition of the aesthetic object. This object is not only produced or executed; it is an object *for* aesthetic perception and is in this respect always per-

formed as well. Nevertheless, when it is imperative to do so, we shall use "execution" and even the compound form "execution-performance" in order to convey more clearly Dufrenne's distinction (made in the next chapter) between the performance of the specialist (e.g., the actor or the musician) and that of the creator (whose very execution or act of creation is a performance). Finally, we should mention that "performance" also translates *représentation,* which refers specifically to a theatrical or operatic performance.—Trans.

2 / The Work and Its Performance

THE WORK must offer itself to perception: it must be performed in order to pass, as it were, from a potential to an actual existence. At least performance [*l'exécution*] is indispensable for those arts whose works endure in the signs in which they are set down while waiting to be enacted [*jouées*]. We can indeed speak in such cases of a virtual existence, even though the work has been completed and its actual performance [*représentation*] adds nothing in principle to what its creator intended. This demand for a concretization, as Ingarden calls it, is one which we feel keenly in the literature of the theater. In reading a play, I am very conscious of a certain deficiency which I may, moreover, try to make good by imagining more or less vaguely, depending upon my familiarity with the theater, the play's staging, gestures, and intonations. This is an imaginary performance [*exécution imaginaire*] but one which gives life to the text and sometimes illuminates it. A certain word may take on meaning because it escapes like a pent-up confession, another because it is blurted out. Here a scene is made dramatic by the presence, unobtrusive or sovereign, of a mute character, there a declamatory speech calls for a certain kind of mimicry and even of costume: "How heavy are these flowing veils and vain ornaments!" [1] If the author has now and then taken care to write out instructions for stage arrangement and acting, he has done so primarily for the reader's sake, to stimulate the reader's imagination to the extent that the circulation of the text permits multiplying

1. A line from Racine's *Phèdre*, act 1, scene 3.—Trans.

the "seen" theater by the theater as read.² But the fact is that this effort of imagination which I exert impairs the spontaneity of my perception of the words and therefore serves judgment rather than perception. In performing the piece with my own resources, I seek primarily to understand, discover, or comment on its meaning. The nature of this reading now becomes clear. Since the work lacks the sensuous presence through which it can become an aesthetic object, reading retains of it only what exercises thought, namely, its structure and signification. Although I yield to its enchantment in the theater, in reading I remain detached, bringing my intelligence to bear upon the text. And in this we no doubt derive a great deal from the work and already pay it respect, the only kind which unsuccessful plays can expect—those, for example, which simply fail to come across the footlights or those in which a "message" prevails. In short, if I do not adopt the aesthetic attitude—in the sense to be described later—it is because I do not confront the work itself, the work which has reached the point where the aesthetic object is disclosable.³ This disclosure is made possible by the performance. Without trying too quickly to specify the change in the ontological status of the work to which performance gives rise, let us see how performance is demanded by certain arts which this demand suffices to distinguish from others.

[I] THE ARTS IN WHICH THE PERFORMER IS NOT THE CREATOR

THE ARTS which call most clearly for a performance are those in which performance is a step completely separate

2. In the plays of George Bernard Shaw or of Saroyan, there is more "nebentext" than text. There is generally more of such commentary in modern than in classic works. This may be because, as in Shakespeare's case, earlier theater, still quite close to its popular origins in the Commedia dell'Arte, cared little about being in print, relying for its performance on a mixture of traditions and improvisations. Or it may be due, as in the case of the French classicists, to a kind of contempt for commentary.

3. We must, perhaps, make an exception for the play which is poetic in its own right, whose reading, like that of a poem, suffices for its performance (somewhat like an oratorio, which calls for singing, not acting). This is the case in *Cantate à trois voix;* and one whole portion of Claudelian theater is perhaps located in an extension of this work. That is why the lyricism of *Partage du Midi,* so beautiful in the reading, seemed to me so hollow and tedious in performance. When a work which is not really for the theater is performed, its performance betrays rather than fulfills it.

from creation. It is true, however, that we sometimes give the name of "creation" to the first performance of a play, in which the performer [*l'exécutant*], though distinct from the creator, [*l'auteur*], may claim the title of artist. The difference between performance and creation is unquestionably greatest in the relation of architect to builder and least in that of choreographer to dancer; for ballet is unquestionably the art which exists least independently of a performer, inasmuch as it does not have a well-defined sign system at its disposal and demands a performance of quality more urgently than the other arts.[4] Let us leave the case of architecture aside. If the actor, instrumentalist, and dancer like to call themselves artists, it is because they are aware of being indispensable to the work. But in what way are they indispensable?

Just as, for Hegel, the idea passes through nature, so here the aesthetic object passes through man. Man becomes its substance or matter [*matière*], a precious matter, more ductile and yet more refractory than ordinary matter, disappearing each time man ceases to be an actor. If the matter of the work is the sensuous, then the sensuous must either be produced by man, as sounds are by the musician, or be found in man's body itself, insofar as it is offered for our viewing, as in the gestures of the dancer and the actor. What, then, is the status of the performer? As the will of the slave, according to Aristotle, resides in his master, so the performer's will is in the work: he is possessed, alienated, submissive to a foreign intention. We know how Sartre has developed Diderot's famous paradox by showing how the actor, caught up by the unreal, becomes unreal in the character he incarnates.[5] For the actor, it is not a question of performing certain gestures on command, of obeying a set of rules. The text is not a schema for assembling gestures or words but must be given life, made to live in itself: the actor who creates a role through the life which he breathes into the work is justified in calling himself an artist. If we wish to revert to Hegelian

4. The building foreman may, moreover, have under him, in addition to artisans from different trades, actual artists as well: sculptors, painters, landscapists, and even poets, as in the case of Valéry at the Palais de Chaillot. The stage director, too, may call upon painters or musicians. But we are then dealing with collaboration in a *Gesamtkunstwerk*, in which artists are not reduced to the role of performers.

5. That is why the actor is always improvising. All his rehearsals serve only to prepare him for improvising in a real performance—which is not an easy matter. [See Jean-Paul Sartre, *The Psychology of Imagination*, trans. B. Frechtman (New York: Washington Square Press, 1966), chap. 2 and Conclusion.—Trans.]

language, we may say that the idea contained in the work asks for more than mere translation. In order to become truly an idea, it must be lived. An idea which remains in the limbo of interiority, giving no proof of itself, is not fully an idea. Thus, thanks to the performer, it is through man that the work is present before me and speaks to me—through man, the meaningful object *par excellence*. To be sure, meaning derives from words which the actor utters or from sounds which the virtuoso produces. But words assume their full meaning only when uttered; language is thereby restored to its true purpose, that of being spoken. For the meaning of the word is not separable from all the bodily components which are added to it, such as accent, intonation, and mimicry. What Husserl calls qualities of manifestation manifest not only psychological content but meaning as well. Or rather, this meaning is bound up with the psychological content: what we say is inseparable from what we mean and from the way we say it. That is why a poem can be fully appreciated only when recited and not read silently; this is even more the case with a play. It is through the voice that language again becomes a human event and that the sign assumes its true office. And the same holds for musical sounds: the violin throbs only if the performer himself does, the instrument being to the performer what the throat is to the singer, namely, an extension of his body. Thus it is still in the human body that the music becomes incarnate, but in a body disciplined by the instrument, obliged to submit to long training in order to become the instrument of an instrument. We see this still better in the case of the orchestra conductor who, like the stage director or the choreographer, is the necessary mediator between the work and the performer. He directs and supervises the performance, for the work finds its unity in him because it unfolds within him as if it dwelled inside his body and because he renders it visible by his very pantomime, however restrained his gestures may be at times. This process is similar to the way in which a dancer realizes a ballet in himself. Even more than music, the dance, being conveyed through man, is a meaningful language.

But for a better understanding of what performance brings to the work, we must realize that the work should be congenial to the performer whom it solicits. Whatever charm it has is measured by the felicity with which it is performed. It is the best of signs when the director considers a play workable, each scene appearing to take immediate shape in a stage situation, each cue in a posture, the whole piece obedient to a certain logic of the body. But it is in music that this corporeal logic best gives us the measure of art: the happier the musician is in playing the work, the happier the result. Even the composer is often "carried away" in his bodily movement while improvising on the piano. We are speaking, of course, of a trained body to which long practice has given full scope to spontaneity, so that its participation guarantees the naturalness of the work. To be sure, the work must also be premeditated and controlled—but only on condition that the effort be concealed beneath the ease of the sensuous, that its mathematics become graceful, that its order be in the service of a spontaneity. We measure by these criteria the difference between a Bach fugue and some of the works of the twelve-tone school, and we realize why music is first of all melodic. When a melody of Debussy's is interrupted, it is by another melody and not by some abstract pattern. We may say that the ear is pleased by what pleases the performer's fingers. And if a dancer were bored in dancing, that is, if his body did not open up possibilities which, however extreme, were nevertheless his, where would the dance in it be? This is why the pitfall of the *pas de deux* and solo lies in their transitions: dead intervals and a purely abstract logic must not be intercalated between any two of their positions, each of which, for a second, nimbly represents necessity. Instead, repose must be a loosening and preparation, a going forward—just as harmonic modulations in classical music are still part of the melody, or as entrances and exits in the theater are still motion and drama.

Thus the performance manifests the quality of the work or at least that master quality, the free play of the sensuous which the performer exhibits. But this is enough to establish the responsibility of the performer. If he reveals the work, he must be faithful to it. But faithful to what? Here we stumble on the problem of the status of the work of art, a problem which precedes a consideration of the work's performance. For the spectator or critic, even for the interpreter, this problem finds a circular expression. When we abandon the aesthetic attitude in order to appraise the interpretation of a work, we judge the interpretation in terms of the work—but only because we know the work from its interpretations. Nevertheless, we do have to grant a *truth* of the work which is independent of its performance or anterior to it. It is less a question here of knowing what the work of art is before its performance than of knowing whether the performance meets the demands of that work—which, as a matter of fact, wants to be performed in order to offer itself as an aesthetic object. That is why we speak of truth, not reality. The reality of the work consists in what it is, regardless of whether it is performed or not. Its truth is what it aspires to be and what it becomes precisely through its performance, namely, the aesthetic object, that object to which we implicitly refer in order to discuss the work and also in order to appraise its performance. The performance reveals the being of the work by completing it, and we have only an inadequate idea of the work so long as we have not attended its performance or at the very least imagined it. But through the performance, we aim at the truth of the work. It is this truth which guides our judgment of subsequent performances or even of the present one. Still, where do we obtain the truth of the work, if not from the performance? It is so necessary that this truth appear that the performance sometimes guides, if not alters, our judgment by imposing too exclusive an image of the aesthetic object. Thus *The Dying Swan* is connected in many memories with Pavlova, *Petrouchka* with Nijinsky, *Doctor Knock* with Jouvet, and *Ondine* with Madeleine Ozeray: embodiments too perfect, as it were, seeming to pass sentence on all the others. But there is a danger here only if such interpretation imposes itself not by its fidelity but because it is recommended by a tradition which has never been challenged. It may then mask the face of the work and distort our judgment. (Even more seriously, it can sometimes influence aesthetic creation to the extent that the latter anticipates the performance and is ruled by it. Lifar had to loosen up too narrow a conception of classical dance without breaking with tradition, just as Wagner and even Berlioz had to give the orchestra a new breadth, and as Debussy had to give back to the piano its eight octaves and to the pianist a new familiarity with his instrument.) But, setting aside these exceptional cases, can we not say that the performance always invents, so to speak, the truth of the work? Performance is interpretation: that is, its truth is not fixed beforehand and several interpretations of the same work are possible, with the result that it changes meaning with the times.

But we must not slide too far down the slope of this aesthetic relativism. Our understanding of a work is undeniably bound up with its performances, which are themselves linked to a particular historical taste. Molière's plays are perhaps not staged as they were by Molière himself or understood or relished as in Molière's day.[6] This point, moreover, goes beyond the problem of per-

6. "The stage directions which we can attribute with certainty to Molière are very few and all are dictated by the action," writes Dullin

formance, and we shall have occasion to return to it. There is a life of the work through history, a life which depends upon the historicity of the aesthetic culture. Each epoch privileges certain aesthetic objects to the detriment of others which it sometimes completely ignores. The work waxes or wanes, is enriched or impoverished, according to the warmth of our devotion to it and the meaning we discover in it. These avatars are closely related to the vicissitudes of the performed work's actual performance, whether as causes or as effects. And we shall have to say of them what we must now say about the historicity of interpretations: within history itself, there appears, or tends to be realized, something which surpasses history and does not have its truth in history. Furthermore, history is illuminated only by the light of these fixed stars. If everything were caught up in the swirl of history, there would be no history at all. Thus the different traditions of performance constitute a history which tends to reveal the truth of the work through multiple trials and errors. But this is possible only because there is already a truth of the work which needs performance in order to appear but at the same time judges this performance.

In order to appraise the quality of a performance, we may indeed refer to the intentions of the work's creator. Music critics do so at times, without being the dupes of what is equivocal in this reference itself. If, for example, they denounce the emphatic and vulgar interpretation of a recording of Fauré's *Requiem* in the name of what is religious in Fauré, they are well aware that Fauré held the post of organist at the church of St. Francis Xavier for twenty years without practicing religion. What is religious in Fauré is found in his work, not in his private life. How do we know this, if not upon hearing this work? And we shall see that the aesthetic experience extends from the work to its creator.[7] Moreover, it can happen that, without previously

---

(*L'Avare,* ed. Charles Dullin [Paris: Editions du Seuil, 1946], p. 11). He also shows how staging was encumbered with traditions which today are obsolete and meaningless and how, even in the interpretation of a leading character like Harpagon, tradition was made and unmade according to the taste of each epoch, as iconography attests in the absence of more precise information.

7. Nevertheless, it is important for the performer to know what the creator thought of his own work and what he intended for it. It is not unimportant to the actor who wants to play Racine to seek out that "natural declamation" which Racine taught so painstakingly to Baron and La Champmeslé, or for the person who wants to play Shakespeare to find out how Elizabethan scenery was arranged and what Shakespeare thought of the fools' nonsense in *Hamlet.* We are not suggesting the abandonment of machinery or electricity in order to restore the performances of the

knowing the work or anything about its creator, we still pronounce an unfavorable judgment on its performance. Is this not because the performance, as it reveals the work, denounces itself? It is further to be noted that we are more sensitive to the defects than to the virtues of a performance. A good performance fades away in the presence of the work, being and appearance coincide, and we wholly attain the aesthetic object. What distracts us are its defects. Something seems to ring false and a lack of harmony becomes evident, the responsibility for which must clearly be borne by the performance. If the tempo of the andante is too fast, the actor's delivery too slow, the décor too brash, or the *entrechat* too heavy, the spell is broken and we take the performer to task—or the work does, for it is the work which has been betrayed.

Thus is the circle closed: the work is completed by its performance, but at the same time it judges the performance in which it is completed. The demand which is being realized—if the work has the being of a demand to begin with—remains a demand with regard to the performance. In other words, the concrete existence which the work achieves is a normative existence: its reality must reveal a truth which makes itself known within this reality. The historicity of its performances does not completely relativize the work's truth. This historicity does not weaken any of that demand which is in the work and which always gives rise to new performances. Since appearance, though necessary to being, is nevertheless not identical with it, a number of different performances of the same work or, from the viewpoint of the public, several interpretations of the same performed work, can all be valid. Henri Gouhier says of the masterpiece: "Each re-creation causes a new image to spring up, so that it [the masterpiece] is endlessly new without ceasing to be the same . . . [it is] complete in each of these images." [8] This is why we cannot assign to history the task of gradually deciphering and revealing a work. Laurence Olivier's *Hamlet* is no truer than that of Jean-Louis Barrault. Nor is it only Hamlet the man, as Shakespeare has him speak, who is inexhaustible in the ambiguity and incompleteness of each of his gestures and words. It is the work itself as a totality—Beethoven's Ninth Symphony or a Braque

Hôtel de Bourgogne or the Globe. We must do for the production what Ravel did for Rameau, that is, recover a certain spirit by new means. And, after all, the return to the creator is not an absolute guarantee. He may himself be mistaken about his work, and, even for the performer, the work must judge its creator.

8. Henri Gouhier, *L'Essence du théâtre* (Paris: Plon, 1943), p. 73.

still life, as well as *Hamlet*—which is inexhaustible because of what we shall refer to as its depth. The work is irreducible to its performances and yet graspable only through them or, rather, in them. We may say that *the* truth of the work consists in being *a* truth. If, instead of being perceiving spectators, we were, as Jaspers puts it, "consciousness in general," able to survey history and all the work's historical truths, there would no longer be any truth at all—the being of the work would have reabsorbed its appearance, and the work would be an eternal truth instead of an aesthetic object.

Thus the work is an infinite demand which wants a finite realization and which is realized each time the work is present for us with sufficient clarity and rigor, without false notes, and whenever everything invites our perception to honor the aesthetic object in it. The truth of the work which we then possess is really the truth which the work imposes and which imposes itself upon us.

If this transcendence has a meaning, it exists first of all for the performer; and yet he performs the work only by imagining a work already performed and reads its text only by imagining it as realized. In any event, he has to perform it in reality. For him, the truth of the work is not something given but a task. And the chief virtue which the work requires of the performer is submissiveness. Great directors and conductors are unanimous on this point.[9] This submissiveness is difficult to achieve and has degrees. It is difficult for several reasons, relating both to the work and to the performer. First, the qualities of virtuosity and intelligence required of a performer are such that he cannot help being conscious of his own importance. Second, his contribution may be not only that of a performer but also that of an artist. Such is the case of the painter who designs the scenery for Claudel's *Christophe Colomb*, the composer who writes the music for one of its scenes, and the set designer who designs a backdrop for it.[10] Last, the work, as it issues from the hands of its creator, does in fact allow the performer considerable initiative. The performance

9. See the four converging testimonials by Georges Pitoëff, Charles Dullin, Louis Jouvet, and Gaston Baty at the beginning of Gouhier's book.

10. The performer is, in such cases, an artist—a title not merited by the stagehand but already claimed by the actor. Yet he remains a performer in the service of the work, even though within that work he is a creator. This raises a new problem which we are reserving for later discussion, namely, the problem of the work when it involves the collaboration of different arts and of the necessity of introducing a hierarchy into these diverse art forms, thereby subordinating them under a "masterwork."

must be invented; it is a creation. Thus the performer is tempted to consider himself instead of the work as his goal. And this is the source not only of certain errors of interpretation—which are appealing and worthy of respect when they stem more from excess of zeal than presumption, as when Baty fails to fit into the role of Bérénice or Jouvet into that of Tartuffe, but which are less appealing when they proceed from incomprehension or awkwardness—but also of what Gouhier calls "heresies," of which he gives a great many examples. (Among such heresies are those of the collaborator who does not want to submit to a discipline, for example, the librettist who would like to throw off the yoke of the music or the musician who would like to overshadow the play. There are also the heresies of the performer who takes too much liberty with the work, either to win acceptance for his interpretation or to get into the limelight. Sarah Bernhardt played *Phèdre* but was superior in the plays of Victorien Sardou, because her genius shone in saving a mediocre text rather than in serving an inspired one.)

With regard to this point but without developing it, we would like to introduce a distinction between the stage actor and the screen actor. The glamour of the screen star is well known, as is the fact that the public is drawn to the cinema more by the star than by the film. This is a phenomenon against which the Soviet cinema reacted in the past and the Italian cinema more recently; and it is noteworthy that the greatest films are known by the director's rather than the actor's name. The actor is in this way relegated to his role of performer, and the creator is . . . well, who is he? Is he the scenario writer, the director, or the editor? The question does not arise when these three jobs are held by the same person. But when it does arise, it must be settled in favor of the director, because, in the art of the screen, presentation is essential, since there is no *re*-presentation (as in stage performances) but only, at each showing, a mechanically obtained reproduction. The performance has all the more value in that it takes place just once, and the director who presides over it assumes a corresponding importance. Moreover, since the work has only a screen on which to be displayed, it impresses itself much more forcefully upon our vision, its appearance being inscribed more exclusively within the visual. The expressive values belonging to what is seen are more intense in it, because on the screen nothing is familiar and everything questions us, speaking to us as it questions. On the screen a vase on a table can have the mystery and eloquence of a vase painted by Cézanne, qualities which it lacks on the stage. (This is why the cinema is justified in drawing inspiration from painting, discovering there not only local color but properly pictorial values as well, as can be seen in the film *La Kermesse héroïque.*) Consequently, the action which the work depicts must be conceived in terms of images and movement and must unfold in a much more rapid rhythm than in the theater: *No Exit* is inconceivable on the screen. More generally, the best play, transferred to the screen without precautions, without regard to the laws of this medium, will result in a film which is either lifeless or of value only as a documentary—as a means of reproduction and not as a work of art. In the cinema, the text is only a pretext: the true creator is the director.[11] This promotion of the director in turn benefits the actor. The actor does more than recite a text. He bespeaks himself in order to be seen through and through. He has no room in which to step back from his role and so he finally has only one role, namely, himself—a role which, if we are to believe the new hagiography, he still plays in everyday life. On the screen, the hallucinatory character of his presence, all the more compelling for being fictive, makes him more wondrous. He is far off like a mirage, yet luring like an enchanter. (Adding to this effect are matters extrinsic to the work. The cult of the actor answers to a certain compensatory need, to the desire to live glamorously by proxy. The artist's hypertrophied ego answers to the atrophied ego of his admirer.)

The difference in status between the stage actor and the screen actor would therefore invite us to discern degrees in the independence of the performer, if not in the submissiveness which is required of him. In a word, we would have to distinguish between the performer who does nothing but perform and those who are associated with the performance in creating a work which must be integrated into and subordinated to the whole but is nonetheless a work of art in itself, capable of being exhibited alone. We shall save for later this problem concerning the collaboration of the arts. In addition, among performers [*exécutants*] properly so called—whose art is, with all due respect, still a

---

11. This raises a question: when we want to adapt a novel or a drama for the screen, is not the author of the text truly the creator, compared with whom the creator of the film is only a performer, in the same class as the stage director? No, unless the film has basically failed. But if, in fact, the work has been correctly adapted, it is a new work, which the director can claim to have fathered. Even if he is indebted to the literary work, he is creating a new work with new means. There is kinship, not subordination, between the two.

technique—we would have to discern how closely they are associated with the work and its prestige-value. At one extreme, there is the contractor or mason who executes the architect's plans. At the other extreme (which is a little beyond the screen actor), we have the dancer, who is often his own choreographer and who, in any case, is all the more indispensable to a work that has no signs in which to be preserved and that hardly exists except in the state of a project or tradition until the dancer gives it an unrivalled fullness. His triumphant body is the most beautiful of sensuous materials. But what can we say of the arts in which the sensuous seems in no way to require a performance?

[II] THE ARTS IN WHICH THE PERFORMER IS THE CREATOR

IN TRUTH, all the arts require a performance: the painter executes or "performs" a portrait, the sculptor a bust. Here creation *is* performance, whereas in the arts in which the performance is separate, performance is not considered the creative act. We do not say that the playwright performs a play or the composer a sonata. Nevertheless, in the arts in which the performance is entrusted to specialists, the creator, in order to bring forth or to control his creation, may himself shoulder the burden of performance. Aeschylus, Molière, and Shakespeare appear on the stage. Racine composes *Mithridate* while reciting with such passion that prying persons become concerned about his health. The musician composes at the piano or turns conductor. The architect sometimes becomes a contractor. For nothing can replace the teachings of concrete experience, and performance is for the creator both the best source of inspiration and the most effective means of supervision. But when performance coincides with creation, can we still call it "performance" [*exécution*]?

This matter could draw us very deeply into a psychology of creation, which is not our subject. We shall consider it here only in order to arrive at an understanding of how the work is always given in perception, and we shall do so by comparing the two kinds of performance. When performance is separate from creation and appears as creation's consummation, something exists prior to the performance and imposes a law upon it. In other words, the work exists beforehand, possessed of an abstract existence and, although without a perceptible body, sufficiently real and exacting to command its performance. But when the painter executes his canvas, what exists prior to this execution? Let us note that this question arises in all of the arts, even in those in which the performance of the work is deferred. When does the work begin to exist before blossoming into something perceptible? Here we again come on the notion of an imaginary aesthetic object, which we have ruled out of our inquiry. For, if the work exists before its creative execution or performance, it does so only for the artist and in the form of an image. Does this mean that the artist sees his work beforehand as I see Peter in image form in his photo, or as the dreamer sees figures in his dreams? No, for the execution-performance would then have quite another aspect, knowing neither second thoughts nor hesitations. The creator does not see, he feels. What he feels is a certitude, the assurance of not being unequal to a task and of being bound to a particular path marked out by his previous works. But he also feels a desire which answers to a call: something wants to come into being, something on which he has reflected for a long time as a craftsman. These terms are untranslatable for the layman, both because of their reference to something personal and because of their technical character. It is with himself that the artist debates as he thinks out his colors, harmonies, or characters. What this act of meditation, which is like the labor of childbirth, strives to fix and deliver is something which wants to *be*. The work which the artist bears within him is, on this plane, already a demand. But it is only a demand, one entirely inside the creator. It is nothing he can see or imitate. In preparing himself for the execution-performance, the artist puts himself into a state of grace, and the demand which induces it is the expression of an inner logic—the logic of a certain technical development, of a peculiarly aesthetic searching, and of a spiritual maturation. All this comes together in the artist, who is precisely that individual in whom it all merges. More deeply than other men, he creates himself by creating and he creates because he creates himself.

Let us pause here for a moment to ask ourselves whether this logic is really one of personal development. The objection will no doubt be raised that the artist as a man is often unequal, if not even markedly inferior, to his work, so much so that on meeting him we are surprised that he has created it. It seems that the creator whose act we describe is really the phenomenological creator who appears to the public only through his work. But can we not say that the actual creator harbors, sometimes without knowing it, this phenomenological creator who is equal to his work, so that not only the demand for the work but its creation as well are effected *within* the actual creator and in spite of him? What we sometimes say about the unconscious character of artistic creation would find its meaning here. To be sure, the unconscious is not a creator, and the artist who is creating knows that he is creating, for he brings to bear on his creation all the experience gained from the conscious and voluntary work through which he has acquired his craft, taste, and awareness of aesthetic problems—in brief, the instruments of creation. But, after that, by a ruse of the aesthetic reason, everything happens as if art created itself or mirrored itself in the artist. (From the moment artists became aware of this ruse, they have refused to consider themselves artisans and have felt themselves at times possessed or accursed. But they have not always been aware of the ruse and, above all, they have not always been aware of their unawareness.) This is why the real creator does not necessarily resemble his work. He is a body which, originally indifferent, can become a skillful instrument of the demon who inhabits him and who is alone capable of that spiritual maturation which makes invention possible. His works proceed from him, but they point to that within him which is not himself. Before they have been created, the demand that they exist is a demand which does not come from him. Thus it may be that the artist hears a call without knowing whence it comes: *interior intimo meo.*[12]

But this provides even clearer evidence that at this stage the work is purely a demand and needs the artist as its instrument. If its origin is unlocatable, its content is also indeterminate and does not inhere in transparent images. Everything remains to be done, and the performance is indeed creation. That is why performance here has the character which Alain described so well and is in no way comparable to performance by a specialist. The demand is met, and the desire which acknowledges it is satisfied, only by passing from the unreal to the real. This is a transition, not from an abstract to a concrete existence, but from nonexistence to existence, and it proceeds by way of a creation which, when completed, gives the work concrete existence at a

---

12. We see how the analysis of aesthetic creation, in trying to discover how art uses the artist in order to come into being, could link with a question, raised by Heidegger, which is that of every ontology. How is Being revealed through man, *Sein* by Dasein? And, flowing from that, what is man? We shall rediscover this problem in our analysis of aesthetic experience when we ask what art reveals, for, if art inspires and gives rise to the spectator as well as to the artist, is it not in the service of Being as its very manifestation?

single stroke. That is why, in its act, creation can rely only on itself or, rather, its own product, namely, the work as it takes shape and enters into existence. The meditation through which the artist gathers his forces and wrestles with a certain call (a meditation perhaps absent in the unaware artist, the one in whom the demand arises without his understanding it) is followed by the labor of creation, unless it be contemporaneous with it. It is only through this meditation that the labor escapes being called that of a mere artisan.

Let us express ourselves in another way. For the creator there is surely a reality in the project, if we take "project" to mean either the general plan or the outline. There is a thought which presides at the creation and precedes it. But is this thought concerning the work to be created equivalent to the thought which inheres in the work once it is created? If the "to be" indicates a task and the thought is a program of labor, the project cannot yet give us the key to the work, since it tells us only how the creative operation is conceived by its author. Nevertheless, this program must hold a promise. It is geared to the realization of a certain "idea" which is, in fact, the work demanding its realization. But what does this idea mean, and what is its status? What it implies—and Valéry has perhaps not taken sufficient account of this—is that for the artist himself there is indeed an in-itself of the work, a being which he must promote, a truth which he must serve and reveal. When he is said to be inspired—sometimes to the point of possession—he doubtless has the feeling of being forced to serve the work through a labor whose end he cannot foresee. It appears to him that it is not he who wills the work, but the work which wills itself in him and which has chosen him (perhaps in spite of him) as a means by which to incarnate itself. Thus the inspired artist's project is only the work's will expressing itself through him.[13] In this sense, the work possesses a being-for-the-artist, a being which is anterior to his act. But we must add at once that this being, which is inaccessible to us, is also inaccessible to him, so that he can no longer

13. Let it be clearly understood that we are not trying to introduce a myth about the work to be created. What drives the artist is his own genius, that is, a certain need to express himself, to give stability to a vision of his own world, as we shall see further on. Of course, there is the question of why he chooses to express himself thus rather than in some other way, for example, in speech, in action, or simply in silence. But, in any case, the call of the work is at the same time a call of self to self that is translated into a demand for creation. What the artist must create is a work which is truly *his*. But he is perhaps not aware that he can learn this only by creating it.

arrange for our access to it. Before he has created it, the work makes itself known to him only as a demand, not as an idea which he can think. All that he thinks are his projects, and these, if serious, immediately assume outline form. What happens is not that the idea matures within him, but that attempts multiply and a real work begins to burgeon. While he works, laying out his designs, preparing his sketches, reworking his preliminary forms, he is in no position to measure what he is doing against the idea that he first formed of the work. He simply judges what he is doing, reacting to any disappointment which he feels (and especially to a certain call to which he keeps listening) by thinking "That's still not it," and then he reapplies himself to the work. But what the "it" is, he does not know, nor will he know until the work, finally completed, relases him from further effort. Moreover, he may always have the impression that he is not entirely released, that he is stopping only through weariness or inability, without having carried out his mandate. The works he has created will then appear to him only as halting places on the way to the work which remains to be created and which he has not created because he has not come to know it. His only chance of getting to know it is to discover it by creating it. His only resource is the act of making, for which seeing is one reward.[14]

14. One sees how this analysis could be reconciled with the Bergsonian theory of the dynamic schema. But a psychology of artistic creation would still have to justify the idea of inspiration as an indeterminate call by showing what is special about aesthetic invention. What is common to all invention is its accidental character. It is a historical event and, as such, strictly unforeseeable, as Tarde has realized. But purely technical inventions, relating to ordinary objects, counterbalance this contingent aspect by a peculiar logic immanent in their appearance and diffusion, first in that they answer to a certain need created within the milieu (even though this need is not determining and sometimes arises only as a consequence of invention), and second in that they imply a certain technical level which allows them to mature before being born. In a way, each new invention is prefigured in the preceding one. In fact, except for some great discoveries which are sudden mutations even if not suddenly adopted, the technical world changes more often than not through an accumulation of interdependent details, without the inventor's personality being a decisive element in this progress. The same cannot be said of artistic invention. Symbolism was not prefigured in the Parnassians, nor Fauvism in impressionism, in the way that the jet airplane was in the propeller airplane. If there is a logic in aesthetic development, it can be grasped only after the fact. What the artist experiences when he measures himself against tradition—and indeed this is most often only after the event, as if to justify himself—is not the desire to prolong and complete but to create something different. In short, he knows the work only when he has created it. Until then, he knows only that something new wills itself within him and that, because it is new, he must first create it.

This is why the artist is an artist only through his act. He does not think the idea of the work but rather about what he is making and what he perceives as he creates. It is always with what is perceived that he deals, and the in-itself of the work exists for him only by being identified with what is perceived. He knows what he has intended only when, following creation, he perceives it and judges it to be definitive—that is, when he is at last in the position of the spectator. It is therefore useless to try to look for the truth of the work in the way in which the artist conceives it. Nevertheless, when we have had occasion to examine uncompleted works by an artist, as in the case of certain Rembrandt etchings, the rejected scores of a composer, or the rough drafts of a poet, we are tempted to say, seeing how the work has been created, "This is what the artist intended." But we are then retrospectively conceiving an idea of the work, an idea which we imagine was present at the act of creation and inspired it. For the artist, however, inspiration is merely an indeterminate call which becomes more definite only through repeated attempts and through the awareness of their inadequacy.

This labor, which goes from the first groping to the finished work through a sequence of accidents, retouchings, and renewals, cannot be likened to that of the actor and the instrumentalist. They too hesitate, feel their way, progress through repetitions. They too strain, but only in order to realize a model, not to create something out of nothing. On the other hand, even if the performance is different in the two cases, the results are comparable. If the artist does without the specialist, it is because he takes the place of one. What the mason with his trowel does for the building in keeping with the architect's directives, the painter with his brushes does for the painting. In creating the work, he raises it by the same act to a complete and definitive existence. It needs no more than a look to become an aesthetic object. There is no system of signs here which would enable the work to await a performance. The sensuous is produced once and for all, fixed on canvas, as the painter says, or petrified in stone. In all cases, the sensuous is the very substance of the work. Just as a painting is made up of colors and music of sounds, so is poetry or drama constructed of words which must be uttered or the dance of movements which must be carried out. Yet here the sensuous is not caught and elaborated by means of signs but must be immediately and directly treated. The responsibility for treating it cannot be entrusted to anyone but the creator and for two reasons: (1) because one cannot imagine it precisely enough to give directives before having executed it; and (2) because these directives can never be so precise as to dissociate execution from creation.[15]

The characteristics of execution or performance mark the work. What is required of the performer who carries out the work is required of the creator who executes it in creating it. Here again the sensuous passes through man and displays itself as fully sensuous only if it is created with felicity—as much as the pianist or dancer, the painter must be a virtuoso. The body always joins in, as Valéry has shown in the case of architecture, not only in lending the skill and sureness of its powers but also in communicating to the work, through a kind of connivance, the depth which is in it. That *interior* from which the call of the work emanates now finds its analogue in bodily inspiration. As the idea wells up from a spiritual depth, so the means for its execution spring from a vital depth. The grace of the stroke of a brush or a hammer imparts to the sensuous a charm without which there is simply no aesthetic object. As a dance perishes in an ungainly or tired dancer, so does music that drags and drawing that is hesitant and unsure of itself. The effort may be arduous, but the performance must have a quick and obedient organ at its disposal. In short, the artist must possess craftsmanship. Whatever the delays and retouchings, his gesture must be assured and free.

AND SINCE there is something comparable, at least as to their results, in the two kinds of performance, that of the specialist and that of the creator, we are justified in examining the first kind in order to learn about the second. For the aesthetic object, it is always a question of revealing itself. Therefore, for the work of art, it is a matter of passing into a concrete existence where appearance is equivalent to being. However, the passage is more abrupt in the second kind of performance, that of the creator: existence in idea is not yet *an* existence, and the performance is a creation *ex nihilo*. In the case of the specialist, the passage is effected entirely within existence—a passage which,

15. Thus can one reply, in passing, to the objection raised by work done by studio assistants. When Rubens has one of his pupils execute a corner of a painting—an animal in Paradise or an angel in an Assumption —it must be said that: (1) the canvas has already largely been executed by the master: everything is in place, the composition is everywhere assured, and the rhythmic patterns are established; and (2) the pupil has been so shaped by the master that he adopts his manner without difficulty and is basically already a master, as in the case of da Vinci working with Verrochio.

as such, is difficult to describe. It is not exactly from the possible to the real, because the work as reduced to a body of signs has already been completed. If the possible means only the precarious and indefinable state of what does not yet exist and is waiting to exist, we must point out that the creator has already chosen from among all the candidates for existence and left the others in nothingness. He makes this choice through an act which has perhaps not even taken note of alternatives and in any case is such that, after it, the possible cannot be evoked without our becoming subject to the Bergsonian critique and indulging in a retrospective illusion. Neither is the passage one from the unreal, since the work is already real before its performance and in any event cannot be called unreal if we identify the unreal with the imaginary. Nor is it a passage from absence to presence, for it is not an absent work that I have before me when I read a text. Something of the work is present to me, and the terms "absence" and "presence" designate my attitude toward the work rather than its nature. We have therefore preferred to speak of this passage as one which proceeds from a demand to its fulfillment, for the project by itself has body and being only through what forms it. The written work, by contrast, is already formed and only awaits its metamorphosis, which it imposes upon the performer. The same text awaits both the reader and the actor, and the public performance is only a refined reading which spares the spectator the trouble of reading it himself. What the public performance contributes, then, is the revelation of the work in terms of the two kinds of the sensuous, namely, the visual and the auditory. The passage is from the abstract to the concrete—if we can agree to apply the term "abstract" to the existence of signs whose reading is a means, not an end, and which above all call intelligence into play, and the term "concrete" to the existence in which these signs find a perceptible expression, in which the note on the stave becomes sound or the word on paper becomes the word uttered (it is the same word, but it changes in function by changing in appearance; thus its very meaning changes, if not in content, at least in eloquence).[16] We must, then, admit degrees of

16. Ingarden, in a work to which we shall return, uses the term *Konkretisation* for what we have called "performance." He even includes in this concretization the cooperation which the reader or the public accords the literary work. We shall develop this point in the next chapter. [See Roman Ingarden, *Das literarische Kunstwerk* (Tübingen: Niemeyer, 1965); English translation by George G. Grabowicz, *The Literary Work of Art* (Evanston, Ill.: Northwestern University Press, 1973), §§ 61–64.— Trans.]

existence from the abstract to the concrete: what alters is not the content of the work as analysis can apprehend it but the fullness of its being. The change does not reside in a movement from the unreal to the real which has been forced once and for all by the creative act. The change lies in a movement, within the very heart of the real, from an abstract existence to a sensuous existence, from being to appearance.

Indeed, so necessary is this appearance to the aesthetic object that it can in turn give rise to two kinds of activity. Both kinds can be said to be limiting cases of performance, and the first deserves to be examined now.

[III] REPRODUCTIONS

IN ORDER TO MULTIPLY its appearance or, rather, its occasions for appearing to someone, the work tends to make itself multiple. Each art contrives to find the means for this multiplication of the unique. The principal means is reproduction. These means for multiplying the appearance of the work cannot be considered identical with the execution or performance which produces this appearance. The mission of reproduction is only that of repeating by mechanical means and without reworking, that is, without manual copying, a work already completed and offered to the public.[17] This is why reproduction does not seem to raise the ontological problem posed by performance. Whereas the work acquires a new existence in its performance, reproduction does not alter its being. Instead, reproduction creates a new object which is at least physically and numerically different from, even if it tries to be equal to, the original. It is only the reproduction's resemblance to the original which is in question and not its ontological status, which is the same as that of the performed work. We cannot say that the reproduction assigns to its object an abstract existence analogous to that which the work possesses before its performance, because that would make the reproduction a mere sign—as if it were a mode of writing [écriture] in which the work, which cannot itself be written, comes to be set

17. We must therefore distinguish between the reproduction and the copy; only the latter involves artistic activity. The copy is in turn different from the pastiche, a copying which is not acknowledged as such and imitates a style rather than a particular work. There is a cluster of problems here into which we cannot delve, because they primarily concern creation.

down. If the reproduction raises an ontological problem, it is with regard to the work it reproduces and not with regard to itself: in imitating the work of art, it tries to be that work by proxy or in image. Rather than being a token of the work, the reproduction conveys the work's presence, a presence which is not merely imaginary or illusory. Thus, between the abstract and the concrete existence of the work, we must make room for this existence by proxy. And the reproduction must make every effort to be the work itself because it is not, for me as spectator, an analogue through which I relate to the work, a mere means for forming the image of the work. The reproduction can give me the work only by presenting itself as the work, by inviting me to perceive and not to imagine. For the work is a work only as perceived, and there can be no question of yielding only an image or idea of it: I aim at Peter through his photo, but I do not aim at an original through its reproduction. If the reproduction is untrue to the original, I thus have no further recourse (except to recollect the original if I have seen it; but I would then be comparing, judging, and appreciating, and there would no longer be any aesthetic perception, strictly speaking); and the work too has no recourse, for it then exists only imperfectly, *hic et nunc*, and for me.

The practical problem which the making of reproductions raises is therefore analogous to the problem which performance raises for the performer. The task of accuracy is analogous to the task of fidelity. More precisely, if it is not a question of giving the work a perceptible or sensuous body, which it already has, how do we safeguard this body? How do we transmit what is both unique and sensuous in the work? How do we create likeness?

Before coming to grips with this problem, we must distinguish between reproduction and the many other ways in which the work tends to be communicated. In the case of works requiring a separate performance, reproductions pose no problem. In its abstract state, the work can be multiplied indefinitely. It attains this existence through a type of sign language or writing which signifies the sensuous without itself being sensuous (or, rather, it is sensuous only practically and not aesthetically, that is, without its legibility's being an end in principle) and allows an indefinite reproduction of signs.[18] On the plane of aesthetic

18. Here we must qualify a bit. The statement is true only when writing entirely subserves speaking and makes no claim to being a decorative pattern. An illuminated manuscript is actually a complex aesthetic object in which the text is at one with its presentation, because the writing has

existence, the reproduction of the sensuous creates no problem because the sensuous has not yet been exhibited. The dissemination
[*diffusion*] of a text is neither true reproduction nor performance,
for what is reproduced is not the work as an aesthetic object but
a sign. On the other hand, the performance of these same works
in their concrete existence can be reproduced—that is, repeated,
as in the case of theater performances—because it is an operation separate from creation. Here the problem posed for us by
the historicity of the performance arises again. Since there are
as many interpretations as performances, which is the right one?
They can all be valid, thereby revealing the inexhaustible character of the aesthetic object—providing we remain pliant and
deferential, in an attitude in which the objectivity of this object
is confirmed. Moreover, our age has discovered the means for
fixing a single performance and at the same time disseminating
it. These means are the film and the phonograph—film, in this
instance, is not the instrument of an independent art but a mechanical mode of reproduction comparable to that of a printing
press in relation to a written text.

Nevertheless, radio broadcasting [*diffusion radiophonique*] is
not reproduction. It transmits but does not recommence. No new
object is created—and yet is it really the integral aesthetic object which exists at the end of the operation? One can say that
the cinematic record of a work, e.g., a ballet or an opera, is different from the work and therefore reproduction. But we would
probably not say this of a radio broadcast, because it is the
sound itself (the same sound, if the reception is good) which is
transmitted. Here our experience of the radio theater illuminates
the case of music that is broadcast: the absence of actors is a

---

value in itself. Its competition with the text is then such that our attention
often turns completely away from the literary in order to contemplate the
pictorial. More generally, we must take into account the importance at-
taching to the physical presentation of the text, to the quality of the paper
and the type. We like to read our favorite poets in fine editions. Does this
mean that the literary object changes from one edition to the next? Of
course not. The pleasure we gain from a fine edition is in fact of the same
order as our pleasure in listening to music while sitting in a good armchair rather than in a folding chair. Purely aesthetic pleasure engendered
in us by the presence of the object mingles (to the point that sensualism
can confuse the agreeable and the beautiful, for want of sufficiently discriminating between them) with a myriad affective echoes awakened
either by the object *materialiter spectatum* or by its context—which confirm aesthetic pleasure without constituting it or which render us more
receptive to it. A beautiful Japanese print in no way makes a poetic text
more beautiful, it only makes reading the text more pleasant. In the same
way, a crystal glass does not render the wine nobler but only allows us to
savor it with greater relish.

distinct loss, as is the absence of a surrounding audience. The work is present—more so, surely, than when I simply read the text or the score, but less so than when I attend its performance. There are, therefore, degrees of presence even within the concrete existence or sensuous presence of the work.

In the case of the arts in which performance, inseparable from creation, is completed once and for all, the problem of reproduction is primarily practical: how is likeness to be created? No definitive answer can be given, and each case must be considered separately. The reproduction is not the work, but it can approach it asymptotically, depending upon the material character of the work to be reproduced, the level of technique, and the technician's understanding of what he wants to reproduce. The chief virtue of reproduction is likeness. It must give us as exact an idea of the work as possible—an idea, not an image in Sartre's sense of a magic power of evoking the presence of an absent thing. What I ask of the reproduction is the truth of the work, for my instruction rather than my pleasure. Reproduction is an instrument of inquiry and work. The paradox is that the truth of the work as an aesthetic object is given in the presence of the work because it is immanent in the sensuous. I cannot have a true idea of a painting—though I can of an engine—by looking at a diagram which shows it disassembled. An equivalent of such a diagram is the rough sketch outlining the composition of a painting, or the thematic analysis of a musical work, or the summary of a play. These schemata enable me to know the structure of the work as a created object—and we shall see how important this structure is—but I do not know it as an aesthetic object, for in the latter the sensuous is irreplaceable. But without claiming to compete with the original, the reproduction does claim to be something more than a means for conveying a purely objective and abstract knowledge. That is, it also strives to deliver truth to us through a presence which saves something of the sensuous. A hierarchy is thus established among reproductions, based on how well they provide an equivalent of the sensuous original.

We must now make place for those works whose material, as the bearer of the sensuous, is such that, following a first treatment by the artist, it can be treated mechanically for purposes of a reproduction which is a perfect copy.[19] Thus we have the art

19. A greater proportion of the mechanical or the fortuitous (for example, in the baking of enamel) and a lesser proportion of manual or intellectual creation help determine the minor character of certain arts.

of engraving, in which the design is made to be reproduced, as well as the arts of ceramic and porcelain. We can hardly say that the cups of a Sèvres service, for example, are the reproduction of an original cup. The same holds true of the woodworking arts, where reproduction is not done mechanically but the share of artisan's work is so considerable that imitation can be perfect. An excellent copy of a piece of period furniture is an aesthetic object deserving the same respect as the original, and it is only for nonaesthetic reasons that an art collector will refuse it the same market value.[20] Similar too is the case of marble copied in bronze—by means of casting, a new aesthetic object is created which, moreover, acquires this status only because it differs, however slightly, from its model. For the technique of casting, which ensures the likeness, nevertheless leaves the sculptor a margin of initiative, so that his labor makes of the bronze a unique work. Let us add that the matter of the work, through which this casting is marked off from the simple plaster cast or clay model, helps to give the object the standing of a work of art through its own qualities of resistance and pliability to the sculptor's file. In such a case, we can say that the reproduction is at its limit the work itself.

This is already less true of the piano transcription of an orchestral work, even though the transcription also presupposes the cooperation, if not of an artist, at least of a man of taste, capable of judging what parts of a score to sacrifice in transcribing but not capable of inventing like the composer who rescores a piano piece for the orchestra. Something of the sensuous is still preserved here—harmony, if not tonal quality. In the same way, a good color reproduction of a painting is obviously superior to a black-and-white reproduction which, aside from exhibiting the composition—which is more structural than sensuous—preserves only the tones of the painting. Reproduction in black and white is to color reproduction what, in sculpture, the photograph is to the plaster cast (the bronze copy not being comparable) and, in architecture, the photograph to the scale model.[21]

20. The reasons are nevertheless aesthetic, if the prestige of the genuine work stems from respect for the creative act whose trace we want to possess. And the same is true if, when the original is antique, this prestige derives from the feeling that it makes a difference in the being of the aesthetic object to have lasted so long and to have provided so many aesthetic experiences.

21. More exactly, to full-scale plaster casts, like those of the monuments reproduced at the Palais de Chaillot or of the Temple of Angkor at the Colonial Exposition of 1931. For the architectural model is, in fact, different. In the model's shrinking of all the dimensions of the archi-

Admittedly, all these reproductions make us see and not think. But the sensuous which they set before us is doubly impoverished, both qualitatively and spatially, so that we can no longer lead that sort of ritual dance around it through which, in multiplying our perspectives, we physically experience the inexhaustible nature of the object—a nature which is, in the case of the aesthetic object, the symbol of a spiritual depth of which we always have a presentiment. The art of reproduction consists, then, in concretizing, from among these innumerable angles of vision, the one which is the most significant or evocative, thus teaching us to see while providing us with the occasion for seeing. The ingenuity which reproduction displays in "artistically" using the mechanical means at its command makes up for the impotence of these means. In the absence of the plenitude of the sensuous, the reproduction conveys instead its character, which is both surprising and complete—e.g., in the absence of tonal quality, there is melody. This is why the photographer can be called an artist with as much right as the actor. He does not create a new aesthetic object[22] but, in placing himself in the service of the object which he is reproducing, he exists on its level.

Thus a reproduction does more than acquaint us with the aesthetic object, although this by itself is by no means unimportant. The reproduction initiates us to the aesthetic object through a process not of analyzing but of showing. But here the reproduction encounters its limits—how quickly depends on its means. For the presence which it provides is not that of the work, which is why the reproduction always has a lower price and value than the original.[23] In most of the major arts—especially painting and architecture, but also the dance, theater, and recorded music—the fate of the reproduction, given the present level of

---

tectural object, the sensuous is considerably altered. Gestalt psychology has demonstrated this in the course of opposing the intellectualism which improperly transfers to perception the relativism which belongs to logical judgment.

22. Unlike the art photograph properly so called, which creates its object. But can it not be said that something new is created by a close-up or crop, as in detail photographs? No, for the details may be beautiful in themselves and undoubtedly interesting to observe, but they still do not constitute a work of art, because they have been composed not for themselves but rather for the whole from which they have been lifted. They do not constitute a form having its own foundation—like a portrait, for example—unless they are already an independent work, like a sculpture in a building, a gargoyle, or a stained-glass window.

23. This does not apply to works which come to us in the form of indefinitely repeated signs. An original edition is not an original at all. Pursuing one is a mania like any other and is without aesthetic significance.

technique, recalls that of mnemonic reproduction. Memory gives us more than a knowledge of the past but never quite gives us its living actuality. Memory oscillates between reconstruction and actualization. Pure memory, the dream which would be knowledge, is lost in the nothingness of the unconscious. The presence of the painting in the photograph of it, like the presence of music or drama on the radio, is a bloodless presence. In the first case, it is a real but diminished presence. In the second case, there is a fuller presence, but it exists by proxy and is always imperfect. Before it I am obliged to make an effort to be myself completely present to it in some way other than through intelligence or taste alone.

Hence there are avatars in the appearance of the work which are the result of the means employed to make it appear, whether in creating or reproducing it. Its being is not affected insofar as it has already been created and thus preexists as a demand on those who produce or multiply its appearance. But, since it is of its essence to appear and to exist for us, so long as it appears only through artificial signs or awkward performances or imperfect reproductions, it enjoys only a diminished existence. In other words, the sensuous is irreplaceable. There can be no true idea of a work of art (we can, of course, have true ideas *about* it) but only a more or less true perception of it. The being of the work of art yields itself only through its sensuous presence, which allows me to apprehend it as an aesthetic object. This is why it is so vulnerable and so open to betrayal by whoever betrays its appearance. Its being is no more affected by the vicissitudes of its existence than the being of Kant's 100 thalers. However, unlike the thalers, the work must exist fully in order to be known and to become an aesthetic object. And that is why, outside of its appearance, and, for example, for those who have to perform it or reproduce it, its being is solely that of a demand which can give rise to endless interpretations. On the other hand, for those to whom it appears, the work's being is that of a sensuous presence which is inexhaustible: a being whose reality is incontestable but whose truth, tied to appearance, is ungraspable. It is a being for which appearance is a requirement, since it cannot find its truth elsewhere; whereas in the case of an ordinary perceived object, it makes no difference whether it is present in one way or another, because a true idea of it exists in principle and because for it perception is not everything.

But if the work of art wishes to appear, it will appear to me. If it wishes to be totally present, it is in order that I may be present to it. The performance takes place in front of a spectator who participates in it. We can say in all seriousness that the spectator actually is a performer, indeed, the only performer, when he is a reader; for the reader is one who perceives, but who, in uttering sounds, presents himself to himself to be perceived. Thus we can realize that the spectator is driven by the same duty as the performer—namely, to be submissive and faithful to the work—and that all aesthetic perception is a task. This point could be examined further here, but it will be done more opportunely in the next chapter, which treats the work and the spectator—where we shall still not take up aesthetic perception as such but, rather, deal with the spectator's contribution to the work by adopting the point of view of the *perceptum* instead of the *percipiens*.

3 / The Work
and Its Public

IF, AS WE HAVE JUST SEEN, the work tends to multiply its presence, it is in order to offer itself to the spectator. The aesthetic object needs a public. We are all well aware of this fact, but the artist who values his work feels it the most keenly. An unexhibited painting, an unpublished manuscript, and an unperformed play are objects which do not yet have standing in the cultural world, which do not yet fully exist. To be sure, the artist can say that they are his works and that they exist, since he has created them. However, he would also like them to exist for others, to have their existence ratified by a public judgment. If this judgment is slow in coming, he cannot escape the anguish of self-doubt. He can only appeal to "his own," like the solitary Nietzsche, or, like Stendhal, to the superior judgment of posterity —which means still being dependent on a public.[1] Now, when the work thus awaits a public, is that not evidence of the fact that it exists for our sake? Yet, at the same time, it is through the spectator that the work finds its *own* full reality. Of course, it can be said of any object that it has no right to the title "object" unless its existence has been established by an objective knowledge which certifies that it is not an illusory phenomenon existing only in the radical solitude of a single consciousness. Every

---

1. This does not necessarily imply that the artist creates for an audience, as Sartre asserts is the case for the writer. We shall bypass this question, which touches upon the psychology of creation. But even if the artist creates for himself, that is, tries to solve his own artistic problems in becoming an artist, his work, once it has been completed, detaches itself from him. It is a rare artist who decides of his own free will to remain his work's only spectator, as in Balzac's *Chef d'oeuvre inconnu*.

object demands to be perceived and to effect a convergence upon itself. But in the case of ordinary objects, we can make up for the absence of such knowledge either by hearsay, no matter how deficient, or by an imperfect knowledge which may, nevertheless, be adequate to it. These means are not available, however, for the aesthetic object: the reality of this object can only be revealed, not demonstrated. It has no other guarantee than to be attested to by a perception and to be situated at the crossroads of a plurality of perceptions. Precisely how the work is perceived by the spectator and what he discovers in it will be discussed later. For the present, we shall continue to examine the work and to ask only how it is affected by the spectator and how, in turn, it affects him.

[I] WHAT THE WORK EXPECTS OF THE SPECTATOR

WHAT THE WORK EXPECTS of the spectator is its consecration and, simultaneously, its completion. Drawing on Scheler's distinction between objectivity and universality, we may say that the objectivity of the value which the work bears can be felt only on contact with the object, and its universality can be established only empirically through unanimity of opinion and the test of time. But the public does not merely contribute to the work the consecration or confirmation of this value. Such confirmation is important, of course, and the artist is right in expecting it. No matter how great his self-confidence he is well aware that he cannot be both judge and client, that he is never the wholly impartial spectator of his work, and that only the verdict of the public matters. But the work has value only as long as it has being, and the primary task of the public is to fulfill this being. What the work expects of the public is, first of all, its completion. It is for the sake of this completion that the artist needs the spectator's collaboration, as Hegel had already seen. And we know why: if the aesthetic object can only be shown or revealed, if no knowledge can be its equivalent and no translation into concepts substituted for it, it is because its primary reality is found above all in the sensuous, as we have suggested. A painting, a dance, a musical work, and a poem are felicitous and necessary arrangements of colors, movements, musical sounds, and words which must themselves be converted into sounds, respectively. Let the sensuous recede into the background, become a mere accident or a sign, and the object ceases to be aesthetic. Now, the sensuous is an act common both to the sensing being and to what is sensed. What happens to the colors in a painting when they are no longer reflected in a look? They return to their ontic status of things or ideas; they become chemical products or light vibrations and are no longer colors. They are colors only through and for whoever perceives them, and the painting is truly an aesthetic object only when it is contemplated.

But without entering into the secret of perception, we must state precisely how the spectator contributes to this epiphany of the aesthetic object. He does so doubly: he is both performer and witness, and the emphasis shifts from one of these functions to the other according to whether or not a given work of art requires a performance which is separate from its original creation.

(a) The performer

First of all, the spectator cooperates in the performance and, when it takes place in his presence, figures in an audience. The work needs an audience to the extent that the performer himself needs one. Here we use the narrower term "audience" instead of "public" to denote the compact and transitory group which attends a performance. Public celebrations help us to understand this contribution of the audience. Whether he is at the pageants of Versailles, religious processions, or Nuremberg parades, the spectator is at the same time an actor, moved and delighted by these events. It is as if the total event, with its discipline and solemnity, had been molded by the will of some stage director into a kind of work of art. If some spectacle is not offered it, the crowd turns *itself* into one, for all is in readiness for a show, and we would venture to say that there is in this case aesthetic perception without an aesthetic object. (This is especially so if we agree with Alain's analysis that the discipline of body and imagination—resulting in a beautiful human form, composed and free, which will be a favorite subject of art—constitutes an essential condition of aesthetic perception and perhaps of aesthetic creation.) We meet the same crowd again in the theater auditorium, a crowd which is a spectacle in itself and which understands itself. In Alain's words, "this great sea of flesh within which signals ceaselessly rebound, ever more powerful because of its mute dialogue," is necessary first of all to the performer himself.[2] Claudel thinks so too, making the actor speak in the same terms as Alain: "I look at them, and the theater is nothing but living, clothed flesh. . . . They listen to me and weigh what I say; they look at me, and I enter their souls as into a vacant house." [3] The actor is supported by this exchange. It is thus that he lives his part and is possessed. During rehearsals, he thinks about the exchange and works at it. Then, because he has worked so hard, he improvises before the audience, he no longer thinks of his part but only of the audience, and it is thus that he is fully present and, through him, the work as well. The text finds a voice which is fully a voice, since this voice is addressed to an audience whose silence is the most moving response.[4] Thus the attention which bears initially on the actor carries over to the work. Moreover, it helps in the work's comprehension—here, to "comprehend" is indeed to grasp-together. If it is true, as we shall see, that the very height of aesthetic perception is found in the feeling which reveals the expressiveness of the work, a prime form of this feeling is discoverable in the kind of human warmth and emotion which a rapt crowd exudes. "The rich physiological depth which creates in the theater, as in ceremony (where it is everything), what professionals call atmosphere," to quote Alain again.[5]

What we have just said of the theater can also be said of the dance, for the good dancer is the one who is sufficiently sure of himself to convert the movements imposed on him into signs directed to the audience. In other words, he can surpass himself in his performance by putting not only grace but also spontaneity into what is nevertheless precisely determined and preordained. And what of music? Here it is less certain that the spontaneity of the soloist is called forth by the audience, and, in the orchestra, the instrumentalist is aware only of the conductor. But it is at least left for the audience to collaborate in the performance by forming a backdrop of pure silence, a human silence charged with attention, and for this attention, by reverberating from one

2. Alain, *Vingt Leçons sur les beaux-arts* (Paris: Gallimard, 1931), p. 124.

3. Paul Claudel, *L'Echange*, act 2.

4. Here again we measure the difference between the theater and the cinema by the fact that the screen actor must make his meaning much more explicit than his colleague in the theater, addressing himself first of all to the intelligence. In addition, the absence of an actor is complemented by the absence, as it were, of an audience. Both the darkness and the design of movie theaters prevent the formation of an audience.

5. Alain, *Vingt Leçons*, p. 126.—Trans.

consciousness to another, to create the most favorable climate for aesthetic perception.

But the examination of music invites us to introduce into this description of the audience a nuance which will prepare the way for the broader term "public," which we shall soon have to utilize in considering a morphologically dispersed group of people. Is this homogeneous gathering, which resounds and reechoes, which plants a single emotion and a single attention in the heart of each one, similar to the group which expresses itself through a collective consciousness born of the fusion and even of the alienation of its individual members? To be sure, there is communion here, but one which we must doubly qualify. First of all, the communion is magnetized by a ruling object which is the aesthetic object. Instead of the group's needing only itself, it needs the performance of the work, as an audience of believers needs the performance of the religious service. This is why emotion, instead of being released inordinately, as in a panic, is guided by the allure of the object and is measured by it, thus remaining a property of attention. And this object itself is careful to repress emotion even while arousing it. By a thousand ruses the dramatic work reminds the spectator that he is, in fact, a spectator and must not allow himself to take part in the performance.[6] Second, through this attention to the object and its properties, the play, shaping man into the tranquil and sovereign form of the spectator, invites him to be himself and not to become alienated. It is thus, as Hytier points out, that the theater must create, not than a mass communion but "the accord of a multiplicity of personal admirations."[7] This is what Alain means by saying that the theater is a school for the consciousness of self. By losing himself in an audience which is directed by the object, the spectator gains himself. The audience invites him and prepares him to be himself. And we shall likewise see that, by alienating himself in the aesthetic object, the spectator asserts himself no less, since this object reflects his own image back to him.

In other words, the spectator participates in the play doubly.

6. We shall return to this point. Let us, however, note what happens in a certain art of oratory which is not productive of an art work, where intonation and gesticulation aim to convince and sometimes to unleash passions, making the spectator a party and not a witness. The true actor, on the contrary, does not harangue. He plays a role, and the result is a "play."

7. Jean Hytier, "L'Esthétique du drame," *Journal de psychologie* Vol. XXIX (January, 1932).

As a member of an audience, he collaborates in the performance of the work at the same time that he "gets into form" to apprehend it. However, it is as a solitary and meditative consciousness that he communes with the work for the sake of its metamorphosis into an aesthetic object. In the latter instance, he is already, as Souriau says, that witness required by the work, that subjectivity who, in order to be fully a subjectivity, can only be singular, to whom the appearance refers and through and for whom this appearance is expressive. We are going to consider this function of being a witness in the case of the arts which are not performed separately and which also happen to be those which are performed in private. It is there that this function is preponderant, when the reality of the audience fades into the background and takes on another meaning.

But first we must return to a question which we have left hanging. In those arts which are appreciated in solitude, is not the spectator who will be the witness first of all a performer? To be sure, the performance has been assumed by the creator himself once and for all, and it is only a question of the spectator's collaborating in it as he does in the dramatic presentation. But, in the plastic arts, we may be tempted to give the title of performance to that kind of "game" [*jeu*] which the spectator must play or act out [*jouer*] in front of the work in order to select or multiply his perspectives on it. This gambit of the spectator is not unimportant, as Hegel has suggested.[8] The work is a forceful lover who draws the spectator to precisely those points where he must place himself in order to become a witness. But it is too much to call this sort of activity performance, for it is not a question of creating the sensuous but of perceiving it. The assistance which the spectator provides—indeed, any spectator in any art—is that of an aesthetic perception which reveals the aesthetic object. What is common to spectator and performer is simply the homage which their docility pays to the work—in the performer's case, in order to incarnate it; in the spectator's, in order to grasp it.

Nevertheless, the same problem remains unresolved in the case of reading. A play, for example, must be presented. When it is not, the reader can penetrate its meaning only by imagining the performance in his own way—in short, by being a performer, if only vicariously and in imagination. But does not every reader have to be a performer in order to make words pass

8. Hegel, *Esthétique*, trans. S. Jankélévitch (Paris: Aubier, 1944), III, 210.

from the abstract existence of the written sign to the concrete existence of the uttered sign, at least if the sign takes on its full meaning only when uttered? Without creating a whole theory of language at this point, we must at the minimum distinguish between the arts of prose and of poetry. The prose arts treat the work as an instrument of meaning without paying too much attention to the sensuous qualities which the work manifests when it is uttered. Instead, the sensuous qualities which are sometimes foreshadowed in reading form, as it were, a halo around meaning. The word sounds good because it is the right one, and it sounds strange if the idea which it introduces is surprising. Far from the meaning's being immanent in the sensuous, the sensuous, when it appears, is like an effect of meaning. What usually appear in prose are signs on paper whose purely visual display is without glory or importance of its own, on which one's look does not alight as a look but rather as an instrument of the understanding. Knowledge glides over the words and monopolizes our attention.[9] The reader goes straight to the meaning. Without undertaking a performance which would bring a sensuous element into being, he is above all a witness. Since meaning or the represented object is preponderant in prose, the reader is a witness who derealizes himself or makes himself mental in order to take his place inside the represented world rather than being a witness situated in the real world where the sensuous is displayed.

But it is not the same with poetry. If we grant that the poetic word signifies only in being recited—that it is a foreign and impenetrable "nature" (and not a familiar instrument) which is as striking and opaque as the sensuous in sculpture and paint-

9. In pursuing this idea, we are reduced to saying that the novel, whatever its craft and creative power, is not quite an art, because the sensuous is short-changed or subordinated in it. But there is another side to the reading of a novel, which Sartre has clearly pointed out. We do not read a novel as we do just any book, because in the novel knowledge turns from signifying to imaging. The word is then not merely a tool, the neutral bearer of a meaning. It is "representative," and this function confers upon it a certain density and personality (to which we may add a certain affective function, whose examination Sartre by-passes). Consequently, the novel is a work of art all the same, but a special one in that, instead of causing meaning to appear in the sensuous, it gives meaning abstractly. The novel strives to "realize" this knowledge in images by prompting the reader not so much to become a spectator in a virtual drama as to identify himself with the chief character and to become a partner in his perceptions, an accomplice in his acts. But this contribution of the imagination is not the equivalent of a performance. (See Jean-Paul Sartre, *The Psychology of Imagination*, trans. B. Frechtman [New York: Washington Square Press, 1966], pp. 81 ff.)

ing and in which meaning has been caught and becomes nature itself, as it were, so that it is revealed rather than stated—then we must grant that the poetic word requires a special kind of reading.[10] The reader must associate himself with the effort which the poet makes to wrench the word out of its character as a familiar and unnoticed tool and to restore to it an unwonted aspect and a power to express, not as a sign but as a thing. He must therefore read aloud in such a way that the sound carries and acquires force. Is an inner reading, in the sense in which one speaks of inner speech, sufficient? Yes, if it has the motor character of inner speech which confers upon the latter enough externality for us to be able to read our thoughts in it. Even this muted reading associates our vocal apparatus with our eyes for the purpose of testing the resistance and qualities of the word. If the gesture does not accompany the spoken word, as in the case of the actor, it is because the poem is not drama and because the word says everything, providing it *is* said.[11] But is this not a performance all the same? And must we not say that the reader is at once actor and spectator—which is, after all, the condition of any speaker?

Croce objects that "the declamation, and even the recitation, of a poem is not poetry, but something else, beautiful or ugly, which we must judge in its proper sphere. . . . Poetry is an inner voice to which no human voice can be equal."[12] We may

---

10. Regarding the character and function of the poetic word, the analyses of Sartre (*Psychology*, pp. 85 ff.; *What Is Literature?*, trans. B. Frechtman [New York: Harper & Row, 1965]) rejoin those of Mallarmé and Valéry on the incantatory power of speech: "I say: 'a flower.'" Not only does the word precede the meaning, it bears the meaning within it. The object is encased in the word like the swan in the ice, like the "dead nude" in "the frozen oblivion of the mirror." On the other hand, one may ask whether this analysis agrees with that of Heidegger, for whom "poetry never takes language as a raw material ready to hand, rather it is poetry which first makes language possible. . . . The essence of language must be understood through the essence of poetry." (Quoted from Martin Heidegger, "Hölderlin and the Essence of Poetry," trans. D. Scott, in *Existence and Being*, ed. W. Brock [Chicago: Regnery, 1950], pp. 283–84.) We shall have occasion to return to the Heideggerian conception of poetry, whose import is essentially ontological.

11. See Paul Valéry: "A poem is a duration during which, as a reader, I breathe by prescribed rule. I lend my breath and the machinery of my voice, or simply their power, which harmonizes with silence. I abandon myself to the delightful prospect of reading and living wherever the words lead." [Valéry, *Oeuvres*, ed. Jean Hytier (Paris: Gallimard, 1957), I, 95. —Trans.]

12. B. Croce, *La Poésie*, trans. D. Dreyfus (Paris: Presses Universitaires de France, 1950), p. 99.

grant that the recitation may be abstracted from the thing recited and judged for itself, much as we might judge an actor's performance by itself, and that the recitation would then seem like a "practical act" separate from "poetical expression." It is thus that Croce opposes the technical to the artistic. However, the question is whether the practical act, even though distinct from creation, is not necessary to the coming into being of the created thing as an aesthetic object. We say "coming into being" and not "constituting," because phenomenologically it is the hearing of the poem which is truly constitutive. But the practical act *is* presentative, for it allows the sensuous to be born. One can deny this only if one denies the total immanence of sense in the sensuousness of the aesthetic object. And Croce, though Hegelian in his notion (itself rather confusedly developed) that art universalizes the particular, is not sufficiently Hegelian to assert this immanence as such, even though he speaks in his *Aesthetic* of " the unity of intuition and expression" in which the inner and the outer are speculatively identified.[13] He is biased against immanence because he never places himself systematically at the viewpoint of the spectator and because, in any case, he looks at art rather than the work of art. What he seeks to grasp is the very principle of art, that is, what he calls "intuition."[14] The whole first chapter of his *Essence of Aesthetic* is a commentary upon his assertion that "art remains completely defined, if we define it as intuition," where intuition is truly intuition "because it represents a feeling and arises from it."[15] This is why he seeks out the poetic rather than the poem and why he finds it as easily in the novel or tragedy as in the epic or elegy. We may wonder whether this quest does not imply a more precise ontology similar to the one we shall find later in Heidegger. But, in any event, such an ontology does not eliminate the need for a phenomenology of the specifically poetic work which is put forth by a culture and which a reader grasps. And it is to the actualization of this work insofar as it is distinct from prose that reading (a reading distinct from ordinary reading, in which the eye is the immediate organ of the intelligence) seems to us necessary.

13. *Ibid.*, pp. 5, 183.
14. This is why beauty is the only aesthetic category for him.
15. See B. Croce, *The Essence of Aesthetic*, trans. D. Ainslie (London: Heinemann, 1921).—Trans.

(b) The witness

If the reader turns performer, it is, in every case, in order to confront the work, to be its witness. The work takes him as its witness because, just as man wants to be recognized by man in the celebrated Hegelian dialectic, the work needs man in order to be recognized as an aesthetic object. In opposition to every subjectivism, we must state that man brings nothing to the work except its consecration. Moreover, in studying the aesthetic attitude, we shall see that, without giving up being himself, he must have before the work the clear and impartial attitude of the witness as well as the special intelligence of a witness who is at one with what he registers and who is an accomplice rather than a judge. How is this harmony possible, this "form" composed of spectator and work? How can the spectator be simultaneously outside and inside, and this with respect both to the sensuous and to meaning? At this point, we must outline an analysis of the spectator's presence to the aesthetic object.[16]

It seems, and especially in the plastic arts, that the witness is first of all a registering apparatus placed at one point or another in space by the work as it organizes its own way of being viewed. A painting is created to be seen at a certain distance and from a certain viewing point. It organizes itself under our gaze. The drawing becomes more precisely defined, the colors harmonize and become alive (taking on shape and themselves suggesting shape), and the represented object appears more lucidly. This is particularly true of works composed in accordance with classical perspective—a centered, static perspective which roots the spectator to the perspectival center, the only viewing point. But it is still true of all works which in a thousand different ways reject this perspective. In reestablishing a pictorial dynamism, they do not compel the spectator's body to move for the purpose of correcting appearances. As Charles Lapicque says, "we must attribute those opinions according to which a Cézanne fruit dish is drawn askew to our refusal to move." [17] In fact, the movement

16. We shall return to it in the investigation of perception, but we must show even now what the object demands of us. We encounter here Souriau's analysis in *La Correspondance des arts,* in the chapter entitled, "Essence of a Cosmological Structure: The Viewing Point" (Paris: Flammarion, 1947), p. 264.

17. Charles Lapicque, "Espace de la peinture et espace de la nature," in *La Profondeur et le rythme* (Paris: Arthaud, 1948), p. 9.

which the work imposes on us is a nonphysical one. There is always a certain point from which appearances, even if not for the purpose of conveying meaning, organize themselves best, and from which colors in particular are at their most expressive. With respect to a piece of sculpture, there are likewise, as Waldemar Conrad states, "privileged perspectives" on which the sculptor has decided. And the monument makes the visitor move in accordance with its architectural logic, so that at each moment it is wholly present and yet inexhaustible. This inexhaustible character appears even to the motionless spectator, at the opera or ballet, who has chosen his seat with regard to his purse rather than the work, as well as to the observor of a painting who is tied to the spot by its perspective.

All of this serves as a warning: no more than perception resolves into a schema of subject and object external to one another (in the way that stimulus and sensory organ are externally related to the physicist) does the presence of the witness to the work reduce to physical presence. He must enter intimately into the work. Music is instructive here. At a concert, I face the orchestra but exist in the symphony. To designate this reciprocal possession, it could just as easily be said that the symphony exists in me. But to avoid all subjectivism, we must speak rather of an alienation of the subject in the object and perhaps even of a bewitchment by it. Our presence to the aesthetic object has something absolute about it—not at all the absolute of a transcendental *cogito,* which would be out of play, but the absolute of a consciousness which is entirely open and as if possessed by what it projects. In short, the witness is not a pure spectator but an involved one—involved in the work itself. And despite the distinction which Maurice Pradines underscores between the visual and the auditory, this point holds even for works which call the visual into play. Thus a painting demands that I allow myself to be haunted by its color. When, in that state, I look at a painting which rejects classical perspective, I am able to penetrate its space, even though such a space is built out of the debris of vital space, whether through a piling up of objects (as in some of Braque's still lifes) or through the alteration of spaces (as in cubism) or through the confusion of planes and the rejection of apparent sizes (as in Western primitives). Painting which is called "abstract" is instructive in this regard. It is still to be distinguished from the merely decorative, which is content to decorate an already given space, say, the periphery of a tapestry or the margin of a manuscript. For, through colors, abstract painting creates its own space, which it compels us to assume. It is a space which does not make a hole in the wall because it orders its shapes pictorially instead of conceptually, and also because, disarming our ordinary habits and predispositions, it invites us not to act but to contemplate. To dream, says Lapicque (making very ingenious use of Bergson), means to substitute, for an efficacious predisposition which mobilizes the body, an imaginary one which no longer interests it.[18] But we must be careful here. In this context, to dream in no way means to beget extravagant images which becloud perception and disqualify the witness. On the contrary—and is it not thus that Bergson understands the image?—it means to coincide with the object.[19] Such dreaming is not, however, a complete relaxation in which consciousness is engulfed. That is why we would not say, as Lapicque does, that the body "retires from all activity." For it is through our body, through its vigilance and experience, that we remain in touch with the object. But instead of anticipating action and trying to make the object submit to it, our body submits to the object, allowing itself to be moved by the object.

Thus the witness, without leaving his post in physical space, penetrates into the world of the work. Because he allows himself to be won over and inhabited by the sensuous, he thereby penetrates into the work's signification—we may say that the meaning penetrates him, so close is the reciprocity of subject and object. In front of a figurative painting, I am *with* the characters represented: I am *in* Canaletto's city or *under* Ruysdael's oak. No lighting is impossible, because the lighting belongs to the painting. No monster is teratological, no untidiness calls for the broom, and the fruit dish has a right to be lopsided. This does not mean that the painting partakes of the unreal. It means that I have derealized myself in order to proclaim the painting's reality and that I have gained a foothold in the new world which it opens to me, a new man myself. But we must see clearly that, in making myself unreal, I forbid myself any active participation. By becoming disinterested in the natural world which I have left,

18. Lapicque shows very clearly that ordinary perceptual experience already plays its part in the dream and that lived space is basically dreamed space. Hence it follows that "what is inevitably dreamed in the natural world, space properly so called, glides smoothly into pure pictorial space" (*ibid.*, p. 25).

19. The Bergsonian theory of the image falls in with what, in a quite different language, Merleau-Ponty describes under the heading of existence, namely, a basic, prereflective accord of subject and object at the level of the body proper. We shall return to this at some length.

I have lost the ability to be *interested* in the aesthetic world. I am within it but only to contemplate it. Moreover, this is all that the work expects of me—that I stay in it and get to know it from within. I watch a play or read a novel in the same way. The personal relationship which I maintain with the work in the theater, where I am part of the audience, does not oblige me to renounce my function of spectator but rather to belong to the work while remaining a spectator. I am with the characters, I know about any one of them what the others know of him and what he knows about the others. Yet I do not identify myself with any of them. Rather, I take the threads as given to me and recompose the action in which the characters are involved. It is with the ensemble as a whole that I am on a level, as the conductor is with his entire orchestra. This is why the theater is essentially action and not psychology.[20] Because my look takes in the whole scene, what I witness is an event which, as Gouhier has very ably shown, creates a situation for characters in such a way that the characters are defined in terms of the situation.[21] I am contemporaneous with the total situation rather than with the characters. I enter the world of the work by the main gate, for the situation is the totality of this world, like the compositional whole in a painting. Here we have the difference between the theater and the novel. The novel proposes, in a manner of which contemporary novelists have been acutely aware, to identify me, even while I remain a spectator, with one of the characters and to see the others through his eyes—this character being able, moreover, to remain the same or to change in the course of the work. I am not in this case privy to the work's secret, or at most I am privy to the secret of only one consciousness.[22] The world I penetrate in this way has the fragmentary character, indeterminate and open, of the natural world. Nevertheless, I am still *there*, in the world of the novel.

We shall return at length to these problems concerning aesthetic perception and the nature of the world of the work. But

20. This idea has been developed by Touchard in *Dionysos*. Of course, this in no way means that the theater cannot be psychologically true. [See Pierre Touchard, *Dionysos* (Paris: Editions du Seuil, 1948).—Trans.]

21. "The dramatic categories refer to *what is happening;* they qualify the action as an *event* creating a situation" (H. Gouhier, *L'Essence du théâtre* [Paris: Plon, 1943], p. 168).

22. This is why the novel is tempted by psychology. But to psychologize is always a risk, and many novelists have decided on a psychology which mocks psychology. In their novels, even the leading character is exhibited rather than explained. It is thus, to boot, that they obtain the greatest participation from the reader, for the reader sees instead of thinking.

it was necessary to make clear what the work expects of its witness: it expects him to play the game. The work expands within him, but only if he takes the role it assigns him. With all its being, it prepares this role: later we shall see how, through the structural organization of the sensuous, it disposes the body to a felicitous perception. At the same time that he perceives or, in the case of the novel, that he imagines, the witness penetrates the world of the work, not to take action in it or to be acted on by it, but to bear witness, so that this world may take on meaning through his presence, and the intentions of the work may be realized. And it is still the work which, within this world, assigns him a perspective—either a physical perspective on an object or a nonphysical [*spirituelle*] perspective on a meaning (e.g., the perspective of the theatergoer or of the novel reader respectively). Because this meaning is given in the sensuous, the nonphysical perspective can harmonize with the physical perspective governed by perception. This is especially true in visual works, where the meaning of a painting or monument appears in terms of the place where the spectator is stationed. Nevertheless, presence to the world of the work is not to be confused with physical presence to the sensuous. Mere physical presence can be a matter of indifference, as when I decide where to sit at a concert. But if I am truly before a work—truly present to it—it is in order to be with it. The *Da* of Dasein is a nonphysical *Da*, but it is still a *Da*. I coexist in this world of the work of which I am a witness. I do not view it from above, and I am in it as much as I am in the physical world. I obey the time of the music, I wait for the characters in the novel to reveal themselves, I can never know what is behind Cézanne's *House of the Hanged Man*. This is because, always a spectator, I am in the service of the work, which seems, in Souriau's term, to "posit" me.

The work therefore has the initiative. What it expects of the spectator corresponds to what it has planned for him. And that forbids any subjectivism. Far from the work's existing in us, we exist in the work. To be a witness is to be prohibited from adding anything to the work, for the work imposes itself upon the spectator as imperiously as it does upon the performer. Of course, the public also has the freedom to interpret. The public has this freedom not in performing but in understanding, and it has it to the point where the meaning of the work and even its density vary according to what different spectators find in it. But it is in the work that they find this meaning, not in themselves as something to transfer onto the work. We must be on guard here against the theory which, assuming that we can never know anything but our own representations and can understand only ourselves, holds that the work is within us. To be sure, it is not enough to say that this psychologism has been refuted by the theory of intentionality. For it remains true in one sense, as we shall verify in studying *Homo poeticus*, that we always discover in the work what we are. But we must add at once that it is the work which awakens us to ourselves. It is the work which releases in us the play of memories and associations which we must, moreover, repress rather than encourage in order to remain faithful to the work; for it is the latter that crystallizes this inner precipitate. And if the work gains lucidity in each of us, it is only through what it calls forth in us. The ideas it suggests, the feelings it awakens, the concrete images—*Ansichten,* as Ingarden calls them—which nourish its meanings vary with each spectator. But they vary like perspectives which converge at the same point, like intentions which aim at the same object, or like languages which say the same thing. The identity of the work is not altered, since its content appears and is refracted differently in different consciousnesses. All these views only display or exfoliate its possibilities, minting the capital which it conceals. It will be said, and rightly, that the same holds for any object which never confides itself except in *Abschattungen* and which is at the limit nothing but the target of an infinite series of intentional acts. Yet the difference is that the truth of the aesthetic object is both richer and more pressing—richer, because it is not a question merely of a physical reality to be mastered but of an expression to be grasped; more pressing, because it seems to us that this truth involves us and that it is up to us to assume it.

[II] WHAT THE WORK BRINGS TO THE SPECTATOR

IT IS BECAUSE the truth of the work is present to us as soon as we are present to the work that the work acts upon us. The work does so even if we cannot articulate this sense of dual presence. We would like now to point out two modalities of this action which relate to its presence alone and which converge in the notion that, by inviting man to be a witness, the work develops the human in him, or at least that aspect of the human which is exercised in contemplation.

(a) Taste

First of all, the work forms taste. Here we must distinguish between two conceptions of taste. Generally, taste expresses the arbitrary and peremptory aspects of subjectivity in its inclinations and preferences. It is a fact that I prefer classical to Romantic music, as it is a fact that I prefer well-done meat and dry wine: *non disputandum.* An existential psychoanalysis could perhaps demonstrate that each of these choices expresses and confirms a unique manner of being in the world, i.e., the nontemporal choice which seals my fate. In this case, my tastes would be irreducible, because they would be seen as part of an irreducible whole which is, fundamentally, my nature[23]—as well as a testimony to my finitude. But subjectivity thus understood, even if we still define it as a project in a world, is recognized by its contents or its reactions. It refers to itself rather than to the world. Aesthetic tastes thus express the reaction of my nature to the aesthetic object. They imply that I am more attentive to myself than to the object, and to my pleasure first of all; for they are measured by the pleasure I find in aesthetic experience, a pleasure which proceeds not so much from the object as from me—or, rather, from the object's agreement with me, from the feeling I experience of being confirmed in my existence or of being revealed to myself. The judgment of taste decides what I prefer by virtue of what I am.

Now, this return to the self, even through the mediation of the aesthetic object, is not the root of the aesthetic experience. Alain suggests the same in saying that pleasure is not a necessary ingredient of aesthetic experience and that beauty awakens not pleasure but a feeling of the sublime. The sublime would thus be, in a slightly modified sense, our feeling of alienation or being lost in the aesthetic object, the sacrifice of subjectivity to something toward which it transcends itself and which transcends it—in short, the feeling which arises when we renounce

---

23. It matters little at this point to know whether this nature is still an act of freedom, as Sartre insists. For it is then a freedom which is still not mine. The first choice is not a genuine choice, that is, one which was thought over and then assumed, and therefore authentic. True freedom implies a radical conversion with respect to that choice. Jeanson has stated it very well: "It is already a free choice in fact and one which is mine but, paradoxically, it remains for me to make *from* it a free choice of myself" (Francis Jeanson, *Le Problème moral et la pensée de Sartre* [Paris: Editions du Seuil, 1965], p. 305).

all feeling, all return to self, in order to exist in the object through the sublimation of subjectivity. Thus subjectivity becomes a projection of a world rather than a return to self. This subjectivity *is* its own singularity instead of merely positing it, and it occupies itself with knowing rather than with preferring.

We are now in a position to define taste as such in its opposition to a plurality of tastes. Taste can give direction to tastes but can also run counter to them. Even if I do not like this or that work, I am capable of appraising it and of recognizing it. Whereas tastes are determinate, taste as such is not exclusive. To have taste is to possess a capacity of judgment which is beyond prejudice and partisanship. As Kant saw, this judgment is capable of universality. But why? Because it requires only my attention to the object, and not a decision. It is the work itself which appears before the tribunal and judges itself. Let us note that in this court the just judge is the one who allows the truth to unveil itself and is content to pronounce his sanction. It is the defendant who sentences himself (Hegel would add that he needs punishment precisely for his act to be recognized). To judge rightly is therefore to abstain from judging insofar as judgment is biased and arbitrary. It is to prefer the preferable only because it reveals itself as such and to do so without formulating a preference or, rather, by forcing ourselves to lay aside our preferences. To have taste is not to have tastes. That is why good taste resides in nonchoices rather than in choices. Admittedly, taste can inspire a sort of hierarchy among works, but only on the condition that the work avow itself as major or minor and claim its proper place.[24] And it is worth noting that good taste is readily eclectic, and it is so without bad conscience. It consists above all in avoiding the mistakes to which individual tastes are often subject. Thus good taste must not be taken in by works which lack validity because they strive for effect, seek to impress, or flatter our subjectivity—precisely where subjectivity is most vulnerable—so as to seduce us in the very name of taste, as we see in sentimental poetry, in moralizing or erotic painting, or in the Grand-Guignol.[25] Authentic art turns us away from ourselves and toward itself.

24. Nevertheless, we do ask critics to exercise their judgment, and we know that their function is not unimportant. But what we expect of them are judgments of existence rather than of taste: judgments as to what the work is, how it was created, what it says insofar as it can be explicated, and what it brings forth that is new.

25. The Grand-Guignol is a theater in Paris which specializes in the presentation of melodrama.—Trans.

And that is how the work of art forms taste. As Alain has shown at great length and as the arts of ceremony as well as music and poetry clearly illustrate, the work by its very presence disciplines the passions, imposes order and measure, and opens up the soul in a calmed body. Further, the work represses the role of the particular (whether it is empirical, historically determined, or capricious) in subjectivity. Or, more exactly, it converts the particular into the universal, enjoining the witness to be exemplary.[26] It invites subjectivity to constitute itself as a pure look, as a free opening onto the object, and it invites the special content of this subjectivity to enter the service of understanding instead of obscuring it by causing its own preferences to prevail. The work of art is an education in attention. And to the extent that our capacity for being open is exercised, the capacity to understand develops—to understand what must be understood, that is, to penetrate into the world which the work opens up. We shall probably say that comprehension can be furthered by prior thought and apprenticeship. But ultimately the important thing is to communicate with the work, beyond all knowledge and technique. And precisely this defines taste, to which the amateur can lay claim with as much right as the expert.

Through taste, the witness raises himself to what is universal in the human, that is, to the capacity of doing justice to the aesthetic object—which is not a constitutive capacity, but which allows the judgment of taste to become capable of universality. This universality is going to be revealed in a second mode of action belonging to the aesthetic object: the creation of a "public," where this term has a broader meaning than "audience."

(b) The constitution of a public

And, in fact, we shall grasp the power of the work still better in observing that its witness, even when solitary, is not alone. He is part of a public, and the constitution of this public, its

---

26. In the same way, in accord with what Croce says (following Hegel), it universalizes its own content not by making an abstract essence out of it but by wresting it from the determinations which, in the natural world, ceaselessly disguise and alter it. Van Gogh's chair is both *a* chair and *the* chair, something which possesses meaning in itself without anything's being able to strip it away. But we would point out that this universal is not yet the universal of the logos attained by absolute knowledge, if this is accessible, but a revealed universal which finds expression only aesthetically.

peculiar nature (which is not reducible to that of an audience present and necessary to a performance), testifies to the reality of the work and to its effect on its witnesses. The important thing, therefore, is to see how this public tends to embody the universality which is already found in the solitary witness. For such a public is the indefinite multiplication of the witness, a witness who is indefinitely multipliable and who becomes the counterpart [le semblable] of every human being by surpassing particularity.

This public is undoubtedly desired by the spectator or witness himself. If the solitary reader vaguely experiences the reality of an invisible public, if he is conscious of adhering to a secret society whose password is the work or of cooperating in a culture whose end and means are the work, this consciousness answers to a need within him. The aesthetic emotion wants to communicate and spread. It seeks confidants and cowitnesses. And it seeks guarantors as well. The demand for a public corresponds to a craving for security. The judgment of taste which ratifies and concludes the aesthetic experience feels sure of itself only insofar as it has supporters. For the judgment of taste, the homage of a public or of a tradition is the best assurance.

But it is the work which wants and creates this public. The work needs this public. And yet is not a single witness sufficient? Indeed it is; yet, because the meaning of the work is inexhaustible, the aesthetic object profits from a plurality of interpretations. The deciphering of its meaning is never finished, and its public has always to expand in order to begin this deciphering again. To be sure, if the work is thus insatiable, it is not in the manner of an object whose determinations relating it to the external world are never exhausted, or of a historical event whose meaning, even if its subject has been incontestably established (as when we say, "King John slept here"), can always be called into question as a result of being completely understandable only in relation to all of history. The work, by contrast, is detached from its spatiotemporal context. The work is in universal space and time, as though instituting a space and time of its own. It is rather in the manner of a person that the work establishes itself as inexhaustible. Not that it enjoys a special freedom. It does not have the questionable character of the lie or the unforseeable character of the free act, being completely equal to itself. But the face it turns toward us seems, like the human face, to express something beyond our grasp. And we can already guess why this is so. It is that the work's meaning is not exhausted in what it represents. The work's meaning is not anything that can be defined, summed up, and explained as the objective meaning of an intelligible object can be, or as the meaning of prose language can be exhausted. What it represents is conveyed only through what it expresses; and expression, even when immediately grasped, is still elusive.

But the most important point here is that the aesthetic object gains being from the plurality of interpretations which attach themselves to it. The aesthetic object is enriched in the measure that the work finds a vaster public and a more multifarious meaning. Everything takes place as if the aesthetic object were metamorphosing, gaining in density or depth, as if something of its being has been transformed by the cult whose object it is. That is why we cannot say, with Sartre, that it is indifferent whether the work survives its author and earns a "subjective immortality." It is a matter of indifference only to the author who is no longer present to congratulate himself upon this immortality. Such immortality is not merely sanction but enrichment. Nor should we believe that it disarms and renders the work innocuous. The work which does not die continues to affect us— perhaps not in the same way as the freshly completed work (composed by a living creator for a living public and working at times like an explosive) but doubtless with as much efficacy, because it acts in depth, inviting man first of all to be and not immediately to do. The difference is somewhat like that between the tract and the literary work. Thus we could say that the public continues to create the work by adding to its meaning, as if respect and ardor were themselves creative. Can we not say, moreover, that these latter are similarly creative in interpersonal relationships? What I hope for in my friend, what my friendship expects of him, that he be himself, he ends by being. In like manner, the work becomes self-assured and grows in stature through the conspiring of its public.

But how does it create this public? And then again how does it happen that a public can be formed and felt even when the circumstances of aesthetic perception render it invisible? It is because, in the first place, this public is not fundamentally an assemblage of individuals or the indefinite extension of the relations of an I and a thou, but the immediate affirmation of a we. Even at the theater, glances neither meet nor question one another, and the dialectical process of recognition is not entered into. Our gazes remain fixed upon the stage and intersect only there. The other does not appear in his provocative singularity but as my counterpart, whose existence reduces to the personal act which he performs in common with me. On the other hand, let me for a moment become attentive to my neighbor, and he again becomes that concrete individual whose presence cramps me, whose reactions differ from mine, whom I even suspect of not having understood anything. The public dissolves to make way for a mutual relationship of consciousnesses which operates on another plane. The group is a group, "essentially social," as Raymond Aron says, only when the relations of I and thou are surpassed. And, as it happens, the aesthetic object enables the public to be constituted as a group because it proposes itself as an eminent objectivity which wins individuals to itself and compels them to forget their individual differences. If the group, as social, involves a system of feelings, thoughts, or acts to which the individual is conscious of adhering as if submitting to an external norm, then the public is a typical group. The public forms a real community, founded not on the objectivity of an institution or a system of representation but on the eminent objectivity of the work. The work obliges me to renounce my own differentness, to make myself the counterpart of my fellow by accepting, like him, the rule of the game, which is to look and, as it were, to admire. The person who hisses at a concert instead of trying to understand or shrugs his shoulders at an exhibition of paintings rather than really looking at them breaks the pact which forms the public. At the same time, he evades, as we shall see later, the aesthetic experience. The objectivity of the work and the demand which goes with it impose and guarantee the reality of this social bond.

But this guarantee is also a limiting point at which the indefinite character of the group becomes apparent. For the public tends to become ever more open in character. First, since the work becomes a work only when contemplated, it does not give rise to norms which call for and regulate a definite activity. It creates a participation, not a cooperation. In this sense, the cohesion of the group is precarious, for it is experienced only on contact with the object. Second, the group itself is indefinite in extent. The counterpart whom I rediscover there has traits all the more undifferentiated in that he is not the collaborator in a common enterprise. He is defined in terms not of an activity to be pursued but of a perception to be experienced in common. Defined as the associate in a perception, he is still only vaguely defined. That is why anyone may enter the circle of a public. Yet it happens that the public is under the impression that it constitutes a privileged society to which only the initiated have access: hence cliques and coteries. And perhaps these sects should not be scorned—not only because snobbism, which is nothing other than the concern to portray the public as an elite, can serve to awaken taste (even if it is by creating a scandal), but also because it is perhaps under that willfully restricted and limited form that the public becomes aware of being a public. And it is inevitable that the public be thus restricted when the work is recent and has not had enough time to circulate, or when it guards an esoteric feature and seems to want to keep its secret.[27] The public then feels itself to have been determined and selected by the work. But this particularization of the counterpart, who is almost an accomplice, is a moment of a dialectical movement which must lead to a concrete universality. The counterpart must include singular determinations, so that as the universal notion stretches further away from him this notion does not become lost in a formal abstraction. Thus must the idea of man include that of citizen, as the idea of nation must contain that of region. It is by taking on concrete contents that the idea or notion can develop without losing its substance and that the group can expand without ceasing to be a group. And indeed, as the work grows older, its public expands, both horizontally and vertically.

Vertically, the generations form a kind of relay team in standing guard over the work. And we see here what the antiquity of the work is worth. Looking at the work, I am joined today to those generations and civilizations through which, motionless, it has passed. I follow in their wake and continue a tradition. There is no tradition without something's being transmitted which, at the same time, transmits the past. This is the office of the work, which is in effect historical not only in bearing witness to the past from which it arises but also in connecting past to present through a chain of viewings.

Horizontally, as time enhances the prestige of the work, its field of influence grows. If Racine, who wrote for a few Versailles courtiers, is now read by the whole bourgeoisie, it is not only because the bourgeoisie succeeded the aristocracy or because the French system of education has been democratized. It is also because we are in a better position today to understand Racine.

27. Let us observe that hermeticism is a feature of the work itself which we must not measure by the incomprehension of the public. Even when understood, the obscure work remains obscure. It is not at all like a hieroglyph which can be translated or a dream which can be interpreted. For it is the meaning itself which is obscure. It is not a case of form's being inadequate to content. Aesthetic feeling has to do with dim evidences.

A new work is often received with indifference, sometimes with scorn or anger—signs of obtuseness, which permit its defenders to band together and unite. After a while, if the work has not disappeared from the cultural scene, and even if it is always contested, it expands its public. And what matters to us here is that this public, as it grows, tends to stop being a public and merges with humanity, where counterparts rejoin one another beyond their particularity. And this metamorphosis of the group has a double meaning, both for the individual who is called to humanity and for the group which is transcended.

Man in front of the aesthetic object transcends his singularity and becomes open to the universally human. Like the proletarian for Comte or Marx, a man without ties, freed of the shackles and prejudices which enslave his consciousness, he is capable of rediscovering the stark essence of man within himself and of directly joining forces with others in the aesthetic community. What divides men are conflicts on the vital plane. That is why the struggle of consciousnesses in Hegel is a struggle for life. But the aesthetic object brings men together again on a loftier plane where, without ceasing to be individualized, they feel themselves to be interdependent. We may say, then, that aesthetic contemplation is in essence a social act, much as are, according to Scheler, loving, obeying, and respecting. Aesthetic contemplation is an act which includes at least an allusion to the other as my equal, because I feel supported by him, approved by him, and in a sense answerable to him. Even if the implicit presence of the other is not that of a being for whom I am responsible, it is that of a being with whom I am united. This demand for reciprocity which aesthetic admiration involves is one of the meanings of Kant's formal universality of the judgment of taste. In the same way that love expects love in return, and authority, obedience, admiration provokes further acts of admiration. And whereas the intersubjectivity founded upon primordial experiences like those of sympathy or love is not yet sociability—because the relation of person to person is not yet a social relation, for the other remains a fellow creature who is at once irreducibly distinct from and yet linked to me—the public is a social group because the work serves as a common denominator for consciousnesses who feel themselves counterparts.[28]

28. We shall later rediscover this unity of singularity and universality. Man does not join man by denying his difference, yet it is not by cultivating his difference that he becomes most profoundly himself, but by realizing the human within him.

We see thereby what "aesthetic sociability" is. If we make use of Scheler's terms, we shall say that the public is not a "society" because it is in no way bound by a contract and does not enlist any interests. It is also not a "community" because there is no stream of collective *Erlebnisse* in which individual consciousnesses are immersed. It is the identity of the object which assures the identity of its representations. Thus it is not a question of a collective consciousness but of a consciousness directed by a common object. And it is to the "cosmos of spiritual persons" that we would have to compare the public, a city of spirits in which is revealed, outside of any physical or contractual bond, a spiritual solidarity. The public is perhaps only a degraded form of this cosmos, but it is a form of it all the same, as in Kant the universality of the judgment of taste symbolizes the reality of a realm of ends by attesting to the spiritual kinship of rational beings.[29] If it is true that the demand for a community of persons is what animates every genuine social structure and the end toward which it strives—if it is true, in other words, that the closed is not opposed to the open but tends always to open itself, like the individual who rejoins mankind—we can say that each group tends toward humanity.[30] And perhaps this indefinite enlargement of the public, this open group which is defined more by its power of appeal than by its exclusions, is the best sign and the best instrument of this human vocation. In any event, we can begin to see the humanist significance of aesthetic experience. We shall confirm this later by showing how aesthetic perception calls on the spectator to realize the human within him at the same time that he recognizes the human as surrounding him in the public.

A final remark: no matter how large the public may be, even if it tends to be identified with humanity at large, we cannot confuse it with the masses, with the living community, because the work could direct itself to this community only on condition of accepting and defending the community's values, of entering the service of another cause than that of art. To be sure, there

29. See Immanuel Kant, *Critique of Judgement,* trans. J. C. Meredith (Oxford: Oxford University Press, 1952); and Max Scheler, *On the Eternal in Man,* trans. B. Noble (London: SCM Press, 1960), and *Man's Place in Nature,* trans. Hans Meyerhoff (Boston: Beacon, 1961).—Trans.

30. This movement is outlined in the thought of Comte as well as of Kant. [See Immanuel Kant, *The Critique of Practical Reason and Other Writings in Moral Philosophy,* trans. Lewis W. Beck (Chicago: University of Chicago Press, 1948); and Auguste Comte, *Système de politique positive* (Paris: Dunod, 1880), esp. Vol. III.—Trans.]

has been an art of the masses. Indeed, all art has been an art of the masses until very recent times, since basically, as we have stated, art has only just become aware of itself. Art for art's sake is a new idea. Before this point, the artist spontaneously entered the service of the *Weltanschauung* peculiar to his community, acting in the service of his faith during periods of faith. The work had no public, but the mass of faithful recognized itself in it and came to learn from it about its faith. People in the Middle Ages did not come to admire the sculptured tympanum over the portal of Moissac, but to worship Christ as he will appear on the day of the Last Judgment. Must we say that today the work has no other bond with the public than the taste for art which the work communicates to the public? Not quite, for the work still brings the public a message. But the work's harmony with the public is not a preestablished one, and art creates a communion which does not exist prior to it. What is more, the beliefs and values which cement the community are not necessarily—indeed, are far from being—those which the aesthetic object expresses in its own way. The beliefs and values found in the latter hardly touch the masses but instead create a public.

Does this mean that an art of the masses is not possible to-day? We are tempted to believe so when we think of examples which suggest themselves: tawdry religious art, Hollywood films, or detective stories. Yet in these cases we are dealing with a com-mercialized art whose works are turned out serially, indeed, with an encroachment by merchants on the techniques of art, and that is not enough to banish the idea of an art of the masses. But if today the dialogue between art and the masses does not manage to establish itself—not even in literature, as Sartre con-fesses—it is because the meeting ground of a common faith is lacking.[31] Let a living faith pass through the community and it will touch the artist and reverberate in the aesthetic object. We saw this for a moment in Russia, before art was dictated there. Eisenstein's films are related to the Russian Revolution as Peri-clean Athens is to the Persian defeat at Marathon. But as long as that faith does not exist, the artist can never propose anything but his own faith to whoever wants to listen. His public is only a public and not the masses in general, but it is still a public which tends toward humanity.

And this movement of the public toward humanity is possible only through the work. If the aesthetic object expects of the

31. See Sartre, *What Is Literature?*.—Trans.

public not only its consecration but also its completion, conversely the public expects of the work its promotion to humanity. Therefore, the aesthetic object brings no less to the public than it receives from it. The public must be a public for it and raise itself to the universal. And, of course, it can constitute itself in this way only because the work first acts on the individual and by itself invites him to an attitude of attention and respect. We shall see this at closer hand when studying aesthetic perception in Part 3. But it was first necessary to underscore the fact of a public, because the public extends the influence which the work exerts over the individual, and because the public is so characteristic of the aesthetic object. Other objects have no public, or, if they do, it is in no way comparable to that of the work of art. And recognizing this fact of the public renders us more sensitive to the ambiguous status of the aesthetic object, which exists both for us and in itself.

4 / The Aesthetic Object amid Other Objects

WE MUST NOW COMPARE the aesthetic object with other objects which perception encounters in the world and among which, however naïvely, it discriminates. In other words, we must, in a quite empirical manner, compare the aesthetic object with living beings, natural objects, objects of use, and signifying objects. This will be the best way to approach the being of the aesthetic object as we know it from the perception which it solicits and through which it becomes this kind of object. But a preliminary, twofold objection may give us pause. Is it legitimate to compare the aesthetic object as a perceived object with other objects? Yes, because every object is perceived and, for its part, the aesthetic object is not less real for being perceived. When an object which we find beautiful becomes aesthetic under our gaze, our perception by no means creates a new object but only does justice to the original object, which must lend itself to this aestheticization. In becoming aesthetic, the object becomes nothing other than it was, even though perception reserves a peculiar fate for it. In short, it is metamorphosed only into *itself*, for it is into itself that its appearing finally changes it. Yet if all objects, aesthetically perceived, can become aesthetic objects, how can we oppose them to "the aesthetic object"? Did we not agree that we must not, except for reasons of method, too strictly circumscribe the domain of aesthetic objects which, as such, admit of beauty? But we also agreed that the work of art is the aesthetic object *par excellence,* so that, if we identify the aesthetic object with the work of art, we have the right to contrast it with other objects which are aesthetic only potentially or incidentally. Thus, we can seek what distinguishes the aesthetic object qua work of art from other objects which are aesthetic only *per accidens*. It is on condition of privileging the work of art that we can conceive an adequate idea of the aesthetic object. At the same time, we shall have to dwell upon what is nonaesthetic in other objects without forgetting, however, that they may become aesthetic and sometimes even claim to be so. But if we want to understand how they can become aesthetic, we must examine them in the light of the work of art. Our primary purpose, nevertheless, is limited to describing the features peculiar to the aesthetic object and to emphasizing its differences from other objects, rather than following the opposite path of trying to find out how life, nature, or industry imitates art and produces objects which solicit an aesthetic perception.

[I] The Aesthetic Object and the Living Being

THE COMPARISON OF THE LIVING BEING or creature [*le vivant*] with the aesthetic object will not detain us long. Even if we are led to discover an analogy between the aesthetic object and the living being, and even if the living being harbors aesthetic qualities, it is impossible to confuse the two. For the living creature constitutes a well-defined sector of the real—at least if we think of it as existing in the characteristic form of the self-moving being, since plants do not seem so "alive" for the naïve consciousness. It is only for the reflective consciousness, which rejects first impressions and simple distinctions, that the question arises of a continuity of matter and life and of hybrid forms which, in space and time, can assure this continuity. But we know that the child very early behaves differently toward a person or an animal than toward an inert thing. Even at this point, the living creature appears before the child in its own guise, unchallengeable. Is he not tempted, however, to extend to the inanimate the characteristics which he observes in the animate? But we can show that the child's animism is nevertheless metaphorical or, if we prefer, in bad faith. The little girl who plays mother with her doll distinguishes quite clearly between the doll and a real infant, just as the hallucinated individual distinguishes his hallucinatory experience from an injection which a doctor has just given him. The child who strikes the table into which he has bumped—like Xerxes lashing the sea—is not unaware that the table is made of wood and is incapable of feeling pain, since he knows at other times how to use it as a thing and does not think that he is inflicting wounds on it when he nicks it with a knife. The child, like the adult, is simply able to experience emotions which, for a moment, upset established features of the world. The same is true of the adult animist. Modern ethnologists are unanimous in recognizing "positive" thinking in primitive man, that is, first and foremost, an aptitude for differentiating the various sectors of the real. And Comte, defining fetishism by his statement that "the primitive notion of external order makes no distinction at all between the material and the vital," showed "the inner breakup" which star worship wrought in this system and the immanence of positivity in the primitive mentality.[1] A phenomenology of animism would have to distinguish between: (1) the aspect of truth—the foreshadowing of the idea of law in the idea of cause, which, as Comte indicates, is at first conceived anthropomorphically; (2) the aspect of play, of which emotion may be the extreme form; and (3) the aspect of metaphor, by which one is even less likely to be taken in but which is accounted for by the experience which is the ground of all animism—the awareness that things can, like faces or behavior, have an expression. We shall treat lengthily the notion of expression. Suffice it to say here that in no case does this expressiveness efface the characteristics, to which it is added, of the natural object as distinct from the living being.

The aesthetic object cannot be confused with the living being as thus specified. This is so evident in a painting or a monument that it hardly needs mention. However, we must mention it with regard to objects which call on man, on the human body, in order to appear. Is not the dance in the dancer? Would it still be a dance if the dancer were to become a robot or a marionette, as Gordon Craig dreamed that the actor would some day become in a theater where the director would finally be king? Let us halt at this example. It is certain that there is no dance whatever without a dancer. We can make things dance, as Chaplin did with pieces of bread in *The Gold Rush*, but this is a dance only to the extent that we still imagine a dancer whose feet are here represented by pieces of bread. It is no longer a dance, except in metaphor, when, for example, colored shapes are made to dance

1. See Auguste Comte, *Système de politique positive* (Paris: Dunod, 1880), III, 123.

on the movie screen.[2] But the ballet itself, as long as it exists
only in the imagination of the choreographer, who is unable to
confer the same existence on it as is conferred upon a theatrical
work by the very paper on which it is written, is not yet an aesthetic object. Furthermore, the qualities of the dance are those
of the dancer. There is no grace if the dancer is not graceful, no
nobility if he is not noble, no transport if he is not transported.
"It is unpardonable for a dancer to be ugly," said Théophile Gau-
tier. Better still, it can be said that the dance is nothing other
than the apotheosis of the human body, the triumph of life. To
imagine a *danse macabre*, we must ressuscitate the skeletons;
and Death, who leads the action in *La Table rond*, is portrayed
by a magnificent living being. Thus the aesthetic object which
offers itself to me is not only composed in this case of living
beings, it even strives to give me the clearest image of life. Each
movement of the dancer is like a living affirmation, the exhibition of life-forces displayed in their proper duration. But if
the dance provides an image of life, it is only because the dance
is not life itself. The living beings the dance employs are in its
service, lending it their quality as living beings in order to
represent life. And life treated aesthetically is not life *simpliciter*,
any more than the dancer is an ordinary living being, or Dullin
the real Julius Caesar. And if the dancer is in the service of the
dance, if he tries to identify himself with it, it is because it is
distinct from him. The dance for him is what the text or scenario
is for the actor, and the score for the musician. The spectator
perceives the dance as realizing itself through the dancer, as
having an absolutely imperative need of the dancer in order to
appear, yet not as identifying itself with him.

What, then, is this aesthetic object? A thing, an idea, something imaginary? Let us again refer to the spectator's naïve
experience of it. He sees a ballet: members of the cast execute
movements in time with a certain piece of music. Do these
gesticulations against a background of sound constitute the
whole spectacle? No, for through the movements and forms, the
spectator perceives a certain logic, which is often that of an
action: the ballet bears a title and often tells a story, of *Phèdre*
or of *Oedipus*, a fable, a tale. In the dancer's performance, the
spectator follows the story as if it were an account given to him.

2. As in the effect of "mobile light" created by the "clavilux." About
this instrument, see Thomas Munro, *The Arts and Their Interrelations*
(New York: Liberal Arts Press, 1949), pp. 506 ff.

Is this, then, the ballet? Not yet—at least not in its entirety. The forewarned spectator guards against becoming too interested in the anecdote lest it overshadow the dance. He does not want the dance to be reduced to a pantomime. He avoids judging the ballet in terms of its story, for the story is only a pretext that is much less important than the libretto is for the opera. Instead, he judges the action in terms of the ballet and appreciates it for the way in which it calls forth choreographic expression and serves the cause of the dance. The dance is not sacrificed to what it represents. The spectator grasps its movements and figures as obedient to another logic, which may be inspired by the music but belongs no more to the music than to the narrative subject. The ballet follows the music without submitting to it. "The dancer dances to the music as if over a carpet," says Roland-Manuel. It is noteworthy that great works written for the dance which take the dance as a pretext (to the point where these works can very easily be performed for their own sake) nevertheless allow the dance to take them as a pretext in turn—as when Isadora Duncan dances to Schumann or Janine Solane to Beethoven or Bach. Any music which attempts to dominate the dance in the manner of military music that dominates a march step kills the dance instead of inspiring it.[3] The logic of choreographic development is, therefore, above all a logic of bodily movements, but one which is conveyed through rules (as is musical development, from which it borrows its terminology) and which, also like music, can develop a thematic structure. We see this logic in the arabesque of Wilis in the second act of *Giselle* or in the elevation movements in *Icare*, for which Serge Lifar invented the sixth and seventh positions that momentarily suppress movement outward. As Lifar states, "I had to interpret choreographically the flight and fall of the hero, his disembodiment, and his human end [*fin*]."[4]

This last example shows best what the spectator perceives, namely, a certain atmosphere in which subject, music, and choreography cooperate and which forms the soul of the ballet. This atmosphere is what the dancers aim at. It is the aesthetic object itself as they bring it into being. This atmosphere is perceptible even in the pure dance, where expression is not prompted and fortified by a specific subject. The dance always expresses, even when it does not narrate. It is grace, lightness, innocence.

3. See Serge Lifar, *Traité du danse académique* (Paris: Bordas, 1949), p. 215.
4. *Ibid.*, p. 44.

In this sense, the dance triumphs as beyond all representation, as an absolute language which bespeaks only itself.[5] That is what distinguishes the dance from pantomime—a theater without words—and also from acrobatics, to which it is incorrect to reduce the pure dance. For if pure dance expresses only itself, it is at least *self*-signifying and subordinates the dancer to this self. The acrobat, on the other hand, assumes responsibility before the public only with regard to his own body, whose capabilities he exhibits. The dancer dedicates his body to the dance. His movements proceed from his trunk as if they obeyed some secret impulsion from the deepest recesses of his being. The acrobat, in contrast, employs his body in precise actions that are often regulated by some object such as a rope, bar, or rings. He must succeed in his feats, reach a goal, and not express anything. In the acrobat the body is body, not language. No matter how thrilling it may be, the acrobatic spectacle does not constitute an aesthetic object, as the ballet can. The ballet *Forains*, staged by Roland Petit, exhibits this difference: the circus performers, conceived in dance terms, cease to be acrobats. Even the exercises which figure in it are not means for exhibiting bodily prowess and individual talent but gestures which fit into an ensemble and combine into an expression. When purely acrobatic figures are introduced casually and integrated into the ballet cautiously, as in *Le Bal des blanchisseuses*, they take on expressive values—for example, joy, freedom from care, or "the derangement of all the senses"—and thus submit to the meaning which animates the ballet as a whole. And if certain choregraphic movements are borrowed from acrobatics—like the *entrechats*, which derive from circus performers of the Italian school —they aim at an effect in which their athletic character is lost. "With us," Lifar writes, "grace and grandeur are substituted for athletic stunts. . . . What distinguishes the dancer's leap from the acrobat's is the famous halt in midair, the feat of 'touching the curtain tops and staying there,' which is clearly an optical

5. That is why, as Henri Gouhier states, "A choreographic critic in love with pure dance will always denounce the action ballet as the most beautiful of heresies" (*L'Essence du théâtre* [Paris: Plon, 1943], p. 148). Ever since Noverre invented the action ballet, the history of the classic dance has been, as Lifar states, "a perpetual hesitation between two great poles of attraction: on the one hand, the pure and objective dance, as we find it in operas, comedies, and even in certain choreographic works; and, on the other, pantomime, which claims to express *everything* and in which the dance plays an ever less important role" (*Traité*, p. 214). But we would not say that the pure dance is inexpressive; it simply lacks a subject.

effect obtained by means of certain movements of the torso and feet." [6]

Even if the ballet expresses nothing other than life itself—at least, when its expression is not particularized by a definite subject (which, we may add, inspires expression without constricting it)—it is *life* with which we are dealing and not the living being. Living beings are called on only to bear witness to life, "that universal indestructible substance, a flowing essence equal to itself," as Hegel puts it. The living being disavows life whenever "it asserts itself as not resolved in the universal," whenever it pursues its particular aims and in its awkwardness and infirmities lets the death which it bears within it show through as the sign of its finitude. The dancer, on the contrary, proclaims life through movements which are pure movements, which no aim particularizes and no fatigue alters. But precisely in expressing life, the dancer forgoes appearing as a mere living being. He forgoes it both in giving his movements a character of gratuitousness, fluidity, and totality (a character emblematic of life as universal) and in giving them a sculptural or architectural character by the poses he takes, in what are called attitudes or arabesques, or by the groups which he composes with others. This sculptural character suspends duration only to make us feel its tremulousness and its upsurge more fully. For even if dance is an art of synthesis, it "nevertheless remains more rhythm than form, more musical than plastic." [7] The plastic element in dance is movement gathered up into itself as a promise of movement. In the dance, the living being is always surpassed in his particularity. And why is this, if not because the dancer submits to the ballet and becomes the instrument of the aesthetic object which he is incarnating? This object, which the spectator discerns in the dancer, is no more a living being than a painting is oil paint or a monument is stone. The living being is the material from which the aesthetic object is made and the organ of performance through which the aesthetic object appears.

In other arts which require a performance, the material is not the living being himself but the sound or the word, and the living being is only a performer. In these arts, the aesthetic object is still less identifiable with the living being.

But a difficulty analogous to that which the dance has presented can be found in the art of formal gardens. Does not the

6. Lifar, *Traité*, p. 95.
7. Raymond Bayer, *L'Esthétique de la grâce*, 2 vols. (Paris: Alcan, 1934), II, 212.

aesthetic object in this case consist merely in plant life? When winter extinguishes this life, what is left of the park? At least *something* is left: a certain structure which is still discernible in the layout of the clumps of shrubs, the flower beds, the paths, and the grouping of the trees. It is emphasized by a basin, a vase, or a statue at certain central points. (By the same token, when the park surrounds and solemnizes a monument, something is left of the harmony which it must realize with this monument and in which it is the subordinate member.) This structure, which is properly the work of the landscape architect as opposed to the gardener, is to the park what the text is to the theater, or the score to the music. When the leaves sprout again and the flowers bloom, we can say that this flowering, prepared for and supervised by the gardener, executes the work of art. At the same time, along with the ground itself, whose accidental features he must utilize and organize, the flowering furnishes the gardener with his appropriate material. The aesthetic object appears fully only when this work has been executed, when the vegetation lends its volumes and colors. However, the aesthetic object does not reduce to this. When I go for a walk in the park, it is still an idea that I perceive, but one that is perceptible to the eye and delivers a certain expression: nobility and measure here, abandon and caprice there, intimacy and tenderness elsewhere. The aesthetic object is always a language. Even if it makes use of the living being in order to be transmitted, this function forbids us to reduce the aesthetic object to the living being.

Since this function also distinguishes the aesthetic object from other objects, we must stress it in our effort to discern the specific traits of this object.

[II] The Aesthetic Object and the Natural Object

(a) The natural object and the object of use

Among objects which contrast with living beings, perception spontaneously distinguishes between natural objects [*les choses naturelles*] and artificial objects, between those which do not bear the mark of man and those which do, between a stone and a hammer, a branch and a cane, a cave and a house. This distinction, it will be said, is less apparent than that between natural objects and living beings. We can in fact treat the natural object as an instrument, use a rock as a hammer, or find shelter in the cave as in a house. Moreover, the first hammers were stones and the first houses were caves. This is true, and the intelligence which is at work in human perception—and not equally in the perception of Köhler's apes—can have a presentiment of the implement in the natural object and readies far in advance that peculiarly human technique which has recourse to tools (for there is indeed a vital technique in regard to which we hardly dare speak of intelligence and which does not invent the tool).[8] But this only means that we may adopt the same behavior with regard to the natural object that we display toward objects of use [objets usuels]—yet without erasing the difference between the two. Surprised by rain, I seek shelter in a cave, without the cave's turning into a house for me. The opposite is true for the troglodyte who, no matter how hastily he furnishes his cave, impregnates it with a visible humanity. Then the natural object is metamorphosed so as to be integrated into the cultural world— like the branch I cut to make a staff. Then, too, ownership is established, for possession humanizes the object: this dog is mine because I have fed it, this field because I have enclosed it. The human object exists to serve man. Made by and for man, it belongs to someone and is capable of becoming an object of exchange. In this sense—and this is all we mean here—property is perceived in the object itself, because this object brings the mark of man immediately before me, making a cultural world immediately present and perceptible. The object of use speaks to me of others, as it were, before I even encounter them.[9] First

8. We must still distinguish, among objects that are made, between objects of use (a house, a cultivated field, a roast prepared by a butcher) and instruments (fork, pen, violin) which are means in the service of objects of use, as production may be in the service of consumption. But this distinction imposes itself only after reflection. It makes no difference in our behavior, for it is in both cases taught by tradition and regulated by the object.

9. We do not have to wonder here whether the experience of the other must exist prior to the experience of the presence of the other in particular objects. Merleau-Ponty, who raises the problem of solipsism generally, does not expressly distinguish, in the movement of transcendence toward others that is peculiar to subjectivity, between the relation to the other as singular and the relation to the social as "the generalized other" in Mead's expression. He is, above all, concerned with placing the experience of the world and of the other in parallel: "our relationship to the social, like our relation to the world, is deeper than any express perception or any judgment" (Maurice Merleau-Ponty, *Phenomenology of Perception*, trans. C. Smith [New York: Humanities Press, 1962], p. 362). It seems to us, as we shall try to demonstrate later, that, at least in theory, the experience of the "human" precedes and directs the experience of others. The encounter

of all, by a certain tautness and air of finality, it points to a making which has produced it. While the natural object bears within it the impress of the accidents of which it is the precarious result, the man-made object bears the seal of the norm to which it has been subordinated and which has presided at its making. An order appears in it, in the geometry of its forms, in the equilibrium of its proportions, in the firmness of its foundations. This order, instituted by man, has been able to command nature and has violated the anarchy of chance. The object has been made, and it can be unmade and remade in accordance with the particular order which has brought it into being. What is human in the object is, above all, the law which governs it as a result of having governed its creation. At the same time, this law expresses the possibility of a use, since the object reveals itself as made to be used. Even if I do not know this use, as with certain objects brought to light by excavation, I know that the object has been conceived for use and that I would be able to recapture the behavior which accounts for this object if I were to use it myself. There is, then, a look of finality about the object of use, but of external finality, since its *raison d'être* lies not in itself but in what is done with it. Finally, this object is also human in that it can show the mark of use, as a bed retains the imprint of a body which has lain in it or as the handle of a tool can be worn smooth through repeated usage.

This human character enables us at first glance to pick out the object of use from among natural objects, exactly as we can tell the domesticated animal, a docile creature, from the wild animal who refuses by his unpredictable actions to be integrated into the cultural world. But we must notice that the human here is not yet the expressive, in the sense in which a look or a gesture is expressive. The human is, indeed, that which speaks to man, but without resembling him or saying anything inward to him. The human accords with the hand and the project but not yet with feeling. It announces a real and active man but not his deepest possibility. (Whereas the human which we shall later see revealed by aesthetic experience falls short of the objective enterprises and techniques of man; it is that through which man becomes man.) The natural object is, in contrast, nonhuman and, as it were, wild. Just as it rebuffs our glance by what is

---

with the individual is clearly that by which this idea of the human is constantly tested and nurtured. But this encounter is perhaps understood only through the idea, which is also tested in the wider experience of a human world.

disorderly in it, so it rebuffs our attempts to grasp it, and we see no use in it. A possible aspect of the nonhuman is the sublime which challenges man by that grandeur, as Kant states, "by comparison with which everything is small." But the nonhuman can just as well be experienced as menace, indifference, or disorder—always as that which is not to the measure or at the mercy of man. In another connection, we can accept it as a test or trial, thinking sometimes to acquire new strength through contact with an object or landscape which has not been tamed or emasculated by man. The pleasure of the vacation that involves leaving the city where everything is human, too human, is often the pleasure of a return to nature. But it is important to see clearly here that this difference between the natural object and the object of use, between a cityscape and the *Urwald,* between the arid Causses[10] or an unruly sea, is given directly in perception. And it is immediately noted in different behaviors. The cultural object is that of which Bergson's famous saying holds true: "To recognize an object of use consists above all in knowing how to make use of it." I know that there is a norm of use just as there is a norm of the object, because the object was intended for use. Even if this norm is proposed by the object through its structure and its modes of apprehension, it is a norm which has had to be or must be learned. Thus the object of use calls for social behavior, since learning is something eminently social—the method of trial and error is, for man, mostly passional in character, and self-instruction is only a last resort.[11] The object of use therefore introduces me to the cultural world, where the other is present in filigree form both in the object and in the use which I can make of it, that is, in the meaning which the object has for me. For it is really meaning which has been conveyed to me in this suggestion for behavior, a meaning which is more familiar when the suggestion is lively and the behavior free. Perhaps this is why scientific explanation tends

10. The limestone plateau in the south of France.—Trans.
11. Of course, this in no way warrants the coercion which a norm-setting like that in the Taylor system means to foist on the man at work. (The ineffectualness of this system has been exposed by George Friedmann in *Problèmes humaines du machinisme industriel* [Paris: Gallimard, 1946].) It is still less warranted inasmuch as we are then dealing with norms not only foreign to the individual but at least partly foreign to the machine, as in time-study. True learning in no way excludes—on the contrary, it favors—the adjustment, which each individual must discover for himself, of his own norms to the norms of the object. It is in this way that the individual takes on a social dimension through the instruction of the example furnished him.

toward the construction of a mechanical model, that is, toward the substitution of an object of use for the natural object. Yet the object of use induces action rather than intellection. Its familiarity leads us to a connivance in which perception is lost in gestures. It revives our attention only when it poses a problem and again becomes a thing for us. For the thing calls forth a different behavior. The nonhuman in it is at first upsetting. Aggressive tendencies may be awakened in order to counter this foreign presence, to accept the challenge it hurls, and to give evidence of our mastery. What would be vandalism in the case of the object of use, because this use is regulated, learned, and official, excites no protest here.[12] Destructive acts, whose psychoanalysis can always be ultimately undertaken, are the natural expression of an inevitable curiosity awakened by a thing for which we have no use. Of course, this curiosity may express itself differently. However, more often than not, at the core of our surprise there is the desire to take possession of the thing, which is unamenable to norms, and to deal with it by force. Thus snow invites us to press it together, a mountain invites us to carve it, the sea invites us to plunge into it. The pleasure of swimming probably stems from that dominion which I exercise not only over myself in adapting to a new milieu (felt even more in underwater spear-fishing, where the spectacle of depths is at first as oppressive as the physical pressure of the water) but over the very thing which I make support me when it should be engulfing me. To be sure, such behavior with regard to the natural world is often learned and can even be institutionalized. Its difference from behavior toward the object of use then tends to fade, and the natural world tends to become familiar. Indeed, the natural world is already cultural in a certain sense—through the social tradition of tourism and through the "feeling for nature" which is itself a cultural product. But there remains in it something alien and unyielding which always offers us a challenge.

12. Who has not seen almost unbearable examples of this during the war? This is because war, thrusting the individual into an inhuman adventure where he must leave everything behind him—including whatever inspired tenderness and nurtured hope—invites him to break his ties with the cultural world, to profane whatever inspires respect and elevates man.

(b) Aesthetic object and nature

The work of art is encountered in the world of objects, where the natural and the cultural, the natural object and the man-made object, mingle inextricably. Let us first compare the work of art with natural objects, those nonhuman things which come and go at the whim of chance and over which man has no control. But why do we need to do so? Is it not obvious enough that the work is a human object? Here we must be careful. The aesthetic object does not repudiate nature but may well be in harmony with it, like a church in the heart of a village or a fountain in a garden. Likewise, a pier is beautiful when it hugs and exactly continues the shoreline, and roads and viaducts are rightly called works of art for the way in which they adopt and bring out the lines of a landscape. The French term for engineering [*génie*] is not at all inappropriate.[13] No doubt this argument is open to reservations, for it can be said that nature, when it is marked by the work of art or the work of engineering, is no longer nature. As we shall see, it is aestheticized and falls into the orbit of art. Moreover, we cannot ignore the difference between the work of art [*oeuvre d'art*] and the work of engineering [*ouvrage d'art*]. The former presupposes a nature already tamed, a village already built, a garden already planted. Above all, the work of art converts from nature whatever lends itself to being aestheticized and can appear aesthetic by itself, for example, a quality of light or a color of the sky that watercolor can capture, or a pattern of forms. Thus does the creator of stained glass, bringing the glass into harmony with light, make something aesthetic out of the aesthetic. On the other hand, the engineer does violence to nature in order to realize his abstract plan and takes no notice, in the struggle which he conducts against the physical obstacle, of the sensuous aspect of things. And nature, to which he has had to yield in order to vanquish it, aestheticizes his work to the extent to which nature is itself aesthetic. However, whether as aestheticized or as aestheticizing, nature, when it enters into alliance with art, keeps its character as nature and communicates it to art. In this character, nature possesses a countenance which defies man and reveals an unfathomable otherness.

13. The word *génie* can mean, among other things, "genius" as well as "engineering."—Trans.

We can thus say that the aesthetic object is nature in that it expresses nature, not by imitating it but by submitting to it. Alain has stressed this point at length.[14] The nature to which art submits is the physiological structure of the human body as well as the force in things. And not only does art submit to nature in order to create a lasting work—wherefore architecture is the art *par excellence,* and Michelangelo was right in saying that painters or sculptors should be architects first—but it even proclaims this submission: the aesthetic object accommodates itself to nature. Whether it becomes integral with an environment, like the Parthenon on the Acropolis or Notre Dame on the banks of the Seine, or whether it does not hide the natural laws of the material which it shapes and yet obeys, it confesses to being a thing among things and is not ashamed of being nonhuman in its humanity.

Even the arts which are separated from nature, those whose works are sheltered in monuments which culture builds for them—music in the concert hall, painting in the museum, poetry in the library—harbor within them something of nature. And what do they harbor? They harbor the aesthetic object, which is always there and which, quite simply, expects of me only the tribute of a perception. It has the stubborn presence of the natural object. It is there for me, yet as if it were not there. It has indeed been created by someone who beckons to me through his work, but not to invite me to some joint action, to warn me of a danger, or to give me an order. What this object

14. "Resemblance to a man, an animal, or a plant, is only an external rule, almost mechanical, and closer to industry than to art. Nature must be revealed in the work itself, and altogether differently, through the conditions which an incompletely submissive material imposes, a material retaining something of its own forms; hence through all the conditions of the craft which, as soon as they are evinced, heighten and embellish the forms of the work" (*Vingt Leçons sur les beaux-arts* [Paris: Gallimard, 1931], p. 222). We know how this idea leads Alain to mistrust taste: "A work of bad taste, which is perhaps taste [itself]," because taste is pleased by an ornament which tricks nature and is ashamed of it. "For, when we trim yews into the shape of birds or people, we feel good, although we lose the beautiful and fall into arbitrary ornament" (*ibid.,* p. 184).

On the other hand, industry does violence to nature by imposing a premeditated idea upon it. The beautiful must be natural: "miracle of nature revealing and sustaining the idea." It is weight itself which creates the Romanesque vault, and the law of the spirit appears as the law of nature. Alain's whole aesthetic, an aesthetic based on the image of the stonemason, is thus an annotation of the *Critique of Judgement* as well as of Comte's *Politique positive,* for it appears that Humanity is the artist. True art is a popular art, the art of the man who is nearest to things and follows a tradition. "It is the mason who has created these forms" (*Système des beaux-arts* [Paris: Gallimard, 1926], p. 194).

says to me is left in the secrecy of my perception and does not move me to do anything.

It moves me to do nothing but perceive, that is, open myself to the sensuous. For the aesthetic object is, above all, the irresistible and magnificent presence of the sensuous. What is a melody, if not a stream of sound which washes over me? But also what is a poem, if not the radiance and harmony of words by which, once again, the ear is delighted? And what is painting, if not a play of colors; or even a historic building, if not the sensuous qualities of stone, its mass, shimmer, and patina? If color grows dull and fades, the pictorial object vanishes. If the ruin is still an aesthetic object, it is because in it the stone remains stone, its very erosion manifesting its stoneness. But if the monument loses all its elements of line and color, as happens in a fire, it then ceases to be an aesthetic object. Similarly, if words become no more than signs without sensuous quality— as if they were mere mathematical algorithms—and are reduced to their meaning, then the poem ceases to be a poem.

Thus the aesthetic object is the sensuous appearing in its glory. But in this the aesthetic object is already distinguishable from the ordinary object which *has* colors but is not color, which *makes* noise but is not sound. For perception goes straight to what interests it, proceeding through colors and sounds, through the sensuous qualities whose meaning it at first seeks to grasp. It aims at the useful, as Descartes realized, or at knowledge, which itself on this level seeks the useful and strives to make an object of use out of the object of nature. The noise of a locomotive does not interest a mechanic in the way it interests Honegger, nor does the noise of the sea interest the sailor in the way it does Debussy. For the former person in each case, the object is not enjoyed for itself, and its sensuous properties are not appreciated. We shall see how, in contrast, these properties are sought out and ennobled through the artist's operation and through aesthetic perception. Through art, the sensuous is no longer a sign, unimportant in itself, but an end. The sensuous itself becomes an object or, at least, inseparable from the object which it "qualifies." The relationship between the matter, which is the body of the work, and the sensuous is no longer what it is in the object of use. In the case of the ordinary object, perception, by a spontaneous movement which Aristotelian physics investigates on its own account, distinguishes between the matter and its sensuous qualities, because what interests it in the object is its substance as a thing, that by which stone becomes stone and can serve for building, that by which steel can be used in a machine, that by which words have meaning and enable communication to take place. Art, on the contrary, rejects any distinction between matter and the sensuous: matter here is nothing other than the depth of the sensuous itself. This rugged and encrusted massiveness is stone. That high-pitched, slender, probing sound is the timbre of a flute, and "flute" is nothing but the name given to that sound. The sound itself is the matter. In speaking of woodwinds and brass, we are not referring to the instrument but to the materiality of the sound. Likewise, when painters speak of matter, they are not concerned with a chemical product or the canvas upon which it is brushed but with the color itself apprehended in its thickness, purity, and density—in short, the color as it affords an avenue to the work, but without loss of sensuous quality and reference to perception. Thus, for the perceiver, matter is the sensuous itself considered in its materiality, or, as one may also say, in its alien character. There is no need to invoke a substratum for the sensuous, since the sensuous is an object in itself. It is enough for perception to register this miracle of the sensuous given in its plenitude and bearing witness to a matter which is in no way ashamed of itself.

This uselessness of the aesthetic object and the primacy which the sensuous enjoys there lead us to discern in it a radical exteriority—the exteriority of an in-itself which does not exist for our sake and which imposes itself on us, leaving us no other recourse than perception. In this respect, the aesthetic object differs from the object of use and resembles the object of nature. Let us ponder for a moment this naturelike element in it. We could certainly bestow the title of nature, in a sense closely related to Heidegger's sense of "earth," upon that massive presence of the object which almost does violence to us.[15] Berlioz's Faust sings of nature as immense, impenetrable, and proud, and so can the symphony, the monument, or the poem. Thus we can understand why Emmanuel Levinas invokes the aesthetic object to convey some idea of the fundamental fact of existence as the "there is [*il y a*]"—in which are mingled the subjective sense of existence found in existential philosophy and the objective sense of classical realism. For it is the aesthetic object which gives us the experience of the nakedness of the given,

15. See Martin Heidegger, "The Origin of the Work of Art," trans. A. Hofstadter, in *Poetry, Language, and Thought* (New York: Harper & Row, 1971).—Trans.

that is, of that essential otherness which instrumentality masks, just as clothes in the world of society mask the disturbing alterity of the other.[16] "Art, even the most realistic, communicates this character of *otherness* to the objects represented, which are nevertheless part of our world." [17] The efforts of contemporary painting are here singularly illuminating. "Objects no longer matter as elements of a universal order which our gaze is given like perspective. Fissures disrupt the continuity of the universe throughout. The particular stands out in the nakedness of its being." [18]

But this transmutation of the object, this thickening of its in-itself, bears not only on the object represented in the work (which the act of representation extracts from perception of an orderly world) but also on the being of the aesthetic object, that is, its very material. Perhaps Levinas does not lay enough stress upon this. What we are calling nature here is not exactly the "there is" or *natura naturata* as these are revealed in the privileged experiences which every philosophy seeks and invokes in its own way, e.g., as the intellectual grasp of necessity, as the feeling of anguish, or as the experience of horror. Instead, nature is our experience of the necessity of the sensuous, that is, of a necessity internal to the sensuous—where necessity is not reduced to the contingent advent of a sensation which takes me by surprise, as when a sudden light blinds me or an odor invades me, but is, through form, the consecration of the sensuous and of the evidence it gives concerning being.

The aesthetic object is also nature—this especially concerns what it represents, a point we shall develop later—in that there is something incomprehensible about it, a characteristic which the plastic and poetic arts of today have systematically emphasized and exploited. But even the most facile art conceals something mysterious by the mere fact that it is addressed to our perception rather than to our understanding. As soon as we wish to make the content of the work explicit, the unfathomable

16. We shall see, however, that the aesthetic object has a form which is like a garment for it. "The statues of antiquity are never truly naked," says Levinas (*De l'existence à l'existant* [Paris: Vrin, 1947], p. 61). Through this form, the aesthetic object, unconquerable as it is, submits itself to perception, and its "there is" becomes a perceived existence. So we would not say that "the discovery of the materiality of being is the discovery of its formless swarming." Aesthetic nature is not an amorphous nature.

17. *Ibid.*, p. 84.

18. *Ibid.*, p. 90.

is revealed. When we have stated the subject of a painting or a poem, we have still not said anything; and what can we say concerning the subject of music or of architecture? It is in this respect that the aesthetic object is like a natural object, yet it is even more refractory, for when we try to grasp the natural object through its history and context, even if the quest were in principle endless, we gain the impression that there is nothing else to seek and that knowledge is the truth of perception. This is not so in the case of the aesthetic object. The aesthetic object is an unjustified presence or one whose justification is not amenable to the intelligence. Yet it is an imperious presence, because the materiality of the object is heightened by it and because the sensuous finds its apotheosis in it (through special efforts and artifices which we shall explore). This is why, in Heidegger's view, the work of art brings forth a world and at the same time reveals the earth. "The work moves the earth itself into the open of a world and keeps it there." [19]

But the sensuous is material only to the extent that it is given form, and the qualities of this matter are strictly tied to form. It is in this that nature is surpassed. For we shall see that, without returning to an intellectualist psychology, we cannot grant that perception delivers the sensuous in its primordial state, or that in the aesthetic event—which is, as Levinas states, "the event of the sensation as sensation"—sensation returns "to the impersonality of its elements." [20] Art does indeed rehabilitate the sensuous by altering or suppressing the shape of the object to which in ordinary perception the sensuous immediately refers, but this "dis-qualification" of the object is not the renunciation of all meaning. A sense is always immanent in the sensuous, and this sense is, above all, the form which manifests both the plenitude and the necessity of the sensuous.

Of course, signification does not consist solely in setting the sensuous in order. This is evident in the case of literary works and even in the plastic arts—a point to which we shall return when we compare the aesthetic object with the signifying object. But in here identifying the form of the sensuous with signification (a signification which signifies only the sensuous), we perhaps gain by seeing that, conversely, signification understood as sense or meaning (explicit or foreshadowed, intelligible or affective) can itself be form—contrary to the view of form

19. Heidegger, "Origin," p. 673.
20. Levinas, *De l'existence*, p. 86.

which we hold when we oppose it traditionally to substance and forget the immanence of sense in the sensuous. We shall have frequent recourse to this central notion, and we are going to see throughout the present chapter different aspects of form defining themselves more clearly. Each new determination that is added to the sensuous constitutes a form with respect to preceding determinations. At this point, however, form is still only the immediate and immediately perceived organization of the sensuous (the objective analysis of the work will later reveal the schemata which control this organization). The aesthetic object is an object in which the matter abides only if the form is not lost. Painters know that colors have intensity only through the harmony they compose and that colors fade if this form is mutilated. The word has its full brilliance, and also its richness of meaning, only in the strict order of the poem, where it plays its part like the violin in an orchestra and where sometimes, on the occasion of an *enjambement* or a breach of syntax, it rings out like the clash of cymbals. Similarly, sound is fully sound only through a melodic form whose presence is felt even when the melody has been interrupted or reduced to rhythmic pattern. Such form is still present when musical sound approaches noise, as we observe in listening to the brass instruments and to massive orchestral effects. The hardness of stone is convincing to our gaze only if it is perfectly in place and visibly assumes its function, which is to control weight while being obedient to it. (To be sure, in the case of architecture there is at times a desire to disavow this obedience and to create illusion. Then, at the same time that we seem to trifle with weight, we hide the nature of stone, compelling it to become festoon, lace, astragal. We camouflage its structure with ornament, its form with a wealth of forms, as in flamboyant Gothic and English Gothic. What saves this enterprise is that the medley of forms still constitutes *a* form. The eye senses a law hidden in the tangle, a symmetry and a regularity stand out which replace the mechanical order of weight by a geometrical order. Even in this proliferation of symbolic art, there is always the abstract beauty of which Hegel speaks. And ornament puts us on notice that form is not for use but for contemplation.) At bottom, the apogee of the sensuous only marks the blossoming of form. The sensuous appears through form, but it also makes form appear—form being that through which the sensuous becomes nature, that necessity which is inside the sensuous, not outside it like the necessity which governs the object of use and which is the logical necessity (immediately understood by the body) of a use. When Hegel undertakes to "separate the formative element from sensuous, external reality" [21]—form being characterized by regularity, symmetry, and equilibrium, and the sensuous by its purity—in order to seek a twofold and abstract determination of unity (which itself remains abstract, because it is the unity of a natural object merely perceived and not yet inhabited by a meaning), he confesses "that we are dealing with dead abstractions and a unity which has nothing real about it." [22] These abstractions unquestionably take on a meaning if we consider the aesthetic operation, and especially our reflection on this operation, since the treatment of the matter can be distinguished from the elaboration of form. But if we consider the perceived object, the unity of the sensuous-as-matter and of form is in fact indecomposable. Form is form not only in uniting the sensuous but also in giving it its *éclat*. It is a quality [*vertu*] of the sensuous. The form of music is the harmonization of sounds together with the rhythmic elements which it includes. The form of a painting is not only the design but also the play of colors by which the design is emphasized and sometimes even constituted. It is on condition of not separating form from the sensuous that we subscribe to the analyses of Jeanne Hersch, who places the accent on the exteriority and fullness which form confers upon the aesthetic object in promoting "artistic existence as such." [23] Because of form, the aesthetic object ceases to exist as a mere means of reproducing a real object and comes to exist by itself. Its truth is not outside it, in a reality which it imitates, but within itself. This ontological self-sufficiency which form bestows on the sensuous which it unifies allows us to say that the aesthetic object is nature. The sensuous as fixed, given form and life, finally becomes an object, constituting a nature which has the anonymous, blind force of Nature. The aesthetic object is there, and the first thing it requires of us is the avowal of its presence, not through nausea but, as we shall see later in detail, through joy.

Thus the aesthetic object is nature through the power of the sensuous within it, but the sensuous is powerful only through form. Form itself is, in the first place, the form of the sensuous.

21. Hegel, *Esthétique*, trans. S. Jankélévitch (Paris: Aubier, 1944), I, 168.
22. *Ibid.*, p. 178.
23. Jeanne Hersch, *L'Etre et la forme* (Neuchâtel: La Baconnière, 1946), p. 121.

Now, this form has been imposed on the object by the art of its creator. Paradoxically, the aesthetic object is natural only because it is artificial. And it is with the artificial object that we must now compare it.

[III] THE AESTHETIC OBJECT AND THE OBJECT OF USE

ON THE BASIS of what has just been said, one already suspects that the aesthetic object cannot be completely identified with the object of use [*l'objet usuel*]. It does not solicit the gesture which uses it but the perception which contemplates it. With respect to the imperatives of need, the aesthetic object seems absolutely gratuitous. The painting adds nothing to the solidity of the wall, the armchair may be comfortable without being beautiful, the poem teaches me nothing about what calls for my enterprise in the world. Thus, art has been considered in some epochs as a superfluity reserved for an idle class, a luxury refused to those whom work confines in the world of tools. Through art, seeing, hearing, and reading become disinterested modes of behavior which seem dedicated to the greater glory of perception and lack any outcome of consequence. The aesthetic object promises nothing; it neither threatens nor cajoles. It has no power over me, except through the attraction which it exercises and from which I can always hide. I have no power over it except to escape it or destroy it—actions which I know are not permissible, since the object is recommended to me by a tradition which forbids me to destroy it and which invites me to lend it my attention. I cannot, without cheapening myself, become a vandal or a Boetian. Thus the aesthetic object remains, quite simply, *there,* and it expects of me only the tribute of a perception.

Yet cannot the object of use be aesthetic, and cannot the aesthetic object serve certain useful functions?

(a) Usefulness

Certain misunderstandings must be cleared up here. Surely, the object of use, as indeed any object, can be aesthetically perceived and judged to be beautiful. It is beautiful if it manifests the fullness of the being which has been imparted to it, if it answers to the use for which it was intended, and if it shows by its appearance that it does answer to it—e.g., a plowshare, a locomotive, a barn. However, such objects are not essentially aesthetic but are so only incidentally, since they do not solicit the gaze which aestheticizes them. Certain objects of use nevertheless do solicit this gaze. Without renouncing their usefulness, they seek to please by the manner in which they are ornamented or decorated. Here the minor arts (and the term has an axiological significance) offer a host of examples. Two questions then arise. To what extent do these objects succeed in pleasing? This is a question of taste which depends on whether or not we like the ornament, whether or not we agree to its overloading the object sometimes to the point of camouflaging it. But, more objectively, to what extent must we take these objects for works of art, that is, for essentially aesthetic objects? We are confronted here with borderline cases with which we do not wish to encumber our study. But we can affirm that: (1) in such objects aesthetic quality is not measured by usefulness, e.g., the most beautiful vase is not the least porous, and the most beautiful armchair is not the most comfortable; (2) if the object is primarily aesthetic and is only incidentally useful, the use we eventually make of it ought not to turn us entirely away from its aesthetic perception, or at least the object ought still to remind us in some way that it is aesthetic without allowing us to confuse it with any object of use.

We are going to try out this interpretation through exploring the most impressive of the arts, architecture. For it is beyond question that every building, be it cottage or palace, barn or temple, has a use. Is it by reason of its use that it becomes an aesthetic object? To be precise, let us say that, like everything in nature, it can be aestheticized, but that, apart from its depending upon us, this metamorphosis depends more on its context than on itself. A cottage intrigues the artist's eye by the harmony it realizes with half-wild flowers, the hollow of a valley, the shade of an oak. It is as an element of nature that it is pleasing and not as what it is. But what if the architectural monument is a hallowed work and claims to be an aesthetic object? Undoubtedly, it has still been erected for some purpose—e.g., habitation, ceremony, or prayer—which it agrees to fulfill; and this purpose is not unimportant. The architect finds in such purpose, which is joined to nature's laws of weights and materials, one of those constraints without which there is no art at all, because nothing is created where everything is possible. While the poet makes his own rules, the architect simply receives his from a client. But the use of a work is not in itself enough to make it an authentic work. Of two churches which equally shelter the faithful and assure them the same meditation, one may be aesthetically lacking. It is still necessary that the work impart its destination to our gaze without ambiguity, "that it speak clearly," as Eupalinos states.[24] Thus it is with certain buildings, and also with roads of which we actually say that they climb a mountain, as if the motion which they invite and facilitate resided in them, or with those breakwaters which conform so well to an estuary that they shield the calm of its basins: "How clear to the mind!" "But," adds Eupalinos, "let us place above [them] the buildings of art!"

Here Valéry parts company with Alain. Objects which are beautiful in a natural way because their intended use forces them to harmonize with nature, so that the useful in them becomes natural, may serve as models for works of art. As Alain states, "In northern Italy, it is quite clear that palaces imitate cottages in the form of their terraces and colonnades as well as in their search for shade." [25] But they are not works of art because of this. It is not enough that they assume their function. They still must "sing," in Valéry's word. But how so? In Valéry's perspective, the music hides the word. What do the Pyramids say? Do they tell what they enclose? And what does the Parthenon say? The temple shelters the god, but the god, according to Hegel, comes after the temple. It is strange that, on the verge of explicating the song, Eupalinos slips away (even if he is to be revived in the person of Socrates) and that a theory of creating comes to be substituted for a description of what is created. This act of substitution advises us that the aesthetic object refers us back to the artist as he expresses himself in this object. But let us first try to say in what respect the work of art extends beyond the useful and becomes capable of singing.

The building which possesses a clear language during the time in which we listen to it is aesthetically perceived. However, here we come upon the difference between mere works of engineering and authentic works of art, that is, between the

24. Eupalinos is an architect in Paul Valéry's *Eupalinos*. In this pseudo-Platonic dialogue, he advocates the idea that the aim of architecture should be a clarity of structure that is comparable to the lucidity of forms in music.—Trans.
25. Alain, *Système*, p. 194.

building which speaks and the building which sings.[26] We can understand this language only if we suspend our own activity, but we must also face the object from a certain privileged place, as when we are before a canvas. As soon as I am on the road, it is no longer the road which climbs the slope, but myself. When I cross the bridge, I no longer admire the bend of its arches. The country house is beautiful only from the outside and from a certain perspective which weds it to garden or field. These objects so close to nature are aestheticized, as is nature itself, by a look which fixes and relates them as in a painting and remains before them as if before a painting. In contrast, if the architectural work of art invites us to be a spectator, it authorizes us to be one more completely. The object is aesthetic through and through, as I can verify by a stroll which leads from one discovery to another and which has no end. As Alain states, "the monument opens up when we walk [through it], but it closes up as soon as we stop." [27] Here the power of the aesthetic object is such that it involves the spectator in a sort of dance wholly given up to contemplation, a dance to a music and a melody which each new perspective keeps unfolding without any resolution to bring it to a close.[28] Moreover, if we cease to be a spectator, if we use the monument instead of contemplating it, its power still asserts itself. What is aesthetic in it still compels our recognition in the demeanor of our daily affairs and, so to speak, aestheticizes us. At the theater, the audience which comes to acclaim a play participates in some way in its performance. The same is true of ourselves in the presence of the architectural work. The ordinary structure, built to our needs, moves us, but only to attend to our needs and without special consideration for it, whereas the architectural monument obliges us to play a part, even when we merely act according to our needs. He who lives there places himself on exhibition, even if no spectator is present. Louis XIV at Versailles can only be majestic, and the

26. This distinction between engineering work [*ouvrage*] and art work [*oeuvre*], like the one between artisan and artist, which Alain refuses to make—loyal as he is to the aesthetic of the time in which language had not introduced this nuance—is recent. It dates from art's self-consciousness, of which the art-for-art's-sake credo has been a prime expression and whose results must today be recorded by a phenomenology of aesthetic experience.

27. Alain, *Système*, p. 177.

28. Was Souriau thinking of Eupalinos when he wrote of the cathedral that is "a symphony of forms in deep space, yielding, to the extent that I move within it, arpeggios of colonnades in changing perspective, rich harmonies of vaults and arches, flagstones, or altars"? (*La Correspondance des arts* [Paris: Flammarion, 1947], p. 64).

archbishop at Notre Dame is always attired with ecclesiastical gravity. The monument answers needs, but by creating a theatrical, urbane behavior. It is a triumph of art: in ceasing to perceive the work, man himself becomes a work of art.

It is in somewhat the same manner that poetry, another form of music, moves us. The words it employs are often everyday words taken from ordinary language—a language which is also an object of use whenever I employ it, without paying attention to it, to communicate and act, making use of words as I use a welcome armchair or a thirst-quenching drink. But let the word become poetry and I am unable to consume it in this way. It compels recognition with such power—it is so pressing and novel—that I can recite it only with respect. I must become a poet. Last, we may again cite the minor arts. For example, even if a beautiful vase serves practical ends, it assumes its true role only in ceremonies. The needs it satisfies are rather those of the gods in a temple or of the dead in a tomb in which it is sealed. The cape worn by an officiating priest, the jewel which sparkles on a gown, the mask worn by the black dancer—all these objects are associated with ceremony and sometimes regulate it. They, too, participate in the spectacle.

(b) The presence of the creator

Granting that the true aesthetic object, even if it may answer to demands for use, is not merely an object of use, then we must note the difference between these two objects with regard to a second point. Both in effect tell us that they are works of man—not things born of chance but man-made objects. We know how much contemporary aesthetics dwells upon this characteristic of the aesthetic object. Alain invokes creating [le faire] as a means for restoring imagination and purging emotions, while Valéry sees creating as the principle of a technique capable of revealing man to himself. Souriau opposes the will to create to the will to express and dwells upon the instaurational function of art. Bayer formulates the idea of a metatechnique, inscribing it in a theory of operational realism. This relation to creating may indeed help to determine the ontic status of the aesthetic object, to find a guarantee for its objectivity in the creative activity of the artist. But at present we are trying only to determine why this activity appears differently in the aesthetic object from the way it appears in the object of use. Now, form is what is human in both and attests to their creation by man, and it is form which organizes matter and thus triumphs over nature. Pondering this form in its relation to matter, we can immediately point to a difference between the two objects, a difference on which Alain, for example, dwells. The object of use does not hesitate to do violence to nature in order to realize its plans, and the idea which directs its manufacture is in no way hidden. Thus we have to do here with naked intelligence and an abstract object. The aesthetic object, in contrast, in no way presents a violent or separate form, and for the following reasons: it is made by hand rather than by machine in mass production; it does not stem from one fixed idea but from an inspiration which feeds on the progress of the work itself and welcomes the happy accident; and, finally, time's long patience concerning the most venerable objects has given the finishing touches to the artist's original patient labor, thereby harmonizing art with nature. All happens as if nature were becoming spirit. Thus we come on a familiar idea through an unfamiliar route, by showing that the sensuous here has the weight of nature and that form is on a level with the sensuous as that through which the sensuous becomes sensuous. But one may still examine the language of this sensuous form, seeking for what it proclaims about the gesture from which it arises. It is at this point that the distance between the object of use and the aesthetic object begins to increase and that, at the same time, form begins to become style.

In the object of use, the form certainly expresses the fact that it is manufactured but says nothing about who manufactured it. The maker has been the abstract means by which an idea has been realized in an object which itself remains abstract. Is this not the bitter fate of the factory worker and even of prehistoric man as he chiseled flints? Nothing is more moving than those stones which bear the mark of human toil from the most remote ages, and yet what do they tell us about the man who made the first tool from them? Nothing, except that he was there.[29] On the other hand, the paintings of Altamira tell us something about the man who, serious and filled with wonder, outlined them on the rock. Thus they give us access to the world in which he lived. We must now try to describe this living presence of the artist in the work—a presence which is not comparable to the anonymous

29. That it gives the historian certain information about this man's culture, from which he will be able to deduce or learn a great deal, is another matter. We are concerned now with the being of this man—and of his culture only to the extent to which it may itself express this being.

presence of the worker in the product of his craft but reveals instead the profound humanity of the aesthetic object.

Let us consider for a moment the vast question of the relationship between the work and its creator. This relationship is subject to serious ambiguity, since it can be conceived in two ways. On the one hand, we can attempt to explain the creation and nature of a given work by its creator, a creator whom we know in certain respects and who then becomes a principle of explanation of the work, since he is known independently of it. Here the explanation goes from the creator to the work. On the other hand, we can examine the work by itself and proceed from the work to its creator. Now, it is precisely the virtue of the aesthetic object not to explain but to reveal its creator. Except by accident, the aesthetic object gives no information about him which we cannot glean elsewhere and which the historian gathers. Yet it does place us directly in communication with him, providing us with a presence which history cannot supply, revealing a countenance which history could not reconstitute. It is this second approach which we must describe. It is completely involved in the aesthetic experience, while the first approach assumes, on the contrary, that we may at least provisionally abandon aesthetic experience in order to look elsewhere for information. There is still another reason for giving priority to the second step, a reason which has different aspects, depending on whether we ask about the aesthetic object or about its creator. If we are asking about the object, we must say that it cannot be entirely explained through its creator. The truth of the work is in the work, not in the circumstances of its creation or in the project which directs it. Is it not to steer from Charybdis into Scylla to seek to grasp the being of the object in the being of its project? Is there such a being as the latter, that is, a work prior to the work? We have already mentioned these difficulties in connection with the performance of the work, but we are now asking about its creator. And we can affirm that, just as the aesthetic object alone tells us about itself or at least about what is aesthetic in it, only it informs us about its creator or at least provides an irreplaceable image of him. Therefore, just as there is a truth of the object (a truth which is delivered to perception and is not reducible to explanation), so there is a truth of the artist which is present in the work, which is not reducible to history, and which history itself must take into account.

Let us stress this point, first by considering biography. Assuming that it is faithful, a biography confides the history of the artist. But does it give us his essential countenance and tell us why he is the creator of a particular work? If biography seeks to explain his activity as an artist by the acts which the individual has experienced as his own, it looks for causes which, even when forming part of his psychological personality, remain outside that complex of decisions in which the individual recognizes himself. In this sense, biography decomposes the life which the individual experiences as a continuous and unique destiny into a powder of events and acts whose unity, no longer that of a single meaning, is reduced to that of a causal series. Biography dissolves individuality into an aspect of the objective world. It is tempted to do so because a life which is completed and which is hence without a future reenters universal time and thereby submits to schemata of objective knowledge. But an interlacing of anonymous forces or partial determinisms cannot restore the shape of a being, the unity of a personal style.[30] It is undeniable that this method is not useless, for man is an object in his involuntary being and is therefore open to an objective explanation. But he also insists upon being grasped as a man. It is this demand which a truly comprehensive method tries to satisfy, seeking to grasp the unity of a life through the acts and emotions by which a person is revealed. A comprehensive method tends to restore the presence of the individual, together with everything immediately meaningful and coherent which this presence includes. It seeks to attain, beyond the ambiguities peculiar to every presence, what Sartre calls an "existential project" or what could also be called, in Kantian language, an intelligible character. It is this project or character that we express by saying "that's just like him," that is, when we rediscover in all of the individual's attitudes a family resemblance, indefinable yet inescapable. Only by being comprehensive in this sense can a biography place us in communication with the artist. But can it really do so? It tells us not about the artist but about

30. This idea, which has found favor, was first expressed by Raymond Aron, in *Introduction à la philosophie de l'histoire* (Paris: Gallimard, 1938). He has shown that "to know oneself is not to know a fragment of one's past, neither one's intellectual attainments nor feelings. It is to know the whole and the unity of the unique individual that we are" (p. 59). Moreover, Aron has shown how knowledge of the other, always acted upon by the multiplicity of interpretations, "is neither more nor less privileged than self-knowledge. It makes its way toward a goal located at infinity and, in distinction from the positive sciences, it is ceaselessly called into question" (p. 71).

the man, the whole man. If biography is true to itself, nothing gives it the right to select certain privileged moments or characteristic acts, as the novelist does continually. Even if biography does arrogate this right to itself, there is no certainty that it should privilege these moments and acts of creation or that the truth of the man is in his activity as an artist—even if this is, in fact, most frequently the case, since, encouraged by the public, the artist thinks of himself as an artist and of his art as a vocation. If biography thus seeks its center of gravity in the creative activity of the artist and is polarized around a certain image of the artist, it is because biography has, to begin with, felt the attraction of the work and because the image in question has been elaborated in commerce with the work. The biography of the artist therefore finds its inspiration and justification in a prior acquaintance with the creator through the work. It is his work, not his biography, which informs us concerning the creator. Biography can instruct us only if it has itself first been instructed by the work. Thus, in the titles which certain biographies adopt—titles which aspire to express the truth about the creator in one word—we should shift the epithet from life to work. The life of Balzac appears "prodigious" only because his work has something prodigious about it, Rimaud's is "adventurous" because his work is an adventure. The truest biography is the one which, faithful to the work rather than to the circumstances of its creation and the accidents of life, has found in the work the means for orienting its understanding and for interpreting a life.

Should we lend any greater credence to confessions or intimate journals, in which the creator claims to show himself without disguise in order to free himself or to appeal to us? We cannot accept this testimony on faith. It is not solely a question of the mistrust—legitimate enough—of a historian who accepts as accurate only what he can verify. It is the portrait itself which is offered us that we must question. Such questioning is constantly present in my relations with the other. I never fully adhere to what he tells me about himself. I can believe his words to be sincere without believing them to be true, and I set myself up as the judge of his own confession. This spontaneous mistrust is probably due to my feeling of the powerlessness of the self to know itself and, at the same time, of the feeling of incommunicability of consciousnesses. The other is simultaneously, and indissolubly, obscure to himself and to me, and is perhaps defined by this very obscurity.[31] I can know him only by measuring the image of himself which he proffers to me against the image which I form of him. This makes for a kind of misunderstanding which cannot easily be cleared up and is antecedent to any suspicion of ruse, concealment, or lie. I can accept his confession only as a document, as one testimony among others which leads me to form an opinion by which I shall decide about its truth and sincerity. Whenever the other tells me about himself, I adopt toward him the attitude of a psychoanalyst who, in deciphering the latent content of my associations, claims to know better than myself what I think or what I am. This does not imply that I objectify the other but only that I oppose my truth about him to the one which he offers me. And whence do I derive this truth about the other? From the very first contact which I have with him, simultaneous with or even antecedent to what he may tell me. Because he appears immediately meaningful, I have an idea of him which owes nothing to his confidings. He reveals himself to me through his whole presence, and I judge him spontaneously by his appearance. The other's appearance appeals to my judgment and yields a preconceptual knowledge by acquaintance on which I must rely as soon as I enter into the game of intersubjectivity. I am with the other as I am in the world, in accordance with what Husserl calls "the natural attitude."[32] Far from constructing him or reducing him to the status of an object, I experience him as alter ego and thereby discover an idea of him by which I can measure what he tells me about himself. This is particularly perceptible when the other speaks to me. I keep appealing from what he says to what he expresses. We shall return to an analysis of language, but we can already observe how language reveals the speaker. The word has a double function; as Husserl says, it designates, but it also exhibits.[33] Just as a signpost shows the

---

31. See Merleau-Ponty: "Behavior is not a thing, but it is no longer an idea. It is not the envelope of a pure consciousness and, as the witness of behavior, I am not a pure consciousness" (*The Structure of Behavior*, trans. Alden L. Fisher [Boston: Beacon Press, 1963], p. 171).

32. See E. Husserl, *Ideas*, trans. W. R. Boyce Gibson (New York: Humanities Press, 1931), §§ 27–32, pp. 101 ff.—Trans.

33. The idea of this *Kundgabe* has been developed, following Husserl, by H. Schmalenbach in "Phénoménologie du signe" (in *Signe et symbole, Etre et penser*, ed. P. Thévenaz, Vol. XIII [Neuchâtel: La Baconnière, 1946], p. 52). [On the notion of *Kundgabe*, see Husserl, *Logical Investigations*, trans. J. Findlay, 2 vols. (New York: Humanities Press, 1970), I, 276 ff.—Trans.]

way while also expressing the solicitude of a tourist association or the generosity of Peugeot, so language is first of all the interpreter of an objective meaning which it transmits to us, but it also harbors another meaning which we discover indirectly in accent, intonation, and mimicry—in short, in all the artistic potential of music or dance contained within the spoken word. And such potential is all the more eloquent in that it is spontaneous and is not voluntarily addressed to us. The discourse of the other therefore informs us about him without his even being aware of it.

Likewise, when I read the confession of an artist, I compare what he tells me about himself with what I already know. Whence does this prior knowledge come? It comes either from what his works have already taught me (and in this case we return to the situation of biography, which has to be informed about the works of an artist in order to inform us about the artist), or else from the confession itself. In the latter case, we regard the confession as we do any other work, that is, we refuse it any special privilege with respect to a knowledge of the artist. Privileged it evidently is in its objective meaning, since the artist is talking to us about himself. But it is not privileged in its secondary meaning—in terms of which the artist appears as a transparency, as the artist and not as the subject of a book. Thus the *Nouvelle Héloïse* gives us Rousseau as clearly as do his *Confessions* or his *Rêveries;* indeed even better, because in the *Nouvelle Héloïse* the secondary meaning does not enter into competition with the objective meaning, which is that of an impersonal narrative. It is the image of Rousseau which the *Nouvelle Héloïse* gives us which is, for us, the interpretative instrument for, and the measure of the truth of, his *Confessions.*

We must therefore return to the idea that it is above all through the work itself that we are acquainted with the artist— not in his real act (for we may know nothing about the circumstances of creation, and in any event, we are told about them only independently of the aesthetic experience) but in a certain truth of his being which aesthetic experience alone reveals. How does it do this? Here we must remind ourselves of the difference between the aesthetic object and the object of use. We may infer that the difference is the same as that between the two functions of language, that is, the transmission of an impersonal meaning and the expression of a person. By its very form, the object of use attests to an act of making. I am clearly aware that, unlike the natural object, it was made by and for man. But the object of use does not tell me anything about the person who created it. It tells me about the gesture I have to make, and it is completely absorbed in the use I make of it. The aesthetic object, in contrast, neither solicits nor serves any practical undertaking. It leaves me free to discover its creator and speaks to me of this creator. But how does it thus speak of him? We can clarify this question by stating that the aesthetic object manifests a style. What, then, is style? It is a certain procedure which is recognized by the stylization which it produces, that is, by the substitution of forms intended by the spirit for the inchoate proliferation of forms in nature. The *splendor ordinis* revealed by an acanthus leaf, by a Pascalian sentence, or by the tonal order of a sonata betrays a pattern [*dessin*] answering to a plan [*dessein*]. Style is therefore the mark of an organizing activity which rejects accidents and seeks the purest form. To attain style is to arrive at mastery and to do what we want to do.

(c) *Style*

Thus we must distinguish between style and craft. To be sure, style, insofar as it defines the creative activity of the artist, involves craft as well, and it is as such that style is open to evaluation by the critic. And, undoubtedly, all art is craft in the beginning: the painter's brush-stroke, the sculptor's blow, the poet's manipulation of words are matters of craft. And we may say that craft is even anonymous to the extent to which it is taught. Despite the distinction stressed by Malraux between the artisan who imitates and the artist who, manifesting a will to power, refuses to imitate, a psychology of creation must combine tradition with invention, apprenticeship with rebellion.[34] In dwelling too much upon the will to power, one risks underestimating the technical side of art. It is true that invention does occasionally stem from rebellion, but nevertheless a continuing apprenticeship is required. For the artist to be himself he may have to rebel against others, but he must be a good worker first of all. Moreover, concern for craftsmanship in no way prevents self-expression, as we can see in the case of the anonymous works made in the huts of African medicine men or of the equally anonymous works made in medieval workshops. The considerable part which imitation plays, through the organization of apprenticeship or initiation, firmly establishes the

34. André Malraux, *Psychologie de l'art* (Geneva: Skira, 1947), II, 128.

importance of artistic formulae. Here the aesthetic object is the product of a school which preserves and transmits the secrets of its craft, as opposed to an individual who invents his own way of working. And yet works of craft are not really anonymous, because they still have something personal to say. The artist who has submitted to all the demands of a craft tradition is still entirely present in his work. In contrast with academic art—from which the artist is always absent and in which only a hand without a heart is present—we feel that the Dogon who carves a mask of himself tells us, in his work, "And I have seen at times what men thought they saw." Even if he has blindly followed the prescriptions of a mysterious code, he has entered on a creative act. His craft may be made up of formulae which are binding, immutable, and impersonal, yet these become transfigured and take on a sacred character in the eyes of those who enact them. Then we feel that the artist has been the prey of his art and that the motions he performs betray a necessity to which he has completely subjugated, if not sacrificed, himself. In our eyes, he thus appears as the repository of a secret, a secret which is not his own and of which, in contrast with the modern artist who is lucid and self-willed, he is not even aware that he is the custodian. He is like the naïve consciousness in Hegel's *Phenomenology of Mind*. He conveys a truth which can be stated only by *us*, providing that we are as submissive to his work as the Hegelian philosophy is to history. This artist, who is buried in the anonymity of remote ages and who, without knowing it, becomes the ground of an incomparable experience, really has something to say; a humanity in search of itself stammers through him.

Style is therefore craft, but a craft which permits the artist to express himself and to be himself. We would not be illuminating the problem if we posed questions like, "Can one premeditate being oneself?" or "Can one will not to be self-willed?" But we do perhaps illuminate it by saying that premeditated acts, which require diligence and aim at an effect, end by bringing forth human spontaneity at its best. To comprehend this, we need only renounce the idea that nature expresses itself best through the elementary, the primitive, and the unthinking. What is truly primitive in us—the most automatic, uncoercible behavior, as well as our physiological apparatus with its reflexes and instincts (insofar as we can isolate and observe them)—manifests a kind of life-wisdom of which we are the beneficiaries but which bears no mark of individuality at all. On the other hand, what truly reveals the foundations of a personality, its impulsions or tendencies, cannot be called primitive without our misconstruing the term. An emotional outburst may reveal a trait of character, but it is by no means a primitive reaction. Psychoanalysis has amply shown that the most apparently spontaneous behavior, as soon as it is elucidated, is the result of a life-history and gives information about the self only because it originates in it. It is no longer possible to confuse the primitive with the unconscious or even, if we understand Ravaisson, with the vital automatism which is often a failed freedom.[35] Thus we must handle with care the notion of the primitive and realize that we cannot find in the primitive, even in rudimentary form, the characteristic signs of a personality. We must, on the contrary, look for these signs in the most elaborate and highly organized behavior. It is in the same way that we must seek in art, and precisely in its craft component, for the singular nature of the artist.

Style is therefore the locus in which the artist appears. And this is due to what is strictly technical in style: a certain way of treating matter, of assembling and arranging stones, colors, or sounds. In order to create an aesthetic object, style gives the appearance of urgency to these arrangements, simplifications, or combinations by which man keeps adding to nature and asserting his freedom from all accepted facts and models. But it is still necessary for these technical means to appear to us as subserving a singular idea or vision. Monet dissolves the hard stone of cathedrals in an acid of light; Cézanne, in contrast, makes the gnarled articulations of Provençal hills stand out. It is clear that the impressionism of Monet and the latent cubism of Cézanne bring different techniques into play, bearing on the composition, the blending of colors, and the attack of the brush, and corresponding to different doctrines of perspective or color vision. But for me as the onlooker—if not for the painter himself —technique and doctrine do not suffice to define a style. They must still appear to me as if demanded by a certain vision of the world, a vision which makes an adventure and a confession out of creation. If Monet has a style, it exists to the degree that his work invites me to attribute to him a certain way of considering the world as the realm of light, as that openness of which Rilke sings and in which all things become transparent to and consubstantial with the gaze. And if there is a style of

35. Félix Ravaisson (1813–1900) was a French philosopher who wrote, among other things, on the nature of habit.—Trans.

Cézanne, it is insofar as I attribute to Cézanne an obsession with a Spinozan fullness, vigor, and immutability. There is style when I discern, even without being able to articulate it, a certain vital relation of man to the world, and when the artist appears to me as the one through whom this relation exists, not because he brings it into being but because he lives it. And it is the incomparable quality of this relation to the world, this "style of life," which I immediately grasp in the work, looking straight through its craft characteristics without paying attention to them and, in all strictness, without even seeing them. Or, rather, these characteristics appear full of meaning and as if transfigured by it, in accordance with that immanence of meaning in the sign which defines expression and which we shall continually single out. Thus Van Gogh's touch *is* his tragic quality. For Van Gogh, to adopt a certain technique is equivalent to uttering a certain cry, thereby, as Artuad says, "evoking the abrupt and barbaric atmosphere of the most moving, emotional, and impassioned Elizabethan drama." [36] Likewise, Caravaggio's lighting, contrasted and arrayed in depth, is not merely a means for representing an isolated scene in high relief but involves a whole way of seeing. It signifies both a certain mystery and a certain brutality, a resistant world which is not pleasant or smooth and for which we must be armed with the nonchalant courage of conquistadors. What we shall call technical schemata are means not just for creating the work but for expressing a world. Craft is therefore a signature, as we can see in Wagner's ninth chord, in Chagall's donkey and rooster, or in some key word for a poet. On the other hand, if these features of craft are reduced to a method, the attempt to draw attention to oneself by an arbitrary sign seems inauthentic. We want the mark of the worker to be on his work and to be seen as his most spontaneous and hence most necessary act—in short, to be recognized for what it is and not as some label or other. We easily distinguish the artificial employment of a formula which is like a factory stamp from the necessary repetition of a stroke which

36. From Antonin Artaud, *Van Gogh* (Paris: K. Editions, 1947). Artaud has seen very clearly why Van Gogh is first of all a painter: "This is what strikes me most in Van Gogh, the most painterly of painters, who, without leaving his tubes, brushes, or the framework of motif and canvas in order to resort to anecdote, narration, drama, and the intrinsic beauty of subject and object, succeeded in emotionalizing nature and its objects in such a way that none of the fabulous tales of Poe, Melvin, Gérard de Nerval, or Hoffmann says more on the psychological and dramatic plane than do these two-penny canvases."

bears witness to the self-fidelity and sincerity of a work. We accept a resemblance between works by the same artist when this resemblance does not stem from the serial application of the same recipe and when, instead of the cleverness of the mercenary artist who is always sure to earn money, it bespeaks the emotion of the man who seeks to express himself without trickery. It is in these terms that we see the difference in Reuben's work between his *Paradises* or those enormous mythological "machines" which seem to be mass-produced in the painter's studio, and the portraits or *The Return of Philopoemen*—a difference which is especially prominent when we compare the completed paintings of *The Life of Marie de Medici* and its maquettes in Vienna. Here the sketch is truer than the finished work, because it is closer to the creative gesture. In the sketch, craft does not efface style.

This comes down to saying that style reveals a twofold necessity. While the object of use reveals only the necessity of a form that in turn expresses the demand inherent in an end external to the object and to the artisan's person as well, the aesthetic object manifests both the necessity of a sensuous form subject to a strictly aesthetic norm and the necessity of a meaning experienced by the artist "as a living fate," in Malraux's phrase.[37] When comparing the aesthetic object with nature, we pointed out that the sensuous has all its *éclat* there only if it is controlled by a form clearly immanent in the sensuous, since form is nothing other than the harmonious organization of the sensuous. Style reveals another aspect of form. Style defines a form capable of attesting to the personality which created it, a form which is a meaning and which, at this level of our analysis, means its creator. And it appears at the precise point where the two necessities combine, that is, where the aesthetic norm which regulates form (a norm which in a painting imposes certain distortions, a "plastic" rhyme, and a *passage* of color values, or, in poetry, a jingle of words and a break in rhythm), far from appearing arbitrary, lets us view a certain aspect of the world which is peculiar to the artist and by which the artist is recognized. A certain woman in a Picasso painting has the face of an insect, not merely because cubist technique calls for it but because Picasso himself breathes in this stifling and grotesque universe which is also expressed by Kafka's *Metamorphosis*. This is why Negro art does not touch me so long as I see in it, as the West

37. Malraux, *Psychologie*, I, 82.

did for many centuries, only a barbaric or clumsy technique, a miscarriage of art. However, I discover a Negro style to be as authentic as any other as soon as I believe, as the ethnologist invites me to do, that it says something which it alone can say and that there is adequation between its form and content. Now we can understand why the decorative does not truly attain to style. Ornament has nothing to say, it indicates only the labor of an artist and not his *Weltanschauung*, unless the ornament achieves a cosmological quality, as in cathedral tympani or baroque art—unless, in other words, it expresses, in its own way, the world of the artist. We shall return to this notion of expression, thus extending our analysis of style.

But a final problem poses itself here. If it is the aesthetic object that is expressive—so much so that we judge the artist's sincerity by it and re-create, as it were, the artist in the image of his work—are we justified in generalizing and speaking of a collective style? We are already generalizing when we speak of a style of Mozart, instead of speaking of the style of the *Jupiter* symphony or the Concerto in A. We are justified in this to the degree that all the works of Mozart resemble one another insofar as they are all consubstantial with Mozart.[38] But the same is no longer true when we speak of genre or type and invoke a classical, Negro, cubist, or Italian style. We may be compelled to retain such terms when we have no information about the genesis of the work and its creator. Thus we speak of Dogon art, Etruscan art, and the art of the Steppes. But we may also refer knowingly to genre, without the excuse of ignorance, as when we speak of Russian ballet, symbolist poetry, or the impressionist school. What validity, then, can a characterization of style have which seems systematically to be making an abstraction from what is personal in it? At first glance, it appears that to subsume the work under a type or genre is to make an abstraction of the artist as an individual and therefore as a subjectivity. To say that a poem is Romantic is to neglect the fact that it was written by Novalis or Vigny and make it impossible for ourselves to rejoin the poet through his poem. We then have no more communication with him than an entomologist with the insects he classifies—which can in fact be the situation of the historian or

38. We know how Proust stressed what Bergson called "the resemblance of an artist's works to one another": "Thinking back on the sameness of Vinteuil's works, I explained to Albertine that the great men of letters created only a single work or rather only refracted through different surroundings the same beauty which they brought into the world" (*A la recherche du temps perdu* [Paris: Gallimard, 1923], VI, 225).

critic. But let us not forget that type can also be interpreted as a Hegelian idea (and perhaps also as an aspect of a typology, à la Max Weber). Type then points to a spiritual reality with which I can enter into communication and which is still singular, even though not inscribed in the unfolding of a subjective consciousness. This idea offers itself to me with the same insistence as the gesture or word of a singular person. It has the same power of signification, and it reveals in the same way a certain vital relation with the world—outside of this relation, style is only formalism. In this case, we are justified in speaking of a type, because here type does not annul the subjectivity constitutive of style. Type merely introduces a new form, nonpersonal yet unique, of that subjectivity.

It will nevertheless be said that we have arrived at this notion of a collective style only by methods which in the end appeal to a power of abstraction that depersonalizes the work. Malraux has noted that the comparison of markedly different works brought together by photography—causing stained glass, bronze, canvas, or tapestry to lose their specific qualities as objects—made it possible to discover a parent style which the material of these objects sometimes hides. Resort to the photograph makes one think of Galton, but it is a question of something entirely different from a generic image. Our concern is with what is identical in a search or a vision, with what has the same accent in different voices. The photograph merely has the effect of enlisting our attention. It does not extract from the works a character which is common to each of them. Instead, the photograph makes us penetrate the depths of the work more profoundly by uncovering its visible aspect and restoring to vision its prerogatives. Thus encountering the genius which inhabits each work, we can discover the affinity which connects them and constitutes a collective style. This style is generic, not general. It expresses a certain vision of the world which I can rediscover in different works and which constitutes the source of an endless number of possible creations—a force which can externalize itself in a thousand ways. It is not a question here of arts which correlate with each other but of a certain identical creative emotion which diversely embodies itself in them. It is through this emotion that style always remains personal: style reveals a secret which we must indeed personalize. It is impossible for us not to imbue an authentic work with life, not to sense a consciousness behind it which is affiliated with ours and calls out to us. To understand the language of the work is always to understand someone.

Consequently, when we speak of a Gothic, baroque, or Negro style, we presume a consciousness' inhabiting and giving life to this Gothic or baroque world which we are invited to enter. The aesthetic world specified by a style is always a human world, a world of things which is there for us as an enchanted world disclosed only to the initiate. The Gothic style is the style of Gothic man. I care little about whether in a given case this man has a proper name or is merely one of millions. What is important is that he is always a man and that he invites me to be his counterpart.

Moreover, there are certain creators who claim this status of the anonymous and yet unique artist, whose work we subsume under a type without sacrificing anything of its humanity and without dimming its brilliance. We can discern two kinds of immanence of the artist in the aesthetic object. There is the work in which the artist, conscious of his vocation (sometimes to the point of pride), imposes his presence and himself solicits a dialogue with the spectator. There is also the work in which the artist takes a back seat to the school, becoming the instrument of a tradition and the echo of a secular effort. Still present, personalized by the task to which he is dedicated, he is no longer named. Does this mean that he no longer claims his work to be unique? We are indeed tempted to give the prize to works which are truly unique. There is only one Mozart, but an endless number of classical musicians seem dethroned in being unable to leave their anonymity. Great works are incomparable works which we cannot subsume under a genre without doing them a radical injustice. Proust insists on this. "That unknown quality of a unique world which no other musician had ever made us see constitutes, I said to Albertine, the most authentic proof of genius, rather than what is found in the content of the work itself." [39] The genius is the one I recognize among a thousand, the one who, even if he has not desired it, has no equal. But let us be clear. In listening to Mozart, I must recognize Mozart; and if, having recognized him, I say that Mozart belongs to a certain classical style, then I perform the critic's task, I lose touch with the work. I stop perceiving aesthetically in order to know objectively. The passage from the individual to the type is very much the result of an abstraction, especially if I effect this passage externally by comparing techniques, influences, and the entire history of the works. But, on the other hand, I am not in-

39. *Ibid.*, VI, 235.

fallible. If I have not been advised that the *Masonic Funeral Music* is by Mozart, I may believe it to be by Beethoven. I may mistake a Mozart symphony for one by Haydn. Would I be doing an injustice to Mozart if, questioned about the authorship of the symphony, I prudently replied that it is a work in the classical style? I may have listened to it as faithfully, penetrated its world as deeply, appreciated it as fully as if I had known it was by Mozart. Accordingly, in saying, "this is a classical work," as in saying of a bronze that it is Scythian or of a fresco that it is Byzantine, I would all the same have experienced what is unique in the work. I would not have generalized. The name I give to it is not a proper name, but the artist I discover is a singular artist, and I am not insensitive to what is unique in his work. Yet this uniqueness can be repeated, the incomparable compared—not by a logical comparison but, as when two faces resemble each other, by a community of expression. Just as the unique music of Vinteuil evokes "the fragrant silkiness of a geranium," so music can evoke architecture or poetry. For that matter, Haydn can evoke Mozart, or Vermeer, Pieter de Hooch. This means that there is a world common to both terms of the comparison, as well as a common soul which is nevertheless a singular soul and which, in the aesthetic experience, is as real, present, and meaningful for me as Mozart or Vermeer himself when I have identified him.[40]

Therefore, we must not think that the work is less expressive or less valuable when the artist is unknown to us (whether because we are ignorant of him or because he is hidden in his work) and we append the name of a type or genre to his work. On the contrary, we would say that the highest expression is the most modest one and that the most authentic subjectivity is that which rejoins the universal. And we may also say that the unsigned work attests no less to a creative subjectivity. This proposition is not, we may add, the exact opposite of the preceding one, for the generality of the type is not the universality of the human. Rather, the work which is reduced to a type is still singular in that it expresses a certain singular vision of the world. Precisely because of its singularity, it can lay claim to universality. And it can do this quite effectively insofar as this singularity is essential to the work. As we have just seen, it does not depend

40. When the critic or expert determines a collective style by generalizing, he is guided by the discovery of a spiritual identity which does not result from a generalization. The generalization justifies this identity only after the event.

on conspicuous detail or an overly systematic formula; instead, it expresses itself discreetly. Consequently, the work loses nothing in being anonymous. Of course, we do have the feeling of a greater familiarity with the work when we can evoke its creator and recall what we know of him in other respects. Biographies find their function here. But this very intimacy is a danger, because we may become diverted from the work itself, bringing into the countenance which the work intimates irrelevant traits which the work does not suggest. This is to say that aesthetic perception perhaps gains in purity by ignoring everything about the creator, while still experiencing his presence. As long as we adopt the aesthetic attitude, Mozart is not more concretely present for us than classical man, and classical man is not less present than Mozart. The difference between them is not the difference between individual and type. Both are real insofar as they are required by real works, and both are imaginary insofar as I apprehend them only through the work and without any reference to history. The division between them deepens only when I renounce the aesthetic attitude. Then classical man again becomes the product of a generalization and Mozart remains an individual about whom I know factual details which pertain only to him. But when I am genuinely present to the work, neither the abstract man nor the concrete individual is really the artist, the person whose true countenance is found in the work itself.

We cannot reiterate too often that the truth of the creator is in no way the historic truth of the real individual who is the subject of biography. It is, rather, the truth of the man who is present in the work and whom I know only through the work. If the Comtean idea of subjective existence ever had meaning, it is precisely here. The artist is the man who sacrifices objective existence for subjective existence, who chooses to exist in his work rather than in the world and in history. If he sometimes shirks the norms of daily life, it is because he vaguely believes that it is not on his behavior in this life that he can be reached and judged. And perhaps the individuals who believe this most clearly and bitterly are those who experience themselves as alienated, dispossessed, or lost. For them, true life lies elsewhere, in the universe of the work which is disclosed whenever the work meets the public. A meager immortality, perhaps, but in it man attains the status of man. We know what Sartre has done with Malraux's dictum that "Death transforms life into a destiny for man." [41] In like manner, the work is a destiny for the artist, for it alone is cited at that last judgment which humanity pronounces. In vain does the artist sometimes attempt to dissemble, *larvatum prodere*. He is that man whose best aspect does not exist in the mode of the for-itself but in that of the for-others, that is, in the consciousness of a public. The artist is that man on whom every man has claims and who has no way of resisting these claims. "Prostitution of the actor," the phrase goes; prostitution of the artist, we would have to add, but a sacred prostitution. This is why the artist can so easily be mistaken about himself. Boris de Schloezer has clearly noted this, but to explain the "anomaly" he proposes to distinguish between the man and the artist, identifying the artist with *Homo faber*—as soon as the man begins to create, "he becomes another person." [42] And this other, who creates, cannot be entirely conscious of his act of creation. But perhaps we should also distinguish not only between man and artist but also between the artist and his created image. Of this image, which the work provides and which is reflected in the public, the artist cannot be conscious. If this image is his truth, we can say in this precise sense that he is not conscious of himself, even if he is still conscious of his creation—and we must probably agree with de Schloezer that he is not always fully conscious even of that.

The man-made object thus places us in a human world in which it elicits a technical behavior and invites us to become human through the use of tool or implement. The implement embodies the human in general as sedimented in an object, but it enables us to enter into communication with its creator only indirectly. The aesthetic object, on the other hand, places us on the plane of the I and thou without opposing one to the other. Far from the other's usurping my world, he opens his world to me without compelling me, and I open myself to it. We say "his world"; and it is indeed thus that the artist reveals himself in his work, not only because the work bears witness to a singular act of creation but also because it evokes a world which can be ascribed only to a subjectivity. We know the artist through this personal world which his work expresses. Thus the analysis of

41. See Jean-Paul Sartre, *Being and Nothingness*, trans. Hazel Barnes (New York: Philosophical Library, 1956), pp. 540 f.—Trans.
42. Boris de Schloezer, *Introduction à J. S. Bach* (Paris: Gallimard, 1947), p. 300.

style must be followed by an analysis of the expression peculiar to the aesthetic object. We shall enter this analysis through the investigation of another essential aspect of the aesthetic object, its capacity to signify or mean [*signifier*]. This investigation will be conducted by comparing the aesthetic object with another category of objects, objects which we can say are intrinsically signifying [*signifiants*] in character.

[IV] THE AESTHETIC OBJECT AND THE SIGNIFYING OBJECT

EXCEPT IN THE CASE of certain minor arts such as pottery, weaving, or woodworking, the aesthetic object is not usually confused with objects of use. But we must carefully distinguish the aesthetic object from another species of object, a species which itself falls under the genus of objects of use. For lack of a better term, we shall call this new species of object "signifying." The function of such objects is not to subserve some action or to satisfy a need but to dispense knowledge. We can, of course, call all objects signifying in some sense. However, we must single out those objects which do more than signify merely in order to prepare us for some action and which are not used up in the fulfillment of their task. Scientific texts, catechisms, photograph albums, and, on a more modest scale, signposts are all signs whose signification engages us in an activity only after having first furnished us with information. In a cultural world which, like ours, attaches great value to positive knowledge and to the means of solidifying and distributing such knowledge, these signifying objects constitute an autonomous and prestigious group of objects whose influence extends dangerously far, even down to the most degraded offshoots of our culture, such as the daily papers and advertising. Certainly, none of these objects threatens to usurp the function of the aesthetic object. But wherever there are no libraries, where science remains bound to religion, and where the only knowledge considered to be of any value is taught by the church—in such conditions, does not the aesthetic object assume the function of the signifying object and transmit information? The Abbé Suger was well aware that the stone carvings on the tympana and columns of the cathedral at St. Denis would assume the function of a catechism. Even today we learn the Sumerian religion by way of bas-reliefs, the Achaean religion from the Homeric poems, and the Dogon religion from their masks. Indeed, all the arts which are sometimes termed "representational" in a wide sense seem to have, as their aim, signifying by means of representation. Only modern art makes use of the same term to designate a certain optional and nonessential characteristic of the arts, conceiving of painting and poetry on the model of music. The main question for us, therefore, is whether or not the aesthetic object is primarily a signifying object. Consequently, we must also query whether reading the aesthetic object's signification is not what is primarily expected of us. Particularly today, these questions pose a supreme problem for aesthetic reflection.[43]

Our discussion of the distinction between the aesthetic object and the signifying object will be our first attempt to consider this problem, which we shall subsequently reexamine in specifying the structure of the work of art and in describing aesthetic perception. We shall leave aside those arts which are apparently nonrepresentational, such as music or architecture, and limit our discussion to the arts which seem to be naturally representational, such as painting, sculpture, and the literary arts.[44] It is in these last three cases that the aesthetic object seems most often to hold a signification before us. A particular painting, for example, is a still life depicting pears on a compote dish. A particular statue represents Hercules or Apollo. A novel, a play, a movie usually contain the story of some individual who does such-and-such. But what *is* signified in these works and how is that signification presented to us?

43. In an important article which anticipates many of Malraux's analyses, Pierre Godet is surprised that this problem "has not been examined and investigated for itself" ("Sujet et symbole dans les arts plastiques," *Signe et symbole*). It has, of course, been broached in artistic production and increasingly in public taste. Art is always ahead of reflection on art. However, Etienne Souriau has begun to consider the problem of the represented object and "the universe of discourse" of the work in terms of his concept of the "reified or thingly existence" of the work of art. Our own distinction between signification and expression, which will appear throughout our work, reflects Souriau's distinction between reified and transcendental existence. (See Etienne Souriau, *La Correspondance des arts* [Paris: Flammarion, 1947], p. 48 n.)

44. It is not strictly correct to call the literary arts representational. Their materials are words. They speak, they do not let us see. They depict only by metaphor. But what is important for our purpose is that they have a subject or subject matter [*un sujet*], and, unless the mode of representation is specified, this subject can be considered as a represented object.

(a) From signification to expression

As opposed to the natural significations which our everyday utilitarian perception deciphers in the world, the signified object is first of all unreal. The aesthetic object can conjure up an absent object but cannot force it to be present. The word "flower" in a poem by Mallarmé does not announce the presence of a flower in the same way that a perfume announces the presence of a flower which I have never seen. And even though a statue may *be* the god it represents, it is not this god in the same way that a cloud *is* the rain which is about to fall. This character of unreality is often emphasized by an artist's very choice of subjects, which may be borrowed from antiquity, legend, or myth. The Trojan War or the adventures of Gargantua, the amorous escapades of Jupiter or of Don Juan, the shepherds of Arcadia, or the martyrs of primitive Christianity —none of these themes appears to concern us directly. Yet information in the newspapers, in economic charts, and even in scientific discussions matters to us because it claims a truth which in one way or another is of concrete importance to us. This observation hints at a first peculiarity possessed by the aesthetic object. Even if it is capable of truth because of what it represents, its truth is not comparable to the truth of the intellectual object. We suspect that such truth is internal to the aesthetic object and that it cannot be verified in the world of objects. It is a truth which is attached not to *what* the object represents but rather to the *manner* of representation. Any possible application of the content of the aesthetic object to the real world, that is, any truth extrinsic to the work (however important that truth may be), is given in addition to the intrinsic truth of the work and as a recompense for the work's fidelity to this intrinsic truth. Any work which attempts to be true in terms of the external world and not in terms of itself, that is, any work which claims that its meaning is verified in reality because it takes account of reality (either by calling us to know the real or by inciting us to act in a concrete way), is not an aesthetic object.

Furthermore, the unreality of what is signified is not sufficient to distinguish between the aesthetic object and the purely signifying object. The rain discussed in a meteorological text, for example, is no more dampening than a rainstorm depicted by a landscape painter. In the first place, what is represented is not always of great interest, nor is it necessarily what commends the work to our attention. Classical aesthetics once attempted to identify the virtues of a work with those of its model by claiming that a painting is beautiful because it represents a beautiful woman or that a poem is great because it recounts a great event. All Western art from the Renaissance to the nineteenth century has been founded on this prejudice—a prejudice whose influence has not been disastrous only because artists do not always know what they are doing or occasionally forget this doctrine at the moment of creation and retain trust only in themselves and the work at hand. We realize today, however, that the greatest or most beautiful works are not always those whose subject is the greatest or the most beautiful. And it has been works of art themselves which have persuaded us on this point. The famous Moissac panel shows how a brawl between men and monsters may be an aesthetic equivalent to the sacrifice of Abraham, just as Toulouse-Lautrec's Goulue is the equal of any duchess, or Giradoux's Madwoman of Chaillot is as tragic as Electra. At least, these equivalences are established in a negative sense. In itself, that is, insofar as it is not integrated into the work of art, a given subject is no more important than any other. The signifying object, on the contrary, is judged in terms of what it signifies. A scientific manual, for example, is judged in accordance with its content, and its form is completely subordinate to this content.

How does the aesthetic object affect the subject (a subject which one is not allowed to judge)? The signifying object claims to justify the signification it bears and attempts to gain our conviction as to its truth or at least to present as convincingly as possible its testimony to this truth. The aesthetic object does not demonstrate [*démontre*], it shows [*montre*]. As we know, the theater has renounced didacticism and the novel is not interested in explanation. They limit themselves to recounting a story and leave to the scholar the task of using this story to draw sociological or psychological conclusions.[45] The psychology in Proust lies in the fact that his novel is a novel about the writing of a novel. His hero is a psychologist who is shown

45. That there is no genuine psychology in theater has been shown by Pierre Touchard in the case of tragedy, where the characters are subordinated to the action. This does not mean that they cannot be true; but they are true as norms rather than as realities. (See Pierre Touchard, *Dionysos* [Paris: Editions du Seuil, 1949].—Trans.)

practicing psychology, and the virtue of this work lies not in the psychology explicitly brought to light but in that which is *not* directly exposed.

Are we therefore limited to saying that signifying art imitates and that its peculiar virtue lies in imitating accurately? But the aesthetic object often shows what it shows with a seeming negligence of and contempt for what should be the truth of the act of showing—verisimilitude. We are well acquainted with the liberty plastic art takes with appearances. The novel overturns chronology in the work of Faulkner, mingles hallucination and action in Joyce, mixes a number of different techniques in Dos Passos, and approaches the status of myth in Kafka. The theater, under Pirandello's influence, has become a theater of the theater by duplicating the actor and his role. Finally, what analogues do the so-called primitive arts have in nature? It seems, therefore, that the work of art does not have its truth in verisimilitude. We should not consider the unreal object it represents as a copy of the real object (a copy whose value would be measured by its exactitude). Malraux confirms this point by showing that the artist is not inspired to creation through the contemplation of nature but rather through his admiration for the masterworks of his predecessors. Giotto did not learn painting by looking at live sheep but by considering sheep as painted by Cimabue. Hugo heard the voices of shadows or waves only because he wanted "to be Chateaubriand or nothing." Malraux draws the consequences for the spectator as well. The spectator should not judge the work as if it were a strictly signifying object. He should not compare the represented object with the real object in order to condemn or rectify the former's infidelities, finally turning his back on the aesthetic object in favor of the real one. The aesthetic object is not an organ of knowledge any more than it is a substitute for the original. Whether a portrait resembles its subject or not, it is not an aesthetic object until it ceases to be a portrait and loses the signifying role which is so frequently assumed by the photograph. We should not be tempted to think in terms of a preexisting model. The represented object must appear to result from the demands of the particular painting in which it figures. When we gaze on Franz Hals's portrait of Descartes, we should think of Hals rather than Descartes—or, more exactly, place ourselves at Hals's level.

The aesthetic object is not a sign which points to something else. This does not mean, of course, that we must prevent ourselves from seeing a human figure on the canvas or that Hals should be prevented from representing Descartes. Even in viewing an abstract painting, we perceive something. Even in the most extreme experiments in abstraction, the aesthetic object continues to signify. But signification in this case does not imply that the represented object imitates an object or an event in the world. It merely means that something is being represented or proffered, even if that something is not identifiable. A point which we shall later emphasize is that the work always has a subject. But if this subject does not by itself hold the spectator's attention and if it need not be an imitation of the real, is this not because it functions as a means toward another signification and is in itself no more than a symbol?

Our problem has not yet been solved. How can that apparent contempt for appearances on the part of the aesthetic object still allow for signification, and is not what it signifies the holy? The Last Judgment is no thematic pretext for the sculptor Gislebert, whose name is inscribed on the astonishing tympanum of the cathedral of Autun. Everything on this tympanum is signifying in character: the hierarchical difference in size of Christ, the angels, and men;[46] the key of Saint Peter; even the shellfish carried by one of the elect in his satchel to show that he was a pilgrim to Santiago de Compostela. Gislebert did not produce this tympanum for the public but for the community of faithful to which he belonged. What they found on the stone was the Holy Scripture, and they did not consider it to be an instrument of their pleasure but of their salvation. If we were to look beyond advanced civilizations and established religions, we would find that the primitive mask or fetish is also created in the service of a faith.[47] For the primitive, truth does not lie in the insignificant appearances of the everyday world but in the great cosmic forces which course through this world, in the exemplary events recounted in myth and repeated in ritual, and in all that gives meaning to appearances rather than receiving it

46. And yet the extraordinary elongation of the more important figures in the manner of El Greco, so characteristic of Burgundian Romanesque, means something different. Certain aspects of this work, such as the number and disposition of the characters which fit the form of the tympanum and leave no space empty, answer to purely aesthetic preoccupations, even though they are not personal to their author.

47. In primitive civilizations, even the free arts are religious in some respects. Marcel Griaule has pointed out that, in the case of Dogon art, "even if our primary concern had been free art we could not neglect some of their religious beliefs, since the primary materials used by the blacks are never inert" (*Arts de l'Afrique noire* [Paris: Editions du Chêne, 1947], p. 36).

from them. It is helpful here to recall the remarkable analyses of Mircea Eliade. The work of art, according to Eliade, imitates or permits a "hierophany." It translates the individual's perception of the world, a perception which starts from the fragmentary and insignificant appearances of the world and goes straight to the vital and cosmic forces. It participates in the will to "insert itself into reality and into the holy through fundamental physiological actions which it transforms into ceremony." [48] The same can be said about the totem poles of the Haida Indians, the painted ancestors of the New Hebrides, or the bronze figures of the Steppes. Such works attempt to render the invisible visible. Eugène Fromentin has made much the same observation concerning Rembrandt's work, which manifests an invisible that is much more real and present than the visible and that directs our vision of the visible.[49] Even when performed before whites, the Navajo Yei-Be-Chei, a dance for conjuring up the dead by means of strident chanting and violent dancing before a fire, attests to man's terrifying intimacy with the powers which create his destiny. Thus the primitive arts express a faith which is shared by the entire community. Their signification is mystical and not aesthetic. The work is not meant to be an aesthetic object; it becomes so in spite of itself.

In spite of itself and *by us*, that is, by the men of the twentieth century who bring the vase, mask, or bronze into a museum (or else reproduce it) and contemplate the work without participating in the faith by which it was created. It is like contemplating a portrait of an unknown person without thinking of this person, or looking at the Angel of Reims without praying to it as a guardian angel. Thus the work of art, in Malraux's phrase, "undergoes its metamorphosis." It ceases to be a symbol in order to become an aesthetic object. This is a decisive revolution. It seems that for the first time in history an authentically

48. Mircea Eliade, *Traité de l'histoire des religions* (Paris: Payot, 1964), p. 41.
49. Eliade has shown convincingly for the tellurian hierophants that some primary intuitions (such as that of Mother Earth, the Mistress of the Place, the source of all living forms, the guardian of children, and the womb to which the dead return in order to rest, regenerate, and return to life) precede instead of follow the positive observation of phenomena. Nature is natural only after the fact, and the sacred clarifies the profane. "The drama of Tammus is what reveals the drama of the death and resurrection of vegetation, not the other way around" (*Traité de l'histoire*, p. 363). Analogous views will be found in the psychoanalysis of knowledge proposed by Gaston Bachelard. [See Bachelard, *La Formation de l'esprit scientifique* (Paris: Vrin, 1938).—Trans.]

aesthetic experience becomes possible and promotes to the dignity of art what had never before been considered or created as such. All previous metamorphoses merely modified the aspect of one style because another style had been born. Thus the men of the Renaissance responded anew to Greek art while remaining indifferent to Gothic art, and we think of Paolo Uccello as an unrecognized Cézanne, of Sponde as an unrecognized Mallarmé, and of Guillaume de Machault as an unrecognized Honegger. All such historical metamorphoses, in which the present revives the past so as to exalt or disavow it, are nothing compared to the essential metamorphosis realized in the twentieth century. First of all, this metamorphosis affects the past as a whole, e.g., when patient historical and ethnological research reconstructs the past from artifacts found in tombs and on lost islands. We accept all these works and convert them into aesthetic objects, because there is no single style to which we are intellectually or religiously bound and which has such a grip on us as to cloud our view of all other styles. Malraux writes, "In the twelfth century a Weï statue would not have been compared with a Romanesque statue: an idol would have been compared with a saint." [50] Today the two are reconciled in the domain of art, since our indifference to significations will not allow us to be indifferent to any aesthetic object which appears to be authentic.[51]

As soon as perception discovers aesthetic objects where they had not been perceived before, modern art, according to an easily conceivable reciprocal movement, begins to produce works which present themselves immediately as aesthetic objects. Such works do not attempt to capture our attention by means of an explicit representation or by a symbolic signification; rather, they demand pure contemplation. For this to occur, a certain state of culture must free art from the obligation to signify. The liberation can be the result either of the introduction of a new sort of knowledge (as with treatises on physics and psychology which limit works like Lucretius' *De rerum natura* to the status

50. André Malraux, *The Voices of Silence*, trans. Stuart Gilbert (Garden City, N.Y.: Doubleday, 1953), p. 585.

51. This poses a problem to which we shall return. In an extreme sense, we could argue that a Christian is blind to Christian art precisely because he is a Christian, or else that ethnologists are not to be trusted to understand primitive art. Marcel Griaule, however, objects to this: "It seems both dangerous and absurd to separate the object of thought from its creators and seek only those emotions and seductions which depend on material forms which have been set up by unknown hands" (*Arts de l'Afrique noire*, p. 42). We shall eventually have to take his objection into account.

of a poem or Madame de Lafayette's *La Princesse de Clèves* to the status of a novel) or of more advanced means for the imitation of nature (such as the invention of photography, which frees the painter or sculptor from the necessity of *trompe-l'oeil* effects.) Such a liberation may also occur in the religious sphere, where we have lost our former naïveté. Religion no longer serves as an inspiration for most aesthetic activity either because it has lost the power to do so or because, by becoming highly spiritualized, it no longer concerns itself with art at all. From all this arises the temptation toward a pure art liberated from any necessity for imitation or statement. This is a magnificent temptation, for purity has not been given its due. The vocation of the artist becomes one of an aesthetic sainthood rendered deadly serious by the examples of a few tragic lives which attest to the difference between our type of metamorphosis and that of the Renaissance.[52] Yet the very seriousness of the modern artistic project poses a question. If art is an absolute and has its own martyrs, how can it help but signify? If art were really reduced to the purely sensuous, would it not lose all substance and cease to be worthy of the passions it has aroused? Does not the continuing impact of works from past epochs result from the fact that, in their own time, they were endowed with content and that something of the faith by which they were sustained is transmitted to us through them, however ignorant we may be of the details of that faith? If, therefore, the work does retain a signifying power and the aesthetic object is not something purely sensuous, what then is the place of such signification in the structure of the work and its function in the dynamic of the creative act? Furthermore, how is this signification grasped by aesthetic perception? We shall return continually to these problems, which are in fact the center of all our reflections. Here we broach the first part of our answer by indicating the nature of that signification which we shall call expression.

It is difficult to deny that, as opposed to ordinary signifying objects, the aesthetic object remains expressive. Although the tympanum of Autun may have completely lost its didactic role for those who are not interested in Christian dogma or who do

52. The fact is that the Renaissance, as Frank P. Chambers points out (*The History of Taste: An Account of the Revolutions of Art Criticism and Theory in Europe* [New York: Columbia University Press, 1933]), invented the dilettante, the connoisseur who takes pleasure in the arts for their beauty and not for their moral or religious instruction. But the aesthetics of beauty conceals the problem of the truth of art and thus does not inspire apostles.

not come to identify the protagonists of the depicted drama, it continues to say something in terms of what is immediately visible, in the placing of the characters, their long and nostalgic silhouettes, their solemn and awkward gestures, their serious faces, the folds of their tunics moving in the wind of the infinite. Even though we may be unaware that the Navajo Yei-Be-Chei is meant to beseech the spirit of evil residing in the body of the sick person, we nevertheless sense, through the strange cries and steps of the dance, an association with some tragic secret by means of which the gates of death spring open. We are beginning to realize that ethnological research and, in the case of Christian art, the persistence of the Christian tradition do not constitute an obstacle to aesthetic experience. What is said through feeling can be experienced or confirmed in the objective elucidation of the meaning of the work. Still, this knowledge by itself remains foreign to the aesthetic experience. Only that revelation which we shall call "affective" is truly constitutive of the aesthetic experience. The aesthetic object does not speak to me *about* its subject. The subject itself speaks to me, and in the manner in which it is treated. The subject is an inevitable ingredient in the work not so much for its own sake as for the sake of the form which is given to it and by which it becomes expressive. The Last Judgment as treated in a theological dissertation, or illness as described in a treatise on pathology, is not truly expressive. What is expressive is the Last Judgment as sculpted by Gislebert or illness as mimed in a primitive dance.

Thus the aesthetic object is distinguished from the signifying object both by a difference in nature and by the way in which signification is treated. The relationship between what is signified and what does the signifying in the aesthetic object is not the same as that in natural objects. Natural objects continually point outside of themselves in space and time and in this way gradually constitute the nature into which they are integrated. Nor does the relationship resemble that found in signifying objects, where signs disappear behind the signification they present. We shall emphasize strongly—and investigate the consequences of—the point that, in the case of the aesthetic object, what is signified is immanent in what does the signifying. While ordinary perception seeks the meaning of the given beyond the given, the aesthetic object does not allow perception to transcend the given. Instead, perception stops and remains precisely in this given, which will not let perception break loose from it.

Aesthetic signification does not, in fact, possess an autonomous existence. It exists only through the aesthetic object by which it is revealed. It does not preexist this object. Of course, the Faust legends predated Goethe's poem, and the countryside of the Île-de-France was an inspiration for Corot, Manet, and Pissarro, just as popular tunes provided the thematic inspiration for Haydn and Stravinsky. But although such objects from the cultural or the natural world and events from the historical world provide the pretext for creation, they are not in a strict sense the subject of the work. They are what is specifically identifiable in discussing the work—what the title often names. They belong to the work as something reflected upon by the artist and the spectator. The true subject, however, is in the work itself. It can be perceived only in the work and grasped only in the way the work treats it. Two different works can have the same subject and still differ in what they signify, insofar as the sensuous which they radiate may not be the same. We are inevitably unfaithful to the work in whatever we may say concerning its subject by way of definition, synopsis, or explication. This is best shown in any attempt to give the meaning of musical works. Any musical commentary is itself immediately judged by the work itself. We can easily claim, as Beethoven himself did, that the "Andante" of his Quartet no. 15 in A Minor expresses a prayer of gratitude to God by a recovering invalid. But does this really express what is contained in that movement's infinitely extended chords of ever-changing harmonies? What is said *in* music can be said only *by* music. Even when a painting presents an object which can be identified and described, the object which I name is not equivalent to the object which the painting represents. In a sense, the difference between the work and our relation to it is of the same order as the radical difference between the flesh-and-blood individual and his description in a passport. Neither a verbal description nor a portrait could ever represent a real individual with exactitude. The distance between the real and the conceptual or the represented can never be annulled. But this distance is not what is specifically at issue here. We are concerned with the relationship of one language to another whereby a commentary is forced to reexpress an object already expressed by means of art. Perhaps, therefore, a short reflection on language may help us to grasp the phenomenon of expression.

(b) Expression in language

In a sense, every object constitutes a language and, conversely, every language is a sort of object. Like every object, language must first of all be apprehended. A word must be perceived through an aural or visual appearance which often presents no more than an incomplete or confused aspect of that word. Then the word must be understood and interpreted as a sign of something else which is its meaning. For our purposes, the only difference between a word and an ordinary object is that a word has a mission to signify. A definite meaning is attached by convention to the word that cannot legitimately be replaced by another. An object, on the contrary, signifies only for those who wish to decipher its message. An object can assume, according to the whim of imagination, different meanings —all of which may be valid for the understanding. It would not be impossible, however, to attenuate this difference by demonstrating that, on the one hand, language is like nature in the Comtean sense of having a thematic richness which a single usage could never exhaust, and that, on the other hand, the aesthetic object may end by having an everyday signification and thus becoming a sort of signal.

We must join together the following two themes. Language presupposes comprehension, which implies that thought rules over language. Comprehension presupposes a preliminary agreement between the meaning and the word, that is, a signifying power of the word through its resemblance to the object, which implies that thought presupposes language. (Reduced to epistemological terms, this contradiction is essentially what Comte makes explicit in parceling out language to both biology and sociology.) Like man himself, who lives by identifying himself with his body and inaugurates thought without ever ultimately escaping from this body, language is divided into the monism in which it is rooted and the dualism in which it stands in danger of being abolished once it has been realized. Its status must lie in a continually unstable equilibrium between the being of the gesture by which language becomes expressive and the being of the spoken word by which it becomes rational. Language is both the organ of an immediate comprehension (that *with* which we think) and the means toward a mediated comprehension (that which makes us think *of* something). In short, language is both nature and spirit.[53] This ambivalence is also found in language's function. The word is simultaneously signifiying and expressive. It is signifying in that it harbors an objective signification which is in a sense external to it and requires the operation of the understanding. It is expressive in that it bears an immanent signification within itself which surpasses the objective meaning grasped by the understanding. The word is a sign, but it is more than a sign. The word simultaneously says and shows, and what it shows is different from what it says.

First, however, we must emphasize the word's function of saying, which, as Pradines has demonstrated, cannot be reduced

53. The somewhat Pascalian sentiment about the ambiguity of language is expressed throughout Brice Parain, *Recherches sur la nature et les fonctions du langage* (Paris: Gallimard, 1942). Parain seems to begin with the assumption that the origin of language is hidden from us. Thus we cannot resolve the problem of naming or be sure whether the referent of words lies in a singular thing for which they are the natural sign or in an intelligible essence for which they are a conventional sign. But, even if this problem cannot be resolved, there is another function of language, namely, "demonstration," which when examined does not lead us to the ungraspable beginning of language but to its end. By using language to demonstrate, we in fact reverse the relationship between the word and its meaning. "The object is not what gives a sign its signification, but it is the sign which makes us imagine an object for its signification" (*ibid.*, p. 73). Language is thus a program, i.e., an order or a promise. It expresses the possible, something which needs to be realized, and not the real. How, then, does the idea of an "expressionist" theory of language arise? Parain understands by this idea that, instead of designating an object, language has the function of expressing us, the speakers. (We shall return to this idea.) The future which language opens is our own, because in speaking we make a decision concerning ourselves and reveal ourselves. Furthermore, in order to retain some objectivity in language, Parain also argues, citing Hegel and even Leibniz, that expression must be thought from the perspective "of humanity as a whole" rather than that of the individual (*ibid.*, p. 136). When we speak, we enter into an adventure which surpasses us and is important for the history of the world. Icarus finally found his truth in the aviator and Newton in Einstein. But, in the end, Parain cannot cite history as a justification for the truth of language. Thus he introduces "expressionism," which subordinates this truth to man. He restores language to its authority, without returning to the unsolvable problem of its origin, by suggesting that language is a task for its speakers because it is "transcendent." It is a test and a judge. We judge by it, but we are also judged by it. Thus we tend to silence, as at the end of a test. It seems to us that if we established ourselves in language, we would finally be a universal by which to measure our singularity. Yet language provides cruel evidence of our separation and finitude by introducing a truth by which to measure our falseness. We can understand the power Parain attributes to language and why he even becomes frightened of it. He is at the opposite pole from Claudelian pride, that is, the pride of the Creator.

to its function of showing.[54] The transmission of a thought is not the communication of an emotion. To say "I suffer" is not the same as weeping in order to induce others to weep. Language presupposes an intellectual activity which is not found in vocal mimicry. Even if language borrows its symbolism from an imitation of objects, it still presupposes, in Pradines's words, "a mind capable of understanding and looking for that particular symbolism." (Schmalenbach seems to argue in a similar manner, by placing an understanding of the sign at the origin of language.)[55] Language constantly tends to be a rational instrument of signification and to become a conventional system of algorithms—that is, capable not only of propounding a truth but also of furnishing the norms (at least the formal norms) for that truth. In this respect, language is not downgraded in being institutionalized, for that is how it becomes the faithful auxiliary of a thought which has become conscious of itself and of a communication which is attempting to reach the level of thought. Thought cannot become conscious of itself until it makes language a means and not an end and points out the distinction between what is signified [*le signifié*] and what does the signifying [*le signifiant*]. This is how we learn the words of a foreign language—words which, for this reason, will never possess their complete poetic value for us. Even when a meaning becomes internal to a word, this is because it is deposited within the word and fixed there; but the meaning is neither subordinated to nor created by the word. Hence language cannot claim to be of value by itself. It is devoured by its meaning and is entirely in the service of thought or of an action which presupposes thought. Its only virtue is exactness. Language must say exactly what it has to say in order that we can know precisely with what we are dealing. Other words are always possible if they say the same thing. Translations are also always possible, either from one language to another or within the interior of the same language, on condition that these translations remain faithful to the original meaning and that the words are treated like tools which can be replaced by other tools performing the same function. The word's sensuous qualities do not typically hold our attention. The word's entire function is to signify a meaning which is always presupposed. Following Boileau, we may say that the very definition of

54. Maurice Pradines, *Psychologie générale* (Paris: Presses Universitaires de France, 1946), II, 499 ff.
55. See Schmalenbach, "Phénoménologie du signe."—Trans.

prose is that what is well conceived can be clearly enunciated. In becoming aesthetic, however, language undergoes a radical transformation.

In fact, language cannot have an objective signification unless that signification is already immanent in it. Similarly, language cannot awaken in us the mechanism of comprehension unless it has already realized a sort of organic complicity with the object. Merleau-Ponty discovers this expressive quality, through which language has its primordial being, on a level of behavior at which intelligence and motor activity are identified. The word gives rise to a motor commentary which institutes a resemblance between it and the object. This is not the naïve theory of onomatopoeia correctly condemned by Pradines, which believes in an objective resemblance between word and object. The word is no more a *trompe-l'oreille* device than authentic painting is a result of *trompe-l'oeil*. The resemblance we have in mind is a lived one. The family likeness [*air de famille*] between word and object, through which the word traces the object before designating it, results from the fact that we behave similarly before the word and the object. The way we grasp a meaning in pronouncing the word is analogous to the way we treat the presence of the object.[56]

Language is therefore expressive to the extent that it carries its meaning along with it, offering it to us like the living presence of the object it designates. Merleau-Ponty's notion of originary speech has to do with a meaning directly secreted by the sign,

56. This is why we learn language at the same time that we familiarize ourselves with the world. We know by naming. The fact that society is what transmits our language to us does not change this familiarity. It simply gives evidence of the eminently social character of language. What could be misleading is that we subsequently learn foreign languages by means of an analytical method and consider words as signs in a code. But we should point out that this awkward and reflected usage occurs only in the beginning of the learning process, where we do not speak but rather translate by referring to our native language. It is not a pure thought which is at the root of this process but another word which must be translated. But what happens in this case is that we move to what is nevertheless the rational usage of language—even if only in the sense of Merleau-Ponty's "idea-limit" (*Phenomenology of Perception*, p. 190)—which claims to subordinate language to thought. This is also why we do not think that it is necessary to teach foreign languages in the same way we learn our native language, as certain educators have attempted to do. It is perhaps better to give the mind its opportunity according to the classical method, to allow the mind to manifest its power, and treat language as a sign system conventionally subjected to meaning. This will not prevent our mind from becoming embodied or language from becoming a gesture through habit.

as opposed to the speech which merely translates preexisting ideas and presupposes previous communication between speaker and listener. For this reason, the poetic word is endowed with the incantatory presence hailed by poets. The same is true of other artistic materials. Color for painting is not a sign or an accidental feature, as in the Aristotelian world-view, but an agent which brings forth the object. In the same way, the sounds of a symphonic poem like *La Mer* are not simply the roar of the ocean, they are the ocean itself. Or rather, the ocean has become sound, just as a flaxen-haired girl or a terrace by the light of the moon also become sound in Debussy's work. As soon as it is no longer mere noise, sound ceases to be the attribute of an object in order to become its expression. Hence silence can be sonorous just as the night can be colorful. The aesthetic object seems to conjure up what it designates because the thing is present within it, not in terms of the thing's external being which can be parceled out into distinct attributes, but in terms of what is deepest and least divisible in it: namely, its essence, which art alone can grasp and express with such certainty that imagination and even understanding need not add their commentaries to aesthetic perception.

Language, however, can be expressive in a different way. It is not only a relationship between self and object but also one between two distinct selves. Language is expressive in that it manifests a subject. By the way in which it is spoken and (as we shall see later) written,[57] language is a gesture in which we read a meaning and which indicates to us the intentions of the speaker. Language is not only a means of communicating an idea by a choice of words but also a means of revealing oneself [*se livrer*]. Speaking always means speaking of oneself—it is autobiographical, as Nietzsche observed about philosophizing. Speaking is a witnessing and a promising. Once something is said, it cannot be retracted. "Our words commit us to the extent that they express us and not further, since they are the future of our present." [58] Words commit us as soon as they have a meaning, because we choose this meaning and decide about ourselves by this very choice.[59] By choosing to call "parallel" two

57. Recognition tests prove that writing is expressive independent of one's choice of words.

58. Parain, *Recherches*, p. 171.

59. This could be used to clarify Sartre's idea of committed literature. It expresses a very general commitment which is, however, extremely imperious and of which political commitment is only one possibility among others.

lines which do not meet, a geometer commits himself to a certain type of geometry. A man commits himself when he says "I love you," thereby determining the meaning of a certain troubling unrest which he experiences. Mosca was well aware of this fact when he was frightened lest that same phrase "and all its consequences" appear in the relationship between Fabrice and Sanseverina. Hence it is not difficult to endow words with a magical power to produce certain effects. We are constantly confronted with the efficacy of this power, for example, when a phrase put into circulation can be strong enough to bring down a government. This phrase can enjoy such a career because, in pronouncing it, one takes an oath and decides on one's future. This is why we are sometimes so attentive to someone's very next word. We expect it to reveal an individual to us and we find the truth of this individual more important than the truth of the idea. Any theory of language as a social bond must realize that language is both endowed with meaning—that is, the instrument of objectification or the depository of objectivity—and an instrument for communication through which individuals recognize one another as counterparts. Thus language constitutes an intersubjectivity for which the objectivity of the thing or idea has merely mediatory value.

The feelings of the other are what is revealed immediately by expression thus understood as a type of gesture. For example, a friend signals to me from a distance. I cannot easily understand the explicit signification of this gestured message, and yet I can read impatience, hate, and anger in his gestures, just as I can grasp the same feelings in the intonation of words pronounced in a foreign language. The more gestures try to attain the status of language, the more we need a key to this language, which thereby becomes conventional in character—just as we must learn highway signals or the vocabulary of a foreign language. But, as long as gestures do not claim to make any objective statement, they constitute a spontaneous and immediately comprehensible language. This type of comprehension, however, is limited to what is commonly called feeling, that is, to a certain way of being in the world, of instituting a particular relationship with it, of discovering its character, and of living certain experiences in its terms. It is in terms of feelings that the original relationship of a human being with the world is elaborated and the ungraspable spontaneity of the for-itself is manifested. Our ability to recognize a for-itself is due to this capacity for expression. Such a capacity contradicts solipsism and reveals the meaning of behavior. It is a meaning which can only be perceived and which an analysis can account for only on the basis of that direct and irreplaceable experience. Expression is the mode of revelation for whatever lacks a concept, since there are concepts only of objects. Whenever a subject, or at least that fundamental act by which a subject is constituted (that is, the act by which he relates most spontaneously to the world), is in question, concepts are inoperative.

Thus we come to recognize a new aspect of language, one which extends the notion of language beyond spoken language and perhaps rediscovers the foundation of all language. However, the two aspects of language which are manifested by the two forms of expression must be rigorously distinguished. When we understand a meaning, we follow an idea; by sounding out the word or by allowing ourselves to be imbued with it, we enter into a sphere of objectivity in order to attain a truth. The universe of discourse thus requires that the speaker as well as the listener have a concern for truth: (1) as a will to veracity (for which, as Kant saw, a lie can never become a universal law, because language can speak only in order to say something true); and (2) as a will to give an account and to rationalize. When we name an object, we do not merely invoke it. We bring it into the kingdom of reason. To speak is to commit oneself and others to the formal and even the ethical demands of thought. Even if speech is originally expressive and makes the object arise, speech makes the object arise not as a brute presence but as humanized and subject to reason. The need to speak which we sometimes experience when before a pleasing landscape—a need to describe it or simply to say that it is beautiful—is a need to convert an eloquent but uninformed impression into something lucid and legitimate and also to tame the object by converting its presence into truth and our own rapture into mastery. How different in this respect is a painter's reaction when he says nothing but simply picks up his brush! He wishes to perpetuate and not to clarify the mystery of the object. The poet has the same goal, even if he cannot burst the corset of rationality in which language is bound.

Understanding a human being, in contrast, does not involve invoking a truth. It is rather the experience of a presence which does not bring our power of judgment into play; nor does it appeal to the rules of judgment which are called forth by the gap between the object and its name (a gap that is not overcome even when the name conjures up the object). Between a gesture and its meaning, there is no semantic fissure comparable to that present in verbal language, where rationality is introduced as a demand for adequation between word and thing and as a reflection on the correct and proper usage of words. Instead, the meaning is entirely *in* the gesture. Expression makes the sign and the signified coincide. A shaking voice *is* timidity, and violent and raucous sputtering *is* anger. Error seems impossible in such cases. And yet can we not be deceived by expressions? Do we know for certain whether to attribute a certain sharpness of tone to pride or to timidity, or a particular uneasiness to love or to fear? We should point out here what we shall have to reconsider in discussing the aesthetic object, namely, that we can be hesitant as to the meaning of someone's behavior for two reasons. On the one hand, the behavior's meaning may be truly undefinable. In such a case, we should not be surprised that our perception is confused, since our perception is as confused as if we were attempting to perceive ourselves. For example, does Phaedra know whether her first tremblings mean love? On the other hand, we may not be truly attentive and may fail to make ourselves fully present to the signs which seem to us obscure or ambiguous. In neither of these cases, however, is meaning really hidden as the meaning of a cryptogram can be hidden. We must say simply that we cannot define this meaning. It is not that the meaning is concealed but that we ourselves are blind. It is possible, moreover, that we are not responsible for this blindness, for certain conditions necessary to put us in a state of receptivity may not have been realized. An example of this is the child who may witness gestures of desire but fail to understand them, because his or her sexuality has either not yet been awakened or not yet been differentiated and attached to a specific object. There is also the ethnologist who does not understand a particular ritual mimicry, because he overlooks its object and, not wishing to imitate the first explorers by making fun of primitive stupidity, is reduced to invoking a prelogical mentality.[60] These examples in no way suggest—as was gen-

---

60. Lévy-Bruhl is often criticized on this point, particularly by American sociologists. There is also a difference between the two examples we have just cited. A child needs certain affective and organic abilities in order to understand. The anthropologist, on the other hand, needs certain mental abilities which allow him to understand what is primitive by becoming primitive himself. The two experiences also differ in that the child is satisfied with an immediate apprehension which he does not explicate any more than he explicates his own feeling but can nevertheless experience very vividly, as when he kisses his mother with all his heart. The an-

erally held before Max Scheler—that a subject's interpretation of expression comes solely from referring to himself and drawing conclusions about others which are based on himself. They do, however, provide evidence for a precondition of our apprehension of others. We must be able to feel ourselves intended or affected by others' behavior and not feel them to be completely foreign to us or moving in a universe totally different from our own. This condition is not realized unless we can reapprehend and re-create in our own terms the gestures of others in such a way that they find an echo in our own behavior and are inscribed in our own universe. We understand directly others' experience after being made sensitive by our own experience, and we would remain closed off from others if nothing prepared us to accept their experience and live its meaning. There is no feeling [*sentiment*] without a sort of presentiment [*pressentiment*].[61] But the fact remains that when the conditions required to put us in this state of grace are realized, expression presents its meaning directly to us without orienting us (in the manner of naming) toward the universe of reason. Hence aesthetic language presents us, as we have seen, with the creator of the work. The aesthetic object is expressive because its creator expresses himself in it. He does not exhibit or prostitute himself. Rather, he expresses himself in such acts of expression as the poet's naming of the object, the painter's showing it, or the musician's singing it. In all these cases, a world appears which is, in a sense, the creator's own and which lies beyond what he says or represents. Furthermore, all this seems to indicate that we should unite the two forms of expression which we have just distinguished—that which reveals the object and that which reveals a human being.

These two forms of expression are, in fact, complementary, and it is in language that we most often find them united. For language is both speech and gesture. This is as true for the individual who expresses himself, whose speech underlines his gestures while his gestures put stress on his choice of words, as it is for the individual who receives the expression, for whom speech and gesture are mutually clarifying in their harmony or contrast. The dual character of expression is easily perceived. It

---

thropologist, in contrast, looks for a general system of beliefs, values, and symbols behind the immediate meaning of behavior to which this meaning can be attached. He makes his apprehension reflective in character.

61. This point will quickly lead us to the problem of innateness or reminiscence and again to imagination in its metaphysical function.

is precisely because of this duality that language can appear as the bearer of an objective sense and designate a *Sachverhalt* ("state of affairs") which can be stated and intended in different ways by different speakers. The same spoken word can be said with joy, regret, or fervor, while it is difficult to make angry gestures when in good spirits.[62] But our perception of the duality of expression is due to the fact that the word becomes detached from its gestural context and ceases itself to be a gesture. It ceases at the same time to be expressive in its semantic function, and any expressive qualities become concentrated in the gesture as separated from the word. Thus the gesture is the true seat of expressiveness, and one form of expression must consequently be subordinated to another. Is not language's expressiveness as speech a result of language's having been expressive first as gesture? Is not language's expression of an object due to an expression of a subject who, by expressing himself, confers on language the unique capacity to signify and perhaps to signify a new meaning? Language, of course, cannot be invested with such a capacity unless it is already meaningful. In this peculiarity lies the paradox of language. If it were completely pure, expression would perhaps be simply a matter of enchantment which possesses neither meaning nor thought. For this reason, expression tends to become language and signs tend to become signals. But while expression is a limit of language, it is also the foundation of language, which accomplishes its signifying function only on the condition of being or having been expressive. And language is not expressive unless a subject is manifested in it. The originary speech which names an object is expressive insofar as a subject expresses, through this speech, a gesture he makes, an emotion he feels, a project he forms, or the knowledge through which he becomes consubstantial with the object. In naming the object, the subject speaks of himself and expresses his accord with the object. Only on this condition are words natural. And, similarly, the language of others is expressive only because it blends the other with the object and because, in revealing to us the other person, it also reveals the object through the other person. We shall be able to confirm this

62. We nevertheless distinguish between a distracted and a passionate caress and between a feigned and a sincere emotion. This distinction shows that the gesture may itself become language and receive the status of a sign which is capable of objectivity and is perhaps fulfilled by different intentions, like a word pronounced with different accents.

point when we come to consider the world of the aesthetic object, that is, the world of its creator.

(c) *Expression in the aesthetic object*

Perhaps the preceding brief analysis of language has sufficiently clarified the expressive quality of the aesthetic object. Authentic art is an originary speech which, instead of bringing forth conceptual meaning, simultaneously awakens a feeling and conjures up a presence. An aesthetic dimension of meaning corresponds to the aesthetic dimension of the sign. What happens to the signification in what is said in an untranslatable and irreplaceable manner by orchestral timbres or tonal harmonies? What happens to the represented object through the colors of a painting? Where in a poem are the clarity, logical rigor, and precision which satisfy the understanding? We need only think of such metaphoric expressions as Valéry and Verlaine have used: high noon has been called justice, the sea an incomparable hydra rapturous over its blue skin, and a woman a beautiful autumn sky of transparent pink. The liberties taken by modern poets with objective meaning and those taken by painters with their subjects are well known. We could cite their extravagances endlessly. But are they really extravagances? Not at all. Strange groupings of words and encounters with sound in which only the ear is satisfied are shocking only to the understanding. We cannot doubt that such works do say (and urgently) something which they alone are capable of expressing. It seems hopeless, and in fact would be very difficult, to make explicit the meaning of their expression in precise terms, since these works alone can truly say it. Yet this meaning can be easily grasped, as we shall see, by a natural movement of perception which knows with certainty what an expression means through the feeling it awakens. Thus a child understands its mother's smile, a hiker understands the somber horror of a forest, and a doctor understands the flushed complexion of his patient. We speak of the aesthetic object in the same manner not only in the case of poetic language but also with regard to movements in a dance, the curve of a column, a melodic line, and even the most distant and apparently most undecipherable works. The Rodin bronze which lies on my desk is not simply a bronze which has been molded in a certain manner and whose volumes and contours outline a certain form which is pleasing to the eye. It is first of all *a hand*. But it is a hand in bronze which has not been created to take the place of a real hand in the sense that a copy can replace an original. This hand has no need of an arm which will prolong it and bind it to a body in the world of bodies. When it speaks to me expressively, it says nothing about what a real hand can perform in the world. It is unable to grasp, caress, or bless. If on my own I evoke some gesture or activity of a real hand, I have betrayed the work. What the work says cannot be translated in terms of the world. It expresses vigor, suppleness, and even tenderness in its caressing position and in its two low-ered fingers that are incapable of gripping anything. It expresses human misery, in the prominent veins on the back of the hand, but also the hope of peace and rest. This hand does not, however, point to any real history. All of what it expresses is within it and is true only in the world it opens to me—a world without real hands, where a hand ceases to be real in order to become true, and where force, delicacy, and the longing for rest have an absolute signification and need not be related to objective be-havior in order to be understood. This world is given in the aesthetic object. Beyond this world there is only the real, from which the aesthetic object is absent.

These initial remarks should help us to avoid indulging in a serious equivocation. By laying emphasis on the expression of the aesthetic object and suggesting that the apprehension of this object is a function of feeling, we do not wish to imply that the expressiveness of the aesthetic object is to be measured by the emotions it can arouse. We do not wish to confuse emotion and feeling, the moving and the expressive. The melodrama in which the heroine weeps, erotic painting, effusive poetry, and horror films are not our models. Jeanne Hersch has quite cor-rectly pointed out "the excess of expressiveness" as one of the perils of art and condemned "those two apparently opposed but essentially similar temptations of *Verismo* and excessive pathos." [63] In the same vein, Malraux denounces "the arts of delectation," which have to do with sensations and not with values and "are not inferior arts but . . . anti-arts." [64] True art is not saccharine. It does not grab at the spectator's heartstrings. It associates the body with perception not to titillate but to convince. Furthermore, it never loses a sense of measure. It

63. Hersch, *L'Etre et la forme*, p. 186.
64. Malraux, *The Voices of Silence*, p. 516.

invites us to be spectators and does not compete with the spectacles of life, whose pathos, horror, and seduction lack restraint or a coefficient of unreality. True art gives us access to another world which, though not without relationship to the real world, still does not affect us as if it were itself real. The feeling it awakens in us is a means of knowing this other world, an instrument of knowledge—and not, like emotion, a means of defence or the sign of an upheavel. Such a world, moreover, is not shown but rather *said* by art. What speaks in this world (in the case of the representational arts) is not so much what it represents as the sensuous qualities which are the means of representation. It is Van Gogh's brush-strokes and colors which express despair and love, not the bedroom or the wheatfield he depicts.

In fact, the subject of the work—a subject which is the work's objective meaning in representational art and is tied to aesthetic language—appears only through [*à travers*] the feeling awakened by expression. The represented object appears through the expressed object—the struggles of Achilles through the grandeur expressed in epic poetry, the entry of the Crusaders into Jerusalem through the noble tumult expressed by Delacroix's colors, and places of prayer through the contemplativeness and peace expressed in Romanesque arches. Should we be surprised? We have said that the word bears the thing within it and that this defines expression. When a poet invokes the sea, we genuinely feel the sea's presence. But the sea is not present as it would be for a swimmer or a geographer. For it is not present as an idea, as it would be in the language of prose, or as a material presence (which would be impossible in any case). It is present, all the same, with a presence which we must call affective and with a truth of its own which can be discovered only through art. Thus art truly represents only in expressing, that is, in communicating through the magic of the sensuous a certain feeling by means of which the represented object can appear as present. Art signifies primarily because it is expressive. Moreover, it may well be true that not all art is representational. At least we shall have to consider this possibility in the case of arts like music or architecture, which first attracted our attention to the splendor of the sensuous. By contrast, the literary and the plastic arts invite us above all to consider signification, especially in the form of representation. All this suggests that expression appears more adequately the more adequately the sensuous appears. Art can express only by virtue of the sensuous and according to an operation which transforms brute sensuousness into aesthetic sensuousness.

CONCLUSION: NATURE AND FORM

JUST AS THE SENSUOUS bears a signification which it proceeds to convert into expression, so, conversely, it may be said that this signification in-forms the sensuous. Thus we rediscover form, whose manner of organizing the sensuous we have already mentioned, and style, which gives evidence of something premeditated and personal in this organization. Signification—both representation and expression, which is the meaning of meaning and, in a sense, a sort of form for representation—must be understood in terms of form. When signification reaches its highest point, it becomes genuine form, the soul of an object which has finally been delimited.

The aesthetic object presents itself to us as a totality. The sonata we hear or the statue we contemplate is a sonata or statue in its entirety, which cannot be decomposed. We confront it as if we were faced with a perfect object which is imposed on us and with which we have an immediate communication that cannot be dissected. In this chapter, certain distinctions have been introduced to which we shall continually return. In attempting to offer a first means of approach to the being of the aesthetic object, we have distinguished it from living beings, natural objects, and objects of use. Thus we were able to define three of its aspects: (1) in terms of its matter, that is, insofar as it is offered to perception, it has the being of the sensuous; (2) in terms of its meaning, that is, when it represents, it has the being of an idea; and (3) when it is expressive, it has the being of feeling.[65] This analysis will make full sense when we attempt an objective study of the work. But our investigation cannot end with the work, since then it would omit the aesthetic object in the strict sense and substitute for it a schema which results from an objectifying attitude. This is not an attitude we take spontaneously before the aesthetic object, since it allows this object to

65. We may point to a fourth aspect of the aesthetic object that deserves mention. It is analogous to what Etienne Souriau calls "physical existence," i.e., "the body of the work of art" (*La Correspondance des arts,* p. 46). This body, however, belongs to the work of art as something known and not to the aesthetic object as something perceived.

become lost in a plurality of determinations. When we contemplate it in order to enjoy it, the aesthetic object appears to us as a whole. It is an object unified by its form. But the form is not only the unity of the sensuous, it is also a unity of meaning.

This form is, however, above all the principle which in-forms the sensuous by delimiting it. How does this happen? We first apprehend form as contour, the limit of the object in relation to the background of indifferent and neutralized reality from which the object distinguishes itself. The form is what defines the object by its external relations rather than by what is internal to it. The experiments of Gestalt psychology, and particularly those of Rubin, which emphasize the relation between figure and ground, suggest that a figure is discerned in the field of perception by means of its contour and that it may even be reduced to its contour.[66] Gestalt psychology, however, is careful not to forget that the figure is a totality which, as has been pointed out by Guillaume, "possesses form, contour, and organization" and also "has functional properties" and "internal organization" by which "every articulation of contour is subject to functional modifications." [67] The models proposed by Gestalt psychology could serve to manifest the difference between the ornamental and the artistic, particularly between the decorative and the pictorial. Thus arabesques and geometrical compositions which are suitable for the decoration of walls, rugs, or vases appear, in the light of Gestalt psychology, as figures which lack the flesh of the sensuous. It makes little difference whether or not these designs have been inspired by an object which has become stylized through tradition, such as the ibex of Elamite pottery, the rose-window, or serpentine-shaped jewelry. The original model is not represented or even considered. We confront these designs as we would those purely geometric figures which are perceptual equivalents of a concept. It seems that the pleasure which we take in contemplating these designs results from the fact that it is within perception itself that we come across the secret of their order and the law by which they are engendered. The sensuous is not experienced for its own sake as it is in a drawing where one feels the hand of the artist and his whole being animating that hand. The sensuous is experienced for the sake of the concept it harbors—a concept which, though not explicitly

66. See Edgar Rubin, *Visuell wahrgenommene Figuren, Studien in psychologischer Analyse* (Copenhagen: Gyldendal, 1922).

67. Paul Guillaume, *La Psychologie de la forme* (Paris: Flammarion, 1937), pp. 61, 67.

stated, is nonetheless evident.[68] The idea, as Hegel would say, remains abstract and does not constitute the object. Thus the decorative is not truly expressive, although it has its own physiognomy in the sense that we can feel that a certain line is supple, a particular outline is severe, or a particular figure is heavy. But such characteristics do not appear to be directed or ordered by an individual who is expressing himself through them. They gain their complete meaning only in the aesthetic object, e.g., in Rubens' circular and swirling compositions, which express a sort of cosmic orgy, in the sequential composition of Rude's *La Marseillaise* regarded as an expression of energy, or in Poussin's vertical lines felt as expressions of order. Thus the decorative can serve as an ornament. But since its form is nothing more than contour, it is not itself an object.

Yet the examples that we have just cited indicate that, at least in the representational arts, form is more intimately linked with what it represents [*le fond*] than Gestalt analysis would imply. Form bears on the represented object. Of course, the temptation to define form as contour remains. There are certain arts which would seem to call for such a definition, as, for example, sculpture or drawing—especially line drawing, where form seems undeniably to be found in the line which limits the represented object, since the sensuous in this case is reduced to a minimum. In fact, if our interest is first directed to the represented object, then the work's form will be the object's form, that is, the silhouette it represents, such as the caricature or schematic drawing whose perception has been analyzed by Sartre.[69] In the case of the aesthetic object, however, it is no longer the represented object which must be considered first. A line has value in itself and not as a schema which must be deciphered by intentions—intentions which are fulfilled intuitively by this line through a process of bodily imitation. Since the represented object has been neutralized, a line does not hold

68. This is why it does not seem legitimate to compare the decorative with the musical, as was attempted by Waldemar Conrad in "Das ästhetische Objekt" (*Zeitschrift für Ästhetik und allgemeine Kunstwissenschaft*, III [1904], 41), on the grounds that both involve simple elements such as lines, planes, and sounds. There is an important difference between a line and a sound and even between an ornamental and a melodic line. Because the former merely illustrates an impersonal law of artistic construction, it does not have the sensuous plenitude of sound. Conrad recognizes, moreover, that the decorative, unlike music, does not produce an "absolute object."

69. See Jean-Paul Sartre, *The Psychology of Imagination*, trans. B. Frechtman (New York: Washington Square Press, 1966).—Trans.

my attention as a contour of some object. But the line's purpose is not, as in the case of the decorative arts, to express some abstract law of design. Rather, the line expresses what is sensuous within it, to wit, its splendor, its firmness, its fantasy, and its elegance. If its form is defined as the contour which encloses a space, then the form that we have been seeking to define here—aesthetic form—is in a sense the form of that form. Form defined as the contour of the represented object would be unacceptable in any case, because such a form cannot be found in impressionist painting. It is not found in the work of Georges Braque either (or at least in his most recent works, for which Jean Paulhan's exegesis is no longer entirely applicable). In Braque's work, space itself ceases to be space because it is entirely filled with overlapping forms which shatter and cancel one another in their interweaving. Form construed as the contour of a represented object is similarly not to be found in the sort of counterpoint in which melodic lines are superimposed over one another or in music like Debussy's, which is continually breaking and disrupting its melodic flow. In truth, the form of the aesthetic object is not attached to that which this object represents. Or at least what is represented is taken into the form rather than the form's proceeding from it. This is the case with the characteristic swirling movement in Rubens' work—a movement which carries along the painting and sustains its garlands of angels and peasant dances—just as in the various *Pietas* of Romanesque bas-reliefs a mournful stupor sustains the rigid standing figures placed around the tomb.

Form is, in fact, always the form of the sensuous. This is why it is deeply engaged in the matter of which the sensuous is the effect. The form of ballet is above all its movement, which possesses, according to an irresistible logic, the ornamented bodies of the dancers. The form of painting is the harmony of colors, "that impression which results from a particular arrangement of colors, light, shadow, etc.—all that can be called the music of the painting." [70] This form is already an

---

70. Eugène Delacroix, *Oeuvres littéraires* (Paris: G. Crès, 1923), I, 63. The same idea can be found in an extract from Baudelaire's *Eugène Delacroix,* an idea which can serve as a point of departure for abstract art: "When a painting by Delacroix is placed too far away for you to be able to judge the harmony of its contours or the more or less dramatic quality of its subject, it penetrates you with a supernatural voluptuousness. It seems that a magic atmosphere has come up to and enveloped you. . . . An analysis of its subject performed when you come close to the painting

initial meaning. The logical meaning of the aesthetic object, "what the painting represents," as Delacroix would say, confirms and articulates this initial meaning. The two meanings do not truly differ. This is the secret of the work of art on which we shall lay great stress. The subject—in the sense of the subject matter [le sujet]—is wedded with exactitude to the form of the sensuous; it is the form of this form. A particular splendid tumult of lines and colors must be the entrance of the Crusaders into Jerusalem or at least some equestrian epic. A particular series of situations on the stage must spell tragedy. A particular Gregorian modulation of a mass of stone must be a cathedral. Because the subject finds its exact correlative in the sensuous, the unity of sense and the sensuous in the work surpasses itself and becomes expression, that is, the ultimate form of the aesthetic object and the meaning of its meaning.

Hence form is connected with what is represented only because it is connected first of all with the sensuous in which representation is immanent. Form is the organizing principle of the sensuous and that which exalts it to the level of art. It is no longer simply contour, the external form of the work according to which we can either think the object (and perhaps discover the law of its reproduction) or grasp, manage, and utilize the object. Form is revealed in style. It appears most clearly when no represented object is present to compete with the aesthetic object, as in the case of music. Then its entire function is to unify the sensuous. The sensuous, however, must be unified with more of the sensuous and not with the conceptual— or, rather, it must be unified with a concrete idea. It is commonly believed that ordinary perception does not grasp form, instead occupying itself with identifying the object in order to know and utilize it. Yet ordinary perception does not always stop at mere identification, as Gestalt psychology has clearly shown. This school of thought extends the word "form" to the very expression of objects, which is a stage beyond the spatio-temporal organization of the given by the figure which allows us to isolate and identify an object. "All sorts of persons, objects, and situations have a moral physiognomy. The theory of form . . . admits that objects have by themselves, as a result of their own structure and independent of all the previous experience

_____

will neither add nor subtract anything from this primitive pleasure, whose source is far from all concrete thought" (Charles Baudelaire, *Eugène Delacroix, His Life and His Work*, trans. J. M. Bernstein [New York: Lear, 1947], p. 64).

of the subject who perceives them, certain characteristics of strangeness, terror, irritation, calm, grace, and elegance."[71] The aesthetic object has just such a character, a character which we shall be calling "affective." The aesthetic object speaks not only from the richness of the sensuous but through the affective quality which it expresses and which allows us to recognize it without recourse to concepts. Its unity is not only sensuous but affective. This unity is not a new form which has been added to those we have already discerned. It is rather a new aspect of the object, for the affective itself is immanent in the sensuous, as the verb *sentir* ("to feel," "to sense") indicates.

As soon as we cease to oppose the aesthetic object's form to what is represented in this object and realize how aesthetic perception grasps what is represented *within* form itself, then such a form, which embraces what is represented, becomes the genuine Gestalt and the signifying unity of the object. This is the form which appears first to the spectator, presenting the object as a totality because it is the unity of the internal and the external. (This form, moreover, should be distinguished from the work's objective structure, which is the foundation of the work from the viewpoint of creation and its mere reflection from the viewpoint of perception.) The form of a poem is not simply the ordering of the verbal material by which language rediscovers its musicality. It is also the meaning of the poem. But this form-meaning is not so much the logical meaning which can be extracted from the poem in order to be translated into the language of prose as it is the poem's poetic meaning, which is exhaled like perfume and which is the work's genuine garment. We cannot grasp the form of a painting without taking account of the object which it represents and which is underlined by the title. What perception encounters, however, in that movement which goes straight to the represented object is not a real object which has been transported from the kingdom of things into the framework of the work. It is a new object which is elicited by the force of the colors and which speaks a new expressive language. Such expression cements the unity of the painting.

We would disagree with Hersch on this point, after having approved of her efforts to determine what she calls aesthetic existence as opposed to the practical, contemplative, theoretical, and social senses of existence. (There is an evident relationship

71. Guillaume, *Psychologie*, p. 190.

between her distinctions and those we have made concerning different types of objects.) She is, of course, correct in arguing that "the true problem of art is an ontological problem. . . . The artist wishes to make something *exist* and not to make it beautiful," [72] and that aesthetic form is the "absolute form which is capable of conferring an existence on the work of art that has not been derived [from anything else]." [73] It seems to us, however, that form cannot be defined without taking account of meaning as well as of feeling (insofar as feeling reveals expression, which is itself a type of meaning). Otherwise, form can be only abstract and furnish form to a matter which has been given independent of form. Hence everything would be lowered to the level of matter. Hersch mentions this explicitly in the case of a Dutch still life. "Countrysides, lemons, feelings, all of these, on the level of art, constitute the given, the matter which has no existence by itself." Further, "the representational antecedents of the work do not exist any more than the affective antecedents do." [74] It is legitimate to claim that nothing in the work exists outside the creative gesture of the artist. But through the form of the work—a form which has been received from the creative gesture—the given changes its meaning. The distinction between matter and form is no longer operative, or, more precisely, the entire matter, from which meaning cannot be excluded, is taken up into the form. Form is the soul of the work, just as the soul is the form of the body. The ancient Aristotelian notion of soul rejoins the notion of Gestalt. For it is from the standpoint of perception and the science of perception that there exists a soul as the principle of an organized and animated body, a body which appears as a signifying totality. We see the body *through* the soul. In the same way, we see the body of the work through its meaning and particularly through its expression, which is the highest level of meaning. Form is what gives the object meaning. We were able to speak earlier of an external form as unifying the sensuous because this form offered an implicit outline of the work's meaning. To be a column is an implicit meaning of stone, but to be slender and majestic involves a surplus of sense. It is thanks to this surplus that we truly see the column. Hersch returns to the phenomenological

72. Hersch, *L'Etre et la forme*, p. 189. According to our definition of the beautiful, however, to which Mlle Hersch should not object, to will the existence of the aesthetic object and to will its beauty are one and the same thing.

73. *Ibid.*, p. 164.

74. *Ibid.*, p. 69.

aspect of form when she describes its characteristics in terms which we shall remember in what lies ahead: coherence, totality, limitation, autonomous formality, and the interiority or intentionality of the work with regard to itself.[75] But these characteristics gain their complete meaning only through the meaning which is immanent in the work and constitutive of its form.

Moreover, it is through the very unity of form that the aesthetic object is, as we have asserted above, nature. But we must point out that, on the one hand, this nature is a signifying nature that surpasses brute nature. By bearing signification as it does, the sensuous loses none of its simultaneously alien and triumphant character. It is, rather, confirmed in its sensuous being and thus as nature. On the other hand, the aesthetic object also communicates a character of nature to the signification which it bears. However spontaneously we are able to unravel the meaning of this signification (perhaps we can do so because the signification imposes itself directly on us with its own type of evidence and without having to submit to the demands of understanding), there is something mysterious and irreducible to discourse in the signification. Modern art—both plastic and poetic—has systematically heightened and exploited this incomprehensible depth of meaning. Yet even art which appears easy to comprehend harbors something mysterious, simply because it addresses itself to perception and thus to feeling, rather than to understanding.

Thus we can say that the aesthetic object possesses certain characteristics of the natural object, such as indifference, opacity, and self-sufficiency. Nevertheless, though the natural object does not call to us so insistently as the object of use, it still refers us to a world in which it is rooted and on whose basis it appears. The in-itself of the natural object is stamped with impotence. It is not even completely what it is, since it is delivered over to a world. Furthermore, the only relation perception can have with it is one of understanding, that is, grasping it in its context. We perceive coastal rocks as beaten by the waves, and the sea as constantly beginning again. Thus perception veers toward intellection and is motivated by a desire to discover objectivity in terms of a stable relation between continually changing terms. The externality of the natural object means externality to itself on the part of the physical thing which is purely a thing, not only as thought by a Cartesian

75. *Ibid.*, pp. 164 ff.

understanding but also as grasped by perception. This non-expressive thing, which is not possessed and animated by an internal signification, belongs to being only to lose itself in being. Moreover, the being to which it attests is the indeterminate being which is not the unity of determinations but their abyss, a desertlike being whose image is found in a nature that has not been transformed by the mark of human determinations. This type of externality does not fit the aesthetic object, which is always unified by its form, a form which is a promise of interiority. The aesthetic object bears its meaning within itself and is a world unto itself. We can understand this kind of object only by remaining close to it and constantly coming back to it. Because it illuminates itself in this way, it is like a for-itself. Or rather, it is like a for-itself of the in-itself, that is, a taking up of the in-itself into the for-itself. The aesthetic object is luminous through its very opacity—not by receiving an alien light by which a world is outlined, but by making its own light spring from itself in the act of expression. Thus we shall call the aesthetic object a "quasi subject." We can better understand the ambiguous status of this quasi subject by considering at this point its relationship with the world.

5 / Aesthetic Object and World

WE HAVE SPOKEN of a world of the aesthetic object. But is the aesthetic object not *in* the world? We have said that it is found amid those objects with which we have compared it: the cathedral in the heart of the city, the poem in the library, and the painting in a gallery. Yet if the aesthetic object is not entirely *like* other objects, is it possible to say that it is *with* them? What, exactly, is its place? How is it able to be in the world if it is at the same time the source of a world? Even before we attempt to describe this position, we suspect that it is ambiguous.

Indeed, what is this world where we seek the place of the aesthetic object and which guarantees to us the reality of each thing inscribed in it? The world is the whole of perceived objects, not such that it could be known through a science capable of surveying it, but such that it is given as the horizon of all perceived objects and as the horizon of all horizons. It is the background against which all forms are outlined and which ensures both the truth and the frailty of perception, since everything in it is both real and inexhaustible. Yet if the world is the standard of reality, this is not merely because it is a spectacle surrounded by a horizon, but also because it is the very theater of our actions or projects. All things within our grasp relate to it, whether they attract or repel, tolerate or evade, this grasp. To calculate the distance of galaxies is already to evoke a possible journey. Of course, the glance that Kant casts upon the starry sky is not the same as that of Icarus.[1] Aesthetic contemplation is not the same

1. See Immanuel Kant, *Critique of Practical Reason,* trans. L. W. Beck (New York: Liberal Arts Press, 1956), p. 166.—Trans.

thing as the perception by which the body throws itself into some adventure. But neither is aesthetic contemplation imagination or dreaming, and its object does demand to be perceived. Thus the aesthetic object always appears upon the foundation of the world. Perception is able to outline this object more sharply only by the exclusive attention that it brings to it, as does the theatergoer. But the fascination is not such that the entire context can be totally abolished, for that would be to dream and not to perceive.

Nevertheless, the aesthetic object appears in the world as something not *of* the world. It has the being of a signification. The sign is in the world and signifies to me from it. But must that which is signified—the meaning which the words of a poem, the gestures of a dancer, the perfect harmonies of a Greek temple, or the hieratic figures of an Egyptian bas-relief have for me—be located in an intelligible heaven, a world of ideas transcending the world of things? The nature of the aesthetic object is such that the signification is immanent in the sign, engaging through *it* in the world of things. If this signification were strictly intelligible and if the sign were an instrument necessary for it but nevertheless indifferent to it, we could separate sign from signification and banish the signification to another world open to understanding but not to perception, that is, a world of ideal objects. If, on the contrary, the signification were a natural signification grounded upon some empirical connection which perception could decipher (as an articular pain signifies a passage of time), both the signified and the signifier would pertain to the natural world—which is open to perception—and it would not be necessary to separate them. But in the present case the sign does not announce the signification; it *is* the signification. It is not endowed with an intrinsic or logical clarity of the sort which rationalism accords to simple essences or to eternal truths and which would make of the sign a purely conventional means, invented afterward to signify this clarity. Lacking such clarity, the signification in question possesses only the perceptual evidence given in the very act of perceiving the sign.

By the same token, the sign which bears this signification demands a special status. It is in the world but appears to disown the world, unable to accommodate itself entirely to a contingent and ephemeral existence. It is in the world in somewhat the same way that other people are there for us, as when someone's expression touches or convinces us. This expression acquaints us not only with the being of another subjectivity but also with the possibility of a world which radiates that subjectivity. Thus the smile of a mother indicates to her child that there is an agreeable world—agreeable precisely because someone smiled there. The other person is the source of a world, but that world is still the world where the other has his place. For the paradox of the world is that it is illuminated for everyone with a certain glow, which may be the light of a smile or the darkness of blasphemy. Or, rather, the world *is* the light which each one projects in terms of his own being there. Yet the world is also a place in common, the light of all lights, the horizon of all horizons. Each person is held within it, and yet it is held in turn by each and is never, except at the limit, the world of no one, an in-itself which would not be for me. Insofar as I reflect, the world is mine and is extinguished with me. Insofar as I live, I am surpassed by the world, caught in it like a rat in a trap. Perhaps a truly transcendental reflection would recover this primary assurance by uncovering me as situated. Thus my connection with the world and the world itself are ambiguous. I have my world in the world, and yet my world is nothing but the world. And it is in the same way that we will be able to speak of a world of the aesthetic object. There is nothing but *the* world, and yet the aesthetic object is pregnant with *a* world of its own. Thus one realizes that the aesthetic object is not in the natural world as are other objects. We must show this before describing what its world is like.

[I] THE AESTHETIC OBJECT IN THE WORLD

(a) The aesthetic object in space

At first glance the aesthetic object appears as a privileged object, standing out against a background [*un fond*] of ordinary objects to which it is bound but from which it detaches itself. A painting decorates the wall, and it is well known how seriously modern painters have taken this function. A statue decorates a temple or a park, music is heard in a concert hall constructed for that purpose, and even solitary reading is carried on in a specific framework which is marginally perceived. A genuine reader does not read his favorite poets on the train any more than he would hang a painting in his kitchen or place a marble statue in an unflattering position. But how does the aesthetic object detach itself?

When, in the perception of ordinary objects, a figure stands out against a background, it means that a particular object assumes its autonomy. The inkwell on my table can be moved. Or a diagram on a piece of paper can be considered separately and, if required, reproduced on another piece of paper. In short, the world is composed of distinct objects and is, on the plane of perception itself, "of a fibrous structure." But it is, all the same, a world given to me full of objects and, as it were, in advance of them, for the objects my gaze or my hand distinguishes are set apart from an inexhaustible whole from which they cannot be completely extricated. The background is that through which the world manifests itself as the background of all backgrounds. The cosmological idea is lived as the experience, immediate in all perception, of the horizon immanent in every real object, through which the object gives itself as real and accessible by situating itself in the world. The background is the guarantee of the form because the world is the guarantee of the object. And the object which is silhouetted against the world, far from disowning the world, invokes and confirms it. It is by means of the world that the object is real, not only because its profile stands out against it but because it is supported and nourished by that unfathomable reservoir of beings. All its density comes from this reservoir, from the background of night and silence. Parodying Nietzsche, we can say that it is a being constituted by distance.[2] In this light, determinism would be merely the explanation and intellectual proof of this primeval experience, showing how the object is linked with others through determinations which, step by step, go to infinity. Thus the distinction between figure and ground in perception sanctions both the

---

2. We cannot always interpret this background in a spatial sense. Belonging to the world can have a mystical significance. The most ancient religions call on us to perceive the world (as if it were an incomplete spatial totality and, perhaps, in order to compensate for what that totality lacks) as an elementary power—the Earth-Mother, the Ground—a fundamental force of which myth is the explanation. In such a case, the thing or event integrates itself into the world by participating in it. Each tree, each spring participates in the telluric power which it manifests. It is by means of this participation that they are real, that they are more than episodes or contigent and hollow objects, and that they have being. The world is always the guarantee of reality. Moreover, this ontic virtue of the world (one could easily say ontogenetic) by no means excludes its spatial form. The power of the world extends to all things and all things are one.

independence of the object which gives our technique something to grasp and the necessary relation of that object to a world which constitutes it as an object. But the difficulty of combining the object's independence with its relation to the world increases if the object has even more independence and appears to take the initiative for this relation. This is the case with a living being which separates itself from the environment and unites with it through its own motor activity in changing its place, whereas an inert object is something which I am able to move.

The same is true of the aesthetic object. It refuses, even more vigorously than the thing, to allow itself to be integrated, through perception and action, into the everyday world. In the first place, the aesthetic object often requires its own background, composed of objects explicitly intended to be its heralds and guardians and to inspire respect for the work. Thus a painting requires a frame which separates it from the wall, and sometimes a museum which separates it from the ordinary world. Similarly, drama demands a theater which completely encloses the production both to focus on it and to protect it, just as the church cuts the believer off from the world in order to put him in the presence of God.[3] The environment here appears to be more of a boundary than an intermediary; aesthetic perception is called on to isolate the object rather than bind it to others.

Indeed, the aesthetic object demands that we recognize its autonomy. Our perception must establish a context appropriate to it, a zone of space or time, of empty space or silence, which encircles our attention like a nimbus. This context is seen in the silence which precedes a recital or in the way we prepare to read, sheltered from all distraction: "I wish to read Homer's *Iliad* in three days; therefore, Corydon, close the door tightly." As one constructs a museum for paintings or a theater for plays, our behavior creates the psychical [*spirituel*] environment of a fervent attention. And yet this environment is not to be understood as the mere fact of our having taken precautions to prepare ourselves. It is so strongly required by the aesthetic object that it appears to be a property of that object. The silence which ensues in the concert hall when the conductor's baton is raised or three taps are heard is not merely a silence which the audience creates by keeping quiet. It is a silence which the work

3. We do not speak here of the scenery, which we shall discuss elsewhere, because it is already an integral part of the aesthetic object and does not have to be made aesthetic.

carries as its forward messenger and is part of the work in the same way that a frame is part of a painting. It is perceived as an object or, rather, as the commencement of the aesthetic object, just as the silence of the forest or the night is also perceived. And the same is true of the solitude, stillness, and comfort we seek in order to read—all of which combine with the work, much as the scepter, cortege, and solemnity accompany the pomp of royal majesty. Such a psychical environment is not so much the background against which the object stands out as it is the radiance of the object itself, the aura of its presence. Moreover, even *our* presence is united with the work. Though spectators, we are also the actors of the aesthetic object. To the extent that the work is ceremonial in character—and it is well known what importance Alain gives to this aspect of the arts— not only is the attention of the audience required to furnish the work with its psychical background, but the very presence of the audience is necessary to provide it with its physical background. A half-empty auditorium is as unbearable as an inattentive audience. Thus we see the ambiguity of the relationship between the figure and the background as well as the tentacular nature of the aesthetic object. The aesthetic object aestheticizes its sur- roundings and integrates them into its own world. It makes them into provinces of its kingdom, servants under its authority.

All this represents another, more certain way for the aes- thetic object to detach itself and claim its autonomy. The ob- ject's outer limit—its "frame"—is never completely isolated. The wall is always present around the picture's frame, and the city surrounds the theater. Furthermore, certain arts are not able to possess material frames. In any case, it is difficult for perception to isolate the aesthetic object from the perceptual field. This is especially true for the temporal arts, which have a peculiar duration that, as we shall see, confers on them a more obvious independence and a more palpable interiority. One can listen to music or to a poem with his eyes closed. Similarly, the arts with the most eloquent signification, such as the literary arts, carry us more easily into their own world and force us to cast off the everyday. But the spatial arts are the least amenable to such a separation. The spatial object has its place in everyday space, through both its materiality and its thinglike structure. How, then, does the aesthetic object assert itself? It does so by annexing its unwary neighbors and exercising its aesthetic privilege upon them. Consider an architectural monu- ment, such as the palace of Versailles. I circle it, enter it, examine it. I conduct a sort of sacred dance around it, through the avenues which it opens to me. I take up many positions from which to view it, some by choice and others by chance, so that I can say I truly see it from the esplanade, the gaming table, or from any other point where I may station myself. Music or drama transports me on a magic carpet and puts me down in another place which is no longer in the world, but an architectural monument fastens me to the world while manifesting itself as an object of the world. Nevertheless, it stands out sharply against a background. What sort of background? It is a park from which I contemplate the monument or which I see through its windows, a city which exists in its image, or the unexcelled skies of the Ile-de-France. But the park is not merely a setting [*décor*] associated with the monument. While a setting announces the entry of the work into the world where it has its justification for existence (and in that way thrusts aside the natural world), the park clings to the natural world by all the roots of its trees. Arising from the forest which borders it and which renders homage to it, a true park has its reality in the world of seasons and vegetal powers which it simultaneously governs and obeys. The park binds the palace to nature. The park puts the palace in the world, as the public square with its linden trees and its stone fountain does for the village church and the Beauce Plain does for the spire of Chartres. But then a transformation takes place. In binding itself to the world instead of separating itself from it, the architectural work annexes the world and aestheticizes it. Through the magic of the palace at Versailles, the park, the sky, and the city take on a new quality; I am no longer able to perceive them as ordinary objects.[4] Even history, of which the monument perhaps speaks to me, is promoted to aesthetic dignity. Its truth is no longer to be found in the narration of events whose mechanisms are infinitely complicated. Its truth is in the image—in the images of the court, of a refined world with extremely punctilious cere-

4. As Focillon has observed quite rightly, "Greece, for instance, exists as a geographical basis for certain ideas about man, but the landscape of Doric art, or rather, Doric art as a landscape, created a Greece without which the real Greece is merely a great, luminous desert. Again, the landscape of Gothic art, or rather, Gothic art as a landscape, created a France and a French humanity that no one could foresee: outlines of the horizon, silhouettes of cities—a poetry, in short, that arose from Gothic art, and not from geology or from Capetian institutions" (Henri Focillon, *The Life of Forms in Art*, trans. C. B. Hogan and George Kubler [New York: Wittenborn Schultz, 1948], p. 14).

monies, and of postures noble like those of statues—which gives a clear countenance to the past and represses the scruples of the historian.

The work becomes the subject of the objects where it reigns. It magnetizes the environment the way the other's look does in Sartre's description. Everything converges on the work and is transformed by it. In the same way a wall is glorified by a painting which is hung on it, as the Isba is sanctified by the icon. Undoubtedly the wall is joined to other walls, to the house, to the city. The wall has the world for a background and links the aesthetic object to the world. But as aestheticized by the presence of the work, it ceases to belong to the world. I no longer perceive it as the wall of a room, forming a partition, a resistant mass through which I am able to drive nails or open a door. It becomes an independently existing wall, incorruptible and intangible. It comes to be cut off from the world. But why not the other walls and the neighboring house? Where does the magic influence of the aesthetic object end? Quite simply, it ends at the point where the look ends, because the aesthetic object, with its dependencies, is at one with the look. To be aesthetic is to count aesthetically for the look. But are the boundaries of the aesthetic precisely those of the look? When I isolate and magnify a ballet dancer with my opera glass for an instant, I realize that I arbitrarily isolate an element of the performance, just as I may ignore what I see in order to concentrate on the music. In the same way, I know well that the monument, the park, and the sky are not held wholly within my present perceptual field. Like an ordinary object, the aesthetic object overflows my look, although it gives itself as totally present. But it is nevertheless the look, or at least a possible look, which assigns to the aesthetic object the limits of its influence, since it is for the look that the object is aesthetic. Moreover, if it is futile to try to locate the exact boundaries of the object, this is because they are not objectifiable. The aesthetic object separates itself from the world less in erecting boundaries within the world than in denying the world as a whole, in denying as worldly even that which it integrates into the world. When I am at the theater, the everyday world that I will rediscover on coming out is thrust into nonexistence. Everything which is not accessory to the aesthetic object, not in the service of the experience that it offers to me, is bracketed. Everything that recalls me to reality appears to be troublesome and disloyal.

Such is the relationship of the aesthetic object with its surroundings. The real world cannot be totally abolished for me, for then I would dream the aesthetic object instead of perceiving it. I relate to the aesthetic object only on the condition of being in the world, of feeling engaged in an inexhaustible given, and of being assured that nowhere will the ground disappear from under my feet but will always be experienced in its rigidity. The silent consciousness of an indeterminate horizon guarantees the presence of the aesthetic object, which is not present to me unless it places itself in space where all things stand before me in their radical externality. The necessary separations by which it attracts my attention are as much a way of embodying as of detaching—witness the frame around the painting which is not seen as an intermediary between it and the wall, the white around the page which is not perceived, and the silence which is not heard. But these separations themselves and the whole environment to which they allude are transformed by the work into its own substance. The aesthetic object exercises a sovereign imperialism. It makes the real unreal by aestheticizing it.

But it is always on the condition of becoming incarnate that the aesthetic object appears in the world and at the same time actualizes its being. This is proof that it is important that the aesthetic object be in the world, precisely because nothing is perceptible, and possesses a meaning immanent in the perceptible, unless it is in the world. And yet it exists there only by keeping its distance. Something in it denies the world. Now, having considered the aesthetic object's position in space, we may see this point more clearly by considering its life in time. We shall see the same effort of the aesthetic object to free itself from its condition as a thing, as well as that in it which articulates this effort.

(b) The aesthetic object in time

How does the aesthetic object act in time? As in space, will it not be by simultaneously dominating it and withdrawing from it, by entering it unwillingly? But first, what sort of time is in question? Since the work is the product of a style, it is first and foremost historical time. Every aesthetic object is "a historical monument." How does the aesthetic object situate itself in history? It does so less through its matter, which belongs to the time of things, than through its form and its meaning, through that which man perceives and reads in it, and through what it says of man and what man says of it. Thus its relationship to human time has all the ambiguity of historicity.

In the first place, the work affords a hold for history. It solicits the intervention of the historian who assigns it a date and fastens it securely, as if he may wish thereby to explain the work, making it both the product and the illustration of its times. This is particularly true when the work is anonymous, since then it can be explained only through its relation to its epoch, to the extent that it can be dated. Such explanation is of the same order as our explaining the work by its author. It is precisely such explanation which is in question. One renounces entering directly into relation with the aesthetic object and fails to consider the specificity of the work. Thus the explanation bears only on external and insignificant features of the work, on certain technical details which are strictly the choice of the subject. But the being of the work itself, that through which it is perhaps a masterpiece, is overlooked by the historical determinism to which one tries to subject it. Pointing out that Ingres and Delacroix, Debussy and Franck, Valéry and Apollinaire are contemporaries suffices to show the limits of such historical exegesis. Nevertheless, the work continues to belong to history throughout its lifetime. For, as Ingarden says, there is a life of art works. The aesthetic object, since it is dated by the human gesture which has created it, is brought into historical time by human apprehensions, and it meets with a varied fortune according to the intention of these apprehensions and their aptitude for grasping it fully. In compliance with civilizations, the aesthetic object dies or is reborn, disappears or revives. It also depends on new aesthetic objects which appear in history to orient aesthetic perception. Interest in African art revives because of Picasso, and Picasso is fecundated by African art. The public, through the tradition which it transmits and the transformations which it brings about, enriches or impoverishes the signification of the object. And finally, the aesthetic object depends on performers, since each new production is not only an epiphany but a discovery and sometimes a fountain of youth for the work. It is in this way that certain works grow old and others are rejuvenated at the mercy of history. Have these works themselves changed? It suffices that their public or their servants have changed. The aesthetic object appears only with their cooperation. Undoubtedly there is a nontemporal truth of the object, but it is the fate of that singular essence to be phenomenalized, to surrender, as Heidegger says, to its guardians, who are not always able to be faithful to it or, rather, who are faithful to it only by transporting it into their own world, delivering it over to the vicissitudes of history. But it is appropriate to point out that, within the history which carries it along, the aesthetic object leads a relatively autonomous life. Its future is not entirely explained by its historical context, any more than its creation is entirely explained by the circumstances which surround it (not even by the psychology of its author). Through the eddies of universal history, art appears to be the source of a history of its own. At any rate, its relations with universal history are not fixed by a strict determinism.[5] However, in history, as in the world, the aesthetic object is unable to claim a total independence. It has its own life only in and through history, because the men who have made or who perceive it are also in history.

The aesthetic object is historical just to the extent that it allows itself, not without resistance, to be dragged along and explained by history, while in turn expressing history in some way. The critical attitude which tends to explain the work through history is evoked by the aesthetic object itself. The aesthetic object bears its age and speaks to us of history, of the epoch in which it was born. What does it tell us about this epoch? Not much, but perhaps the essential. "The museum without walls," says Malraux, "is the melody of history, not its illustration."[6] Undoubtedly we would have a quite different idea of extinct civilizations if we did not know their art. The idea which their art gives to us can anticipate and orient the investigations of the historian. We knew Sumerian art when it was called Chaldean, that is, before Sumerian civilization was circumscribed: "an urgent poetry emanated from the obscure zones which receded in the face of history, before it had reached them."[7] But poetry is not knowledge, and that which history teaches does not so much undermine the testimony of art as

5. In addition to the possibility of a history proper of the work and thus of art as a category of culture, there is, more profoundly, a time proper to the aesthetic object. This is an idea which we can here only predelineate. In addition to being *in* time, the aesthetic object can be the source of a time of its own. The world which it reveals can have a temporal dimension. But then it is a question of a duration which is interior to the aesthetic object and unrelated to history, since it reveals itself only in the aesthetic experience where history is in some way suspended. We shall try to describe this sense of duration in what follows.

6. André Malraux, *The Voices of Silence,* trans. Stuart Gilbert (Garden City, N.Y.: Doubleday, 1953), p. 610.

7. *Ibid.,* p. 109.

limit it to what it confidently is—the testimony of a man who is capable of being at war with his epoch and not necessarily the herald of it. What different ideas the future historian who wishes to judge our times by our art will have depending on whether he turns to the Prix de Rome or to the galleries of abstract art, to Valéry or to the surrealists! We know that even the artist whom the aesthetic object delivers to us is not the real artist but the one who belongs to the object. And the same is true of his epoch, except that the epoch is even less present in the work than is the author, because it is only presented through him and as that which, one supposes, has made him possible. We return to the age of Louis XIV through what Lully and Mansart reveal in their music and their architecture. It is an anonymous Gothic man who answers to the Gothic style by invoking the whole Gothic age, in much the same way that Mansart reveals a different epoch through Versailles. Similarly, the man of Benin [Nigeria] is responsible for the civilization of Benin. Perhaps it is the truth of an epoch—just as it is the truth of the creator—which the work delivers to us in this way, assuming that the truth of an epoch lies in what it has produced or has permitted in the first place. But the historian has good reasons not to think of an era in this way. A civilization is not able to exist simply through its artistic masterpieces. The truth of the age of Louis XIV lies as much in the misery of the workmen who perished in draining the marshes of Versailles as in the splendor of the palace, just as the truth of the Middle Ages lies as much in its plagues as in its cathedrals. However, it is advisable that we listen to the voice of the cathedrals; if it is *the* truth of the medieval master builder, it is *a* truth of the Middle Ages, that which there is in it of music, as Malraux says.

The work speaks to us about its times in the same way that it speaks about its creator, for the times are only the creator generalized. A period is marked by a style to the extent that a collective style appears through an individual style, that is, where the style has its period. But it is not insignificant that a certain form of historical man, even a partial and sublimated form, is given in the art object. For in this way an aesthetic humanism is possible, indeed inevitable, assuming that the object is historical and bears witness to the mark of man. It gives evidence of its creator and, through him, of the civilization which has inspired him. This is true above all—and here we are brought back to history—of periods of religious faith, when the artist, however personal or even rebellious he may be, does not question his culture and consequently is a living (though often unaware) expression of it. Maurice Blanchot appears to reproach Malraux discreetly for having abandoned the theme of the museum without walls, a theme which should have led him to consider art truly for itself, as a closed universe, directed to itself, impervious to all foreign value, and animated by a duration punctuated only by its own discoveries and transformations. Yet Malraux breaks down the doors of this universe, reintroducing into it the values of culture and the figures of history and thereby making of it "no longer the temple of images, but the shrine of civilizations, of religions, of historical splendors." [8] This critique appears unjust to us. It is true, however, that "Malraux is concerned not only with painting, but also with man; yet he has not been able to escape from the great temptation of trying to save the latter through the former." [9] But why speak of this temptation as if it were a matter of a sin or an error? Is the concern for rendering justice to modern art and to the modern conception of art incompatible with a humanism when this concern, while manifesting itself in and through that art, has nevertheless permitted the revival and the comparison of all the significant varieties of world art? Blanchot is able to suggest such an incompatibility only in the name of a metaphysics of art which is impressive but equivocal. Art can be considered an absolute bereft of all value and of all human and historical meaning only on the condition of being "nowhere" and only if "the work is its own absence." But from the obvious fact that art manifests itself outside the world, in the absence of the world, can one infer that "its task is to realize absence, not only the absence *of* the world, but absence *as* the world"? [10] And what is this absence? "Absence alone is eternity." Blanchot seems to expect that, in order to pass over into eternity, the work commits suicide by reducing itself to a spot of color where the painting destroys itself. But must the work renounce itself in order to contribute to the well-being of art? And why does anyone think that "art joins forces with nothingness and absence"? We rediscover this negative ontology of art every time we inquire into the being of the aesthetic object. [11] What

8. Maurice Blanchot, "Le Musée, l'art et le temps," pt. 2, *Critique*, VI (January, 1951), 31.
9. Blanchot, *ibid.*, pt. 1 (December, 1950), p. 205.
10. Blanchot, *ibid.*, pt. 2, p. 37.
11. But it may be necessary to pose the problem in terms of art rather than of the work. One may say that art, when it becomes self-conscious,

Blanchot calls absence is that which is inexhaustible in the work and that to which its transformations attest. It is also the infinitely exacting in art as witnessed by its history. If this is the case, absence would be the reverse of a presence, and nothingness would be the expression of the plenitude of being. How else can nothingness be evoked with respect to the work? How can one deny Malraux's view that the work is in the first place a creation? The other world which it bears in itself is not nothingness. It is the negation of the everyday world, a negation which it is necessary to credit very positively to man himself and to the origins of the human. And if this negation implies nothingness, we must understand nothingess in a Sartrian sense which will not affect the aesthetic object.

Thus it cannot be denied that the object is real and historical. The object cannot isolate itself completely from history by creating a history which would be that of its own transformations alone and which would emanate solely from its own being, a being that is described by Blanchot as "restlessness and motion." That is why the object attests to the history into which it is inserted—not only to the epoch when it was created but perhaps also to the periods which it spans and in which it experiences its own life.

But there is more to be said. There is no human history without a becoming of things. Although the work is caught up in human time, it also belongs to the time of things in terms of that part of itself which is a thing in the world. For even if there is time only for a subjectivity capable of temporalizing, and strictly for an object capable of opening a history, nevertheless subjectivity exists in time along with objects which have no history. The world is always the kernel of time—of a "natural time [which] is always there" [12] and which acts to support me before I constitute it. (It is in the same way that the aesthetic object is always latent in the work before I perceive it, and that the world is the world in itself before being my world or for me.) Hence the work endures along with things in a time which is not yet temporality because it is not experienced by a subjectivity. This time enacts the drama of its presence to the

when "today for the first time it is revealed in its essence and its totality." succeeds through its very drive toward the highest purity in denying its own existence, becoming impossible, and giving rise to works which display a sort of will to nothingness. However, such works are nonetheless real and are caught up in the fabric of history.

12. Maurice Merleau-Ponty, *Phenomenology of Perception*, trans. C. Smith (New York: Humanities Press, 1962), p. 347.

world and of its impetus toward the future, but it is also a repetition and reapprehension which leaves its mark upon things. The aesthetic object changes and sometimes perishes within such time.

How is this possible? It would now appear that the work has the frailty of things, and yet it is not exactly subject to the same destiny. At least in its aesthetic dimension, the work neither changes nor perishes as things do. How, then, is the aesthetic object vulnerable to the ravages of time? Cathedrals were destroyed by lightning many times in the Middle Ages, the Alexandrian library was burned by Omar, Miller's novels were burned in Philadelphia, and the frescoes of the Papal Palace at Avignon were defiled by Napoleon's cavalry. Are all the ways in which the work of art succumbs to the force of historical events equivalent? Here we must point to a crucial distinction. A book condemned and burned can be republished secretly and circulated underground. It survives destruction if a single copy is saved. It is different with a painting, of which there is but a single example. This confirms the distinction that we made in the Introduction between the aesthetic object and the body of signs into which, in the case of works which must be performed, this object withdraws and is thereby perpetuated. This distinction allows us to understand how the literary object is nearly invulnerable. As long as one copy of the novel remains, the destruction of all the other copies does not touch it. But what if the last copy is mutilated or destroyed? The work may still survive in someone's memory and reappear as soon as it is uttered or enacted. This is proof that it exists through its bearer only by proxy, that is, as the possibility of being generated anew and of reappearing. It is because the aesthetic object is thus distinguishable from its bearer that it is not liable to deterioration. It does not grow old.[13] It is not changed by decay. Only if its bearer forsakes it does it disappear, and if its bearer is mutilated by some accident, it becomes something else. Fragments of a work on a mutilated papyrus are no longer the same work, any more than excerpts would be. Even if methodically chosen, fragments or excerpts enable me to acquire knowledge of the work but not to read the work itself. Strictly speaking, these parts of a work constitute a new aesthetic object. An isolated verse or melodic movement can be

13. Or, if it does grow old, it is in a completely different sense, namely, as a cultural object caught up in history.

beautiful by itself, as a color can be beautiful by its boldness or intensity, or a line by the simplicity or vigor upon which the effects of decorative art depend. Therefore beauty is, as Hegel says, the abstract unity of the sensuous matter, of which purity is the principal criterion.[14] But the abstract beauty of an element qua element cannot constitute an aesthetic object, since, as we shall see, the aesthetic object implies a totality. Undoubtedly we can call the element itself beautiful only by sensing a totality in it, e.g., in a sound, the commonality of its harmonies; in a color, the wholeness of the spectrum (*pace* Goethe); or in a line, the pure diversity of the space it traverses. In the same way, a verse or a melodic phrase is a sort of totality, without possessing the authority of an integral work.[15] This is why excerpts never provide more than an access to the work. Excerpts are better than a synopsis, in that they already possess an aesthetic character. But they are less satisfactory than ruins, which preserve the mark of the total form imposed by creative art. Thus the work perishes if all its bearers together disappear or undergo serious mutilations. It dies totally, not slowly as ruins do. But the care that culture takes in preserving the signs which contain it (so as to multiply the performances or the reproductions) answers to the aesthetic object's demand that it endure both the powers of oblivion and the destructive forces of nature, without suffering the common destiny of things.

Plastic works are vulnerable through their body. Bound by that body to things and to the flow of the world, the plastic object grows old and wears down with time. There are ruins of a statue just as there are architectural ruins, since the statue is still in marble or stone. The properties of the material are not

---

14. G. W. F. Hegel, *Esthétique* (Paris: Aubier, 1944), I, 77.

15. This raises a particular problem, that of the dimensions of the aesthetic object. What, for example, is the shortest possible poem? A quatrain is only an epigram or, as with those of Mallarmé, a politeness. It is not a poem. Prévert entitled a poem "Paris Bemused"; the text: "A certain Blaise Pascal, etc."; it is a joke, not a poem. Schönberg composed some short pieces of a few measures. Are they musical compositions? A novelette is a work of art for the same reason as a novel is, although it is not more easily appreciable and is, as the publishers well know, more rarely appreciated. But what about a novelette which is reduced to a few lines? It is necessary to allow the aesthetic form the opportunity of displaying itself, of expanding in space and time, providing perception the leisure for penetrating the work and for letting itself be penetrated by it. Finally, it is necessary that the work exist in proportion to man, to his gaze and attention. In contrast with the colossal, the minuscule does not have the capacity to reach the sublime.

unrelated to its beauty, as when the stone is sculpted in terms of its natural veining or even split according to its cleavage. The same is true of painting, at least as long as it is linked to architecture: for example, *The Last Supper,* the frescoes reproduced in the Palais de Chaillot, and even the paintings of Rembrandt which have been restored.[16] Perhaps we shall also speak some day of the ruins of a film. But if the aesthetic object is its body, it is also other than and more than its body. The architectural work is made of stone, but not simply of stone. A painting is not just a canvas covered with a ground on which chemical products are deposited. Once placed on canvas, the color loses its industrial name and its chemical nature—at least for us as spectators, if not for the expert who cleans the painting. It is now color seen and not color manufactured. It is seen as the color of an object, such as the red of the carpet or the blue of the sky.

As difficult as it is to distinguish the aesthetic object from its body—and it is certainly more difficult than distinguishing it from its bearer—the example of ruins allows us to make such a distinction in the case of the plastic arts by showing us that, precisely when the work is changed in its body, it asserts itself as more than body. Ruins, in fact, say a great deal, and one knows how certain epochs have been sensitive to their language. Of course, they inform us above all that the aesthetic object is also a natural thing subject to the vicissitudes of cosmic flux. However, in that very erosion of the aesthetic object, we discover that it is not an object like other objects. For the ruin does not sink back purely and simply into nature. It is still an aesthetic object which awakens in us new feelings aroused by the parade of time. The deterioration attests to the past, and the object then gives rise to the spontaneous respect which gerontocracies feel for old men, which classicists have for the ancients, and which collectors feel for old things. The object that has crossed the ages in order to come to us is stirring. It partakes of that profundity of time from which it arises. The ruin's prestige comes both from the allure of the distant, to which man is always responsive because the distant is like an image of what is primordial, and from the ruin's ability to illustrate time in

16. For Hegel, sculpture and painting are linked to architecture as if they were conclusions drawn from a premise. Even for Ruskin, the architectural object is essentially a setting and a background for painting and sculpture. (See Ruskin, *Seven Lamps of Architecture* [New York: Willy, 1890], p. 11.)

submitting to and surmounting it. Stars and rocks are not truly temporal. They are only what they are, a blind and opaque present, and if they serve to measure time, it is because they have a kind of immobility. They are ageless things, fixed points, landmarks from which the understanding is able to reconstruct objective time bit by bit. Like people, ruins have an age. Their past is bound up in their present. They do not stem from the immediate but come from elsewhere. They are historical, recounting their history themselves. It is sufficient that they have, as in *Le Cid,* "let time pass," a time whose scars they carry in their flesh. But in order that a ruin should still be aesthetic, it is clearly necessary that the initial object be so. A tenement house in ruins is not beautiful. Lacking style, it does not possess any genuine age—it has no assignable date of origin, just as it fails to carry the mark of a creator. The object which bears a date of origin must also show that it has faced time bravely. The most beautiful edifice destroyed by some cataclysm does not leave aesthetic ruins. Here the object is destroyed, not molded, by time. It dies without having ever grown old, and its ruins are incomprehensible.[17]

Time does not do such violence to the aesthetic object. On the contrary, the external necessity which time exhibits makes the necessity immanent in the object appear—its lines of force, its points of intersection, its proportions. The aesthetic object is preserved in the ruins because it erodes according to its own standards, and it does so without becoming deformed. That is why restoration, when it is visible, always arouses indignation. It is necessary to take careful precautions in order to struggle against time. Besides, what good does restoration do if the aesthetic object continues to appear in the ruins—as does the temple in the column, or the castle in the turret—and if time, far from acting by chance, reveals the essence of the object in uncovering its inner structure? The half-obliterated friezes of the Greek temples still show rhythm of movement in a thrilling way. The mutilated busts of Apollo still express nobility. Thus it is sometimes desirable for sculptors actually to imitate the action of time in making a bust, a torso, or a hand. In making something new, they aim at the same effect that the temporal avatars realize. Restoring the represented object to the state of the natural thing, they give it a new visage, more inscrutable

17. The aesthetic object does not die as does a living thing, but it grows old as a living thing does, while integrating into its own nature the influence of the world to which it is delivered.

and more expressive. A hand which, in Rodin's studio, springs from a crude stone is more astonishing than one which is affixed to an arm. Like a vine or a spider, the sculpted hand paradoxically takes on an animated character, as if it truly existed in the service of a live body. Likewise, where better than in Greek basaltic busts, unified in themselves and not distracted by limbs, do we learn that the chest shelters the Platonic *thūmos,* the seat of courage and indignation?

It is not inappropriate to infer the truth of actual ruins from that of such artificial ones. The action of time, in addition to emphasizing the lines of strength of the represented object through a true stylization—in creating or stressing a style, in returning it to the world—gives rise to a visage which is all the more meaningful for its being unusual. We know, too, that it is characteristic of aesthetic experience to baffle our habits in order to force a new kind of perception on us. Undoubtedly, there comes a moment when the object completes its demise. Everything finds its end, as the saying goes, and the fallen aesthetic object becomes no more than an ordinary object. And yet one can say that it becomes such an object only because it was one originally, because that which was natural in it was blended with the art so subtly that their duality appears only at the moment when the art is obliterated. The reason that the ruin is capable of being an aesthetic object for such a long time is that the aesthetic object, though natural, is other than and more than natural. How is this so? Through its form. It is through its form that an object's aesthetic character is assured, but only as long as this form endures.

We have not yet concluded our examination of the form of the aesthetic object, a form which is the singular and sensuous essence of the object and bestows on the object something of the eternity proper to essence.[18] This is exactly what ruins allow to appear—a truth of the object which needs a material body in order to be manifested, but which cannot be identified with that body. In the case of works that are performed, it is the same form which each successive new body strives to manifest and which every interpretation endeavors to represent. The form does not create the body but, on the contrary, complies with it.

18. This is a metaphorical eternity, since the essence as real is timeless and not eternal. Moreover, it is in history, as an effect of culture, that it is revealed and is constituted in being revealed. It is thus through reflection that the essence appears, but reflection itself is situated in the historical world. This is why the eidetic must appeal to the empirical.

Thus one can say that the form is the factor of truth and immutability in the aesthetic object—in spite of the interpretations to which it is subjected and even though it needs those interpretations. It is that which appears invincibly the same through different interpretations, that which makes the object the same underneath the changing bodies which it assumes. In other words, the form is the truth of the aesthetic object. The form has the virtue of timelessness which belongs to truth conceived as the being of the true and not as events produced in history. Of course, it is necessary for truth to manifest itself. But the truth of the aesthetic object can appear only in the sensuous, in the immediate being-there of nature. This truth, wholly linked to the aesthetic object's appearance, bound to its expression, is thereby temporal. There is no refuge for it in an intelligible heaven. Through its form, the aesthetic object is nontemporal; but because its form is the form of a body, it is consecrated to the world and to time.

We shall better understand how the aesthetic object can exist in the world in such an ambiguous way if we consider the world proper to this object. Within its own world, the aesthetic object will again show its difference from the ordinary object. The ordinary object appears against the background of the world. It is from the world that the ordinary object takes its being, and it is through the world and in the world that I am able to grasp it. It has only a relative independence; perception ascertains it by always seizing it in its context; understanding seeks its meaning outside of it by emptying time and space from it. The aesthetic object, in contrast, demands attention, continually recalling this attention to itself because it offers itself as constituting its own world and not as being *of* the world. What Heidegger says of the world—*die Welt weltet* [the world worlds]—is above all true of the world of the aesthetic object. Even if this object is not able to secede completely—when it remains a thing of the world and is perceived as a thing of the world—it still transcends its thinghood by opposing its world to the world.

[II] THE WORLD OF THE AESTHETIC OBJECT

WE NOW PROCEED to confirm and develop what has already been suggested by the confrontation between the aesthetic object and the ordinary signifying object. The aesthetic object signifies neither in the manner of a history or physics book nor as a signal would. The aesthetic object addresses itself neither to the will so as to inform it nor to the intellect so as to instruct it. It *shows* and sometimes shows only itself, without referring to anything real. In any case, the aesthetic object does not claim to imitate the real (even if some aesthetic theories prescribe such imitation). When the authentic artist draws his inspiration from the real, he does so in order to measure himself against it and to remake it. Even when he celebrates the Creation he competes with it or, like Claudel, at least does not hide the fact that he collaborates with and completes it. In signifying, the aesthetic object does not exist to serve the world. It is, rather, the source of a world which is its own. The justification for speaking of "world" here will be given below; at present we are content with describing it.

What is this world? Is it only a portion of the real world transposed into the work in such a way that the work represents it? Is the world of Balzac only the world of the Nucingens, the Vautrins, or the Chouans? Is the world of Rouault that of clowns, judges, and Crucifixions? And then what would be the world of Mozart or Chopin? When we name the world of the aesthetic object by its creator, we emphasize the presence of a certain style, a unique way of treating a subject, of making the sensuous serve representation. The Romanesque and the Gothic master builders have the same object; they both wish to erect God's house. But do Saint-Séverin and Sainte-Chapelle produce the same impression? How many painters have treated the Crucifixion? From Rembrandt to Rubens, it is the same Christ, but it is not the same Christianity. On the other hand, when Giraudoux shows us Bardini or Electra, when Bach writes cantatas or a concerto, when Goya paints a festival or a nightmare, it is to the same world that they give us access.[19]

19. Is this still true when one compares Van Gogh's *The Potato Eaters* or his first landscapes, inspired by Corot, with the Arlesian canvases? Does it hold when one considers Rimbaud's first poems (which imitate Banville) alongside *Illuminations*? Certain creators are like Proteus. There are two remarks which must be made in this connection. First, when it is a question of the phenomenal creator, the one of whom the work speaks to us, and not of the actual creator, it is not, strictly speaking, the world of the creator to which one refers but the world of the aesthetic object. It is not the world of Racine but the world of the author of *Phèdre*. And if we do speak of a world of Racine, it is after the fact, when we have discovered an essential kinship between the world of the author of *Phèdre* and that of *Athalie*. Besides, it is noteworthy that modern culture strives to establish

Sometimes it is even by means of that world that we identify the work, as surely as we do by the style, since the world is that which the style expresses.

These considerations suffice to inform us that the creator's world cannot be described according to norms valid for the objective world or even for the represented world. The world of the creator is expressed and not represented. It is not without relation to the represented world, but it is not identical with it, since two different subjects can participate equally in the same world, as when Phaedra and Athalie, who live before us on the stage in two different worlds—in two different plays—nevertheless communicate in the same world of Racine. It is not easy to see what this world is, yet we are immediately sensitive to its presence as soon as the aesthetic object introduces it to us. It is not a world of identifiable objects. One can neither explore it nor survey it, because one does not have to take distance into consideration with respect to it. In truth, it is less a world than the atmosphere of a world, in the sense that we say an atmosphere is tense or lively. Thus it is a matter of a certain quality of objects or of beings, but a quality which does not belong to them in their own right, since it is not they that bring it about. The quality in question is like a supervening or impersonal principle in accordance with which we say that there is an electric atmosphere or, as Trénet sang, that there is joy in the air. This principle is embodied in individuals or in things. It is somewhat like the collective consciousness which governs individual consciousness in times of agitation. Whether or not it is a principle of explanation, it is at any rate a reality that we feel keenly when we come into contact with the group from which it emanates. We have much the same experience in a dark forest. It seems to us that individual shadows are not the result of shade, but, on the contrary, that the shadows create the leafy summits and the entanglement of underbrush along with the entire vegetable mass in its damp mystery. The forest prevents us from seeing the tree, and the forest itself is seen only through its atmosphere. But here the

---

that relationship, in offering the complete works of an author or in collecting the chief works of a musician on recordings or of a painter in a museum. Then the style of the creator appears. The effect of the aggregate thus produced is incomparable. Each work is understood alongside the others, without losing its uniqueness. All of them fade away as if each were a voice in a single choir, a province of the same world. This is why we are able to speak of a world of the creator, but always on condition that we do not forget that the creator is revealed only through his works, and that his world is the one expressed in his works.

atmosphere refers to the real world of men or things. To what does it refer in the aesthetic object? It is not a quality of the real world but of the object itself. The world of the aesthetic object is a world interior to the object. It is as such that we must describe it, leaving until later the examination of its coefficient of reality and its truth with respect to the real world. At the very moment when it proposes the real, the aesthetic object seems to exclude it or to convert it into its own substance. We become engaged in its world only by being diverted from *the* world, even if we do not leave it altogether and if the environment is always *mitgemeint* [cointended]. On the one hand, it is necessary that perception not degenerate into a dream, and there is perception only if we are in the world. On the other hand, the aesthetic object itself must be real in order to thrust itself upon us and to draw us into the world which it opens to us and which is its highest signification.

(a) *The represented world*

In order to understand the world of the aesthetic object, we must grasp it in its opposition but also in its quite limited relationship to the world as strictly represented. Are we not tempted to identify this latter world immediately with the subject of the work? Let us, therefore, first consider the represented world.[20] At first glance it thrusts itself upon our attention and appears to be the very substance of the work. But does it truly create a world by itself? Does the represented object raise itself to that height? The nature of the world, in fact, is to be open and to refer continually from object to object, extending all limits. The world is the inexhaustible reservoir of being which is attested to quantitatively by the infinite nature of space and time, but which is also symbolized by the myths of an inexhaustible creative power or of an eternal return of forms and kinds. Undoubtedly, the world can be adumbrated by the most humble object as soon as I realize that I cannot coincide with it entirely, that in its very presence it escapes me in some way, and that it is joined to something beyond itself which I am never able to reach or wholly master. In this respect, when the aesthetic object is considered as a thing, it attests to the world. If the world is to take shape in my sight, I must undertake to explore it or

20. We shall limit ourselves to the representational arts. Whether there are truly nonrepresentational arts can be determined only by studying the nature and function of the subject in the structure of the aesthetic object.

let my gaze lose itself at the horizon. I must have some contact with the unlimited. But does the object as aesthetically represented furnish a represented world? Yes and no. Even if the representation does not imitate, it tends to make the object leave its framework, to confer on this object the power of evoking the world in which the object is able to take its place. The real object, in contrast, possesses a plenitude by which it accords with the world as with that which surrounds and extends it.

I read a novel. Some characters evolve before me who have, by virtue of art, a certain density of being and constancy. These characters are present to me as is the hidden side of a cube, which ensures that the cube is more than a superficial spectacle and exists inviscerated in a perceptual field. The characters themselves live in a world which I experience as spatial and temporal density and as a peculiar style.[21] The art of the novelist may, however, take many different paths. It can, for instance, represent the world of things and events, the cosmic and human context, as an independent and primary reality—a sort of Great Being à la Comte, where individuals are sometimes caught in a trap, receiving their fate according to the place they occupy. The classical novel unfolds in this way, even if it depicts the context only in light strokes and reserves the bulk of the work for psychological design. But the novelist can, in contrast, according to a totally different perspective, subordinate the context to the individuals or to one special individual whose consciousness becomes a center of reference which is itself referred to no other. The contemporary novel most often operates in this way. Finally, one can, as it were, merge the two perspectives, obtaining a world which has a cosmic density through an entanglement of diverse aims, as if its substance were made of many adventures, decisions, fears, and hopes. Such appears to be the special unity of Dos Passos and Sartre. At any rate, there are no heroes except those engaged in a world. To conceive a hero of a novel is not only to recognize in him the opacity, the fullness, the secret property of a consciousness, it is also to grasp him in relation to a world which is both a correlative and a destiny, according to the ambiguity of the human condition. The world is suggested

21. How that is possible we are not able to discuss here. The imagination plays a role in it, perhaps not only in Sartre's sense but also in Kant's. The world as an idea of reason would have its root in the imagination as the unlimited power of disclosure. But the imagination opens up, whereas reason demands the possibility of closure, of achieving synthesis. Imagination poses an entirely valid standard, although one which is always on the horizon of knowing or acting.

in the work by scattered indications whose synthesis we continually effect. This synthesis is realized, not in the manner of a judgment which collects and compares, but because each indication offers more than it is, as when a detail set apart within a whole is corroborated by other details. Yet the whole is never reducible to the sum of the parts, as Balzac sometimes seems to believe. It is in this sense that the indications in a novel are truly expressive, always saying more than their literal meaning. They are the inverse of clear and distinct ideas in which the meaning is rigorously coextensive with the signs. It is possible that the novelist's art—indeed, that of all artists—consists of choosing, of cutting out as much as of adding, for he is not interested in the prodigality of appearances or the indefiniteness of horizons. He retains only that which interests him. What he retains must suffice to allow us to reach a world of which we easily accept the fact that certain aspects are clear and others obscure, but which has the shape of a world all the same. This mixture of the implicit and explicit exists, moreover, in the image of the perceived world.

The represented world also possesses, in its own fashion, the spatiotemporal structure of the perceived world. Space and time here fill a dual function. They serve both to open up a world and to ordain it objectively by creating a world common to the characters and the readers. Even if they are centered in a character who experiences them, they also have meaning for the reader. They possess enough objectivity for the represented world to be identifiable and objective in the manner of the real world of which it is the image, although the represented world can be presented as lived and dominated by a central subjectivity with which the novelist identifies (and does not merely consign to a place in an impersonal world). This world is still subject to the requirements of representation and must appear objective enough for the reader to become oriented there. In the novel, space and time transfer the objectivity of the real to the represented elements. In fact, they appear according to the norms of objectivity, even when there is a flying carpet or seven-league boots to make light of distance. These distances are measurable, and we know it. Paris is at the same distance for heroes of novels and for the real traveler. Undoubtedly that space can be qualified by the restlessness of the hero as well as by his means of locomotion, but, as in the case of the real traveler, it is from an objective given that we understand the restlessness or that we appreciate the airplane he takes. Similarly, the time of the represented world imitates the time of the real world, to the point of reproducing it in the novels which explore the interior monologue, where the time of the reading and the time of the story recounted coincide in a certain fashion.[22] Even the time of legends and myths has the aspect of real time, as when heroes are engaged in adventures. Even more often the time of the novel makes reference to the time of objective history. The story unfolds between dates which exist on a calendar, referring to events which are localized in both history and geography.

There is at the least a sort of osmosis proceeding from the real world to the represented world, even for novelists who have abandoned the naturalistic illusion. Nevertheless, it will be said that the techniques of expressing time vary considerably and that certain novelists make free with objective time. This is certainly so, but it is not because such novelists abandon the time of the real world and claim to invent another time for the world which they represent. Rather, it is because the notion of a real time is itself ambiguous and gives rise to treatments and explanations which are quite diverse. Between objective time and lived time, between time-space and time-duration, the choice is always open. At least time can be described and recounted according to these two perspectives. One perspective orders time according to the causality of things, and the other orders time according to the spontaneity of a consciousness. Thus the novelist is able to choose the most appropriate means to indicate time, depending on whether he writes a story of a consciousness or a story of the world. Wherever he puts the accent, he strives to restore to time, within the world that he represents, the allure which it possesses for him in the real world. And he cannot entirely sacrifice the expression of objective time. Even if the time of the story is nothing but an objectified time and consequently is unable to claim ontological priority, it is nonetheless the means by which we gain access to a subjective time and to a necessary aspect of duration as well. A novelist like Faulkner, who abuses chronology (symbolized by Quentin's watch-smashing in *The Sound and the Fury*) in order to reveal the inanity of a present which is always the replica of a past and has meaning only in reference to the past, cannot prevent the reader from putting time in order so that he can recognize himself in it and give an objective meaning to the lived categories of before and

22. Jean Pouillon points this out in *Temps et roman* (Paris: Gallimard, 1946), p. 186.

after. Moreover, the novelist himself must provide the means for this act of ordering, e.g., by utilizing grammatical moods. It is due to our ability to reconstitute an objective structure of lived time that what is represented in a novel appears to have the density of a world.

The same holds true for all the representational arts. Each one makes certain privileged objects comply with an over-all scheme and places behind these objects backdrop which gives them, in contrast, more consistency and at the same time the indeterminacy of a world. Undoubtedly this backdrop itself can be minutely represented, as in the novels of Balzac, in early Flemish canvases, and in palaces surrounded by gardens in the French style. Such art neglects only what is intentionally omitted. The same precision attests to an effort to associate the world with the represented object in order to force the world into the structure of the work. One may say that this is a naïve effort. Does not a uniform background, an Elizabethan setting, suffice? Why encumber the aesthetic object and make it compete with the real? The setting [*le décor*], particularly in the theater, serves a double function. One function can be emphasized more than the other, but neither should be wholly neglected. The setting surrounds and delimits the aesthetic object in its sensuous body, and it gives to the represented object the aureole of a world.

In drama, as in the novel, the characters who live before me are also bound up in a world. In Racine's play, Phaedra, the daughter of Minos and Pasiphaé, is caught up in that dark Dionysiac universe in which Theseus, the heroic founder of cities who is freed from the Labyrinth, triumphs, but which condemns her to the infernal gods. Not only do I know of this world: I see it. Phaedra moves in a setting, but the setting signifies much more than it represents. Behind the palace suggested by a porch, a city exists for me from which noises sometimes arise in the wings. Indeed, all of Greece is present, as well as the distant shores— though no more distant for me than for Phaedra—where the survivor Theseus disembarks. But it is not necessary—in fact, it is impossible—that this fabulous geography be offered to the eye. It suffices if it is suggested to the mind by the indications of the text. Thus the signification remains for the most part confined to spoken words. One may here establish a comparison between the setting in the theater and in the film. In the theater, the words are what order the setting and give it its profound truth. It is not at all necessary that the setting create the illusion of reality, since it need only please the eye. Thus it need not compete with the dramatic object, for it is not empowered to constitute in itself an autonomous pictorial or architectural aesthetic object. However lively and pleasant the colors are, they do not possess the dignity of colors in an authentic painting. One covers the set with distempered paint, using the same elementary technique as the house painter. Moreover, the scene designer has no right to use stone, only cardboard and stucco. The setting, in principle, signifies only through the text which it is entrusted to illustrate.[23] In other words, the world of the dramatic work is as much presented to the mind as it is to the senses. It suffices to make only a discreet allusion to the senses, filling them up effortlessly rather than exciting them. For the scenery must not divert the eye from the actor. The scenery acts as a costume for him rather than as a geographical landmark. One of its functions can be seen in the kind of scenery which Christian Bérard composed for *Don Juan* and which involved the division of technical space to regulate the movements of the actors and the unfolding of the action. The setting is to the actor what the stadium is to the athlete or the race track to the horseman. At the same time, the setting encloses the space of the stage, separating it from the wings more strictly than from the audience. The setting is to the play what the frame is to the painting, though it also continues to function as the background. This is particularly evident in the ballet, where the dancers create, through their posture and their grouping, plastic shapes which often serve as a background for a solo or a duet and which themselves need a framework in order to be consolidated and to produce their effect. The setting is the framework of the performance [*représentation*] before becoming the framework of the represented object. It delimits the choreographic space before opening the space of the world where the action unfolds in the ballet. A few curtains suffice for this delimitation, unless the setting is more intimately associated with the aesthetic object.

The setting in the case of film is different. In fact, certain shots can stand out like a tableau—indeed, are sometimes specifically inspired by a pictorial work, so that the setting is first of all the means of framing the composition. Care in composition is required more or less explicitly in all visual art—architecture is the chief example. But the vocation of the cinema that corresponds to its technical possibilities is one that uses all the resources of the image in order to extend the field of represen-

23. We shall see, however, that it is able to signify by itself and thus to be more directly associated with the aesthetic object.

tation to the dimensions of the world. Then the represented world, especially in exterior shots, gains the breadth which Van Eyck or Breughel present in their painting without their precise detail. In film, the setting assumes more responsibility than the spoken word for presenting the represented world, since the spoken word cannot have the same importance on the screen that it does on the stage. That which the text says, the screen is always able to show. This does not mean, however, that the value of the film's scenery is measured by its ability to create illusion. In fact, the cinema has taken over all the tricks of perspective that painting has abandoned. *Trompe-l'oeil* is king in the cinema. The height of film art is all too often to make the corner of a studio hold a city. It uses miniatures of houses rapidly diminishing in size to obtain a truncated perspective. If necessary, it places extras in the background, among the houses with reduced dimensions—small children ridiculously dressed up in mustaches. Are these artifices still art? In this respect, film, so often eager to imitate the theater, may have something to learn from the latter. Without going to the extent of installing a prompter's box in a corner of the image, film should remember that art must never be ashamed of its medium and of its limits. Film can enlarge our vision without having to deceive us.

In other words, even when it is used to connect a world with the represented action, the setting must be selective and not try to show too much. Moreover, it always acts as some sort of frame. The setting limits the world which it evokes to the dimensions of the aesthetic object, closing it off as much as opening it up. Thus, if the represented world is an image of the real world, it is an image which is inevitably and voluntarily mutilated. That which the work gives us of the real world is only what is necessary to situate the characters or to illuminate the action. Its purpose is not so much to represent a world as to single out some determinate and meaningful object from within it, making this object its property and taking us back to it untiringly. In practical perception the horizon is like a challenge which we must take up, or like a question to which knowledge will provide an answer through an investigation that gradually moves it back. But the world which is the backdrop of the aesthetic object, instead of soliciting our attention, directs it immediately to the foreground, to the essential. Crete, reeking with the blood of the Minotaur, interests us only as a means of understanding Phaedra. The city which spreads out toward an enormous horizon in Van Eyck's *Madonna with Chancellor Rollin* requires only a sidelong look from us. Like the landscape of high rocks behind the *Mona Lisa,* the city is there only to offer the Madonna the same homage that we are supposed to give her. Thus the represented world is not truly a world by itself in the sense that the real world is. It cannot compete with the real world insofar as: (*a*) the represented world claims (and we agree to apply to it) the norm of objectivity; (*b*) one seeks in the represented world the image or the interpretation of the real world; and (*c*) the real world itself is conceived as an objective world which is the measure of all objectivity. If the aesthetic object offers us a world, it is in another manner and according to a mode which should be common to all of the arts, representational or not.

(*b*) *The expressed world*

The represented world does not allow us to speak yet of a world of the work which is original and singular. Undoubtedly it is a world distinct from the real world, with all the distance which separates the real from the represented. But it still imitates the real world, even if it is fantastic, since it always forms identifiable objects with the help of elements borrowed from the real, as studies on creative imagination have clearly shown. That is why works which do not raise themselves to the level of expression exhaust their entire ambition in copying the real. In contrast, if the work shuns imitation and constitutes an original creation on the level of representation itself, it is through its desire to be expressive, and, as we shall see, it is the expressed world which animates the represented world.

Moreover, the represented world is not truly a world. It is not self-sufficient; it is indeterminate. This is not only because it is represented and not real but also because it is incomplete. The work by itself affords us only sparse information about itself. However much we may know about this world and however precise our descriptions of it, there is always a beyond, just as there is a third dimension absent from a painting which the imagination tries vainly to fill out by lengthening and enriching the appearance. Undoubtedly this indeterminacy is characteristic of the world. It is that which escapes apprehension and cannot be totalized. It is the possibility of a perpetual progress or a labor of Sisyphus. Space and time, which form its structure, are the source of its indeterminacy. But we must add something else to this negative cosmology. What is the source of our ability to speak of a world if we are doomed to this infinite disorder, continually forced to relate one object to another? We must somehow obtain the idea of a possible totality, a unity for the indefinite. Within the objective world which science seeks to master, we may think that the idea of such unity comes from the very principle of unification. That which assures the unity of the world—that which allows one to think of a world—is the fact that all things are equally subsumed under the conditions of objectivity. What determines the indeterminate is, at the least, the fact that it is indefinitely determinable. Is this fact the source of the idea of world? We shall see. In any event, it cannot be the source for the idea of a world proper to the aesthetic object. We do not perceive the aesthetic object under the sign of determinism, that is, by confining to the understanding the task of pursuing indefinitely the unification of the world. It is deficient works—the ones that offer only an incoherent representation—which hand over to the understanding the chore of ordering the elements which they offer. Genuine works, even when they baffle the understanding, bear in themselves the principle of their unity. Their unity is both the perceived unity of the appearance as rigorously composed and the felt unity of a world represented by the appearance or, rather, emanating from it in such a way that what is represented itself signifies totality and is converted into a world.

What is the source of the unity by which the expressed is able to assume the shape of a world? We already know, from the fact that the consciousness of the artist is expressed through it, since there can be expression only of a subjectivity (and that is why we are able to identify the world of the aesthetic object and the world of the creator; the creator as revealed by the work is the guarantee of what the work reveals). The unity of an atmosphere is thus the unity of a *Weltanschauung;* its coherence is the coherence of a characteristic or quality. This *Weltanschauung* is not a doctrine but rather the vital metaphysical element in all men, the way of being in the world which reveals itself in a personality. We are not surprised that it can turn itself into a world, the world of an aesthetic object, since each man already radiates a world. There is a nimbus of joy around the joyous man. We say of another that he exudes boredom. The effect is such that ordinary objects can change their appearance through the mere presence of someone. But while expression ordinarily remains indistinct, its world blurred, the aesthetic object expresses the world of the artist with greater power and precision and gives it bulk and unity.

Therefore, a higher principle of unity comes to the aesthetic object from the fact that it is capable of expression, that is, from the fact that it signifies not only by representing but, through that which it represents, by producing in the perceiver a certain impression. Thus the aesthetic object manifests a certain quality which words cannot translate but which communicates itself in arousing a feeling. This quality proper to the work—to the works of a single creator or to a single style—is a world atmosphere. How is it produced? Through the ensemble from which it emanates. All the elements of the represented world conspire to produce it, according to their mode of representation. Take the novel, for example. It evokes a world. In its way, the novel establishes a setting in which characters evolve (with the reservation that, except in certain classical novels that are not entirely set free from the theater, the setting is only for us; for the character, it is a context to which he is dialectically bound). But the setting, the characters, and the events which are recounted, with varying degrees of emphasis, are chosen by the novelist, set apart from the undetermined story or outline in order to produce a certain total effect. Moreover, the precise intention which presides over that choice matters little. Whether the novelist wished to demonstrate the motives of a character in showing the hero subject to various tests, wished to sketch a sort of fresco, or simply wished to tell a story, the work, if it is successful, manifests a unity which transcends the detail of the representations. In one instance, the unity will proceed less from the unity of a character than from the unity of a life, a unity resulting from the indefinable resemblance between the actions of one man and thus between the situations in which he is caught and the visages which the world offers to him. In another instance, the unity will arise from a certain allure, from a rhythm common to events, from a style of the world as creating a style of life and not the converse—as in the swarming of bewildered insects in the incoherent universe of Dos Passos, or in the indifferent cruelty of Zola's universe regulated by laws which no Providence promulgates or amends, or in the proliferation of a voluntaristic world in Balzac's works. In still another case, the unity will proceed from the very rhythm of the story, as in the ardent or peaceful breathing of a world which hardens into fatality in the short stories of de Maupassant. In every instance, the choice of the novelist is justified by an identical result, that of producing a certain total effect like that which painters obtain (so obviously that there is no need to stress it) by the rigor with which they harmonize the values and colors of a composition.

What we have said of the setting can now be reconsidered in the light of the idea of the work's unity. The scenery in a play contributes to creating a world, first by enlarging the perspectives of the presentation, by giving a horizon to the represented objects as well as a framework for the actors. But, while assuming this indispensable function, the scenery is also able to combine more directly with the work by participating in its expressive function. Consider a setting like that of Bérard for *Les Bonnes*. Because it is presented as stuffy, sumptuous, and suffocating, an apartment is able to become the principal personage in a play. So, too, is a forest filled with mystery, especially when contrasted with the liberating sea, as Valentine Hugo has demonstrated in the case of *Pelléas et Mélisande*.[24] In such instances, the affective quality of the world matters more than its geography. Things are no longer a mere locus of action, they truly have a meaning by themselves—a meaning which is not their utilitarian meaning. They are aestheticized. The scenery ceases to decorate because it has undertaken the responsibility of expressing the world rather than leaving it to the care of the text. (However, the scenery must remain scenery and avoid deception; itself aestheticized, it belongs to the world of the work and not to the natural world.) The same is true for the architectural setting. If it is the real world which is annexed by the monument, it is more easily converted into an expressed world than into a represented world. For the architectural monument introduces us into a world of its own. Undoubtedly, the elements of this world are less easily distinguished from one another than those of the world of the play. Just as the real mingles with the aesthetic, so that which is represented—for example, the architectural signification, the historical context evoked by the style—mingles with what is expressed: nobility, fervor, majesty, tranquillity. Not to know the

24. This is the way that Gordon Craig conceives of the scenery: "It is idle to talk about the distraction of scenery, because the question here is not how to create some distracting scenery, but rather how to create a place which harmonizes with the thoughts of the poet. . . . Take *Macbeth* . . . I see two things. I see a lofty and steep rock, and I see the moist cloud which envelops the head of this rock. That is to say, a place for fierce and warlike men to inhabit, a place for phantoms to nest in. Ultimately this moisture will destroy the rock; ultimately these spirits will destroy the men" (Edward Gordon Craig, *On the Art of the Theatre* [New York: Theatre Arts Books, 1956], p. 22).

interior life of the architectural monument is to refuse it aesthetic quality. Versailles speaks to us through the rigor of its layout, the elegant equilibrium of its proportions, the discreet pomp of its embellishment, the delicate color of the stone. Its pure and measured voice expresses order and clarity and sovereign urbanity in the very countenance of stone. In such a building, man gains stature and solidity by the majesty which resounds in him, rebuking all dissonant emotion like a perfect harmony. And the surroundings—the park, the sky, and even the town—which the palace annexes and aestheticizes speak the same language. The setting is like a bass accompaniment to the clear voice of the monument.

Expression thus establishes a singular world. It is not the unity of a perceivable space, of an addible sum; it is not a unity which can be grasped from the outside, surveyed, and defined. It proceeds from an internal cohesion which is amenable only to the logic of feeling. The unity manifests itself both in what it integrates and in what it excludes. To see what it excludes, let us consider the problems posed by the mingling of genres. When we say that a certain tragic art, like that of Racine, excludes the comic, we mean that the world expressed by the tragedy is a closed world. It is open through the indefinite multiplicity of objects that is able to qualify, but closed—closed inwardly, so to speak, and according to the internal requirements of cohesion—because of what it rejects. And who is the judge of it? How is it possible, except through feeling, to condemn the false notes or to approve the harmony? That is why the problem of the unity of style is unable to receive an objectively and universally valid solution. But, when the work is done, one does know whether there is a unified feeling such as one experiences upon arriving in a coherent world, in a world which is truly a world. And it is notable that, if the internal unity is missing, there is no longer any expressiveness. There are only represented objects, which may be interesting or tedious but which are so diverse that they no longer form a world. This is the case in certain of Hugo's melodramas, or in those novels which "end well" in order to please the reader. The danger is great, especially for composite works.[25] Moreover, the unity of the expressed world must include as much elasticity as rigor, perhaps because it is not ratified by an explicit logic. That the expression is total does not imply repetition or monotony. The cruel can alternate with the tender, as

25. See Benedetto Croce, *The Essence of Aesthetic*, trans. Douglas Ainslie (London: Heinemann, 1921), pp. 36–37.

the tragic sometimes does with the comic, without destroying the unity of expression. Tenderness and buffoonery in Mozart's *Abduction from the Seraglio* form a precious mixture that constitutes a world of smiling liberty where the action delivers love from agony and restores it to innocence. Similarly, the sublime and the vulgar combine to form a world which one can only call Homeric. Just as different modes of behavior of the same man, provided that the behavior is not superficial and mechanical, possess an indefinable resemblance which attests to the reality of the person, so too in the same novel different scenes with different characters can exhibit, beyond their diversity, a subtle resemblance, like objects subject to the same illumination or movements transfigured by the same emotion. Such resemblance is the seal of the creator. It is also perceptible among the movements of a suite or a sonata. It is a long way from a minuet to a jig, from an adagio to a presto, and yet, in the presence of great works, we feel the unity of an atmosphere for which it would be vain to seek the reason in a thematic structure (as we would for cyclical works). The atmosphere changes and yet remains the same, sustaining a kind of organic development which does not change its essence. If the Ninth Symphony possesses such prestige, it is perhaps because of the admirable movement from a muted atmosphere in the beginning of a joyous sense of triumphant and fraternal freedom at the end—while passing through a frantic and then measured scherzo and a meditative adagio, without which the force of the movement would be broken and the spiritual unity destroyed.

Because expression is as much a principle of integration as of exclusion, we must say further that the expressed world clearly has the volume of a world. Like the Einsteinian universe, it is both finite and unlimited. It has an atmosphere that diffuses itself, not because it is ungraspable, but because it has the positive power of extending itself beyond the particular objects of which it is the quality and of drawing other objects to it in order to disclose itself through them. This atmosphere is like the spilled wine of which the poet speaks, which requires an entire sea in order to manifest its inexhaustible power of coloration.[26] The soft, delicate tranquillity which is expressed by the interiors of Vermeer is not contained between the walls which the paint-

26. Dufrenne is thinking of the poem, "Le Vin perdu," by Paul Valéry. —Trans.

ing encloses. It radiates upon an infinity of absent objects and constitutes the visage of a world of which it is the potentiality.[27] Thus the world of the aesthetic object certainly has the essential world-property of being open. But it is in intension rather than in extension, or, as we shall say, in depth. The world of the aesthetic object is not indefinite in the way that space and time are —in a mechanical way which becomes evident whenever one wishes to give it an objective representation. Rather, it is indefinite in the sense of a potentiality which no actualization can exhaust. It is an indefinite possibility of objects which are linked and reconciled by a common quality, as a sound is pregnant with innumerable harmonic overtones. In this respect, the aesthetic object has the dimensions of a world, dimensions which defy measurement not because there is always more to measure but because there is nothing yet to measure. This world is not crowded with objects; it precedes them. It is like a faint light in which they are revealed and in which everything that is perceptible in this light is disclosed—or, if one prefers, like an atmosphere in which all those things that can display themselves are revealed.

Thus the world of the aesthetic object is not yet structured in accordance with space and time but is rather the potentiality of space and time—as it is of objects as well. It cannot possess an objective space and time, since there is objectivity only in relation to objects which serve to order such space and time. Here we are not yet on the level of objects which the work can represent. Nor does the world of the aesthetic object possess a lived space and time. For space and time are lived only by appealing to objective space and time and through individual consciousnesses, and in the expressed world we fall short of represented personages. This is why we must try to catch space and time at their roots, where they are different from what they are in the represented world—a world for which they may lay the foundation. For representation as such flattens out space and above all stops time. Time as represented is time comprehended, and one can comprehend time only by invoking chronology. That is why the novelist often chooses the lazy solution of merely following chronology. At any rate, if the novel is incapable of

27. And that is why we are able to recognize it elsewhere, when we come back to the real, in the peacefulness of a landscape, in the serenity of a countenance, or wherever else. If it is possible that in a sense the aesthetic is the truth of the real, we shall see that it is because of this potentiality.

expressing time, tricks designed to make living time appear, such as those which appear in Pouillon's analysis, are in vain. We return in the end to chronology.[28] For objective time to become animated, we must feel it spread through the aesthetic object, the aesthetic object must itself become temporal, and we must take charge of this temporality. We shall explore later in more detail the idea that the aesthetic object is able to be the source of its own time and space. This idea is posed to us now under another aspect, namely, that in expressing a world the aesthetic object already expresses a preobjective space and time *as* this world. And it is certainly the same idea, since the aesthetic object is capable of expression only in terms of its being. If it expresses space and time, this is because it is capable of spatializing and temporalizing in some way and not simply because it represents space and time objectively defined. Nor is it the case that the aesthetic object locates itself through its matter in the space and time of the ordinary world. Rather, the aesthetic object is the covert source of a space and time of its own.

In fact, the aesthetic object clearly manifests such space and time in its expression. The architectural monument has a grandeur or a loftiness incommensurable with its surface or its height. The symphony or the novel has a rhythm, a force, or a restraint of which an objective measure like the metronome gives only an impoverished image. We should realize that, in seeking to grasp expression, we disclose an unpopulated world, one which is only the promise of a world. The space and time which we find there are not structures of an organized world but qualities of an expressed world which is a prelude to knowledge. We already have this experience in the real world, where the first determinations of space and time—the far and the near, the absent and the present, the repeatable and the irrevocable—appear to us in impatience, dreaming, nostalgia, astonishment, and repulsion. In this way space is animated and hollowed out, and we respond to it through movement or through a plan, the rough draft of a movement. And it is thus that the aesthetic object possesses a spatiality of its own. In the presence of the Winged Victory, we are at first aware of an animated atmosphere of wind and of upward movement, creating a space

28. This is perhaps what distinguishes a novel like Aldous Huxley's *Eyeless in Gaza* from a novel like Virginia Woolf's *The Waves.* In the latter, we feel a certain quality of time whereby we are taken into an atmosphere of the unchanging, to the extent that the story communicates the lightness of childhood, the heaviness of memories, and the sclerosis of aging. [See Pouillon, *Temps et roman.*—Trans.]

which is that of taking flight and which has the dimensions of an ethereal world. The space of the garret where the dancer Babilée struggles like an animal caught in a trap (in the ballet staged by Roland Petit, *Le Jeune Homme et la mort*) is a closed and asphyxiating space which only death is able to open up and join to the horizons of the city, to the everyday life illuminated by the Eiffel Tower. Similarly, in Mallarmé's work, the feeling of emptiness which is communicated to us by the mysterious and chilling aspect of the verse hollows out space as the locus of a perpetual absence, and this emptiness precedes the being through which it speaks.

But it is above all time, in its preobjective form, which the aesthetic object manifests in its expression. There is (and we shall return to this point) a duration peculiar to the musical object. This duration is always movement, a movement which includes the movement of a soul fascinated by sound and immersed in a certain atmosphere. Objective time is still only an external means for the object to manifest this internal temporality of a world without objects or referents, and yet a world which is recognizable and imperiously offered. The titles of the movements or the indications of the tempo exhibit both the quality of the duration for the listener and the cadence of the rhythm for the performer—in short, the means of using the objective time which is like the prime matter of the work. In the literary work, there is likewise a temporality of the atmosphere that emanates from the peculiar style of the narrative and is independent of historical time. The rhythm of *Macbeth* is precipitate, whereas the action is spread out over years—twenty years, according to the chronicles on which the play is based. The rhythm of Joyce's *Ulysses* is extremely slow, whereas the action unfolds in twenty-four hours. Thus the atmosphere, depending on whether it is tragic or liberated, light or heavy, cheerful or suffocating, suggests a duration which shrinks or slackens, drags or quickens. Undoubtedly, if the expressed belongs inevitably to the represented, one could say that the duration is a function of the way in which the represented characters live time. Because Macbeth is fascinated, then corrupted, by crime, his will hurls him toward his own destruction; the fall of a soul into the snare of fatality is thus a movement uniformly accelerated. It is Macbeth's time—that of the evil project which he forms and of which he is captive, caught in its trap like the consciousness of a dreamer—which guides the theatrical time. Similarly, it is Bloom's time which guides the rhythm of the novel, a way of living without the future in an inconsistent universe whose only truth lies in a past which is more legendary than historical and which one recounts instead of repeating. But, conversely, one can say that there is a temporality of the tragic or of the aesthenic, that is, a temporality of the atmosphere which governs represented space and time and prepares us to grasp the space and time lived by the characters and even a sense of objective space and time. In truth, if there is a time peculiar to the work, it is not easily distinguishable from the time represented in the work. And yet the distinction is necessary, since represented time is a time which is said or shown but is not lived. At the limit, represented time is a time without temporalization, an arrested time such as we find in a painting representing dawn or twilight, or in Leconte de Lisle's poem, "Midi, roi des étés." It is time as an object, a time which is no longer time. Expressed time, in contrast, is a genuine time, since it is truly lived and grasped by the spectator capable of associating himself with the aesthetic object. It is in the spectator that the atmosphere temporalizes itself, that the quality of the world awakens the promise of time. In fact, the spectator experiences this temporality only because he also participates in the historical time which the characters live. Conversely, the spectator participates in historical time only because he is taken up in the atmosphere and is sensitive to its own duration.

(c) The represented world and the expressed world

The fact that it is difficult to distinguish between these two types of time, the nascent temporality in the expressed world and the time of the represented object, alerts us to the close relationship established between the expressed and the represented. We have said both that the expressed is like the effect of the represented and that the expressed precedes and heralds the represented. Both propositions are true. The relation of the expressed and the represented can be compared with that of the *a priori* and the *a posteriori*. The expressed is, as it were, the possibility of the represented, and the represented is the reality of the expressed. Together with the style which gives them body, they compose the world of the aesthetic object. We shall confirm this when we examine the structure of the aesthetic object, since in it the signification is immanent in the sign. Meanwhile, we shall concentrate on the element of signification in order to specify the relationship between the represented and the expressed.

The verb "to express" requires a subject, and in the present case the subject is the work. It is the *work* which expresses. Yet the work is first of all that which it represents. For this reason, the unity of the expression also depends on the represented objects—which tells us as well that the reflection attached to those objects will be an indispensable moment of aesthetic experience. In arts that are wholly representational in character, represented objects have a primary place, and it appears that they bear the expression in themselves and in such a way that we can read it directly. There is a world of *Hamlet* on the condition that the drama recount a story in which the characters meet, and events link up, in a certain setting. All the features furnished by the creator are here the witnesses and guardians of the expressed world, for example, the cock and donkey of Chagall, the dishonest soubrettes of Molière, the elongated bodies of El Greco. In the case of the writer, it is a matter of his key words, the system of images peculiar to him, and the arsenal of his adjectives (though he is not always so poverty-stricken in this regard as claims the professor in Giraudoux's *Juliette au pays des hommes*). With his treasure of words, the writer strives not so much to describe or mimic a pre-existing world as to evoke a world re-created by him.[29] All that is represented or suggested in this fashion signifies beyond the explicit meaning, as a word does in terms of its intonation. But it signifies still more radically, because the affective coefficient with which the magic of style endows the representation not only tends to emphasize the meaning but also to free it. The represented object becomes a symbol, but a symbol that is not swallowed up in an external signification (as happens in allegory), since this object does not pretend to translate a concept whose comprehension would render it useless. The represented object is not a springboard which one abandons at the moment of leaping from the sensuous to the intelligible. The expressed world is not another world but the expansion of represented objects to the dimensions of a world. When Valéry sings of the palm, a world opens to us where everything is palmlike—softly curved and fecund, patient, and rich with the grace of

29. For "there are no adjectives in nature," as Claude Roy remarks in his *Descriptions critiques* (Paris: Gallimard, 1949), a book which he dedicates to Colette.

gesture and fulfillment.[30] But in the nonrepresentational arts, the work is expressive through the form of the sensuous, and the reading of expression cannot traverse the level of representation. This conclusion brings us to the second, and essential, form of the relationship between the expressed and the represented.

For the represented world has, conversely, need of the expressed world. More specifically, represented objects constitute a world only on the condition that the expression present a unity in multiplicity, somewhat like Claude Bernard's notion of a controlling idea which presides over the constitution of an organism. This primacy of the expressed is explicable in two propositions. First, it gives rise to represented objects. We have said that the atmosphere was produced by the objects, and we must now add that the objects are produced by the atmosphere. The paradox of this dialectical relationship tends to be blunted if one restricts oneself to the example of a nonrepresentational art like music, for then only one of the terms is entirely true. Musical expression does not result from represented objects. On the contrary, musical expression tends to arouse representations in the form of images which are often undesirable and which are a way for the atmosphere to crystallize into a world. This happens needlessly, because the work does not require it and the expressed world should suffice by itself. We even risk losing sight of the multitude of imaginary objects. But we must add that imagination is not responsible for this temptation— to which, however, it easily succumbs. Expression naturally solicits representation as a complement, yet expression is able to do without representation. This solicitation is authorized, on the contrary, in representational arts, where, paradoxically, the atmosphere seems to give rise to the represented world. Is this not what Malraux wishes to say in terms of the psychology of creation when he writes, in reference to Faulkner's *Sanctuary,* "I would be not at all surprised if . . . the work were for him, not a story of which the unfolding determines tragic situations, but, on the contrary, a story born of tragedy, of the opposition and the crushing of unknown persons, and if the imagination serves only to lead logically from the characters to this original situation"?[31] Aesthetic experience confirms this observation. It is often through a certain atmosphere into which we are initially

30. Dufrenne refers to Paul Valéry's poem, "Palme."—Trans.
31. See André Malraux, *La Psychologie de l'art* (Geneva: Skira, 1947).
—Trans.

thrown that we apprehend the represented object. In the theater, for example, the first scenes directly instill in us a certain emotion which orients our entire comprehension. It is not sufficient that a problem be posed or an intrigue outlined, for it is also necessary that there be communicated to us a certain world-quality within which the problem or intrigue takes on meaning.

In other words, the expressed has primacy in a second sense. It transfigures the represented and confers on it a meaning through which it becomes inexhaustible—an inexhaustibility differing from that which it enjoys within reality. One may believe that this transformation occurs through the object's becoming unreal by being transported into the work, as if one were transplanting it, like a living species. To be sure, this conversion from the real to the unreal is important. We have already ascertained its effects in speaking of the innocuous character of the represented object. We may add here that the techniques peculiar to each art, the material conditions of the representation, are able to alter the shape of the object and even its affective character. One knows, for example, how in film a quite insignificant object is able to move us—a tear becomes unbearable, simply because its presence on the screen is unexpected and insistent. But in the present case, it is a matter of a metamorphosis which does not derive from material conditions but from the fact that the represented object is integrated into a new world. Heidegger says that "Being is unable to manifest itself in any fashion if it is unable to find some way of entering into a world." [32] It is through the transcendence of Dasein that this *Urgeschichte* is realized. One can say that the same unexpected event happens to the represented object, imparting to the aesthetic object something like the transcendence of Dasein. To express is to transcend toward a meaning, and the luminescence of the meaning—the quality of the atmosphere—gives rise to a new countenance for the object. What strange fragrance the fleurs-de-lis of medieval Annunciations take on in illuminating an immediately present world of purity and faith! And when it is Rimbaud who evokes illuminated manuscripts in the secret and amazing world which is peculiar to them, with what color they adorn themselves! Even the cinema in this way can convert the objects which it represents, and not only by exiling them on

32. See Martin Heidegger, "What Is Metaphysics?," trans. R. F. C. Hull and Alan Crick, in *Existence and Being*, ed. W. Brock (Chicago: Regnery, 1950).—Trans.

the screen. One thinks of the furnishings of a room in Rune Hagberg's astonishing film, *Après le crépuscule vient la nuit*. And we must go even farther. Not only does expression confer on what is represented that "aura," in Focillon's term, by which it becomes expressive (it is understood that the relation is dialectical, and that at the same time it is because what is represented is expressive that there is an expression). Furthermore, expression consecrates that which is objective in what is represented, that in it which imitates the real. It is because we are sensitive to that which the palm in Valéry's poem expresses, to that surplus of meaning with which it is charged, that we go straight to its vegetable existence, perceive its fullness, glimpse its solemn and peaceful curve, and make it truly a palm for us. When Rimbaud writes, "O seasons, O castles!" in order to express the world of the helpless and miserable soul in a universe too full and too beautiful—to which the soul can become equal only in an act of denial—then seasons and castles are there in all their glory.[33] It is in like manner that the space and time of the novel or of theater can become veridical. They are objective at the level of the represented, but we have observed that the novelist can experiment with this objectivity without obscuring or annulling it (and thereby depriving space and time of their most pregnant meaning). For space and time form the matrix of the world insofar as the world is external to us and resists us. The novelist experiments in order to animate space and time, allowing us to seize again, on the level of expression, the movement through which they originally reveal the subject. The temporality or spatiality which the aesthetic object expresses, both by its structure and through the contrivances of representation, and with which the spectator is invited to associate himself, establish rather than destroy the objectivity of represented space and time and thus bring about the intelligibility of the narrative. Similarly, an adjective can found a substantive, creating an object by means of the expression which the adjective confers on the substantive—unless the substantive, poetically employed, contains its own adjective in the way that a sound vibrates with its harmonic overtones. The expressed thus confirms the represented in its objective being. The expressed founds the represented while at the same time being founded on it.

33. Arthur Rimbaud, "A Season in Hell," *Rimbaud: Complete Works, Selected Letters,* trans. Wallace Fowlie (Chicago: University of Chicago Press, 1966), p. 201.

In short, the expressed world is like the soul of the represented world, which is, as it were, its body. The relationship which unites them renders them inseparable, and it is together that they constitute the world of the aesthetic object—a world through which this object gains depth. And it is due to their conjugal status that we are able to define the world of a work or of a creator in terms of what it contains. We can say that the world of Balzac is defined by a given social group in which a certain character circulates, or that the world of Cézanne is Provence, an osseous and ardent land, a land of persons who have the motionless opacity of that land. But then we must not forget that there is still another factor—that these landscapes, natural or human, express a certain vision of the world, composing an atmosphere to which a nonrepresentational art like music gives us direct access. In short, the world of the work is a finite but unlimited totality, a totality which the work shows through both its form and its content, while soliciting reflection as well as feeling. This world is the work itself, considered not in its immediate and meaningless reality as a mute thing without a soul but as a thing which surpasses itself toward its meaning—that is, as a quasi subject.

(d) The objective world and the world of the aesthetic object

One question still remains in abeyance, whether it is legitimate to use the term "world" in order to designate that which the aesthetic object signifies, in particular the surplus of meaning by which the expressed overflows the represented. We have not inquired into the extent to which the world of the aesthetic object testifies to the objective world. We shall have to confront the problem later, when we inquire about the truth of the aesthetic object. But now we must justify the use we have already made of the notion of world. One objection is likely to be raised immediately—is this notion not applicable exclusively to the real? Is there not in the end a single world, the one in which representations and significations are given? Is not a world which is a function of signs a myth? For the understanding, the only world is the objective world. And reason, even if it is responsible for the *idea* of the world— the "cosmological idea"—only carries understanding to its limit. Furthermore, an existential conception of the world which subjectifies it in linking it to the work of art, and through the latter to a concrete subject, would be nonsense. Must we accept this objection? That the world of the work is not a real world, in the sense that the objects among which I live are real, is evident. But for all that, does it deserve the title of world?

First of all, we may observe with Jaspers that the notion of an objective and total world is unspecifiable. As soon as I analyze it, I discover that it returns me to my own world, the world where I am and that I am—a world which is for me at one and the same time a correlate and a destiny. The earth is both the planet that revolves around the sun according to astronomy and the earth which sustains me ("precious firmness, o feeling of the earth!") and which, as Husserl says, "does not, qua *Urarché*, move." Thus "if I speak of 'the world,' I immediately allude to two worlds which remain in spite of all distinctions." [34] It is notable that science itself meets with this ambiguity (and has on occasion pointed it out to philosophers) when it finds itself obliged to renounce the idea of an objective world which is unique and universal. Indeed, biologists, and even sociologists who follow suit, orient their investigations toward the world as environment, as that which constitutes living beings, but also as that which is constituted by them through an irreducible reciprocal causality. It is here that we encounter the notion of a world which we can call "subjective" in order to oppose it to an impersonal objective world which could be known only by a disembodied reason and which natural science strives to elaborate. But it is necessary to recall that, for the individual who lives it, his world is by no means subjective. It is real, pressing, and irreducible. For this reason, when reflection discovers such a world, it can no longer accord a monopoly to the objective world, the world that physics, or rather the metaphysics of nature in Kant's sense, knows. This "subjective" world is neither the true world with respect to which other worlds would be only illusory nor the total world of which the others would be mere parts. On the contrary, it derives its value from the fact that it is deeply rooted in the human experience of the world which is the common world of coexistence. The world of the subject is not a subjectified world but a world in which and on which the subject harmonizes with other subjects. Such a subject is not an inalienable subjectivity but an existence

34. Karl Jaspers, *Philosophy*, trans. E. B. Ashton (Chicago: University of Chicago Press, 1969), I, 58 f. Jaspers returns here to Heidegger's *Being and Time*, "which has said the essential on the question"; and we shall ourselves call upon Heidegger in a moment.

"given to itself." [35] Thus this world appeals to an objective treatment which makes it appear as common to all subjects and thereby rejects the claims of the solipsistic *cogito*—in short, it appeals to science. But not even science challenges the initial experience of the subjective world. On the one hand, to the degree that science gets rid of its prejudice of scientism, it takes the subjective world seriously. Ought not the biologist who studies the spider's world in relation to its behavior have a feeling for its world through a kind of sympathy with the spider? In any case, such sympathy is quite evident when the question is, for the psychiatrist, that of grasping the perceptual field of a patient, as in Gelb's analysis of Schneider, or, for the sociologist, that of grasping the cultural field of the primitive.[36] On the other hand, it is possible that the reflection which is associated with a properly objective world is experienced only on the condition of first feeling it. Of course, reflection is conscious of feeling only to reject it, and the objections of Valéry and Pascal to this strategy of reflection pertain. But perhaps it was first necessary to contemplate the sky and be frightened by the silence of infinite spaces in order to conceive subsequently the astronomical world.[37] Similarly, it may be necessary first to feel chemical bodies, even at the price of the deviations with which imagination exploits this feeling, in order later to constitute a positive chemistry.[38] And when the theory of relativity teaches us that, by virtue of the mechanical equivalence of rest and uniform rectilinear transformation as stated by the principle of identity, all observation is dependent on the observer, such a theory appears to give a scientific transposition of the idea that all apprehension of a world is linked to a feeling of the world.

The objective world thus has no other prerogative than that of being the limit toward which each subjective world tends when the latter ceases being lived in order to be thought. It is an unspecifiable limit, because thought is always the thought of someone and is brought forth from an initial experience.[39]

35. One finds this expression in the work of both Jaspers and Merleau-Ponty.

36. See E. Gelb and K. Goldstein, *Psychologische Analysen hirnpathologischer Fälle* (Leipzig: Barth, 1920).—Trans.

37. "The eternal silence of these infinite spaces frightens me" (Blaise Pascal, *Pensées* [New York: E. P. Dutton, 1958], no. 206).—Trans.

38. Bachelard has demonstrated this clearly in *La Formation de l'esprit scientifique*, 4th ed. (Paris: Vrin, 1938).

39. Conversely, the fact that the subjective world (at least in terms of human intersubjectivity) tends toward that limit prevents us from thinking that there is a numberable multiplicity of such worlds, and, for

It is in the subjective world, then, that we must seek the root of the notion of the world and the fundamental relation of the world to a subjectivity—a subjectivity which is not a pure transcendental subjectivity, but precisely a subjectivity that defines itself by its relation to a world through the style of its being in the world. And it is thus that the idea of a world peculiar to the aesthetic object is justified as the expression of a creative subjectivity.

In fact, if we now stop short of the distinction between the subjective and the objective, what does the idea of the world signify? Kant tells us that it is an idea of reason which presupposes the establishment by understanding of an order among phenomena. For reason "applies itself to understanding . . . being the faculty which secures the unity of the rules of understanding under principles." [40] So close is the relation with understanding that Kant, after having said that "the pure concepts of reason . . . which are *transcendental ideas* . . . are imposed by the very nature of reason itself," [41] adds that "pure and transcendental concepts can issue only from the understanding; reason does not really generate any concept; the most it can do is to *free* a concept of *understanding* from the unavoidable limitations of possible experience," [42] so that the transcendental ideas are "simply categories extended to the unconditioned." [43] Thus the idea of the world is strictly unconditioned: "What reason is really seeking . . . is solely the unconditioned." [44] The idea of the totality of phenomena is only an application and an illustration of the idea of a primordial unity. It is because "this *unconditioned* is always contained in the *absolute totality of the series* as represented in imagination" that "reason here adopts the method of starting from the idea of totality, though what it really has in view is the *unconditioned.*" [45] Thus the unconditioned is not the last member of a series, the final and inaccessible object of representation. Rather, it is the soul of the series, that by which the series is a

---

example, as many worlds as there are particular consciousness. For to suppose a countable plurality would be to suppose a totality, and, consequently, to come back to the idea that the subjective worlds are set apart from an objective world given or conceived previously.

40. Immanuel Kant, *Critique of Pure Reason,* trans. Norman Kemp Smith (New York: St. Martin's Press, 1929), B 359, p. 303.

41. *Ibid.,* A 327, B 384, pp. 318–19.

42. *Ibid.,* A 409, B 435, p. 386.

43. *Ibid.*

44. *Ibid.,* A 416, B 444, p. 391.

45. *Ibid.,* A 417, B 445, p. 391.

series. The principle "to which all experience is subordinate, but which is never itself an object of experience," [46] cannot be determined by a logical derivation analogous to that which allows the categories of understanding to be derived from judgments. Can we not say, then, that although the unconditioned is inaccessible to understanding, it nevertheless reveals itself to feeling—that the idea of the world is in the first place a feeling of the world (just as the moral law, a practical expression of reason, is grasped first through respect)? Furthermore, can we not say that the unconditioned proceeds from the very being of subjectivity? If the world is not the indefinite totality of phenomena but rather their unity (a unity which is like the quality that generates the series), and if the unconditioned is above all a mode of openness, is this not because subjectivity is itself an openness and, as Heidegger would say, transcendental?

As a matter of fact, on this precise point, which alone concerns us here, Heidegger carries on from Kant. He distinguishes, with Kant, two meanings of the term "world," one properly cosmological and attached to traditional metaphysics, and the other existential and found not only in the *Anthropology* but also in the *Critique of Pure Reason*. For the world, as the totality of phenomena, is an unconditioned that is still relative to a finite consciousness, and Kant distinguishes it from the transcendental ideal, which is the totality of all things as the object of the *intuitus originarius*.[47] He alludes at the same time to the finitude of consciousness and to the being of man, whose fundamental structure is finitude. Heidegger's interpretation consists in adding to this allusion the analysis of the *Anthropology*, where, as Kant says, "the concept of the world designates the concept that involves what necessarily interests each man." [48] In the last analysis, "the world designates Dasein in the ground of its being." [49] But we cannot call the world, even when

46. *Ibid.*, A 311, B 367, pp. 308–9.
47. Dufrenne here refers to Kant's distinction between a derivative (*intuitus derivativus*) and an original intuition, which, as Kant says, "seems to belong solely to the primordial being." See *Critique of Pure Reason*, B 72, p. 90.—Trans.
48. Cited by Martin Heidegger, *Kant and the Problem of Metaphysics*, trans. James S. Churchill (Bloomington: Indiana University Press, 1962).
49. By slipping from the cosmological to the existential, Heidegger rejoins the general interpretation which he gives of Kant in returning the transcendental to transcendence, and he illuminates the world by the notion of being-in-the-world. A world appears, a being "enters a world," because Dasein transcends toward it in a movement which constitutes it. It

it is defined as correlative to the transcendence of the subject, "subjective." Heidegger takes care to stress this: the subject is not subjective. Nor is that which corresponds to it, since it is defined precisely by the movement of transcendence: "The world does not become a being within the sphere of the subjective." [50] By producing the world "before itself," the subject discovers himself as belonging to a world. Thus the possibility arises of an objective treatment of the world as a world where I am (and not as a world that I am)—a treatment which will denounce the world as subjective from the outset and will consider the subject as merely one being among others, thereby neglecting the subject's power to transcend. The tension between the subjective world and the objective world has its source in the original experience of the world, which still falls short of the distinction between the objective and the subjective. In any case, the fact that the subject finds himself bound to the world, although suggesting an objective conception of the world as the locus or the totality of phenomena independent of subjectivity, does not disqualify the subjective world for the benefit of the objective world which rational thought strives to elaborate. It is thus that the aesthetic object can appear both as being in the world and as opening up a world.

But with what right do we invoke the aesthetic object here? Is it a subjectivity, a Dasein? Undoubtedly, the interpretation of the subjectivity of the subject which Heidegger proposes seeks above all to "make possible the problem of Being." Viewing the being of subjectivity as transcendence, Heidegger is led to propose that transcendence is itself an adventure of being.[51] But

---

is clearly toward the world and not toward such and such a being that it transcends, for it is from the totality that Dasein is able to enter into relation with such and such a being. (Provided that one understands the world not as an ontic series but as ontological totality. Heidegger warns us on that matter in *The Essence of Reasons* [trans. Terrence Malick (Evanston, Ill.: Northwestern University Press, 1969)]. The analysis of *Umwelt* in *Being and Time* gives an initial characterization of the phenomenon of the world which only facilitates the transcendental analysis.) Thus Dasein "finds itself in the midst of being and enters into relation with it"—whereas we shall say that Dasein has the feeling of a world, especially in view of the fact that Heidegger himself refers to the *Befindlichkeit* where that relation is expressed. In other words, "that human reality transcends amounts to saying: in the essence of its being, human reality is the *shaping of a world*" (*Essence of Reasons,* pp. 109 f.).

50. *Ibid.*
51. See Martin Heidegger, "Letter on Humanism," trans. E. Lohner, in *Philosophy in the Twentieth Century,* ed. W. Barrett and H. B. Aiken (New York: Random House, 1962), III, 270 ff.

it remains that phenomenology is also able to lead to an existential psychoanalysis, on the condition that one accept the transition from the transcendental to the empirical, from the ontological to the anthropological.[52] The fundamental project which constitutes the subject as transcendence and discloses the world can be made determinate in singular projects, each of which discloses a peculiar world. In this case, the world is the singular world of a subject who loses nothing of his quality as subject when his project is the concrete project of a singular being in the world. We can thus speak of the world of a subject. But what of a world of the aesthetic object? We may speak of this too—if the aesthetic object is a quasi subject, that is, if it is capable of expression. In order to express, the aesthetic object must transcend itself toward a signification which is not the explicit signification attached to representations but a more fundamental signification that projects a world. In aesthetic experience, the unconditioned is the atmosphere of a world which is revealed by the expression through which the transcendence of the subject manifests itself. Moreover, we are justified in treating the aesthetic object as a quasi subject, because it is the work of a creator. A subject always appears in the aesthetic object, and that is why one is able to speak indifferently of a world of the creator or of a world of the work. The aesthetic object contains the subjectivity of the subject who has created it and expresses himself in it, and whom in turn it manifests.

Furthermore, the immanence of the creator in the aesthetic object guarantees the reality of the world of this object. For we are now facing a final problem whose answer we can only begin to sketch: is this world real? The question is in fact ambiguous but nevertheless cannot be evaded. For the question poses itself with persistence, whether it be when one opposes the singular world to an objective and total world, or whether it be when one considers that what the aesthetic object says or suggests is unreal or make-believe (because that which is represented only imitates the real, with more or less success, but is not itself real). Thus two implicit affirmations come together to disqualify the truth of the aesthetic object, that of the primacy of the objective world and that of the vanity of art, all of whose resources and ambition should go into imitating the world. The first affirmation leads to the view that the world of the aesthetic

52. In our own view, this transition is, for ontology, a decisive and inevitable trial. It is necessary to return to the cave.

object is unreal, since it constitutes a personal interpretation of a world which is in itself impersonal. Reality is measured in terms of objectivity, so that night, for example, is real as an astronomical phenomenon but not real as gloom, as horror, or as that great peace of which Péguy speaks. To this view, we have replied that, even if the world does indeed authorize that quest for objectivity which entails that subjectivity deny itself— or at least make itself, as Jaspers says, exact—the notion of the world nonetheless has its root in the singular disclosure which is effected by subjectivity. The real then becomes what this subjectivity makes real, and the horror or the serenity of the night is as real as the astronomical fact of night. And the objective world cannot be invoked as embracing or explaining the subjective worlds—any more than optics explains vision when it substitutes a mechanical schema for vision, or than the world of the doctor comprehends the world of the sick, or than the world of the economist reconciles the worlds of management and proletariat. Nor can the world of the aesthetician reduce or replace the world of each creator. Moreover, the world of the aesthetic object is not unreal just because it is make-believe. Certainly, the represented object is unreal. Even for those who believe in hell, the demons of Bosch are unreal. The most exact portrait is unreal, since it does not proffer the subject himself. But the represented is not the essential element. The represented is only a means of saying something. And that which is said is real as soon as the objective world is no longer regarded as the absolute norm of the real. Even if demons are unreal, the world of Bosch is real—as the world of Mozart is real, even though nothing is represented in it. And if one is persistent, one can find a basis for the reality of these worlds in the objective world, since the aesthetic object is after all installed there. The creator has lived in the objective world. Yet it is the subjective worlds which finally *speak* and express a world that is as real as any other. The problem which remains is that of knowing to what extent this world is true and whether, in order to be true, it must be compared with the objective world. We shall approach this problem later.

It suffices for us to have shown that the aesthetic object is, like subjectivity itself, the source of a peculiar world that cannot be reduced to the objective world. We suspect that this world cannot reveal itself except to a subject who would be not only the witness of its epiphany but also capable of associating himself with the movement of the subjectivity which produced it—

in brief, a subject who, instead of making himself a consciousness in general so as to think the objective world, responds to the subjectivity of the work through his own subjectivity. We have pointed to the form which aesthetic perception takes in this case—feeling, the specific mode of apprehending the expressed world. The study of aesthetic perception will attempt to establish this thesis in greater detail. But meanwhile, we must return to the being of the aesthetic object, which is in the world and contains its own world.

6 / The Being of the Aesthetic Object

THE DESCRIPTION OF THE AESTHETIC OBJECT, which we shall complete and justify through a brief examination of the work of art, now calls for systematization. What is the being of the aesthetic object? The aesthetic object sends us to the public, but the public returns us to the work, since its perception (for the same reason as its performance) includes a demand for truth which runs the risk of never being fully satisfied. The aesthetic obejct likewise sends us to the creator, but the genuine creator is always a creator *for us* and is immanent in the work. Finally, the aesthetic object bears a world within it, but that world vanishes as soon as the feeling which provides access to it dissipates. The aesthetic object thus claims both unity (especially the unity of sign and signification) and autonomy, since it bears its meaning in itself, although the unity and autonomy which consecrate the excellence of its form count upon being recognized by and manifested in perception. Must we say that they really exist only in perception? That would be to surrender to a psychologism which aesthetic experience belies, for this experience meets with the reality of its object and refuses to reduce it to the being of a simple representation. But an aesthetics which is strictly and simply antipsychologistic does not resolve the difficulty; or, rather, it resolves the difficulty for the work, urging consideration of its genesis and structure, but not for the aesthetic object, for the work as perceived (for one is unable to treat the work without appealing to the experience which apprehends it and referring implicitly to the aesthetic object of which it is the promise). The problem which is posed and made precise by the aesthetic object is that of the status of the perceived object. But it happens that certain philosophical doctrines, through clinging to the aesthetic object itself, avoid the difficulty by refusing to attribute to the aesthetic object the intellectually equivocal being of the perceived object. Let us begin by recalling at least those doctrines which draw their inspiration, directly or indirectly, from phenomenology and make the aesthetic object into either an imaginary or an intellectual object.

[I] THE DOCTRINES

IT MAY BE TEMPTING, even if paradoxical, to define the aesthetic object as imaginary. Is this not a way of saying that its being cannot be reduced to that of an ordinary thing and that it requires from us a unique attitude which eventuates neither in reflection nor in action? Sartre's theory is familiar.

(a) Sartre

Sartre settles the debate between realism and psychologism by trying to find a third course. The aesthetic object has the being neither of a thing nor of a representation. It is imaginary. It "is constituted and apprehended by an imaginative consciousness which posits it as unreal." [1] This theory arises from a general theory of imagination which identifies imagination with freedom and sees it as the power both to negate and to posit the world. Imagination "is the whole of consciousness as it realizes its freedom," that is, as it surpasses the real and thereby grounds it. [2] One can immediately object that the unreal can be anything, such as what one sees in a dream or in a delirium. If the aesthetic object is an unreality, why would not all unreality be an aesthetic object? In this sense, all dreaming is artistic, and there is no need to visit a museum or a theater where we would run the risk of perceiving something real. But Sartre evidently would not agree that every act of dreaming constitutes an aesthetic object. The aesthetic object appears only to one who is in the presence of

1. Jean-Paul Sartre, *The Psychology of Imagination*, trans. B. Frechtman (New York: Washington Square Press, 1966), p. 249. [This translation will be occasionally modified in what follows.—Trans.]
   2. *Ibid.*, p. 243.

a work of art. As a matter of fact, this object links imagination to perception, even though it is the nature of imagination to refuse perception. Consciousness does not arbitrarily exercise this power of denying the perceived through an act of imagining. The advent of the imaginary is always motivated by the "situation in the world" of consciousness.[3] It is the real as perceived—what Sartre calls the *analogon:* colors, sounds, words, whatever exists as a thing and is thus perceivable—which invites consciousness, without doing violence to its spontaneity, to imagine the unreal. For the real functions as *analogon* when it ceases to be perceived for itself. The image exists only against the background of the world, and the imagination presupposes perception at the same time that it rejects it. Even though Beethoven's Seventh Symphony is unreal, it is still necessary that I be at the concert and that my ears hear the sounds so that this unreal can manifest itself in me. But if the imaginary is the negation of perception, the perceived is able to serve only as a catalyst for the imaginary. The perceived can neither orient nor limit the imaginary. If the Seventh Symphony is what I imagine when I hear and not *what I hear,* what prevents me from making it responsible for the outlandish reveries which it may awaken in me? If it is Charles VIII who is the aesthetic object and not the painting which I see, why not extend the dimensions of the object to include the procession of associations which can present Charles VIII to me?

This consequence can be avoided only by a kind of equivocation. The perceived *analogon* does not act only as the incentive which induces consciousness to imagine. The imaginary also mingles with it and benefits from its qualities. The aesthetic object "is apprehended through its *analogon,*" it "functions as an *analogon* of itself." [4] Thus, if the performance is accurate, "I am confronted by the symphony itself. But now, what is the Seventh Symphony itself? Obviously it is a *thing,* that is, something which is before me, which endures, which lasts. But is that 'thing' real or unreal? . . . It is completely beyond the real." [5] In being conceived as an unreality, the aesthetic object is still not any less a thing. But how can this object function in two paintings at once? Has not the unreal previously been defined by qualities which oppose it to a thing? What causes the confusion is that when one speaks of a thing, one thinks of what is real in the aesthetic object, of the impasto or the glaze of the painting or of

3. See *ibid.,* p. 241.—Trans.
4. *Ibid.,* p. 253.
5. *Ibid.,* pp. 250–51.

the sound produced by the orchestra. And when one speaks of the unreal, one thinks of a distant region which overshadows aesthetic experience through a seemingly inexhaustible plenitude of meaning which remains even if contemplation continues indefinitely. The confusion is thus created by the ambiguity of the perceived object, totally present and yet unable to be grasped, simultaneously given and rejected, present through its thinghood and elusive in its meaning. And ambiguity is at its maximum in the aesthetic object, where the meaning is entirely immanent in the appearance. Sartre thoroughly identifies the unreal with the meaning and even with what is most elementary in the meaning —that is, with the represented object, the real thing to which consciousness "refers" in "intending": Charles VIII or a bouquet of flowers, Hamlet or Ophelia. The nonrepresentational arts immediately present a problem. "Is a cathedral anything more than a mass of *real* stone which dominates the surrounding housetops?" [6] To this objection, which Sartre himself poses, he replies only indirectly by examining another less embarrassing case, that of music. Music, even if it represents nothing and does not allow the distinction between matter and meaning, at least allows for the distinction between the work and its performance. But one can answer for Sartre that, since the cathedral, like the Seventh Symphony, represents nothing, there is in it, as in the symphony, a certain idea which it seeks to express through the entire bulk and force of its stone, an idea which may be only the idea of the cathedral itself. This idea is not the concept, which is the general and impersonal definition, but the singular soul of the object. That is why the object which allows a concept to appear (an object of daily use is the best example) is a commonplace object and not an aesthetic one (as Valéry says of a house in comparison with a temple). Thus, at the moment they express, there is a subject in all the arts, even when they represent nothing. It is, finally, this subject which is properly the aesthetic object for Sartre. It is important to distinguish it from the work's matter, which is the real thing that is perceived as such—the canvas of the painting, the stone of the cathedral, or the words and gestures of the actor. To be sure, there is still a relationship between the perceived and the imagined, since the first is the *analogon*. "The painter did not *realize* his mental image at all: he has simply constructed a material *analogon* of such a kind that everyone can graft on the image provided that he looks at the *analogon*. . . .

6. *Ibid.*, p. 250.—Trans.

The painting should then be conceived as a material thing *visited* from time to time (in fact, every time that the spectator assumes the imaginative attitude) by an unreal which is precisely the *depicted object.*" [7] The thing made by the artist, sometimes brought into being with the collaboration of performers, is thus only a means for the imaginary to appear. And perception is only an occasion for imagining.

But how is it that the perceived thing can evoke precisely the same image which has obsessed the artist and not some other? If aesthetic contemplation is "an induced dream," how does one control this dream? [8] Must not the imaginary be somehow inherent in the perceived thing, in the same way that a subjectively grasped form corresponds to an objective structure, that a melody is in the perceived sounds in order to be grasped as an idea, and that Charles VIII must be on the canvas in order to be apprehended as Charles VIII? In other words, the relation between a real and an unreal thing cannot be the essentially contingent connection between the perceived and the imagined. The relation must be the connection between the sign and signification. The opposition between figure and ground should not be hardened into the dualism of the perceived and the imagined. The unity of the aesthetic object must not be destroyed for the sake of the imaginary, which would then monopolize the aesthetic. It is the whole object which is aesthetic, even if its unity harbors an insurmountable ambiguity to the extent that the meaning tends to become detached from it. There are thus two points on which we would challenge Sartre.

The first is that, having formed the theory of "the image-portrait," he extends it to the portrait as aesthetic object and founds an aesthetics on a theory of the imagination. He assimilates the aesthetic object to the represented object, itself conceived as imaginary in the fullest sense. The portrait refers to the original which is "reached as an image" by the mediation of the painting so that "the relationship . . . between the portrait and the original is nothing short of magical." [9] He could at least have diminished the influence of the represented object by following instructions which he gave at the beginning of his analysis:

We know that there is a type of imaginative consciousness in which the object is not posited as existing; and another in which

7. *Ibid.*, p. 247.
8. *Ibid.*, p. 252.
9. *Ibid.*, p. 30.

the object is posited as not existing. . . . But when I look at the photographs in a magazine they "mean nothing to me," that is, I may look at them without any thought that they exist. In that case the persons whose photographs I see are reached through these photographs, but without positing their existence, exactly like Death and the Knight, who are reached through Dürer's engraving, but without my positing them.[10]

It is in the same way that the represented object is reached in every aesthetic object, that is, as a neutralized meaning which is not posited or referred to an original. And here it is precisely of neutralization rather than of imagination that we must speak.

The second point we challenge is the identification of the unreal with the imaginary. It can be said that the meaning is an unreality—it is even a banality, if one means by this only that the subject of the work is not situated in the real world, as Hamlet played by Laurence Olivier or Barrault is not the true Hamlet, and as one does not raise his umbrella when he hears the storm in Beethoven's Sixth Symphony. One can say more profoundly that this unreality results from an excess of reality and is unreal because it is inaccessible or unexpressible. There is in the Hamlet who is presented to me or in the symphony which I hear something that I am never certain of understanding or making explicit, because the work is too rich and my sensibility too poor. In any case, the unreal does not originate from an imagining, that is, a distracted, consciousness. The unreal requires a realizing consciousness which is attentive to the perceived. If contemplation is a type of alienation, if the return to the everyday is an awakening and a disenchantment, the initial fascination comes from perception, not from imagination. It is in the perceived that we tend to lose ourselves (we shall see that it is, on the contrary, in the everyday world of action that the imagination exerts itself). Since the unreal, as the meaning of the aesthetic object, does not constitute an imaginary realm, it resides within the aesthetic object and must be grasped in it. The meaning is immanent in the thing. The aesthetic object is one, and the unreal is a "thing" only because it is found in the real, in the perceived thing, just as the soul is in the body and is manifested through the body. To be sure, a reading [lecture] is necessary— a reading of whose correctness we are never entirely certain— for the meaning to appear. This is why the aesthetic object is completed only in the consciousness of the spectator. Although

10. *Ibid.*, p. 31.

consciousness does not constitute the meaning, consciousness discovers meaning in what it perceives. The relationship between the painter and the painted object is not a relationship of "visitation," an arbitrary relationship suddenly constituted by a consciousness which decides to imagine. If an act of consciousness is necessary, it is in order to complete the painting by discovering the object in it, and not in order to deny the painting by replacing it with an object. In fact, it remains the case that this is a necessary act and that the unity of the aesthetic object is held in abeyance by perception. If, by introducing the dualism of the perceived and the imagined, of the material *analogon* and the properly aesthetic object, Sartre succeeds only in underlining and accentuating the problem, we shall not be able to resolve it by defending an aesthetic monism and substituting perception for imagination, because one must understand that the aesthetic object can be both this thing and this meaning—thing and meaning existing at once outside of me and through me.[11]

If we deny that the aesthetic object is imaginary yet admit that it is not reduced to the being of a thing, can we not say that it is an ideal object? It is important that we emphasize that the aesthetic object surpasses perceived being, and we can do so in two different ways. We can show that the aesthetic object involves an ever present demand for perception, as Waldemar Conrad does. Or we can attribute to the aesthetic object the being of a signification, by making it what we have called an intellectual object. It is this latter way that Roman Ingarden has chosen

11. If we challenge the theory maintained in *The Psychology of Imagination,* it is in the name of what Sartre himself has written in *What Is Literature?* (trans. B. Frechtman [New York: Harper & Row, 1965]). For if the aesthetic object is imaginary, one no longer understands how it is able truly to engage the spectator, as Sartre recommends in this latter work. One realizes, strictly speaking, that a word is "a particular moment of action," "the moment of reflective consciousness," at least if it is a commonplace word. But should one extend this efficacy to all art and say, for example, that "the aesthetic object is properly the world insofar as it is intended through the imaginary"? Here we would be more Sartrian than Sartre, saying that what is intended in the aesthetic experience is not *the* world but a world whose relationship to the world remains to be discovered. As for the aesthetic object, it is not itself this world. The aesthetic object expresses this world. It is a certain sensuous reality which, for the artist as well as for the spectator, is a goal, as Sartre himself has said very well. The two theses of *The Psychology of Imagination* and *What Is Literature?* are compatible only if one allows that the unreal holds the key to the real. We shall see that this thesis, valuable for ordinary perception, is not admissible for aesthetic perception. Art does not act on the authority of imagining, because it presents its meaning within the sensuous and dispenses with seeking beyond the given.

in a study bearing on the literary work that is particularly pregnant with signification. We shall see that we can, with the aid of
Boris de Schloezer, extend the same interpretation to an art like
music.

(b) Ingarden

It is true that Ingarden, who, like Conrad, follows the directives of Husserl's phenomenology, speaks neither of an intellectual object nor of an ideal object. He even takes exception when
Conrad uses such a term. But Ingarden speaks of "the purely
intentional being" of the aesthetic object, and he makes this being
depend on significations, which are ideal objects. In fact, his
phenomenology of the literary work, conceived as a "polyphonic"
structure, merges with a rationalist conception of language that
distinguishes the sign, the thing signified, and the apprehension
of the signification. It also rests upon the equally rationalistic
affirmation of the primacy of signification. For Ingarden, a word
is, in the first place, vocal material to which a signification is
added. This signification is separate from the word, and it requires a particular act of consciousness for the word to take on
its meaning and exercise its function—a process that is gradual
in character. The intentionality of an act of consciousness imparts intentionality to the word, which is thus a secondary and
derived intentionality. Ingarden states that the layer of the work
formed by its significations, without being made identical with a
psychologically lived content, does not have autonomous ideal
being, but is relative to the subjective operations of consciousness.[12] Moreover, the unities of meaning, which are constituted
by sentences, form "represented objects" which create the plot of
a story or a drama. Thus unities of meaning are related to these
objects as what represents to what is represented. This difference
between the two factors comes into play within signification itself, since what represents—the "state of affairs" as intentional
correlate of the sentence—is already, with regard to the sentence
as vocal unity, unified with what is represented. The represented
object keeps us clearly within the plane of the intentional; it is
truly "the purely intentional object." [13] Moreover, the representa-

12. Roman Ingarden, *Das literarische Kunstwerk* (Halle: Niemeyer,
1931); English translation by George G. Grabowicz, *The Literary Work of
Art* (Evanston, Ill.: Northwestern University Press, 1973), § 18.
13. *Ibid.*, § 30.

tion of these intentional objects may be sharpened by the "imaginary aspects [*Ansichten*]" which provide an intuitive grasp of them—these aspects being parallel to Husserl's "profiles" [*Abschattungen*] of perception, which fulfill intentions of perceived objects. But all this is not of great consequence here, since Ingarden does not specify the status of the imaginary. For [according to Ingarden] the authentic and primary determination of represented objects resides in the intentionality of the unities of meaning which deliver the intentional states of affairs.[14] The imaginary aspects, in making these objects visible, provide only supplementary determinations.[15]

The literary object is heteronomous. It is at the mercy of subjective operations which intend it and through which it is constituted. The equivocal term "constitution," which provides so much difficulty for Husserl, is implicit in Ingarden, who sometimes employs it in affirming that the literary work has no autonomy at all because it is above all a system of significations. In truth, this affirmation rests upon rather different arguments spread throughout Ingarden's work. One argument is that the work of art is always a "schematic formation" (*ein schematisches Gebild*), that it includes blank spaces, "points of indetermination" or allusions, potentialities which are actualized only when reading makes them concrete (by filling the gaps and animating the images).[16] Similarly, we would add that, just as movement in a plastic work of art appears only when the gaze animates the represented object, so here the narrative fills the gaps and offers the fullness, coherence, and insistence of lived experience only for the consciousness who lives it. On the other hand, if the

14. *Ibid.*, § 42.
15. Nevertheless, this discrimination of four "layers" [*Schichten*] of the work—vocal material, verbal meaning, represented object, and imaginary aspect—is of interest inasmuch as it helps Ingarden to distinguish the aesthetic object from its "concretizations." A certain act of consciousness corresponds to each of these layers, and we are free to perform whichever of these acts we like. In other words, our attention can shift from one layer to another so that the work is always grasped "in an abridged perspective" which varies with the dispositions of the reader, the interest he brings to the work, the intelligence he brings to the understanding of its meanings, or the vivacity of the imagination which animates those meanings. This means that the reading is never absolutely faithful and that the aesthetic object always overflows the perception or the consciousness which one has of it. It is open to a plurality of interpretations which can be opposed to each other and which are transmitted in the same way as a tradition of staging, of declamation, or even of comprehension, and which compose a history, a "life," for the aesthetic object. But the work is beyond these concretizations, because these latter are themselves intended by the work.
16. *Das literarische Kunstwerk* (*Literary Work of Art*), §§ 20, 63.

represented object contains something unfinished, it is because it is in a sense imaginary. The sentences of a literary work are not *bona fide* judgments which claim to grasp the real and come under the jurisdiction of the true or the false, as in a scientific work. The sentence, "the pen is on the table," does not have the same resonance and validity when I read it in a novel as when I pronounce it in response to a question which has been asked. Undoubtedly the represented object is always affected by a certain mode of existence, such as the real, the ideal, or the possible. I easily grasp the difference between the two sentences, "John saw his pen on the table," and "John remembered having seen his pen on the table." But in order for the represented object to be represented as real or imaginary, past or future, this positing of existence is, as it were, neutralized and impossible to take quite seriously. It is accomplished in the unreal, like the conversation of characters who are real for those to whom such conversation is addressed but who, as is shown by quotation marks, are not entirely real for me. It is in this respect that the represented object is a purely intentional object. Herein resides the deepest reason for the heteronomy of the aesthetic object.

It appears to us that Ingarden is guilty of two equivocations here, one with regard to the notion of intentional object and the other with regard to the notion of heteronomy. In both respects, Ingarden is unfaithful to Husserl. When he identifies the represented object with a purely intentional object, Ingarden appears to be tempted to make this identification by virtue of the fact that the represented object is in effect rendered neutral and, in this sense, unreal. But the unreality of the represented object is certainly not the same as that of the intentional object. In fact, the intentional object is not unreal. As Ingarden himself says, it is an appearance which, moreover, is not a pure nothing.[17] Nor is it a double of the real object that is somehow severed from its reality. Husserl has carefully avoided separating the real object situated in nature from the intentional object immanent in perception and situated in lived experience.[18] When I perceive a tree, there is not, on the one hand, an intentional tree deprived of reality and existing only in my perception, and, on the other hand, a real tree which I will rejoin through the intentional tree. The very purpose of the doctrine of intentionality is to avoid this ruinous distinction, the pitfall of all psychologism. The character

17. *Ibid.*, § 20.
18. See Husserl, *Ideas*, trans. W. R. Boyce Gibson (New York: Humanities Press, 1931), p. 263.

of reality must not be excluded from the intentional object. Even if it does not penetrate to the noematic kernel which defines the tree as such and constitutes its meaning, it belongs to the complete noema of the perceived, just as the quality of unreality belongs to the noema of the imagined (as do also "attentional modifications"). This integration into the noema of diverse theses of existence, varying according to the species of intentional experience, thus forbids the separation of the intentional object from the real object. Fundamentally—and perhaps Ingarden has not been careful enough in this connection—the intentional object appears only through the phenomenological reduction. The reduction creates nothing. It simply suspends the thesis of the natural attitude. The reduction does not constitute a new object or subtract anything from the real object. To "bracket" is not to subtract. All that the reduction asks of us is not to "operate the thesis" (of reality or unreality), that is, not to participate in it and to give ourselves free play. To practice the reduction is to adopt the attitude of the philosopher who, in Hegel's *Phenomenology of Mind,* looks over the shoulder of naïve consciousness and comprehends what it experiences. The intentional object is not different from either the real or the unreal object. It is either one of these objects grasped from the perspective of the reduction, which leaves belief intact and refuses to participate in it.

But then one can no longer say that the object represented by a word or a sentence is specifically an intentional object. The fact that it is unreal does not imply that it is reduced. The seizure of the represented as such is not a reduction that we practice without knowing it. Inasmuch as it is not reduced phenomenologically, the represented object is no more an intentional object than is the object which is perceived, recollected, or awaited. Consequently, one can no longer attribute to the represented object the heteronomy of being which one can attribute to intentional objects and which one discovers through the reduction by bringing to light the noetic-noematic structures. Moreover, does the mere correlation of an object with an intending act certify its heteronomy? If this were so, it would be necessary to attribute heteronomy both to the perceived object, which implies a special perceptual intention, and to the real object, which implies a thesis of reality. If one situates oneself on the plane of the reduction, one does not have the right to oppose, as Ingarden does, the heteronomy of the represented object except by subordinating it to foundations which have an autonomous being. [According to Ingarden] whoever grants the heteronomous existence of sentences (and thus of the literary work), must also accept all its autonomous foundations and must not be content with pure acts of consciousness[19] (which are sufficient to define the heteronomy of the intentional object). These supplementary foundations are, on the one hand, the subjective operations which preside over the creation of the work. On the other hand, and above all, they are "ideal concepts" to which the sentences of the work refer and which are actualized in them. Ingarden states that just as a sentence cannot be formed without the operation which forms it, it is not able to exist in the mode of heteronomy without ideal concepts.[20] But the intervention of these ideal concepts runs the risk of distorting the interpretation of the aesthetic object. We must affirm here something which Ingarden does not specify because of his polyphonic conception, namely, that what characterizes the literary work and opposes it to ordinary writing is the fact that the signification, even if it refers to ideal objects, is given in the word. Words have sufficient power for this because they carry their meaning within themselves. Thanks to words, the work achieves autonomy. It is in words that the work has its root.

And, in fact, one does not read a poem, or even a novel, as one reads a scientific work, an essay, or a news story. In the latter, significations are primary and cannot be neglected. In literary works, in contrast, one does not go straight to the significations through the words, conjuring away perception of these words and immediately substituting knowledge in their place. Sartre articulates this point when he says that, while the sphere of objective significations becomes an unreal world, knowledge, by a radical modification of intention, becomes "imaginary knowing." We prefer to say perceptual knowing, so that we may avoid introducing the dichotomy between perception and imagination, and because imagination appears to us to be repressed rather than stimulated by the aesthetic object. To read is to perceive. This is a truism, if we mean that the reading implies perception of signs written on paper. But we mean that, in the literary arts, the words which these signs deliver to us, far from being reduced to the function of signifying and to being obliterated by their signification, are perceived as things and end by bestowing on their signification this same quality of the perceptible. Indeed, the words assume importance here. They have a peculiar physiognomy of gravity or of brightness and not the discreet virtues of an

19. *Das literarische Kunstwerk* (*Literary Work of Art*), § 64.
20. *Ibid.*

algorithm, which must be clear and precise. Their meaning receives stability only through their sensuous virtues, and thus their significations become concrete. But how? Not because images come to graft themselves on them. Sartre himself has observed that images, properly so called, appear only during an interruption or failure of the reading, when the reader is not truly "taken" by the text. Abstract terms are not explained by images or diagrams. When Verlaine says "behold these fruits, flowers, leaves, and branches," he no more awakens botanical images in me than does Satie's "Melodies in the Form of a Pear" or a still life by Bazaine. What is concrete here is not the signification insofar as it is imaginary but its presence. The signification obtains from the word a type of insistence and density. It expands into a world, a world which we have the impression of constituting but which is given to us. The fruits and flowers of Verlaine are concrete, not because they are visible to our eyes, but because they introduce us into a certain atmosphere which is not the objective sphere of significations.

It is the immanence of the signification in language which Ingarden's conception does not clarify sufficiently. Perhaps it is necessary to understand the literary arts apart from the other arts and not to accord a special privilege to the represented object, that is, to "the level of meanings." Undoubtedly, one attraction of a novel lies in what it allows us to understand. We often measure a novel's value by the ideas which it propounds and the reflections to which it gives birth. It is also indubitable that there is often more material of depth in a novel than in a psychology textbook or in a history book. If what a painting represents is finally of no great importance—although one would have thought otherwise before painting came to a full consciousness of itself, that is, when one gravely discussed the representation of angels or the morality of the subject matter—it is not the same with regard to what a novel recounts. But the manner in which a novel recounts is also important. When it is done, we can conceptualize it by reflecting on it. We can express what a novel says in terms of science or philosophy, or we can integrate it into a system. But it is in this respect that we are not novelists and are limited to partial perspectives on the novel. If the novel suggests certain reflections to us, it is more by the way it represents than by what it represents. It is because of the art the novel contains that we are thus instructed—that is, if we are willing to forget afterward how it has acted on us. What is aesthetic in the literary work finally derives from the means of representation which it brings into play and on which the represented object depends. It depends on what is graspable in it from the outside, that is, on the choice and arrangement of the words. Thus one could say that, even in the literary arts, the aesthetic object, far from being a represented object or, as Ingarden says (through an identification which seems ill-advised to us), an intentional object, is still a perceived object. Knowledge of it is rooted in the perception of the sensuous aspects of the work, culminating in the feeling which thrusts us, within the heart of meaning, into a world immanent in the work.

Therefore, by stressing significations, Ingarden preserves the objectivity of the aesthetic object. But he does so only by cutting it off from the perceived through too radical a distinction between the word and its meaning, and by making the aesthetic object depend on a sphere of ideal being. From this he concludes to the heteronomy of the aesthetic object. Yet if we wish to do justice to the reality of the aesthetic object, it is not sufficient to insist on its meaning. We must also show that it bears this meaning within itself in order to present it to perception.

(c) De Schloezer

Boris de Schloezer, a student of the musical object, has not achieved the recognition he deserves. The importance of his remarkable book, *Introduction à J. S. Bach,* is found above all in his view that the meaning of the aesthetic object does not necessarily consist of representations like those which the pictorial or the literary object offer. To be sure, music has a meaning which grants it an autonomous being and which each performance strives to manifest in order to be faithful to the work. Lacking this, music would be only an absurd collection of sounds, a disconcerting accident, an appearance which would never cease to negate itself. De Schloezer discerns three aspects of this meaning, rational, psychological, and intellectual. The rational meaning does not properly belong to the music, except in the case of program music or the music which accompanies a text. It is overlain by the music itself: "Music succeeds in absorbing the rational meaning (of verbal systems) because it does not attempt to contain it—since, by its very nature, it ignores it completely. I say this expressly of the music and not of the musician." [21] If the

21. Boris de Schloezer, *Introduction à J. S. Bach* (Paris: Gallimard, 1947), p. 269.

words which are sung still have a meaning for the listener, "this meaning is not the one which they had before being put into music, but the one which the musical phrase confers on them." [22] With regard to the psychological meaning, which resides in the expressive character of the work and is conveyed in affective terms, de Schloezer shows clearly that it belongs to all music, even the most austere, the most impassive, on the condition that one not confuse what is expressive with what is moving. The psychological meaning is rooted in the structure of the work and receives an objective reality from the work, provided that one not psychologize it by identifying it with the emotions or the reveries which it can awaken in the listener. But for de Schloezer, the authentic meaning, of which the psychological meaning is but the obverse side or degradation, is the intellectual [*spirituel*] meaning, the "concrete idea" of the work, its being as an organic totality. The musical object has an intellectual meaning because it is a complete system of sounds. This meaning is the unfolding of an interior necessity, of a nontemporal unity which emerges through the diversity of forms or movements. [23] In brief, de Schloezer offers us an aesthetic Spinozism. Thus the work requires being "understood" by an operation of intellectual synthesis which transcends the merely sensory. This does not require that the listener know music theory, any more than the poem

22. *Ibid.*, p. 273. Perhaps we should express some reservations concerning the idea that the words which are sung are absorbed into the music and concerning the general thesis which one may be able to infer from that idea, namely, that the alliance of two or more arts necessarily accrues to the benefit of only one of them. The words of a poem or a libretto—when the libretto is not merely a pretext and when it possesses an aesthetic value of its own, as in *Tristan and Isolde*—have not only a rational but also a poetic meaning. This is the kind of meaning which we reproached Ingarden for having neglected. Between the poetic meaning and the musical meaning, just as between the musical meaning and the choreographic meaning (that is, between diverse expressive values), an affinity may be established which makes the two equal. More accurately, they are the same, constituting an identity, precisely because the meaning situates itself beyond the rational.

23. Indeed, de Schloezer says that the musical work is nontemporal. This affirmation does not have the same meaning for him as for Sartre. For Sartre, the musical object is nontemporal because it is an imaginary thing which can slip away only into an unreal time. "The time of unreal objects is itself unreal. It has no characteristics whatever of perceptual time. . . . It can expand or contract at will while remaining the shadow of the object, with its shadow of space" (Sartre, *The Psychology of Imagination*, p. 169). For de Schloezer, music is nontemporal because it substitutes, on the part of the composer who produces it and the listener who understands it, an organization of time by the intellect. "To organize time musically is to transcend it" (de Schloezer, *Introduction*, p. 31).

demands that the reader be a grammarian or a philologist. On the contrary, the layman, who is not hindered by academic habits, sometimes adapts himself better than the expert to the unprecedented. His very ignorance renders him open to the music and aids his understanding. To understand is nothing other than "to grasp the series of sounds in its unity," that is, to restore the work as a totality which is sufficient in itself. The meaning which one grasps in this way is truly the being of the object, that which constitutes the object as such and prevents it from being dispersed into an absurd diversity. Intellectual meaning, then, is immanent in the work. "The musical work is not a sign for something else but signifies itself. It is what it says to me, its meaning being immanent within it. And this meaning exists as embodied, not as signified, in the work." [24] It is in this way that such meaning is a "concrete idea."

More adequately than Ingarden, de Schloezer accounts for the unity of the aesthetic object. To this object, one can apply the formula which Goldstein applies to the organism—"the meaning of an organism is its being." But if meaning can thus unify and constitute the aesthetic object, it is because meaning originates from the depths of the object and not from the representations which the object provokes. A work is truly *one* work only on the condition of possessing a unity more profound than the logical coherence of a rational meaning, a unity which brings together both the signified and the signifying elements in the work and which gives the work its personality. It is this unity which constitutes the final peripity of the meaning of the aesthetic object. Lacking such unity, the aesthetic object has only the being of a sign and loses its rigor and fullness. Now, it is only the nature of this meaning, not its function, that one may question. The primacy accorded by de Schloezer to the intellectual meaning over the psychological meaning appears debatable to us. If the psychological meaning denotes expression, is it not itself the highest signification of the aesthetic object? It is not at all clear how the affective element, to the extent that expression is directed to feeling, can be a degraded form of intellectual meaning. For de Schloezer, the priority of intellectual meaning is backed by an intellectualist theory of perception. In this theory, to understand music is to bring about a synthesis by means of judgment—it is to grasp, or rather deform, an idea which governs the sensuous and which, because it presides over its development,

24. De Schloezer, *Introduction*, p. 27.

is itself nontemporal. But can an idea so linked to an act of judgment still be a concrete idea? Does it not transcend the sensuous, whose meaning it is? If, on the contrary, we renounce the theory according to which concrete ideas are graspable only by an intellectual operation, we can simultaneously reconcile the intellectual with the affective and assure its immanence in the sensuous. Finally, if music acquires its being from the meaning which dwells in it, how is this being given, except in perception? In what is the meaning immanent, except in the perceived? And in the case of music, is the perceived not the sonorous, sensuous element which imposes its presence on us and communicates its expression to us—rather than our imposing a law on it?[25] It is the sensuous itself which is expressive, and de Schloezer himself says that "one learns how to understand music by listening to it." [26] This means that music is not an intellectual object. Like all aesthetic objects and the literary work itself, music is a perceived object. What distinguishes aesthetic perception from ordinary perception is that, if we are to have access to the aesthetic object, nothing else is asked of us than that we perceive, since it is in the perceived that the meaning and being of the object are revealed. In aesthetic experience, the entire attention of the subject is oriented toward perception, and the materiality of the object is destined to elicit this perception and to efface itself before the triumphant sensuous element.

(d) Conrad

The aesthetic object is not an intellectual object, and the meaning in it cannot be distinguished from the sign so as to attain ideality. If the aesthetic object is to be an ideal object, then it must be so entirely. Even the perceived, as the bearer of the meaning, must be ideal. This means that perception is always an approximation. The ideal is not the intelligible but that which is beyond the actually perceived as constituting a task for perception—an *Aufgabe,* in Conrad's term.

Let us follow Conrad's analysis. The symphony is not reduced to the perception I have of it. Far from being an imaginary thing

25. Intellectualism is not, however, entirely false, and we shall return to it later. It is possible for reflection to cooperate with aesthetic perception. But reflection does not constitute aesthetic perception. The meaning of the perceived object is not dependent on an intellectual act. It is only tried out in its presence.

26. De Schloezer, *Introduction,* p. 26.

to which I would have access by breaking with perception, the symphony exists at the boundary of perception. Thus, regardless of whether I whistle a piece, play it as an arrangement for four hands on the piano, or hear it played by an orchestra more or less well conducted, it remains distinct from these performances, which give me only an incomplete or imperfect grasp of it.[27] This is not because in itself the symphony ceases to be a perceived object, but because it requires an adequate perception in which to be truly presented. When, in order to remind a friend of the Seventh Symphony, I hum its themes, I do not pretend to place him in the presence of the work. I give him a description of it, as one may summarize a novel or describe a painting. Yet I find that I am unable to convey the admirable counterpoint of the second movement, the harmony, or the tonal qualities. In short, I cannot convey what the work is in itself. All this is delivered only by a certain perception in the determinate circumstances of a given performance. (Sartre appears to say the same thing, but he qualifies it with the naïve statement that "this is due to my desire to hear the Seventh Symphony 'played perfectly,' because the symphony will then be *perfectly itself*." [28] In fact, it is difficult to see why, according to Sartre, a complete performance is required at all. A sketch can suffice to conjure for me the imaginary presence of the aesthetic object, and a photograph can possess the same power of evocation as a portrait.) Similarly, music demands a certain quality of performance in order to make possible a certain hearing. A plastic object demands a certain perspective on it—one could almost say, a certain quality of behavior on the part of the spectator—in order to permit a certain vision.

Thus we must speak of a privileged perception, a perception by which the aesthetic object is distinguished from the natural object. In the first place, such perception excludes diverse meanings for the sake of one meaning. A statue does not have to be touched but only seen. Even for a blind Michelangelo, a statue which is touched and not seen ceases to be an aesthetic object and becomes a known object—unless, by a miracle of imagination and (even more) of memory, touching it awakens an imaginary vision. And the mass or the quality of the material is aesthetically important only to the extent that vision can ap-

27. Waldemar Conrad, "Der ästhetische Gegenstand: Eine phänomenologische Studie," *Zeitschrift für Ästhetik und allgemeine Kunstwissenschaft*, III (1904), 77.
28. Sartre, *The Psychology of Imagination*, p. 250.

preciate it and lay claim to its authenticity. Second, the aesthetic object demands a certain point of view. A painting must be seen under a certain lighting, from a certain position, in conditions prescribed by the object which assure the best vision. In contrast, it does not matter from what perspective I see a photograph or under what conditions. It suffices that I recognize the object which the photograph designates. If I work hard at it, it is not in order to see for the sake of seeing but in order to know or to use something. Likewise, in the case of an architectural monument there are, as Conrad says, a *Hauptansicht* and certain *Nebenansichten*. Perhaps the perception of an architectural object is never wholly complete. We need to see the flying buttresses and the transept of Notre Dame, as well as the three portals and the towers. Thus the architectural monument, through its three dimensions, calls for a walk around it rather than an immobile view—a walk which requires stopping at various points which offer perspectives, as a camera may put together different successive views of the same work. Here we meet again with the idea that the aesthetic object, controlling the performance, calls for and governs perception and, as distinguished from the natural object, provides a perception which has no goal other than itself. Its prescriptions allow a certain latitude for the performer as well as for the spectator. But when this latitude is exceeded—e.g., when the reader stammers, the instruments are out of tune, the painting is covered with dust, the architectural monument is seen from too far away—the aesthetic object will disappear. To say that we have only an approximate image of it amounts to saying that it is no longer *it* which is present.

The essential thing for Conrad is to distinguish the aesthetic object from the performances to which it gives rise, and, above all, from the perceptions which we have of it. Since the aesthetic object is distinct from its epiphanies, it is an ideal object. But is this not true of all perceived objects? Not exactly. To the extent that we are content with experiencing the presence of an object, any perception which attests to this object is valid. On the other hand, to the extent that we wish to know the object in its truth, no single perception is sufficient to grasp it in its totality and to explain it by joining it to its context through necessary relations. There are two levels. In one, perception is always valid without anyone's imposing a norm upon it. In the other, perception is always considered invalid. Perception does not possess degrees of adequateness, because, as soon as perception has acquainted us with the presence of the object, and unless we adopt the aesthetic attitude, perception is surpassed toward action or intellection. The aesthetic object is destined for perception alone, not for utilization or knowledge. As a result, one must have one or more privileged perceptions of it. But this means that perception provides not only the object's presence but also its truth, and that this truth is the truth of a perceived object. Consequently, to say that the aesthetic object is ideal is not to say that it is ideational in character. The being of the aesthetic object is not the being of an abstract signification. It is, rather, the being of a sensuous thing which is realized only in perception. This is the essential point, which Conrad fails to emphasize. To make the aesthetic object the ideal limit of perception is not to exclude it from perception. It is to say only that this object is a norm for perception. Undoubtedly it is a norm only because it has the being of an in-itself. As de Schloezer says quite clearly, if music is reduced to what is perceived, "all performances are of equal worth." But even if music should not be reduced to what is perceived, it is only from within the perceived that it surpasses the perceived.

[II] The Aesthetic Object as a Perceived Object

This evocation of several doctrines inspired by phenomenology allows us to close in on the problem of the status of the aesthetic object. The aesthetic object is an object which is essentially perceived. This means that it is destined to be perceived and is completed only in perception. And it is precisely with regard to the being of the perceived object that the doctrines examined above falter and differ from each other.

(a) The perceived object

In fact, the perceived object offers a difficulty for reflection which is not easily resolved. Let us consider this for a moment. From where do the meaning and being of the perceived object come? Does the being reduce to the meaning which it has for me? Does it have a meaning through itself or through the idea which gives me a grip on it? Is its being independent of the representation which I have of it—is it grounded in itself or, on the contrary, on this very representation? It is in regard to this problem that idealism and realism have always been opposed. Even the doctrine of intentionality is involved in this long debate, which it cannot escape at the outset. To say with Sartre that the perceived object is both external and relative to consciousness is to compress the difficulty into a formula and not to resolve it at all. It is not sufficient to deny that the object is in consciousness and to affirm that, in its essence, consciousness transcends itself toward the object. To the extent that Husserl's notion of intentionality leads to hardening the opposition between the for-itself and the in-itself, the debate cannot be overcome. It can be settled only in favor of the idealism which is characteristic of Husserl's published works and is seen in the central theme of "constitution." The problem of perception remains as a splinter in the flesh of idealism. It is significant that Sartre has avoided approaching it in *Being and Nothingness* and that his other phenomenological works deal with the imagination and the emotions, that is, with domains in which one can bring to light the constitutive, *sinngebend* (sense-giving) activity of consciousness (this activity is conceived as a power of nihilation, through which the opposition of the for-itself and the in-itself stands out; for Sartre's originality lies in having shown, through interpreting certain Heideggerian themes, that it is because consciousness is nothingness and is able to nihilate that it is constitutive). The fact of perception, on the contrary, bids us dissolve the dilemma whereby the opposition of subject and object has brought all reflection to a standstill. It suggests that the object is not the product of a constitutive activity and yet that the object exists only for a consciousness capable of recognizing and studying it. The face of perception calls on us to conceive of a relation between subject and object such that the one exists only by means of the other—such that the subject is relative to the object in the same way that the object is relative to the subject. In other words, the subject can encounter the object only if it is first on a level with it, if it prepares for the object from within its own depths, and if the object is offered to it with all its exteriority. This reconciliation of subject and object takes place within the subject himself, in whom the body as lived and the body as object are identified. Such is Merleau-Ponty's thesis.[29] This gives phenomenology a new orientation, one which began in the unpublished works of Husserl. The reduction no longer culminates in the discovery of a constitutive consciousness but in the discovery of its own impossibility. To endeavor to suspend the thesis of the world, to renounce the natural attitude along with its spontaneous realism,

29. See Maurice Merleau-Ponty, *Phenomenology of Perception*, trans. C. Smith (New York: Humanities Press, 1962), Pts. 1, 2.—Trans.

is to realize that one cannot do it—no one can abstract himself from the world so long as he is in it, and the prereflective relationship with the world is always already given. Intentionality is this continually renewed project of consciousness by which consciousness achieves an accord with the object before all reflection. It is in this way that Merleau-Ponty also restores meaning to Gestalt psychology: the form is not the figure of the object immediately given as an articulated and meaningful totality but the totality that the subject forms with the object, in which one can only artificially distinguish between subject and object. Perception is precisely the expression of this close bond between object and subject, a bond through which the object is immediately lived by the subject in the irreducible experience of an original truth which cannot be assimilated to the syntheses effected by conscious judgment. This living relationship is presented by Merleau-Ponty in analogy with the relationship between an organism and its environment.[30] (This analogy is a dangerous one, since conceiving of perception as a mode of behavior may lead to neglecting the "representational" element in it; for the analogy takes account only of what is present to the body.)

In fact, the thing is not only the correlate of psychophysiological behavior and bodily teleology, it is also a reality which is imposed on us for which the psychophysiological setting is a response. The thing is a norm for us as much as we are a norm for it. If it were not such a norm, we would return to a transcendental philosophy wherein the transcendental, instead of being a constitutive consciousness, would be the lived body. In this case, we would have been successful in locating perception on a level with lived experience, but we would remain within the perspectives of an idealism. Merleau-Ponty has realized this himself: "One can-

30. The whole question is that of knowing what this relationship can mean when it designates not only the reciprocity of the lived body with the world, the organism with its environment. Moreover, how can one transpose this reciprocity from the vital order to the psychological order? Is there a plane of pure perception which is no longer lived experience as such, yet not reflective in character either? Is there a kind of perception which is not attached to understanding? Is the body transcendental other than at the level of behavior? Merleau-Ponty's theory in a way combines Heidegger's metaphysical theory, according to which Dasein reveals Being because it is in-the-world, with Sartre's phenomenological theory, which takes up this analysis in terms of consciousness, and with Goldstein's biological theory, which considers the relationship between the organism and its environment. But, if one can dispute the transposition from Dasein to consciousness, as Beaufret has done, there is all the more reason to dispute the transposition from consciousness to the organism. We shall return to this question in the analysis of perception.

not conceive of any perceived thing without someone to perceive it. But the fact remains that the thing presents itself to the person who perceives it as the thing in itself, and thus poses the problem of a genuine *in-itself-for-us*." [31] What does "in-itself" signify? In the first place, it means that the object does not rely upon me in order to exist and that there is a fullness of the object which remains inaccessible to me. In this way, the thing in itself in Kant's Transcendental Aesthetic—like the noumenon in the Analytic and the idea in the Dialectic—attests to the finitude of man, his inability to acquire an original intuition in which seeing is creating. For in perception there is nothing but the temporal, and temporality, like spatiality, forbids our grasping a finished totality. That by which there is a world for us is the very thing that prevents the world from being definitively knowable by us. But in-itself also signifies that there is a truth of the object whose presence alone is given to perception—a truth which attracts perception yet prevents it from ever being satisfied, and which leads to a reflection in which perception itself is placed in question. To say that the object is in-itself is to say that this object has an objective being which we are not able to grasp absolutely, because all knowledge begins with perception and because this in-itself cannot avoid being for-us.

Thus perception is perpetually the theater for a drama. Perception never ceases going beyond itself toward another form of consciousness which attempts to free itself from subjectivity and to seize the objectivity of the object. The distinction between subject and object is the result and the goal of this effort. At the same time, perception never ceases returning to the initial experience in which the assuring presence of the object is given to it, because in this experience object and subject are not yet distinguished. This drama is echoed in the status of the perceived object, which exists not only as lived by me but as independent from me, refusing the complicity which binds it to me in perception and urging on me an objectifying attitude which upholds the truth of its objective being. The perceived object is the object whose presence is indubitable because I am present to it. But, since I am present to it only by bringing into play temporality and spatiality—by accepting my being thrown into the world and my lostness in it—this presence is both assured and precarious. The object appears to me as that which is beyond appearance, totally present, and never totally known, thus

31. Merleau-Ponty, *Phenomenology of Perception*, p. 322.

suggesting (as empiricism and intellectualism both postulate implicitly) that there is somewhere a total knowledge of it. The object thus claims the very distinction between subject and object which sanctions its autonomy. If its presence is signifying, there is a truth in this signification which lingers at the horizon of the presence and invites us to grasp it. The experience of perception is clearly the beginning of all thought and the root of all truth, but it seems to come marked with an original defect: what it reveals is still only a promise. Thus the perceived object is a transcendence in immanence, not only in the sense that consciousness transcends itself toward it, but also—and perhaps Merleau-Ponty has not stressed this strongly enough—in that it includes a truth which continually eludes perception, although perception always has an inkling of it. The immediate comprehension of the object always calls for an explication of it which would be an explicitation of its objective structure. And if the perceived object is not only real but also true—possessing a truth which perception proclaims yet cannot grasp—it calls for conceptual understanding.

Therefore, the perceived object has an ambiguous status. It is the object which I perceive because it is present to me, but at the same time it is something else. It is that strange reality which perception does not exhaust, which appeals to a knowledge that wishes to owe nothing to perception, and which always obliges me to place naïve evidence in question by decentering knowledge in order to desubjectify it. This means that perception includes a demand for truth and must be aware of its own limits. A theory of perception must remember these limits and prepare a path to reflection which seeks the truth of the object whose presence is experienced in perception. It must accord priority to the in-itself over the for-us, and it can do so by understanding the in-itself in a sense which is not specifically Kantian. In this respect, the crucial thing is to avoid reducing the object's *esse* to a *percipi*, while still not allowing the object to escape the grasp of consciousness altogether.

(b) The aesthetic object and form

Although the distinction between presence and truth sheds some light on the problem of the perceived object, one cannot capitalize on it to resolve the problem of the aesthetic object. For the aesthetic object is an object whose truth manifests itself only through presence.[32] If the ordinary object invites us to transcend perception, the aesthetic object brings us back to it invincibly. If the ordinary object undermines Merleau-Ponty's thesis to a certain extent—or, more precisely, obliges it to account for the possibility of the movement from what is perceived to what is thought—the aesthetic object confirms it, or at least forces us to return from thought to perception, from the in-itself to the for-us. The aesthetic object is essentially perceived. For its epiphany to take place, sometimes its performance, and always a witness or the public, is required. It manifests the sensuous in its glory. However, if it realizes itself in perception, does it not have merely the subjective being of a representation? No. For it is also a thing, the result of an "instaurative" activity, as Souriau says (a thinker whose entire philosophical and aesthetic work is devoted to meditation upon this activity). Or we may cite Bayer, who describes the aesthetic "effects" registered by perception only in order to seek what is "typical" in perception and to disclose its "structure." [33] Thus we will say that the aesthetic object is the work itself, the work as the product of an act of creation which is open to an objective analysis. But we must add that the work in question is a work only insofar as it is aesthetically perceived. In this respect, we shall no doubt be subject to Souriau's critique: "Art is, above all, *action*—instaurative action—as I never tire of saying; and those who place the aesthetic fact solely on the side of contemplation create an aesthetic in which art is forgotten!" [34] But a theory of the aesthetic object certainly must give proper place to contemplation. The work itself calls for a type of perception which discovers in it (or realizes through it) the aesthetic object, so that the very analysis of the work continually refers, at least implicitly, to this perception. Thus the aesthetic object compels us to maintain two propositions which spell out the formula "in-itself-for-us." On the one hand, there is a being of the aesthetic object which forbids its reduction to the

32. This is a question, as before, of the truth to which the object is amenable as far as its being is objective enough to afford a grasp of the true, and not of the truth of which the object is capable so far as it says something and compares what it says with the real. In any case, this problem will be treated in our final chapter.

33. Raymond Bayer, *L'Esthétique de la grâce*, 2 vols. (Paris: Alcan, 1934), II, 328.

34. Etienne Souriau, "Introduction à J. S. Bach," *Revue d'esthétique*, I (April, 1948), 205.

being of a representation. On the other hand, this being is dependent on perception and is attained in it, for the being at stake here is an appearance.

That there is a being, and consequently a truth, of the aesthetic object can be confirmed in two ways. In the first place, the object puts forth demands which manifest a will-to-be that acts to assure its being. It is on perception that the object first places a demand. Far from waiting for perception, the aesthetic object elicits it and governs it—which suggests that the object needs perception in order fully to be. Not only does the aesthetic object, as Conrad has shown, offer to its witness a certain place and behavior; it also demands a certain attitude through which the witness offers it all his inner resources. In this sense, far from being simply for us, it is we who are for it; and it is in-itself precisely because it opposes itself to us. This character of demand is also addressed to the performer insofar as the work must be performed, for the performer knows that there is a truth of the aesthetic object to which he must be equal. If, through his failure, this truth is not made manifest, it still continues to exist. One could even say, as we have already said, that the aesthetic object demands its own creator. But the argument for a being of the aesthetic object that is anterior to creation cannot be accepted here. We can grasp the aesthetic object's being only by giving this object every chance and by supposing the work to be already created. The demand which manifests this being addresses itself to whoever must grasp the aesthetic object through the work, not to its creator.

It is on this condition that the work has its full meaning. By this, we certainly do not mean that the aesthetic object is an imaginary thing, any more than America was purely imaginary before Columbus discovered it. The aesthetic object can be abortive or absent, through our fault or through that of its interpreters, without being unreal on that account. If its appearance is falsified or goes unrecognized, it is nonetheless real. And one can say that, if the aesthetic object has a will-to-be, it is because there is a being *of* this object. This being is the being of a demand and not the being of a possibility or of an ought-to-be, that is, of something which is not yet and perhaps never will be. As a member of the class of works not yet performed or not aesthetically perceived, the aesthetic object exists *already,* and it is in this way that it has the being of a truth. But this being is not a being to be discovered beyond the given. It is the being of a presence which we must proclaim or realize. Thus the aesthetic object's presence is pregnant with its truth. This presence must be the presence of the object itself and not of a sham. The aesthetic object is not external or transcendent to its appearance, since it is realized only through them, and in this way it differs from the ordinary object. For it does not matter whether the ordinary object is well or poorly perceived (the difference is felt only by the person who is mistaken and who suffers the consequences). Nevertheless, the aesthetic object cannot be reduced to its appearances, since it is able to disown them by itself. The painting itself informs us that the lighting is poor or that our position is unfavorable. Music itself indicates that the movement is poorly timed or that we are not in a position to be able to hear it. The architectural monument itself informs us that its setting betrays it, that time has defiled its stone, or that we have an inadequate view of it. The aesthetic object is only appearance, but in appearance there is more than appearance. The being of the aesthetic object consists in appearing, but something is revealed in this appearing—its truth, a truth which compels the spectator to yield to its revelation.

If he does yield to it, the being of the aesthetic object is no longer that of a demand but that of a fullness. This fullness or plenitude is the second mark of its in-itself character. Thus the aesthetic object is a thing, and one can say that a symphony or a ballet is just as much a thing as an architectural monument or a piece of pottery. The fullness which the aesthetic object possesses is always that of an appearance, that is, of the sensuous which is the act common to the sensing being and to what is sensed. But there is an in-itself of this sensuousness (where the in-itself continues to be opposed to the for-us). Above all, aesthetic perception does not grasp the sensuous as if it had an accidental or subjective character and had to be immediately interpreted and surpassed toward a pragmatic signification, in the manner of secondary qualities. Aesthetic perception grasps the sensuous as imposing itself and as valid for itself. The sensuous exerts a kind of sovereignty over perception. As we have said, the sensuous has the force of nature, and the nature it evokes is not that of merely natural things, but rather the elementary power which primitive religions strive to conjure, the mysterious splendor of being which precedes men and objects. For the aesthetic object in itself is not a natural object. It becomes one only when it is abandoned to itself, reduced to the being of a sign. From the standpoint of its material substance, the architectural monument is a natural object, just as it can become an object of use if it is inhabited or repaired. But as an aesthetic object, the architectural monument is nature of another sort, as we can see through the overflowing, confident, and imperious character of the perceptions which it awakens. It is the sensuous itself which is massive, not the stone as a material. The same is true of the colors of a painting which have a persistence, a luster, and a firmness which characterize nature in the deeper sense. The same holds for the words of a poem with their timbre, iridescence, and resonance. To speak of an in-itself of the sensuous is thus to indicate its fullness and its insistent quality, by which the aesthetic object is distinguished from ordinary objects, which present themselves through impoverished sensations, dull and transient, and promptly hide themselves behind a concept. One could say that the aesthetic "virtue" of the object is to be measured by its power of exalting the sensuous and of blotting out everything else. An opera of which I retain the summary, a poem which pretends to instruct me, a painting which attracts me by its subject, an architectural monument which speaks instead of celebrating—all these are objects which are imperfectly aesthetic. It is necessary that the object exert a kind of magic so that perception can relegate to the background that which ordinary perception places in the foreground.[35] The sensuous fascinates me and I lose myself in it. I merge into the shrill melody of the oboes, the pure line of the violin, the din of the brass. I merge with the thrust of the Gothic spire or the dazzling harmony of the painting. I merge with the word and its peculiar countenance and the savor which it leaves in my mouth when I pronounce it. I am lost—literally, "alien-ated"—in the aesthetic object. The sensuous reverberates in me without my being able to be anything other than the place of its manifestation and the echo of its power.

However, it is not necessary to believe that the sensuous gives itself as a pure sensuousness. The sensuous has a meaning, whose pregnant import helps to structure it and to impose it on us as an in-itself. But it is important to recall how the sensuous is the instrument of this meaning. When ordinary perception does not result in gesture, it transcends itself toward

35. There is always some bad faith in magic. We pretend that we do not matter, that it is only Venus attached to her prey, or a fairy's wand. But our consent or our effort is also necessary, in this case, our consent to the sensuous, our accepting the rules of the aesthetic game. But it remains the case that the sensuous surrounds us and that our estrangement in it pays homage to its power.

knowledge. It is attentive to the sensuous only to the extent that it is instructive in character. In the case of a face, I remember the color of the cheeks because that tells me something about health, but not the color of the eyes, unless I wish to give a precise description for which this color will count. Here the sensuous is present only for the sake of its meaning, that is, for that which it represents. It leads to knowledge and disappears behind it. It is from knowledge that we must descend again to the sensuous—if this knowledge invites us to do so there, through its deficiency. In this case, perception must have lost the spontaneous confidence which it has in itself. The subject has begun to reflect and to ask himself exactly what is it that he sees. "Sensible quality, far from being co-extensive with perception, is the peculiar product of an attitude of curiosity or observation." [36] The aesthetic object, as we have described it, calls for the opposite course. If, being present at the opera, I am interested only in the story which is recounted, I have missed the essential thing, which is to hear the music. In the presence of the music, I must first discover, and in some way isolate, the sensuous—which is the entire reality of the aesthetic object—in order subsequently to grasp its meaning. Thus I shall verify that this meaning is both immanent in the sensuous and proper to it, the represented object being but one of its aspects.

The meaning instilled in us by the sensuous is more than the explicit signification of the represented object. Through this object, the aesthetic object says something else to us. The aesthetic object does not say it explicitly but by introducing us into a singular world of its own, a world for which the represented object is only a symbol. Van Gogh's bedroom is not merely a room where someone lives. It is a room which is haunted by Van Gogh's spirit and which, in the light of day, urges us to sense the mystery of a night which the painter could not enter without being utterly overwhelmed. The aesthetic object carries the world which it reveals within itself. Rather than referring to the world outside itself, as things do—e.g., as a cloud refers to rain —the aesthetic object refers to itself alone and is for itself its own light. We have expressed this point by saying that the aesthetic object is a quasi for-itself. We shall verify it through the analysis of this object's structure when we discern, in the very movement which animates it, a relationship of this object with itself which is constitutive of its own temporality. For the

36. Merleau-Ponty, *Phenomenology of Perception*, p. 226.

moment, it suffices to observe that this character of the aesthetic object, which is equally opposed to the for-us, confirms its in-itselfness. For the for-itself no more excludes the in-itself in the aesthetic object than in the human person. The for-itself always qualifies that which is a thing and yet more than a thing.[37] The quasi for-itself thus attests that the aesthetic object possesses the autonomous existence which its creator intended for it and which one is unable to make dependent on ideal significations in Ingarden's manner. The aesthetic object bears its own signification within it, and by entering more profoundly into communion with the object, one discovers its signification, just as one understands the being of others only by virtue of friendship.

This communion is indispensable. Without it, the aesthetic object is inert and meaningless, just as without performance (when it requires one) it is still only imperfectly existent. It is not difficult to imagine a civilization of Boetians or Vandals in which the aesthetic object would disappear as such, where works survive as things without any meaning. The steeple is not an aesthetic object for the artilleryman who aims at it, nor is a painting an aesthetic object for someone who consigns it to the attic. Just as man awaits recognition by his fellow man and does not fully realize his being in the state of nature, as Rousseau said, so too the aesthetic object waits for a perception in which the sensuous will be displayed and, through the sensuous, its meaning as well. It is for and through the spectator that the aesthetic object has the independence and objectivity of the in-itself. It is in presence that the aesthetic object has its truth. As soon as it is intended by an impersonal consciousness, of the kind possessed by the scholar when he is no longer interested in the sensuous for its own sake and does not seek in it the secret of the object, the aesthetic object fades away and falls back to the rank of a commonplace thing. It is truly itself only in aesthetic experience. It thrusts itself on perception, and yet it has being only through perception.

We may illuminate this paradox (though without overcoming it) by returning once more to the notion of form. It is through form that the aesthetic object affirms both its unity and

37. Is this not the principal advance which Merleau-Ponty has made over Sartre by establishing a reflection upon the dialectical being of the body and behavior? The "in-itself-for-itself" does not designate an impossible god. It designates that demigod who is man—and also, by adding a "quasi," the aesthetic object, the most human of man's works.

its autonomy. Form, in fact, is not something which determines the aesthetic object from the outside. Form manifests the being which the creative act has conferred upon it. The aesthetic object does not have a form; it *is* form. To be sure, form must be given to the aesthetic object by a creative act, according to unifying spatiotemporal determinations. If Kant's Transcendental Aesthetic is correct, a sensuousness that is pure diversity could not be perceived. *A priori* forms of sensibility must confer a unity upon this diversity. We shall see how the artist himself organizes space and time in ordering the sensuous. In neither case are space and time a framework external to the sensuous and merely added to it. For it is the same thing to produce the sensuous in the first place and to organize it spatiotemporally, to produce sounds and to order them in melodic phrases according to rhythm and harmony, that is, to constitute a meaningful totality. Furthermore, music is not in time, it is *of* time, that is, it has a duration of its own, which is like a form of respiration and for which measurement is only an external dimension. Similarly, the architectural monument in space is *of* space. Instead of being measured, it does its own measuring. It creates height by the upward force of its columns or the boldness of its arches, depth by the receding succession of its parts, and breadth by the majesty of its façades or the width of its portal. We shall see that space and time are so well integrated into the aesthetic object that they seem to proceed from it. Spatiality and temporality become the dimensions of the world internal to the object, the forms which the object, far from receiving, invents for its own world.

Thus form is not an external principle of unity which would come from the outside to structure the sensuous, as one puts shoes on a shoe tree or wine in a bottle. Form is, on the contrary, internal to the sensuous. Form is nothing other than the way in which the sensuous proclaims itself and offers itself to perception, as the composition in a modern painting expresses the way in which the colors are organized as colors, or as the action in a ballet expresses the way in which the movements are connected. This is why form is not accurately considered when it is reduced to contour or outline. Form is rather the totality of the sensuous insofar as, on the one hand, it constitutes itself as an object and, on the other hand, it represents something. Because it gives form to the object and confers a being on it, one can say that form is both meaning and essence. Form is the idea which is incarnate in the appearance and imparts to it something of its eternal character—a character which one senses in the presence of ruins. But here we must make two further clarifications.

The first is that such an idea is not amenable to logos or reason. The aesthetic object expresses the idea through its own power of expression, and it is communicated to feeling without allowing itself to be dominated by the understanding. In this way, the idea affords access to a world. The unconditioned is revealed only through affectivity. This is why aesthetic experience may lie at the heart of being in the world. At least it always brings us back to the original experience of this being in the world. But by the same token, aesthetic experience cannot usurp the prerogatives of philosophy. Art possesses another language, and it is up to every individual to know which kind of discourse he prefers.

The second clarification is that the idea, which is so completely incarnate in the aesthetic object and so inseparable from the sensuous that is revealed only to feeling, emanates from this object itself, which thereby constitutes itself as a for-itself. We rediscover here a theme of Henri Focillon's: "A sign signifies an object, form signifies only *itself*." [38] Such is the intrinsic character of expression, and an irreducibility to logic is its corollary. The aesthetic object provides its own meaning, and that which unifies it is at the same time that which assures its autonomy. One could say that the form is the "soul" of the object, in keeping with the Aristotelian meaning of the word. Thus, when we speak of the in-itself of the aesthetic object, we are not opposing it to the for-itself but to the for-us. When we say that it is nature, it is not so much to identify it as a natural object as to stress the imperious and independent character of its reality.

38. Henri Focillon, *The Life of Forms,* trans. C. B. Hogan and G. Kubler (New Haven: Yale University Press, 1942), p. 3. Throughout this remarkable study, which anticipates both the psychology of form ("An architectural mass, a relationship of tones, a painter's touch, an engraved line exist and possess value primarily in and of themselves. Their physiognomic quality may closely resemble that of nature, but it must not be confused with nature" [*ibid.*, pp. 3–4]) and certain themes from Malraux ("Plastic forms are subjected to the principle of metamorphoses, by which they are perpetually renewed, as well as to the principle of styles, by which their relationship is . . . first tested, then made fast, and finally disrupted" [*ibid.*, p. 6]), Focillon suggests the idea that the aesthetic object, through its form, is pregnant with a world: "It [form] prolongs and diffuses itself throughout our dreams and fancies: we regard it, as it were, as a kind of fissure through which crowds of images aspiring to birth may be introduced into some indefinite realm—a realm which is neither that of physical extension nor that of pure thought" (*ibid.*, p. 3).

We have still not grasped the final peripety of the notion of form when we have thus acknowledged the sovereign form which inhabits the aesthetic object and which is both the arrangement of the sensuous and the signification that is immanent in it (since the unity of the aesthetic object and its plenitude are determined by the pregnancy of this form and by the distinctness with which the sensuous contour of the object, as well as its demeanor and expression, stand out). For we cannot forget that this form must be read by perception. Hence it is still a form in the sense that Merleau-Ponty understands it, namely, something in the object which must be experienced and recaptured by the subject, thus presupposing an affinity (and sealing the alliance) between subject and object. The form is less the shape of an object than the shape of the system which the subject forms with the object, of that "rapport with the world" which expresses itself unfailingly in us and is constitutive of both the object and the subject. Already, we may suspect that this solidarity of the *percipiens* and *perceptum* is particularly evident in aesthetic experience, since the form of this object is especially pregnant in character.

But this very pregnancy forbids us to devalue the in-itself in comparison with the for-us. In the relationship which unites the aesthetic object with me and subjects me to the aesthetic attitude, it is, after all, the aesthetic object which has the initiative. I am only the occasion for the logos of feeling to deliver itself and to speak through me. Everything takes place as if the object needed me in order that the sensuous may realize itself and discover its meaning. But I am only the instrument of this realization. It is the object which commands. This is why aesthetic perception, inasmuch as it is feeling, is a form of alienation.[39] This alienation itself is a task for me, since I must surrender to the enchantment, deny my tendency to seek mastery of the object, and conjure up the sensuous so as to lose myself in it. Then I recognize in the object an interiority and an affinity with myself. I intend the aesthetic object, but I intend it as consubstantial with myself. While penetrating into it, I allow it to penetrate into me, rather than keeping it at a distance. It does not cease

39. To this alienation of the spectator, a psychology of creation would show what corresponds in the alienation of the creator—he also sacrifices himself in order for the aesthetic object to exist. These two acts of alienation are complementary and symmetrical. That which I recognize in the object in becoming alienated in it is what the artist himself has put there. The work is thus the cementing force of intersubjectivity.

being an object while it mingles with me. The distance which it has is not abolished because I am absorbed in it, since it remains a rule for me and imposes its meaning on me. Such is the paradox: I become the melody or the statue, and yet the melody and the statue remain external to me. I become them so that they can be themselves. It is in me that the aesthetic object is constituted as other than me. In other words, the phenomenon of alienation here modifies the usual notion of intentionality. I cannot say that I constitute the aesthetic object. Rather, it constitutes itself in me in the very act by which I intend it, since I do not intend it by positing it as outside myself but by vowing myself to its service. Thus one can see why consciousness is not the provider of meaning. Instead of positing the object, consciousness embraces the object, which affirms itself in this embrace.[40]

We can now realize the importance of examining aesthetic perception, since it is perception that brings about the metamorphosis of the work into the aesthetic object—an object in which the work is completed and in which it delivers its authentic meaning. Such an examination will be forced to repeat the themes which distinguish it from a description of the aesthetic object. By this means, we shall also verify that the aesthetic object requires a special type of perception which, even if it traverses reflection, does not terminate in it. Rather, this perception returns to itself in the guise of feeling, because the aesthetic object can manifest itself, in its truth and not only in its presence, to perception alone. But first we are going to outline an analysis of the work, whose sensuous presentation is found in the aesthetic object. This will afford a confirmation of the description which we have just given, particularly of the idea that there is an in-itself of the aesthetic object. In fact, we already understand how the work is able to enlighten us concerning the object. The aesthetic object *is* the work insofar as it is perceived. The only difference between them stems from the intervention of consciousness—a consciousness which is discreet and docile but makes the object pass from night to day, from the state of being a thing to the state of being perceived. It is in the work that the in-itself of the aesthetic object must find its ground. If this object draws its being from the work and is clarified by reference to it, then, conversely, the work has its

40. Dufrenne refers here to Husserl's notion of consciousness as *sinngebende*, literally, "meaning-giving." See *Ideas*, trans. W. R. Boyce Gibson (New York: Humanities Press, 1931), § 55, pp. 168 f.—Trans.

truth in the aesthetic object and must be understood through it. That is why an analysis of the work is meaningful only if it refers constantly to a possible perception, thus showing that the work exists in order to be perceived.

PART II

Analysis of
the Work of Art

Now WE BEGIN the objective study of the aesthetic object. We are authorized to do so precisely by what is objective in this object. The sensuous element which constitutes the aesthetic object does not present the object as an unintelligible diversity but as an organized and meaningful totality. And we know why this is so. The aesthetic object is the product of an act of making, and this making creates structures and meaning. Instead of describing the steps of this creative activity, we must grasp the *results* of this activity more accurately. In other words, we are going to move from the aesthetic object back to the work. For it is the work which is created and is thus a thing—a privileged thing which supports the aesthetic object and converts itself into this object at the instigation of perception. The work is what is subject to an objective study. The work is what authenticates any attempt, scholarly or otherwise, at analysis and interpretation. When we speak of the work, furthermore, this implies that we are also speaking of the aesthetic object. We have seen that, in a sense, the two can be identified. But to rediscover the work behind the object, it suffices to renounce the aesthetic attitude and to adopt an attitude of objectification that is appropriate for an objective analysis. Instead of considering the work as something perceived, we shall consider it as something known, as something which precedes perception. Yet what we shall have to say concerning the work will overlap in two ways with what we said concerning the object. The study of the work both explains (insofar as we find the "why" of this object in the work) and presupposes (insofar as it is our grasp of the aesthetic object that orients our analysis of the work) aesthetic experience. For this analysis can be conducted only in reference to aesthetic experience and thus by not forgetting that what our analysis discloses has meaning for perception alone.

As we have already seen, the work presents multiple aspects for analysis. For reasons of clarity, we shall eliminate from consideration

[237]

a material factor—a system of graphic signs—which in certain works serves to transmit to performers the instructions which are necessary for actualization. But it remains the case that the work, as a thing, possesses a basic matter from which it is made and which the artist organizes in his own manner. The reality of this matter is what confers the character of being a thing on the work as well as on its sensuous elements, which assume in the work the role of this matter insofar as it is perceived. In addition, the work possesses a subject around which its matter is organized. This subject represents or signifies something which must be understood for itself. In the end, it possesses an expression which is capable of giving it a unity beyond material coherence and logical rigor and of conferring upon it a temporality—a being-for-itself. These diverse aspects of the work do not, however, exist in isolation. They appear to us only by an act of abstraction—an abstraction which is, moreover, inevitable when we consider the work in its status as a thing and seek out its structure, that is, when we neglect the fact that the aesthetic object also exists for us. We shall show that we have a right to distinguish the elements of the work only by remembering that in fact aesthetic perception abolishes these distinctions and goes straight to the total work. It is the same thing to show that the work exists for perception as to show that all of its elements tend toward a unity, a unity which is not merely the unity of sign and signification in a signifying thing, but also the unity of a quasi for-itself.

7 / The Temporal Arts and the Spatial Arts

How SHALL WE BEGIN the analysis of the work? We can pursue this analysis in a fully satisfactory manner only in terms of a specific work, or at least of a specific art. Every art involves its own techniques and calls for a peculiar mode of composition. A painting is not composed in the same way as a novel, or a ballet in the same way as an architectural monument. What our analysis will uncover at first will be the formal schemata which regulate the composition of the work in terms of its artistic genre and which are imposed by that genre on the work's creator. Every work implies the choice of a form—where "form" is understood simply as the totality of the very general determinations which allow us (in accordance with prevailing cultural norms) to classify a work as a certain form of art and in a certain artistic genre.[1] An aesthetic object cannot be just anything indifferently. It must be a sonata or a symphony, an epic or a sonnet, a fresco or a miniature, a pantomime or a classical dance, a tragedy or a farce. It must yield to a formal schema which ties it down to certain rules and grants it an official status. There are, of course, works which mix various art forms, such as the opera, and others which mix genres, such as tragicomedy. But because such works constitute a distinct object which can be identified and defined—an object that is clearly

1. Why the artist chooses a particular art, that is, a particular language, is a question which rightly belongs to psychology. If what he says can be expressed only by the language he chooses, then the problem belongs to a comparative aesthetics and to a theory of the analogy of expressions.

different from the sort of ambivalent and suspect object which confounds perception as well as understanding—they are still obedient to norms. Thus the aesthetic object is defined both by what it wishes to be and by what it refuses to be.

The norms which rule over an artistic genre or type are indissolubly material and cultural. They express both the unique nature of the particular art and certain cultural demands which systematize and orient technical requirements. Thus the theater requires that the words be heard past the footlights, that the action be intelligible to the spectator, and that the scenes not change so quickly that the audience's attention is dispersed or the performance interrupted by set changes. The rules of unity as observed by classical theater systematize these requirements by determining the structure a theatrical work must have. Similarly, but more elastically, the dimensions of a painting are determined both by the conditions of perception and by the dimensions of the wall on which it must hang (in this latter respect, by a certain state of architecture). And in architecture, the look of a building is dependent both on the nature of its materials and on the purpose for which it is built. Thus it is dependent on the culture, which determines this purpose by asking for a temple for a god or for a palace for a prince, and also on the state of that culture's technology (a technology not of construction alone but, as is too often forgotten, of scaffolding as well). In other words, within a given culture certain rules are imposed on every art, and they are all the more authoritative insofar as they take into account the possibilities inherent in each individual art and constitute the schemata of the genre. We shall not, however, study these schemata. They belong to the historian of art and escape the grasp of an eidetic investigation. But they do suggest an important problem. Will the diversity of art, which is found both in its plurality and in its history, allow us to speak of the aesthetic object in general? We have assumed that we can do so, but this assumption must now be justified. This justification is crucial if our analysis of the work of art is going to be able to discover structural elements common to all works—that is, not only formal but also, so to speak, organic schemata. We shall not discover these schemata through an increasing amount of abstraction. On the contrary, we must take an even closer look at the being of the work and at that which, beyond the general determinations which characterize artistic genres, makes the work truly a work of art.

Nevertheless, we must for this very reason take into account the diversity of artistic genres. We shall accordingly outline an analysis of the aesthetic object which pertains first to music and then to painting. These two arts are chosen because of their contrasting character—a character which we may observe in the following fashion. On the one hand, music represents nothing, and in this respect has no "subject," while painting which is not simply decorative or else "abstract" does represent something. On the other hand, music unfolds in time while painting manifests itself in space. Yet the examination of these two arts will allow us precisely to diminish such differences. First, we shall be able to establish that, even though music is an autonomous organization of the sensuous, it nonetheless involves a higher unifying principle which permits a subject to function. Painting, conversely, even though it is primarily figurative, involves a treatment of the sensuous which is not solely ordered by a concern for representation, with the result that representation never appears as the exclusive aim of a work or as the sole proposition offered to perception. Second, we shall establish that the aesthetic object implies *both* space and time, even though in a given case it appears to be only spatial or only temporal. Thus painting is not without relationship to time, nor is music unrelated to space.

This final point calls for a preliminary reflection. We need to digress here in order to outline a few basic notions. This digression will not be without a certain usefulness, because the liaison between space and time at the heart of the aesthetic object possesses a dual importance for our project. In the first place, it allows us to lessen the opposition between the spatial and the temporal arts and to take into account their analogies, the "correspondence of the arts"—a problem which we shall not discuss but for which we hope to prepare the way.[2] Second, our discussion could clarify the status of quasi subject enjoyed by the aesthetic object and the fact that it is both for-itself and in-itself. In this connection, we should emphasize two points. One is that we must recognize the solidarity of space and time, a central theme which is too often neglected by transcendental reflection as well as by cosmology. Next, we must understand the characteristics of space and time as they are related to the aesthetic object. For it is not a matter here of the space and time of the objective world—in which the work is situated by age or by the place of its exhibition—but of the space and time

2. Dufrenne refers indirectly here to the title of Etienne Souriau's book, *La Correspondance des arts* (Paris: Flammarion, 1947).—Trans.

which the work *is*. We shall thus reinforce what we have said concerning the primary dimensions of the expressed world. It is a question of a temporality and spatiality which are constitutive of the object and of a certain active relationship which the object in its being entertains with space and time. This relationship, in terms of which the aesthetic object is a quasi subject, can be clarified only by reference to the subject.

It is, in fact, in relation to the subject that the solidarity of space and time can be grasped in the first place—that is, of an originary space and time which are the source of the objective space and time which are considered the framework for phenomena. The human self implies both temporality and spatiality, and the *Da* ("there") of Dasein ("being-there," "existence") has a meaning which is both temporal and spatial. Heidegger finds the origin of this idea in Kant. Primary time is not an empty framework, a form understood as something which contains and in which previously given sensations become ordered.[3] By discerning an act of imagination in our intuition of space and time and by distinguishing formal intuition from the form of intuition, Kant suggests that form precedes any formalism.[4] Time is seen as a relationship of the self with itself or, as Kant says, of the self as "affected by itself."[5] It is a pure movement of departing from the self in order to return to the self, thereby hollowing out an interiority. Instead of the total coincidence of self with itself which is found in the *mens instantanea*, which has no being-for-itself, a process is set into motion which constitutes an "I" in a sort of interior distance where the self is distinguished from itself, thus establishing itself as a self. In Heidegger's terms, temporality is not an ecstasis but the unity of ecstases, a perpetual return to the self. The self is what endures and what remains the same in becoming other. Without this return to the self, there would be no diaspora or dispersal of instants.[6] Objective time, in contrast,

3. Jean Nabert has demonstrated that brute sensation cannot constitute brute material which preexists a formative synthesis. (See "L'Expérience interne chez Kant," *Revue de métaphysique et de morale,* XXXI [April–June, 1924], 205–68.)

4. The word "form" does not have merely a logical meaning as the condition for the possibility of any experience whatsoever. It also has an ontological meaning, by which it designates a mode of being on the part of the subject. "Formal" is the term we apply to an originary act.

5. Immanuel Kant, *Critique of Pure Reason,* trans. Norman Kemp Smith (New York: St. Martin's Press, 1929), A 49, B 68, p. 87.

6. See Martin Heidegger, *Being and Time,* trans. J. Macquarrie and E. Robinson (New York: Harper, 1962), pp. 377 ff.—Trans.

is what does not belong to the subject. It is a decentralized time which is no more than externality, while temporality retains by loosening and returns by departing. Temporality is the being of a subject.[7] In the end, the subject, who is defined by temporality as a relationship of the self with itself, constitutes an organic totality. Being a self means dividing oneself in order to be united and to form a whole. The meaning of the time proper to living beings differs from the meaning of clock time, which is borrowed from physics. Clock time arises out of objective time, whereas the time proper to the living being expresses the interiority of life and what Kant calls its internal finality. We shall see how the aesthetic object also involves such internal finality. It is itself "living" not only because it enters into history through the historicity of judgments of taste but also because it is animated by a sort of internal movement.

Just as time is the form of inner sense and thus lies at the source of subjectivity, space is at the origin of externality.[8] And if we conceive of an act of spatialization which is analogous to temporalization, we shall discover the notion of an originary space. Not even Heidegger has attempted this[9]—perhaps because he attributes to time what should be reserved for space (particularly the power of providing the elements of a "figurative synthesis," although Kant realized that "inner intuition yields no shape")[10] and because he interprets the *Da* of *Dasein* in purely temporal terms. Merleau-Ponty is probably closer to Kant on this point when he shows that "space is existential; [and] we might just as well say that existence is spatial."[11] Of course,

7. For this reason, we shall understand time to be the dimension of human depth. Our experience of the past and of childhood is what affects us most deeply, and the future is what exalts us.

8. It is a different problem when Kant goes on to say that knowledge of the self is subject to temporal conditions and that we thus know only a phenomenal self. In this case, we are dealing with an objective and previously spatialized time. Perhaps Pierre Lachieze-Rey is correct in criticizing Kant in the name of a philosophy of the subject (*L'Idéalisme kantien* [Paris: Alcan, 1931], p. 184). But it should be enough to distinguish between a temporality which is constitutive of the being of a subject and a time which is constitutive of an objective knowledge of the subject, i.e., between the movement by which the subject posits himself as existence and the movement by which he knows himself as essence.

9. Heidegger alludes to this only once in his *Kant and the Problem of Metaphysics*, trans. J. Churchill (Bloomington: Indiana University Press, 1962), § 34.

10. Kant, *Critique of Pure Reason*, A 33, B 50, p. 77; on figurative synthesis, see pp. 164 f.

11. Merleau-Ponty, *Phenomenology of Perception*, trans. C. Smith (New York: Humanities Press, 1962), p. 293.

Merleau-Ponty criticizes the Kantian notion of space according to which space locates things because it is a system of relationships determined by the mind. But Merleau-Ponty blames Kant particularly for a rigid notion of form. Thus Merleau-Ponty is led to contrast a "spatialized" space, which is fully constituted in the mind, with a more open "spatializing" space. Yet it seems that Kant anticipates this objection by making space a form *of sensibility,* a given which precedes all other givens. He thereby wishes to discover a primary space by which all our concepts of space and constructions of spatial objects will be possible. What kind of space is this? For Merleau-Ponty, it precedes every constitutive operation and is always itself previously constituted. Thus it attests to "a communication with the world which is older than thought" and to the very fact of our corporeality: the hold our bodies have on the world.[12]

Such a phenomenological description as Merleau-Ponty's can be understood in a transcendental sense, according to which space posits the given as given. Even though the body sustains a fundamental relationship with things by opening itself up to them and, as it were, spilling over into them, we can say that, short of embodiment, the subject constitutes itself by opposing itself to the object, turning toward something which it is not, and preparing to receive it. This expectation, reception, or movement-toward is what Heidegger has analyzed so brilliantly—however wrong he may be in attributing it to temporality. Space is what is designated in this movement of opening up—space as the aspect of otherness, as what is always outside (whether it is far or near), and as an elsewhere opposed to the here which we are. For this reason we believe that the *Da* should be understood in terms of space as well as time. If the *Da* signifies the upsurge of an absolute presence, this presence can be given to itself only by constituting a presence—not a punctual instant, but a plenitude in which the for-itself gathers itself together and the ectases are united. This presence has a spatial meaning as well. It is a presence *to,* the threshold of a space in which the subject can enter into relation with an object and, at the limit, become himself an object among others. Heidegger's celebrated formula that "insofar as Dasein temporalizes itself, a world *is* too" would be clearer if "spatializes" were substituted for "temporalizes."[13] In other words, we can

12. *Ibid.,* p. 297.
13. See Heidegger, *Being and Time,* p. 417.—Trans.

use Heidegger's own language to say that Dasein is indeed a "light" but that, in order to illuminate a world by being reflected back from objects, this light must open up a space. Consciousness of the world can take place only insofar as the self withdraws and creates a distance. Is this not the function of originary space, namely, to place us before [*en face de*] a being which we are not or, more precisely, to render this situation of being-before possible?

On the foundation of this coexistence of both an originary temporality and an originary spatiality in the subject, and moving now from the phenomenological to the noetic level, we can understand the solidarity of space and time in the object as it is revealed and established by consciousness. Kant can again be of help here. According to Kant, temporality and spatiality collaborate to the extent that they are both necessary to that "pure synthesis of the imagination" whose unity, "prior to a perception, is the ground of the possibility of all knowledge." [14] Does Kant not say, in a "reflection" quoted by Heidegger, that "Raum und Zeit sind Formen der Vorbildung in der Anschauung"? [15] His notion of schematism seems to give the advantage to time, because the schemata are movements internal to the imagination of the subject which render the apprehension of an object possible—an apprehension, as it were, from the viewpoint of the subject and not from that of the object. The schema "concerns the determination of inner sense in general according to conditions of its form," and not the external sense. [16] But is it not in space that the *Anblick* ("aspect") of something in general can become perceptible? Moreover, when time and space as forms of intuition become themselves objects and then tools of knowledge, they can be determined only by one another.

Time, the kind of time which "cannot be perceived in itself" (something that should not surprise us, because even "if everything moves, movement itself cannot be perceived," and because time is the space of subjectivity), "cannot be determined without the representation of space," as Jean Nabert has demonstrated. [17] Thus we encounter the problem of the schematism. The transcendental determinations of time do not belong to an originary time understood as a form of intuition. They originate in an act of understanding (or of imagination) which itself refers to

14. Kant, *Critique of Pure Reason*, A 118, p. 143.
15. Heidegger, *Kant and the Problem of Metaphysics*, p. 180.
16. Kant, *Critique of Pure Reason*, A 142, B 181, p. 183.
17. See Nabert, "L'Expérience interne," pp. 254–56.

external intuitions. Thus the inventory of schemata presupposes the table of categories, and their definition appeals to the object which will be given to external perception. The representation of time not only arises from the prompting of external perceptions but also depends on the particular content which it represents. It will be argued that, according to the Transcendental Aesthetic of the first *Critique*, time involves a dimension which is unique to it and which owes nothing to space, namely, succession. For Kant claims that different periods of time are successive and not simultaneous, whereas different stretches of space are not successive but simultaneous. Yet this is to imply that time is specified only in relation to space. We should add that the irreversibility characteristic of temporal succession and the idea of a temporal order appear only in the light of causality. As Nabert also shows, the validity of causality, in turn, can be demonstrated only through phenomena in space—which means only through the irreversibility of movement. In sum, time has fewer intuitive properties than space. This is why temporal relationships can and must be expressed by an external intuition. And it is for the very reason that it can be illustrated by space that time is, in Kant's eyes, an intuition. From this follows that spatialization of time through which time is detached from the subject. Lived time then becomes, through the intermediary of space, a known and measurable time—a time which we can control. Instead of a flux which *we are,* it is a time which *we have.* And it is also a time which *has us,* since, by knowing ourselves as objects, we inscribe ourselves within this time and take our place among its events.

The converse is also true. Space cannot be determined outside of time. A straight line is the figurative representation of time, but the line must be drawn, and it can be drawn only successively. In the same way, coexistence in space can be revealed only to a look capable of simultaneity. Our looking at a group of objects implies that we are looking at all of them in a single moment. Finally, like a traveler who appreciates what distance can mean, we measure space with time. Hence space is in turn a symbol of time, just as, a moment ago, time was a symbol of space. Any voyage through space—including the drawing of a straight line—leads us back to ourselves and to the act of a successive synthesis through which self-consciousness is established. Space can be ordered only according to schemata, that is, by acts, such as counting, in which a subject engages itself and mimics, in time, determinations in space. Without that primary synthesis which constitutes time, we would think nothing, because there would be no one to think. Similarly, without the spreading out of space as the locus of objects, we would also think nothing, since there would be nothing to think. Thus there is a symmetry between the spatialization of time and the temporalization of space, a symmetry which affects the destiny of knowledge. We know only space, which is the principle of all objectivity, but we know only *according to* time, that is, only so long as we are actually engaged in knowing and attain knowledge in a given period of time. The intuition of space is a successive act, and space must be run through in an internal movement. Furthermore, knowing annexes the other to ourselves and thus temporalizes it. Space is animated by time. Thus space becomes the locus of external movements, since movement establishes the liaison between the time which we are and the space which we are not.

In fact, this solidarity of space and time is expressed best in the very notion of movement. "Considered as the describing of a space [as opposed to the movement of an object belonging to the domain of empirical science], motion is a pure act of the successive synthesis of the manifold in outer intuition in general by means of the productive imagination, and belongs not only to geometry, but even to transcendental philosophy." [18] This means that: (1) space is described on the basis of time; and (2) this connection is established in the interior of an object. Consequently, movement can be apprehended in the world only because movement is first of all the act of a subject who manifests himself by positing the possibility of a world. The subject-object relationship is prefigured, at the very core of the subject, by the relation of time to space. And movement, which exists in the subject before appearing in the object, expresses this relation in terms of the object itself.

Thus the solidarity of temporality and spatiality in the subject leads us to comprehend how, in the object, time is spatialized and space is temporalized. This reciprocal relation appears most clearly in the aesthetic object. But reflection should then proceed in an opposite direction. Reflection should start from the objective time and space which have been built up in the work thanks to structural schemata, through the spatialization of time and the temporalization of space, and from there discover the aesthetic object's own time and space. Space

18. Kant, *Critique of Pure Reason,* B 155, p. 167 n.

and time in this latter sense are internal to the object and assumed by it. It is they that make it a quasi subject capable of a world which it expresses.

We shall now undertake such a course of reflection by considering the musical and the pictorial work. This reflection is not central to our discussion but nonetheless finds a natural place in it. In seeking the structure of the work and particularly of sensuous matter (which is the element in the work that lends itself best to analysis), we are led to consider and confirm the solidarity of temporal and spatial determinations. By the same token, we shall understand that the same structural categories—namely, harmony, rhythm, and melody—can be discovered in all art. It is for this reason that the digression which we have just taken may be of some value.

8 / The Musical Work

MUSIC PROVIDES US with an example of an art that is nonrepresentational and of an essentially temporal nature. Yet, as we shall see in considering the role of the sensuous in music, music does contain something like a "subject"—a subject which neither represents nor imitates reality. We shall see further that, since space is called upon by musical time to elaborate the matter of sound, it is an integral part of the musical work and an essential dimension of its being.

[I] HARMONY

FIRST, how does the musical work present itself to us? It is presented as a discourse in sound, one which is not meant to say something, to convey an explicit signification, but simply to exist as the interplay of sounds. If there is a subject, as in program symphonies or in compositions with specific titles, it is not readily apparent. What *is* apparent is the gradual unfolding of the sensuous—the sensuous being both the means and the end of the work, its matter and its final result. Yet undoubtedly, the very notion of the sensuous or perceptible in music is equivocal, as the dispute between Boris de Schloezer and Robert Francès demonstrates. De Schloezer upholds an intellectualist theory concerning the perception of the musical object. This theory is based on an ontological thesis which holds that the unity of the musical object, as conceived by the

[249]

composer, is not dependent on perception but resides in the non-temporal being of an intellectual meaning. "The work exists outside time and as an absolute unity, an undivided whole." [1] Francès, on the other hand, cites experimental research to support the theory of form suggested by Merleau-Ponty's interpretation of the notion of Gestalt. According to this theory, the form of the object is subordinate to the "constitution of an object-subject totality having its own laws." [2] Francès writes:

> Music is not concerned with constructing systems of elementary objective relationships; it seeks to construct systems of forms dominated by tendencies—such as the essential polarity of certain moments, a burst of unexpected melody, a particular contrapuntal figure—never conceived in objective terms but always with constant reference to the universe of perceived structures.[3]

De Schloezer responds by observing that music is at once "meaning *and* form." He points out, quite correctly, that "the difficulty here lies in the fact that to maintain such a thesis, Francès must place himself in the position of the listener and thus neglect the composer. . . . The musician's relationship to the music he creates is quite different from that of a listener to what he hears." [4] We can clarify this ambiguity by distinguishing between the work as produced by the composer and the same work as perceived by the listener. We must agree with Francès that sound is intended for the ear, and that perception actualizes sound. The ear is the judge not only of the attractiveness of the sound but of its particular qualities, which it relays to the physicist. And the composer who writes with a listener in mind does so by consulting his own ear, not a treatise on acoustics. However, to write music at all is to presuppose a being of sound prior to perception, to acknowledge the reality of a sonorous matter having sufficient consistency and flexibility for the composer to produce the sounds himself. It is this fabricated character of sounds which justifies objective analysis by the musical theorist, who seeks to define the sound without questioning its perceived being, in contrast with the physicist, who separates sound from its relation to perception.

1. Boris de Schloezer, *Introduction à J. S. Bach* (Paris: Gallimard, 1947), p. 251.
2. Robert Francès, "La Structure en musique," *Les Temps modernes,* XLIII (October, 1948), 730.
3. *Ibid.*
4. Boris de Schloezer, "Sens, forme et structure en musique," *Les Temps modernes,* XLIII (May, 1949), 939.

In other words, it could be argued that sound is perceived only within the field of perception as opened up by the subject-object dyad. Sound is apparent first to the ear, then to the rest of the body. Thus its signification would be primarily motoric. This is verified by the Abraham experiments to which Francès refers, as well as by the earlier Werner studies: "The sound interval is the final form taken by a tension felt by the entire body."[5] All this brings us back to the fact that we are disturbed and moved by the harmony of the music, and even more so by its rhythm—i.e., the organization of movement within us which corresponds to sound or, more precisely, the means by which sound is constituted as sound in us. But the function of being a perceived object cannot be fully assumed by the aesthetic object unless the artist is aware of this necessity and isolates, determines, and rationalizes his material. For us, musical sound is simply perceived. But for the artist, it must first of all be produced. The artist enacts a dialectic of the perceived and the produced, of the spontaneous and the formalized. The objective nature of sound implies a technical precondition. There must be an instrument, for example, the piano (which is to the musician what oil paint is to a painter, in that both media allow for broad possibilities of expression).[6] There is an intellectual condition implied also, which is both historical and cultural—the rational explanation of sound, the "theory of music."

The cultural reality of the matter of sound is similar to that of a language. It possesses the same consistency and cohesion. The writer calls on language, that is, on a system of words which, because they have meaning, are defined by each other and are brought together in a sentence. Since the words have their own sound structure, they attract or repel one another according to rigorous demands of signification. In the same way, the musician has to do with a codified system of sounds perpetuated by a long-standing and prestigious tradition, in which the varying possibilities of timbres are themselves determined by the technique of the instrument or, as in vocal polyphony, by as many vocal possibilities as the performers

5. Heinz Werner, *Ueber die Auspragüng von Tongestalten*, cited by Merleau-Ponty in *Phenomenology of Perception*, trans. C. Smith (New York: Humanities Press, 1962), p. 211.
6. The dialectic of the perceived and the reflected is found in playing the piano. The body plays with a natural spontaneity and invention. Yet there is also an element of thought present which exercises control over the playing—but a kind of thought which is almost completely immanent in the body.

offer. A playwright too must always bear in mind the interpreter for whom he is writing, both in designating the role and in choosing his vocabulary. Therefore, just as a writer must first be familiar with his language, the composer must understand musical notation and, when necessary, instrumentation. And what of the untrained musician, one who has not studied counterpoint? We would maintain that such a person, by playing an instrument or familiarizing himself with musical repertoire, has indeed acquired a practical knowledge and a spontaneous command of musical language similar to the command and knowledge of writers who have forgotten or neglected the rules of grammar and rhetoric. Within this milieu of sound, each sound is a note, an element of the whole, and is assigned a certain function as a degree in the scale, regardless of which key the scale is in. The note exercises certain powers of attraction or repulsion toward the other notes and assumes meaning only by functioning in the whole. Yet the artist can assign it a function, because systematic musical rules exist which he may or may not follow himself.

Obviously, such a system lacks the internal logic of a rational construction, and it is difficult to distinguish the necessary elements from the contingent ones or, better, the natural ones from the artificial ones. The ways in which the raw material of musical sound has been treated in the course of Western civilization have often been inadequately described in musical treatises, because the end is presupposed from the beginning. Formally speaking, music owes much to a kind of rational thinking, which is inspired by a desire to order and to codify and sometimes appeals to principles of physics, particularly in the case of the tempered scale. Still, the harmonic system is not constructed with the premeditated rigor of the rules of Esperanto but, rather, with a desire to retain the suppleness and spontaneity of a living language, where reflection is preceded by usage or invented to justify it. The ear—educated through repeated contact with musical works—must make the final judgment, so that rational thought must submit to aesthetic judgment. Etienne Souriau has emphasized this point in his critique of Becquerel's thesis, which postulates "an accord between the artistic function of pure sounds and the mathematics of vibratory frequencies which produce them."[7] For the

7. Etienne Souriau, *La Correspondance des arts* (Paris: Flammarion, 1947), p. 228.

term "natural" may be interpreted in two different ways, according to whether the norm is perception or physics. Ambiguity is always possible when the laws of a system of sounds are invoked, depending on whether its laws are sanctioned by the ear or by acoustic measure. Since acoustics is usually invoked post facto to verify the spontaneous judgment of the ear, the true dichotomy is between the natural and the artificial, between a procedure which relies on tradition and thereby perception and a procedure which, without necessarily being revolutionary, still wants to subject the system of musical sound to rational elaboration. This is a legitimate demand in the Western world, where, as de Schloezer observes, the course of music is not so closely linked with the structure of instruments as in Eastern culture.

This opposition, springing from the dialectic of the in-itself and the for-itself, reappears in all our analyses of the aesthetic object and manifests itself throughout the de Schloezer-Francès debates. Gisèle Brelet expresses the terms of the opposition in a slightly different way, namely, by juxtaposing empiricism and formalism. According to her, Hindemith, as an empiricist, must denounce what is arbitrary and artificial in the classic tonal system, a system which defines chromaticism as the introduction of foreign chords into the established tonality and bases its harmonic progression on the "natural structure" of different chords or, better, on the harmonic value of the intervals involved and on the position in the scale of the root of the chord. In contrast, Schönberg, as a formalist, holds that "the natural forms immanent in the matter of sound should serve as the point of departure for a generalization which frees them from the auditory expression which had initially revealed them." [8] Superimposed thirds, fundamental to classical harmony, become superimposed fourths in atonal harmony. The perfect triad C-E-G becomes C-F-B, a "synthetic chord which differs considerably from the original scale harmonies," as Schönberg admits.[9] Brelet also shows that in this dialectic between content and form—between sound as perceived and constructed, and by extension, between the aesthetic object as perceived and the work as created—the terms "formal" and "empirical" are interdependent. Brelet observes that Hindemith's empiricism is based on the natural forms apparent in the sonority: "[This

8. Gisèle Brelet, *Esthétique et création musicale* (Paris: Presses Universitaires de France, 1947), p. 59.
9. *Ibid.*, p. 60.

empiricism] remans an aesthetic and predetermined conception of sonorous facts and not a simple tabulation of these facts." [10] On the other hand, Schönberg "creates original auditory facts: each new form brings with it new revelations of the sensuous in sound . . . and this is its final justification; for the constant transformation of sounds, through the continual imposition of new forms, is one of the principal aims of music." [11]

We can say, then, that harmony defines a certain milieu of sound whose imperious reality is acknowledged by the ear and perpetuated by tradition. Great musical works constantly explore and enlarge this milieu. These works cannot exist as works except in relation to this milieu. From within such a milieu, the musician selects his field of action, which, in classical composition, would be a mode or key—a complete tonal scheme—unless, as in the case of the fugue, the formal pattern and thus the key of each statement of the subject are already predetermined. Even an innovative or revolutionary composer is governed by rules as rigid as those he denies, insofar as the new rules define a space which must be maintained in order to prevent music from disintegrating into noise. In analyzing classical music, we can easily identify what Vincent d'Indy terms a harmonic schema, that is, the tonal basis of the entire work. D'Indy himself bases much of his musical analysis, particularly of Beethoven, on this principle. But he cautions us that "the music we see must not be confused with what we are hearing, for hearing alone constitutes musical experience." [12] Music is first of all duration and movement, melody and rhythm. Harmony has no meaning unless we continue beyond the simple study and classification of chords to consider them "genetically." [13] To harmonize, in the strict sense of the term, is to construct a chord, to define the role of the scale tone in relation to a certain tonal field which is itself taken from the milieu of sound. Whether the chord expresses stability, as a major chord does, or whether it conveys an uncertain transitory effect, as does a seventh chord, its role is always defined in terms of possible movement. The material of music is defined by the

10. *Ibid.,* p. 51.
11. *Ibid.,* p. 62.
12. Vincent d'Indy, *Cours de composition musicale,* 4 vols. (Paris: Durand et fils, 1909), II, 163.
13. "Chords are too often considered the aim in writing on music, when they should be treated as the means" (*ibid.,* I, 117). This statement contains an implicit criticism of Schönberg's formalism.

constitution of a field of tonality which serves as a theater of future adventure. Thus harmony, far from being a static state, supports the movement of melody.[14] Through the dynamism of perception, melody sets the tonality in motion. The best example of this occurs in the late works of Franck, especially his D Minor Symphony, in which there occurs "a kind of battle of tonalities, with the music's acting as a stage on which thematic characters move savagely between two poles or between two opposing powers, warring among themselves until one is ultimately defeated."[15]

As music has become increasingly complex—progressing from constant modulation either to final rejection of a tonal center or to retention of a tonal center (though a polytonal one, as in Stravinsky's case)—harmonic analysis has been rendered practically impossible. Still, the fact remains that a note must always be conceived in relation to other notes, whether the scale is a five-tone or twelve-tone one. As a field for his work, the musician selects a certain region of the field of sound. In this respect, we can consider the harmonic schema as the tonal basis for the musical work. This harmonic schema is readily apparent when major and minor keys are juxtaposed, yet it may pass unnoticed when we consider the work as a whole. It then seems less important, of a secondary nature. Like the Kantian schema of quality—and harmony is the quality of sound—the harmonic schema is a certain way of filling the field of sound. This schema awakens in the listener an activity which Kant would attribute to imagination, an activity that does not mechanically tabulate but seizes the harmony as it presents itself. Harmony makes sound into a graspable reality—as opposed to noise, which startles us initially but fails to hold our attention. At this point, the intellectual sense of harmony merges with the ordinary sense of the term. All music is harmonious, because harmony is the primary condition of musical being. Harmony defines sound as sound, as well as the work itself as the totality of sounds. Just as in Platonic justice, where man is man and a city a city, harmony renders the musical object an authentic

14. In addition, harmony influences the destiny of the melody. De Schloezer has shown this, using Bach chorales as examples in which the same melody is harmonized in two different ways (*Introduction*, p. 187). The milieu of sound defined by harmony is never indifferent to the melody unfolding within it. The work is an interlocking totality to those who can perceive it as such.

15. D'Indy, *Cours*, II, 161.

object which can be grasped as such, though additional schemata must be introduced if the musical object is to be seized fully.

An important thesis is thus confirmed. The artist, in working with his raw material to create his work, presupposes perception. Moreover, all the structural elements in the work invite this perception, which serves in turn to dissolve these elements in their separateness. Further, harmonic analysis reveals the relation of music to space. We have mentioned the milieu of sound. Harmony in a musical work, as de Schloezer has noted, is the relationship of the composition to the milieu in which it is realized, and "harmonic analysis consists in transferring this process to an active state by making becoming into being, and time into space." [16] This ideal space, defined by specifiable intervals and considered apart from the duration and intensity of sounds, is a space presupposed by all the activity of *Homo faber*. This space renders musical reality accessible and manipulable. Although not constituting this reality, the space in question makes its mastery possible. But this space is still more than just an artificial language, and the term "milieu of sound" is more than a metaphor. Indicated here is a spatiality which is constitutive of musical being. Whatever in this being is objective, constructed, and commanding for perception finds its natural expression in spatial terms. We could say that music calls forth space in order to manifest to what extent it is irreducible to the subjectively perceived.

[II] RHYTHM

THE ABOVE OBSERVATIONS also apply to rhythm. On the one hand, rhythm is a characteristic of the total work and can be thus perceived. It denotes the very movement which animates the work. As such, rhythm is undefinable and cannot be apprehended separately from the work—although it may be felt and imitated by the body, as when one taps his foot in time with the music. Even in this latter case, however, rhythm is perceived as incorporated into and blended with the work. As de Schloezer has pointed out, this is why pitch and timbre variations affect rhythm in the same way as a change in time or

16. De Schloezer, *Introduction*, p. 176.

stress would. This means that rhythm participates in the total musical work, acting as its heartbeat or, better, as the secret law of its internal development. Consequently, rhythm is not reducible to the algorithm of a succession.[17] On the other hand, this very movement of the work must be premeditated and constructed. It is by analyzing the work that we can discover just how it was composed. This composition again implies the necessary presence of space. Just as establishing a milieu of sound allows us to reduce the melodic line to a series of articulated points of varying pitch, establishing a rhythmic milieu allows us to reduce the style of a given duration to a schema of spatial progression. This analogy did not occur to de Schloezer, who defines rhythm as "the translation of form into the terms of becoming." He believes that the temporalization which makes the rhythm of the work apparent is already a translation or a reduction. However, he does not realize that the true reduction effected by critical observation is itself a spatialization. He holds that the musical object transcends time, and that to express this object in terms of becoming is to alter it. But it seems to us that, even if we grant the nontemporality of the musical object, the becoming in terms of which this object expresses itself rhythmically must be spatialized to be analyzed. Moreover, we cannot agree that the immanent unity of the musical work is static and that our examination is what confers dynamism on it. The self-movement of the work is, rather, genuinely part of its being, and this movement is manifested in its rhythm.

De Schloezer distinguishes between two kinds of rhythm—external rhythm, which he sometimes unfortunately calls "natural," and organic rhythm. External rhythm is measurable or, rather, it is a principle of measurement which, by means of a schema, permits us to scan the movement and to classify the multiplicity of sounds. This can be done only by abstracting from the quality and pitch of the sounds and by reducing the work to its skeletal framework. In this connection, Mathis Lussy compares rhythm to a drawing which melody and harmony embellish with color, just as we can invent a colorful melody to accompany the rhythmic noise of a train. But we must

17. Therefore rhythm, like melody, is a unified whole. Polyrhythm exists only upon analysis—an analysis which isolates the different rhythms occurring in the different voices. To emphasize, as Bartok sometimes does, polyphony by the use of polymetrics—which separates the accents of each rhythm—seems to us to ignore the primary rhythmic unity of the musical work.

remember that rhythm as an isolated element has no more reality than a sketch in relation to an actual painting. It is only one moment in the composition of the work. It can become a useful tool in the analysis of the work but can never be distinct from the total work. (This is why the choice of a system of rhythmical analysis is ultimately arbitrary. Musical notation, like the precise determination of musical space, derives from a long tradition, although it is noticeably absent from Gregorian chants and many modern compositions.) Any analysis which attempts to discover the rhythmic schema of a musical work must progressively complicate the elementary pattern which establishes the beat, until the singular movement of the musical object as a whole is discovered—that is, until external rhythm merges with organic rhythm to express the very essence of this object, although in its initial form external rhythm is only a schematic means of access. For these are the two functions of rhythm: (1) as a schema, it allows perception to obtain a basic grasp of the work; and (2) when perception seizes the aesthetic object, rhythm espouses and expresses the very being of this object.

How does the rhythmic schema become more complicated and gradually charged with positive determinations, merging more closely with the actual rhythm of the work? In its elementary form, the schema is first a formal principle of measurement. Time is divided into equal parts, beginning with a simple yet multipliable unit, as in Gregorian or Greek music. Or the procedure may be reversed and the unit itself subdivided, as is often done today. Such measurement structures the relations of duration. For in music we always have to do with duration, with a gradual flowing, which one renders perceptible by means of rhythmic markers. And thus a spatial element inevitably enters. For Kant, succession is already a second determination of time qua form, and it is defined in terms of formal intuition. In order for us to apprehend succession, it must be rhythmical. This does not mean that it is altered or changed—that we reconstitute the successive by adding instants together—but that we associate ourselves with the flowing of duration. Counting, beating time, and marking bar lines are naïve ways of participating in the rhythm and absorbing it. As soon as succession is involved, it must be organized by the regular return of temporal units. Isochronism is the elementary principle of rhythm. Music conforms scrupulously to it, except for an occasional use of the agogic accent which some specialists see as the basis for the French verse line. Thus the primary rhythmic schema introduces the notion of number into our considerations.

But number as such does not constitute rhythm. Rhythm implies not only a stretch of time—the measure—which is divided into units but the possibility of identifying equal intervals between the units and of referring to their repetition. The ear demands this, just as the eye needs the bar line in music or the indented line in poetry. A series of equally spaced points is not rhythm, either, but is only the basis for a sinusoidal curve from which we derive maximums and minimums. Thus is established the necessity of the rhythmic ictus or stress. The measure is defined and experienced through the duration which separates each downbeat. And the rhythmic schema then takes on a second aspect. The measure is an indication not only of the proportionate length of duration but of the alternation of accents. Adding intensity to quantity not only clarifies quantity, it brings out a new factor, a primary determination of the musical object. While the measurement of time in terms of measure and beat gives us an external indication of this object in a way that could be applied to any object (even though the absolute lapse of time of the components of the measure, indicated by the metronome, depends on the tempo of the piece and acts as the first introduction to the work), the accents fall specifically on sounds, just as they bear on words in prose and in so doing create the allure of the particular word. In other words, measurement encroaches on the aesthetic object, which in turn lends itself to being measured. Moving from extensive to intensive quantity, one appeals to the object as capable of possessing a kind of quality which is governed by laws of extensive quantity. Henceforth, the rhythmic schema takes on its full meaning, and the specific kind of rhythm can then be discerned—as a ternary rhythm (3/4) is distinguished from a binary rhythm (2/4). Numerous musical terms are used to refer to the distribution of accents. Anacrusis and masculine and feminine endings are determined by the relation of a given note to the downbeat of a measure. In the same way, syncopation contrasts metric accent with strictly rhythmic accent. Obviously, rhythm changes completely for us once harmony is added to it. Still, even major chords and strong resolutions are not wholly significant harmonically unless they are prepared by the beat. Harmony clarifies the beat but also presupposes it.

Building on this fundamental rhythmic schema, we can construct other schemata which bring us even closer to the rhythm of the work. Given only a time signature of 2/4 or 9/8 or a metronome marking of M = 100, we do not know a great deal about the tempo of a musical work. But seeing the notation "waltz," "mazurka," or "minuet," we know at once that the composer has confined himself to certain standard patterns based on the three-beat measure. Just as the composition of a work is dictated by certain formal genres (*lied*, rondo, or theme and variations), its rhythm is also governed by a type, even though the same rhythm may be found in quite different compositions, including those written in free form, like Ravel's "Valse" and some of Chopin's mazurkas. Thus the rhythmic schema provides a supplementary determination of the work, even though it cannot account for the particular allure of any work.[18] It is also possible for a composer to invent a rhythmic schema of his own rather than using a traditional one. An unusual rhythm draws us deeper into the work, makes us more aware of the harmony and melody as well as the length and intensity of sounds. No analysis can grasp the rhythm of the entire work at the outset. We must proceed slowly by studying characteristic aspects of the work, as, for example, the rhythm of a subject or countersubject, of a theme or its development. The choice of these rhythmic elements is important. It should not be an arbitrary selection, for example, the first eight measures of a piece. We should choose in accordance with what we already know about the work, at least about its composition, because these elements perform an important function in the work, either as an organizing principle or as an episode in its development. To do this involves a consideration of the whole structure of the work. How could we analyze rhythm on the basis of an isolated phrase? It is not certain that the accents or the rhythmic figures will coincide with the metric accents and figures. The ear alone must judge. Only the ear understands the work, which is written for the ear. This is stated in the empirical rules formulated by Lussy in his discussion of values and silences. He concludes:

18. The fact that those schemata occur most often in the dance indicates to some extent their organic character. If they answer to a particular plastic movement of the body, they will awaken certain echoes in the body. We are most conscious of the movement of an object when the movement is within us. Marking time involves not only the intellect but the body as well, and together they make rhythm more immediate and more noticeable. Yet even if some isolated rhythms do retain a certain dancelike quality, they do not negate the reality of the over-all rhythm of the work. Two minuets in the same form may have two very different rhythms, if the harmonies and keys also differ.

"Finally, and most important, one must listen for the hesitation which precedes the repose of the last note of each group to see if it will be a temporary pause anticipating what is to come or whether it is indeed the final repose." [19] Relying on the ear as the sole judge may seem arbitrary, but analysis must have recourse to perception to judge the work as an aesthetic object. We may speak of musical impressions, such as a sudden rush forward, complete repose, tension, relaxation, or hollowness or fullness of a chord. Yet these are not purely subjective impressions. They designate, on the contrary, the reality of the musical object, which by its very nature is known only through impressions.

Rhythm helps to determine melody when thus considered as detached from the beat, which serves only as a means. Rhythm now characterizes the structure of the phrase and even the entire work. At least, it does so if the subject or theme is able to impose itself on the whole work, as happens in Beethoven, in whose work a major theme is often intentionally more melodic. And it is even more true if we consider the totality of rhythm in a polyphonic work whose various parts may each have a different rhythm, just as in counterpoint each part unfolds its own melody (and the rhythm of the accompaniment in the bass often opposes rather than supports the melody). By analyzing the music, we discover a polyrhythm which the trained ear would recognize immediately. Does the presence of polyrhythm mean that the over-all rhythmic structure of the work is destroyed? Not at all. The diverse rhythms constitute one unique rhythm, and the work thus safeguards its unity. Maintaining unity in variety and vice versa, making variety contribute to unity, is the secret of the art of music, just as it is the secret of all life-producing organisms. And just as one can understand such an organism at a glance, one can perceive the rhythm—the inimitable measured movement—of the musical work.

But if we depend continually on perception, what purpose is served by an analysis which reveals schemata within the work? If rhythm is ultimately the very movement or the duration of the work as perceived, why introduce a rhythmic schema to fragment this movement? In a certain sense, rhythm is opposed to rhythmic schemata in the same way that Bergsonian duration is opposed to time. The rhythm of the musical object—which is not foreign to it but depends on harmony and melody—is its

19. Mathis Lussy, *Le Rythme musical: Son origine, sa fonction et son accentuation* (Paris: Heugel, 1883), p. 55.

very being. This rhythm expresses its own duration by measuring, not the time which contains the object, but the time which it *is*, the internal becoming which constitutes it. The musical object imposes its own tempo and organizes its own future development rather than submitting to it. In comparison with this internal and singular time which the musical object unfolds according to its own logic, the rhythmic schema, at least in its elementary form, seems to indicate an objective and artificial rhythm, unrelated to the melody. Nevertheless, the distinction between rhythm and the rhythmic schema diminishes as soon as the schema—while retaining its formal character—is swallowed up in the qualitative structure of the work. The schema is never completely external to the musical object's living duration. The schema participates in objective time insofar as it is a numerical order based on the infinite divisibility of a spatialized matter; but it participates in musical duration to the degree that it has a tempo, a unity defined in absolute value. It participates even more when it points to the qualitative points of reference borrowed from the very body of the work, that is, to the intensity of the sounds and to their harmonic signification.

In fact, the schema has a double relation to the musical object. First, it gives access to the object's duration. The movement of the work is apparent to us only if we can appreciate and follow it. Bergson suggests that we should "listen to a melody and allow ourselves to be lulled by it." [20] But this is impossible. To do so would be to allow the musical object to crumble away and dissolve. We can reach it only by participating in it through an act of imagination which is defined by the schema and which is the first stage in an act of understanding, for the rational aspect of the musical object is already present in the schema. Counting and measuring are schemata in which imagination serves as a prelude to understanding. We must attentively follow—even sometimes in a numerical way—the rhythmic pattern of the melody rather than allow ourselves to be lulled by it. In other words, we cannot apprehend duration except by means of time. We have no pure intuition of duration. The rhythmic pattern allows us to attain duration through time, because of the prerational movement of the schematizing activity awakened in us by the rhythmic schema. We imitate the movement deep within ourselves in order to grasp it in the ob-

20. Henri Bergson, *La Pensée et le mouvant* (Paris: Alcan, 1934), p. 164.

ject. We put ourselves in harmony with the imperious becoming of this object. We introduce order not by an act of understanding but by a movement that imitates number in traversing a succession. Without this element of order, we would become lost in the movement and unable to identify it properly. In this respect, the rhythmic schema objectifies and orders the movement in a very Kantian sense, for it is a question, as in Kant's schema of quantity, of "producing time in the apprehension of the object." The schema is a method—a means of finding oneself within the musical object—and the imagination presiding over the schema and one's bodily activity are closely linked in this effort. Schematizing is an art deeply hidden within the human body. Thus rhythmic schemata are necessary for the apprehension of the work. They need not be explicitly indicated, as in a musical analysis. They need only be felt. They present themselves as an invitation for us to make the necessary inner movement to place ourselves on the level of the musical object. Certain experiences show how this is so. When listening with difficulty to a complex musical work, we suddenly hear a familiar rhythmic pattern, and our whole apprehension of the work changes—we suddenly understand it. Yet, if the rhythm is too insistent, as in a march or a dance, we find ourselves too close to the musical object. It is then no longer attractively elusive and mysterious to us. It is of interest only to the body and is so heavily rhythmic that it has no real rhythm of its own. It is thus tyrannized by the beat, void of any inner life of its own. Rhythmic schemata thus serve to stimulate imagination and put us in accord with the musical object. These schemata allow us to move in step with the musical object, to participate in the same adventure.

But rhythmic schemata must belong to the work itself and not simply act as a gauge for measuring duration. In this, we have the second relation of rhythm to musical duration. Rhythmic schemata penetrate the musical object. We have seen that, in their more complicated form, they are determined by accents, the genre of the work, or its thematic structure. Yet this only indicates that the work complies with the rhythmic schemata, that its development is ordered and can be followed, and that its duration forms a composed whole. Even if we do not know anything of the actual circumstances surrounding the work's creation, we still know that rhythm is an essential moment in its construction. The choice of the rhythmic structure— a choice which we can imagine only in terms of our experience of the work—is a fundamental decision to be made by the composer.

Rhythm attests to the fact that there can be no duration which is unrelated to the universal order of time. Is this not reminiscent of Kant's view that an event is perceived only by means of the law regulating the passage of time? In the same way, musical duration is not perceived as such unless it contains, in its contours or its accents, some means of relating to objective time. Thus we reach a conclusion which is by no means novel: the aesthetic object is a composed or constructed object. No matter how much freedom it may display, this freedom must be earned and exercised in terms of a rule. No matter how supple or how singular the rhythmic structure of the musical object, this structure must be supported by schemata or else risk annihilation. These schemata are both means of access to the work and constitutive elements of the work. In this way, they contribute to the work, considered as duration, consistency and plenitude—consistency and plenitude which call forth spatiality insofar as space signifies externality to consciousness as well as the reality of the object. For this reason, music, though a temporal art, does not exclude space.

In fact, the presence of rhythmic schemata involves a spatialization of time. We become aware of this when we realize that schemata can be easily translated into spatial terms. Obviously, space could not represent time if the measurement of time did not already possess a spatial character. The relationships between duration and intensity which determine the basic schemata are not only represented in the score but can also be easily illustrated by presenting intervals (horizontal, not vertical, intervals) and accents in terms of lines or colors. In his *Essai sur les principes de la métrique anglaise*, Paul Verrier analyses diverse "varieties of rhythm" by supplementing each musical example with a spatial image in the form of a colored drawing. But do we really need this confirmation? Time can be treated only by first being spatialized. We know time cannot be measured except by movements in space. We should reiterate what we said earlier of harmony—this temporal space has been defined and explored by ancient tradition. Tradition has also determined the system of time measurement which has been used for centuries in Western music. Thus the spatialization which confers objectivity on time is also a humanization. Moreover, such temporal space is the raw material which furnishes the matter of the musical object. Just as the harmonic milieu confers on the note its proper status and value, the temporal milieu confers rhythmic character on the becoming or development of the musical work. Duration is made up of time and springs from time, even though duration is entirely different from time. The musician cannot create an object with an authentic duration except by situating it in objective time, the only kind of time on which he has a grip and the only one within which he can measure movement—a movement which, in the completed work, ultimately transcends all attempts at measurement and becomes its own standard of measurement. And it is because the aesthetic object participates in space through measurable time (by which it constitutes its duration) that it has the insistent and graspable reality of the in-itself—a reality on the basis of which it becomes perceivable. At the same time, however, the aesthetic object acts as a for-itself insofar as it is duration, that is, to the extent that it is the origin of its own becoming and is animated by its own self-propelled movement.

[III] MELODY

NEVERTHELESS, one musical element seems unreducible to space. This is melody, precisely the term which Bergson uses to describe duration. Melody should not be grouped with rhythm and harmony, as it often is. Rhythm and harmony are indeed aspects of the total work, but they are also, to the degree that they give rise to schemata, elements in the composition of the work and instruments in its creation. In contrast, melody seems to defy analysis. Melody is what appears spontaneously in the work when we yield to it, when we sit back and let it sing. Melody is the work itself qua duration. This is why it can be read only horizontally. Of course, melody is not meant to be read but to be heard. It can be read only if the reading does not turn into analysis and only by those who are able to evoke the song in the presence of the written sign.

This song, in its sovereign unfolding, is the very meaning of the musical object, a meaning that cannot be apprehended except through perception of the work. But can we speak of meaning where there is no explicable signification, no represented object, and no discourse? Meaning here immediately surpasses itself toward expression. Music unveils a world invisible to the eye, undemonstrable to the intellect. Yet this world can be expressed only by music, for it is a world which vanishes once the music ends. It exists in the music insofar as it is perceived, and nowhere else. Anything we may say of it in another language is pitifully inadequate to express what music expresses. Thus we encounter, once again, the special relation of form to content in aesthetic expression. But this ineffable meaning still deserves to be called meaning, for it is what the musical object says. The musical object exists only by expressing this meaning. Meaning informs music, making it music rather than an incoherent succession of sounds. Melody is expressive, and, conversely, expression is melody. Melody is the way in which sounds are molded into a musical entity, just as the parts of a face form a physiognomy, and psychological traits a personality. Melody is the meaning of music because it is the essence of music: the meaning of music is music itself. This is why melody should be given a privileged position over rhythm or harmony. Melody incorporates these two elements and cannot be reduced to them. Rhythm based on beat and presenting quantitative relations is not, by itself alone, music. It characterizes a duration but does not produce it. Melody alone is duration. Rhythm is insufficient to engender and fully determine music. Rhythm occurs in all art as an element of composition—and in all reality bearing its own duration, that is, in living beings and perhaps in historical events. The same is true of harmony. The harmonic schema assigns each note a particular status within a static system, just as we may construct a scale of colors or of lines (harmony exists outside music just as rhythm does). But music is not just a mass of notes. Specifying the matter of a given art is not enough. Stone is used in both sculpture and architecture, and language is the basis for both prose and poetry. Only melody manifests and characterizes music.[21] Rhythm and harmony are properties of melody, and melody alone is music. Rhythmic and harmonic schemata are constituent elements in the work only to the extent that they relate to the melody and

21. D'Indy reduces harmony to a secondary position: through the principle of tonality and the cycle of fifths, it does indeed span the whole scale. But even tonality, in its active function, is itself linked to melody. D'Indy speaks of melodic modulation. Carried one step further, this concept would mean the destruction of the theory of chords and of vertical writing and thus of practically all modern music. Is such an extreme measure a necessary result of subordinating harmony to melody? It would seem that a series of successive chords could very well create a melody of their own.

express certain aspects of it. They account for the singularity of a work, not its musicality.

But if melody can claim this status, is analysis then rendered unnecessary? If melody can be apprehended only by perception, which uncovers it in the meaning of the music, must it not be constructed to be heard? And could this meaning not be further broken down into smaller elements which—like the topics of a discourse, the acts of a play, or the scenes of a ballet—are means of making it explicit, and yet not reduce it to the level of the intellect? Yes. The "themes" are to the melody what the schemata are to harmony and rhythm. They assume a double function: (1) they provide a subject, a nucleus of meaning which the melody develops; and (2) in organizing the music, they guarantee the presence of spatiality, without which the musical object (though not itself spatial) would have no objectivity and would thus risk complete disintegration.

In fact, we can always provide a melodic analysis of a musical work. D'Indy gives examples. It is noteworthy that he tends to identify melodic schemata with rhythmic schemata, thereby emphasizing what we have said of the rhythmic schema, namely, that it is deeply involved in the content of the work because music is essentially duration and rhythm is thus brought to bear on the destiny of the melody.[22] The rhythmic schema is so closely linked to the melodic schema that sometimes it is given the function of a theme, as in both Beethoven and Stravinsky.[23] Although rhythm does not encroach on the privileges of melody, there can never be a melody devoid of rhythm. Rhythm thus profits from this association with melody and becomes an element of the music's signification. (We speak, for

22. But d'Indy does distinguish between melodic and harmonic schemata. Even if "the harmonic schema is subject to the same conditions as the melodic schema," it is not so necessary as rhythm to characterize the melody. "We should note that the most beautiful musical phrases are the ones which derive their force from their own *rhythmic melody*, and therefore do not need an accompanying harmony to preserve their beauty" (*Cours*, I, 43). De Schloezer would agree with d'Indy's designation of melody as more important than harmony, but he would classify harmony as a melodic element, whereas for d'Indy a theme or musical phrase can be beautiful in itself.

23. "The theme of Stravinsky's *Sacre du printemps* seems to consist entirely in repetition. . . . The only form of development is rhythmic, and it proceeds either by elimination or by metrical amplification. On rare occasions, Beethoven experimented with rhythmic development, but he never used rhythm as the immediate matter of musical language so extensively as Stravinsky does" (André Schaeffner, *Stravinsky* [Paris: Gallimard, 1951], p. 52).

example, of the "blows of fate.") Melody also profits by becoming able to unfold in duration. However, the rhythmic schema represents a higher degree of abstraction than the melodic schema. Rhythm never constitutes the whole melody, and harmony still less so, even though the harmonic *Stimmung* may act as a theme, as it often does in impressionistic music. Furthermore, d'Indy suggests identifying the melodic schema with what he calls elsewhere the musical idea generative of the work.

It does not seem, then, that the function of the theme can be entirely abolished, in spite of the contentions of René Leibowitz and the partisans of atonality. "Athematism" has, in fact, rarely been used by any composer. Of course, impressionism in music set out to break up and disperse the traditional melodic line, but if Debussy rejected the melody and its traditional form—as straightforward, precise, and aggressive—he did so only to restore it in the form of a continual arabesque, a perpetual upsurge. What could be more melodic than the andante of the G Minor Quartet or *La Mer*? In the same way Wagner suppresses the aria but exalts the song. There can be no nonmelodic music, because all music is made up of themes (even if they may not be treated and developed in the traditional manner).

But if there is a melodic schema, which is to melody what the harmonic schema is to harmony, such a schema is unique and cannot be classified with other schemata. The musical work is not made up of schemata in the same way that it is based on themes. A theme is, as d'Indy says, a musical idea in the strict sense of the word. Not only does the theme provide the impetus for the whole musical creation (Beethoven's theory of the musical idea is similar to Valéry's belief that the first line of poetry is a gift from the gods) but it also exerts considerable influence on the psychological history of the work. In short, the theme is the *eidos* of the work, its substantial form, or, better, its formal cause. We identify a musical work by the themes we discover in it, but not at all in the same way that we would identify a poem by a particular line or stanza, or a painting by a specific detail in its design or color. The theme is given as engendering the whole musical work. The work consists in the development of various themes, either in terms of classical rules of thematic development, like the regularly reappearing refrain of a rondo, or according to rules of solemn restatement at crucial points of the musical discourse, as in Wagnerian leitmotivs (which, as one critic has observed "exclude the usual spontaneous development of musical time").[24] In any case, it is the presence of themes which etches the physiognomy of the musical work.[25] Moreover, the dialogue between two or more themes confers on the work's expression a dialectical aspect. The character and efficacy of these themes may be so strong, that, instead of merely succeeding each other in the foreground of the work, they form a single resultant melody, as when they are evoked together in counterpoint. Still, they require that we hear and recognize them as distinct from each other. Their distinctness no more weakens the unity of the work than the presence of two dancers destroys the unity of a *pas de deux* in ballet. In brief, the theme, the generative principle of the melody, is also the main character of the work, like the hero whose tragic destiny imprints itself on the events of the drama or epic. The rhythmic and harmonic schemata are also generative principles of the musical work, but only insofar as the work is considered as a composition. If the work is considered a signifying unity or as pure becoming, these schemata tend to become muted, as both rhythm and harmony blend with melody, becoming inseparable from it. The melodic schema, however, does not fade away at all. It participates in the final triumph of the melody which it produced and which it continues to animate. For the melodic schema is the generative principle of the work, insofar as the work is organized into a musical unity and to the extent that it thus constitutes a signifying object. It is, in fact, the schema of meaning, the elementary expression of what the work is saying, its subject (in the sense that we would speak of a "subject" of a fugue). We can therefore affirm that the theme is not related to the melody as a part relates to a whole.

Finally, because the schema is both meaning and duration, the signifying aspect of melodic temporality is assured. Gisèle

24. Souvitchinsky, "La Notion de temps et la musique," *La Revue musicale*, no. 191 (May, 1939), p. 315.

25. Can an aesthetically inferior musical phrase function as a theme? Often a popular song or earlier classical work becomes the basis for a new composition. Sometimes, too, the main theme of a particular work seems insignificant because of its brevity. Franck's cyclical D Minor Symphony is based on a three-note theme, the Wagnerian leitmotiv is only four or five notes. Thus the musician is creating something from nothing, and the development shows us how he does this; hence its importance to the work as a whole. However, it is always possible for a well-constructed theme to undergo a very mediocre development. The difference is that between inspiration and mechanical composition. Although the theme does not wholly determine the quality of a given work, it does influence its general character. The theme's aesthetic quality or lack of it is therefore important to assess.

Brelet declares that the type of development which is inspired by the theme is an "unfolding in time," as the term "development" indicates.[26] But what seems to us even more important is that the future implied in the theme is a future of meaning. The theme is pregnant with possibilities for opening up time, and these may be said to be logical possibilities as explicable as harmony itself.[27] Thus meaning and time are inseparable in musical reality, as they already are within the melodic schema. Time manifests meaning only because meaning calls for time. This is why we cannot agree with de Schloezer that the musical object is nontemporal. Nor is it pure duration. On the one hand, duration must be organized (and this is the function of rhythm, as we have seen). On the other hand, duration is meaningful; it is not an unpredictable adventure but a necessary future.

All of which brings us once again to the necessity of the theme. Brelet has clearly shown that without a theme, duration would dissolve into nothing, and that a becoming which refuses form is no longer a becoming at all. In Romantic music, however, we see manifested "the contradiction at the heart of Bergsonian duration, a duration which cannot be posited either by intelligence or without it." [28] What gives consistency to the duration by organizing it is not merely the rhythmic or harmonic schema but the theme understood as meaning. The melodic schema allows access to the work insofar as the work is a duration which is not amorphous and unintelligible but meaningful.

Yet if the melody, in which all music fulfills itself, is made up of melodic shemata, can it still be spatialized through the intervention of these schemata, as rhythm and harmony were? The uniqueness of the melodic schema requires a qualified answer. To the extent that the schema is melodic, it is itself duration and it supports the melody qua duration. In this re-

26. All of which still does not, in our judgment, justify a more controversial claim bearing on the psychology of creation, namely, that musical time, the length of time required to execute a work, is identical to the duration subjectively experienced by the composer at the time of writing it and that "the creator imprints on the development the reality of his own intimate sense of duration" (Brelet, *Esthétique*, p. 78). Brelet does avoid, however, the subjectivism to which such a position could lead by stating that "lived experience is possible only through form" and that duration must be constructed (*ibid.*, p. 82).

27. This is why the theme can be broken down into leitmotivs which announce the development. This fragmented character of the theme identifies it not only as having duration but as possessing intelligibility.

28. Brelet, *Esthétique*, p. 102.

spect, it cannot be the instrument of spatialization. The harmonic and rhythmic elements associated with the melodic schema dissolve in it. But insofar as the schema is truly a schema, it introduces, if not a quantitative element of composition, at least a logical element of organization which is foreign to duration, because it constitutes, at the very heart of duration, an atom of duration. In its atomic character, it permits us a certain orientation within the duration of the work, and, because it can be scanned, a spatial element is thereby introduced. The schema can only confer its plenitude on the melodic duration by filling a space. Thus melody fills the concert hall and penetrates us through and through. We must not assume that this metaphor is based on a scientific theory concerning the displacement of sound waves. Music is not made up of waves, although it does possess its own volume, as Bergson and others have observed. Being voluminous, music can be said to occupy the concert hall. It is essential that anything spatial be experienced in the depths of the imagination, as Kant would say. This is why we can simultaneously follow both the melodic development of the work and its accompanying harmonic and rhythmic movement. One's body is always involved here. In recognizing themes and in imitating them, as in counting rhythm and sensing harmony, it is the body which orders duration and unites with it. Thus the schema accomplishes its goal in and through the body. The body also delineates space. It cannot function as an intermediary between *cogito* and world except by furnishing the space for this world to take shape. Obviously, it is questionable whether we can speak of spatialization where space is not represented and intended by intelligence, but only experienced on the ambiguous and obscure plane of imagination—the plane on which the aesthetic attitude places us. Let us speak then of an implicit spatialization. We must acknowledge its presence as a basis for explicit spatialization, which occurs either when we imagine a spatial counterpart to the musical object or when we undertake a systematic analysis of the work. We must also be aware that what the scientific attitude effects is rooted in what the aesthetic attitude experiences and that, for example, the schemata disclosed in analysis are first experienced as incitations for the body and as suggestions for the imagination. How else could we understand that the musical object can become accessible to us? It has objectivity only insofar as it is composed and organized and thus only insofar as it lends itself to spatialization.

Clearly, we are not concerned with a translation of the musical into the spatial but rather with the spatiality inherent in musical temporality, that is, in a duration which is itself constructed. This spatiality, experienced by the body upon hearing the music, cannot be given a definite form or measured. No spatial representation intrudes on or alters the purity of the music. But analogies and correspondences are at least possible between musical and plastic arts, based on the secret affinity between the temporal and the spatial. The often mentioned similarity between music and architecture is a case in point. In this instance, the schema plays its most exacting role. It distributes the object that it organizes according to proportions possessing monumental solidity. Music evokes architecture, not because of its material character but because architecture occupies space more imperiously than any other art and assures the triumph of order. Architecture fills space by organizing it in compliance with secret and invisible laws. It is this organizational nucleus, resulting from the efficacy of a theme, which is the common element in music and architecture. It is the organization of musical duration which is translated into the organization of architectural space. Nevertheless, duration as such suggests an arabesque shape, because, as Kant noted, a straight line allows us to represent time by spatializing it. What the arabesque adds to the straight line is, perhaps, the signifying character of musical duration, which is itself constituted by an unfolding of meaning. Ordered by a particular linear theme, the arabesque manifests a power of signification. Perhaps the arabesque figure, in contrast to the straight line, closes the distance between duration and time—not only because it can possess meaning but also because it is organic and continuous. To speak, as Debussy does, of melodic arabesques is to spatialize duration but nevertheless not to betray it. Yet whether we analogize music to architecture or the arabesque—depending on whether we consider the organization or the duration of the musical object—is such spatialization really anything more than metaphor? We would find it difficult to designate a particular monument or decorative line in architecture which has its precise counterpart in a given work of music. We may evoke these spatial objects as illustrations of the order and course of temporal development, but they are not definitive. Evoking them merely has a suggestive value which is difficult to resist.

Nevertheless, there have been attempts to clarify these analogies between the arts. Souriau's theory, the most significant to date, attempts to "discover a common essence [between different arts] which is located beyond the difference between time and space." [29] It is outside our present scope to discuss this theory, however intriguing it is. We shall simply observe that correspondences can be established either at the level of the aesthetic object's material organization or at the level of expression. In the first case, the correspondence is based on a function of illustration, as in the instance of the melodic arabesque which Souriau constructs from mathematical symbols that "reproduce the exact structural properties (both physical and aesthetic) of the musical groupings." In the second case, the correspondence is an analogy, as when Souriau discusses music and colors and analyzes quite convincingly the "chord" formed by the colors in a Veronese painting. We can pass, as in language, from pictorial tonality to musical tonality if the colors and notes are understood in terms of their "aesthetic function" rather than of their physical nature. This function, it seems to us, is inseparable from the effect which colors and notes produce, that is, from their psychological signification and, consequently, from their expression.

But at the root of these correspondences lies the phenomenological solidarity of time and space. We shall now consider painting, a spatial art, in an effort to see how this solidarity is manifested by a temporalization of space which is symmetrical with the spatialization of duration. [30]

29. Souriau, *La Correspondance des arts*, p. 212.
30. Most of the problems which we have considered in this chapter and in certain previous chapters are treated in the noteworthy book of Jeanne Vial, *L'Etre musical* (Neuchâtel: La Baconnière, 1952). We regret that we did not know of this book early enough to take account of it in our own discussion.

9 / The Pictorial Work

OUR REFLECTION ON PAINTING can begin with a reflection on the temporality of pictorial space. Once that notion has been clarified, an analysis of painting can commence and follow the same route as that of music. By posing this first question, furthermore, we are at the same time beginning our consideration of a second question which was the original motive of our examination, that is, the question of the "subject." For, at first sight, painting is defined, and is contrasted with music, in terms of two characteristics—the importance of the represented object and the preeminence of spatiality. In addition, these characteristics are linked together. The problems of space originate in a concern for representation, and the articulation of a concrete space within the two-dimensional space of the canvas is imposed by a representation which wishes to be faithful to its object. Whenever the represented object comes to occupy the foreground, monopolizes the spectator's attention by virtue of being the exclusive bearer of expression, and masks the properly pictorial object in which content is completely immanent in form, then the temporal dimension of painting cannot appear. Our attention is involved in the domain of concepts, i.e., in the nontemporal. Strictly speaking, temporality can still be articulated as a property of the represented object, but it no longer belongs to painting itself in the sense that duration belongs to music. Thus we must determine and limit the importance of the subject in order to conceive of the possibility of an authentic pictorial temporality.

[274]

[I] THE TEMPORALIZATION OF SPACE

LET US TAKE a closer look at these matters. It is obvious that painting is an art of space. The painter draws and places his colors on the surface of the canvas for the sake of a perception which will take in the aesthetic object in a single look instead of following it in the flow of a duration. Moreover, to the extent that painting is figurative, it represents concrete space and invites us to evoke the third dimension in which the represented object resides and through which we can identify this object in order to appreciate the representational powers of the painting. This act of evocation is not difficult. Inasmuch as we were looking for a representation of an object in the painting, we go straight to the object and immediately reconstitute it. We behave in relation to it as we would before a real object—that is, in the way that we sense the missing side of a cube, the indefinite extension of a road, or the size of a man we see at a distance and whose real height we do not perceive. In Sartre's words, "I always perceive more and otherwise than I see." [1] Or, as Husserl would say, the constitution of the perceived object involves a group of empty intentions which adhere tightly to perception and, once fulfilled, complete it. Or we may say that these fulfilled intentions realize the perceived object's meaning so as to make it into a real and meaningful object. In this respect, we could almost say that the men of the Renaissance worried over imitating depth to no avail. Insofar as we look for an image of a real object in the pictorial object, we perceive it without difficulty. Indeed, the painter should react against this facility on the part of the spectator. If the painter wants to turn us away from the represented object in order to return us to the pictorial object, he must discourage and paralyze our tendency to perceive perspective and pitilessly lead us back to two dimensions. We know that modern painters who return to the grand tradition of architectural painting attempt not to disturb the integrity of the picture plane. In the same way, they renounce *trompe-l'oeil* effects and traditional perspective, which presents the illusion of depth invincibly and with little difficulty.

1. Jean-Paul Sartre, *The Psychology of Imagination*, trans. B. Frechtman (New York: Washington Square Press, 1966), p. 154.

Such a decision founds the very possibility of painting. It should be understood that this decision does not exclude all representation or all perspective. But it does reject the use of purely technical means, especially when they are merely mechanical, for guaranteeing exact representation. It subordinates exactness to expression and the represented object to the pictorial object, that is, to the painting itself as an aesthetic object. The pictorial object is still the represented object, but it is no longer considered for its own sake as if it belonged to an abstract universe of discourse. The pictorial object is the represented object insofar as it is (1) incarnated in and inseparable from design and color, and (2) the bearer of expression and of a meaning which surpasses it and is expressed in the arrangement of the pictorial matter. To remain with the represented object is to embrace an abstraction. It involves forgetting that the represented object has reality through an autonomous matter and meaning through a transcendent expression. It involves reducing the aesthetic object to an object of use, which ordinary perception by-passes in order to go straight to its signification—searching for the rational or manual hold which this signification has over the object without considering the object in itself. The work of art, in contrast, demands consideration for its own sake. Diderot's *Salons*, and in a wider sense, many critics, have suggested this theorem: the coefficient of painting in a painted work is inversely proportional to the number of commentaries inspired by its subject. It may be more correct to add that aesthetic intelligence is inversely proportional to the attention devoted to the represented object. When a picture attracts attention as a result of what it represents, all the worse for the picture. When a critic allows himself to be fascinated by what is represented and does not look beyond the picture itself, then all the worse for him as well!

What, therefore, can be the meaning of time for pictorial space, which is to represented space what the pictorial object is to the represented object (where the latter is an object which has become part of the painting without being dominant in it)? Let us treat this problem theoretically before confirming our answer by an analysis of the painted work. We can pose two questions here. What can be the meaning of time? In what form can time be manifested? Objective time concerns the work only as a historical object and does not belong to the work's substance. Its effect on our aesthetic judgment—as, for example, when we are conscious of communicating with the past through the intermediary of a long tradition—results from causes which are of no importance to the work itself or to our perception of the work. It is true that painting is bound to history in an even more precise sense. Colors exist in an evolving time as a result of their chemical structure. A good part of pictorial craft is occupied in struggling against the erosive effects of this sort of time. In this regard, the Italian and Flemish primitives had greater success than the classical artists. Veronese and Titian were more successful than da Vinci, and Rubens more than Rembrandt.[2] But the fact that the pictorial object possesses a history through its matter, that is, that it is tied to objective time, does not imply that it bears this time within itself. In contrast, the time which animates pictorial space must belong to the structure of the painting. But how does it do so? It has to enter by proxy, under the guise of movement. We know that movement can act as a delegate for time in this way. Movement is the side of space which is turned toward time, and it is the means by which space manifests time and, when necessary, measures it. But we must distinguish movement from the trajectory of movement. Movement is a temporal adventure, but it has a trajectory and thus leaves a wake that attests to its occurrence in space. To claim this is no doubt to revive the notion of trajectory which had been discredited by Bergson, for a trajectory is a representation of time. But does it also betray time? Not if we admit that time can be known only on the condition of being objectified and thus spatialized and that duration can be grasped only as the limit to this objectification. Moreover, we may consider (deferring to Bergson by linking movement with mobility) the trajectory as something that moves itself.[3] In other words, pictorial space becomes temporalized when it is given to us as a structured and oriented space in which certain privileged lines

2. It is remarkable that modern painters seem willingly indifferent to this problem. There is little doubt that some of Léger's and Matisse's washes, whose base has been diluted, will quickly yellow at the same time that the parts of the canvas which have been left colorless will brown. In many of Braque's works, as another example, the sort of grounds he uses will eat away the paint, especially the yellows and the lighter whites, applied to them.

3. Bergson himself invites us, in his *Creative Evolution* (trans. Arthur Mitchell [New York: Henry Holt, 1911]), to consider spatial trajectory as a distending of duration and the relaxation of a rhythm. The trajectory is no longer considered as an instrument of knowledge but, from the ontological viewpoint, as a formal determination of space. It is not what moves but the result of movement and, in a sense, movement's repose.

constitute trajectories that, instead of appearing to us as the inert residue of some movement, appear as filled with a movement realized in immobility.

The work, however, cannot manifest this movement which is imprisoned in the immobile unless there is a consciousness which is capable of deciphering the work and thus of breaking the spell which holds movement captive. Such a liberation requires that movement be first of all lived by the spectator. Let us remember Kant's lesson: movement in the subject precedes movement in the object. This is the meaning of the transcendental schematism, and this is why we perceive melody as a duration which has been schematized by rhythm. Time must thus intervene in the subject as well as in the object, and the subject is given priority in this respect. It is not necessary that we be conscious of time, but we must at least live it in the depths of our imagination. We are well aware that, in all visual perception, simultaneity is mediated by succession. The look wanders over the object and never comes to a complete stop. It is by this movement of the look that the movement of the object appears. Most important, it is by this movement that the object is an object for-us and penetrates our intimacy. But this quasi-imperceptible and unregulated movement hardly awakens in us the feeling of duration. Rather, we feel inert before inert things. The pictorial object becomes animated only by affecting us more deeply than this. Painting is an art which is difficult to understand and to savor. It is the most abstract of the arts because, by limiting itself to two dimensions, it rejects the means of persuasion which are employed in the other plastic arts and which move the spectator by actually setting him into motion or at least suggesting possible movements. Painting presents an object which is so external to the spectator that it often tells him nothing, as if it were not meant for him. It invites him to become immobile and orders only the movement of his eyes through the allure of contrasts and transitions. We shall return to this point later, in attempting to comprehend the spell which the painter casts.

This burgeoning movement within the spectator corresponds to a movement in the creator which finds its way into his work. In this latter case, it is a question of a movement within the object itself and immanent to its very matter. It is a movement in the lines and colors, as if lines and colors were not simply trajectories in an inert space but awakened to a life unique to them. The plastic element vibrates as if it retained something of the movement of the hand which placed it on the canvas. (This is especially the case with modern painting, which does not seek to cover with a glaze the traces of its work but allows the brush-stroke to appear and occasionally draws with it.) In a drawing which retains evidence of sketch lines, erasures, and new attempts, we feel the uncertainty and the power of the creative gesture. The decorative drawing—for example, the type of very pure drawing of which Matisse and Picasso are such masters—may efface all the gestural qualities of the work and thus seem colder (for here, too, movement engenders warmth and, conversely, warm colors suggest movement). Even this calm and clean pictorial writing harbors movement in the geometrical quality of the line which confers on it a deliberate character, whether straight or sinuous. This sort of movement has a psychical aspect, like the duration of which it is a witness. Frozen instead of unfolding in space, it seems to be caught in an inner dimension like a Mallarméan swan whose paralyzed flight returns it only to itself and awakens consciousness.[4] Thus we can understand that the movement in the work which answers to a parallel movement in the spectator and reproduces the movement of the creator is not simply the movement of the represented object. A picture which represents running figures or a storm can be inert and silent. Van Gogh's olive trees, desperately twisted in the soil by their convulsive roots, are more actively in motion than Gericault's horses. In architecture as well as in painting, the baroque is often more motionless than the Byzantine.

The fact that painting tends to represent movement is the result of what de Waroquier has called the "cinematic idea," which has continually haunted painting and is fulfilled only today with film.[5] But if the only ambition of painting were the representation of movement, the invention of the cinema—"dynamized painting," as it has been called—would leave painting without any practitioners and ready to lay down its arms.[6] In reality,

4. This is closely linked to the Bergsonian cosmology of movement and space. What is deposited in the space of the canvas or, rather, what becomes that space is the creative duration of the demiurge. What is proper to the aesthetic object is to retain and manifest something of the creative movement in its soul and even in its matter. Pictorial space is thus a degraded duration but one which remembers having been duration. The object of use, on the contrary, has definitely fallen to the level of the thing. It is mere exteriority and has no redeeming quality.

5. See the meeting of the Société d'Esthétique reported in the *Revue d'esthétique*, Vol. I (1948), no. 2.

6. In any event, film is distinguished from painting in that movement

representing movement and *being* movement are two quite different things for painting, and they can be distinguished as soon as the represented object is distinguished from the pictorial object. The truth is that, since the represented object is itself a moment of the pictorial object, one sort of movement can contaminate the other. Represented movement tends to communicate its dynamism to the aesthetic object, which not only represents it but assumes it (in the same way that semantics influences phonetics or the prose sense of a word affects its poetic value). And if the movement of the creative gesture appears more clearly to the extent that it seems to be identified and unified with an external movement (which it in turn determines), it makes a difference whether an artist chooses to represent motion or immobility, a storm or a still life. It may even seem that he must make himself tempestuous or calm and that his brush-stroke will then feel the effect. But represented movement is no more than a suggestion of the genuine movement of the work, which is not simulated or imitated but real (although, at the same time, congealed). The movement of the represented object is an arrested movement. It goes from motion to immobility. The movement of the pictorial object, in contrast, is a congealed movement which tends to unfold. It goes from immobility to motion. More exactly, immobility appears to us in this case like those halting motions which are simply phases in an over-all movement, e.g., a rest in music or a pause in the dance. Such immobility is the end of a movement and retains a certain vibrancy. We could almost say that immobility magnifies this movement by fixing and suspending it, just as a magic spell cast over Sleeping Beauty suspends a life which will eventually be taken up again as if no time had elapsed. Similarly, the plastic tableau formed for an instant by a dancer is also the apotheosis of a movement, the résumé of a movement which has just unfolded, and the call to another movement which will be pursued until a perfect cadence is achieved.

Such a movement, however, which manifests the duration of the creative gesture in the work, is not only a movement-*from*—as, for example, from the creative gesture whose impetus it retains—but a movement-*toward*, that is, toward a signification. André Lhote has grasped this point clearly. In his commentary

---

is its very matter and its means, as is the case with dance. Movement is what appears to us and serves to represent something else, telling a story as in the theater (but not in dance). Film is the novel in movement, and it is in movement because it exists in the form of images.

on Ingres's notion that movement is life, he states: "This is obviously not a case of the displacement of limbs or of some vain mimicry, but of an internal gesture, an *aspiration to the status of sign* possessed by every form as soon as the spectator is enraptured."[7] We are well aware that this aspiration to the status of sign appears only under the gaze of the spectator. No work is itself unless it appears before a consciousness, and even the becoming of music is a becoming only for its auditors. But what is essential here is that the work *appear*. Its forms and colors mean something and tend toward expression. The words of spoken language are inert because their meaning is external and indifferent. The aesthetic object, on the other hand, is meaningful by nature and seeks, in its very being, to signify. This movement toward meaning, moreover, is not unique to the plastic arts. It is common to all the arts, but it is masked in the temporal arts by the sensuous movement of the aesthetic object. In the arts fated by their materials to immobility, however, we can more easily discern, in the object's sovereign tranquillity, its impatience to be heard, the convergence and impulsion of all of its elements toward meaning. It will be argued that this is an unreal movement which can be called movement only by metaphor. So be it! This is certainly true for the inert objects for which spatiality is an irremediable destiny and whose movement can only be a displacement in space reducible to a trajectory. But genuine movement, which is a self-movement, is not simply a spatial displacement. It is also an unfolding of meaning, just as in musical movement. Or, if we wish to put it this way, it is an affirmation of the self. Movement strives toward the other and yet is constitutive of the self. At the same time that it is visible, it is also an invisible movement of the self toward itself—through which movement it participates in duration, defined as interiority. This movement of a work's elements toward meaning is a movement toward the accomplishment of the aesthetic object. It directs itself not toward a final chord [*l'accord*] of resolution, as in the temporal arts, but toward the state of accord [*l'accord*] which composes the work and presides over its unity. The use of the vanishing point is not to order perspective but to draw various lines toward it and visibly certify the unity of the design. In the same way, colors ordered around a few principal hues, as around a keynote, produce a harmonic unity in their assemblage together. We shall take account of the procedures which make possible this movement of the object toward its unity and glory.

7. André Lhote, *De la palette à l'écritoire* (Paris: Corrêa, 1946), p. 171.

We must say once again, however, that this meaning which structures and animates matter is itself duration or, if you prefer, melody. The claim will be made that meaning is nontemporal and, citing Plato and Spinoza, that the idea must be thought *sub specie aeterni*. But, let us repeat, this is a case of a signification which is not logical, in contrast with that of the represented object (an object concerning which a great deal of discourse is possible). Instead, we have to do with a signification which is, strictly speaking, inexpressible, because it resides both in the form and in the content of the pictorial object like the soul of a living creature. The sense of truth involved here is not inscribed in a nontemporal sky of intelligibility but is found in the object whose being it expresses. In other words, the truth of the pictorial object is not a relationship of the self to something else, but a relationship of the self with itself. This relationship initiates temporality. It should not be claimed, in this connection, that temporality implies the movement of a consciousness or of life, since it would then be necessary to dispute that music is duration—which no one will attempt to do. But such a claim may simply be saying that the duration of the aesthetic object can be perceived only if it is integrated into our own duration. This condition holds for every object. It merely means that we do not attribute duration to things unless we experience it and that things endure for us only insofar as we are enduring beings ourselves. It is precisely this sense of the work's movement which necessitates that our look rest on the work long enough for it to blossom before us—just as music comes to fill our ears—while, at the same time and by an inverse movement, we penetrate further into the work. It is our look which endures. But this duration is demanded by the pictorial object—not so vigorously as by the musical object, which bends us to its own tempo, yet sufficiently for us to feel that we have betrayed the work if our attention has been too brief. We must allow the work to attain to itself, to deliver its message, and above all to display its melody.

[II] THE STRUCTURE OF THE PICTORIAL OBJECT

LET US TURN to analysis and consider the work in its theoretical genesis. Is it possible to justify the impression of duration which enters into aesthetic perception and to discover how time is portrayed on the basis of space and how movement is communicated by means of the motionless?

(a) Harmony

As in the case of music, we should begin with a harmonic analysis (understanding harmony in the rigorous sense defined by Boris de Schloezer) in order to discern the matter of the pictorial object. At first sight, the distinction between harmony and rhythm seems incongruous for the plastic arts. Vitruvius' notion of *symmetria* includes both harmony and eurhythmy. "When all parts are in accord with a total symmetry in a building which has been agreeably proportioned, then there is eurhythmy." [8] But such a confusion of the two terms seems justified only through a very broad definition of their meanings. It neglects the dynamic aspects of rhythm, and, most important, it understands harmony in the vague sense of a fortuitous accord of parts, a unity. If harmony is thus understood, rhythm becomes merely a means to obtain it. But besides the fact that the means should be distinguished from its effect, it is necessary to determine the matter of the pictorial object and to uncover the harmonic schemata which preside over its use and thus constitute the object as matter.

It is possible to contend that the painter's materials exist objectively and have no need of being defined. After all, they are bought at an artists' supply store. This argument, however, overlooks the difference between materials and matter and neglects the fact that matter must be given a structure and meaning within the framework of the aesthetic enterprise. Matter must involve laws which allow it both to resist and to submit to the projects of the artist. The argument has some pertinence, however, in the case of drawing. While rhythmic analysis is essential to this sort of art, it is difficult to perform a harmonic analysis and find the harmonic schemata of a drawing, for ultimately drawing has no matter. There are, of course, a piece of paper and a pencil. But are these instruments anything more than material causes, tools, means of transcribing signs, just as they are for musicians or poets who write their works? And the signs at work here do not have their own matter or, at best, they have an indifferent matter. They are of value only for their signification,

8. See Luc Benoist, *Les Rythmes et la vie* (Paris: Flammarion, 1949), p. 316.

and this signification is that of a mere description, the most abstract sort of signification, because the sign does not even make use of the sonorous plenitude of the word. In this respect, drawing is a sort of writing. Thus we understand how equivocal its influence on painting can be. Because of the stylization to which it is impelled, drawing certainly suggests a style and permits the emergence of art. Yet it imposes the fatal prejudice of imitation, and it seems that its entire vocation is to create an ever more exact representation. This prejudice controlled painting in the West for a long time. Western art found it extremely difficult to admit the importance of the element of color by which it finally gained its autonomy, because it labored under the impression that drawing can say everything. Even then, color was at first tolerated primarily for the sake of coloring the drawing and adding to the resemblance, as in children's coloring books. For a long time painters continued to have recourse to values which result, according to Alain, from draftsmen's demands for good "modeling," that is, for nuancing colors without daring to treat color for the sake of color and brush-strokes for their own sake. In these ways, art followed the lead of ordinary perception, since ordinary perception goes straight to the thing without passing through its colors. Concentrated attention and an analytical frame of mind are needed in order to recognize colors as such. As the theory of forms has demonstrated, the object is given to us as a totality which signifies through its sensuous aspects, and in such a way that each sensuous aspect is organized around this totality without any individual aspect's becoming privileged. When we see a rose, we see it as real, sweet, moist, and soft. Each quality points to all the others as to its equivalents. No single quality constitutes a privileged theme which the others would serve only to translate. Moreover, as Katz has shown, unless a special effort is made we perceive only surface colors which adhere to the thing while other modalities of color, such as *Glanzen* ("luster"), *Glühen* ("glow"), and *Leuchten* ("gleam") escape us. A special effort is needed in order to give color a privileged position, to make it the center of reference for perception, and thus to arrive at Cézanne's conception of seeing: "when color realizes its proper richness, form is fulfilled." It is with this insight that painting is at last emancipated. When we want to pick out a sensuous aspect of an object, we usually choose the one which we understand most easily, that is, contour, with which drawing concerns itself. Contour is not only the most readable sign, it is also that which can most easily pretend to represent the essence of the object. In relation to contour, color seems only an accident, a secondary quality. During the long debate between colorists and draftsmen, the apostles of drawing have always had the support of rationalistic thought. It is in Descartes's time, at the Académie Royale de Peinture et de Sculpture and during discussions in which the works of Titian and Poussin were compared, that we can find the most solemn affirmations of the primacy of drawing. "Drawing imitates all real things, while color represents what is merely accidental. For we all still agree that color is only an accident. . . . In addition, color depends on drawing because it is not capable of representing or portraying anything without the ordering effect of drawing."[9] Is this claim not exactly the opposite of Van Gogh and Cézanne? Drawing will exercise supremacy and tend to exclude color as long as the pictorial object is confused with the represented object and painting gives itself the mission of signifying a rational truth.

It is from painters that we learn to see colors. It has been claimed that, since painters are not satisfied with what they learn from the practice of ordinary perception, they have had to elaborate a pictorial language just as musicians had to elaborate a musical language. (Is it not music which teaches us to perceive sounds?) Besides, there are no pure colors in nature except in certain unique and immediately admirable objects, such as precious stones or flowers. There is usually no more than the visual equivalent of noise. Like sounds, colors must be invented both by the proper technical apparatus and by a theoretical (and in a sense doctrinal) foundation for the sensuous. The result would be that color would become a kind of matter. Here we must note an objection similar to that which was leveled against the definition of sound as the matter of music. Can color be an object whose nature is to be conceived? Is it not essentially a perceived object? Would we not misunderstand color by making it the object of a theory and exiling it from the field of perception by disturbing its attachment to the human body (an attachment which has been described by psychologists like Werner and Katz)? Our claims satisfy this objection completely. The vocation of color is to be perceived and experienced through our look by offering to our body a certain hold on the world and predisposing our body to certain movements. Later we shall emphasize the motor signification of colors by which painting becomes

9. A discourse by Le Brun, quoted by Lhote, in *De la palette*, p. 82.

animated in response to our bodily movements. It is also the case that, insofar as color appears in ordinary perception, it is not perceived for itself. It is not yet an autonomous quality but, as Merleau-Ponty points out, "an introduction to the thing."

Therefore, if the painter wishes to invite us into the kingdom of color, he must perform an act of reflection on perception, an act of which his work itself will relieve us. As a singular and expressive quality, color can appear to him to be transmitted to the spectator only on the condition that he adopt a new attitude —*Einstellung auf reine Optik*, as Katz would say—shatter the immanent unity of the field of perception by blinking his eyes, break down the intricate structure of vision, and destroy his natural communication with the spectacle precisely so as to un-cover its secret. This is a symbolic gesture. The painter blinks his eyes and undoes what nature has done for him. His conquest of the sensuous, however, is precarious. At the end of the effort to determine color, color can impose itself upon us with such force that it completely fills us and no longer deserves the name of color. Since it is not blind, this experience appeals to the con-cept of order. Precisely because the perception of the sensuous as isolated is, in a sense, against nature, such perception needs the help of the idea. Thus the theory of colors comes to sup-port the experience of color. This is all the more necessary be-cause the painter must not only discern the nuances of color but also reproduce them in order to communicate them to the spec-tator. He can do this only by his art. Color must become objec-tive on canvas, where it will resume a dialogue with the subjectivity of the spectator. But this emancipation of color pre-supposes a number of revolutions, both mental and technical.

First of all, this emancipation of color cannot come about mentally unless it opposes drawing, for drawing tends to impose the law of imitation. Wherever this law is not in force, as in decorative art, color has long been freed and in certain cases has dominated drawing. But this "pure painting," as Souriau calls it, is not yet painting, because it does not yet intend to signify and seeks merely to be pleasant. It does not resolve the problem posed by the duality of the represented and the pictorial object but simply eludes it. Such an escape will always be a temptation for authentic painting once it has become conscious of itself, and it will constantly seek to sidestep the problem in the same way and return to the decorative. In any event, for color to be constituted, drawn form must be disposed of in favor of the form of color. An object must be created which will demand perception rather than interpretation, an object before which all the commentaries of the Académie Royale—commentaries which insist on finding symbols everywhere—will seem ridiculous. Presupposed here is a new idea of both art and perception. Art must be considered as a will to creation and not to imitation. And, in order that art can be justified in exalting secondary quality without falling back to the level of the decorative, it must be admitted, with respect to perception, that appearances can present a truth which differs from but is no less than the rational truth attained by understanding. Perception must be rehabilitated—if not as the homeland of all truth, at least as capable of a certain truth. At the same time, credit must be given to aesthetic significations (whether affective or practical) which are immanent in perception and which are left unaccounted for by rationalism.

It is true that painters did not have to be explicitly conscious of this conversion of the meaning accorded to perception. But to confirm the advent of color a technical revolution was also necessary—a revolution which would allow artists to become conscious of the conversion in their very activity. This revolution was the discovery of oil paint. Weak paints, which had been employed in distemper and fresco from earliest antiquity, have a certain technical virtue. Water is inert and evaporates without leaving a residue, while with oil the work is at the mercy of accidents which come with slow dessication, such as cracking, warping, and fading. But this very virtue of water-based paints has its corresponding defects. A medium which does not "work" and which offers no menacing pitfalls does not invite the painter to work. This is all the more the case because erasures and retouching are not possible. Thus the painter is urged to seek a definitive version immediately, with the paradoxical result that fresco offers an appearance of being more finished than oil painting (and it is remarkable that water color has not really gained the right to be listed among the arts except as a medium for sketching, as in Cézanne and Dufy). In addition, weak paints have their limits. Although water color and tempera assure greater freshness in tones, their spectrum of colors is highly limited. Fresco excludes red madder, vermilion, and a brilliant blue which cannot tolerate the toxic action of lime. These limitations join with another to prevent the full advent of color. By emphasizing the wall, fresco is subservient to architecture. It is little more than bas-relief. As a nonliberated form of sculpture, it seeks the sculptural allure of forms, as we can see with Giotto, and returns naturally to drawing. With oil, in contrast, "a painting is no longer a colored surface but is now a pictorial matter." [10] Oil confers a substantial and manipulable reality on color. The painter can dig into his materials and realize in pictorial matter those dreams of power which have been so well described by Bachelard.[11] Color is no longer an ephemeral and weightless matter, a sort of sensuous quality which the eye barely grasps. It is now embodied in a thick and unctuous matter to which our hands can relate as easily as our eyes. In the same way, the composer details the universe of sounds with his harmonic science, but also with the aid of his entire body in accord with the piano. The brush-stroke, the sign of a project which unites the human body with the body of a noble matter, becomes an intrinsic element of painting. More discreet in the transparent areas, it is affirmed in the impasto and proclaims the power and the movement of the creative gesture. The painter can sculpt colors, and the play of strokes becomes a mode of drawing. As we shall see, with only a little more effort color will be able to assume the functions of drawing.

We should realize first, however, how color can be subject to a harmonic analysis. When it has acquired its independence and objectivity, it must still receive the sanction of the mind. Knowledge in the form of a theory of colors is to painting what harmony is to music. It would not be impossible to find, in the history of painting, an effort parallel to that of musicians to establish, sometimes in the very vicinity of science and with the same illusions as to the legitimacy of a scientific explanation (we need only think of Serusier or Seurat), an objective status for colors and laws which would regulate their combinations, harmonies, and contrasts. This treatment of colors is, of course, less difficult than a parallel treatment of sounds. It is also less necessary, because pictorial matter has a more sensuous reality. The apprenticeship of the painter is shorter but just as indispensable as that of the musician. This is all the more true because the painter decides not only the nature of his colors but also their material function, that is, the role they will be assigned and sometimes their explosive value as well. Now, it is light which has occasioned the most debate. Is it white, yellow, or pink? Perception cannot decide. Perception goes directly to the illuminated objects and rejects the notion of *Raumfarbe:* "Illumination and

10. René Huyghe, *La Poétique de Vermeer* (Paris: Tissué, 1948), p. 94.
11. Gaston Bachelard, *La Terre et les rêveries de la volonté* (Paris: Corti, 1948), p. 74.

reflection assume their role only if they become discreet intermediaries and guide our gaze instead of stopping it." [12] Light is the zero degree of color in relation to which the colors of things are positive. The Venetians, however, discovered that light has a soft gold color. Illuminated manuscripts and the works of "primitive" painters had long been painted on a base of gold. The impressionist revolution consisted in decreeing that light was orange, not the lightest tint (as in the pale yellows of Poussin and Turner) but the warmest. Also, shadows for the impressionists are this tint's cool complement, blue. From one extreme to the other, a painter can stress either red-violet and violet-blue, as did Cézanne, or the other end of the prism, yellow-green and green-blue. We often forget that Delacroix had discovered much earlier, but without applying them in the same way, the conclusions that shadows are violet and reflections green. "Nothing exists without these three colors, violet, green, and orange." [13] Thus in the last resort, colors are defined by the pictorial function assigned to them and even by their expressive value, as we see in Van Gogh and Gauguin. Is expression any less effective in these cases because it is premeditated? What is reflective in character is founded on unreflective experience—the living experience of the painter—and returns to the unreflective level in the spectator. But the detour through reflection was nonetheless necessary.

We must add finally that this elaboration of pictorial language is the result of a cultural history. There is color for the painter only through the progressive humanization of the sensuous. Once again we find art on the road to intersubjectivity. Aesthetic creation and aesthetic perception are possible only in a cultural milieu. We are never alone. When we perceive a picture, our very look, which involves a connivance with the object, is guided by the artist. And behind the artist stand all those who created a given tradition, all those for whom color became an idea in order that, for our eyes, it can be a triumphant explosion on the canvas.

Since color is subject to an analysis which we must call harmonic, we can discover in the pictorial object harmonic schemata which seem to preside over its composition and affect the choice of colors, their role, and their treatment. We cannot be

12. Maurice Merleau-Ponty, *Phenomenology of Perception*, trans. C. Smith (New York: Humanities Press, 1962), p. 343.

13. André Lhote, *Treatise on Landscape Painting*, trans. W. J. Strachen (London: Zwemmer, 1950), p. 156.

sure whether the work conceals a "tonal plan" similar to that of the musician, but certain particularly lucid painters give evidence of this. Emile Bernard has made note of Delacroix's choice of colors for each of his pictures. Gauguin wrote to de Monfried, regarding one canvas, "General harmony: somber, sad, violet-blue, sad and chrome 1. The linen is chrome 2. because that color *suggests* night without always being explicit and also serves as a passage between yellow-orange and green which completes the musical chord." [14] Every authentic picture is built on a certain harmony of colors which sometimes haunts the painter to the point of enabling us to identify his canvases. We recognize Vermeer by a yellow-blue tonality and Bonnard by a violet-green-orange tonality. We may say that the "chord" they thus strike involves a tonic which establishes the tonality as well as a dominant by which a complete color scale can be determined. All chords prepare for the major chord and do so discreetly, for there are few great painters who do not apply Rubens' precept that a third of the hues should be luminous and two-thirds neutral, like the often subtle and precious grays dear to Velasquez. Thus a painter decides on the relative importance of his colors by choosing his scale and then decides on the manner of treating them, either by modeling them, that is, by playing on their values from clear to dark, or by modulating them, that is, by multiplying the various hues and tints from warm to cool. Colors are modulated for the purpose either of animating various areas of the canvas and articulating the design by means of color or of obtaining the greatest intensity of color. Thus Delacroix appreciates the fact that the brilliance of a Constable landscape is due to the diversity of different hues of green and claims that he could express the freshness of a virginal face with mud. This will later be opposed by the predilections of those who favor flat colors as prophesied by Gauguin, who said "A kilo of green is more green than a half-kilo and young painters should meditate on this apparent truism." [15]

These diverse techniques have a single aim: unity in diversity. This unity is expressed in terms of light. Light is naturally a melodic reality in that it transcends harmonic organization, even though in a sense it is the result of this organization. In ordinary perception we experience light only by aestheticizing it and becoming sensitive to the atmosphere of a spring morning

14. Quoted by Lhote, *De la palette*, p. 301.
15. Quoted, *ibid.*, p. 308.

or an evening in autumn. But in art, light must appear as light. It must appear in the painting itself and be its own light, a *lumen naturale*. The painting is not only an illuminated object which receives light, so that we must choose the best position before it in order to view it. The painting is also, considered in itself, an illuminating object which gives rise to its own light, a light whose mission is not only to "guide the look" but which *is* the look and thus constitutes the pictorial object as a quasi subject. There is no need for the source of light to be represented in the painting. When La Tour paints a torch, and even when Lorrain represents the sun, they are aware that their images are merely a play of values or colors in the totality of the picture which composes this light. Every pictorial work embodies and spreads light, even those depicting shadows and even prints and drawings, or else it is blind and empty. But this light appears to its best advantage when shadows do not imply somberness and, above all, when painting is not reduced to imitation and color ceases to be subordinate to drawing. Then light appears as color, as the flower of color. It is true that light can devour color. For painters who are faithful to light values, like Caravaggio, La Tour, or Rembrandt, rendering light presupposes that a considerable portion of the surface is covered with deep shadow and that day reigns only through night. For colorists, day alone reigns. Shadow itself is a color, and it is in light at the height of its power that color ends by losing itself. Through color, light is everywhere, even in the midst of darkness. There is no illumination which is imposed on the represented object as if from the outside and is plentiful on the canvas only to disappear at its source. There is a light which has the power of radiating from the pictorial object like the living heat it diffuses. Thus light is not so much the unity which results from harmony as the unity which renders harmony possible. It is the sensuous *a priori* of the work by which the work can become a theater of movement.

(b) Rhythm

What we have just said about harmony should make it evident that harmony is the principle of movement in painting— just as it is in music, whose sensuous qualities need a keynote and where dissonance calls for a chord of resolution. Such movement is ordered by rhythm and thus manifests a duration which is born of the animation of space. It is true that rhythm can animate only space. It cannot inscribe a real becoming in objective time. Rhythm does not preside over a temporal progression but over the unification of a spatial manifold. Yet space in this case is no longer the inert space of geometry. It has become a field of action where something happens, contrasts are resolved, and conflicts arise and pass away. As a result, rhythm is here inseparable from harmony, whereas in music the two can be kept separate if necessary. In painting, rhythm does no more than organize and animate the manifold which is obtained through harmony and whose nature and use are determined by the harmonic schema.

Before showing how the rhythmic schema fulfills its task, we must point out that rhythm belongs to drawing in the same way that harmony belongs to color. Color in itself, as harmony strives to grasp its essence and to give it form, cannot constitute a pictorial object. Drawing gives form. Only drawing gives consistency to an object, only drawing establishes discernible and measurable relationships in space where colors can be measured, contrasted, and grounded, and only drawing distributes these relationships and proportions into an order which requires movement. Thus drawing is irreplaceable. Are we therefore championing drawing in its ancient debate with color? Not at all. But we must distinguish between drawing as an artistic technique (e.g., pen, pencil, and charcoal drawing) whose goal is to represent the contour of objects and whose ambition is most often to imitate, and drawing as a means of composition, such as it appears in a diagram or sketch manifesting the plan that presides over the arrangement of the object. The latter sense of drawing is what interests us here. Every work needs such drawing [dessin], because it proceeds from a plan [dessein] in the mind of the artist. This drawing expresses the law which regulates the fabrication of the object and confers a structure on it. (It is only insofar as the intention to represent, aiding in the progressive elaboration of the object, is present that drawing appears in the sense of a technique of representation.) Now, the function of drawing in the larger sense can be taken over by color. "The proper work of the painter is to present form by color alone." [16] For color can be a type of writing, the only type which is aesthetic and in which the sign in itself possesses a fullness of meaning that allows the sign to be regarded as an end as well as a means. [17] Drawing becomes an art as soon as the sign is em-

16. Alain, *Système des beaux-arts* (Paris: Gallimard, 1926), p. 248.
17. Calligraphy does not attain the level of the aesthetic. It gives evidence only of neatness and assiduousness. It becomes aesthetic only if it

bodied in it through color, that is, as soon as the pencil line, even without the aid of shadows which strengthen it, becomes black in color and animates the paper, which then becomes white in contrast. Drawing then culminates in painting, where form becomes color without ceasing to be form—as in the works of Van Gogh or Rouault, but also in impressionism, where form arises from a multitude of brush-strokes and where cathedral stones, corroded with light, never cease to be monumental. The object represented by drawing in terms of its contour can also be represented by color—perhaps even better, since pictorial matter has enough body and value to render the sign more imperious and suggestive. But then the sign becomes valid in itself and constitutes a pictorial object whose represented object is no more than an element and whose richness of signification no longer results from exactitude of representation alone. As soon as we arrive at this pictorial object, drawing exists only in the second sense which we have distinguished. Drawing is the structure of the pictorial object, and as such it can never be suppressed by color.

An analysis of the pictorial object can uncover rhythmic schemata attesting that its composition is the result of an act of making. Here we may distinguish formal schemata from typal schemata and show that the formal belong to drawing or construction while the typal belong to the properly pictorial element of the work, and that the formal animate "plastic form" while the typal animate "pictorial form" (these distinctions are those proposed by Lionello Venturi).[18] Formal schemata, furthermore, establish the general architecture of the work, the orientation of its lines of force, and the distribution and balancing of its masses. Analysis can discover, in every plastic work, a general shape of the lines (straight in classical, curved in baroque) which forcefully direct the eye and distribute space into different regions whose surfaces sustain various relationships among themselves. This general shape reveals an order—and almost a logic—of relationships and proportions which can sometimes be

---

succeeds in making us forget its function as writing and allows letters to be considered for themselves and to bear a meaning by themselves, as in manuscripts when the initial capital of a chapter is fully ornamented with spirals and vines and becomes a cosmic figure which provides its own meaning.

18. See Lionello Venturi, *Painting and Painters: How to Look at a Picture* (New York: Scribner, 1945), *passim*. This distinction is also found in Wölfflin, where it is drawn between the linear, which is the principle of classical art, and the painterly, which is the principle of baroque art. But, unlike Wölfflin, we would not make the distinction the basis for an opposition of styles.

stated in simple numerical terms. This order can be all the more easily referred to and defined because certain painters conceived it in accordance with rigorous principles. The works of Matila Ghyka have provided evidence for this mathematization of forms which we cannot afford to ignore, although Ghyka's research concerns plastic art in general. The results of this research are, however, subject to three reservations. (1) The mathematical formula discovered in the construction of a work is often only approximated. (2) No formula can be invoked to explain the beauty of a work. A schema, whether numerical or not, instructs us concerning the structure of a work, reveals to us the procedure of its fabrication, but tells us nothing of the total work, which can be considered only on the condition of relegating the results of our analysis to a second level. (3) We must not believe that this formula is indispensable to artistic creation. We could discover an order in a picture which is rigorous and subject to mathematics without that order's having been deliberately willed by the artist. Inspiration can lead to the same results as calculation, and an artist can incorporate geometrical shapes into his work while having no thought of geometry as such.[19] (It is possible that Ghyka's Pythagoreanism would not dispute our interpretation. If number regulates nature and is found in all of nature's products, number can also regulate the artist, who is a "force of nature," and be found in his works without the artist's becoming conscious of it.) It is noteworthy that a painter like Lhote, who is particularly careful about composition and whose masters are Poussin, Ingres, and Seurat, should write that "the procedure which consists in drawing the cage before forcing one's captive forms into it has no right to claim priority."[20]

With these reservations in mind, it is fascinating to follow Ghyka, especially in his commentary on Hambridge's theory concerning Greek vases. For Hambridge refers to "dynamic schemata" in considering certain rectangles whose module is an incommensurable number, principally $\sqrt{5}$ or φ.[21] He calls these rectangles "dynamic" as opposed to static rectangles whose module is a whole number or a fraction (the rectangle with a

19. Distinguishing the role of spontaneity from that of calculation in the creative act is one of the most difficult tasks of a psychology of creation. We will not take on this task here, since we shall invoke the artist only to the extent that he is invoked by the work.
20. Lhote, *Treatise on Landscape Painting*, p. 62.
21. See Matila Ghyka, *L'Esthétique des proportions dans la nature et dans les arts* (Paris: Gallimard, 1938), pp. 221 ff.

φ module is characterized by the property of having squared gnomons). He then effects the "harmonic decomposition" of these dynamic rectangles, through dividing their surface into rectangles and squares by means of diagonals, lines perpendicular to these diagonals and lowered from the summit, and lines parallel to the sides and drawn through the points of intersection obtained from the first two lines. By these means and others somewhat more complicated, he determines surfaces which are all a function of the module of the initial rectangle. And the contours of these surfaces themselves determine a certain number of points which can be seen in the silhouette of the object under consideration. The rectangles which enclose the aesthetic object are termed "dynamic" precisely because they contain, potentially, the allure of the object. We cannot ignore such sophisticated research any more than we can ignore Lund's research on architecture. We can oppose to it only the reservations cited above. In the first place, we cannot be sure whether potters and architects consciously employed these formal relationships in their works. Also, the geometric schema often applies only roughly. Finally, there is always something arbitrary about the very choice of the dynamic rectangle and the mode of harmonic decomposition. The researcher finds what he was seeking because one tends to look for what one wants to find. Nevertheless, the continual reappearance of what Hambridge calls "the non-mixture of dynamic themes" is a remarkable fact. Once a rectangle has been chosen, it is impossible to decompose it by introducing a different module—with the result that, even though decomposition enjoys a certain freedom (as is evidenced by the figures constructed by Hambridge), it exercises this freedom only within the limits of the chosen theme and must rediscover the object within these limits. This rule, it seems to us, provides the meaning and value of the analysis of "dynamic symmetry." It makes the reality of a law of generation appear in a mathematical language whose conventional character is of little consequence. It confirms the organic character of the aesthetic object. A law for the generation of form can be found in every work of art, more or less deeply dissimulated but always as an active ingredient. The freedom which this law authorizes and the variations which it tolerates do not affect its reality.

Thus we find in these dynamic themes or schemata privileged examples of what we have called rhythmic schemata. Rhythm here is the constancy of a law which organizes space. This law furnishes the element of repetition which is indispensable to rhythm as a means of giving form to movement. What is repeated is the fundamental form of the work in its subdivisions. The work unfolds by making its unique formula explicit and not by indefinitely repeating the same design through mechanical addition, as in decorative art. Thus the work engenders a diversity in the unity of its being. Movement is nothing other than this development of an essence, the adventure of an entity which remains equal to itself throughout all its metamorphoses, like a theme through its variations. It seems, however, that we are far from living movement and closer to the logical than to the organic. For we are placing a mathematical formula at the source of the aesthetic object. But this is because organic growth cannot be represented [*figurée*] except by a logical development, nor can living movement be represented except by a logical movement. The movement of the aesthetic object can be only a psychical movement toward a plenitude of meaning and not a physical movement toward a spatial object. Most important, this is still only a case of the external form of the object and not of its total reality. Logical rhythm measures the growth of the aesthetic object and manifests the way it has been composed, not its total effect. The melodic elements which result from the subject of the work will eventually mask the rigor of formal determinations and restore the fantasy and exuberance of life, as does ornament in architecture. A strict formality can characterize vases or temples, especially when we are establishing their profile, but it is less characteristic of the pictorial object, whose design is, in a sense, submerged by color and whose signification involves an element of representation. Thus in architecture these rhythmic schemata can also be called melodic. The melody of the architectural object resides in the rhythm which presides over its composition. To speak in musical language, we may say that the theme developed by the work must be a rhythmic unit. This gives further evidence of the impossibility of radically distinguishing between the elements of the aesthetic object. Even in painting, melody is not easily distinguished from rhythm; but we may at least point to another aspect of rhythm—an aspect through which rhythm tends to become confused with harmony.

This aspect is manifested by typal schemata which guide the organization of the properly pictorial elements. These elements can be classified according to either the intensity or the hue of their tonalities. The schema of relief or outline distributes light and dark and arranges their interaction so that the light planes will propel the dark planes toward the spectator and the dark planes will drive away the light planes indefinitely until another dark plane is pushed forward. As Lhote has written, such a system of contrasts, rhythmically unfolded, "gives the work not only its framework but also its movement." [22] This is a fictive process, for it is also a psychical movement. Depth belongs to the description of the represented object, which is itself just one component of the plastic idea incarnated in the painting. (This is why depth must be indicated in deference to the represented object, yet without detracting from other plastic components, which require that the work submit to the verticality of the wall and expand its two dimensions.) But the painter can also animate the surface and suggest depth through the use of color contrasts which play on the opposition of complementary colors or of warm and cold hues. Thus, through the play of light and shadow, the rhythmic schema determines the movement of colors, their transitions, and their return to an earlier state. Relief is signified by drawing if the painter remains faithful to the local tone and if movement is expressed by subtle color inflections, as in Tintoretto's *Susanna* or Ingres's *Odalisque*. After the impressionist revolution, however, which extends the role of color to the point of submerging the drawing, cubism as heralded by Cézanne rediscovered construction by color and depth. Cézanne wrote: "For human beings nature exists more in depth than on the surface; thus the necessity of introducing into the vibrations of light represented by reds and yellows a sufficient amount of bluish shades to give the feeling of the air." [23]

Thus, whether it is brought to bear on intensities or on hues, the rhythmic schema regulates the unfolding of pictorial elements. It suggests depth through the movement which it impresses on these elements. This movement animates every component, and it moves from the truth of the represented object toward the truth of the pictorial object. Once again, rhythm is the agent of melody or, in other words, the means by which the total work can reveal its intimate meaning and the plastic idea can appear. As with musical rhythm, however, this movement is present on the canvas only because it communicates itself to the spectator. Unless the spectator's look is animated, the canvas remains inert. But the canvas leads the look. Its privileged lines, its major axes of construction, and its diagonals and arabesques all invite the spectator to explore it. An unfolding of fields of values

22. Lhote, *Treatise on Landscape Painting*, p. 28.
23. Quoted by Lhote, *De la palette*, p. 255.

and colors directs him. To the extent that he remains unshaken and unmoved by rhythmic schemata, his perception is not true. The work must resonate within us. The work must be taken up again within us by an active participation of our bodies, so that it can finally be given in its sensuous truth and in the unimpeachable purity of its appearing. This is what schemata answer to in all perception. They determine the structure of the object only because they give rise to a sort of connivance within the spectator. In one and the same movement, the thing gives itself to him and he opens himself up to it.

(c) Melody

It is in this way that melody, what Delacroix calls "the music of the picture," is discovered. But can analysis isolate such a melody and attribute its development to melodic schemata? It is here that the difference between music and painting seems most pronounced. We have just observed that in painting rhythmic schemata can be called melodic and that melody in painting seems to be reduced to rhythm. In fact, the properly melodic schema can appear and claim a certain independence only where melody, as in music, can be conceived as the subject of the work and analyzed as such—providing that, on the one hand, analysis confess its limits and that melody finally appear as bound to harmony and rhythm, and, on the other hand, melody bear the expression in which the work is revealed as a totality. In painting, as in all the arts where the subject is presented in a plastic representation, the subject does not lend itself to analysis. In itself, the subject is subordinated neither to a law of composition nor to a development. The work is what is composed and not its subject—which, moreover, is easily apprehended in a single look.[24] Therefore, there is no melodic schema in painting, and melody cannot be assimilated with the subject. The only use which the notion of melody may retain is that of designating the total effect produced by the aesthetic object—an

24. In the literary arts, the subject is apprehended successively through reading or hearing. Thus it lends itself to analysis, and we can discover themes in the work and follow their movement. But these themes cannot be identified with musical themes, that is, melodic schemata, because they are under the sway of language and allow themselves to be reduced to intelligible formulae. Hence they do not belong to melody but instead help in its production, insofar as melody results from the total effect.

effect which is presented only to perception and which resists analysis, that is, once again, what Delacroix calls the music of the painting and Valéry the song of the monument. Such a melody involves no schemata and is unreducible. All that can be discerned by analysis are those elements which help to produce the melody—the matter of the work treated according to harmonic and rhythmic schemata, as well as the work's subject. But the subject, whether or not it lends itself to analysis, can no longer be promoted to the dignity of melody. It is not anything more than an element in the total work.

Nevertheless, the difference between music and painting is in this case more apparent than real. For we can consider the melody as the subject in music precisely because the subject *is* a melody, that is, because the subject is not in itself simply a concept or a representation but is finally expression. And if music contains an explicit subject, as in program music, it becomes clear that this subject can no more be considered a melody than can the subject of a painting or a drama. The subject truly deserves the title of "melody" only insofar as it is the soul of the musical object. The privileged position of music lies only in the fact that music's melody is more easily grasped because it can be constituted by themes. In the other arts, in contrast, analysis attaches itself to the subject, often to the point of losing sight of the aesthetic object. In music, analysis can come closer to the essence of the musical itself. In any event, melody is the expression of the total aesthetic object, the subtle language which the work adopts in order to speak and which introduces us into its world. It is essentially what we have called expression.

Temporality, which is evident in the arts of time and secret in the arts of space, resides in the internal movement by which the work unifies itself in order to appear and deliver its song. Rhythm manifests and marks off this movement. But such movement can be motionless—in which case, it will not be brought forth in an objective and measurable time. The time at the heart of the aesthetic object is only an index of its interiority and of the relation of the self with itself which constitutes this object as a quasi subject. Such time is not a dimension of the objective world but rather a temporal atmosphere which corresponds to a world-atmosphere, to the world expressed by the work. The measured time of the temporal arts—a time which we must follow in order to apprehend the aesthetic object—is like an image of the more secret time in terms of which the aesthetic object is meaning. Similarly, the space of the spatial arts is like an image of that more secret space which is unique to the temporal arts and through which the aesthetic object possesses an invincible presence and can proclaim its own world.

Consequently, the arts of space and time are not absolutely heterogeneous. There is a certain affinity between them which in the end stems from the fact that they present fabricated objects which appear as organic and meaningful wholes. From this basis in observation, we can now summarily indicate the invariant characteristics of every aesthetic object.

10 / The Structure of the
Work of Art in General

THE AFFINITIES between the arts of space and of time that we have just been investigating allow us to attempt to find the invariant characteristics of the work of art. These are the general conditions common to all the arts through which the work can: (1) assume formal determinations, especially spatiality, which will constitute it as an object by giving consistency and harmony to the sensuous; and (2) say something and manifest (through an internal movement which confers on it a certain temporality) its aptitude for a type of expression which surpasses the explicit significations which the work sometimes presents. We can specify these conditions by further distinguishing the three aspects of the work to which we pointed at the beginning of this book and whose differences impose themselves on analysis independent of any psychological account of creation.

[I] THE TREATMENT OF MATTER

EVERY WORK POSSESSES a matter which constitutes, properly speaking, its sensuous nature. This matter is to be distinguished from the materials by means of which the sensuous is produced. The matter of music is sound and not the instruments which are the means for engendering sounds. In the same way, the matter of poetry is that particular sound which is the spoken word and not the voice which speaks the word or the actor who delivers it in the theater with his whole body. The materials of the work—its human or material instruments—are, in a sense, the matter of the matter. They are in the service of the aesthetic experience, but in principle they behave like a discreet servant and do not stand out. Thus the orchestra is concealed in the pit. But are not the singers occupying the stage? This is true. For the most part, art does not attempt to hide the materials it employs. It can integrate them into the spectacle on the condition that they be neutralized. That is, they must not be perceived for themselves but as a support for, and as an extension of, the sensuous. Thus the acting of an actor, insofar as is is seen, is associated with spoken words insofar as they are heard. Hence a new sensuous element comes to reinforce the first. In the same way, the playing of a virtuoso adds visual qualities to the hearing of a musical performance and emphasizes the visual as well as the sonorous, even though such an effect had not been explicitly foreseen by the composer. (We should, moreover, point to a difference between actors and musical performers. Actors lend their voices and entire bodies to their task and become themselves genuine materials for their words. Musical performers make use of materials in the form of instruments.) There are also arts in which the sensuous is inseparable from the materials by which it is produced. Architecture and sculpture cannot conceal their stone.[1] Yet stone is not truly the matter of this type of work. Just as a violin exists only for its sonorous quality and a violinist only for his virtuosity, stone, in a sense, exists only for its sensuous qualities, for its rigor, its polish, its dullness, or for the pink of the "three steps of pink marble." Certainly stone also helps in embodying an object, such as a temple or a statue, in the same way that a painted canvas embodies a landscape or a portrait. But the Albi Cathedral is not built of bricks, or the Petit Trianon of marble, or some Romanesque crucifix of ivory, in the sense that shoes are made of leather and certain tools of steel. Of course, if the architect wants his work to succeed, he will no more cheat with his stone than the shoemaker would with his leather. However, he uses his materials with ostentation, because they are more than a mere means of building a palace or a temple (themselves conceived as objects of use), just as leather is both means and

1. Hegel's classification of various arts is, in fact, based on this importance of materials—materials which are considered to be both a burden and an indiscretion. For Hegel, the arts realize *Geist* to the extent that sensuousness becomes disentangled from materiality.

end for the shoemaker. The artist's materials are not chosen only for their use-value, which is tested in utilization and which is not manifested for its own sake. They are also valued for their uniquely sensuous qualities, which are capable of constituting the aesthetic object because they offer themselves to perception. Aesthetically, the artist's materials do not exist simply as materials, that is, as what they would be for the artisan as well as for the artist, but as a support for the sensuous in its actuality. They are present in order to appear and to compose an object of contemplation and not an object of use. Instead of the sensuous's leading to the intelligible, properties to substance, or individual stones and their splendor to the quality of "stoneness," substance must manifest *itself*. The intelligible exists only for the sake of the sensuous. Stone must reveal itself as stone. Whatever reveals itself in this way constitutes the genuine matter of the aesthetic object, the sort of matter which will be informed and unified by the specific subject treated in the work of art. The artist wrestles with his materials so that they may disappear before our eyes as materials and be exalted as matter. Ultimately these materials become aesthetic by advertising themselves instead of keeping themselves hidden, that is, by displaying all of their sensuous richness. The artist's materials negate themselves as things by *appearing*. This paradox is perhaps more easily understood through a counterproof. The task of the false is to attempt to convince us that it is true. Thus a cardboard model or a theatrical set (although scenery performs other functions and is not solely directed toward deceiving) strives to indicate and suggest the presence of stone and attempts to be truer than nature through the multiplication of signs.[2] Not being stone, they seek to impose the concept of stone. Actual stone, on the contrary, proclaims itself shamelessly by means of its very appearance. Such stone has no need to convince us of its truth. The result is that we are left free, not to forget that it is stone, but to neglect this fact in order to attach ourselves to the appearances it presents to our eyes, its peculiar masses, the harmony of its proportions, and light's effects on its surfaces.

Nevertheless, when the sensuous is strictly tied to its materials, it seems not to have so much autonomy and reality as, for example, sound, whose vocal or instrumental origin is less

2. Experts often unmask counterfeit paintings more through the overabundance than through the lack of an artist's characteristic traits. The false errs from an excess of zeal. Lies betray themselves by imitating the truth too well, as in the false alibis common in detective novels.

apparent and which occupies a secondary position in aesthetic experience. This is because, in these cases, the sensuous is less independent, and we are tempted to accentuate the represented object, as in sculpture, and attribute to *it* the virtues of the sensuous. The beauty of a particular mass will be interpreted as the beauty of a breast, the beauty of a line as that of a profile. The specific texture of the stone will be seen as the splendor or firmness of flesh. Thus there arises the aesthetic heresy which claims that the beauty of a work is judged by the beauty of what it represents. To combat this heresy, the sensuous qualities of sculpture must triumph over the natural prestige of the subject. Abstract sculpture provides the best evidence of this combat, since it invites the eye to be filled only with the appearances offered by the stone or the wood. Thus abstract sculpture enables us to realize that these materials are not primarily destined to furnish signs which will function as imitations but rather to give rise to the iridescence of appearances.

In any event, in sculpture or architecture the conquest of the sensuous cannot be achieved so systematically as in arts such as painting and music, for the two reasons which we have just glimpsed. The first is that, in sculpture and architecture, the represented object seems to solicit all creative activity. The second reason is that, in these two arts, materials are so ponderously present that they seem to be employed precisely for the sake of representing the object rather than for setting forth their own inherent visual qualities. By their very excess, these qualities do not possess so pregnant a character as colors and sounds. They are on the order of primary qualities rather than secondary qualities and closer to the intelligible than to the sensuous. Thus they are found above all in the interplay of geometric givens and possess the numerical character of surfaces and volumes. Other types of quality, such as color and value, are not always effective or evident. We know that, in the ancient world, the arts of stone had recourse to color not so much to ornament the aesthetic object as to constitute it more fully. Thus the use of color helped a temple to be seen as a work of art and not as just another building. There are cases where ornament is more than ornament and where its extravagance is necessary in order to compensate for the austerity of the materials and to vivify the total spectacle. It is true that contemporary sculptors no longer make polychrome or even chryselephantine statues. We know now that a curve or a mass can be a spectacle to which the eye is as sensitive as it is to the most refined harmony of colors. Those architects who design in concrete have taught us to enjoy empty space or a large clear surface as much as the antiquated grace of the rococo. Yet cabinetmakers willingly return to inlay work and ceramicists continue to paint their vases in colors. They do not believe that the values of contour alone are sufficient to constitute an aesthetic object. To geometrize is not necessarily to aestheticize—otherwise industrial tools, propellers, automobile bodies, and skyscrapers would also be works of art. This points to the idea, to which we shall return, that the represented object may be, after all, an indispensable element of aesthetic experience. But without examining this notion further, we can at least argue here that geometrical qualities must be enveloped and hidden in the work of art, or else only an abstract beauty which is not yet genuine beauty will be exhibited. A cathedral is beautiful because each perspectival view of it shatters and overturns symmetries and regularities and because the light diffused through the stained-glass windows makes the stone sing—in short, it is beautiful because the geometrical qualities of the building are no more than a *basso continuo* in the orchestration of the spectacle. In sculpture, geometrical qualities are disturbed or distorted by the fantasy of the artist or by the demands implicit in the model. The sensuous is affirmed by the rejection of abstract laws and by the abundance of the unforeseen. But it remains true that, except when appearing as ornament, the sensuous does not display the same magnificence in the arts of stone as in the other arts. The sensuous retains the same poverty as drawing does in relation to painting. A statue is a drawing in space. It resembles drawing precisely because it retains an abstract character, even when geometrical regularity is thrown into disorder by a swirl of forms which obey no apparent law. We can understand why this is so. In the arts of stone, sensuous qualities adhere to the materials. Sensuous qualities are not produced on the basis of the materials, as timbre is produced from a musical instrument, but *in* the materials. And it is form in its visual aspect which tends to prevail. Thus we see that, in the arts of stone, the sensuous cannot be ordered in a system so vast and coherent as that possessed by the sensuous in music and painting. In the case of music and painting, the sensuous is more independent of the materials involved and offers the spectator much more extensive resources.

In every art, however, the sensuous must be arranged and ordered in such a way as to be perceived unequivocally. The work is always composed of harmonic and rhythmic schemata.

Every work involves harmonic schemata which elaborate with precision the unique language in which the work will be expressed. Or, more exactly, such schemata serve to articulate the materials which serve as a language for the work, although this language is never perceived as language or independent of its sense. These schemata fulfill two functions. First, they define and classify the elements of this aesthetic language. In fulfilling this function, they determine certain exclusive rules for these elements and grant certain privileges to some of them, either in the name of a generally recognized tradition or in the artist's own name (even though he draws his own resources from a common treasure). The fulfillment of these options is what often gives the work its unique character. The act of selecting these elements and putting them in order constitutes a scale or spectrum of possibilities. Thus a scale of sounds is constituted in relation to which noise is excluded (as well as certain sounds, such as quarter-tones, which were allowed into Greek music but are no longer permitted in modern taste, and even some chords, such as chains of fifths in classical music). Similarly, a scale of colors is constituted which differs greatly from one palette to another and which becomes more crowded and more nuanced as painting is pictorialized. We can also isolate a scale of choreographic movements—rigorously limited in classical dance, it becomes suppler when, with expressionism, dance comes into contact with pantomime. Here again, do we not recognize the master ballet dancer by his predilections as well as by what he rejects? Do we not identify Lifar, for example, by movements which become carried away with themselves and seem to spring from visceral depths, Platonic gestures which build on a basis of anger? Or Petit, by the emphasis which renders his gestures imperious or cerebral? Or Lichine, by a certain neutrality? In literature, a spectrum of words is constituted in terms of a prodigality or sobriety of vocabulary, ranging from the modesty of classical authors to the ostentation of the moderns. Each poet has his key words. There is no more reason to scoff at the fires of Corneille or at Hugo's shadows than at Lautréamont's bestiary, Valéry's gold, or Mallarmé's mirrors. In architecture and sculpture, a gamut of lines and surfaces is constituted. For, as we have just seen, their material is stone insofar as stone bears the stamp of man, is susceptible to being geometrized, and can integrate itself into the general movement of the building. The movement of lines and the organization of surfaces determine the style of these works. The

Romanesque statue is recognized by its fixed linear character. The stiffness of its lines is compensated for by their animation. The Gothic statue is recognizable in its modeling effects, since the weakness of its lines is compensated for by the equilibrium of its masses. Finally, a scale of theatrical characters is constituted, since the repertory of characters is, in a sense, the prime matter of dramatic art. It is evident that the theater has gained self-consciousness by establishing a certain number of types which can be contrasted, compared, and correlated according to rules which are at first elementary—types which are for Molière what colors are to the painter and notes to the musician. However replete with meaning these characters may become, they are never more than pawns on the chessboard of the stage. The theater is poorly understood if one does not realize that it is primarily a game of entrances and exits and a certain manner of joining and separating different characters, of submitting them to the experience of presence and absence, and of seeing *in vivo* the significance of *Mitsein* for various types of human being.

The second function of harmonic schemata follows immediately from the first. They establish accents in, and thus organize, the kind of scale just described. These accents also confer upon the work its particular allure. Such is the function of the tonic and the dominant for the musical scale and of the principal tonalities in a musical work undergoing modulation. It is also the task of the principal tones which are established in a painting and (unless the painter systematically uses flat tints) which never possess the purity of musical notes (this is especially noticeable in pointillist techniques, which add the optical mixture composed by the juxtaposition of spots to the material mixture of pigments on the palette, but which appear clearly when the work is seen from the right distance). A similar accentuating role is fulfilled by certain poses and movements that constitute the poles of choreographic gesturing, such as the girl's stamping movement in Petit's presentation of *Le Jeune homme et la mort* or the weighty march of death in Goos's staging of *La Table verte*. In drawing or in architecture, accents are embodied in certain privileged vectors, such as the spirals of Rubens and Van Gogh and the inert horizontals of reclining figures in their paintings. Finally, accents are found in great theatrical scenes where crucial meetings are arranged and decisive speeches delivered. These scenes are so important that they involve the destiny of the characters while condensing into a single moment the life of the work. In relation to these accents, the rest of the work serves as background, preparation, and filling-out. Every work of art has a background which is the horizon of its meaning. But there is also a material background which is the work's elementary matter and which, in a sense, can always be further elaborated (although in fact it is as carefully elaborated as all the rest). Against this material background appear the accents which confer on the sensuous its most forceful intensity and its most pressing presence. It is this function of presenting the material background which is assumed by the *basso continuo* in music or by the accompaniment that harmonizes the melody and gives it consistency without actually constituting it. This may even be the function of the orchestra's tendency toward pandemonium, so prominent since Wagner, as Alain has noted, and produced by introducing or stressing certain instruments whose sound is constantly on the verge of noise. In painting, we find the material background presented through certain colors, especially through those grays which are put to such a refined use by the great painters. In drawing, the material background is the very whiteness of the paper. In dance, the material background is the marching which Valéry rightly calls "the high point of art" but which is at first no more than the promise of a leap. The poetic backdrop is presented by the murmur of the unemphasized words which serve to frame a few striking words. Theater has the coming and going of characters, those swirls of life which suddenly become motionless at critical moments and which are subject to the halting of destiny. Finally, the material background of architecture exists in the stone's very countenance and in the masses suddenly animated by columns or windows.

In addition, every work involves, through its specifically rhythmic schemata, a disposition of the elements which articulate and order its movement—a movement by which the work is temporalized (sometimes secretly) and becomes an animated being. Because it is the result of a making, such movement is constructed on the basis of the motionless, that is, the temporal on the basis of the spatial. The element of measure engenders movement, and rhythm proceeds from number. The elementary rhythmic schema is the measured beat which governs the unfolding of the object and imposes a unity on the diversity of its forms or movements. This is the case in music and in poetry—and also in the theater, which is a sort of ballet whose movements are regulated by destiny and follow, as we know from Shakespeare, the pitiless march of time. Because the temporal arts have vanquished time by means of measure, they can regulate its flow directly. Their mastery of time—a mastery which is acquired by playing on the contrast of same and other —allows the temporal arts to restore duration. As the principle of unpredictable newness, time can be known only through permanence or through the return of the same. Sheer novelty would be maddening. Rhythm is a means of taming time without betraying it and reducing it to the repetition of the constantly identical. For the element of measure inherent in rhythm involves the measuring of diversity, and rhythmic repetition does not exclude variation. It is thus through the agency of rhythm that we are able to grasp the cyclical character of works of art. The most classical expressions of this character are found in the refrain in music, symmetry in architecture, and the alternation of lines and stanzas in poetry. But these cyclical patterns, which are so effective in calming the spirit, cannot be mere repetitions. The musical refrain becomes imitation or variation, symmetry is broken by the different heights of a building's floors, the plastic rhymes of a painting are only distant echoes, and poetic rules can be relaxed even in the most rigorous poems. Everywhere, variety forces unity to be the unity of a variety.

It is thus that the spatial arts suggest time by means of progressions in space. They propose a particular pattern for the object by which its general allure is determined and by which the free play of its appearing is regulated in accordance with certain laws. We have seen how this obtains in the case of ceramics, painting, and architecture, where rhythm serves less to measure and order time than to give rise to time. Rhythm gives movement to the motionless object which gathers itself together, tends toward itself, and envelops an indefinite duration. The result is that, if the object survives the centuries, it is because it triumphs over them and not because it submits to them. The centuries are the witnesses of this mute affirmation or frozen movement which represents the object's insistence on uttering what it has to say. This movement is so true that it seems to have its own tempo. The agogical element is equally valid for the temporal arts, where it expresses a presentation's relative rapidity, whether this rapidity is that of a melodic, a choreographic, or a scenic movement. But this game of acceleration and delay animates even plastic works. The slow mass of a cathedral's buttresses contrasts with the yearning of its spires. A column's capital checks the impulse of its shaft. Everywhere inertia is opposed to movement and slowness to swiftness—even in pictorial works, where straight lines and curves balance off each other's sense of velocity and where colors advance or recede in different cadences, depending on whether they are warm or cold, pure or mixed. Thus rhythm is internalized and integrated more deeply into the structure of the sensuous, and the aesthetic object is endowed with a temporality which we could call potential. As opposed to inert things which do not deserve the attention of a look because they are only what they are and are not animated by a relation of the self with itself, this sort of duration indicates a movement of the object. A movement toward what? As we have said, toward its meaning. But in this respect we must distinguish between the signification which is declared by the "subject" and the expression which emanates from the work as a totality. Let us now consider the former.

[II] THE SUBJECT

ART IS NOT LIMITED to an exhibition of the sensuous. But we cannot deny that this function is essential, since the aesthetic object is a perceived object and its vocation is to rehabilitate and exalt the sensuous to such an extent that what the aesthetic object says is valid only in terms of how it says it. A subject may not always be necessary to impose organization on the sensuous and confer on it a signifying character. Even when the aesthetic object excludes all representation, it is nonetheless still an object. It presents itself by means of a form which unifies it and makes it into an object. In this way, decoration is ordered by motifs, music by tunes. Sometimes a simple contour is enough to constitute an object in terms of a figure contrasted with a ground. Through the aesthetic process, the sensuous has a sufficiently solid structure to possess by itself an objectlike consistency and consequently to be endowed with expression. The result is that, strictly speaking, the sensuous can be sufficient unto itself and bear its own meaning within itself without pointing to anything else. Yet the work of art frequently does represent something. It has a subject [un sujet], that is, a specific subject matter. It is by means of this subject that it becomes signifying. Instead of presenting itself simply as a property of materials, such as the timbre of an instrument, the color on a canvas, or a design in rock, in the same way that a scent belongs to a rose or blue is sky-blue, the sensuous quality of matter becomes a sign. The naïve perception of a work goes straight to what is represented in the work—i.e., to the represented object—and is often content (in spite of the possibility of eventual regret) with the most summary indications of this object.

However, a problem is posed for aesthetic experience by this intervention of a subject, an intervention which is often imperious and fascinating. What should be the role of the represented object in this intervention? Do the interest of the work and the measure of its truth reside in what it represents? There are also problems for objective analysis. What is the function of the represented object in the general economy of the work? And, first of all, is there always a represented object?

This last point is, of course, subject to dispute. A painting can represent a temple, but what does a temple represent? Novels and operas tell stories, but does a symphony? We know that Souriau bases his classification of the arts (which is the most ingenious effort in this direction so far) on the dichotomy between representational and nonrepresentational arts. It is incontestable that the seven "first-degree arts" which he lists are not representational.[3] But we must first come to an agreement concerning the meaning of representation. Painting can imitate to the point of making quite exact copies, while sound is suggestive to the point of the most nuanced of allusions. Pantomime does not represent the way theater does, or sculpture the way painting does, or film the way the novel does. Speaking in words is not similar to speaking with gestures or by drawings. It is quite a distance from evocation to imitation and from suggestion to reproduction. Within a single art, furthermore, representation can occur in quite different ways—sometimes to the point where a particular art seeks to transgress its own limits. Imitative music strives to enter into the domain of the representational arts, while pure painting, in contrast, moves in the other direction. Such achievements can be realized in many ways. There is no limit to the liberties painting can take with its model, as soon as painting rejects *trompe-l'oeil* effects. There is also no limit to the liberties poetry may take with the logic of discourse once it rejects the rationality of prose. When, therefore, can we speak of the represented object, and what is the minimum of meaning that we can give to the word "representation"?

3. See Etienne Souriau, *La Correspondance des arts* (Paris: Flammarion, 1947), *passim*.—Trans.

The represented object is not necessarily a real object which would serve as a model for the creative enterprise. It can, obviously, also be a creature taken from the universe of the fantastic or the legendary. It can even be a completely new imaginary object. And a given representation is not necessarily a copy, reproduction, or exact statement of this object. If we wish to understand representation in the widest sense of the term, we must say that there is representation whenever the aesthetic object invites us to leave the immediacy of the sensuous and proposes a meaning in terms of which the sensuous is only a means and essentially unimportant. That is, we must explicate this meaning according to norms which belong not to aesthetics but to logic. What characterizes representation and makes it contrast with feeling is not so much the reality of what is represented as an appeal to concepts. The represented object is an identifiable object which demands recognition and which expects an unending analysis on the part of reflection. It invites us to turn away from appearance and to seek its peculiar truth elsewhere.

If we understand representation in this way, we shall realize that not all the arts are representational. They do not all have a subject in the sense that we speak of the subject of a novel or a bas-relief. Outside the purely decorative arts, the most notable arts in this category are architecture and music. But are they incapable of possessing any subject whatsoever? This point has often been debated, all the more passionately because the absence of a subject can just as often be an advantage as an inconvenience, depending on the importance one attaches to the presence of the subject in the other arts. For this reason, we should defer for a moment our consideration of this debate in order to underline the importance of the subject in those arts in which it is clearly present.

The subject's importance cannot be disputed in the literary arts—especially in the arts of prose, where words cannot be deprived of their signifying function. The subject is less crucial in poetry, where the word retains the character of a thing of nature and is expected to manifest its sensuous qualities. We cannot imagine a novel or a play which would not signify anything and which would prevent us from seeking a meaning in its written or spoken words. Even in the plastic arts, the subject's importance was never disputed until after that aesthetic revolution of which we have spoken and which directs attention to style rather than to content, that is, to the expression presented by the sensuous rather than to any explicit signification. Here, the value of the work is no longer measured by the import of its subject or its beauty by the beauty of its model. A still life claims the same dignity as a religious painting or an epic. Neither the imitation nor the idealization of objects is any longer of use as a criterion. Pure painting and pure poetry dream of losing their subservience to the subject. They wish to be music. This is due to the fact that, whenever art becomes most forcefully conscious of itself and thus becomes most specifically art—that is, whenever it invents its own language of sound, color, form, and even its own poetic vocabulary—it also becomes conscious of the danger posed to it by representation. Representational art risks being no more than a means in the service of representation. For the prestige of the represented object—and our own predilection for grasping it—is so powerful that it often monopolizes all our attention and clouds over the aesthetic experience. Thus we find ourselves asking questions. What does this mean? What is that man doing in the corner of the picture? Is this dancer's gesture a declaration of love? What will happen to the hero of that novel? In such instances, art presents itself as a sort of ordinary language that requires that we understand its meaning. Art exists not so much for contemplation as for comprehension. How many spectators believe themselves finished with a painting when they have recognized the mountain, the Holy Family, or the rustic scene which it depicts, or with a play after they have followed the plot through to its denouement? They use the work of art as a geographer uses a map, a botanist a flower, or a motorist a signpost. Similarly, whoever uses a fetish for conjuring a god, a temple for praying, or a painting for evoking a beloved presence shirks aesthetic experience. Representation is a trap even for the artist himself, as can be clearly seen in academic art. It is all too easy and tempting to try to convince or seduce others, especially when the public willingly embraces this effort. And thus we can understand that authentic art, refusing to fall back on the subject as a basis for determining aesthetic value, tends to press this refusal, to the point of wishing to expel the subject from the structure of the work altogether.

However, the danger posed to the work by representation is perhaps the ransom for a unique advantage, one which is so indispensable that the nonrepresentational arts may well have to invent some equivalent for representation. If the subject can command our interest to such a point that it leaps to our eyes—

that is, if we must admit that portraits and busts represent someone in particular, that a novel is a narrative, and that in its own way a ballet tells a story by which we are fascinated— can we effectively deny that the subject may play an unreplace-able role in the work, or perhaps many roles, both for the specta-tor and for the artist?

The first of the subject's roles consists precisely in satisfying an irrepressible urge on the part of perception to know the sensuous as the sensuousness *of* something—to discover things, not an inchoate realm of the sensuous, and to relate the sensu-ous to these things. The *hyle* does not offer itself as such but as animated by intentions which constitute an object. Aesthetic perception can become acquainted with the aesthetic object only if it is an object and its sensuous qualities are attached to a support which they qualify. The natural support of the sensu-ous, its material base, is what is most often concealed. We do not usually perceive color as the color of a canvas, or a word as a word written on paper. More frequently we neutralize this perception, which presents merely an object in the world and not an aesthetic object. The sensuous must, therefore, attach itself to a new support, which is precisely the represented ob-ject. Blue on a canvas becomes the blue of the Virgin's tunic or of a mountain on the horizon of a landscape. The sensuous thus assumes its natural function of providing information. It designates and qualifies an object. In the same way, words and sentences designate a "state of affairs" and perform their func-tion as signs. The sensuous, however, cannot be exhaustively identified with this function, nor can it show itself to its best advantage through the exercise of signification. For where it qualifies a real object, the sensuous is, as it were, absorbed into this object and is not perceived for its own sake. It then is valid only as a descriptive predicate of the object, and what is important is to identify the object itself in whatever capacity it interests us. In relation to the more or less present but always convincing reality of this object, the sensuous is something unreal. Or else it becomes real if the represented object to which it refers is unreal. In such a case, it is the sensuous itself which constitutes and dominates the object. Of course, we still intend the object as providing the sense of the sensuous, but we intend it as something represented. This is sufficient to rehabilitate the sensuous. We must pass through the sensuous in order to arrive at the object. We must, for example, make words sound in order to evoke things, or follow the contour of a design in order to recognize it. Thus the represented object offers a way in which the sensuous proves itself to be of use without being obliterated in this use. And, in turn, the represented object aids in the exaltation of the sensuous. The represented object confers on the sensuous the unity of a signification, that is, a unity which draws its rigor from logic. The unity of a novel, or of a poetic meditation, or even of a statue or a painting, is the unity of a meaning which can give rise to reflection because it is the unity of a concept. However external this unity may be with regard to the sensuous, it is nonetheless pregnant with the sensuous.

The subject's second role derives from the fact that the work discloses a world through its expression. This world is an expression which has become boundless and which has detached itself from the perceived (of which it was the countenance) in order to become an affective structure and a cosmological category. Now, it is possible that this cosmological dimension can reveal itself only if there is a represented object which allows expression to solidify or crystallize. Certainly the world which pervades the represented object is a world which remains represented and not expressed. There is a background surrounding the focal planes of a painting or a novel. The Winged Victory evokes space and the wind and the prow of a ship. But this world, which imagination sketches around the subject and which perception grasps only marginally, serves as a witness to the expressed world. Expression clings to what is represented, even though it signifies beyond the represented. An austere, implacable, heart-rending Byzantine Crucifixion presents an entirely different expression from a sumptuous and theatrical Crucifixion by Rubens. Nevertheless, the common theme of Crucifixion involves a general expression which differs in theme from holiday scenes or still lifes. The Byzantine fresco masters did not paint holiday scenes and Fragonard did not paint Crucifixions. This implies that expression, as the artist experiences and presents it concretely through his work, controls specific subjects and, at a deeper level, always needs *some* subject over which to rule.

Thus a psychology of creation would show that a subject is for the most part indispensable to the creation as well as to the perception of the work. For the modern artist, the subject is no more than an "occasion" or a "pretext." Delacroix was, paradoxically, the first to recognize this and also the last genuine painter to work with "grand subjects." But this point must be clearly understood. The pretext in question cannot be any pretext whatsoever, It is chosen by the artist, from a thousand others, in such a way that the artist's predilection for certain subjects becomes noticeable and occasionally can be used to identify his work. In this sense, Christ is not a pretext for Rembrandt or Bach, nor is Guernica for Picasso or Malraux (the authentic Malraux of *Man's Hope* and *Goya*). An artist chooses a particular subject because he is consubstantial with it and because the subject awakens a certain emotion within him and even seems to interrogate him at times. It is not a matter of copying this subject but of furnishing, through [*à travers*] it, a sensuous equivalent of the affective and intellectual signification of this subject for the artist. Rouault does not paint a Christ but a pictorial equivalent, through the depicted Christ, of what Christ signifies for Rouault. The object is represented in its truth (at least in the form of truth with which the artist is acquainted) and not in its flat and meaningless reality. It is thus that the artists least attached to representation, even those who today practice pure painting and pure sculpture, refrain from renouncing a subject altogether and often continue to give their works titles which announce the subject.

But we must insist that this is not a question of repeating a certain reality which is objective and can be objectively transmitted. As soon as the perceived world is objectified, it is no longer of interest to the artist and cannot inspire the creative gesture. All that can then be done is to reproduce it, formulate it, or add some action to it—none of which is part of the artist's task. Once a face has become a well-defined object, all that can be done is to photograph it. Art can add nothing to what is already constituted, identified, and officially known. Art can only alter, deform, or interpret it. Thus we have the classical formulae: *Homo additus naturae,* nature as seen through a particular temperament. As Malraux points out, however, "Art is no more nature as seen through a particular temperament than music is a nightingale as heard through a particular temperament." [4] It is not so much a matter of interpreting as of creating, for, if the object has already been given and the world is completely formed, why should we interpret it? In truth, what interests and stimulates the artist in mundane objects is what has not yet been created and awaits creation. It is that ungraspable dimension of reality which manifests itself only

4. André Malraux, *La Psychologie de l'art* (Geneva: Skira, 1947), II, 152.

through affectivity and which art alone can crystallize and communicate. Whatever geographers have excluded from landscapes, historians from events, and photographers from faces—whatever it is at which perception only hints and is banished by an objectifying consciousness—*this* is what the artist must say. His task, therefore, is not to copy the object but to say it, or rather to let it say itself, by lifting the restrictions placed on it by objective knowledge and giving it a voice. Only in this more exact sense is the artist an interpreter. He furnishes a language to the object and helps it say what it wishes to say, that is, what it means. Thus he does not repudiate the object even when he seems to negate it. He always represents it, but he does so in terms of a truth which is not that of objective knowledge.

We are now in a position to realize that the represented object, invested with the virtues of the sensuous which manifests it and gives it a voice, says something other than what it says prosaically to utilitarian perception. The traditional hierarchy of subjects no longer has any sense. There can be more grandeur in Van Gogh's *Peasants* than in a *Grand Army* by Meissonnier,[5] more fervor in a Picasso *Harlequin* than in Ingres's *The Vow of Louis XIII,* or more mystery in a Cézanne still life (where, as Lionello Venturi remarks, "inanimate objects are transformed into a cosmic tragedy")[6] than in a landscape by Hubert Robert. Art liberates a strange power in the humblest things it represents, because representation surpasses itself toward expression, or, to put it another way, because in art the subject becomes symbol.

But, before showing how expression integrates itself into the structure of the work, we should decide whether there is some equivalent of the subject in the nonrepresentational arts. First, we must distinguish between two functions which are united in representational arts—representing an object, and ordering the sensuous by arranging it in terms of an object. By a movement which is the converse of that which impels the plastic arts to convert themselves into music, music occasionally attempts to represent something. We find this, for example, in nonvocal

5. Van Gogh himself writes: "We can give an impression of anguish without looking straight into the garden of Gethsemane. It is not necessary to represent the characters of the Sermon on the Mount to convey a gentle and consoling motif" (quoted by André Lhote, *De la palette à l'écritoire* [Paris: Corrêa, 1946], p. 328).

6. Lionello Venturi, *Painting and Painters: How to Look at a Picture* (New York: Scribner, 1945), p. 151.

program music or simply in music which has been given a title.[7] Yet whether or not an artist furnishes a program or a title for his work is of little importance. The only danger is that he may be tempted to create literature, or a sort of sound painting, instead of music. If he escapes this danger, he has every right to tell us the motif which inspired him or the image which presented itself to him. The danger is more grave for the spectator. He may believe that the work's title is not simply a matter of the author's confiding in him the subjective circumstances surrounding the work's creation but of an imperative concerning what must be understood before he hears the work. In this case, the spectator runs the risk of no longer hearing at all, that is, he may distance himself from the sensuous in order to form a concept or wander in a realm of images which weaken his attention instead of stimulating it. The same is true for vocal music. If we focus our attention on the words and the representations they suggest, we turn away from the song.[8] The point is that, if music does represent, it is in a more subtle way. Music represents by expressing and by not allowing the auditor to become distracted from the kingdom of sounds. It can be treated as a representational art only insofar as it ceases to be perceived as music. On the other hand, the ordering function of the subject cannot be denied. How is this function realized? By means of two different elements. First, there is the formal schema of the work. What constitutes the unity of a sonata is primarily the fact that it is a sonata, that is, a piece of music which is composed according to certain rules and which can be divided into certain movements. A formal schema is present in every art, but it assumes a special importance in the nonrepresentational arts, because in them it can take the place of a subject. Second, there is another source of unity in the musical work which is more internal to it. This is found in the melody, which is itself organized around themes. The theme of a fugue is even called the subject, and the theme of a sonata's development is sometimes called the motif. But, as we have said, the

7. We shall return to this point in our discussion of the truth of the aesthetic object.

8. The same is true whenever two arts are conjoined. When our attention is focused on the dance, it turns away from the music. And the same applies in the case of film. Does this mean that, in such an association, one art must always be sacrificed to another because of the weakness of our attention? Not exactly, at least not if we by-pass the level of representation. We can then be sensitive to an expression which arises out of both arts joined together and which is the same in each of them.

melody is the expression of the work as it is apprehended by perception. Here the expressive takes the place of—or, rather, avoids passing through—the representational in order to give the aesthetic object its highest form.

The same holds true for architecture. In architecture, too, the subject does not reside in representation. A temple may be (in Valéry's words) "the image of a daughter of Corinth of whom Eupalinos was the fortunate lover," but this image exists only for the creator, because it is subjectively associated with his creation. In a more general sense, as Michelangelo said, architecture may have a relationship with the human body. However, this relationship functions only as a vague rule for the architect and does not mean that monuments must evoke in the spectator the image of a particular human body, any more than a pastoral symphony must evoke the image of meadows or herds. The subject of a temple or palace is above all the temple or palace itself, whose idea is set forth and exalted by the work. The work is its own subject. And it is all the more profoundly so when it sings —then the subject is melody, that is, expression. But the representational arts also acquire, by means of expression, their highest signification and the highest unity of the sensuous.

[III] EXPRESSION

(a) From the subject to expression

Expression is, in fact, the third element of the work's structure. Expression is, however, inseparable from the subject, which in turn is inseparable from the sensuous. For this reason, even if analysis fails to define expression objectively, analysis can still lead up to expression by means of reflection on the subject—especially in the narrative and representational arts, where the subject is sufficiently present and distinct to lend itself to reflection.[9] And if we attempt to define the subject of the work, we soon find it to be inexhaustible. It is a remarkable characteristic of the aesthetic object that it offers a plurality of meanings which are not juxtaposed but, rather, superimposed on each other hierarchically. This plurality testifies to its depth.

9. We shall take up this matter further in the description of aesthetic perception, that is, when we leave the aesthetic object and consider the individual who reflects on the work he perceives.

But we must immediately distinguish between ambiguity and depth. It is possible that the signification of a work may be simply ambiguous or uncertain, even for the writer himself. This is because the work is, as it were, entangled in its own sign-character, as we see in works which invent a new use for language and whose meaning is baffling. They involve a sort of ambiguity by default. In this sense, there are objects which are ambiguous for lack of clarity, just as there are ideas which are confused for the same reason. But there is also an ambiguity by excess, which results from a superabundance of meaning. This, in any case, is the sort of ambiguity which we encounter in the most authentic works.

A first example of a simple duality of meaning is given in the evangelic parables, which often relate a story which is intelligible in itself but at the same time alludes to another meaning. This is, in fact, more than an allusion, since the other meaning is declared and offered with as much precision as the first, provided that a necessary transposition is performed. Such a transposition will not be a word-for-word translation but an active appeal on the part of the literal meaning (even though it is sufficient by itself) to another meaning within itself which is discovered precisely when we cease to hold ourselves at a distance, to explain, and to judge. There is a parallel to this in what Alain says about the truth of fables. We go beyond the status of literal narrative and arrive at the fable when we give up disputing, refuting, or scoffing at the fable and especially when we give up explaining its literal content through psychological or sociological reasoning. This is not to condemn explication but only to claim that the true meaning escapes it. What the fable says by a sort of natural wisdom, like the budding flowers which express spring or the voice of the Pythic oracle which bespeaks an indwelling god, is closed to explanation. The truth of the fable is found in the witness it bears. A witness concerning what? Concerning the man who, by telling the story, tells *himself*, expresses his anguish, his desires, his joys, the work and the days. . . . Recognizing what the fable witnesses to does not mean explaining the fable by the man but finding the man in the fable.[10] In addition, the truth of fables is not necessarily a single, exclusive meaning. Quite different interpretations can

10. It seems that this is the direction taken by Gaston Bachelard in his works after *The Psychoanalysis of Fire* (trans. Alan C. M. Ross [Boston: Beacon Press, 1964]). He is always more anxious to give credit to the works he discusses than to psychoanalyze them.

each claim to be correct, as we can see from the considerable disparity between the claims of a Hegel and an Alain.

The same is true for the authentic work. It always possesses a fourth dimension, an aura of meaning which we sense in advance and which constitutes its depth. What is the meaning, in Kafka's writings, of the quest for an unattainable truth which would fulfill and justify the individual? Is it the anguish of a consumptive, the dereliction of the Jew, or the search for an unachievable transcendence?[11] Here, again, all interpretations are true at one and the same time. This situation is the same as that which we experience before any human fact and is discouraging only to the understanding. Consider the example of historical fact. War is at once the ruse of a desperate capitalist system, a conflict of cultures, an irruption of the natural into the artificial, and the passionate approval of the inhuman by man. All are correct: Marx, Hegel, Bergson, and Alain. All their theories are true, because the human fact is inexhaustible. Signification can be developed on different levels, on each of which it is both complete and insufficient. (In what does this plurality of meaning originate? This is a very large question. Perhaps it originates in the ambiguity of man, who is never what he *is*, who is nature and forms a human, social, and cultural nature, but who never allows himself to be identified with it. Or perhaps it originates in the fact that human existence is always placed before its own transcendence, as Jaspers says. By surpassing itself, human existence provides testimony of something beyond itself which may be illusory but nonetheless gives every great undertaking a religious meaning, as could be shown in the case of the aesthetic object.) The aesthetic object is not always so manifestly ambivalent as the novels of Kafka. But it does constantly leave reflection unsatisfied and often allows us a presentiment of a religious dimension of meaning. Thus the actor's part is often to suggest that the drama we are witnessing is somehow the projected shadow of another drama in which the same protagonists are involved, protagonists who deliver the same words but with a different meaning—as if the truth of what happens on earth were somehow to be found in heaven. (This is something that Jean-Louis Barrault was unable to express in the role of Mésa, while Jean Renoir succeeded in the role of Turelure by suggesting that Turelure is not only an

11. See the excellent analysis of the double meaning of Faulkner's novels in C. E. Magny, *L'Age du roman américain* (Paris: Editions du Seuil, 1948), pp. 209 ff.

ignoble character but a man who has been haunted by resentment following his brief encounter with Sygne, and who says: "I am more Coufontaine than you.")[12]

Let us try to clarify this overflow of meaning which is discovered by reflection when reflection directs itself to the aesthetic object. Does it not involve what one calls a thesis, and in such a way that what is added to the primary meaning would be an implicit philosophy to be grasped within the work? The problem is of a critical character. When philosophers can no longer be scientists because science has fallen into the hands of specialists, they become novelists, dramatists, or poets, and philosophy's center of gravity is thereby displaced from cosmology to anthropology. The danger here is that the implicit philosophy in question may not be given at first, and that the work is then seen as devoted to exhibiting or demonstrating this philosophy in a refusal to be "without concepts." This danger is not real for the artist unless he is not an artist at all, that is, not primarily a creator. If he is a genuine artist, it makes no difference whether he has ideas and even an entire system. He creates out of what he is and will not amputate any part of himself to complete his work. The danger does, however, exist for us as spectators. We may believe that the doctrine is the key to the work, and, under the pretext of searching for this key, we may distance ourselves from the work. Then reflection would separate us from the work by putting a doctrine in the work's place. We constantly run the risk of misunderstanding the true relationship of doctrine and work. It is not that the doctrine is the truth of the work but, rather, that the work is the truth of the doctrine. For the work does not need to be proved; it does the proving itself. Ideas are formed on the basis of the work and possess value only if they can be rediscovered in the work.

Let us, in passing, consider two points more closely. First, all art implies a philosophy insofar as philosophy is understood as a certain manner of expressing oneself through deciding about oneself and the meaning of all things, that is, as a mode of comprehension which is a project both of the universe and of the self. To the extent that philosophy can be viewed as this type of decisiveness, that is, as a prereflective comprehension which is implied in a certain style of life, it corresponds to the overflow of meaning that pervades the work construed as a

12. In this parenthetical remark, Dufrenne refers first to the character of Mésa in Paul Claudel's *Partage de Midi* and then to the characters of Turelure and Sygne de Coufontaine in Claudel's *L'Otage.*—Trans.

witness to the decision of its creator to bring it into being. But philosophy cannot clarify this meaning, because philosophy is just as ambiguous and polyvalent as the meaning itself. Philosophy can be expressed by means of art, but only because it is not yet properly philosophy, that is, capable of being stated and communicated objectively. Moreover, when philosophy has fully realized itself and assumed the systematic form to which it naturally tends, it then exists in tension with art. Art cannot consent to be placed in the service of a doctrine without denying itself, as we know from certain unfortunate attempts at philosophical poetry. On the one hand, art would no longer have its end in itself. On the other hand, it would eventually be reduced to logical significations of which it would be the mere interpretation. Art involves a philosophy only to the extent that philosophy has a genuine need of art and can disengage itself from artistic expression without imposing itself on art, that is, precisely insofar as it is not yet a genuine philosophy. Conversely, philosophy no longer requires the services of art and has no need of a merely approximate expression when it believes it has found its own adequate expression. The attitude philosophy adopts with respect to art is quite different. A presumptuous philosophy tries to control art, as can be seen in various dogmatic systems of aesthetics. A wiser philosophy takes art as an object of reflection but transposes into its own language and integrates into its own system only what it discovers to be true in art. Such a philosophy may, further, retain a nostalgia for art, whose freedom acts as a continuing provocation. Art, conversely, can dream of being philosophy. But their destinies diverge to the degree that aesthetic expression bursts the bounds of understanding and rejects rational rigor. For the philosophy immanent in the work is still not truly philosophy. Or, more precisely, it is a philosophy which has passed into man. An artist is an artist *with* his philosophy and not in the name of his philosophy. He expresses his philosophy in expressing himself. But this philosophy is not fully philosophical, and the spectator need not ponder it as such. Rather, he should associate with it and live it, or feel it by participating in the work. Philosophy does not give rise to the work. The work is what gives rise to a philosophy and gives such philosophy its depth. As soon as we seek to subordinate this philosophy to the rational logos and simultaneously to make it a constitutive although independent element of the work, it can no longer exhaust the meaning of the aesthetic object. For it then becomes clear that this object is something else or something more—not an idea, but a source of appearances.[13]

Second, the inexhaustible character of the meaning of the aesthetic object does not derive from what is inexhaustible in the object represented by it, any more than it derives from a philosophy which it might aim to embody. By themselves, represented things have the opacity which characterizes worldly things. This opacity results both from what is irrefutable in their facticity and from what is indefinite in the causal explanation to which they may be subject. When worldly things are brought onto the canvas or into the novel, they lose none of this opacity. A Cézanne landscape is as inexhaustible as a landscape in the natural world—indeed, even more so, because it has withdrawn from the indefiniteness of external existence, where every form is devoured by change and no single thing exists except in terms of all things. Once on canvas, a natural landscape is taken out of circulation and is, in a sense, promoted to a superior existence where it can no longer be put into question. From the act of representation, the represented thing acquires an irrefutable character. At the same time, the represented thing retains the inexhaustible character of the worldly thing. Similarly, individual human beings represented by art conserve within the work the ungraspable and secret character which belongs to human freedom. We know that, ever since novelists have refused to present themselves as the judges of their personages, they have left us, without warning or precaution, face to face with these personages—allowing *us* to judge them if we want to. These authors no longer make themselves accessory to our reflection, they no longer even furnish a Homeric epithet which fastens onto characters like a sort of signal. In the same way, the playwright forbids himself from violating the secret of his characters. We see the hero desper-

---

13. We have said the same thing, in passing, concerning religious art. What is currently called religious art—e.g., maudlin, tawdry curios—is not art. This involves a debate which is no longer worth debating. We know with what good intentions bad literature is often created. But we should remember why this is so. Good intentions, are, in general, animated by an apostolic will in such a way that the work is no more than a means in the service of a "good cause" or a type of propaganda. The work tries to exhort, seduce, or convince, but its truth and its virtues come from what it represents—and these are not aesthetic virtues. Yet all authentic art is, in a sense, religious. It bespeaks a faith, just as it can bespeak a philosophy. Yet this faith is not a credo which must be defended or even illustrated but, rather, a challenge or an act of assent, a means of hope or of despair, an act of love or revolt—all of which are consummated in the work itself.

ately question himself about the meaning of his act or the authenticity of his being, as in Sartre's *Les Mains sales* or Marcel's *Un Homme de Dieu*. We should not, of course, confuse indeterminacy with depth. Some characters can be ungraspable for the simple reason that they offer us no grip. We do not know what they are simply because they are nothing—somewhat like those students who pretend to be paying attention while their heads are empty. But there are also people in whom mystery is not vacuity but rather the expression of a freedom which rejects every form of determination. It is through excess rather than deficiency that their overflowing reality eludes our grasp.

Even though this humility on the part of the creator confers on the work a character of authenticity, by granting to the represented object every possibility of development, the depth of this object cannot by itself guarantee the depth of the work. Indeed, on the contrary, art transfigures the objects it represents. Art converts their inexhaustibility into its own depth. Art integrates these objects into the world it secretes, a world where they metamorphose and become tempered, like steel. A landscape painted by Cézanne acquires the depth of a sign which points to nothing other than itself. We cannot explain the writhing soil of a Van Gogh landscape by the force of erosion, or by contractions, plications, or fissures—eventually, by the entire universe—any more than we can explain man in the same way that Darwin explains the animal. The painting must be understood in itself. We must restrain our understanding as much as our imagination, to discover in the painting the depth of facticity. But, thanks to art, this facticity is not the brute necessity, the fruit of myriad turns of fate, which is identical with pure contingency. It is an impenetrable necessity, by virtue of its very meaning. Writhing soil, Greek gods, ballet figures, and Roman porticoes do not have merely the literal meaning to which an imitative art would reduce them—just as the story in a parable does not have the simple sense of a narrative. This is because the writhing soil becomes an element and a witness of the world of Van Gogh, the bust of the Greek world, and the *entrechat* of the frenetic, gracious, and tragic world of ballet. The same is true for personages in literature. They also become witnesses, and whatever they have that is secret or ungraspable takes on a new accent in the work of art. Hamlet not only represents the enigma of a lucid yet diseased will but is also an element of the suffocating world which has been rendered in film by the obsessive image of a staircase which is finally mounted only when the action is consummated. Hamlet's world is a world where purity is sullied and truth corrupted, because every person in it is tainted and fools embody truth. Thus represented objects are placed in the service of the total expression and sacrifice themselves for a meaning which surpasses them. They do not cease to be true, and it is on this condition that they can be of use to expression. But they are truer than nature, because they are incorporated into a world which they open up to the spectator.

(b) The unanalyzability of expression

Thus analysis discovers expression as its limit. The work of art says something directly—something beyond its intelligible meaning—and reveals a certain affective quality which may not be easy to translate but can nevertheless be experienced distinctly. Does not a particular painting, even if it has no subject, express the tragic, just as a piece of music expresses tenderness or a particular poem anguish or serenity? We should remember, moreover, that the eloquence of a work is not measured by the intensity of its pathos. A discreet, cold, and delicate work can be as expressive as one which is violent, uncontrollable, and immodest. "Expressive" does not mean "exciting." On the contrary, emotion ravishes and shatters us and prevents us from reading expression.

When faced with expression, analysis must not immediately give up. It can at least attempt to define, and in any case to name, expressions. We most often name an expression in accordance with the name of the creator of a work, because the characteristic quality of that work also appears to designate its creator. It is common to the work and the creator, and it functions as a sort of living bond. The characteristic quality is not only the mark of the worker on his work, it is also the mark of what is genuinely human in the work. By the same token, and because humanity is immediately accessible to man, this quality is what speaks to us immediately. Our comprehension of the work consists in a dialogue which we take up with its creator. In this respect, expression is the foundation of intersubjectivity. Furthermore, analysis can identify the function of expression in the aesthetic object. This function is one of conferring on the object its highest form, because expression is the object's highest signification. Expression has the unity of a physiognomy or even of a form of behavior. Just as we identify

an individual by a certain air which he has and which no particular sign can determine exactly, so the work has a certain
quality which it radiates and by which it is animated through
and through, even if we cannot delimit this quality with exactitude.

Can analysis, however, seek a structure in expression itself
and discover schemata in it as it discovers them in the sensuous? This is the point at which analysis meets its limit. Expression is a quality, and, as Bergson has shown, qualities do not
allow themselves to be either decomposed or composed. Just
as we cannot determine those precise patterns which constitute
a person's unique style, we cannot isolate those specific patterns
which constitute a work's expression. We cannot reduce to their
elements the melancholy grace of Ravel's *Pavane pour une
enfante défunte*, the glory of Franck's chorales, or the tender
sensitivity of Debussy's *La Fille aux cheveux de lin*. We could
possibly fasten epithets to substantives which designate this
quality, but such an effort signifies simply the impotence of
our language and not a real diversity. Expression is grasped in
a single act and is apprehended as an indecomposable unity.

Yet the analytical spirit does not give up easily. Instead of
seeking the components of the feeling revealed by the work—
instead of a conceptual analysis whose artificiality cannot be
denied even if it is legitimate—analysis can seek the elements
which produce this feeling and are particularly expressive.
When we admire the striking serenity of someone's face, do we
not seek the characteristics which produce this impression in
us—the contrast between the lines of the forehead which speak
of passion and struggle and the calm gaze, the vivacity of the
pupils, or the firm outline of the mouth? It is in the same way
that we refer to expressive traits in the work of art. De Schloezer
mentions a large number of these traits in his study of Bach.[14]
Similarly, is it not the return of the opening themes, their re-
absorption in a movement constantly more rapid, and finally,
the splendor of the transition from a minor to a major key which
are responsible for the power of affirmation in Franck's *Prélude,
choral et fugue*? Is it not the indecisiveness of the rhythm and
tonality that is responsible for the strange grace of *La Fille aux
cheveux de lin*? In every musical work, there are privileged
chords or modulations—just as there are key words in poems,

14. See Boris de Schloezer, *Introduction à J. S. Bach* (Paris: Gallimard,
1947).—Trans.

or principal hues and forms in plastic works—which are particularly laden with meaning and return insistently. Moreover, these traits can be extremely diverse. They are, for example, particular visual shapes, details of the mode of writing, or melodic themes which, as we have observed, cannot be aesthetically indifferent and must thus be expressive in themselves.

Let us, however, be cautious here. It may be that we discover certain particularly expressive traits or characteristics in this way only because we have already discovered the expression of the whole work. We refer to these traits only after the fact, and they do not bear the burden of expression by themselves. They are expressive only in relation to the entirety of the work. Would they remain expressive if they were isolated or inserted into another context? A musical development can modulate from minor to major without producing the effect created by Franck's *Chorale*. Musical syntax can be rambling and apparently relaxed without producing the effect of Debussy's *Préludes*. One and the same stroke of the pen can possess very different expressions, depending on the context, and thus no single stroke is expressive by itself. Conversely, all the elements of the work can converge in the same expression. This means that the work as a whole is what bears expression. In order to locate precisely the traits to which we would like to assign an expression, it is necessary to go from part to whole. These traits are not elements on whose basis we could reconstitute the whole. They are not schemata, that is, the elements of a structure or the generative agents of a totality.

Furthermore, when such traits are collected together and systematically exploited, they cease to be expressive, as a result of this very effort. Genuine expression, as we have just seen, is discreet and does not tolerate rash efforts. To strive to express by all the devices at one's disposal is to place oneself outside the realm of expression altogether. Like Sartre's waiter who plays at being a waiter, a person who tries to present a parody of himself is in effect seeking to become his own statue and to petrify himself in the in-itself.[15] He employs his spontaneity—only to become congealed within it. In the same way, a work loses the expressiveness which is the sign of its quasi spontaneity when it asserts its own expression and plays at being expressive. Therefore expression must not be willed and obtained by procedures which can be discovered by analysis or imitated in

15. See Jean-Paul Sartre, *Being and Nothingness,* trans. Hazel Barnes (New York: Philosophical Library, 1956), Pt. 1.—Trans.

pastiche. The fact remains, however, that we can still search for expressive traits in the work, but solely on the condition of not forgetting that: (1) we can attempt this inquiry only after having experienced, in the presence of the total work, the singular affective quality which the work expresses; and (2) these traits are not schemata capable of engendering expression through their own development or their synthesis. Strictly speaking, expression can be analyzed only insofar as it at first escapes analysis.

Thus analysis encounters its own limits and sends us back to perception, through which the aesthetic object is grasped in its unity and with all its meaning. In this way, analysis substantiates what we have said of the being of the aesthetic object. It shows, first, that the object exists as for-us because it is through perception that the object is enabled to fulfill itself, and that the expression in which the object attains its highest form can reveal itself. However, by disclosing the object's structure (a structure which results from the fact that it is created), analysis also shows that the object is in-itself. This is confirmed by its spatial qualities—where "spatial" is understood as the characteristic of givenness possessed by the given. Finally, analysis shows that the aesthetic object is for-itself. Its power of expression confers upon it a quasi subjectivity. The schemata which preside over its composition give rise to an invincible movement within the sensuous—which displays itself in a secret, inner temporality—while at the same time furnishing form to the sensuous and giving it a force akin to nature. Because the aesthetic object is thus endowed with a sort of interiority, it is capable of expression. But the temporality of this object is revealed in our own ongoing duration. For, once again, the aesthetic object is a quasi subject only for the authentic subject, that is, for the perceiving spectator. Thus it is perception which we must now consider.

PART III

Phenomenology of
Aesthetic Perception

THE PHENOMENOLOGY of the aesthetic object must now give way to the phenomenology of aesthetic perception. In fact, the former both prepares for and presupposes the latter, because of the especially close relation of object and perception in aesthetic experience. Yet it is not through an artifice of method that we have been able to introduce the distinction between perception and object. In analyzing the work of art, we have observed and confirmed that the aesthetic object claims the autonomy of an in-itself and merits separate consideration. Nevertheless, the aesthetic object finds its completion in perception, to which we have made continual reference. For this reason, we can be briefer in our study of aesthetic perception. We already know that its goal is the appearing of the aesthetic object, and we know by now what this object is. The crucial task will be to delineate the intrinsic characteristics of aesthetic perception by contrasting it with ordinary perception. This contrast will be maintained throughout our description.

Thus we shall set forth here a general theory of perception. In accordance with this theory, we shall distinguish between three successive moments of perception: presence, representation, and reflection. These moments parallel the three elements of the aesthetic object: the sensuous, the represented object, the expressed world. We should not be surprised at this, since the aesthetic object is also a perceived object. Yet we should beware of a too facile assimilation. It will soon appear that the object represented by the aesthetic object—that is, its subject—is not the sole occupant of the plane of representation. The sensuous must also be represented and not merely lived. Also, it may already be surmised that, by appealing to feeling, the reading of expression in aesthetic perception is substituted for, or in any case conjoined with, reflection rather than being identified with it. Moreover, we must not forget that, beyond the plurality of aspects which analysis distinguishes within it, the aesthetic object is

[333]

one. It is unitary as perceived, and perception itself is unified insofar as it is unifying. The moments which we are going to distinguish within perception do not really divide it. Instead of a chronological genesis, these moments spell out the deepening which perception can undergo and through which it becomes aesthetic perception. The parallelism of the three moments of perception and of the three elements of the aesthetic object will therefore serve to specify the singular aspects of aesthetic perception as well as to underscore their originality.

11 / Presence

EVERY COMPLETE PERCEPTION involves the grasping of a meaning. It is thus that perception engages us in action or reflection and is integrated into the course of our life. To perceive is not to register appearances passively—appearances which are meaningless in themselves. To perceive is to know—that is, to discover—a meaning within or beyond appearances which they offer only to the one who knows how to decipher them. To perceive is also to draw from this knowledge the consequences that accord with the intention guiding our conduct. But how is this meaning deciphered? How do we effect the movement from the sign to the signified? To say that this is done by judgment is to invoke intelligence as a *deus ex machina* without showing its origin or advent, as well as to presuppose an object already given to this intelligence. And to say that it is the result of learning and that nature teaches us from the repetition of contiguities, as when we learn the meaning of a signal, is still too simple. For one thing, certain meanings appear to be understood at once, in an immediate experience. Thus the child is in accord with the world, comprehending the gestures or the language of others as soon as he is capable of certain modes of behavior, long before repetition has been able to establish stable associations and fix them in him. Then again, the mechanical link between sign and thing signified does not constitute a signification. There is signification only if two conditions are fulfilled. First, this link must be realized in behavior by acquiring a certain urgency or authority. Meaning is not primarily something that I think with detachment but something that concerns and determines me, resonating in me and moving me. The pure signification that I contemplate without adhering to it will arise from this more primitive signification, which convinces me because it sets me in motion. Meaning is a demand to which I respond with my body. The second condition, which underlies the imperious character of meaning, is that the meaning be grasped immediately in the sign. The duality of sense and sign will appear only on the basis of their unity, as we have seen in the case of language. Sense and sign are distinguishable only when I become capable of interrogating signs and seeking their signification, and when the sense is more to be thought than lived. But I can decipher signs only when I have already had the experience of signification. I am capable of effecting a higher synthesis of the signified and the signifying only because this synthesis is given to me (in the Gestalt formula) "in the emergence of an indissoluble signification." The fact that we thus perceive significations is the primary message of Gestalt psychology. The object is meaningful by itself, bearing its meaning within itself, *before* the relation constitutive of signification is shown and made explicit.

Consequently, a theory of meaning must begin by describing an existential plane of perception in which presence to the world is realized and in which there is manifested an ability to read directly the meaning borne by the object—that is, in living it without having to decipher or explicate a duality. This theory should beware of the convenient and dangerous notion of "representation" which results from the notion of a closed consciousness. To penetrate the palace of consciousness, the thing would have to undergo a metamorphosis in order to be presented to us.[1] Representation would then be an event which occurs inside one's mind and to which the object is admitted—like a private spectacle within closed doors which consciousness furnishes to itself with the means at hand, namely, the images registered by memory and stored in the unconscious, and the innate ideas which are also interior to the mind.[2] But, in fact, things are

1. As Arthur Rimbaud says in "A Season in Hell": "The thing is in your soul as in a palace emptied so as to avoid seeing a person as undistinguished as yourself." [See Rimbaud, *Complete Works, Selected Letters,* trans. Wallace Fowlie (Chicago: University of Chicago Press, 1966), p. 200.—Trans.]

2. Now everything is false in this imagery, at least to the extent that it now proceeds from the feeling of an "inner life." But the inner life has a moral connotation, indicating that certain of our acts or thoughts answer more closely to ourselves and that this occurs between us and ourselves— or between "*Existenz* and its transcendence," as Jaspers says—without any

present to us in perception, and there is no screen between them and us. We are both of the same race.

The plane of the prereflective has been acutely analyzed by Merleau-Ponty. In his view, the object has no commerce with a transcendent mind which would comprehend it by assembling scattered images furnished separately to each sense. The discovery of the object is not like the solution to a riddle or a case of hidden identity, in which diverse and abstract pieces of information are given concerning the object—strictly speaking, a task of the understanding. Instead, the object that I perceive is revealed to my body insofar as my body is myself, a body permeated with soul and capable of experiencing the world. Thus my body is not an anonymous object which reveals itself only to an act of knowing. Now, objects do not exist primarily for my thought but for my body. Perhaps this is the meaning of the "judgment of perception" which Kant distinguished from the "judgment of experience" and which corresponds to a primary contact with things.[3] If the thing does not possess *de jure* a secret for me, this is because the thing is on a level with me or, rather, because through my body I am on a level with *it*. My body has power over things, since it reigns over them and yet opens itself to them. My body is, as it were, a branching out from things and is capable of recording their presence or absence. The transcendental activity which intellectualism assigns to the mind can also be attributed to the body. Where Lagneau spoke of a rapid judgment dulled by habit, we may talk of a corporeal intellection.[4] As living and as mine, the body is itself capable of knowledge, and this fact represents a scandal only for those who consider the objective rather than the animated body.

Yet we cannot limit all perception to the level of the body. Once a corporeal *cogito,* whose relation to the world is no longer effected by a constitutive consciousness but by the course of an existence, is substituted for a reflective *cogito,* and once it is admitted that "consciousness can live in existing things without reflection, abandoning itself to their concrete structure which has not yet been converted into an expressible significa-

---

witness other than those capable of comprehending and aiding us. But it is useless to found a psychology of interiority on a morality of interiority, since the inner life must itself be experienced openly and in the light of day.

3. See Immanuel Kant, *Prolegomena to Any Future Metaphysics,* trans. Lewis White Beck (New York: Liberal Arts Press, 1950), § 18.—Trans.

4. Jules Lagneau (1858–94), French philosopher.—Trans.

tion"[5]—can it then be pretended that perception is truly conscious? This objection in no way aims at restoring the alternatives of either total or zero consciousness, nor does it contest the reality of a primitive plane on which one's own body exercises its powers as a prelude to knowledge. It seeks only to uphold the rights of reflective perception as a moment of aesthetic experience and also as a prelude to science, whose advent must be shown and which should not be smuggled onto the plane of the unreflective.[6] On the plane of presence, everything is given, nothing is known. Or, if you will, here I know things in the same way that they know me, that is, without explicitly recognizing them. Conscious perception will thereby gain the impression of plenitude, of *Leibhaftigkeit*, which consecrates it. But conscious perception must add to it the power of seeing, of detaching itself. On this plane, signification is experienced by the body in its connivance with the world. The object as seen says something, just as a certain heaviness in the air indicates a tempest to the sailor, or a strident intonation expresses anger. However, on the one hand, the object says these things by itself without suggesting the representation of anything else. On the

5. Maurice Merleau-Ponty, *The Structure of Behavior*, trans. A. L. Fisher (Boston: Beacon, 1963), chap. 4.

6. Moreover, this is the same objection that we would be tempted to direct to Bergson when, at the beginning of *Matter and Memory*, he starts with images—"we must begin with representation itself, that is, with the totality of perceived images" (p. 53)—and identifies them with things. What may justify this move is a Hegelian concern to identify nature and mind, in this case the physical and the psychical. This is why Bergson says that "representation is already drawn into things," that "the universe is a kind of consciousness," and that "the removal of all memory allows us to pass from perception to matter, from subject to object" (p. 64). Yet Bergson distinguishes between presence and representation, just as Merleau-Ponty differentiates between presence and truth. We are among things whose meaning is to be present to us, and our present resides in our adaptations to them. But we are not among things as one thing among others. We are our body and our body is the organ of a freedom, a center of indetermination. Through its ability to introduce a sort of choice, our body effects "a discernment already manifesting mind" (p. 252). But this description of presence as a corporeal kingdom made comprehensible by its spontaneity becomes meaningful only on the basis of the postulate that perceiving is acting, not knowing. Bergson may be unfaithful to this postulate when he tries to insinuate representation, a form of contemplation, into presence, which is action: "our representation of things is born from their coming to be reflected against our freedom" (p. 214). This reflection of bodies on my body may not be mechanical, since my body is already freedom. But can it be identified with the reflection from which representation arises and which makes us pass from action to knowledge? (The quoted passages are from *Matter and Memory*, trans. N. M. Paul and W. S. Palmer [Garden City, N.Y.: Doubleday, Anchor Books, 1959].)

other hand, the object says them to my body without eliciting, through some representation, an act of intelligence other than that of the body. It is thus that we are in the world—by forming a subject-object totality in which the subject and the object are not yet distinguishable.

Such is the plane of presence. A theory of perception cannot remain there. It must break open a pathway from a comprehension lived by the body to the conscious intellection effected at the level of representation. Nevertheless, perception does begin in presence, and it is precisely aesthetic experience which confirms this. The aesthetic object is above all the apotheosis of the sensuous, and all its meaning is given in the sensuous. Hence the latter must be amenable to the body. Thus the aesthetic object first manifests itself to the body, immediately inviting the body to join forces with it. Instead of the body's having to adapt itself to the object in order to know it, it is the object which anticipates, in order to satisfy, the demands of the body. The analysis of the work of art has shown this. The schemata organizing the sensuous seek to confer on it not only brilliance and prestige but also an ability to convince the body. It is primarily our body that is moved by rhythm and that resonates with harmony. It is through the body that the aesthetic object is first taken up and assumed in order to pass from potentiality to act. And it is also through the body that there is a unity of the aesthetic object, especially in the case of composite works, such as opera or ballet, which appeal to several senses at once. The unity which is in the object and which is, as we have suggested, the unity of its expression can be grasped only if the diversity of the sensuous is first gathered together in a *sensorium commune*. The body is the always already established system of equivalences and intersensory transpositions. It is for the body that unity is given before diversity.

One may even say that the virtue of the aesthetic object is largely measured by its ability to seduce the body. If the idea of an aesthetic pleasure has any meaning, it is in terms of a pleasure experienced by the body—a pleasure more refined and discreet than that which accompanies the satisfaction of organic needs, yet one which still sanctions self-affirmation. For it is born from a felicitous use of the body, when the object, instead of disconcerting or menacing the body, offers itself to the latter so that it can exercise its powers freely, without embarking on some questionable adventure. It appears that the aesthetic object anticipates the body's desires or gratifies them insofar as it awakens them. Thus we follow a melody, or promenade in the park, by confidently entrusting ourselves to the object. The pleasure we feel is basically one of innocence. And it is remarkable that the aesthetic experience always has this accent. Of course, this is in part due to the fact that this experience implies leisure, transporting us into a world where all is play and where that which is represented is unreal. But it is also due to the fact that aesthetic experience helps us to realize an accord with the object which stops short of discords and demands, allowing us to renew with the world a pact that evokes a golden age. We may cite here Alain's analyses of the operative catharsis on the part of the spectator as well as the creator, effected through the contemplation as well as the creation of the work of art— analyses which show that Alain's psychology does not reduce to an elementary intellectualism.[7] The aesthetic object takes us back to innocence by repressing emotions and imagination, which exasperate themselves over the nothingness of the imaginary, and by composing the beautiful human form through which the spectator in turn imitates art.

The experience of the spectator exists in the image of the creator's experience. The aesthetic object must be created and performed with equal felicity. A lugubrious dancer ruins a ballet. A painter whose touch is hesitant or discouraged, or a musician who does not trust his piano as if it were a friend, fails in his task. The aesthetic object can certainly express despair or the tragic, but it must express it felicitously: the aesthetic object should not fail even when it expresses failure. Felicity belongs in the body of the artist if not in his soul. Thus the relationship between creator and spectator first manifests itself, through the intermediary of the work, as a sort of corporeal complicity—which may be the case in all human relations. A psychology of creation would insist on this. The phrase "thinking with one's hands" applies to all artists, but especially to the composer improvising at his piano, or the painter at his easel. All that either one knows has passed into his body, which has made itself into music or painting, and this body can now take the initiative and *invent*. It cannot be doubted that inspiration proceeds from the body, if by "inspiration" we mean the spontaneity of enthusiasm, the air of sincerity, freshness, and joy possessed by all great works of art—even when they bear

7. See Alain, *Système des beaux-arts* (Paris: Gallimard, 1926), bk. I.— Trans.

a grave or desperate expression, to which a felicitous creation often secretly imparts some atom of joy or accent of innocence. Nothing compensates for the absence of this inspiration in certain contrived, stiff, and finally tiresome works which were not conceived with the hands. In these, the artist has failed to establish with his body the most valuable of alliances. In contrast, a mere sketch resulting from an improvisation can be beautiful, more beautiful than a work too painstakingly finished. Moreover, it is not always true that the signs of labor must be erased from the aesthetic object. The architect certainly gets rid of his scaffolding, as the writer negates the words he crosses out, but the architect cannot make weight itself disappear, as we see in the case of flying buttresses. Rodin was not ashamed of the mark of his thumb, or Cézanne of his brushstrokes. The same holds for the performer in music. The pianist knows the work with his hands, and all of it has a place in his motor field. Each inflection of the melody awakens an echo in his body, as do the subtleties of harmony which mean as much for the hand as for the ear. He hears with his fingers. Similarly, the conductor hears with his arms—with his whole body, through which the music flows and becomes dance. The same is true of the theatrical director with his eye. For him, everything becomes situation, encounter, movement—spectacle. And, faced with the aesthetic object, every spectator is a performer in his own fashion. It is not a question of being a virtuoso or knowing the object as intimately as the virtuoso who produces it. But the spectator participates in this production. Even a plastic work, having no need of incarnating itself in duration, is at least allowed to expand within the spectator. Just as a scientific object may be known only if a mechanical model is made of it, so the spectator knows the aesthetic object because a dynamic model surges within him, where the object is remade.

Therefore the presence of the aesthetic object to the body is necessary. As immanent in the sensuous, meaning itself must traverse the body. Meaning can be read by feeling or elaborated upon by reflection only if it is first received and experienced by the body, that is, if the body is intelligent from the beginning. Yet the reading of expression presupposes another engagement in addition to that of the body. I do not yet understand a poem when I merely let myself be carried along by the words and rocked by their rhythm. In fact, close inspection reveals that rhythm is itself grasped only to the degree that the words are understood. But, conversely, the meaning of the word—at least of the poetic word—is understood only by means of the resonance it awakens, and the movement it induces, within me. The experience of signification occurs through the experience of the sensuous virtues which the word has for the mouth proffering it or for the ear hearing it. Hence the body is always linked with perception. It is thus that the perceived possesses both the irrecusable character of the given through which the aesthetic object is naturelike and the air of familiarity by which it is closer to us than any other object.

Nonetheless, the aesthetic object does not exist for the body alone. If it did, the most beautiful work would be the most flattering one. It is even dangerous for art to be no more than the occasion for bodily excitement or emotion. The music transporting us, the monument crushing us, the poem uttering itself mechanically, the painting flattering the eye speak too vividly to the body to move the mind. We have spoken of works of art that fail through their very excess of expressiveness. They can also fail—and it is basically the same phenomenon—through an excess of corporeal eloquence. And in fact the great works do not make any considerable advances toward, or concessions to, the body. Of course, they have a structure which makes them apprehendable by the body, but again we must make an effort to seize this structure, which is not always revealed on first contact. The body positioned in front of the aesthetic object must be equipped with habits and capable of discriminating judgment. Perhaps such virtues, inscribed in the body, do not proceed from it. If the body were unaided in its activity, the aesthetic object could well lose its patience, as it were. To be sure, in making the body the instrument of our presence to the world and of the knowledge by which this world has an immediate meaning, we already confer on the body powers that an objectifying perspective cannot recognize in the body-as-object. In no event must we underestimate these powers in grasping the aesthetic object. But if the lived body carries the mind in it, can the mind not react on the body in turn? It is not prejudicial to the body to show (if one can) the advent of mind, that is, how the body surpasses itself. The body's function in aesthetic experience will be better understood when the dialectic of which it is the seat and the power of which it is the organ are finally known.

Thus if the body must bring us and the aesthetic object into accord, and if the body pays homage to this object even in the pleasure that it sometimes experiences in its presence, this does not occur in terms of its normal proclivities. The contact that the body makes with ordinary objects usually ends in an action of using them rather than in a contemplation which consecrates them. We recall the famous formula of Bergson's *Matter and Memory:* "Recognizing an ordinary object consists above all in knowing how to use it." Must we reproach Bergson, who understood the role of the body in the actualization of images, for having believed that the body is materialistic because it is material? Maurice Pradines has shown that all Bergson's examples are chosen from the realm of artificial objects, in which gnosis reduces to *praxis.* Thus Pradines opposes, to the perception of the chair or the fork, the disinterested perception of a flower, the blue sky, a tree at the horizon.[8] We would add the aesthetic object to this list. The body may have a certain way of relating itself habitually to the farthest and most inoffensive or useless things, a phenomenon which a pragmatic theory of perception cannot explain. Perhaps the body is capable of gratuitous acts. Yet it is unarguable that aesthetic perception somehow goes against nature. Perhaps this is why aesthetic perception leads us back to a golden age. Such perception often fails because the body is naturally needful and because it seeks to know so that it may act rather than contemplate. However indispensable its role in aesthetic contemplation, the body cannot carry out this contemplation by itself alone. It adopts the aesthetic attitude only by virtue of a decision that it does not itself make. This suffices to explain both that the body must be educated to contribute to aesthetic experience and that the work of art itself, if it is made for the body, is not made for the body alone and may at times even thwart it.

Moreover, when we remain at this first contact of the aesthetic object with the body, and even if the body gains intimacy with the object immediately, the only signification deciphered is one for the body. What the work represents, at least in the representational arts, is not yet truly known. But it is already present, since to grant the body an elementary power of comprehension is precisely to preclude both the distinction between the sensuous and its meaning, and any consideration of the sensuous as a senseless stimulus to which the sensory organs react in accordance with a natural law. The sensuous is seized as the sensuousness *of* something, and the first movement of perception is to apprehend an *object,* whether this object is real (e.g., a vase or a building) or represented (the subject of the

8. Maurice Pradines, *Traité de psychologie générale* (Paris: Presses Universitaires de France, 1946), I, 192.

painting or the story told by the novel). Does the body suffice for this act of apprehension? Can a reflection on meaning which discovers it to be inexhaustible be carried out by the body? It becomes increasingly evident that we cannot remain on the plane of presence alone—nor can a general theory of perception.

12 / Representation and Imagination

[I] IMAGINATION

PERCEPTION IS NOT wholly confined to the level of the prereflective. Thus we must move from the lived to the thought, from presence to representation. Can this movement be theoretically justified? Of course, the mind can no more be deduced than the body, but the perpetual oscillation between the reflective and the unreflective, the perceived and the lived—an oscillation best exemplified in aesthetic perception—can at least be observed and described. In any event, the advent and the perpetual rebirth of the reflective *cogito* oblige us to evoke a new transcendental factor. In the last chapter, the transcendental was, as it were, the capacity of being-with assumed by the body. In the present chapter, the transcendental will be the capacity of seeing assumed by the imagination, the self as *lumen naturale*. The image, which is itself a *metaxu* or middle term between the brute presence where the object is experienced and the thought where it becomes idea, allows the object to appear, to be present as represented. The imagination somehow creates the liaison between mind and body. Even if imagination is the capacity to suggest and make us see, it is rooted in the body, as the examination of the schemata involved in music and painting has already indicated. By invoking a higher level of perception, we do not reject the plane of presence. We shall see that even unconscious knowledge located within presence nourishes representation. As a result, the body is not absent from

[345]

the higher level. Representation is the heir to what the body has experienced. Moreover, the body itself prepares for representation. As the center of indetermination, the body indicates in advance the movement by which we shall arrive there. The body reconciles us with the object instead of separating us from it, but we should not think that its activity is exhausted in possessing and consuming. Pradines has shown that "a quality without exteriority, as it is described by Berkeley and J. Müller, is impossible. . . . An impression cannot assume a quality or, in other words, cannot begin to qualify an object without putting it *at a distance* from us." [1] The schematism by which the object can become an object for an intelligence is attributable to the body. In this view, the body does not merely respond to the object. It imitates the conditions under which the object can be thought and located in a world. Yet the advent of representation cannot be grasped without first of all evoking characteristics of a for-itself.

We must distinguish between the transcendental and the empirical aspects of imagination, even though these aspects are ultimately conjoined. As transcendental, the imagination is seen as the possibility of a look [*regard*] having a "spectacle" as its correlate. This look presupposes both an act of opening and an act of withdrawal—a withdrawal, in that the totality formed by subject and object must be disintegrated in order that the intentional movement of the for-itself, by which it opposes itself to an object, can be accomplished. An opening is involved, insofar as the detachment of consciousness from object hollows out an empty space, which is the *a priori* of sensibility and in which the object can take on form. In fact, the withdrawal *is* an opening, the movement one of illumination. But how is the detachment which creates both the withdrawal and the opening possible? Through temporality.[2] To withdraw from activity is to take refuge in the past. On the psychological plane, this is seen

1. Maurice Pradines, *Traité de psychologie générale* (Paris: Presses Universitaires de France, 1946), I, 414.
2. We cannot resolve here the metaphysical problem which arises at this point. As Heidegger has shown, the affinity of the for-itself and temporality is such that one can ask whether it is temporality which constitutes the for-itself (as when I am the beneficiary of a duration that I serve to display) or whether it is the for-itself which temporalizes itself (as when the upsurge of a consciousness makes time appear). If all consciousness is consciousness of time, is it not time itself which is consciousness? [See Martin Heidegger, *Kant and the Problem of Metaphysics*, trans. James S. Churchill (Bloomington: Indiana University Press, 1962), *passim.* —Trans.]

in the phenomenon of attention. To be attentive, to give representation its full due, is to transport oneself into the past in order to grasp the object in its future, for there is a future for myself (a future of the world, my speech, or my gesture) only if I am already in the past. I perceive only *from* the past and *into* the future; in the present, I can only act. To contemplate or think is to return to the past in order to surprise the future. Only by detaching myself from the present where I am lost in things do I cease being one with the object through presence. The *re* of "representation" expresses this interiorization, just as the *con* of "contemplate" expresses the possibility of a survey and a simultaneity which summon up space.

For space is contemporary with time, symbolizing it immediately.[3] The opening created by withdrawal defines space, which is the milieu where the other can appear when I have withdrawn into myself. (This is why all allusion to otherness has recourse to spatial metaphors.) Temporality constitutes only the relationship of the self with itself definitive of an "I." It is by means of space that appearances appear and that seeing becomes possible. Every image possesses a spatial background. I contemplate what is in space from the depth of the past. If, on this basis, I can follow the movement of time—lie in wait for the future and anticipate it—this is because space somehow contains the future. Space is always there, and this "always" inscribed in space compensates for the "no longer" or the "not yet" of temporality. And if space is the condition or, rather, the nature of everything represented insofar as it is given, we have evidence that the given is always appearance, that it is always presented imperfectly, and that there always remain an elsewhere and a beyond. Space, born from a movement toward the past, calls forth the future. The dialectic of subject and object is predelineated in the dialectic of time and space.

The advent of representation occurs with the upsurge of space and time. In agreement with Heidegger's interpretation of Kant, we shall attribute this upsurge to the transcendental imagination. The empirical imagination prolongs this movement, converting appearance into object. The transcendental imagination prefigures the empirical, making the empirical possible. Transcendental imagination expresses the possibility of representation, while empirical imagination accounts for a given representation's meaningfulness and its integration into a total

3. We have already indicated the sense and importance of this solidarity. [See chap. 7 above.—Trans.]

representation of a world. As transcendental, the imagination sees to it that there is a given; as empirical, imagination makes certain that this given, enriched by possibles, possesses a meaning.

What is the source of these possibles? How do they intervene in the form of an image? That which imagination actually contributes to perception by way of extending and animating appearances is not created *ex nihilo*. Imagination nourishes representation with modes of implicit knowledge [*les savoirs*] previously constituted in lived experience. More precisely, imagination plays a dual role. It mobilizes such knowledge, and it converts what is acquired by experience [*l'acquis*] into something visible. In the former case, we must consider knowledge as an aspect of imagination. For knowledge is a virtual state of the image, whose intentional correlate is the possible. Imagination mobilizes the knowledge which it furnishes to representation. Hume's analysis is relevant here. Imagination constitutes the associations which form the indispensable commentary on present impressions and which enable us to know an object. The only problem is that Hume's analysis is warped by the sensationalist prejudice which inspired it. Associations appear as a mechanical miracle, because they are effected between ideas that are the residues of heterogeneous impressions. Synthesis is achieved through habit, which, even though natural (not premeditated or organized by a transcendental activity), still remains somewhat artificial. To avoid this artificiality, we must look to the experience of presence, in which what Husserl calls "passive synthesis" operates naturally by means of the body.[4] Thus, through our body, we are on an even level with the object, though without fully realizing it. We acquire a familiarity with the object which no act of thought can supplant and which is indispensable for all knowledge by acquaintance [*connaissance*]. In affirming this, we are only taking Hume at his word. But we refuse to interpret habit as a mechanical means of associating ideas. Rather, we envisage habit as the organ of an inner condition and, in accordance with its etymology, of a mastery of the corporeal object. Therefore, if imagination mobilizes modes of implicit knowledge, it does so not so much by taking the initiative in an unpredictable outburst as by following the course of a previous experience undergone by the body on the plane of presence.

4. See Edmund Husserl, *Analysen zur passiven Synthesis,* ed. M. Fleischer (The Hague: Nijhoff, 1966), *passim.*—Trans.

As a result, the essential function of imagination is to convert this experience into something visible, giving it the status of representation. We could say that representation is that which makes us think *of*, but we should place the emphasis on the evocative capacity suggested by the "think," not on the connective capacity suggested by the "of" (a capacity belonging to the body). The crucial matter is always the transition from presence to representation. On both the empirical and the transcendental levels, imagination is a force which strives for visibility. The transcendental imagination having opened up the area in which something given can appear, the empirical imagination fills out this field. This is done without multiplying the given. Instead, images are elicited to form a quasi given. These images are not, strictly speaking, images of the visible. However, they put us en route toward the visible by continually appealing to perception for decisive confirmation. For we must realize that the modes of implicit knowledge with which imagination seeks to dominate appearances are neither perceptual nor conceptual. They exist in a prior form in which they can be annexed to a representation.

When we perceive, these modes of knowledge are not evoked *as* knowledge, that is, as supplementary information added to the perceived from the outside, or as a gloss adjoined to a text. They are there as the very meaning of the perceived object, given with it and in it. This proximity of knowledge to the perceived is the work of imagination, for knowledge thus integrated should be termed an "image." If I *know* that snow is cold, I can actualize the memory of experiences that I have had of this coldness; but when I see snow, it appears cold to me without my effecting this actualization. This means, first, that the cold is not known by an influence which would summon up a previously constituted knowledge of cold. Yet it is not felt in the way that white is seen (though we may, instructed by painters, doubt that white itself is seen, and it could be shown that white is not itself seen without the aid of imagination). This sort of immediate presence, nonconceptual and yet nonsensuous, is the "image" of cold which accompanies the perception of snow and renders it eloquent. My implicit knowledge is converted into an abstract and yet real presence *of* something sensuous which is adumbrated but not wholly given. The same holds for the symbolic images in which comprehension is occasionally made determinate. In Sartre's example, the tumultuous and endless sea is an image of the proletariat; it gives neither a true nor an objective comprehension of the object designated by it.[5] Comprehension in the form of an image is an image of comprehension, just as the cold of unfelt snow or the flavor of a roast evoked by a famished man is the image of an unsensed sensuousness [*un sensible non senti*].[6] Second, the cold can be anticipated only because it has already been known. When memory takes the form of an image, anticipation becomes reminiscence. Finally, the image adheres to perception in constituting the object. It is not a piece of mental equipment in consciousness but a way in which consciousness opens itself to the object, prefiguring it from deep within itself as a function of its implicit knowledge.

Therefore, the world is present to us in flesh and blood only because it is at the same time implicitly present in images. To unfold the empirical content of these images, we must appeal to the modes of implicit knowledge which constitute experience. However, in perception such modes of knowledge remain in a latent state of "empty intentions." Consequently, we cannot assert that perception is composed of sensations to which judgment adds modes of knowledge. Modes of implicit knowledge are not *known* [*connu*] as such. Rather, as latent in the form of images, they are incarnate in objects. In this manner, imagination comes to the aid of perception. There *is* an irrecusable given which elicits and directs the imagination: perception is not wholly imagination. But this given is only appearance, since it is contemplated and not lived. Under its transcendental aspect, the imagination allows the given to arise, but as empirical, it restores on the plane of representation a degree of the density

5. See Jean-Paul Sartre, *The Psychology of Imagination,* trans. B. Frechtman (New York: Washington Square Press, 1966), pp. 133 ff.

6. We shall, perhaps, be criticized for juxtaposing the examples of a man who perceives cold in the whiteness of snow and of a famished man who dreams of food. But it is incorrect to restrict imagination to the second case. Insofar as the snow is not in contact with my skin, its coldness is as absent as food is to the famished. The whiteness alone is given to me. Of course, it is the whiteness *of snow,* for perception goes immediately to the object, and its coldness is then given with the object. Yet the coldness is not given in the same way as the whiteness: it is implicit, i.e., a manner of being absent in presence. In contrast, the food which obsesses the famished man is radically absent. Nevertheless, it is present enough to make his mouth water. Without being deluded, he at least realizes the implicit savor and taste of meat and thus enters the universe of food. In the first case, we have an absent presence; in the second, a present absence. It is the context provided by the world which determines whether the image is illusory or valid. All depends on the extent to which the image adheres to perception. In both cases, however, the image is something implicit which blossoms forth on the basis of the real—whether to confirm or to betray it.

and warmth of presence. Thus, instead of saying that the imaginary *is* a quasi present, we prefer to say that the imagination *furnishes* a quasi present, the equivalent of lived significations at the level of representation. It is in this fashion that, for example, the word *flower* designates "l'absente de tout bouquet." [7] But the designatum is nevertheless a flower whose look, fragrance, jocund spontaneity, or naïve pride exists in the margin of our consciousness. Imagination, guided by the text, creates a possible flower which blossoms forth from the word which names it. Similarly, the imagination makes the stone of a monument appear in its hardness, obstinacy, and coldness. These qualities are present as a halo around what I see, enriching my perception without encumbering or altering it.

We can now verify the ultimate unity of the transcendental and empirical imagination. The empirical imagination, which exploits the concrete knowledge [*le savoir concret*] that structures perception, can be clarified only in terms of the transcendental, which founds the possibility of seeing. The unity of two makes the ambiguity of imagination evident—an ambiguity which is finally that of the human condition itself. In fact, imagination appears to possess at once the two faces of nature and mind [*esprit*]. It belongs to the body to the degree that it animates the modes of implicit knowledge inherited from the experience of presence, while opening up reflection to the degree that it allows us to substitute the perceived for the lived. In this latter role, imagination interrupts the intimacy of presence by introducing not so much an absence as the distance within presence which constitutes representation, in terms of which the object confronts us at a distance, open to a look or to judgment.

This crucial ambiguity of imagination can be expressed in two ways. First, we can show that the planes of presence, from which imagination issues, and of representation, which it opens up, are reciprocal and complementary. Indeed, to the extent that it nourishes representation, the experience of presence provides an originary source of all knowledge by acquaintance and even of all consciousness, a source on which we constantly draw. Representation itself, that is, the transformation of the unreflective, is established by a mentalization of the corporeal whose principle is given by the imagination. But conversely, there is a perpetual corporealization of the mental. Our implicit modes of knowledge are continually sedimented into habits. The

7. This is a well-known phrase of Mallarmé, the French symbolist poet. —Trans.

mathematician gains familiarity with algorithms by means of a special lucidity, very much as the engineer becomes familiar with his machine, the composer with his piano, the speaker with words. Thus the unreflective is itself nourished by the reflective. Only by becoming degraded into *savoir-faire* do our implicit modes of knowledge become fully efficacious, for we possess a hold on the object only by conniving with it. As Valéry's Eupalinos says, we are doomed to impotence in all forms of creative activity in which the body plays no role. We must feel ourselves at ease with the object, even if it is mathematical or ideal, through the grace of our body. Yet the body possesses this wisdom only because it is the legatee of modes of implicit knowledge, and it is capable of action only because of the prior advent of ideas. Without such knowledge or ideas, the body is prone to panic or incomprehension, as in the first hearing of a musical work or in our first contact with a foreign language. In this sense, we could even say that the experience of presence, far from being originary, is in fact secondary. Nevertheless, we should not privilege either term by conferring a special priority on it. Any genesis must be, in Pradines's term, a "reciprocal genesis" whereby we oscillate from one term to another, confirming one by the other.[8] We are not a mere mind grafted onto a body or a body which is the precipitate of a degraded mind. We are always and simultaneously a body which becomes mind and a mind which becomes body.

In other words, at the threshold of representation we must posit imagination as the root of space and time, which form the *a priori* structure of all acts of appearing. But imagination can assume this function only if it is already capable of synthesis, thus of mind. The look is a look only in unifying, as Kant showed in his example of the house.[9] Space and time together form the field in which a synthesis can be effected. To open them up is to constitute the possibility of this synthesis. Moreover, they are themselves representable only because of the synthetic act which gathers together a pure manifold. They are, in this respect, nothing other than the ever possible liaison of places and of moments, the other-than-pure objects of a pure synthesis. Thus the imagination helps us to see only because it can unify. This point becomes even clearer when we move from

8. See Pradines, *Traité*, Vol. I, *passim*.—Trans.

9. Immanuel Kant, *Critique of Pure Reason*, trans. Norman Kemp Smith (New York: St. Martin's Press, 1929), p. 220.—Trans.

the transcendental to the empirical imagination, which is capable of extending the space of the given beyond the given only if it can assemble associations around this given. As we have seen, these associations are due to the activity of the body on the plane of lived experience. This indicates that the imagination, as a faculty of synthesis, can be seen as the beneficiary of the body, and thus that the transcendental is, by the same token, corporeal. Hence imagination is both nature and mind, bearing within it the characteristic antinomy of the human condition. As nature, it brings us into accord with nature; as mind, it allows us to survey and think nature. But we can sever our connection with nature only on the condition that we continue to recall it and remain faithful to it. Only as *naturata* are we *naturans*, and we are just as much constrained to make ourselves into objects in presence as objects are constrained to become mental in representation.

[II] PERCEPTION AND IMAGINATION

PERHAPS we are playing with fire by suggesting that imagination may lie at the root of perception. There are two objections to this suggestion which we must consider and which will lead us to specify aesthetic perception more carefully. The first, which can be considered more briefly, consists in the claim that to stress the role of imagination in perception is to make perception into a spectacle, and that such a form of knowledge, separated from praxis and labor and having no grip on the real, is merely free-floating and succumbs to the illusion of idealism. For, it is assumed, imagination is at most a manner of imitating an object's use, instead of actually creating it. Thus imagination always places us under the menace of the imaginary. Our response is to admit this objection. By insisting on the distinction between presence and representation, we have already accepted the notion that perception is first of all contemplative. This holds especially for aesthetic perception, which is more luxury than labor. The *work* is done by the artist; but this work is only presupposed by aesthetic contemplation, which is concerned with results, not effort.

The second objection proceeds from Sartre's well-argued thesis that perception and imagination are unreducible attitudes of consciousness which necessarily exclude one another.[10] For Sartre, the imagination is always empirical. Imagination makes an object appear which, in spite of its unreality, is so convincing that it seizes and engulfs consciousness. Since imagination is said to manifest the capacity of consciousness to nihilate the world, the imagining consciousness is totally involved in this activity and cannot negate its own negation. Only by a sudden turn of events, such as an awakening from deep sleep, can it break the enchantment and return to the real. Similarly, thought which relies on images always risks becoming lost in them. Sartre shows clearly that only a considerable reflective power enables one: (a) to avoid being the dupe of symbolic schemes which purport to give the solution to a problem; and (b) to refuse to lose oneself in images. Thus, for Sartre, imagination is unreducible to perception because of its characteristic charm. Imagination is opposed to perception as magic is to technique.

Perception, in contrast, aims at the real and puts us in the presence of the spatiotemporal object. Sartre grants that we see more than we perceive. However, following Husserl, he attributes this "more" to the empty intentions which complete the visible aspects of the object, conferring a certain richness on it. He admits that such intentions can initiate images which will be fully given when the intentions are fulfilled, but he maintains that, so long as they are empty, the intentions are heterogeneous to the images. But is this not to play on the terms "full" and "empty"? The image is said to fulfill the intention, but how can anything be fulfilled by the unreal? Conversely, are the intentions which enter into the constitution of the perceived object really empty? I do not perceive the opposite side of a cube, and my idea of the cube is quite different from the perception which I will have on turning it around. Yet the unseen face does count for something. It is *there*, and so am I (in intention). Can we say that there is no sense of plenitude here? Do we not have to invoke, precisely in this case, the imagination as a capacity to fulfill? Sartre cannot do this because he has defined the imaginary as unreal. Of course, we cannot deny the marked difference between the dreaming and the perceiving man, that is, between a consciousness which turns away from the real and one which aims squarely at the real. But does imagination find its culmination in dreaming?

10. See Sartre, *Psychology of Imagination*, p. 153; and Sartre, *Imagination*, trans. F. Williams (Ann Arbor: University of Michigan Press, 1962), p. 136.

When imagination is restricted to the single power of denying the real in favor of the unreal, one risks ignoring another manner of denying the real, namely, by surpassing it in order to return to it, just as we may hold ourselves in nothingness to make being emerge. There is an unreal which is a prereal—the constant anticipation of the real without which the real would be, for us, a mere spectacle lacking the depth of space and duration. I am in the world by virtue of always bearing the world within me, and yet I do so precisely so that I may discover it outside myself. (Perhaps it is in this sense that Bergson calls things "images" and that he can say that, at the limit, our perception is in things rather than in us. Perception is in things because things are images—because perception is finally in *us*, since the term "image" leads ineluctably back to us.) Thus the essential function of imagination is to preform the real in an act of expectation which allows us not only to anticipate and recognize the real (as Alain showed) but also to adhere to it. In comparison with this function, the fascination with the unreal on which Sartre insists appears as a sort of aberration in which the unreal, no longer a legitimate means of attaining the real, is posited as an end in itself. In fact, it is most often the real which is aimed at and elaborated upon by the imagination. But even when the imagination does roam—e.g., when I dream that I fly—the purity of my imagined flight, the freshness of the air, the vertigo of height in the dream are still virtues of the world and define the real—a real which frequently is felt only insofar as it is given value by the powers of imagination. Bachelard has shown how this is so. Do we have the right to charge with bad faith the child who dreams of flying and the poet who recreates infantile or dream images of flight?[11] They still reveal an aspect of the real. Even if labor remains the supreme measure of the real (as Hegel and Marx showed), revery can inspire work, as it often inspires scientific investigation in its early stages. The unreal is never entirely aberrant, and no fiction is wholly feigned. The wildest adventures imaginable—journeys which I can never take, landscapes traversed only with closed eyes—still retain an element of the real. Not only do they provide an event or object in the cultural world for the anthropologist or historian, but they furnish the fabric of the real—a countenance, sometimes unforgettable, of

11. See Gaston Bachelard, *L'Air et les songes* (Paris: Corti, 1943). —Trans.

the world—for the consciousness which lives them. The imaginary that seduces us is as instructive as it is ravishing.

Nevertheless, we cannot afford to ignore the warnings of rationalists from Lucretius to Alain. The errant imagination will naturally appear aberrant when compared with the strict notion of the real, which is most clearly exemplified in Cartesian extension and which science elaborates and praxis confirms. Moreover, it is essential for rational purposes to separate assiduously straightforward perception from leaps of imagination. In this respect, the opposition of perception and imagination is called for not only by doctrine but by ordinary wisdom. Consider Alain. Does he not agree with our attempt to rehabilitate imagination, even in its excesses, and to assign it a constitutive role? For him, imagination, though false when conceived as mere corporeal excitement, is still true as a human project. Imagination is, finally, an affirmation of a value which, though not real in itself, bestows sense on the real. This sense does not aid us in perceiving or in immediately completing the object (here Alain is to be distinguished from Bergson). Rather, it takes us beyond perception toward the achievement and completion of man himself. Imagined gods are valid insofar as they represent the meaning of the choice by which I realize humanity, not the immediate sense of the real. Thus work and art confirm imagination as much as they deny it. They give a thicker consistency to the invisible and create man through engendering the gods. Furthermore, does not a need to struggle unremittingly against imagination proceed precisely from the fact that it is always present? We can denounce its illusory character only if it is already in the process of creating illusions, and to create an illusion is to adhere closely to the real and to form a compact with it.

None of this should lead us to deny that there may be a fundamental difference between *Einbildung* and *Fantasie*, "imagination" and "fancy," imagining [*imaginer*] and supposing [*s'imaginer que*]. In the last of these verbal forms, the reflexive pronoun indicates a possible intervention of subjectivity and suggests that the image is here only the echo of our passions or inward structure. Also, the substitution of *que* for the direct object undercuts the intentional character of the imaginary object and discredits its truthfulness. In this regard, imagination would have two avatars, and its aberrations would form the ransom of its freedom. We would reach the unreal blindly or passively, because we have the capacity to attain the real, that is, because the real proposes itself to us on the condition that we somehow anticipate it. In other terms, there is an imagination which derealizes and one which realizes. The latter gives full weight to the real by assuring us of the presence of the hidden and the distant. The derealizing imagination is one which operates from zeal. It realizes only at random, inventing unprecedented worlds which experience will belie.

Whatever form imagination may take, it is always linked to perception, and its snares are dangerous only in this connection. From the very fact that perception represents an unceasing effort to overcome the seduction of images, we see that images are primary and that we reach the real through the unreal. It is because imagination continually enlarges the field of the real which is offered to it and furnishes its spatial and temporal depth that appearances gain a certain stability and that the real becomes a world—an inexhaustible totality in which appearances arise through the disposition of my body and the direction of my attention. Imagination is the *naturans* of the world. Understanding thinks an essence [*une nature*], but imagination opens up a world. The real loses its flatness only through the unreal, which puts the real into perspective and situates us in the midst of things—in a world which displays itself around us in all directions. In the last analysis, then, the imagination is turned toward the real. Derealization is only a partial function, and Sartre takes the part for the whole. To imagine is first of all to open up the possible, which is not necessarily realized in images. Imagination is to be distinguished from perception as the possible is distinguished from the given, not as the unreal is from the real. Imagining is reproductive, not productive. If imagining produces anything, it is the possibility of a given. Imagining does not furnish the content as perceived but sees to it that something *appears*. Its correlate is the possible, and this is why it can get carried away at times. In the kingdom of the possible, anything is possible. But when imagination functions normally—and especially when it functions aesthetically—the possible constitutes a prereal. It is for this reason that imagination is constantly in touch with the real, surpassing the given toward its sense.[12]

12. At this point there begins the movement from imagination to understanding, which thinks the necessary, i.e., the possible plus the real. This will be treated in detail below.

[III] IMAGINATION IN AESTHETIC PERCEPTION

EVEN THOUGH IMAGINATION is thus indispensable to both the advent and the richness of perception in general, its role in aesthetic perception is less important. The function imagination assumes there is similar to what we have called its "transcendental" aspect. The aesthetic object, too—indeed, especially —must be perceived at a proper distance and not simply lived in the proximity of presence. Pradines's distinction between distance and contact senses is again relevant here.[13] It is clear that there are, strictly speaking, no arts of contact, e.g., of odor, taste, or touch. When one speaks of an art of perfumery or of cooking, "art" signifies technique. But perhaps Pradines's distinction assumes its full meaning only with reference to the capacity for withdrawal which we have attributed to the imagination instead of to the senses. It may be necessary that spatial and temporal distance be first projected by a for-itself, in order that sight and hearing may illustrate this distance and cease to merge the object with the subject. In any case, it is evident that the aesthetic object, more than any other object, must become a spectacle for us. Our very behavior before it shows this necessity, e.g., the auditor at a concert who virtually enthrones himself. In such comportment we see once more the ambivalent nature of imagination, which exists within the body and yet is more than the body. For the body itself imitates this detachment. The schemata which structure the object and which energetically invite the body to associate itself with the object are at the same time the means by which the body is extended in relation to the object. Measuring, numbering, or qualifying time by arranging space—activities lived by the body and elicited by the aesthetic object—allow us to link up with this object in a sort of synchronism, while also detaching ourselves from it, though we still maintain a measure of domination over it.

The paradox of aesthetic perception at all levels is that one is at once *Zuschauer* and *Mitspieler,* both contemplator and participant.[14] But the participation, which we shall clarify further at the level of feeling, is never total. The attitude of the

13. See Pradines, *Traité,* I, 226, 404.—Trans.
14. See Richard Müller-Freienfels, *Psychologie der Kunst* (Leipzig: Teubner, 1912), p. 66. Müller-Freienfels takes up Groos's distinction between *Zufühlung* and *Einfühlung.*

spectator at the theater is in a certain sense midway between the attitude of the believer and that of the atheist at a religious ceremony. For the believer, each gesture of the officiant possesses a meaning which moves and engages him. For the atheist, derision is the only proper response. In aesthetic experience, the spectator must be sufficiently interested in the spectacle to follow it but not so much as to be taken in by it. He may sympathize with characters in a novel or play, but not to the point of identifying with them. If he is transported by the action, he should not intervene in it as if it were real. In short, aesthetic perception requires a certain detachment which is lived by the body and its senses, but whose principle is found in the transcendental imagination as a capacity to create distance.

In contrast, the empirical imagination, which completes and animates ordinary perception, is more repressed than aroused by aesthetic perception, and its flightiness is thus avoided. Why is this so? The briefest answer is that the spectacle provided by the aesthetic object is self-sufficient and needs no reinforcement. Imagination may give rise to perception but need not enrich it. First of all, the aesthetic object derives its primary sense from what it represents, that is, from an unreal which per se has no need for elaboration by the imagination.[15] The object as known by ordinary perception is a present and real object which calls for action on our part. Imagination projects the possible lines of this action (or passion), which confirms and develops the object's signification. But the object represented by the aesthetic object (whose function lies precisely in this representation) has a purely represented, hence inoffensive, being. The represented objects exists only by virtue of appearance, which itself exists only in order to signify this object. Moreover, to comprehend an object in ordinary perception is to locate it in a world of external objects in which action manifests itself. When I perceive a lamp on my desk, I grasp it as a possibility of illuminating the paper on which I am writing and of leaving the wall behind me in shadow. Or if I hear a barnyard noise, I interpret it as a hen who has just laid an egg in some particular place to be discovered later. However, the object repre-

15. It is for this reason that we have proposed, in opposition to Sartre, that it is a matter of an unreal, not of the imaginary. It seems to us that imagination is less radically foreign to perception than Sartre believes. But this does not mean that the aesthetic object—a perceived object—can be considered an imaginary entity. On the contrary, we hold that, at least in its empirical aspect, imagination does not play a preponderant role in aesthetic perception.

sented by art does not refer to anything external. It is not *in* a world but constitutes a world which is internal to itself. Of course, as a *thing*—e.g., a painting exhibited in a gallery or a play presented in a theater—the aesthetic object exists in the world. Yet we know that it tends to separate itself from the world in order to constitute a world apart and that what isolates it is precisely the fact that it designates another world. (We see here a sort of reciprocal contamination. The unreal represented object belongs to the real through the appearance which manifests it. Yet the real aesthetic thing is derealized in being the means of representation.) Imagination is directed to the grasping of this other world, not to the control of the real world.

Second, instead of transgressing the given, imagination must always return to and die away in it. The represented object appears through the deepening, not the surpassing, of the given. Appearance is finally self-appearance. The sense of appearance is found only in appearance itself, and this sense confers on appearance an internal necessity by which it becomes at once intelligible. In other words, the represented object is discovered directly through appearance, which by itself *says all*. The only commentary which imagination has to furnish is a literal one. In this case, imagining is limited to perceiving a given appearance better and does not anticipate the perception of something else. Imagination always provides the possibility of seeing—seeing the sense in the appearance, not outside it.

For these two reasons, both derived from the primary fact that the aesthetic object represents something, we must refuse to accord any adventurous character to imagination. This is not to deny that imagination does animate appearance in giving a certain consistency to the represented object—the lines of a drawing must become arranged in a design, the words of a novel into a narrative, the leaps of a dancer into a choreographic suite. The constitution of such meaningful totalities certainly requires the imagination, and we must agree with Kant that a totality can be grasped only by the movement of consciousness in encompassing a portion of space and time and that the schema of the represented object as thus determined is the work of imagination. But even though imagination intervenes here, as in all perception, to stabilize the represented object, its operation remains a modest one. It does not inspire images which pretend to enrich perception but in fact encumber it, nor does it attain the imaginary. In particular, it does not seek to enlarge the field of significations to the point of fabricating a world which is a *second* world. As we have said before, the world of the work exists in comprehension or intension, not in extension.

Some examples may help to clarify this interpretation. Let us turn first to painting, which perhaps furnishes the most obvious example. To perceive a darkened cloud as meaningful is to apprehend rain as something whose consequences concern me. Such a cloud perceived on a canvas manifests *itself*, not rain. The object "cloud" is only represented, and imagination spontaneously allows the possible to arise. Now, a fictive cloud indicates an equally fictive rain. I know this, but such knowledge remains implicit, for to conjure up an actual image of rain is to lose sight of the aesthetic object. Similarly, when I let myself dream in listening to music—e.g., by evoking the sea upon hearing Debussy's symphonic poem, whose form and content seduce me—I will understand of the music, as Souriau says, only what those who do not understand it understand. It is for this reason that we cannot speak with Sartre of "the aesthetic object 'Charles VIII.' " [16] Charles VIII is not an aesthetic object, a term which must be restricted to the painting, that is, to an ensemble of appearances which signify Charles VIII. But Charles VIII is signified in such a way that he is inseparable from these appearances. He is, for them, the means by which they realize themselves as meaningful. Conversely, I fail to achieve contact with the painting when I refuse to consider it as representing someone, thus depriving it of its meaning and conceiving of it merely as a thing with a thinglike signification. In this case, I cannot even say that I adopt a perceiving (instead of an imagining) attitude. For I no longer perceive the spots as colors or the lines as patterns. I perceive only something inchoate on the canvas—which is still to perceive, but not to perceive the painting. As soon as I perceive the painting as such, its subject must appear to me, and thus I imagine the painting itself as appearing to me. But if my act of imagining means a refusal to perceive, the aesthetic object will vanish. In aesthetic experience, imagination is involved only as collaborating with perception, not as the correlate of an image-consciousness which demands the cessation of perception and hence the abandonment of the aesthetic object. By regarding Charles VIII as a historical being, I turn away from the work and treat the painting as if it were a photograph serving as an *analogon* evoking an absent presence. It may be that the painter of the portrait

16. Sartre, *Psychology of Imagination*, p. 246.

himself espoused precisely this sense of truth, which he used to justify a client's demand for resemblance. But if the painter was truly an artist, he accomplished something quite different from the demand of his client—who was not the aim of the work but its occasion. The portrait would then possess truth in another sense, the truth of a creation and not of a reproduction. It is worth noting that, when the photograph is a work of art, it no longer refers explicitly to a model as if to cue the imagination. As art, it possesses enough reality and sense in itself not to appeal to another reality. It is undeniable that a photograph, like a portrait, is always a photograph *of,* just as a dark cloud is always heavy *with* rain. But in aesthetic experience the object of the photograph is contained within the appearance, and there is no need for imagination to make this object explicit or to grant it the quasi-autonomous existence of an imaginary entity. The represented object exists only as the sense of appearance, and in aesthetic perception it has no existence outside appearance.

The immediacy of ordinary contemplation indicates that here the constitutive activity of the represented object is reduced to a minimum. Such minimal activity may not obtain, however, in the arts of space and time, where contemplation must be able to retain a past and anticipate a future. Let us consider the arts of space first. Sculptural or architectural objects which manifest themselves in three spatial dimensions seem to require imagination to open out space in terms of future perspectives and to grasp the object in its plenitude as more than a truncated appearance. Do we not perceive a temple or a statue as we perceive a house or a cube, by enlivening the experience of presence through imagination? Certainly. Yet even here imagination is held in check. First, I do not relate to a temple as I do to a house. I do not live in it or enter it to find my desk or my bed. The palace in which the prince lives is not a palace for the prince. The person who enters a cathedral to worship there is no longer in the cathedral. Of course, in spite of himself, he may be sensitive to the solemnity of the edifice, its forceful columns, altitudinous vaults, and echoing capacity. Everything about the building conspires to move him to piety. Like Stendhal, he may not be able to prevent himself from becoming momentarily a believer. But in doing so, he ceases being a spectator to become an actor. The cathedral has absorbed him in its universe, ensnared him in the trap of its beckoning portal, open aisles, and processional movements. Thus caught up, he no longer confronts an aesthetic object but is, through his participation, himself an aesthetic object, an element of a ceremony whose form is delineated by the cathedral as an architectural monument. But if the ceremony is, for the participant, a potent means of discipline and exaltation, it is an aesthetic object only for the spectator who does not participate in it. Alain would say at this point that even the spectator takes part in the ceremony, since each person in the cathedral is at once actor and spectator, through a reciprocal relation in which an absolute language is communicated. But the aesthetic object calls for a pure spectator who does not believe—or, rather, who believes only with his eyes. Such a spectator does not *use* the cathedral. When he enters it, he does not do so to engage himself in any future enterprise. He enters to *see*. His visit will be constituted by a series of discontinuous present moments, as many as the number of times his look reposes on and isolates the totality of the object. In this type of exploration, there is no imaginable future as such—not only because each look uncovers a new spectacle, but also because each glance is self-sufficient and is not linked with others by the continuity of an action.

It may be objected that diverse viewings of the cathedral are distinguishable only if the building is wholly given in each of them. This would require the imagination to come into play as supplementing direct views through the recollection or anticipation of lateral and hidden presences. All this would lead us back to ordinary perception. But the question is precisely whether aesthetic perception delivers the object in its material plentitude. We do perceive the cathedral as a real edifice which cannot be reduced to an optical illusion or a theatrical set. Each of its aspects arises from the massive totality of the whole, and allusion is continually made to this whole in such a manner that each viewing calls on imagination by referring to what is not now seen and yet could be seen from another position. But to seize the aesthetic object as such means that it must, as we have said above, appear as embodying a represented object. In the present case, this object is the idea of the cathedral as it reveals itself through the building's appearance. The representing and the represented elements mingle objectively, since the cathedral has no subject other than itself. Nonetheless, they are distinguishable subjectively in that the element which represents requires an infinite and unique exploration by imagination, while the represented element is grasped as immediately given in each perception. The vocation of the building as a total object is to be a cathedral in each of its parts or aspects and to allow the idea of the cathedral to be represented in each viewing. This is why aesthetic perception of an architectural object, though open to the overflowing character of this object, typically stops short of its givenness. One could say that, at the limit, we perceive here what a photographic plate would record, a flat image which is the correlate of a pure look, a pure spectacle for a pure spectator. This image is what the building has to say. It tells us why the cathedral is made as it is, just as a novel is written to narrate a story or a ballet is danced to present a movement. The image is the truth of the cathedral, which in aesthetic experience is nothing other than the possibility of being such an image enclosed in stone. Sartre would reject this interpretation by considering the cathedral to be imaginary. But it is not imaginary. As a thing, it overflows and escapes us by its mass and must be filled out by imagination. As a signification, it is wholly present in each self-sufficient perception.

Turning now to the arts of time, we observe that they seem at first glance to demand a pronounced constitutive activity in order: (a) to regulate time by keeping the past immanent in the present; and (b) to give continuity to represented objects. A painting can manifest itself in a single viewing, but a sonata and a novel reveal themselves only successively; their contemplation involves both a past and a future. Thus to read a work of literature is to be transported into a world in which the protagonist acts and which Balzac, for example, carefully describes before beginning the story proper. The protagonist, along with his milieu, must be presented to me without being reduced to a particular comportment of which I have only a snapshot impression. In fact, this comportment belongs to someone whom I come to know and who possesses his own projects, history, character, and destiny as realized in a certain milieu—in brief, someone who is a meaningful totality. When I confront a painting, it satisfies my curiosity to know simply that the subject is Charles VIII. As his portrait is before me, I need not believe that he is there himself, imperiously present in person. Charles VIII remains in obscurity as a nonactualized possibility which haunts perception. He is present only because of the colors, existing as both their means and end, and in no way does he *refer* to the world of history, even if he is ultimately related to it. The truth of the Charles VIII who concerns me aesthetically is present in the portrait, and *this* Charles VIII suffices for himself. He possesses the shadowy existence of a represented object, not the inexhaustible existence of a real object which imagination decks out with possibilities. But if Charles VIII were the hero of a novel, I would need more information about him—information which would be present to my mind whenever he appears in the novel. The depth of the world in which he develops must also form a presence, and this presence is accepted and affirmed by imagination, as it is in visual perception.

The circumspect character of such presence must, however, be underlined. My reading is not interrupted by obtrusive images. The signification of the text remains in a state of suspension (just as I may respond in a conversation without bothering to weigh words; I may simply yield to the experiences they suggest or spontaneously evoke images to illustrate their sense). The represented object is not truly imagined, but neither is it simply comprehended as if it were part of a scientific text. Sartre, who grants us here what he refuses to allow in the case of painting, expresses this point by saying that we rarely imagine when we read a novel. "The reader prepares himself to discover an entire world which is not that of perception, but which is not a world of mental images either." [17] But whereas Sartre considers this world the correlate of an imagistic knowledge, we would prefer to say that it presupposes virtual and undeveloped images which are woven into perception. What precisely is the role of imagination in this process? Imagination functions as little more than an implicit memory which retains the past, realizing it without imposing it on us, and enables us to sense the future without actually anticipating it (for there is no future of the represented object, except the future of its comprehension). Similarly, in music we comprehend and appreciate a certain phrase only if its context is immanent to the phrase. Indeed, all arts in which perception is successive require the aid of an imagination which operates as memory. But we must recall that the time of the work of art is not the ordinary time which imagination enlivens by memories or projects, and that it does not call for the same activity. Even if the time of the work must possess a certain logical structure, it is not fully real and does not interfere with objective time. The time of reading or listening is detached from a vaster time from which it is excluded, as a painting stands out from the wall on which it is hung. When I read, only the time of the work exists for me. When I adhere to the work, objective time vanishes along with the objective world.

17. *Ibid.,* p. 82.—Trans.

The time of the work does not enlist my imagination or understanding as does the time of my mundane enterprises. The work's time can hardly be called duration. It is more like the pure present of contemplation, except that we cannot break it off. If it has a future at all, it is one which is uniquely its own, uncontingent, and immanent to its present. The unity of the work is so closely knit and its fabric so tightly woven that its future is like the unfolding of a meaning whose chronological dimension only illustrates a deeper logical dimension. My own future projects and my hopes, which would normally incite the imagination to transgress the bounds of the work, have no relevance here. We miss the aesthetic object altogether if our imagination transports the work's content into the ordinary universe of objective time. The past which comes to give meaning to the present is not invented or sought in the depths of the spectator's experience. It is given immediately in the work. Instead of anticipating, imagination need only follow the thread of the text without losing itself in seeking external significations. The appearance—the text—says all. The work succeeds precisely when it restricts imagination within the work's limits, discouraging any further elaboration (unless only to show the impotence of such elaboration)—in brief, when the work becomes its own world. Of course, a given work may be extremely stimulating to reflective analysis, as we see in the case of Alain's interpretations of Valéry's "La Jeune Parque." [18] But, beyond the fact that the imagination is no longer operative here, the work is no longer treated as an aesthetic object. The genuine work of art spares us the expense of an exuberant imagination, since to understand and follow the work all that is required is its presence to the mind and to the senses. Aesthetic perception does not need the kind of completion which we give to an obscure and ambiguous perception from the everyday realm.

Two objections may arise at this point which will apply to all the arts. The first concerns precisely the question of obscurity in aesthetic perception. It will be maintained that, for example, a painting may be obscure. This is to be granted, but the point is that we do not have to overcome the obscurity by sifting out the exact outlines of a represented object, as if we were looking for a hidden pattern in a puzzle. There is no need to reinterpret or rearrange the appearances which are offered to us, just as we do not have to seek for artichokes under

18. See Alain, *La Jeune Parque* (Paris: Gallimard, 1953).—Trans.

acanthus leaves or antelopes on Elamite pottery. In short, we have to perceive only what we perceive. When Cézanne paints a slightly misshapen bottle, we are not called upon to correct him. When Renoir makes the hair of a woman disappear imperceptibly into the background of his painting, we do not need to know precisely where this hair comes to an end—it is not our task to comb it. The irritation felt by some people before the deformations, elisions, or abstractions of modern painting and sculpture derives from the prejudiced notion that resemblance is the sole norm of aesthetic truth. The prejudice itself proceeds from the fact that imagination normally operates without hindrance. This operation is unimpeded by an object which merely resembles another object—indeed, here its activity is encouraged—but it becomes uncertain before a unique object which resembles nothing at all. It is undeniable that we can recognize and name the represented object in paintings which are not merely decorative. But we do this precisely to avoid the flights of a restless or bewitched imagination. The real task of imagination in aesthetic experience is therefore to grasp the represented object *in appearance,* without substituting for it (considered as an *analogon*) an imaginary object held to be more or uniquely true. We do not consider silhouettes in a Dufy water color or lines in a Rembrandt engraving as fodder for the imagination. They are not comparable to illustrations in a book on calisthenics. Illustrations are signs to be utilized and not worthy of respect in themselves. The aesthetic object, in contrast, is to be respected precisely insofar as it does not form a pretext for unrestrained acts of imagining.

A second objection is found in the apparent fact that the work itself seems to invite us to complete it when it involves calculated elisions, as C. E. Magny has shown for the novel and the film.[19] The same question arises in theater, where intermissions allow the author to arrange space and time as he likes. Even in music, a practised ear can apprehend crucial ruptures when there are abrupt changes of modulation. The same holds for painting, and, indeed, wherever a smooth transition is removed or information concerning a transition is not given. This objection, which takes the form of an observation, calls for several remarks. First, we know that all art requires sacrifice of detail: witness the successive stages of a Rembrandt engraving. This is because art strives for the essential

19. See C. E. Magny, *L'Age du roman américain* (Paris: Editions du Seuil, 1948).—Trans.

and cannot lose itself in detail. The essential is what the artist means, what he wants to say. It is this which determines what is eliminable as mere detail. (What is detail for one artist is essential for another. For Van Eyck, for example, the essential is precisely the infiinite detail of creation.) But such sacrifices of detail impose no sacrifice on the spectator, for what has been eliminated is of no help to him anyway. These sacrifices can be regretted only if one holds that art is supposed to give an exhaustive account of reality—as if the value of a portrait were to be measured by the fidelity with which it rendered the creases and wrinkles of a particular human face, or the value of a dance by its reproduction of certain human gestures. What the artist sacrifices is not the real but the barnacles which cloud his vision and alter the purity of his creation. We betray him if we do not accept a certain asceticism on his part, for otherwise our look will reintroduce into the work impurities from which it has already been cleansed.

But the narrative arts make use of omissions which do seem to require us to reestablish continuity. Here two kinds of omission must be distinguished. In one case, the omission signifies that nothing has happened. It delimits an empty time and forbids us to imagine what could fill the lacuna, for example, the fifteen years in the life of Frédéric in Flaubert's *L'Education sentimentale*. There is nothing further to comprehend in a case like this except a sheer absence of events, a dreary unfolding, an empty activity. Even to speak thus is too descriptive—rather, we should turn the page. In the case of a second kind of omission, we must reestablish a continuity, because something has occured which is crucial to the course of the story. Thus we ask ourselves what has happened when, after having left Isée in the arms of Mésa at the end of the second act of Claudel's *Partage de Midi*, we rediscover her in the third act with Amalric in a ruined house. We have the right to know what happened, but we do not need to imagine it, since it will be shown to us. In the theater, elision is inevitable. Not only must the playwright choose the most significant scenes and the most highly charged situations, but duration, suspended in the drama's present, can be restored only during the intermission—just as a real event can occur only in the wings. Even in this case, however, all that we need to know of a theatrical event is expressed by the work, without our having to speculate on the course of the work or slow down its rhythm.

It may happen that by a series of careful omissions—by

drawing the curtain on certain events or by withholding essential information—the author leaves us in a state of uncertainty about the content of the play as well as the personality of the characters. Should we then accuse him of betraying our trust, as Sartre accuses Faulkner?[20] The accusation is merited if the omission is a device designed only to lure us, as in a detective story. But it is to be dismissed if the omission is integral to the work, attesting to a certain vision of the world which the author imposes on the reader because it has imposed itself on him as a way of expressing himself. In this case, we must accept the obscurity and consent to losing ourselves in the eddies of the narrative or to being astonished by the behavior of the characters, as if we were before strange beings. Astonishment is our attitude before Picasso's incredible harlequins or before the demonical forms with which Bosch surrounds the figure of St. Anthony. As soon as I attempt a psychoanalysis of the monstrous or try to see alchemical symbols in the toad carrying an egg, the hollow oak, and the flying fish of Bosch's painting, the aesthetic object is lost from sight, and I become insensitive to the effect which it aims to produce in me (even if the author did not think of this effect), for then I claim to comprehend instead of simply seeing. Perhaps, moreover, sight accommodates the fantastic or the incomprehensible more easily than reading. On the canvas, the represented object possesses an irrefutable presence, whereas the narrative, not requiring us to see and appealing to our implicit knowledge, needs a certain logical clarity, without which it may baffle us. Also, narrative time—the time of the plot—must embody a certain order, or it will become radically incoherent.

In this appeal to order, we can see one way in which aesthetic perception also solicits the understanding. We shall develop this point further. However, we must first show how the same process operates in the case of perception in general. In ordinary perception, imagination acts as a prelude to understanding. But the reflection on the perceived object which may subsequently arise can also turn in the direction of feeling, through a movement that is characteristic of aesthetic experience.

20. See Sartre's essay on Faulkner in *Literary and Philosophical Essays,* trans. Annette Michelson (New York: Macmillan, Collier Books, 1967).—Trans.

13 / Reflection and Feeling in Perception in General

[I] UNDERSTANDING

JUST AS AESTHETIC PERCEPTION restrains imagination, so ordinary perception also guards against it. Imagination effects the passage from presence to representation; but imagination can be purged from representation, to which it constantly presumes to attach itself, only by the controlling power of understanding. Now, between imagination, which allows representation to come about, and understanding, which exercises judgment, there seems to be the same distance that we have had to observe (and yet question) between presence and representation. This is so, first, because the function of understanding seems to be to correct imagination. To the extent that imagination is suspect, owing to its capacity for disorder, the mingling of the perceived and the imaginary must be continually undone. To reflect on a given perception is to regain self-possession and to look more closely, that is, to recover the appearance in order to discover new significations. To ponder a starry night, the scene of a crime, or a painting is to look behind the spectacle, to undo appearance in order to search for its law. Similarly, philosophical reflection returns to a primary power of thinking which preexists lived thoughts. Therefore, to reflect is to restrain, at least provisionally, the imagination, which is at the source of lived experience, and to loosen the bond which it weaves between the world and myself. Thus we discover something primary which is logical and unlived. For it is not the same thing to experience the solidarity of two objects in the imagination and to think a necessary link through the understanding. One must admit that only the understanding, by promulgating a necessity which uncovers and excludes fantasy, can sanction the objectivity of nature: "Of all representations *combination* is the only one which cannot be given through the objects . . . since only as having been combined *by the understanding* can anything . . . be given to the faculty of representation." [1]

But, conversely, the understanding can do nothing without the imagination. Recognition cannot be effective without reproduction. And what is true on the transcendental level, where the unifying synthesis establishing the concept of the object is possible only by means of a reproductive synthesis which alone gives consistency to representations, is also true on the empirical level, where the statement of a law presupposes the collation of many terms or many objects. Thus, if understanding is to order nature, imagination must first set forth a world through its power to unite or join the thing signified to the sign. Only then can reflection ratify signification or give the force of law to an association in explaining it by a logical link of identity or causality.

Yet the truth of the matter is that as soon as imagination is given so is understanding. For whenever the opacity of presence is broken, it is possible for the subject (who discerns objects and distinguishes itself from them) to define itself concurrently as a relation of self to self—through what Kant calls self-affection —thus as the unity of movement whereby it detaches itself from objects and returns to itself in anticipation. This relation of self to self constitutes the subject as a unity of apperception. It is through this self-repossession that the subject escapes the dispersion of lived experience where it is only a reflected and not a reflecting being, an echo and not a voice. And the object, in turn, is an object only as a correlate of this unity of the subject. Since the manifold is always a many in a one, the object must itself somehow be one. An object is the unity of appearances, and necessity as a category of modality is the cement which makes unity from appearances and binds objects together in an intelligible nature. As the organ of the unity of apperception, understanding stamps on the flux of appearances the seal of necessity, converting into a necessary unity the contingent unity

1. Immanuel Kant, *Critique of Pure Reason*, trans. Norman Kemp Smith (New York: St. Martin's Press, 1929), B 130, pp. 151–52.

of associations suggested by lived experience. Understanding is the imagination as conscious of itself and as imposing a rule on the spontaneity of its associations. Understanding is the "faculty of rules" through which the represented object becomes an object for the "I think." Understanding is the imagination as capable of thinking what it represents, because it can now control and, if necessary, restrain its spontaneity. In short, between imagination and understanding there is the same ambiguous relation as between presence and imagination. Nature and mind, the lower and higher, continue to unite and differentiate themselves within us. We do not cease to be one, even when we divide ourselves in order to subdue ourselves. And the dialectics of rupture which we perform in order to be mind raises us to the level of the mental without shattering our unity.

In any event, the progress of perception undoubtedly proceeds through disciplining the imagination, which by itself is always prone to stray. If imagination imparts richness to the given, understanding guarantees its rigor and confers on it that objectivity whose first characteristic is the distance we take in regard to the object, and whose second characteristic is the necessity according to which we seize this object as *one* object in *one* world. In this way, the domain of experience unfolds, even though the progress of perception requires a continual victory over the deviations of the imagination. The peril continues because perception must constantly nourish itself on the experience of presence, thus harboring within itself an element of finitude and opacity which it cannot annul except by ceasing to be perception. But it remains true that, insofar as perception is prolonged and purified within these limits and under the impulse of understanding, it augments our mastery of appearances and our grasp of significations.

But this activity of the understanding does not exhaust reflection. In Kantian terms, we may say that understanding employs only a determinant judgment. Now, determinant judgment is in no sense the whole of judgment. It is not at all the type of judgment which the *Critique of Judgement* isolates in order to discern its proper *a priori*. Determinant judgment is, as Kant shows in the example of the perceived house, the intellectual activity through which the categories assume their function in the most ordinary perception. As such, "the determinant judgement determines under universal transcendental laws furnished by understanding and is subsumptive only; the law is marked out for it *a priori,* and it has no need to devise a law for its own guidance to enable it to subordinate the particular in nature to universal." [2] Thus Kant touches on the problem of subsumption: how does it come about that what is given empirically and is contingent in respect to "the universal laws of nature" of which "understanding is no doubt in possession" [3] can yield to the formal exigencies of knowledge and of action? We must presume an "adaptation of nature to our cognitive faculties," [4] an agreement whose principle is found in the Transcendental Deduction (where the empirical affinity of phenomena appears to be a consequence of their transcendental affinity) but which finds sanction only in the *Critique of Judgement,* where the maxims of judgment attest that judgment accepts this agreement as an *a priori* principle for its own use. In other words, the Transcendental Deduction establishes the possibility of a given, and the *Critique of Judgement* establishes the necessity of postulating that this given agree with the *a priori* exigencies which make it possible, affirming a principle of the unity of the manifold which corresponds to the synthetic unity of apperception. It is reflective judgment which decides as to the possibility of subsumption. This is why, as far as its transcendental jurisdiction is concerned, reflective judgment must be distinguished from determinant judgment. Nevertheless, reflective judgment is called forth by determinant judgment. These two kinds of judgment do not stand in an inverse relation to each other, since the universal in determinant judgment is the *a priori* principle of a pure understanding which concerns itself only with "the possibility of nature," while in reflective judgment the universal is a universal law in relation to particular laws. But the universal law of reflective judgment is still empirical and, as such, "contingent as far as the light of *our* understanding goes," [5] because it does not concern the possibility of nature in general but the intelligibility of a nature empirically given. Rather, the two judgments are complementary in character. Subsumption solicits reflection, and it is through reflection that there can arise self-interrogation and the assurance that the object as intelligible can take its place in the world by agreeing with already elabor-

2. Immanuel Kant, *Critique of Judgement,* trans. J. C. Meredith (Oxford: Oxford University Press, 1952), K 179, p. 18.
    3. *Ibid.,* K 184, p. 24.
    4. *Ibid.,* K 185, p. 25.
    5. *Ibid.,* K 180, p. 18.

ated elements of cognition and also by confirming the hope that a total system of cognition is possible. Reflection is, in short, reflection on the possibility of determinant judgment.

We need not follow the route taken by Kant's notion of reflection insofar as it takes the transcendental turn, whereby the subject refers itself to itself as well as to the capacity which it possesses for promulgating the laws of nature and to the pleasure which it takes or has taken in exercising this capacity. Our concern is with the subject as it comes to grips with the perceived object, reflecting on this object instead of on itself. Nonetheless, Kant blazes the trail. He leads us, in the first place, to the idea that the activity of the understanding is neither the only manifestation of judgment nor the ultimate peripety of perception. In addition, he suggest two important themes which are going to guide us to the threshold of feeling. On the one hand, faced with the object, we are able to involve ourselves more deeply than when determinant judgment is in effect. On the other hand, there is a more profound communion with the object than we find in the activity of constitution.

In fact, within determinant judgment, the power of determination is unaware of itself. The "I think" must be able to accompany my representations; but in fact I am not conscious of prescribing law to nature, and I discover only *a posteriori* the exigency and reality of an *a priori*. In contrast, in reflective judgment I cannot forget that I am positing the unity of the manifold "unknown though [this principle] be to us."[6] Here I posit an "as if," an objectivity whose mark of subjectivity I cannot ignore. At the same time, I am conscious of an absolute initiative. I no longer look upon the object as self-evidently proceeding from itself. I call it to account. I expect it to respond to a certain hypothesis which I posit; my legislation is no more than a wish, but I know that I pronounce this wish in the expectation that nature will fufill it. I cannot overlook the fact that the question which I pose is my question and that, accordingly, I put myself into question. I find out what I find out because I searched it out, almost as if my wishing made it so.

If reflection thus implies self-consciousness, that is because I put myself into question. And this means not only that I ask myself whether the law which I claim to find in nature is admissible but also that I bring myself into play in the question

6. *Ibid.*

which I pose as if it were strictly my own affair. I exist not simply as a transcendental subject or as an impersonal *naturans,* but as a concrete subject in contact with a real world, and in such a way that comprehension is like a personal victory: Eureka! This means that I am commited in my reflection. And I commit myself as soon as I open myself up—by participating rather than standing aloof. As we have seen, to open oneself up is the fundamental act through which a subject constitutes itself as a unity of apperception in the presence of an object. But what matters is to open oneself up with all that one is, to set the entire personality into action. Moreover, I maintain a more intimate rapport with the object by reflective than by determinant judgment. I am not contented with ordering appearances or registering meanings proposed to me by the imagination. Instead, I establish that "adaptation of nature to our faculty of judgment"—an adaptation which Kant expresses by the principle of finality. This affinity between nature and myself is not only comprehended in reflection but is experienced, particularly in aesthetic experience, in a sort of communion between the object and myself. And this communion provides a mode of access to feeling.

[II] FROM UNDERSTANDING TO FEELING

AFTER HAVING BEEN CORRECTED by the understanding, perception can certainly reorient itself in another direction— precisely that which aesthetic perception will take. The conversion of the given into something intelligible is not necessarily the last step. Indeed, there is an entire philosophy which affirms that it is not: Gabriel Marcel, in particular, denounces the "care of having" and points out the strict bond between seeing and having.[7] Now, we have attempted to demonstrate, by juxtaposing representation and presence, that thought is inviscerated in being and has its ground in a primary experience of being. But at the level of representation, it is difficult to dispute the fact that knowledge tends to become a form of having. That movement of "loosening, of a provisional rupture which is recognized as such

7. See Jeanne Delhomme, "Témoignage et dialectique," in *Existentialime chrétien: Gabriel Marcel,* ed. Etienne Gilson (Paris: Plon, 1947), p. 132.

through a certain adhesion," and attributed by Marcel to the act of doubt, happens to lie at the root of every representation.[8] In the light of such a movement, in fact, adhesion shows itself for what it was in the first place, a blind and unreflective connivance with the world. The sense of being could not be enlarged, take on life, and raise itself to the dimension of the metaphysical, unless we escaped, by means of reflection, what is merely a being-with experienced in immediacy. But it is also possible for perception—precisely because of its roots in the experience of presence—to return to that experience and branch off from having in the direction of being. Perception will then tend to become communion.

It was observed above that, in contrast to a process of spiritualization, the perceived, in becoming corporal, may descend to the level of lived experience. But this is not the point being made here. In that case, it was simply a matter of renouncing representation and of the possibility of testing out— in contact with things on the level of behavior—the modes of knowledge implicit in conscious perception. It was a question of converting actual seeing [voir] into the power of seeing [pouvoir], of utilizing seeing on a different level, a level on which it disappears as such. But this conversion occurs in such a way that imagination can always restore seeing to its full actuality, provided that one returns to the level of perception. In the present case, on the contrary, we are interested in transforming seeing without negating it and in inaugurating a new relation to being which would not suppress representation or return to pure presence. There is a definite distinction to be made between this new immediacy and the immediacy of presence. Feeling is not simply a return to presence. This is so for three reasons. First, feeling's object is peculiar. Simply described, feeling reveals an interiority. It introduces us to another dimension of the given. It is not only a state or mode of being of the subject; it is a mode of being of the subject which corresponds to a mode of being in the object. Feeling is that in me which relates to a certain quality of the object through which the object manifests its intimacy. (Or rather, we should speak of its reverberation within me, since the language of intentionality applied to feeling obscures the element of the undergone [subi]. Thus Husserl is always tempted by idealism.) Feeling reveals being not only as reality but also

8. Gabriel Marcel, *Metaphysical Journal*, trans. Bernard Wall (Chicago: Regnery, 1952), p. 372.

as depth. Being appears as other than what it is and as un-fathomable, not only (as I learn from imagination) because I can always substitute representations for one another or join them together, but also because I am given something within being which nullifies every representation as well as every action.

Second, feeling distinguishes itself from presence in imply-ing a new attitude on the part of the subject. I must make myself conform to what feeling reveals to me and thus match its depth with my own. For it is not a question of extending my having [*étendre mon avoir*] but rather of listening in on a message [*entendre un message*]. That is why, through feeling, I myself am put into question. Whether or not I am capable of having the feeling will constitute a self-testing and will also provide the measure of my authenticity. Is it not on account of my feelings, their quality, and their penetration that I am truly judged? All of which proves that to feel is in a sense to transcend.

And this is why, finally, feeling distinguishes itself from presence by presupposing that representation has been ex-hausted and surpassed toward something else. It is, moreover, always possible to attain feeling without passing through the stage of representation and reflection. As was the case with the movement from presence to representation, the movement from representation to feeling is not dialectical. Feeling is simply an-other direction which perception may take. We oscillate from perception to feeling, according to the spontaneity of conscious-ness and unburdened by any dialectical necessity. But feeling realizes itself fully only on two conditions. First, imagination (to the extent that it installs and binds us within the unique hori-zontal plane of representation) must be suppressed. But this does not mean that we must give up the perception of appear-ances. It simply implies that imagination, and even understand-ing, must not drag us into the field of purely objective significa-tions which serve only to confirm our power or our indifference. Next (in what must necessarily be labeled an ontological move) we need to open ourselves to a reality which must be experienced authentically from the very depths of our being and which de-mands that we relinquish control over appearances. Aesthetic experience will show us that feeling, in its most elevated form, is an immediacy which has undergone mediation. This is not only because it operates on the level of representation but also because there exists a type of reflection on feeling through which feeling itself is fully realized and which plays a role with respect to feeling similar to that which representation plays in regard to presence. The immediate element in feeling, which is parallel to but not the same as the corresponding element in presence, is not feeling in its entirety. Authentic feeling is a new immediacy.

Furthermore, such feeling, in which perception is realized, is not emotion. It is knowledge [*connaissance*]. Accordingly, the emotion of fear is not to be confused with the feeling of the horrible. It is, rather, a certain way of reacting in the face of the horrible when the horrible is taken as a characteristic of the world as it appears at the time, that is, a means of struggling within the world of the horrible. In the same way, merriment is not a feeling of the comic but the way in which we enter into the world of the comic and make use of it. Similarly, terror and pity are not the feeling of the tragic but, rather, reactions which accompany our entry into the world of the tragic and unite us with the heroes of the tragedy. Fear, merriment, and pity denote movements in the strict sense of e-motions, that is, not only alterations of the subject but also undertakings or beginnings of action, whatever its eventual character. Feeling, on the other hand, is knowledge—even if it be that peculiar spark of knowledge which unleashes the emotions and enters into a circle with them. Conversely, this knowledge is feeling, because it is not reflective and, above all, because it presupposes a certain predisposition to receive the affective. Of course, by exercising our judgment, we could always deny ourselves such a knowledge and thus take refuge in the Stoic ideal of objectivity. Nevertheless, this knowledge involves a certain commitment with respect to the world, through which it is neither thought nor acted upon but simply felt. And this commitment implies a mode of being on the part of the subject—a direction or "sense" [*sens*]—which is most tellingly revealed in the case of the artist. Thus Racine possesses the sense of the tragic, as does Daumier that of the grotesque, and Wagner that of the marvelous. But this sense can also be aroused in the spectator. Indeed, if the spectator were entirely destitute of it (as certain individuals are insensitive to certain values or the blind are insensitive to color), he would fail to have an aesthetic experience or to know the aesthetic object. Thus feeling has a noetic function. It reveals a world. Only when this world has been given can emotion begin to interpret it—either in order to transform it magically, as Sartre suggests (making emotion into a form of dissolute action), or else, as in Ricoeur's view, to engage in a valid action.[9]

Aesthetic experience helps precisely to maintain the functions of feeling in their purity. The world of art is an inoffensive world that we need not take completely seriously. Participation in this world does not go all the way to the level of emotion. Before Rouault's *Le Pendu* I experience all the misery of the world without that element of anguish or fear which, in the real world, leads me to flee or avert the misery. It is not necessary for a spectator at a comedy to feel the same merriment he would experience if he were really in the situation represented. It is sufficient for him to have the feeling of the comic and to laugh with a tranquil laughter which proceeds from knowledge and not from surprise. Feeling is pure because it is a capacity of receptivity, a sensibility to a certain world, and an aptitude for preceiving that world.

[III] APPEARANCE AND EXPRESSION

BEYOND APPEARANCE, which understanding restricts itself to organizing and interpreting, what feeling really seizes on in the exercise of its noetic function is expression. This can be seen if we recall our previous remarks concerning expression in the case of the aesthetic object, and contrast expression with appearance in regard to their respective contents and to the manner in which these contents are appropriated. First, with respect to contents, appearance brings about the knowledge of an object, and expression that of a subject or quasi subject. An appearance is a sign, while an expression makes a sign—gestures—to us. A thing cannot act as a sign, because it is only what it is. A thing hides nothing and it does not institute an interior/exterior dialectic. Of course, a thing has hidden aspects, but these are only hidden for me, and I can always discover them in one way or another. One may also say that a thing maintains an internal privacy to which access is granted only by means of violence.[10] There is, accordingly, something intrinsically fas-

9. Paul Ricoeur, *Freedom and Nature: The Voluntary and the Involuntary,* trans. Erazim V. Kohák (Evanston, Ill.: Northwestern University Press, 1966), pp. 250 ff.

10. See Gaston Bachelard, *La Terre et les rêveries de volonté* (Paris: Corti, 1948), *passim.*

cinating about a project undertaken along these lines. The prestige of speleological explorations, for example, derives in considerable part from that holy terror which was once evoked by a descent into hell. There are, as Rimbaud says in *Déluge,* riches buried in the entrails of the earth: a secret of the interior. That Mephistopheles attributes an entirely human cause to all this and proposes its unearthing is due to the fact that he is Mephistopheles, the profane one. And all exploration, starting with that of the infant who breaks open boxes and smashes his toys to see what is inside, is iconoclastic, just like the surprising spring when (in Valéry's words) the poet "comes to break open the sealed-over fountains." Yet the seal exists precisely in order to inform us of the secret it guards. Though the object does not manifest itself entirely, still it announces that very part of itself which it keeps opaque. The object's own mystery is visible, and its hiding places show themselves *as* hiding places (and such are the only true ones). Even if the object protects itself against my investigations, I still retain the right to approach and examine it. Perception assures me of my power and grants the object to me as a *plenum* which I grasp in an infinite number of ways and with which I have innumerable relations. In the end, we are speaking metaphorically when we talk about the secrets of nature. Even if we strive passionately to discover these secrets, it is not the same as when we are dealing with the secret of a person—the sort of secret that the eyes of Mélisande hide from Golaud. Hence a thing does not need to make a sign, because it is already a sign through and through. It need not exteriorize itself, because it is total exteriority.

Expression, on the other hand, as the capacity for emitting signs and exteriorizing itself, pertains primarily to a subject. Thus it presupposes a will to what American anthropology considers a fundamental human need, namely, self-expression and communication. Signs are exuded even in solitude, where we become for ourselves an imaginary other. A need for self-expression or communication arises from the fact that the for-itself exists only in its self-exteriorization. Mélisande would not have been innocent without her innocent expression and her use of the language of innocence. We are born to ourselves only in our active self-embodiment and in using our bodies not as available equipment to be utilized for preconceived ends but rather as that through which we are what we are. Expression is the revelation of the self, simply because it causes us to actually *be* what is expressed. Expression creates an interior in the very constitution of an exterior, and only at its instigation is the life of the interior rendered possible.[11] Expression can undoubtedly be employed for the sake of deceiving and not for the sake of being. Thus it becomes a language capable of truth and falsehood. But even if we refuse to be the person we express, the other self who we are at a deeper level is still destined to expression. We are always on display and can be deciphered by a sufficiently keen insight. To be is to be visible, whether one is aware of it or not. Thus the reading [*la lecture*] of signification reveals in this case a coincidence of the signifier and signified which is founded on the fact that the signified *is* only by means of the sign. The thing, in contrast, is settled deep into being and has no need to signify. The appearances in which it shows itself do not determine its being but only how we ourselves grasp the thing. It does not have to be visible; rather, we must see *it*. But expression grants a different status to the expressed. Through its self-exteriorization, the interior gains autonomy and distinguishes itself from the exterior in the very moment when it identifies itself with, and is constituted by, the exterior. The exterior is responsible for the interiority of the interior. The eyes of Mélisande are pools of mystery and, although she speaks unreservedly, she says nothing, for the interior which she reveals is revealed as interior, that is, as forever inadequate to expression. Expression appears as inadequate as a result of its very adequacy (only by facing this contradiction will the relation between interior and exterior be truly dialectical, in Hegel's sense). And it really is the case that at every instant I know everything and yet nothing about a given human being.[12] Whereas the thing is unfathomable, the other, because of the dimension of interiority, is simultaneously transparent and indecipherable.

11. In this respect, every action we perform is a means of self-expression. Actions can haunt us because they define us. I am what I do because only through me does what I do take consistency and form. But the expression of my self in my actions is not so much *what* I do as the manner in which I do it. Only in terms of this manner can one find my motivating intention. In this way, the unfashionable ethics of good will regains some of its lost force. But, of course, one can speak of the interior only by means of what is expressed.

12. This is the same antinomy that we noticed in the case of language. To the extent that it is the expression of my thought, it *is* my thought; but it can be so only by not being my thought. Thought as language is a natural fact, but it also receives in this way a mental status. A thought contains a sense and is amenable to a truth. The idea is the word and yet more than the word, and that is why it never ceases to surprise us. In a sense, therefore, dualism is the inner truth of monism, in the same way that Spinoza's attributes are the inner truth of substance.

The other is not, however, other in the sense that nature is the other of mind—and we shall see, in this respect, how a work of art is not indecipherable in the manner of a simple material object.

Hence expression manifests a for-itself as the power to make signs and yet to detach itself from these signs and thus interiorize itself in the act of self-exteriorization, whereas, in the case of appearance, the oneness of the signified and the signifier does not dialectically transform itself into difference. While the redness of embarrassment is such simply because embarrassment means to redden under another's glance, what it indicates to me is an unfathomable interiority. This is so because it tells me nothing, and even if I were to take part in the embarrassment, I could never make it my own or grasp its exact nuance. On the other hand, I immediately perceive the sense of the redness of burning coals as the property of combustibility which these coals possess. But the being of the coals which is in this way revealed to me is in no way the being of an interiority. Even if I attribute a certain substantiality to the coals, their ability to burn, their calorific faculty, is in no way equivalent to the power of saying that one "burns"—an expression which is frequently found on the lips of Corneille's heroes. In this respect, interiority remains, in accordance with Aristotelian physics, an exteriority. Appearance refers me to the thing—which itself, however, is once again just appearance. Thus the progress of knowledge consists simply in discovering new appearances and in clarifying one appearance by another appearance. An idea, in this sense, is no more than an organization of appearances which would allow the substitution of a clear appearance for one that is confused. Thus the differentiation within the identity between sign and meaning is not the same as that between what expresses [*l'exprimant*] and what is expressed [*l'exprimé*]. This opposition of two modes of signification denotes an opposition between thing and subject or, in the case of the aesthetic object, between thing and quasi subject.

We can further clarify this opposition by comparing the activity brought about by the passage from appearance to thing with that effected by the movement from what expresses to what is expressed. Although appearance offers up the thing immediately on the level of presence, this is a corporeal immediacy which is parallel to (but not the same as) the immediacy of expression and in which the reflective is continually infused with the unreflective. And when we pass onto representation, that is, when we step back to let an appearance truly appear, the thing proffers itself through the appearance with the aid of imagination. Then we are enabled to imagine what was at first simply given in primary experience, reviving and mobilizing incarnate modes of knowledge, and thus constantly to surpass appearance in anticipation of the thing. Because imagination, under the imminent control of understanding, takes on the task of developing the signification of what is perceived, that is, of unifying the possible with the actual and thereby according it quasi actuality, it is imagination which is responsible for the given's appearing as a sign instead of simply terminating within itself as no more than itself. Imagination constitutes sense and unites it with the given, which thus becomes more than it is with an excess that constitutes its signification. Understanding intervenes when signs are to be decoded systematically, as in the case of the archeologist or detective, when we become more concerned with intellectual sense than with practical activity—that is, with the future of comprehension rather than with how we will use something. Sense or meaning, therefore, is no longer an inhabitant of appearance, for it is deduced. We move from the sign to what is signified by means of a reasoning which imagination may inspire but cannot justify. We no longer perceive the sign as such. Rather, we consider the object itself as what does the signifying and then decide to find out what it signifies. Accordingly, signification poses a problem and is no longer a solution. Not possessing knowledge, we wonder, what signifies? And we fall immediately into science. We no longer perceive a thing in the world but a phenomenon in nature.

The signification proper to appearance therefore brings us to the object by means of a sort of expectation or anticipation which is itself possible through the memory of lived experience and in the form of an image of the future. But this image is entirely believable only because the object does not harbor surprises. The object says what it is and offers itself, without malice, to the commentaries of imagination and understanding. I am sure of the object first because I know that it contains nothing of the unforseeable (although I may be unaware of certain of its aspects) and next because my knowledge of it precedes any experience with it. Thus I have power over the object, and, since I hold within myself its possible aspects and am able to use imagination to convert the hollow reality of appearance into a complete reality, I no longer experience a presence but, rather, give myself a representation. My sovereignty is, of course, a limited one, because representation comes about only through a preliminary experience of presence. Moreover, my sovereignty in this regard is purely intellectual. Representation is capable of irrigating, by means of images, a bloodless appearance and of naming a given object in its plenitude but not of creating the given. The *intuito* is not *originaria*. Yet, in every case, the movement from the appearance to the object is very much my act. The perceived is the correlate of my perception. And that is why naming is not, as in originary speech, a way of echoing the object or becoming its captive but a way of possessing the object. Speech is the instrument and sign of my mastery, attesting that I hold the key to appearances.

In reading expression by means of feeling, on the other hand, I am no longer deciphering an experience or reconstituting what has already been constituted by the intentionality of my body. I am not exploiting a reserve. I am simply reading. I cannot, of course, read signs unless they are signs for me, that is, unless they awaken a sort of echo in my body. This is why, as we have seen, the reading of expression, like the maturation of an instinct, demands organic condition. But I read a meaning or sense without passing through bodily knowledge which would have to be realized by imagination. What appears to me is the sense itself, to which I have direct access by means of a natural clairvoyance.[13] In the beginning, such a comprehension can only be lived and so bears the same character of bodily (and thus equivocal) immediacy as does the lived comprehension of experience. At this level, it is with my body that I correspond to others. I exist in the human world as I do in the natural world. The child rushes up to its mother when she holds open her arms. Responding to affection with affection and to anger with fear, he does not distinguish between what does the expressing and what is expressed. He lives the sense rather than reflecting on it. We come to perceive this sort of meaning, therefore, by means of the emotion which it arouses in us, just as we grasp the thing successfully by means of the movement to which it gives rise. Like motor activity, emotivity is knowledge. The only difference is that the emotive is a relation with another human

13. It must be admitted that the world of human intentionality is not open, like the world of things, and that the two worlds are distinct. The social sciences are possible only on this condition, that is, if they do not reduce themselves to a science of things through the positivist prejudice. And, since they exist only by an implicit reference to a preliminary comprehension of the human, such a reductive move is incapable of being carried through.

being and not with a thing. Human presence does not behave like the presence of a thing.

But this is not yet the stage of true expression which would imply access to representation, the consciousness of signification. What characterizes this stage and constitutes its specific immediacy is that what is expressed appears there first and instantaneously. The signified traverses the signifier so rapidly that it becomes necessary to rediscover what does the signifying and subject it to interrogation. Is this particular red the red of shame? Is what we had spontaneously perceived as shame, and is now reduced to this appearance of red, really shame? In this way, reflection dissociates what is manifest from its manifestation, just as it also dissociates an object from its qualities. One may say that reflection makes the interior appear as interior. But sense is primary even before reflection comes into play. When reflection does enter, it adds nothing to appearance but rather hollows appearance out and submits itself to appearance. Reflection, in other words, does not mediate what is immediate in expression. That is, expression tends to nullify the activity which attempts to bring about the movement from appearance to thing. To a certain extent, expression paralyzes imagination. This is above all due to the fact that I cannot assume with certainty what a particular manifestation of human behavior is expressing. From an object, I expect nothing; rather, I call on myself for its signification. In the case of a subject, I can expect anything. Since it is an interior which is revealed, it is unfathomable and without common grounds with my own experience. I can, of course, foresee something, but only with an irreducible coefficient of uncertainty which is not found in the apprehension of an object. When I call an appearance suspicious, doubtful, or incomprehensible, my uncertainty comes from a lack of skill or from inexperience. But in the case at hand, it is expression itself, proceeding from the subject and thus at its most transparent, which baffles me as soon as I seek to assure myself of its meaning. Thus I can be only attentive and not active. That is why I cannot imagine a feeling but can only read it. There is nothing hidden in a feeling which may subsequently be discovered, and any future it may possess—which would be revealed in subsequent expressions—cannot be foreseen with precision.[14] Imagination is thus disarmed—as is understanding,

14. It is certainly always possible to analyze a feeling as psychology does, but such an analysis would also lack vitality and hardly be part of a lively reading. It would, moreover, occur only at the risk of gravely altering

to the extent that understanding takes into account and uses that power over the object bestowed on it by imagination. This is true not only because we are dealing with a human subject but also—and these two reasons are the same—because expression has said everything in a single stroke. I need not anticipate—not just because I am in contact with a free agent but also because there is simply nothing to anticipate. Everything is in expression and what is expressed is given to me immediately. I can only return to what does the expressing, in order to open myself more fully to what is expressed and allow it to speak. That would be sufficient to leave room for reflection and also to distinguish what is immediate in feeling from what is immediate in presence. In this light, feeling may lay claim to a dialectic of its own. Aesthetic experience will enlighten us in this respect, because it is there that feeling, as we have just defined it, best realizes its noetic function.

---

the primordial function of expression, which is the revelation of myself as a for-itself. For I would have to transform the for-itself into an object, as when someone denies the expressive character of the gestures of an angry man in order to heed their mechanical character and coldly informs him that he will calm down when he is tired. We shall see that the critic's attitude before the aesthetic object does not differ greatly from such cold contemplation.

14 / Feeling and the Depth
of the Aesthetic Object

IN ORDER TO DESCRIBE the advent of feeling in aesthetic experience, we must follow an itinerary parallel to that which we took in analyzing the structure of the aesthetic object—and, in a more summary fashion, in distinguishing between the aesthetic object and the signifying object. The original move was from the subject of the work to its expression, in an effort to bring that expression (however unanalyzable it is in itself) to light and assign it a place within the structure of the work. We are concerned now, however, with the perceiving subject and not with the object perceived—although we shall have to refer to this object continually.

[I] TWO TYPES OF REFLECTION

IT IS SELF-EVIDENT that the constitutive activity of the understanding is implied by the perception of the aesthetic object. We need not dwell on this point. It will be sufficient simply to note that this constitutive activity is probably facilitated by the structure of the object. This object possesses such rigor and clarity that it seems to adapt itself spontaneously to the rules by which understanding subsumes the variety of the given under the unity of the "I think." This occurs all the more spontaneously because of the proximity of imagination as a transcendental faculty to understanding, whose rules are foreshadowed by the schematism. And the aesthetic object is so constituted by its schemata that it offers itself to the schematizing imagination as easily graspable—just as it does to the body. Perhaps the understanding finds itself at ease before the aesthetic object because of the complicity of the body. The way in which the object occupies space and time, its numerical order and rhythm, the sort of necessity which it manifests—all these things contribute to the satisfaction of understanding by convincing the body.

But the simple fact that constitutive activity is rooted in the body implies that it is unconscious of itself and not the means of access to feeling. Constitutive activity merely orders appearances in order to determine an identifiable object within them and to think that object's relation with other objects. It does not question the sense or meaning of that object. This questioning is the function of reflection proper, which we must now show in operation. For the aesthetic object seeks out reflection and does so all the more pressingly because it is made for us, being a sign through which someone is striving to tell us something. The aesthetic object is a privileged sort of object which, overwhelming us with its imperious presence, demands our attention and poses a problem. We have given an example of such a reflection in operation when we sketched a critical analysis of the work. It remains for us to show the mechanism of this type of reflection, as well as its limit, that is, to see how it flows into feeling.

A preliminary remark is in order. Since the nature of the aesthetic object is to represent something, we begin to suspect that the reflection it arouses may concern itself either with the means of representation or with the thing represented. Moreover, this distinction of form and content (whose limits we foresaw when we observed that content's relationship to form was one of immanence) may well be a product of understanding. But it is certainly true that reflection was at work from the beginning and then oriented itself along two different paths. There is, first, the sort of reflection which treats of the *structure* of the aesthetic object. Then there is the sort which treats of the *sense* of the represented object. Considering a writer's art of composition and syntax is not the same as reflecting on the climate of his depicted universe, nor do we ponder the musician's structure of composition as we do the feelings expressed by his work, or a painter's pictorial techniques as opposed to the atmosphere his paintings may invoke. Reflection on the structure of the aesthetic object is similar to constitutive activity. This kind of reflection defines the object by detaching it from the self so that it may be subjected to a critical examination. To reveal the secrets of its construction, I look into how it is made and, in a sense, supervise it. It is no longer the object as such which subjects me to interrogation, but rather the object as produced by a making whose process and results I can reconstruct and appreciate—that is, an object which I subject to interrogation through my own movements. Hence I detach myself from the work by substituting an analytical perception for a perception of the whole. Reflection always implies a sort of plumbing of the depths, but in this case through decomposing the object rather than gaining intimacy with it. When reflection seeks the elements and the plan of an object's fabrication, it does not treat the elements as the living organs of the object or the plan as the object's animating soul. Rather, reflection conceives both as parts of an arrangement, as elements of a dissoluble unity.

This type of critical reflection is not without interest, since it is responsible for clarifying the object as a perceived reality. It reduces that sense of confused totality in which I seem to become lost and which I experience in first hearing of a musical work, the first reading of certain poems, or even the first contact with a painting. Further, reflection concerning form is capable of increasing our comprehension of the work's meaning and for two reasons. First, since the meaning is immanent in the sign, an analysis of the sign provides access to the meaning. This is particularly true of plastic and musical works, where meaning is genuinely immanent in aesthetic language, in contrast with spoken language, which tends constantly to concern itself with external and conventional meaning. The discovery of a particular musical modulation involves the acquisition of a certain inflection of feeling which runs through the work. Bach's cadences speak of confidence and force. Second, creative activity (whose procedures are made manifest in an analysis of its results) is precisely that sort of activity which does not limit itself to a making which is externally motivated and yet anonymous —as is the case with the artisan—but which takes itself as its aim or posits as its goal the expression of the creator. Thus art is not a technique comparable to other techniques. This is why Van Gogh's brush-strokes *say* something about the message of the work, as does the detail of the Flemish primitives, a writer's personal syntax, or the architect's choice of a particular type of stone or method of procedure. All of which does not negate the fact that there are requirements and traditions for the technique which are independent of the creator and rely on physical and sociological necessities, as we can see in the case of technology. This is why a purely objective examination of the work is always possible. But authentic works have a way of incorporating (and sometimes reinventing) techniques which attests to the presence of the creator and introduces us to his universe of meanings—and to that expression of feelings toward which all reflection tends to surpass itself. But it is presently a question of reflection on objective meanings. Now, reflection on structure can always stop with itself. We can always consider structure uniquely as structure, as the result of an activity examined simply in terms of technique or the material and social conditions which determine technique. But as long as we stay on this level, we have not yet understood the aesthetic object. The sort of inquiry which could provide the key to understanding objects of use (and most certainly does so in the case of tools, which we know how to use on the basis of knowing how they are made) would be of little help in the case of an object which represents something else.

Therefore, the work also calls for reflection on what it signifies. It is an appearance for which we must account, and it has a subject which calls for comprehension. What is the meaning, for example, of the Greek god with his distant smile, which seems to express not so much the joy of one who has conquered the Titans as the apprehensive presentiment that the advent of Christ lies at the horizon of history? What is the meaning of a particular poem whose words are so simple, so limpid and welcoming, so common and prosaic, and yet which can become so suddenly strange? What is the meaning of a certain symphony which sweeps me off into a realm of absurd exploits but must still have some significance? What does Isée mean when she rises before Mésa in Claudel's *Partage de Midi:* "Look at me, I am Isée"? What is the meaning of the oboe and the sound of its plaintive voice? What is the meaning of this shade of yellow which resounds like a fanfare through a painting by Van Gogh? We should note, above all, that such investigations are endless. Is this because they are simply objectless? Is it not an impossible ploy to introduce the conceptual into what properly pertains to the perceptible [*le sensible*] and to find a meaning in a formal flourish, a melodic line, or a patch of color? Is it not true that the literary arts, whose raw material [*matière*] is laden with thought, are the only arts blessed with an immediately communicable meaning? And even the word ceases to have a meaning explicable through reflection once it undergoes a poetic transformation. We become all the more convinced of the correctness of this objection if we believe that the ultimate access to the work lies in feeling. Still, no one really comes to grips with feeling who has not undergone the experience of reflection. The work of art provokes the intelligence as well, and it is not easy to rid oneself of this provocation. Of course, reflection finds itself most at ease in the literary arts, where significations seem to demand explication. From the most ancient times, glossarists have considered textual commentary a privileged activity. But there are also glossaries for painting, music, and the dance—witness the written programs which sometimes come from the hand of the composer or choreographer, the debates waged in the academies of painting or sculpture, or even those simple words of Van Gogh: "I have sought to represent overwhelming human passions by means of color."

And yet, such a reflection on content tends to lose its object to the exact extent that it is faithful to its purpose of moving from appearance to thing—that is, from the work considered as appearance to the represented object—and consequently of transcribing into the langauge of prose what the work says in its own language. This undertaking is ultimately futile, since what is said by the work can be said in no other way, and the immanence of content to form prevents the exclusive employment of the appearance-thing relationship. Such reflection, therefore, is soon surpassed by a sort of reflection whose aim is no longer commentary but explication. This second sort of reflection comes to consider the aesthetic object as a thing in nature whose meaning is to be found in its posterior or anterior context. A cloud's meaning rests in the rain of which it is a herald or in the previous state of the atmosphere by which it has been prepared, and in any case in what it refers to as well as in what it implies. An explication is always the unfolding of an implication. (Whether the implication happens to be logical or real, or whether the logical and real are mutually irreducible, is of little consequence.) Now, as the meaning of the aesthetic object cannot follow after it, since the object does not produce anything, meaning must be found in what precedes it. Thus reflection turns toward the question of the genesis of meaning. When this genesis is considered logically, the investigation concerns the way this meaning develops from certain affirmations or conspicuous beliefs—how, for example, Mallarmé's poetry unfolds from a peculiar feeling of nothingness, the *Brandenburg Concertos* from a certain conception of the musical suite, or the painting of Bosch from an alchemically influenced cosmology. When the genesis of meaning is considered chronologically, the point is to rejoin this meaning to a history—which may be the author's own or that of the culture to which he is heir. The chronological mode of explication often comes to replace the logical. Mallarmé's theme of nothingness will refer to a psychoanalytical exegesis and the symbolical images of Bosch to a tradition by which he has been influenced (the psychology of the artist will refer to an analysis of his milieu and vice versa). In this way, the work appears as overdetermined; or, rather, each key opens a new door for one without one's ever penetrating into the inner chambers. This is due to the fact that a literal commentary (and even more a genetic commentary) neutralizes the aesthetic experience, disturbs its immediacy, and ruins its peculiar charm. Once translated into a different kind of language and reduced to external circumstances, the work is negated in its specificity. It has been left behind, no longer to be recaptured in the investigation of that which it is not. It is now only a natural object which does not find its meaning within itself but in a history of which it is the product. Reflection must be reoriented in order to regain the object—an object which must be accorded anew the essential privilege of sufficing by itself and of bearing its meaning within itself.

WE ARE THUS SEPARATED from the work as a result of having willed to reconstruct it, substituting ourselves for its creator. But there exists another form of reflection which will lead us back into contact with the aesthetic object. Just as Kant distinguishes between determinant and reflective judgment, it is possible to distinguish between a reflection which separates us from and a reflection which makes us adhere to the object. We have just seen the separating form of reflection at work and have also observed its limits. Even an analysis of structure (which would seem to arise uniquely from this kind of reflection, since such an analysis must have the requisite exactitude and precision to account for appearances, just as an architectural plan accounts for a building, or a musical analysis for a symphony) appeared to us to surpass the limits of an objectifying reflection. But the comprehension of meaning incontestably presupposes another form of reflection, the sort of reflection in which I must adopt, from the beginning, a new attitude toward the object. Thus we have said that, by means of reflective judgment, we ourselves were put into question, not necessarily because we reflect on ourselves, but because we consider ourselves *committed* by our reflection. Consequently, such reflection depends on what I am and on the relationship which I inaugurate with the object. By means of adherent reflection, I submit myself to the work instead of submitting it to my jurisdiction, and I allow the work to deposit its meaning within me. I consider the object no longer as a thing which must be known through its appearance—as in critical reflection, where appearance has no value and signifies nothing on its own—but, rather, as a thing which signifies spontaneously and directly, even if I am unable to encompass its meaning: as a quasi subject. And because this thing refers surreptitiously to expression, we shall see that a sympathetic reflection culminates in feeling.

The difference between these two types of reflection is primarily a difference in attitude, since their contents can be identical. In either case, I can search for the meaning of a particular verse in *La Jeune Parque,* or of a particular anatomical deformity in one of the figures in a Gauguin painting, or of a particular grouping of dancers in a ballet. But I restrain myself from questioning in the way that the physicist questions when he searches for the meaning of the distribution of light rays on a spectroscope. In other words, I do not look for a causal agent, whether this be the intention of the creator, the influence of a tradition, or some other circumstance which may bear on the creator's intention. I could still, of course, invoke the creator in order to obtain the meaning of the work. But such a figure would no longer be as distinct from his work as a cause is from its effect. He is not someone whose real personality and whose insertion in a real historical period could furnish the key to his work. Instead, he is someone whom I identify with the work and who does not so much give an account of the work as he is accounted for by it. Therefore my invocation of the creator is simply an explanation of the work in terms of itself. This is what is important: everything I say concerning the work is said in the attempt to remain faithful to it and to find, in it alone, the ground of its being. Thus, were I to maintain the notion of a genesis, it would be that of an autogenesis on the part of the work. An understanding of the work comes no longer from the discovery of who produced it but, rather, from seeing how it produces and unfolds itself. In the end, we probably understand the development and behavior of a living being in exactly the same way. We grasp the phenomenon peculiar to life only by understanding how it reposes within itself and draws its particular substance from all those causes which act on it but which determine it only to be itself. Furthermore, this is how we truly understand other people—that is, when someone's act appears to us to be the expression of his being, when we look within him for an existential, internal necessity, a necessity which is imbued with his personal liberty and not an external necessity which would determine him from the outside. But how is it possible to grasp such an autogenesis? By means of participation, that is, on the condition that we identify ourselves with the object sufficiently to rediscover within ourselves that movement by which the object is itself. Thus the understanding of another person as such presupposes that: (1) there is a sort of consubstantiality between myself and him, so that he is not so radically estranged from me as is the material object; and (2) I feel myself impelled toward this acquaintance, allying myself strictly enough with the other to be sensitive to our mutual affinity.[1] As in Hegel's *Phenomenology of Mind* and Comte's *Social Dynamic,* an understanding of history is a rediscovery of its echo in me, that is, a way of being which is fully historical or fully alive. I must be in accord with history, which must have a

1. This type of assimilation to others is not exactly an identification. Husserl, who calls this assimilation a "pairing" in an "analogizing apprehension," adds that the other as appresented "can never attain actual presence" (*Cartesian Meditations,* trans. Dorion Cairns [The Hague: Nijhoff, 1969], p. 112) in the primordial sphere of my peculiar ownness, since I am not that other—an other whom I would not be able to think except as "an analogue of something included in my particular ownness" (p. 115). But it is through that "analogizing modification of the Ego of mine" that he can be appresented and that "another monad becomes constituted appresentatively in mine." (Here Husserl would like to maintain both the direct and original character of the reading of others and the fundamental otherness of the other. I recognize him as an other but as an other ego; he is "the intentional modification of that Ego of mine" [p. 115] and it is on the ground of my ego that I recognize him as an other.) Husserl himself points out that my past is given to me in the same way. "It becomes constituted in my living present," it "transcends my present," just as "the appresented other being 'transcends' my own being (in the pure and most fundamental sense: what is included in my primordial ownness)." And it may be necessary to extend the idea to the past (i.e., of history or of my own life), which is no more myself than is someone else but is "relative to me a modificatum, an *other* Ego" (pp. 115–16). In any event, I am associated with others through my recognition of them, not only in the sense that this recognition is mine but also in that I recognize them through myself. Pairing presupposes a resemblance, a kinship. But such a commitment of my ego in the recognition of others should not be understood simply from within the transcendental prespective of intentionality. The other does not exist simply in terms of my own aims but also in terms of a transformation of my being. We shall return later to this theme of the two senses in which one opens oneself.

direct relationship with myself. I must experience it at least by proxy. In short, I must recapitulate humanity and bear it within myself. Understanding is the memory of having been, following the lead of the historical object in rediscovering it. The guarantee for this discovery lies in a sense of complicity between myself and the object.

It is in this way that a sympathetic reflection on the aesthetic object proceeds. We can see to what extent it approximates to feeling, into which it flows and by which it is inspired. Such reflection represents a faithful and passionate attention through which I imbue myself with the object by making myself consubstantial with it. Thereby the object is clarified by becoming familiar, and my knowledge is deepened by being incorporated ever more profoundly within me. The questions we asked—e.g., why this particular brush-stroke, this melodic line, or that ornament?—now receive an answer. They are no longer answered through the discovery of a cause external to the work but through the feeling of a necessity internal to the work. This is a necessity which must be called existential, since it is analogous to the necessity we experience within ourselves when we feel bound by the very development of our being to a particular choice or judgment. Why does Isée rise before Mésa to say, "I am Isée"? Precisely because he is Isée, because he is that living and provocative affirmation, that impertinent and reckless audacity, that manner of announcing himself without evasiveness or hesitancy and of breaking through resistances like the grace of a god who says, "I am who I am." Why the monsters in a painting by Bosch? To plunge us into a magic universe where horrors proliferate patiently in a quasi-systematic manner—horrors which are horrible in their detail and not as a whole. Instead of shaking the spectator at a single glance by the subversion of his expectation, a Bosch painting shows us the slow and minute breakdown of the familiar. Why the irruption of the major key in the final movement of Franck's symphony? To usher us into the light. Why the insistent chromaticism of *Tristan and Isolde,* if not to enchant us and to induce the spell of an absurd and impetuous love which rejects day for night? Yet reflection itself gives rise to still further questions. Why the toad rather than the tortoise? Again, why the chromaticism, since the same device plays quite a different role in *Die Meistersinger,* and why the ninth chords rather than Monteverdi's sevenths? Why these particular words in the mouth of Isée rather than some others in another rhythm? But that is exactly the point: aesthetic perception must agree to its limits. For two reasons, aesthetic perception must not reject the evidence of a self-sufficient necessity within the work: (1) because it is the necessity of the work such as it is and not such as it might be; and (2) because this necessity is internal to the work and is not to be explained by traversing a series, or various series, of causes. To understand a work is to be assured that it cannot be otherwise than it is. This is no tautology, since this assurance can come to us only when we are infused with the work to such an extent that we allow it to develop and to affirm itself within us, discovering in this intimacy with the work the will to seek out its meaning within it. For, to repeat, existential necessity cannot be recognized from the outside or be experienced except in myself, insofar as I am capable of opening myself up to this necessity. Such is the necessity of the aesthetic object, which I must at the same time recognize in myself.

This necessity is by no means that which operates in an external way on all worldly things. It is a necessity by which the aesthetic object posits and affirms itself as perfect, immobile, and subject only to its own law—a law which, in turn, confers on the object a sort of inexhaustible quality which reflection discovers to be incomparable. In a sense, inexhaustibility is a quality of any perceived object, which must always be grasped in relation to a fixed point of view and whose appearance must always be filled out by imagination—and in such a way that every viewing appeals to a multiplicity of other viewings and the possible continually lies at the horizon of the real. Nevertheless, though this indeterminacy of the given does belong to the aesthetic object—which is always a perceived object, even if it is never perceived completely—it does not serve to characterize it adequately. But it is not a question, either, of the inexhaustibility of ontic determinations, through which the object is dependent on the entire universe and ungraspable because of the multiplicity of relations by which it is constituted. For this inexhaustibility characterizes even that material object which is the support of the aesthetic object but with which the latter is never to be identified. A cathedral is indeed a mass of stone delivered over to erosion just like any other pile of rocks. But a cathedral is also something else, an incarnate idea for which the stone is merely a means for appearing. It is perception itself which instructs us here, forbidding us to reduce the aesthetic object to the status of an ordinary object. Naïve perception is wiser than understanding, since it acquaints us with the aesthetic object's peculiar stability or, in the case of the evanescent object of the temporal arts, with its consistency and organic nature, its irreducibility to the contingency of external relations.

The first two types of inexhaustibility just distinguished are quantitative or, in Bergson's terms, extensive. They may also be called negative, because they point to both the finitude of sensuous cognition, which is unable to coincide with its object, and the finitude of the object itself, which must be reunited with the universe in order to be completely determined. Accordingly, they define certain characteristics of the object, such as its otherness or externality, or, as it were, its externality to the perceiving consciousness as well as to itself. Yet, far from being appropriate to the aesthetic object as such, these characteristics betray its essential proximity to consciousness as well as the organizing coherence which converts it into a quasi subject. This is so because such characteristics only define the situation of the object with respect to the glance directed toward it or its relation to other objects which, together with it, compose reality. They characterize the being of the in-itself, which cannot be in-and-for-itself and which remains constantly antagonistic to the intelligibility of essence and the sufficiency of the idea. But there is an inexhaustibility of excess as well as of lack, an inexhaustibility which we approach when we consider the multiplicity of possible interpretations of the same object. This multiplicity has a positive significance and attests to the richness of the object. If there is a lack, it is merely in our cognition, which cannot make things rationally explicable. For we are not concerned here with the realm of perception and its indefinite number of necessarily partial perspectives, each of which requires a complement and no one of which can really be true to the object. (The search for truth is in vain at the level of appearance, insofar as appearance is defined by its relativity.) This particular inexhaustibility is, rather, that belonging to a plurality of significations which are (more than the perspectival viewings which we may take on the object) complete expressions of this object. To the extent, however, that these significations remain points of view which intelligence takes concerning the object and are thus comparable to the points of view of perception, they attest to the externality of the object and the fact that it is irreducible to intelligence, in the same way that it is irreducible to the look. Yet, to the extent that these points of view represent an effort to grasp the very nature of the object, their convergence testifies to the depth of the object—a depth which is not simply the opacity of the in-itself but the plenitude of a meaning. And the aesthetic object's inexhaustibility is, in the end, a function of its depth. This object does not exist in the manner of a thing which cannot be fully viewed in the course of a single glance but, rather, in the sense of a consciousness whose depths are unfathomable. Even the image of physical depth tends to mislead, however, to the extent that it suggests measurability and thus extension. The aesthetic object has depth because it is beyond measurement. If we want to grasp it truly, we must transform ourselves. The depth of the aesthetic object is measured by the depth of the existence to which it invites us. Its depth is correlative with ours.

This correlation is characteristic of the kind of feeling in which aesthetic experience culminates. Such feeling may be described by explicating this correlation and demonstrating how man deepens himself and how, in turn, the object appears to him in depth. This demonstration would help to verify what we have continually suggested concerning the being of the aesthetic object, whose depth can be grasped only as the correlate, and also as the image, of spiritual depth. Let us turn, then, to the notion of depth.

[II] FEELING AS BEING-IN-DEPTH

IN FACT, we experience the depth of things in the image of human depth. We are attracted by a deep forest or lake because it gives us the impression that there is some truth to discover, some secret to abduct from the heart of the object. What strange fauna lurk on the ocean floor? What haunted castle is concealed in the sleeping wood? It is the eternal seduction of the hidden. But the hidden is not the merely unexpected, that surprise which one encounters at the turn in the road. However lively the emotions which an unexpected occurrence may evoke or however great may be its power, it still has no charm. The hidden is that sort of unexpected occurrence which one expects, which is coveted as the goal of a long exploration, the recompense promised to the hero of the adventure. Those animals from another world who inhabit our aquariums are not the same for the curious spectator as they are for the adventurer who wrested them from the ocean depths or for those who will examine them through the porthole of their bathyscaphe. The hidden is valued only for its challenging provocation and the courage necessary for taking up the challenge. There is, in a sense, something unswervingly sublime about the hidden. And courage is precisely a primary manifestation of depth in man, a fact which René Le Senne has in mind when he reminds us that courage is the soul of virtue.[2] Courage awakens with the taste for adventure, which is the inexplicable desire for an absent object, and it is confirmed in being enacted on the basis of a strange resolution which in itself derives from something more than the spontaneous motions of anger or fear. For if, as Plato shows, there is anger in courage, or even, according to Alain's suggestion, fear as well, there is also something more—a decision and faith born of freedom, by means of which the conversion of man into hero remains inexplicable. Thus depth as the seat of the hidden summons up the depths in man. This is why it is not simply a matter of extension. Depth is not what is farthest but what is the most difficult. Just as the intellectual object exists as inexhaustible for an intelligence capable of trying out all possible hypotheses, so the hidden exists for courage, and depth for the man of profundity.

Let us try to take a closer look at what human depth involves.[3] The distinction between the superficial and the profound is a simple fact of experience. We are well practiced in weighing a man's character, implementing a spiritual physics of the heavy-handed and the lighthearted, and recognizing the profundity of a person, act, or idea. However, this spontaneous experience can easily degenerate, through the agency of reflection, into a sort of Romanticism of the profound. Thus we must avoid identifying depth with the hidden or the involuntary, that is, with the past and the unconscious. In this respect, any "depth psychology" lays as many traps as it uncovers truths. The past certainly seems to be one gauge of what is profound. The night into which the past sinks is that of a lost paradise whose seductive memory haunts the tales of Genesis as well as of Proust. And it is undeniable that we are affected by the past and sometimes—in the case of certain privileged experiences—more deeply than we would dare to admit. The return to the land of one's birth—whether by elegy or epic—is a pilgrimage to the

2. See René Le Senne, *Traité de morale générale* (Paris: Presses Universitaires de France, 1942).—Trans.

3. Once again, we can define human depth only by means of the double relationship it sustains with the depth of the object. Human depth is the condition for grasping the object's depth while also illustrating the notion of this depth.

origin. We join up with ourselves in an experience of emotional certitude. Nevertheless, what is deep here is not so much the past per se as it is our present experience of uniting ourselves with this past and identifying ourselves with what we have been, aided by a peculiar perception testifying to the past. It is a triple experience. First, we form an integral unit with ourselves and become one, in spite of our temporal diffusion. Second, we take on the extra weight of the past in an experience which is quite the opposite of that of the *Voyageur sans bagages* and by which we are assured of our substantiality without the past's weight dragging us down into the in-itself, since the totality of our past is not the positivity of thinghood but the affirmation of an existence. Finally, we experience the irresistible flow of time, while at the same time possessing something within us that is invulnerable to time, because our past is not abolished and does not become something foreign and distant. It is thus that we experience the dimension of interiority, that which grants us depth—in short, our power of joining ourselves to ourselves and of escaping time within time by founding a new time through fidelity to memory and to promises. But it is not the past by itself which has depth. The past as such does not affect me. What really affects me is the meeting within myself of the past and the present, as well as the sudden and unforeseen nature of this meeting, which the vicissitudes of life arrange. Depth arises, therefore, in the use which I make of the past.

Moreover, just as depth is not quantitative, it is also not a matter of extension. If time comes into the picture, it is time considered as *tensio* and not *extensio,* that is, entirely within the moment. The depth in man is in command of time and is not time's captive subject. The inexorable flow of one moment into the next is no more than an occasion to evoke the past so as to fashion its image and commit oneself to the future. If there is any depth in the passing moment itself, that is, if I am entirely present within it and consecrate it with my presence, then that moment will not pass away. It has become past in my ego and thus an origin from which I can benefit from now on. And with this we are quite close to the analyses of Marcel, who shows how depth confounds time as well as space, rather than leaving them in their familiar form.[4] More precisely, depth is a figure of eternity to the extent that in it the now and the then tend to merge, as do the near and the far, the here and the there. Marcel cites

4. See Gabriel Marcel, "Le Sentiment du profond," *Fontaine,* LI (April, 1946), 586 ff.

the example of those children who seem to be seeking an absolute "here" in their search for a secret hiding place—one may almost call it a metaphysical fatherland. We may also think of the example of that toward which the primitive imagination is constantly striving, namely, the myth, which does not occur in worldly time but rather in an absolute past: Once upon a time . . . a time which has no ancestors but does have a posteriority, an original time continually repeated in worldly time.[5] And there is a certain similarity in the way English novelists (of whom one finds an unexpected echo in Sartre's *La Nausée*) describe the search for moments of perfection. It is not insignificant that such moments of perfection often display an aesthetic dimension. Thus we can affirm two things with confidence. First, although depth has some relationship with time, this relationship is not with the past as such. The prestige enjoyed by the past resists analysis, because contained in the notion of the past are both the idea of the origin as a distant event and the idea of the origin as a court of appeal. In other words, the past involves the idea of the beginning as something first and the idea of the beginning as an absolute—as if temporal distance illustrates and secures the depth of the present moment. (This very confusion may come from what Ferdinand Alquié calls a "desire for eternity," that is, the desire to escape from time that itself is the result of a yearning for completion. It is entirely true, in this sense, that the for-itself wants to be in-itself and that the return to the past is a way of assuring oneself of gaining the security of the irrevocable.) Second, depth can have a relationship with the present moment only to the extent that this moment is filled with my self, arising from a time which I am and not from one *in* which I am. That is, depth refers essentially to the self, to the plenitude and authenticity of my being, and depth is in time only to the extent that time *is* myself.

But the idea of the depth within myself must be purified even further and distinguished from the hidden (or the unconscious), in the same way as we have just distinguished depth and distance—the two themes of the hidden and the distant being, moreover, quite clearly related. There is within me a depth of what I am by nature, and which could be examined by psychology, biology, or genetics. My unconscious, my heredity, my race—all that is carried along in the river of blood spoken

5. See Gerardus Van der Leeuw, "Primitive Man and Religion," in *Religion in Essence and Manifestation*, trans. J. E. Turner (New York: Harper & Row, 1963), pp. 110 ff.

of by Rilke—compose the self's bedrock, which must be brought to light and to which I am bound to acquiesce. In leaning over an abyss of this sort, I experience the same vertigo as the mountain climber at the edge of a crevasse or an explorer at the edge of a tropical forest. But, aside from the fact that this depth of the self's roots appears only to someone who takes it up into his life (just as the fascination of descending into the depths of the earth operates only for someone who has decided to confront the earth's dangers and penetrate its secrets), it is possible that it may not be true depth, which resides in what we do, not in what we are. I am indeed my past and my race, the distant ancestry in which I am joined to the primitive forms of life. However, such an identification poses a seductive problem only if I am also something *else,* even if this be simply my consciousness of my past. For if I am merely a collection of accidents, a product of a sequence of events stretching back indefinitely, a moment of natural history, then all depth is abolished.[6] I must be surprised at being these things, because I know that I am irreducible to them. They are not depth factors except for a being who derives his most authentic depth from elsewhere. Whence comes this depth? From the capacity of being oneself, of leading an inner life whose rhythm is unburdened by external accidents. The depth of objectivity is doubly subordinate to this true depth. For the former must not only be recognized by the self but also be integrated within it. The past of the individual, and even that of the species, is discovered finally within myself—otherwise it

6. Thus, although the horizon of space and time is indeed dizzying when extended by means of cosmology, there is nothing which strikes me as deep in this cavalcade of epochs. It is no more than a manipulation of zeros—until that instant when suddenly I find that it has aroused my interest and discover that in the end I myself am at stake. But I am not at stake as an ego-object—the present result of an immense evolution, in the sense that a mountain would result from the shrinking of the oceans—but as that self which I am and which is found inexplicably tied to the adventures of the animal and mineral world that it experiences as its personal destiny. (Jules Verne's *Journey to the Center of the Earth* brings together many of these themes: the descent into the bowels of the earth, the resurrection of the past, the mingled depths of space and time, all of this confronted by the explorer as a present destiny.) In the same way, the astronomer with his calculations senses no fear before the eternal silence of infinite space. However, for the philosopher who thinks the situation and his place within it, and feels himself to be affected and, as it were, intended by the soundless silence, fear is a very real presence, whatever may be the opinion of Valéry. The heavens acquire depth for the person who measures himself against them and loses himself within them. Man is the center of reference for the cosmically deep, the meeting place of the infinitely large and the infinitely small.

is merely an anonymous chain of events to which I find myself indifferent.

In a parallel sense, psychology tends to accentuate childhood experiences, not merely because they come from childhood but because they are decisive, because the man repeats the child in the same way that the primitive repeats the ancestral tradition. We are authorized to seek depth in the past because we can afterward verify that it was pregnant with a future. But depth can just as easily be contained in the present when the latter instigates the flow of time within us, that is, when an aspect of ourselves is decided and delineated there. It is not enough that experience be engraved within us as an indelible memory; experience must rather bring about our transformation and orient our future. A child who is severely beaten before the boundary post of a meadow (a custom recorded by Montaigne) will always remember the site of that post: there is nothing deep in that. But if this punishment should awaken the child to feelings of injustice or cruelty, or even to more ambiguous feelings, as in the case of Jean-Jacques at the home of Mlle. Lambercier—if thus a new side of the world is shown to him, giving rise to a new aspect of his personality—all this has depth, since it is no longer a matter of passively storing a memory but of a destiny and a commencement. Even here, we are tempted to transcribe what is qualitative into quantitative terms, so that depth comes to reside in whatever attains an impressive number of conditions, as an idea is considered deep when it determines an entire intellectual system, or a passion when it colors a whole array of thoughts or actions. Yet depth cannot be measured by the number of actions which it engenders or inspires. Depth bears these progeny because it is, above all, a certain quality of lived experience, a manner of living of which feeling is the finest illustration.

To possess depth means to situate oneself on a certain level where one becomes sensitive throughout one's being, where a person collects himself together and commits himself. Having such depth can best be understood in contrast with those ways of being indifferent, detached, or superficial when the subject is not really himself. Such a subject lives at the whim of the moment, projectless and without memory, in a time of mere succession which is neither a recovery nor a commitment, as if his actions were no more than movements under the sway of the sort of mechanical causality which is the order of this kind of time. To possess depth means to reject the idea of being a thing, which is always external to itself and is dispersed and practically dismembered in the passing of time. It means being capable of an inner life, collecting oneself within oneself, and acquiring an intimacy. As Pradines remarks, echoes of all this are contained in the word "consciousness," which connotes the emergence of a for-itself, not as the power of negation but as a power of affirmation.

This sort of depth belongs to feeling, particularly to aesthetic feeling. It is what distinguishes feeling from simple impressions, and it is feeling—not our impressions—that corresponds to expression in the object. The only gauge of depth which aesthetic feeling is incapable of offering to us overtly is perseverance. But aesthetic feeling compensates for this lack by proffering a plenitude of the moment—not to mention the fact that, even if it does not openly manifest perseverance by its acts, the waves of its influence ebb only gradually, slowly forming our taste and allowing it to mature. In any event, aesthetic feeling exhibits other signs of depth. It involves, first, a total presence on the part of the subject, for whom the object is present only because he himself is present. As long as all I do is exercise my judgment, I detach myself from the object and become more impersonal—reflection separates. Before the aesthetic object, on the other hand, I am neither a pure consciousness in the sense of a transcendental *cogito* nor a pure look, since my look is laden with all that I am. The aesthetic object does not really belong to me unless I belong to it. This relationship is to be contrasted with the experience of those spectators who give the object no more than a rapid and superficial glance, who understand nothing because they are absent. Aesthetic feeling is deep because the object reaches into everything that constitutes me. My past is immanent in the present of my contemplation and exists there as what I am—it is not the result of a history which would turn me into the final term of a causal sequence, but the seat of a duration in which I am conjoined with myself. This past which I am gives a density to my being and a penetrating quality to my glance. How would I have any sensation of music if my ear were a mere receptacle for sounds, if it were not informed, and, moreover, if it did not allow for the sounds to reverberate and find an echo in this self which I offer them? This does not mean that a particular melody is going to revive a particular moment of sadness within me, conjure up an old love, awaken a particular regret, or evoke a particular chain of thought. In such cases, I would no longer be hearing the melody itself—something that is too often the situation. It means, rather, that all these events from my past have become myself, and that, in hearing the melody, I agree to *be* this self instead of living at its surface. In a similar way, one must, so to speak, have lived in order to be truly present in the world of Shakespeare or Balzac—not that I have to confront the work with a similar experience which I have undergone and wish to reanimate. One need not be a murderer in order to understand Macbeth or a luckless father to understand Lear or Goriot. The work itself will show me the perversion of will that occurs in the murderer or the inner distress of the father, but only on the condition that I participate in the work through something in me which is capable of being affected, through the substantial and yet nonmaterial density of a deep and profound self. The more I lay myself open to the work, the more sensitive will I be to its effects. This is why the experience of my past life is not a matter of indifference in this situation—not because it tells me anything about the meaning of the work itself, but because it allows the work to instruct me by giving the work a greater hold over me, and myself a greater depth.[7]

Aesthetic feeling has depth not only because it unifies us but also because it opens us up. For inner life or the life of the interior [*la vie intérieure*] does not lead the subject into the obscure meanderings of subjective rumination. Rather, the life of the interior is manifested in actions and is no more than a certain quality of these actions, once they have ceased to be soulless responses to the proddings of the environment. In aesthetic experience, inner life is manifested above all in its power of laying open the self. Having depth means being available and receptive, and it is by the same movement that I lay myself open to the object. From a transcendental point of view, we cannot open up a world and open ourselves to that world except in one and the same movement. There is a reciprocity between intentionality and being-oneself. In the present case, such reciprocity is at work at another level. Being oneself no longer designates the pure relationship to the self which constitutes an "I think" but

7. This is one form of the phenomenon of attention. When I pay attention to an idea or an object, it is because I have been sensitized in that direction by my past knowledge. Here we rediscover what we have said about the imagination's mobilization of implicit modes of knowledge on the level of representation. But if we call feeling the attention paid to the aesthetic object, it is because all my affective experiences are present along with this knowledge. Thus it is not only intelligence which is sensitized.

the substance of the self possessing depth. And intentionality is no longer an aim or mere intention *toward* but a participation *with*. And, in fact, to lay myself open is not merely to be conscious of something, but to associate myself with it. Feeling is an act of communion to which I bring the entirety of my being. We have seen, on all levels, the necessity of this participation in the aesthetic object. However, it is no longer simply a matter of the sort of imaginative participation whereby we give a quasi reality to the represented object precisely in order to gain a living representation of it. We are dealing, rather, with the acquisition of an intimacy with what the object expresses. It is no longer a question of pretending that Hamlet is real so that we may become interested in his adventures. Instead, we make ourselves present to Hamlet's world so that it may touch us and flow into us. Feeling has depth, therefore, by this type of generosity, this confidence which it inspires with regard to the object and which does not proceed without fervor. (For the man of depth is the one who is capable of giving credit to others and discovering a hidden dimension in their actions—a nobility in what seems to be small, a personality in what seems to be anonymous, and a freedom in what seems to be determined.) There is even love—a subject to which we shall return—in the aesthetic attitude. Is not love that expectation of a conversion by the attention we pay to the other, to what he is and expresses?

But this is possible only because feeling permits us to read such expressions. The supreme proof of feeling's depth is that it is intelligent in a way that intelligence as such can never be. Precisely because it is a laying open, a mode of attention, feeling operates without forcing itself. The object is transparent to feeling, but hardly with the transparency of clear ideas, which are transparent, in the words of Leibniz, "if they furnish me with the possibility of recognizing the object which they represent." Aesthetic transparency is, rather, the transparency of a sign which is its own meaning, a smile which is tenderness, a motet which is piety. The intelligence of aesthetic expression is alive in proportion to the fullness of our presence and, consequently, to the richness of our feeling. A child knows tenderness in the outstretched arms of its mother, but its response lies in abandoning itself to the embrace. A man knows tenderness in a Mozart andante—that singular nuance of tenderness smiling through tears, that delicate joy which has undergone untold tribulations without becoming lost in them—because his depths have been offered substantial nourishment, as when a hungry fire is offered wood. He penetrates into the meaning just as directly, but this meaning is richer because he lives it more deeply. This is why he can receive and welcome it within himself, instead of responding to it actively and losing himself in his response.

Thus the depth of aesthetic feeling is to be measured in terms of what it discovers in the object. We should now return to the depth of the aesthetic object itself—an object whose notion we have already sketched, if only negatively, by showing that reflection cannot exhaust its meaning. It remains for us to comprehend this notion as correlative with the depth of feeling.

[III] THE DEPTH OF THE AESTHETIC OBJECT

IN OUR ATTEMPT to define the depth of the aesthetic object, we must first, as in the case of human depth, distinguish it from what it is not. In particular, we must either purify or abandon the twin themes of distance and the hidden. The aesthetic object does not possess depth because it is in any sense distant or because there is anything in it which belongs to the past. Neither the exotic nor the antique is a distinguishing mark of aesthetic depth. When we esteem antiquity, we do so for several reasons—none of which bears on the aesthetic. The first is that we take a certain pleasure in reconstituting history. We have a taste for history and are grateful for those objects which can satisfy this taste. Thus the superstition arises that the date is an intrinsic property of the object and possesses a quality all its own. Which is, in a sense, true. The date is often an indicator of style and consequently gives us important information concerning the nature of the object and its place in aesthetic history. But we should not forget that it is style which in the end permits the dating of the object and the founding of a chronology, and not the date which allows the style to be perceived. In fact, however, just as aesthetic perception must be informed and instructed, the date is often our point of reference and allows us to see the object more clearly or at least to subject the object to critical reflection. A second reason, of the same order, is that antiquity is in itself a way of recommending the object to our attention, because its oldness ensures that the object has had to inspire admiration for a long period in order to survive until the present. Just as our perception seeks out reference points and auxiliaries for itself, so our taste seeks out forebears by which it may be justified. Antiquity serves as security for our judgment. But it also (and this leads to a third reason for valuing antiquity) secures the object itself. Is it not a sign of the object's validity as well as its strength that it should have survived the ages and resisted the passage of time? Longevity is a sign of health. Still, although all these reasons may help to explain the prestige of distance, they do not authorize us to measure the intrinsic value of the object by its age. They suggest, moreover, that it is less important to be laden with time than to resist time. The aesthetic object is historical only for critical reflection. In itself, the aesthetic object tends to escape history, to be not the witness of a historical epoch but the source of its own world and its own history.

Nor is aesthetic depth to be found in what is hidden. There is, besides, a mere step from the distant to the hidden. We have just said that only what belongs to nature in the aesthetic object and is thus dedicated to time can partake of distance. In the same way, the hidden pertains only to that aspect of the aesthetic object which acts as a container, in the sense that we say that it possesses a secret. To invoke this aspect would be a denial of the aesthetic object's fundamental law, which is the adequation of appearance to being, as well as a betrayal of the object's interiority (which, as in the case of consciousness, exists only in exteriorizing itself) by weighing it down with an opaque content. Nevertheless, there are two aspects of the aesthetic object which seem to support and justify the idea of the hidden: namely, this object's strangeness and difficulty.

Now, the strangeness possessed by the profound or the deep results from the fact that depth is experienced only on the condition that it exiles and uproots us from those habits which are the embodiment of the superficial self, in order to bring us face to face with a new world which demands a new outlook. Whenever the aesthetic object is incapable of surprising or transforming us, we cannot afford it full merit. It remains an ordinary object which we treat by granting it the distracted response which results from habit and by integrating it within our zone of activity. Thus we turn away from a painting as soon as we have identified the subject, as if the painting's function were no more than the representation of its subject. Or we listen to music with no other end than to tap our feet, as if music's function were no more than to stimulate a march or a dance or simply to create a background of sound for our movements and dreams.

Or we think of a ceramic piece as no more than a receptacle, or read a poem as if it were a piece of prose. In contrast with this is the self-conscious ardor of modern art in its efforts to astonish. It is, of course, possible to provoke astonishment without scandal or violence to the immanent logic of our perception. The aesthetic object is capable of affecting us and converting us to the aesthetic attitude merely by the sort of tranquil necessity with which it imposes itself on us. A portrait by Clouet, a fugue by Bach, and the pediment of a Greek temple all challenge our usual perceptual habits and demand respect through the sovereign character of their simple presence and the quiet interrogation which they direct toward us.

The provocation of astonishment, moreover, cannot be an end in itself—an end which is much too simple to attain. Authentic art is distinguished from its parody in that its desire to astonish remains within the service of the desire to signify, using strangeness only as a stimulant for attention. In this case, the strange is not the arbitrary, although it may seem so compared with our habitual relations with objects of daily use which have become, quite legitimately, norms of activity. With respect to our consciousness of the aesthetic object, this strangeness takes on a sort of necessity. It awakens within us, not our ordinary reactions, but rather the feeling of a necessity internal to the object, a necessity which must be sensed and felt more than understood. Thus surprise seems to be no more than a first moment, however indispensable it is for purging our perceptions and drawing them into the required state of disinterest. It is, however, something more than that. Compared with that wonder which Aristotle calls the starting point of science and which Husserl and his commentators consider to be the inspiration of philosophy as well, aesthetic wonder has the peculiarity of provoking reflection only eventually to reject it. The object requires not so much to be understood (as when we strive to understand an unusual phenomenon so that it may be reintegrated with the established order, thereby disposing of the problem it poses and the perturbation it inspires) as to be experienced in its peculiar depth as an unimpeachable witness. For, to repeat, we are unfaithful to the object to the extent that we remain insensitive to its "outlaw" quality and claim to tame it with explanation and reintegrate it within the universe of our habits. The object must appear to us as continually new. Even when we are familiar with the object, our perception must stay fresh. The wonder it inspires can never disappear entirely as long as we do not reject the aesthetic attitude, in the same way that the presence of a loved one will always affect us as long as we remain in love. And the reason this wonder tends to endure is that the aesthetic object does not surprise us by presenting itself as a problem to solve or an anomaly to diagnose. Nor is its strangeness the result of a comparison with a model with which it must be contrasted, as if it had failed some requirement of resemblance. For we would then be referring it to a foreign standard without remembering its own power of setting standards, that is, its power of being sufficient unto itself without measuring itself against reality. The strangeness of the aesthetic object is an invitation to perceive it better in itself. This strangeness does not fade away, since the strange is an aspect of the profound and not a quality which reflection could banish, in the way that reflection transforms the confused into the clear in the eyes of those philosophers for whom the perceptible is no more than a degradation of the intelligible. Strangeness expresses not so much a lacuna within our knowledge as a positive attribute of the object, which would be falsified were it to be eliminated. Nor can the strange be explained by the hidden, since the aesthetic object hides nothing. The meaning of the work is entirely present, and any mystery it may contain is fully illuminated.

It will also be claimed, however, that the aesthetic object is sometimes difficult to apprehend or comprehend—which is likewise taken to be a sign of its depth. But it is not difficult in the manner of a problem whose solution remains hidden, as if its meaning could be drawn out of it and objectively established. Whenever we call a work difficult, we are too often looking for something in it which is simply not there and insisting on being ourselves no more than pure understanding. Still, such an attitude has its extenuating circumstances. First, aesthetic perception, like any perception, must pass through understanding, since the aesthetic object is also a perceived object. This is why it is no doubt best that the work of art not contradict the natural course of events but instead satisfy the understanding's questioning about what is represented. For the represented object is what falls under the jurisdiction of the understanding, and it is with respect to this object that obscurity is possible. Obscure works are those in which the represented object does not appear and let itself be easily identified. But identification and rational understanding on the part of the subject are in no sense the final end of aesthetic perception. Second, the problem of difficulty is found most frequently in the literary arts, where, because we constantly employ language for everyday use, we are most tempted to seek out an objective meaning. Admittedly, we would be quite clearly betraying language were we to neglect its semantic function (a negligence of which some literary enterprises could be accused). Conversely, the aesthetic use of language takes priority over its utilitarian function, and for this reason semantic difficulty could never be a decisive objection to a poem or novel. We should note, moreover, that what is obscure is not necessarily inaccessible. We may not be able to interpret a particular line of verse, such as "Time sparkled and our dreams are knowledge." We may ask, just what does this mean? But the moment we become sensitive to the line's enchantment and are led into the poetic state (which may have to be the result of a long familiarity but is hardly comparable to the understanding's effort to seek stubbornly the solution to a problem), then the question of meaning is no longer at stake. To comprehend is no longer to explain but to feel, and the poem bears its fruit within us. The same point holds for reputedly simple poems. We are no longer sensitive to their literal sense or conscious of their objective meanings. We are filled, rather, with the evidence of feeling. To recite the verse "Oh lakes, silent rocks, grottos and dark forests" is hardly to establish a geographical inventory. It is, instead, to yield to a sort of enchantment. In the end, we comprehend such a line just as we comprehend the most difficult of texts—by attaining, through the agency of feeling, to a world which cannot be defined. We face all art in fundamentally the same way as we face music, where representation gives way to expression. It is the particular—and formidable—privilege of music to awaken feeling without provoking reflection and to summon us to a depth which is not that of obscurity. There is no obscurity for feeling, which knows the expressed object, but only for understanding, which knows the represented object.

Where, then, does the depth of the aesthetic object reside, if the distant is merely an optional feature for it, and if that which is obscure in it achieves transparency for feeling? The depth must be sought in the object's power to express, through which it is the analogue (as a result of being the proxy) of a subjectivity. This power is drawn from the object's interiority, which must be clarified before anything else. As in the case of man, this interiority is made manifest by the intensity of its being— that is, in a certain manner of existing on a plane which transcends the plane of brute existence, which is under the sway of extension. Conversely, just as there are superficial men, there are also superficial things. They seem to be superfluous and incapable of justifying their own existence—Schopenhauer would say that they are incapable of manifesting that elementary will which moves them toward being—even by the simple demonstration of their usefulness. These objects answer to no need and do not require any action on our part. They do not even stir one's curiosity. Thus they possess no interiority. They express nothing which suggests an internal necessity. They are not meaningful or signifying—or, rather, they signify only what they are not, as reflections in water signify clouds. Undoubtedly, it is liquid matter which best illustrates this superficial existence. This is why the sea is continually celebrated as the instructor of understanding, for understanding alone (i.e., thinking in terms of relations) is related to this radical exteriority. Yet the sea stirs us and speaks to us in its moods of calm as well as in its fury, in the force of its waves and the luster of its colors, and also by its formidable depth. We may say that what is most external is what possesses the most soul, as if the object, in order to arouse us, could in no sense conceal its nature as object—just as the monument does not conceal its mass of stone or the painting the fragility of its canvas. In the same way, the musical sound does not disavow its origins in noise. Even the poem and the literary work retain their character as things through their sonorous nature, their equilibrium, and their density. It is essential that the aesthetic object always possess—on the level of the in-itself —that density of being by which it is nature. It must not play tricks or put on airs. It is as object and without escaping from the grip of understanding that the aesthetic object must speak to us, but in such a way that its power of expression never fails to seem miraculous.

Natural objects seem to be endowed with this privilege from the beginning. The sea is deep not in the sense that oceanography would understand the word but because of its corporeal unity—because the thousands of drops which dance in the spray and defy the understanding rise on an unfathomable totality, eternally one with itself, "a mass of calm and visible reserve." This sort of unlimited repetition, this maintaining of an unalterable permanence through all the eddying which disturbs the surface, all of this is already the image of a certain density of being. But the reality of depth must be sought elsewhere. It is with living beings and with consciousness that we should compare the aesthetic object. For the living creature must constantly mediate its own meaning, and even the most elementary per-

ception serves to assure us that such a being is not entirely reducible to relations of externality. The fact that it is an organized totality quite clearly points to a quality of existence which
is that of a subject related to itself and settled victoriously in
being. We observe here an interiority proper to life as such
which is instituted through the dialectic of part and whole,
through that perpetually endangered and yet eventually rescued
equilibrium which ensures the convergence of functions for the
benefit of the organism. But it is in consciousness that the depth
of an inner life is most evident. The relation of the self to itself
is expressed in consciousness by means of the dialectical movement between the act of reflection and what is reflected upon.
Still, depth must be externalized and manifested by a fundamental relation to a world. Consciousness is, in fact, a relation
to the self and a relation to a world. If we must say that the relation to the self conditions the relation to the world, we should
also say, conversely, that being in the world awakens the consciousness of self. In any event, if the relation to a world is essential to the self and to any depth that it may proclaim, this
relation is not simply that of a container to what is contained.
In order to be relative to the self, the world must, in a sense, be
prefigured in the self. Similarly, the aesthetic object is a relation
to a world. It has depth not only by the perfection of its form
and the internal finality it realizes as if it were a living being but
also by the aura of meaning it diffuses and radiates throughout
a world. Its interiority is that of a thing which secretes a meaning by which it becomes boundless. It seems, then, that consciousness lends to the aesthetic object something of its own
being, since the object appeals to consciousness in order fully to
exist. The aesthetic object possesses a relation of self to self in
the very density of its being. It is identical with its appearance,
but its appearance is the appearance of a world. It is precisely
in this world that is realized—or, rather, is expressed without
being realized—that surplus of meaning which makes the aesthetic object unfathomable. As a result, the aesthetic object's relation to this world, its irradiation of this world, is a manner of
relating itself to itself.

Of course, when we say that the aesthetic object bears a
world within itself, we do not mean to identify this object expressly with a consciousness. But we are justified in conceiving
the aesthetic object by analogy to consciousness, because it is
the proxy of a consciousness. We have remarked often enough
that the aesthetic object expresses its creator, not just because

it is a product of his activity but also because it is the expression of his being. A consciousness is revealed through the object. When we hear the Clarinet Quintet we are present to the world of Mozart, just as if Mozart himself entered into communication with us. The difference between consciousness and the aesthetic object is that, for consciousness, the relation to the world is one of privation. Consciousness is unfathomable because it is ungraspable and because, even at the height of its authenticity and plenitude, it still implies refusal and separation. In short, consciousness is nothing; it is *not* the world toward which it tends and with which it cannot be identified. Even if it is the prefiguration of the in-itself, consciousness cannot be settled in it. Its relation to the world is a relation which it maintains in order to realize without ever in fact realizing itself. The world remains external to consciousness; it is relative to but not identical with consciousness, which is borne by the world without becoming lost in it. Being in the world is essentially ambiguous. The aesthetic object, in contrast, is unfathomable because it *is*, that is, because it exists as a sovereignly real object. The world it brings forth is the expression of the aesthetic object's superabundance and brings about its realization. The relation to self is here a positive relation, comparable to that illustrated by the internal finality of a living being— a finality in terms of the harmony of parts with the whole which constitutes a totality. The relation to the world—to a world which is itself internal to the object— is also marked by positivity and confirms the relation to self. But the aesthetic object is not God, not a *causa sui* which turns creator through an excess of being! It is a perceived object and, as such, subordinate to consciousness. Thus the aesthetic object's relation to self, by which this object is defined, is an as-if relationship, and its world is a world which can only be felt, a world which is not exactly real. The world intended by consciousness is a world which consciousness is not, but it is still a real world. The world of the aesthetic object is a world which it is, but it is an unreal world. It is an unreality internal to the reality of the aesthetic object of which it is the meaning, instead of being an external world which is a reality external to the unreality of a consciousness of which it is the intentional object. Consciousness has depth in the way it continually recaptures itself and (in the very process of self-externalization) fills itself with an existential necessity. The aesthetic object has depth in the way it internalizes, and thereby derealizes, itself. In both cases, the relation to self conditions the relation to the world. In one instance, the process takes place through externalization, and, in the other, through internalization. (We would be willing to add that the living being probably maintains a balance between these two extremes. The relation to self by which it is founded is balanced by its relation to the environment. The living being, located at this intermediary point, becomes consciousness first by negating itself as an individual and then by opposing itself to the world. And it becomes an aesthetic object, as it were, by petrifying itself as an individual and denying the world from which it separates itself in order to substitute for it a new world internal to itself.)

Thus the depth of the aesthetic object is defined by its peculiar property of affirming itself as object while at the same time subjectifying itself as the source of a world. And it is into this world that we penetrate by means of feeling. But just as the expressed world cannot exist without the represented world (at least in the case of the representational arts), so feeling cannot exist without representation or without the reflection to which representation gives rise. Let us, then, consider the relation between feeling and reflection in aesthetic experience.

[IV] REFLECTION AND FEELING IN AESTHETIC PERCEPTION

IT CERTAINLY SEEMS THAT, as the aesthetic object is recognized for what it is in terms of its expressivity, the feelings which gather in expression constitute the decisive moment. Have we not in fact shown how the logic of aesthetic perception leads to this moment? There is, of course, no genuine logic in aesthetic perception, for I can always reject the object and reject the feeling within myself. Perceiving is an act which depends on my personal freedom. To the extent that this act belongs to a concrete "historical" subject, it depends on motivations which are alien to the logic of perception, such as the nature and experience of the subject, or the circumstances which condition this experience. Moreover, the aesthetic object appeals to us in establishing its autonomy, soliciting an objective recognition of its objective being. Were I to neglect its formal perfection or lose sight of the body of the work in order to wallow in its soul, then the soul itself may well escape me, since it is perceptible to me only as conveyed by the matter and the meaning of the object. No presence is felt that is not also understood. The aesthetic attitude is thus hardly a simple affair. It cannot eliminate judgment for the sake of feeling. It is a sort of perpetual oscillation between what could be called the critical attitude and the attitude of feeling.

Since reflection exhausts itself in the attempt to come to know an inexhaustible object, it turns to feeling. The reason for this is clear. Reflection insists on treating the aesthetic object as an ordinary object, and so something about the aesthetic object continually escapes its grasp. Reflection's limitation is that it considers the object from the outside, holds it at a distance (as if it were afraid of losing itself in the object), dragging it down to the level of objectivity. But there are also limits to feeling that should be mentioned at this point. Feeling is encompassed, at both its poles, by reflection. We have mentioned that feeling has an intelligence of its own, yet it acts as if it acquired this intelligence from its proximity with the double reflection by which it is first prepared and then ratified. For, in the end, feeling runs the constant risk of losing itself in the object and returning to the immediacy of presence, or of converting its communion into a blind ecstasy and confusing its reading of what the object expresses with the spontaneous responses of lived experience. Feeling can have a noetic function and value only as a reflective act, in part a victory over former reflection and in part open to a new reflection. Otherwise, feeling would revert to the pure and simple nonreflective level of presence, that is, to what is not knowledge [connaissance] and barely even consciousness.

To speak of a victory over [sur] reflection is to imply that the aesthetic object must be known [connu] and, in a sense, mastered in order to be felt. We are naturally tempted to claim that the object's expression leaps to our eyes and that the feeling by which it is revealed is immediate and spontaneous. Must I, as Stendhal would say, understand harmony or counterpoint in order to be sensitive to Pergolesi or Mozart? Need I know the structure or the history of a work for it to please my taste? Do I have to understand a poem's objective meaning or its implicit metaphysics to be susceptible to its enchantment? To go further, we might be tempted to say that reflection paralyzes rather than provokes feeling, that the most knowledgeable men are not for that reason the most sensitive, and that the kingdom of the aesthetic belongs to the poor in intellect so long as their hearts are rich. Such a theme, which is exploited by various aesthetics of feeling, could be developed further without difficulty. But let us

look a little closer. The truth is that expression offers up its affective meaning immediately. There is nothing hidden in expression and nothing reflective in us. But there is one condition
for such spontaneity of feeling, namely, that the signifier, which
is traversed by the signified, must be clearly given. This is not
always the case when one is dealing with the aesthetic object.
We can hardly emphasize this point too much. Since feeling
shows itself in a flash and with a self-evidence proper to it, we
would like to believe that it arises on our first contact with the
object and is promptly and in its own way intelligent. In the
same way, certain theories of the understanding presuppose that
understanding is immediate. But this notion of the immediate is
highly ambiguous. We can take it as certain that there is in us
a power—which precedes all experience—of decoding expression, as well as an *a priori* knowledge of the affective categories
under which these expressions can be subsumed. But Kant has
shown that I must be given a sensation, and also be able to draw
a straight line, before space can appear to me. In the same way
here, certain conditions of the exercise of my ability must be
realized within me, and the expressive object must be clearly
given to me, before expression can appear and be understood.
These two conditions eventually join together, for my body must
achieve some familiarity with the object before the object can
appear as expressive. It is because we are bodily capable of
wearing a smile that a mother's smile is tenderness to our eyes,
and we find that a ballerina's pose expresses the emotion of love
when we have a certain knowledge of love's gestures. Meaning
is not truly grasped unless my body harmonizes with the sign—
unless, that is, the body is from its very depths present to the
aesthetic object. This lived presence is the condition for feeling
and not feeling itself. And it is not the sole condition, since it is
not sufficient for the object to be present to us. The object must
also be represented. Our bodily hold on the object is no more
than a condition for conscious perception and (through this detour) for feeling. Thus feeling loses its immediacy *de facto,*
even if it retains an immediacy *de jure.* Feeling is immediate
when the object is given to us and when we are ourselves in a
position of readiness, but again, we must be *given* the object.

An immediacy of fact does, of course, exist. There are a beginning to perception and a first contact with the object of such
a sort that the object often seems to offer itself from that first
moment. But this is not an absolute beginning. We go to the object with an entire array of past experiences which form our

particular culture. The musical work is certainly new to the conductor who promptly grasps its structure and meaning in a single reading of the score, but his look is hardly new. Those beginnings which are in fact beginnings—that is, those of the profane—are hesitant and awkward. What I am given at the first hearing of a musical work is more often than not a soup of sound, just as a building may appear at first sight to be a confused labyrinth. So far, I have not oriented myself within the bounds of the object, nor is my body its accomplice. My eye and ear hesitate and go astray. They do not take up the object's rhythm, recognize its refrains and rhymes, or discern its structure. In short, the object has not yet taken form and is not yet expressive. One will say, nevertheless, that even this fledgling perception is receptive to a sort of expression. Every representation, even that of objects of daily use (at least when they are not entirely oriented toward practical application), envelops feeling with an affective quality, and the object turns toward us an expressive countenance. What I discover first in the night is its horror, in a flower its grace, and in a machine its power or elegance. Thus the first perception I have of the aesthetic object, however distorted and confused it may be, is already of the character of feeling. Even if I discern poorly the arrangement and harmony of certain streaks of color on a canvas, they still tell me something and do so without hesitation. But perception thus defined, that is, as extremely close to presence where the subject-object totality cannot be dissolved, is not truly perception. Or we should say that it is not true perception. The immediacy it contains is not yet acceptable, because it is an immediacy of feeling which is awakened by a nebulous appearance of the object. Although this feeling has the sort of self-evidence which attaches to all feeling, there is also something essentially confused in it—not the confusion inherent in that which cannot be mastered intellectually but, rather, a lack of assurance or certitude. It is a feeling which goes only skin deep, is poorly nourished by the uncertain appearance of the object, and does not engage us profoundly because we are not fully summoned. We are as reticent before the object as before someone we have just met with whom we are not yet acquainted.

Thus immediate feeling is not all of feeling. Authentic feeling must be earned, just as (and because) perception must be gained gradually. The aesthetic object must be fully present, and yet it is not always so at first. We have insisted that perception is a task by indicating that there is a truth to the work in relation to which certain perceptions are false or insufficient. The aesthetic object does not yet exist for such perceptions, in spite of its claim to exist. The aesthetic object cannot be satisfied with existing only halfway, in the manner of an inauthentic man. To promote the sort of perception by which feeling in its turn will be true is the task of reflection or of the critical attitude (in our broad sense of the word). Such an attitude could, moreover, adopt ends other than that of directly serving aesthetic perception and thus be expressed by an activity which is not inscribed in the dialectic of reflection and feeling. An example is when the critical attitude reconstructs the history of the work, its genesis, the influence brought to bear on it or which it has itself inspired—in short, when the work becomes the occasion not for an aesthetic perception but for a reflection not expressly attached to its aesthetic character. Even then, however, we cannot be sure that perception, and consequently feeling, do not derive some benefit from such information. Basically, any reflection may contribute to the glory of perception. For what is the point of reflection, if not to render clearer and more perceptible the presence of the aesthetic object? Before it can be present to feeling, this object must be present to the body in accordance with its perceptible character and to the intelligence in accordance with its representational character—where form and content are understood as a unity. Now, how can we bring our eyes to see better, our ears to hear better, and our bodies to associate themselves with the object rather than losing themselves in a chaos of uncertain impressions? How can our bodies be made to seize the object's structure and rhythm, as happens in the sudden grasping of a certain movement when (after a series of attempts in which the body is subjected to violence) the body abruptly understands and takes part as if that movement were natural? The body must find modes of access to the object before it can recognize and accomodate itself to the object. The object must be decomposed, points of reference sought out, its themes and articulations highlighted—finally, an order must appear and a structure emerge from the heart of the initial confusion. In other words, the body must be shown how the work was constructed—not in terms of the actual act of composition (since we are not sure whether its plan of composition was clearly and completely present in the creative act) but, rather, in terms of its perfected state. But is this not the purpose of aesthetic instruction? Whether it be literary, architectural, or musical, such instruction always comes down to an explication of the work, that is, to an exhibition of its parts and their arrangement. Thus the first movement of a sonata appears as the battlefield for two themes, each of which has its own character and enters into an exposition, development, and recapitulation. A poem becomes a sonnet composed in accordance with certain formal schemes, depending on its date. A play turns into a five-act tragedy with an introduction and denouement, certain crises in the plot, and certain dramatic devices to hold our interest. We learn to grasp the aesthetic object by precisely such admittedly scholarly exercises in analysis. When we find ourselves before a new object, it does make a difference whether a certain amount of previous knowledge has prepared our grasp of it and provided us with a means of anticipation—that is, whether we know if the work is of a particular style or from a particular school, if it develops according to certain norms in departing from the rules of the genre, if it has certain characteristic elements, and, most important, if it was composed under peculiar circumstances or with a certain intention. It is the function of the critic to forge ahead of the public's perception in order to orient this perception correctly and mark out its route. The mission of these "competent" (in the Aristotelian sense of the word) critics is not only to pass judgment on the aesthetic object but to facilitate our access to it. Thus armed, our perception acquires intelligence, our attention is no longer surprised and sterile, and our body follows the lead of this critical knowledge (sometimes our body follows so well that it ends by preceding such knowledge).

A better perception is, of course, not a perception of something else. The aesthetic object is still there. But our field of perception grows clearer and more organized. The forms which take shape in the object and which together compose its form are clearer and more pregnant, because from now on they convey a meaning. They are the organs of an organism which are recognized as such by our intelligence. Attention, therefore, is nothing less than reflection at work in perception. Pradines has remarked that attention "is not a separate agency but remains an act just like consciousness itself." [8] Aesthetic perception could be introduced quite readily as evidence into the debate of traditional psychology, the debate between those who believe that

8. Maurice Pradines, *Traité de psychologie générale* (Paris: Presses Universitaires de France, 1946), I, 41.

attention lowers the threshold and increases the intensity of sensations and those who believe that attention merely reveals the characteristics of our sensations by conferring upon them a peculiar "attensity" (in Pradines's term). And such evidence will lead us to agree with the compromise proposed by Pradines. Attention certainly does possess an intensity, but it is not comparable to the intensity of the stimulus. The former intensity is one of meaning, a meaning (if all sensations are meaningful) which is clear as opposed to confused. It is the intensity of an intelligibility which associates itself with sensation, since, again according to Pradines, "the perceptible must have intelligence in order to be felt." [9] A poorly clarified perception ceases to be a perception at all. Once again, every perception bears a meaning once it has reached the level of representation, but this meaning may be misleading. It may be the meaning of a mere haze and not that of the object itself. An adequate meaning is obtained by means of reflection and under the auspices of attention. All this does not mean that attention must be purely intellectual. To be sure, attention does not simply reduce to the body or remain in the *Anstellung* of effort. We realize, moreover, to what extent attention can disturb our motor activity, which becomes more certain of itself the more it can confine itself to habit. But sensory experience is not motoric in character, and in this case attention functions for the sake of the body. An intellectual understanding is also a bodily understanding. The acuity of one's representation reverberates on the level of presence, and even simple sensory accommodation is not just a prelude to attention but also its consequence. Our look is fixed and our ears lend themselves more willingly to their task once they are no longer left in disarray, once they learn how to behave before the object and to possess in its presence that ease which comes from familiarity. The object's presence to our bodies occasionally presupposes a clear and lucid representation, just as the free play of our habits presupposes a methodical and conscious effort to cultivate them. It is the same thing to affirm that attention is expectation or anticipation and to affirm that we are not really perceiving something unless we have already in some sense made its acquaintance. It is thus that reflection can prepare perception, even at the level of bodily behavior. All these procedures are important, even those which seem to

9. *Ibid.*, p. 51.

make use of the work for nonaesthetic purposes. They are all capable of enriching and promoting perception and so preparing for feeling, in which perception is consummated.

But is perception entirely consummated in feeling? Reflection not only prepares for but also ratifies feeling, since feeling can in turn become the object of a reflection which aims to explicate and justify feeling. It is man's permanent vocation to seek to possess what is already given him, and feeling is a gift so transient that it is only natural to want to fix and control it. However, reflection then takes another turn. It seeks not so much to explicate as to name what is expressed, that is, to restate what is said by the work. What occurs is no longer a penetration into the work itself but a penetration into the world of the aesthetic object—and not into its represented world but into the world it radiates. After I have reflected on a poem by Mallarmé, subjected it to a grammatical analysis, interpreted its terms, established its subject—in short, when the work appears to me as clearly as possible—I must still say what Mallarmé has communicated and state, if only half-consciously and to myself, the poem's unique atmosphere, that rarefied world midway between dream and perception where all the edges of reality are blunted in the wave of an exhausted desire and a bitterness which has renounced revolt. Then, if I wish to express the unique affective quality of the Mallarméan world, I can return to all that I learned from my previous reflection, but in such a way that this knowledge will from now on be clarified by feeling, which reveals this quality rather than simply preparing for its advent. Everything merely approached in preliminary explorations is now summoned by feeling to act as its witness— all the rarity and rigor of Mallarmé's rhymes and assonances, the muffled clanging of his words, the secret character of the themes of absence and nothingness, the patient excavation into solitude where nothing flowers except a deserted soul in a desert traversed by shimmerings, the rustling of wings, the touch of a fan. All the elements in the represented world of the work, like the heroes or the setting of a novel, or the subject of a painting, can be invoked to give body to the expressed world and thereby acquire a fresh meaning. They are no longer objects constitutive of the meaning of the work and furnishing the key to its comprehension. They become, rather, objects constituted by the work and serving to illustrate its affective quality. Rather than the work's being discovered through them, it is they who are discovered through the work. Phaedra is from now on a heroine out of Racine. She is explained by the world of Racine, because that world brings her forth in order to be manifested in her. In the same way, it is no longer the ogival arch which creates the Gothic style in architecture, but the Gothic which creates the ogive in order to express in rock the particular Gothic world-view communicated to us on entering Sainte Chapelle or Westminster Abbey. Everything discovered by the critical attitude remains of value but is affected by a change of sign. Reflection is henceforth at the service of, and inspired by, feeling. Our task is no longer to know the techniques and history which explain the production of the work, but instead to understand how the work is expressive. We meet again, therefore, that sympathetic reflection which strives to grasp the work from the inside and not from the outside, and thus to understand what is already understood and to subdivide what was given as a unit in feeling. The questions posed by such a reflection are posed only at the instigation of feeling. Their only function is to clarify feeling's depth. Thus we have said with good reason that sympathetic reflection is always inspired by feeling. Feeling makes use of such reflection in becoming assured of itself, attempting to communicate itself through self-explication, and thus justifying itself. The attention through which reflection is manifested is turned not toward the object whose integrated presence it is concerned to grasp but, rather, toward feeling—and toward the object only to the extent that it gives rise to this feeling. Reflection does not lose anything from what was acquired before its appearance and has now passed to the stage of a partly corporeal knowledge. For we must find ourselves at ease before the work, but from now on the work and ourselves will be equals, and we shall have to take up its profound but not hidden expression.

We can understand, therefore, how the movement from the critical attitude to feeling is not a simple oscillation. Reflection prepares the way for and then clarifies feeling. Conversely, feeling first appeals to and then guides reflection. This alternation between reflection and feeling designates a dialectical progress toward an increasingly complete comprehension of the aesthetic object. It is entirely possible that feeling is what is given first and that all perception begins in feeling, since it may be true that we perceive forms first and that feeling is the soul of form, the principle of unity for a perceptual diversity, or, as it were, the first instance of a meaning which still adheres to bodily presence. And perhaps certain works undertake to thrust us immediately into the stage of feeling. One example is the sort of painting or poetry which rejects the representational aspect of these genres which we had grown accustomed to expect. Another is the type of novel which overthrows normal chronology or plunges us into a magical universe. At first, such works baffle reflection by placing outside its jurisdiction, and thus depriving it of, its principal object, namely, the represented object, and by introducing subversions of technique in such a way as to discourage analysis. But this could be a tactical error on their part. We can never be sure that reflection will surrender in discouragement and abdicate. Reflection on form is always possible, albeit more difficult, since there is just as much technique and rigor in a difficult work if that work is authentic. And, as regards content, reflection is more often provoked than discouraged by the absence of a subject. Finally, a will which is exacerbated by its failure to understand can block the emergence of feeling. The aesthetic object will be seen as a rebus which stirs our interest only as something to be decoded, as is all too clearly the case in the commentaries written by André Breton on surrealist painting. On the other hand, if reflection, unable to find matter for its own operation, does abdicate its position, the feeling which then replaces reflection will be uncertain and confused, since appearances have not allowed themselves to be mastered. But when reflection has ordered appearances and so given the aesthetic object its amplest opportunities to move us, the resultant feeling will be lucid and capable of penetrating to the heart of the object—an object which is no longer an equivocal presence but an articulated reality whose expression is better felt the more we are acquainted with the elements from which it emanates. In the end, the sort of reflection which follows feeling differs from that which precedes feeling. Feeling enriches reflection and, most important, leads it back to the object, from which reflection is constantly tempted to distract itself, since it holds the object at a distance. Only then is the work understood for its own sake, so that the aesthetic object may appear within it. Then all of the work's parts are seen to collaborate in achieving expression and in contributing to the total effect which is encapsulated in the affective quality.

Therefore, aesthetic experience culminates in feeling without being able to eliminate reflection. It is located in the alternation of these two activities. But how is it possible to pass from the one to the other, from a reflective and methodical perception to one which is obliging and enraptured? Here we must appeal to the spontaneity of consciousness, without which perception would not even exist and which can always, as we have said, elude aesthetic experience. This is the spontaneity of the subject himself, who can take the form of a superficial as well as a profound self—that is, of an impersonal as well as a committed consciousness. Moreover, this subject never ceases to be a body—a body which is always present to the object and in which knowledge is made corporeal, taste is formed, and familiarity with the object is deepened. At the same time, there is another basis for the possibility of this alternation. That is the appeal of the aesthetic object itself, which solicits both reflection (because it appears sufficiently coherent and autonomous to lay claim to an objective knowledge) and feeling (because it does not exhaust itself in such knowledge and calls for a more intimate relationship). For the aesthetic object is at once solid, ordered, and distant, and yet also friendly, emotionally moving, and seductive. It can lead either to alienation or to ecstasy. Each of these two aspects continually refers to the other. Its perfection as an object is to be a quasi subject, but it attains this expressive subjectivity only by the rigor and security of its objective being, just as a body possesses or becomes a soul only as a result of being a body with an extraordinarily developed nervous system, or as a man attains the spiritual only by accepting unconditionally his temporal existence.

The aesthetic attitude is therefore not simple. But, in sum, it entertains with the aesthetic object a relationship whose nodal points we have attempted to discern in their dialectical interplay. This is perhaps sufficient to differentiate the aesthetic attitude from those attitudes which the subject may adopt before other objects. It remains for us, then, to consider the aesthetic attitude in a chapter in which our description will be more concise and more rapid.

15 / The Aesthetic Attitude

IN ORDER TO BRING our all too brief study of aesthetic perception to a close, let us compare the attitude we take before the aesthetic object with the attitudes we take before other objects, just as we previously compared the aesthetic object itself with other objects. We shall not spend a great deal of time in this comparison, because our previous considerations in Chapter 4 anticipated much of what can be said here. Furthermore, Basch's well-known analysis of the five possible attitudes that can be held in relation to the world remains generally valid.[1]

We shall not evoke the opposing attitudes that can be taken before the aesthetic object and before the object of use, for our preceding analysis has already adequately contrasted the attitude of contemplation with that of praxis. Moreover, we need only mention in passing the contrast in attitude before the aesthetic object and before the agreeable. *The Critique of Judgement* has said what is essential on this point, and its conclusions have been indirectly confirmed by the psychology of sensory experience as developed by Pradines, who has shown that the experience of the pleasing belongs mainly to the sense of touch, while the apprehension of the beautiful is reserved for those senses which operate from a distance and act as instruments of contemplation, not as organs of enjoyment. The delight taken in the pleasing object does not bring us to *know* it as it is in itself. All I really come to know about it is the way in which it is united

1. See Victor Basch, *Essais d'esthétique, de philosophie et de littérature* (Paris: Alcan, 1934), *passim.*—Trans.

with me. I can gain its acquaintance only through the composite structure which I and it together constitute: "As the fruit dissolves in being enjoyed." In fact, I am more preoccupied with myself than with the object, which I allow to be absorbed within me at the moment of being consumed and enjoyed. Thus the very idea of aesthetic pleasure has seemed to us suspect, to the extent that it continues to evoke enjoyment. The only pleasure which we considered to be a necessary ingredient of the aesthetic experience was that of the body's feeling itself at ease before, and in league with, the object. And we cannot be sure that art provides us with even *this* pleasure unabashedly, since we have observed how Malraux denounces arts of delectation—which recalls Alain's observation that great art calls up the feeling of the sublime, because there is something in it of the sovereign and even of the savage. When the aesthetic object imposes its presence on us, it is not quite so restrained as the pleasurable object. The aesthetic object causes us to yield to it, rather than accommodating itself to us. Does this mean that in aesthetic experience we confront the beautiful as we would the true? Or as we encounter what is lovable [*l'aimable*]? In these cases we have to do with attitudes of the subject which come closest to the aesthetic attitude, and it is to them that we must now devote a more extended discussion.

[I] Our Attitudes before the Beautiful and the True

Is the impassive respect imposed by the aesthetic object comparable to the attitude demanded by what is true? It seems that, whatever else may unite the beautiful and the true, our attitudes toward them diverge on three points. In the first place, I do not assign the same value to the beautiful as to the true. Both can, of course, appear as sheer givens. I am just as disarmed and convinced by rational evidence as by aesthetic evidence, and I can say equally *verum index sui* ("what is true is a sign of itself") and *pulchrum index sui* ("what is beautiful is a sign of itself"). Moreover, if we were to claim that the true, as opposed to the beautiful, presupposes an activity marked by ambition and avarice, nevertheless, we would witness the protests of the apostles of disinterested knowledge, who consider contemplation to be the ultimate end of knowledge. And yet the difference between the two attitudes is to be developed along the following lines: even after it has arrived at a point of purity and abdication of power, the search for the true continues to involve an act of appropriation and lends itself to maneuvers which oppose it to the beautiful. In fact, the contemplation of the true is always the reward for an ascetic activity, and any pleasure it provides is that of conquest. While truth can impose itself on me as some sort of grace—"attention is a natural prayer"—I must nevertheless have merited this gift by opening myself up to it. When the true has been caught in my nets, I can then claim proprietorship over it as a result of having hunted it down. Therefore when, ignoring any notion of the gratuitous, I consider the true as something acquired after considerable struggle, my possession of the true will be marked by avarice. Of course, aesthetic experience also presupposes a certain asceticism: a process of training to refine one's taste and to cleanse one's mind by eliminating every prejudice. The reflection by which we become sensitized to the beautiful also demands an effort. But however constant and determined such an effort may be, it can never take complete credit for the aesthetic experience. Hence the two attitudes differ in just this crucial respect. On the one hand, I have the right to believe that my certainty of a given truth is the result of my own efforts. On the other hand, in aesthetic experience I have the impression that something has been given to me which is quite independent of my own questing zeal. As in the case of Rimbaud, one's Animus can make all sorts of conscious efforts, but Anima will not come until fancy strikes her. In the same way, all the tricks of the artist's trade will not make up for lack of inspiration, just as all the strictures of criticism or arguments of reflection will not, by themselves, induce in the spectator the irresistible self-evidence of the beautiful. "I sought beauty and I found you," says Pelléas, but between the seeking and the discovering of the beautiful there exists an abyss bridged only by its sudden and ever miraculous presence.

Furthermore, I do not treat the true and the beautiful in quite the same way. Any truth I may acquire is treated in the mode of having. It is capitalized, inherited, and exchanged for language as if it were monetary in character. It is I who possess the true, while I am possessed by the beautiful. Yet two different types of truth should be distinguished here—necessary rational truths, and the sort of truth that could be called intuitive and subjective. It is the first sort of truth which we have in mind, the kind which is embedded in knowledge and expressed in time-tested formulae of which I make habitual use and which lose none of their value in intervals of nonemployment. My attitude before such knowledge is like that of a demiurge, and pride is normally part of the experience. Handling the true leads me back to myself and invites me to enjoy my power. The aesthetic experience, in contrast, is not subject to capitalization in the same manner as the true. For two reasons. First, the kingdom of the true is infinite, and knowledge envisions a sort of totality which is never quite fully realized by the various philosophical systems. It is always possible to progress further and annex new territory. But the aesthetic experience cannot progress in the same way as knowledge. Any progress aesthetic experience makes is toward a more refined and sensitive taste which renders us more amenable and docile to the aesthetic object. But such progress does not enlarge the empire of the aesthetic. On the contrary, it tends to restrict that empire by making the spectator more exacting. Moreover, aesthetic experience is irreducible to the sort of concept which the fertility of my intellect can construct by uniting multiple and diverse experiences (future as well as past). For the aesthetic object, as opposed to the concept, is unique and irreplaceable. My generalizations are legitimate when I speak of an artistic genre or school or style, and yet in formulating them I risk losing sight of the aesthetic object itself. As a historian or a critic, I employ concepts which instruct me concerning the nature, composition, or structure of the works I am analyzing. But these concepts prevent any direct communication I may have with the object. Now, the aesthetic object must be constantly present before me, whereas, once I have discovered a truth, it is with me for good. I can continue to be confident of a truth which I am not at the moment consulting or verifying. Indeed, thought can progress only on the condition of not having constantly to retrace its steps, of being able to entrust truth to a manipulable system of signs which safeguard content without the time-consuming necessity of continually fresh explanation. Aesthetic experience, once finished, leaves no more than a pale and futile memory, and the knowledge by which it is replaced cannot compensate for its disappearance. Hence the difference between knowing and feeling—feeling is nourished only by concrete presence. Otherwise, unless sustained by the force of desire (which aesthetic experience is not), feeling tends to waste away. It is conceivable that the feeling of love resists the effects of absence (however difficult and full of dangerous metamorphoses such an ordeal may be), but aesthetic experience cannot survive the disappearance of its object.

Finally, I am not the same person before the true as before the beautiful. The distinction between feeling and knowing is also expressed in the fact that knowledge is anonymous. We have pointed to the pride and pleasure one may take in the possession of knowledge. Yet the self which acquires and boards its treasure of knowledge is not the concrete self, for the truth it possesses is only an interchangeable, not a substantial, piece of merchandise. In contrast, the aesthetic object, to which I commit myself entirely, affects my innermost recesses and awakens a feeling which strikes me at a deeper level than the true ever does. The universality of the true—its essential criterion—derives, strictly speaking, from objects, but above all from the process whereby in acquiring truth the self abstracts from itself: I gain access to truth only by renouncing all that constitutes the self's depth, by reducing myself to the abstract point of a *cogito*. The universality of aesthetic judgment, on the other hand, results from the object's power of affirmation and persuasion rather than from a sacrifice of subjectivity. We have already shown how our reception of the aesthetic object is all the more fruitful the more completely we devote ourselves to it. This is why we are more profoundly committed and bound to the aesthetic object than to the true. I am not someone for whom two plus two equals four in the same way that I am a man who loves Debussy.

Must we, then, conclude that we have burned the bridges between the true and the beautiful and that philosophical reflection can never legitimately seek some sort of truth in beauty? No, because there is at least one other form of truth before which the subject's attitude is closer to the aesthetic attitude. Metaphysical truths, in the widest sense of the term, proceed from an attitude which is not without affinity with the aesthetic attitude. On the one hand, metaphysical truths do not resolve themselves into a rigorous and universally valid knowledge, since they have their fullest meaning only for me. On the other hand, they appeal to me in such a way that they are as much a vocation as a constraint, as much distinct from me as they are internal to me. It is metaphysical truth, and not strictly logical truth, which we will find commingled with aesthetic experience. This is a point to which we shall return.

[II] OUR ATTITUDES BEFORE THE LOVABLE AND THE BEAUTIFUL

THE CHARACTERISTICS which distinguish the aesthetic attitude from the attitude we take in relation to the true are the very characteristics which would seem to show the aesthetic attitude's similarity with our attitude when in love. The aesthetic attitude and love do, in fact, have characteristics in common. Primary among them is our recognition of the power of the other and our acquiescence in his or its rights. A man is as disarmed before his beloved as he is before the aesthetic object, from which he has everything to learn and to receive. He has as little intention of improving the aesthetic object as of transforming his beloved. He would as little dream of using the one as of abusing the other. Someone who is incapable of this sort of good will, however, and who pays greater attention to himself and his own experiences, misses out on aesthetic experience as well as the experience of love. This sort of person degrades the aesthetic to the level of the pleasing and the beloved to an occasion for a series of adventures in which he assumes the role of self-satisfied hero. He is in love with love itself and not with the other. This sort of attitude brings together the two poles of the myth of passion represented in the figures of Don Juan and Tristan, who share a common ground of narcissism in a more or less secret delectation which in one case stems from pleasure and in the other from torment. Moreover, the giving of the self which the aesthetic object requires of the spectator is demanded first from the creator. All creation is an act of love, and it is thus that the lives of those artists we call damned [*maudits*] take on their full meaning. Under the appearance of dissipation, libertinism, or madness, their lives are a testimony to a renunciation of daily concerns and the attention ordinarily paid to one's well-being.

Nevertheless, it is important to point out the differences which subsist between our attitudes before the lovable and the beautiful. First, there is a difference of intensity. The experience of love can take on, quite naturally and from its very essence, a pathetic and tragic character. Why is this, if not for the reason that love is directed toward a person, and aesthetic appreciation toward an object (leaving aside for the moment the situation in which beauty is an attribute of a person and not of a work of art)? This is why we do not search for quite the same thing in the aesthetic object as in someone we love. Aesthetic experience finds what it seeks on the level of appearance; for example, it finds the quality of sadness in the melody or poem itself. This is also why knowledge by acquaintance [*connaissance*] is, at every moment and for every subject, complete in the aesthetic experience. When we learn to see something new in a melody or a poem, this is not progress but conversion. Knowledge of another person, in contrast, is never complete. In other words, because the aesthetic object exists entirely as appearance, it presents itself to us without hesitation, and the only obstacles to our knowledge of it come from ourselves and our own impermeability. The knowledge of another person, on the other hand, presupposes that person's consent as well, for he can always hide, disguise himself, or lie. At the same time, however, the transparency of the aesthetic object involves an opacity. In the very act of presenting itself to us with a certain disdain for what we are and an indifference toward what it itself may be, the aesthetic object remains estranged from us: "I am beautiful, O mortals, as a dream in stone." [2] The knowledge generated by love, in contrast, presupposes that the other is open to me, and that, in the end, the two of us become united. For it is by means of a never quite completed union that such knowledge, itself always incomplete, can arise.

The difference between the two types of experience is most marked at precisely this point. Love requires a kind of union which is not needed by the aesthetic object, because the latter acts on the spectator and holds him at a distance. In love, I am conscious of being indispensable to the other person. All love involves an essential benevolence whereby I substitute the will of the other for my own will in order to assist the other to be himself. Before the beautiful, I assume an attitude of docility, with no intention to affect the beautiful object. Invulnerable and, as it were, eternal, the beautiful has no need of my homage. I cannot pay back or return to it anything of what it gives me, since it is already of such a perfect completeness that any attempt at "improvement" would be a crime. With another person, however, every encounter occurs as dialogue, and love is really a question which calls for a response. The question is a pressing one, and a negative answer will drive love to despair. Hence love submits itself to the judgment of the other and becomes

2. This is the first line in Baudelaire's "La Beauté."—Trans.

preoccupied with how it is regarded. It must prove itself and its good qualities. It does not hesitate to subject itself to the ordeals envisaged in tales of courtly love, with the intention not so much of seducing the other as of convincing him of the strength and sincerity of one's feelings. The very first response which love expects, moreover, is the presence of the beloved. Since this presence has a crucial and inexhaustible significance, love does not succumb to the effects of absence in the same way as aesthetic feeling. Absence takes on a unique aspect in the experience of love: "If a single [beloved] being is absent, the world seems depopulated." [3] Jules Romains remarks in a similar vein: "The idea of absence was no longer an idea like all the others. It had become one of the major categories of a universe suddenly seen from a new perspective. . . . The sound of the ship came to me as a sort of incantation of absence." [4] The point is that presence itself is the condition for my expected gift, the very beginning of that gift which will reciprocate my love.

Love is desire and aspires toward union because it sees the other as indispensable and essentially complementary to oneself. In this attitude we observe the most decisive sign of love, that which gives it the sense of fatality celebrated in poetry. The beloved is felt to be fated and irreplaceable, a being the lover could never leave behind. When his beloved is absent, the lover is no longer himself, and his life has lost its meaning. "For what is the use of life, if not to be made into a gift? And what is the use of a woman, if not to be held in the arms of her man?" [5] The aesthetic object, in contrast, is not really complementary to me. I am, to be sure, transformed and enriched by experiencing such an object, but I undergo this experience without having avidly sought it out, and it is only truly effective when the object is present. Now, because the power of desire is measured during absence, the fact that the banality and urgency of daily living are sufficient to neutralize aesthetic desire—at least in the spectator—shows that the aesthetic experience is not really a phenomenon of desire. It is because I do not experience a genuine desire for the object itself that the pleasure it provides me is different from sexual pleasure. Instead of exciting us to a point at which we are beside ourselves, the aesthetic object lulls and charms. It is as discreet as a lover is passionate, as serene as a lover is tempestuous, as delicate as a lover is violent.

3. This is a line from Lamartine's "L'Isolement."—Trans.
4. Jules Romains, *Lucienne* (Paris: Gallimard, 1922), p. 15.
5. Paul Claudel, *La Cantate à trois voix suivie de Sous le rampart d'Athènes, et de traductions diverses* (Paris: Gallimard, 1931), p. 34.

In the end, love receives its characteristics of insecurity and uncertainty from the fact that love is the desire for a person and not the need for an object. These characteristics are the simple and essential result of the freedom of the other person. The expected gift depends on a liberty continually susceptible to changing its mind and reclaiming what it has given. Hence the familiar themes of inconstancy, the ravages of time, and the waywardness of the heart. Love combats such uncertainty with a faith whose two extremes are confidence and jealousy. Under the title of fidelity, it practices this faith even with regard to itself. For can I be sure of myself unless I am bound by some sort of declaration? But love retains a natural and essential uncertainty in spite of its faith. Love is much too conscious of the freedom of the other to wish to restrain him—which is why, instead of simply presenting its demands, it is torn between its will to union and a respect for difference. And it is through this antinomy that love is condemned to eternal dissatisfaction. Someone in love desires and at the same time rejects union, for total union would be the negation of the other and of oneself. None of this is a problem with respect to the aesthetic object, because the aesthetic object does not demand any union. The presence with which aesthetic appreciation is satisfied does not awaken a desire for possession—a desire which would then have to be suppressed. Aesthetic feeling has no knowledge of the peculiar tension and insecurity which are the stimulants of love. Therefore, we may say that aesthetic experience is at once more and less than the experience of love. It involves less because it does not admit of the simultaneously painful and joyous experience of union and because it does not reveal to us our power of transceding ourselves by making a gift of ourselves. It involves more because, being less demanding, it is more easily fulfilled and is thus more inclined toward serenity. The aesthetic experience involves more, too, because the distance it maintains between subject and object is an assurance of purity within the very fervor of the experience.

These few remarks should confirm what is unique in aesthetic experience, making it incomparable to other experiences. Our next step will be to justify this specificity by attempting a critical analysis of aesthetic experience and by searching out the *a priori* structures which inform its highest and most meaningful moment—the moment, that is, of the reading of expression by feeling. Let us pass, therefore, from the phenomenology to the critique of aesthetic experience.

PART IV
Critique of
Aesthetic Experience

IN AN EFFORT to understand more clearly the fact that aesthetic experience culminates in feeling as the reading of expression, we should now like to show that this experience brings into play veritable *a priori* of affectivity.[1] A *priori* is here to be taken generally in Kant's sense. Just as the *a priori* of sensibility and understanding are the conditions under which an object is given or thought, so the affective *a priori* provide the conditions under which a world can be felt. Yet it is not Kant's impersonal subject who feels this world— even if post-Kantians have subsequently identified this subject with history—but a concrete subject capable of sustaining a vital relationship with a world. Such a subject may be either the artist who expresses himself through this world or the spectator who is linked to the artist through the act of reading this expression.

Aesthetic experience itself calls for the notion of the *a priori*. This is due to the power of the aesthetic object to open up a world through its expressiveness and, though itself given, to anticipate experience. It is not only a matter of calling forth imagination vividly, in the manner of what Bachelard calls "integrating" objects, which dream experience has charged with value.[2] The vivid emotion which such objects often inspire crystallizes itself in images which become a means of entry into a world. Yet this latter world is ephemeral and unstable. Imagination contains the potentiality of a world but cannot carry out the task of realizing it. Thus, while imagination can remove the boundaries of the object, it cannot constitute a totality: it opens but does not enclose. To realize a world, feeling is necessary. Feeling is awakened by an expressive object which not only appeals to

1. The term *a priori* can be singular or plural, depending on the context.—Trans.

2. Gaston Bachelard, *La Terre et les rêveries du repos* (Paris: Corti, 1948), p. 299.

[437]

imagination but is wholly regulated by the function of expressing. This function may be obvious in the case of man, but an object can assume it only through the miracle of art. It is not accidental that Bachelard seeks for examples of integrating objects in literature, where they become aesthetic objects.[3] Aesthetic objects give birth to a world by provoking feeling, not by stimulating imagination. And they do so because of what they are, not because of the associations into which imagination can draw them. If imagination does operate on aesthetic objects, it must first have been released by feeling and be employed to realize the sense or meaning of an expression.[4] We cannot say of every object, as we can of the aesthetic object, that it is expressive by vocation. Moreover, man himself is not always expressive—at least not in the way the aesthetic object is, that is, so deeply that the expression expands into a world. Man is the bearer of a psychical world (as opposed to the material world of which he is the center through his body) only by virtue of possessing sufficient internal force and plenitude. He is expressive as soon as he speaks or smiles—in fact, in all of his behavior—and nothing need be retracted from what we have said of language.[5] Man's expressiveness always appeals to feeling, and sometimes to a form of feeling which is very close to the immediacy of presence in its contingent character. (Such feeling differs from the kind of feeling which engages a total subject in the discovery of a total object.) Moreover, man is fully expressive only when he attains his proper excellence, and then only in rare moments. Such expressiveness does not necessarily occur when he seeks to express himself—when he speaks or gesticulates—but when he is truly himself. This we can also see in art, at least when it represents man.

That which functions as *a priori* is what feeling experiences in the object, a certain affective quality which lies at the origin of the world of the object. But this affective quality has still another function as constitutive. If it is the case that the highest form of the perceived object resides in expression, then affective quality constitutes the aesthetic object. Hence the *a priori*, in the form of affective quality, relates to this object as constituting it. Nevertheless, just as every object does not contain a world, so every affective quality cannot possess such constitutive power. We must again emphasize that

3. What about objects which have not been transformed by art? Here we encounter the problem of natural beauty. We are inclined to think that such objects must somehow be made aesthetic, at least by our very act of looking. Thus Bachelard writes, "for us, the tree is an integrating object: it is usually a work of art" (*ibid.*, p. 299).

4. One may charge Bachelard with idealism for conferring such an important role on imagination. He adopts the point of view of the dreamer and not that of things. But does not the dreamer finally side with things? Also, Bachelard knows perfectly well that science itself begins with the dream, however often it denounces its origin.

5. See above, Part I, chap. 4, § IV.—Trans.

aesthetic objects enjoy a privileged position in this respect. The sexual desirability of a woman or the majesty of an oak are not as such *a priori*. A woman is desirable, an oak majestic, only by accident or excess. We do not accord such qualities any special status as compared with other qualities. They do not constitute these others, and thus they have only relative value. But the sexually desirable may become an *a priori* for the woman who devotes herself wholly to becoming sexy. Precisely at this point, we say that the woman is no longer "natural"; she becomes an aesthetic object. In making herself up, she substitutes artifice, which is already art, for nature. Thus hopeful courtesans prepare in solitude for a career like that of Gigi. If they fail, it may be because they lack Gigi's naturalness and innocence. Similarly, majesty can be as *a priori* for an oak—but only on a canvas of Ruysdael's or for someone who is reminded of Ruysdael in looking at an oak. Only as aestheticized can an affective quality become an *a priori*. For it is in the aesthetic universe alone that an object, determined and fixed in itself by art, can be constituted by means of an affective quality. Only here can Tintoretto's Suzanne be eternally desirable and Ruysdael's oak eternally majestic.

Yet with what right do we speak thus of the *a priori*? And if the affective designates a certain mode of being which belongs to the subject, how can it qualify an object to the point of being an *a priori* for it? The next chapter will treat such questions. Later chapters will attempt to answer the following questions: If affective quality is *a priori* in relation to the world of the aesthetic object, is it also *a priori* for the real world? What is the relationship between these two worlds? What is the truth of the aesthetic object?

16 / The Affective *A Priori*

[I] THE IDEA OF AN AFFECTIVE A PRIORI

WHAT DOES THE IDEA of an affective *a priori* mean? To answer, we must first consider what the affective means if it can be conjoined with the notion of the *a priori*. It should be realized at the outset that affectivity is not invoked here merely as the means by which the *a priori* is revealed. The *a priori* can itself be affective in nature (just as the *a priori* of understanding is rational in character). This point leads to a second. Feeling, itself affective, *knows* the affective as the primary sign of the object. To desire a woman is to know her as desirable, and this quality is as evident as the color of her eyes or the shape of her body. It is for this reason that the noetic function of feeling has a unique value and is not tainted by subjectivity. To deny that a certain patently desirable woman is desirable is to refuse to feel—which is as arbitrary as refusing to see. Yet it is not even necessary to desire. One can judge a woman to be seductive without submitting to seduction, or desirable without experiencing desire. For desire is not simply knowledge [*connaissance*] but, rather, action (or passion). This is why a woman can be desired without being found desirable. What we call "feeling" [*sentiment*] is not reducible to desire. Feeling is only a certain way of knowing an affective quality as the structure of an object, and it is disinterested in spite of the sort of participation which it presupposes. Just as the feeling of the desirable is not a species of desire, so the idea of a circle is not round, or the feeling of the tragic itself tragical (even if it may be oppressive

[441]

or exhilarating). Thus we may say that affectivity is not so much in me as in the object. To feel is to experience a feeling as a property of the object, not as a state of my being. The affective exists in me only as the response to a certain structure in the object. Conversly, this structure attests to the fact that the object is for a subject and cannot be reduced to the kind of objectivity which is for no one. There is something in the object that can be known only by a sort of sympathy in which the subject opens himself to it. Indeed, at the limit, the affectively qualified object is itself a subject and no longer a pure object or the simple correlate of an impersonal consciousness. Instead of being determined from without, affective qualities involve a certain way of relating themselves to each other, a manner of constituting themselves as a totality—in short, a capacity for affecting *themselves*. As a consequence, the affective qualities into which the atmosphere of an aesthetic object is resolved become anthropomorphic. The horrible in Bosch, the joyful in Mozart, the mocking in Faulkner, the tragic quality in *Macbeth* all designate an attitude of the subject as well as a structure of the object, which are in each case complementary. But we still do not know (*a*) how such affective qualities are *a priori,* or (*b*) how an inventory of affective qualities could constitute a table of the affective *a priori* and contribute to a "pure aesthetics."

Before we investigate these matters, we need to review the meaning and function of the *a priori*. When we turn back to Kant's original view, we discover that the *a priori* designates the character of knowledge which is logically, not psychologically, prior to experience and which is both necessary and universal.[1] Thus it is transcendental knowledge which is *a priori,* since for Kant "transcendental" is a term which is "always applied originally to knowledge" and which "in opposition to the 'empirical' is an *a priori* condition of experience that is not given by it." As a result, all research is transcendental which "has for its objects the *a priori* forms, principles, or ideas in their necessary relation with experience."[2] But in Kant's view, the objects of this knowledge—the categories of the understanding as the object of

1. Max Scheler also defines the *a priori* as belonging to knowledge. But knowledge, for Scheler, is intuitive and its content is a "phenomenon" in which the given and the intended converge. (See Max Scheler, *Formalism in Ethics and Non-Formal Ethics of Values,* trans. Manfred S. Frings and Roger L. Funk [Evanston, Ill.: Northwestern University Press, 1973], pp. 50–51.) The *a priori* also defines the object of "material intuitions."

2. André Lalande, ed., *Vocabulaire technique et critique de la philosophie* (Paris: Alcan, 1926), II, 904–6.—Trans.

transcendental principles, the transcendental subject as the object of transcendental apperception, and generally anything that functions as an object in the transcendental philosophy of which the *Critique of Pure Reason* is the "idea"—is itself *a priori*, insofar as it founds the possibility of the empirical object. In this case, the *a priori* is the constitutive, that which lies at the origin of a reality and through which this reality exists for a subject. Thus the *a priori* enjoys a dual function for Kant. First, it determines the relation to an object, creating an objectivity and assuring (as the *Prolegomena to Any Future Metaphysics* shows) the move from the subjective judgment of perception to the objective judgment of experience. Second, the *a priori* determines the nature of this object as the object of a possible experience in accordance with the formula of the Transcendental Deduction: "The *a priori* conditions of a possible experience in general are at the same time the conditions of the possibility of objects of experience." [3] Hence the constitutive is that which makes the object an object—not in itself, but insofar as it enters into experience in such a manner that the subject can relate to it. But we must also observe that, for Kant, the subject constitutes what is constitutive for the object. If the *a priori* is truly *prior* to experience even when it is discovered in the objects of experience, it also belongs to the subject as a structure of knowledge. As the *Prolegomena* says," "thought space renders possible the physical space. . . . This pure [thought] space is not at all a quality of things in themselves, but a form of our sensuous faculty of representation." [4] Kant's critical analysis may begin with the object, but it is the structure of the *cogito* which it uncovers as the condition of the possibility of an experience. It is the subject who bears the *a priori*. Thus Heidegger is not unfaithful to Kant when he sees, in critical reflection, the elucidation of "the subjectivity of the subject" and interprets the transcendental as the transcendence of Dasein. [5] In no way does this imply a subjectivism; rather, it underlines the fundamental reciprocity of subject and object. A philosophy of constitution can also be a philosophy of being, because being reveals itself only to a subject capable of grasping it.

3. Immanuel Kant, *Critique of Pure Reason*, trans. Norman Kemp Smith (New York: St. Martin's Press, 1929), A 111, p. 138.
4. Immanuel Kant, *Prolegomena to Any Future Metaphysics*, trans. Lewis White Beck (New York: Liberal Arts Press, 1950), p. 35.
5. See Martin Heidegger, *Kant and the Problem of Metaphysics*, trans. James S. Churchill (Bloomington: Indiana University Press, 1962), *passim.*—Trans.

Therefore, by beginning with the *a priori* as a characteristic of the object of knowledge (and not of knowledge itself), we obtain three insights. First, the *a priori* is that factor in the object which constitutes it as an object; thus it is constitutive. Second, the *a priori* is a capacity of the subject to open himself to the object and to predetermine its apprehension; as constituting the subject as subject, the *a priori* is existential. Finally, the *a priori* can be the object of a knowledge which is itself *a priori*.[6]

However, since the *a priori* characterizes both the object and the subject (as well as specifying their reciprocity), it can be determined in terms of the forms which the relation of the subject to the object takes. Thus it can be discerned at each of the three levels of presence, representation, and feeling. In each case, an aspect of the lived, represented, or felt object corresponds to an attitude of the living, thinking, or feeling subject respectively. It is at this point that we differ from Kant, who conceived the relation to the object in the form of knowledge alone. For him, the predetermination of the object by the *a priori* as a "constitutive property of the object" is invoked only to found the objective value of knowledge.[7] The real question is whether the transcendental can be conceived in such a way that it is not the foundation of objectivity but constitutive in some other sense. By conceiving of the relation to the object only in cognitive terms and of rational knowledge as alone valid, Kant forces us into a dilemma. Either our thoughts relate only to ourselves and their subjectivity disqualifies them (as in judgments of perception, which possess value only to us individually and some of which relate uniquely to a sensible affection that can never be attributed to the object), or our thoughts are attributed to the object as instances of knowledge (as in judgments of experience whose necessity and universality result from subsumption under a concept of pure understanding). But perhaps a thought may relate to the subject even while it relates to the object—that is, may be subjective without lacking objectivity or intend an object without exiling the subject. To this sort of thought would correspond an object which would be at once subjective and objective—a characterization which we have given to the world of the work. There is a crucial difference between purely subjective judgments such as those cited by Kant—the room is warm, the sugar is sweet—and aesthetic judgments, such as Bach's music

---

6. This last point will be treated in the next chapter.
7. Kant, *Prolegomena*, p. 46.

is serene, Rouault's world is Jansenist, or Matisse introduces us to the nature of light.[8] This difference, which we must not ignore, is the difference between a judgment which makes a representation explicit and one which articulates a feeling. In terms of the relation between the world of the aesthetic object and the subjectivity it discloses, this difference is also one between the way in which anyone may experience the warmth of a room or the sweetness of sugar and the way in which Bach sees and constructs a world on the basis of serenity or Rouault creates from controlled despair.

Consequently, there are a variety of ways in which the subject may relate to the object and vice versa. The subject is constitutive on at least three planes: at the level of presence, through what Merleau-Ponty calls the corporeal *a priori*, which trace out the structure of the world experienced by the lived body; at the level of representation, through the *a priori* which determine the possibility of an objective knowledge of the objective world (it is here that Kant is most relevant); and at the level of feeling, through the affective *a priori*, which open up a world lived and felt by the deep self in the first person. The subject is presented in a new form at each level—as lived body in presence, as impersonal subject in representation, and as deep self in feeling. It is in these forms that the subject successively assumes a relation to the lived, represented, and felt worlds. (We should note here that feeling does not belong exclusively to the spectator confronted with the world expressed by the aesthetic object. Feeling belongs to anyone capable of assuming sufficient personal humanity and depth to experience and illuminate a personal world which is not merely the world of his body or understanding.) The world's threefold countenance is the correlate of the three basic attitudes of the subject, but the relation between subject and world is difficult to conceive because of the ambiguity inherent in the notion of world and constitution. It is always a matter of conceiving a world which is for a subject, but one which is (in Sartre's definition of intentionality) both external and relative to consciousness. This conception of the world is expressed by the unity of the *a priori* in its first two aspects. The problematic character of this unity, within which we shall later seek an ontological meaning, is not fully appreciated by Kant, insofar as he yields to idealism in spite of himself and

8. We do not include "this work is beautiful," for that is not a question of value judgments but of judgments of experience which express the aspect of the world revealed by feeling.

privileges the subjective aspect of the *a priori* by suggesting that, in the object, the *a priori* only reflects the subject's constitutive powers. But in examining the affective *a priori* revealed by aesthetic experience, we cannot afford to ignore the problem of this unity. Thus we must take a closer look at the affective *a priori* in its subjective and objective aspects and in their unity. Only then will we be able to see how the affective *a priori* can be known *a priori* by a subject who is capable of grasping it. We shall also be in a position to ask if a pure aesthetics is possible in which the *a priori* of affectivity would be distinguished and enumerated much as other *a priori* are determined by a pure mathematics, physics, or (perhaps) biology.

[II] The A Priori as Cosmological and as Existential

An affective quality is an *a priori* when, expressed by the work, it is constitutive of the world of the aesthetic object and when it can also be felt independently of the represented world in the same way that we can, as Kant says, conceive of a space or a time without objects. At least this is true in principle, if not in fact. In fact, we know the *a priori* only through the *a posteriori;* and in aesthetic experience the expressed world and the represented world, along with affective quality and objective structure, are always united. But expression as immediately felt animates the world of the aesthetic object, even if it can be recognized as such only by a critical attitude directed to the work. Affective quality is the soul of the expressed world, which itself lies at the origin of the represented world. The total world of the work receives unity and sense only through affective quality—which, as it were, gives rise to the work in order to be, in turn, exhibited by it. It is in this sense that affective quality is constitutive and that the feeling by which it is known enjoys a sort of priority in aesthetic experience. In this respect, we would say of affective qualities what Scheler said of values as "material qualities": they are manifested in objects that are "goods." When a value is only an accessory quality in an object, the object has, so to speak, no personality of its own. It is a mere *Sache,* not a *Ding.* In contrast, when the object is "constituted" or "unified" by a value—"thoroughly *permeated*" by a value—it is a good. But a good reverts to the status of a thing if the value in it is for any reason devalued.[9] Thus a value can precede the object which it constitutes and, like a messenger, announce the presence of the object. "It is as if the axiological nuance of an object . . . were the *first* factor that came upon us . . . a 'medium,' as it were, in which the value comes to develop its content."[10] Hence it seems that value is like a form that creates its own content. A good does not result from the addition of a value to a preexisting thing but instead is incarnated in a thing and constitutes the thing as a good by this very act of incarnation. Similarly, the world of the aesthetic object is structured by an affective quality that acts as its *a priori*.

But once the *a priori* is defined by its proper position in the order of knowledge and by its constitutive power, the question of its singularity arises. As appearing in a work and constituting its world, the *a priori* may seem to be as numerous as aesthetic objects themselves. Can we label as *a priori* a quality of the object which is endlessly diverse and which thus seems unable to be the basis for an apodictic science? This question, to which we shall return, leads us to examine the existential aspect of such an *a priori*. One basis for its singularity is the fact that it is also a characteristic of the concrete (thus singular) subject. After having shown affective quality to be an *a priori* of the aesthetic object, we must now assign this *a priori* to a subjectivity. Now, it is the artist or creator [*l'auteur*] who expresses himself through the world expressed by the work. It is no longer a question of a Kantian impersonal subject who sustains *a priori* which are themselves impersonal and thus objects of rational knowledge. Rather, we have to do with a concrete person who is no longer related to the impersonal world of objective experience but to his own world—into which others penetrate only by communicating with him. The *a priori* expresses the absolute position of a subject confronted with things, and it expresses the way in which he intends, experiences, and transforms them. The *a priori* reveals the way the subject relates to things in order to create his world, just as the corporeal *a priori* may be seen as

9. See Scheler, *Formalism in Ethics*, p. 22. Scheler uses precisely the example of the aesthetic object. A painting ceases to be a good or *Wertding* and remains simply a thing when its colors are removed. The choice of this example does not, however, justify us in identifying value and affective quality.

10. *Ibid.*, p. 18. In this regard, Scheler is not far from the question by which Kant introduces the idea of the *a priori* in the *Prolegomena:* "how can the intuition of the object precede the object itself?" (p. 29).

the way in which a singular body relates to its environment in terms of the imperatives of its own structure. The *a priori* is fundamentally the irreducible factor by means of which a concrete subject is constituted. It is that which Sartre's existential psychoanalysis seeks to discover, except that for us it does not express the pure act of an absolute freedom or a perfectly contingent choice of self.[11] Instead, the *a priori* expresses the nature of a concrete subject who, in terms of the paradox formulated by Jaspers, can create himself only because he is already created.[12] For this reason, in place of the idea of self-choice we prefer the idea of "constitution" as presented by Eugène Minkowski in his effort to oppose psychoanalytic ideology. The only important difference is that, whereas Minkowski's notion of constitution is general and derives from an act of induction, the affective *a priori* is singular and derives from the subject's direct intuition.

The notion of constitution has the further advantage of presupposing "the phenomenon of vital contact with reality." It expresses the basic relation to the world of the individual "torn between two forces: a need to affirm himself and a need to lose himself." [13] In fact, the subject thus defined by his peculiar affective quality always relates to a world, as the transcendental subject defined by the synthetic unity of apperception relates to the object of a possible experience. But the transcendental relation under consideration here is a fundamental act which is the source of all particular acts, one through which a singular essence is affirmed and manifested. It is the necessary exteriorization of an interiority which, in order to exist, is directed and diffused onto what is outside itself. And the world involved in this transcendental relation is a world which is the expression of a subject, not a world which is known as the object of universally valid experience. The experience whose possibility is founded by this *a priori* is one which should be called "existential," and its objects form a world accessible to feeling alone. Such a world emanates from a subject who extends it and makes

11. See Jean-Paul Sartre, *Being and Nothingness,* trans. Hazel Barnes (New York: Philosophical Library, 1956), Pt. 4.—Trans.

12. The philosophical antecedent of the existential *a priori* is not to be found in Kant's notion of intelligible character, which represents the atemporal choice of a transcendental (thus nonconcrete) subject, but in Spinoza's notion of singular essence, which links the subject to his body and to all that he is and which is nonetheless eternal because true in God.

13. Eugène Minkowski, *Vers une cosmologie* (Paris: Aubier-Montaigne, 1967), p. 191.

it explicit. It is not the world which he knows but the world in which he recognizes himself and in terms of which he *is* himself. The subject is so intimately linked with this world that the affective *a priori* which founds it *is* himself: Mozart is serenity, and Beethoven passionate violence.[14] But we should be forewarned that it is not only a matter of the artist [*artiste*], whose creation of the work—giving it a radiant body—makes this world appear as his own expression. The relation to a world which we are considering here is not strictly speaking the relation of a maker [*créateur*] to his product [*créature*]; the latter relation is dependent on an act of making, while the relation in question transforms into appearance the fundamental relation of a concrete subject to his world. This fundamental relation is valid for all men who are capable of expressing themselves by their acts (even if they have no spectators other than themselves) and who possess a personality. The relation is equally valid for the spectator who expresses himself through his appreciation of the work, which he adopts and integrates into his world. Of course, it is undeniable that, whereas the artist creates, the spectator sees. But if (*a*) the work is considered in itself without evoking the historical act of its creation; (*b*) the creator is only the being to which the work witnesses; and (*c*) creation is no more than the sign of a spiritual affinity, we can say that the affinity which is revealed between the work and the creator is the same as that revealed between the spectator and the work which he is capable of feeling and recognizing. (This point will be further clarified when we examine the existential status of the categories by which the spectator knows the affective quality of the work.)

The world to which the subject is thus related, and which is at once his destiny and his own act—like a mirror in which he recognizes himself—is proportionate to his being. Its consistency and reality increase as the subject gains depth and authenticity: We could even say that its objectivity is measured by the extent of subjectivity in the subject.[15] It is not a world which is merely

14. It is not insignificant that the proposition can be inverted to read, serenity is Mozart. This shows that the affective *a priori*, however subjective it may be, is, in a sense, universalizable and thus can become the object of a pure aesthetics.

15. To the degree that the *a priori* still retains an element of objectivity, we should not downgrade the Kantian criteria of universality and necessity in the manner of Scheler, who relegates these criteria to a merely logical status. For Scheler, the *a priori* is a "fact" for the intuition which grasps it. It is true as a fact and its necessity is subordinated to truth, while its universality adds nothing (since it is experienced as such and needs no logical

subjective, nor is it the subjective coloring of a preexisting objective world that occurs when we judge in terms of our moods and dispositions—that is, according to the vicissitudes of the superficial self—that the room is warm or the absinthe bitter. The affective *a priori* constitutes a consistent and coherent world because it resides in the deepest stratum of the subject, as well as forming the most profound aspect of the aesthetic object. But it can already be sensed that it is not possible to speak of the existential *a priori* without comparing it to the cosmological *a priori* and without presuming that the constitutive and existential *a priori* are finally one. Let us next verify this hypothesis by seeing how the world of the work is the truth of the artist.

When we speak of the comic in Molière, we mean that, in attending a Molière play, we are caught up in an atmosphere which orients our comprehension by organizing the sense of all that we will see or hear. This atmosphere is experienced by everyone as a mixture of lucidity and transport, but by anarchists as a combination of bitterness and anger, by poets as a species of tenderness, and by naturalists as a proclamation of faith in man. It communicates the assurances that hypocrisy is the worst of evils and that nature can triumph over the obstacles posed by social artifice. But it required Molière to create this subtle mixture—"subtle" only on analysis, since it is grasped directly by feeling—and he *was* the mixture in person and not merely its fabricator. To talk of the comic in Molière is thus to specify a singular world by giving it a name and contrasting it with other worlds which do not possess a precisely similar atmosphere. It is not only a question of connecting this world with its maker but also of assuring that it exists in the image of its maker (where the "of" designates an existential relation of identity, not a transitive relation of paternity or the real, historical relation between the actual Molière and his work). A singular world calls for a singular subject. We cannot be present to the work without feeling the work as the witness and truth of

___

ratification). (See *Formalism in Ethics*, p. 76.) Although necessity and universality do not acquire a logical sense in the case of the existential *a priori*, they can possess an ontological sense and designate the structure of that which is constituted by this *a priori*. Thus, even if the *a priori* is not logically necessary and universal, it may at least confer a factual necessity and universality on the aesthetic object. Through it, the world of this object acquires an internal cohesion, becoming a universal in Hegelian terms. Kantian criteria are applicable to it no longer in relation to a judgment pronounced from the outside but in relation to its very being or, in Hegelian terms, to the way it affirms itself and judges itself in affirming itself.

a subject. Once again, it is a matter not of the historical act of creation by which a given work has been fabricated, but of a certain existential attitude on the basis of which this world can appear. This attitude is itself *a priori* with regard to the subject, in that it constitutes him *as* a subject.

There are other ways in which we may express the fact that affective quality is constitutive of the work as well as the subject. For example, we may term affective quality "thought," in the sense in which Alain spoke of "a thought foreign to our words, inexpressible and even invisible, and enclosed within the work itself." [16] This may be thought, but only in the Hegelian sense of a principle immanent in (and developing in) the work. It is not thought in the sense of a doctrine or message presiding over the work, seeking to be expressed and verified by it. We have encountered this notion before. Even if the artist has religious or philosophical "ideas," the work does not exist to serve them and its profundity lies elsewhere. Ideas enter into play only by becoming fleshed out through a double metamorphosis. First, the idea in art is not an instance of thought's existing for its own sake. Rather, the idea is lived on the plane of aesthetic creation. If we were writing a psychology of creation, we would have to consider this difficult point and show how the musician thinks with the piano or the painter with his brushes—as, for that matter, every man thinks with words and not with ideas. When the artist who is interrogated answers in an evasive or uncertain fashion, we may be tempted to say that the artist does not think. In fact, he thinks in his own fashion, which is not strictly communicable. He reflects on the object, insofar as he constantly judges his work while creating it, and this judgment is already more than a merely profane opinion. Moreover, even if the artist thinks beyond immediate judgment, his thought is still contained in the work. He may well have an idea of man or a *Weltanschauung*, e.g., Rouault's idea of human misery. But for Rouault, this idea is expressed by the depth of the blues or purples or by a face crushed beneath brush-strokes. It is not that Rouault says to himself "The human face has something derisory in it, thus I will paint it in a certain fashion." Instead, Rouault is not satisfied plastically unless he paints a human face in a certain way, and this signifies that he has a particular idea of man. In brief, the beautiful is the criterion which determines the true. But the true must be rooted in man. It is here that we

16. Alain, *Ingres* (Paris: Editions de Dimanche, 1949), Preface.

find the second metamorphosis of thought. Thought can inspire creation from within (even to the point of becoming one with gesture) only if it is truly internal to the creator, becoming identical with him and, indeed, becoming itself an artist. Then the idea can animate the work by inhabiting the affective quality which is the work's soul. Thus one can say that the work's affective quality embodies thought and even that there is a philosophy in every work, whether it be the bitter and fervent Christianity of Rouault's paintings, Debussy's sensual and sometimes defiant openness to the world, or the Parthenon's Platonic taste for order and measure (not to mention its exaltation of light and its sense of the splendor of the true). But since such thoughts are enclosed within their respective works, they exist in the state of feeling and communicate themselves to feeling. When we reflect on such feeling, we may try to restore it to the state of thought. However, this thought is living for the artist only insofar as it becomes feeling.

It is because this thought incarnates and expresses itself through affective quality that it is capable of producing a world. Thought by itself cannot transform itself into a world. There is no world of Spinoza in the sense that there is a world of Balzac or of Beethoven. Spinoza does present a cosmology, which is not the same thing. A cosmology is a theory of the world, not the feeling of a world, and it strives to account for the objective world, to constitute its objectivity by giving to the propositions which define it a universal value.[17] In contrast, an affective quality can be pregnant with a world, since a world, in the sense in which we have understood the word, is precisely a response to a certain attitude, the correlate of the subjectivity which manifests itself in affective quality. This subjectivity would not manifest itself so completely in thought unless thought were to im-

17. Yet it is possible to speak of a world of Spinoza, if it is the case that Spinoza, like every philosopher, intended to say something which he did not fully succeed in saying, and if we have to understand him not only in terms of his literal text but also through associating ourselves with his effort, affirming what he implies, and trying to coincide with his own point of view—in brief, by invoking feeling. This would be to give philosophy the status of the aesthetic object. Is such a move acceptable? Perhaps it is, but only if we are willing to accept two corollaries. On the one hand, the conversion of philosophy into a work of art is a devaluation, not a promotion. It attests to the impotence of reflection to reach an end of its enterprise and to escape subjectivism. On the other hand, it is reflection itself which determines this devaluation. Only a philosopher can avow the impotence of philosophy. This is why philosophy cannot be a genuine work of art. If it becomes one, it does so only contrary to its own wishes and never deliberately, since philosophy does not itself make such a proposal.

pregnate it totally—in which case, thought would become feeling. As the fundament of a world, thought need not lose all sense of objectivity. Yet it may also express the subject who possesses and lives it, to the point that its truth is, above all, the truth of the subject. (We shall see that this does not prevent the subject from being true in an absolute sense, though still according to nonobjectivistic norms.)

Nevertheless, a trap awaits us when we speak of the world of the subject and are constantly tempted to say that the subject is constitutive. This is the trap of idealism, concerning which Kant was so vigilant, against which our earlier analyses of form in aesthetic perception should have armed us in advance, and which we must still seek to avoid. Aesthetic reflection seems to precipitate us into this trap when we consider the subordination of the work to its creator, but aesthetic reflection appears to evade the trap when the autonomy of the aesthetic object vis-à-vis the spectator is considered. But things are not quite so simple. The analysis of the spectacle of art makes it appear that the aesthetic object is always a perceived object, at one with the spectator in his very being. Conversely, the analysis of the creation of art indicates not only that the work is the act of the artist but that the artist is the act of the work. It is the complexity of the subject's relation to his world which is not fully appreciated in idealism's subordination of the world to the subject, of nature to knowledge, or of environment to organism. In claiming that the cosmological and the existential are only two aspects of the same *a priori*, we no longer accept this subordination. But at what price? We must affirm that the affective quality to which these two aspects belong is anterior to both subject and object, constituting them both. This point can be explicated in two ways.

First, the notion of a world of the subject may be reversed and compensated for by the notion of a subject of the world. "World" and "subject" must be considered equal terms. If we have stressed affective quality as a quality of the world for the subject, we must not forget that it is also a quality of a subject for a world. In other words, just as a world is required by a subject who is a subject precisely in relation to a world, a subject is required by the world, which is a world only in being witnessed. The creator expresses himself through the world of the work, but the world of the work also expresses itself through the creator. In fact, is this not what we mean when we say that a particular artist is necessary for a certain aspect of the world to appear? Was Giraudoux not requisite for the revelation of a

Giraudoucian world, and Racine for a Racinian world? Of course, this signifies that Racine invented the Racinian world, but it also means that the Racinian world created Racine, confirming our impression that certain artists seem to have been summoned and impelled by a truth which does not belong to them and of which they are the witnesses and even the martyrs. Again, it is undeniable that this truth was *their* truth. Only if Racine himself was true can there be a truth of the Racinian world. But it was also necessary that Racine be true because of a Racinian truth which needed Racine. Once again, the creative act should not mislead us. Though the creative act induces us to accord a primacy to the subject, we should also grant an inverse primacy to the object. The artist himself authorizes the latter move when he appeals to inspiration. Acted on as well as acting, the artist exists in the service of a world which seeks to be incarnated in the work through his agency. Moreover, even if the case of the artist invites us to give a special privilege to the subject, we may still invoke the spectator. As we have seen, he is required by the work. In a sense, the work exists only through the public which concretizes and recognizes it. Furthermore, the work imposes itself on the public as it imposes itself on perception, and the public exists only through it. As the Racinian creates Racine, so Racine's work of art—which is still part of the Racinian—creates its public. This is why, instead of saying that a public has a work (as one says that the subject has a world), one says that the work has a public. This public seems to emanate from the work, extending and clarifying it. In this respect, the cosmological seems to have the initiative in comparison with the existential. In fact, however, we must refuse to give priority to either factor, since conversely the public makes the work, which is recognized only if it finds a consciousness that emulates it. Someone must come to express himself in the work or at least find in it an expression of himself.

But we must take the point further. If affective quality as an *a priori* is both cosmological and existential, and neither of these two aspects possesses the primacy or initiative with regard to the other, this quality must be grasped as anterior to the specification of these aspects. For Racine and the Racinian world to exist as equals, they must both be seen as subordinate to an affective quality which we may call pre-Racinian. Naturally, "pre" must not be understood in a chronological or even in a logical sense. The prefix simply invites us to place the accent on the priority of affective quality and to attempt to consider it outside of what it constitutes—as the expressed world can be considered independently of the represented world, or existential commitment separately from the subject. Now, it is through what we have said of expression that we can gain an idea of the primordial reality of affective quality, wherein that part belonging to the subject and that belonging to the object are still indistinguishable. In fact, expression is that which reveals affective quality as total and undifferentiated.[18] Expression exists prior to the distinction between body and soul, exterior and interior. The container and the contained are not yet differentiated within expression. Thus a certain melody *is* tenderness, without our having to effect a *rapprochement* between notes taken as a musical reality and tenderness as an emotional reality. As a word has a sense before being grasped as a phonetic reality and prior to the distinction between phoneme and semanteme, so the aesthetic object has a sense before it appears as a material object or as a signifying object. Affective quality is precisely this sense as immediately given through the sign. But to be prior to the distinction between interior and exterior is also to be prior to the distinction between subject and object, for the interior refers to a subject and the exterior to an object. Tenderness is at once a quality of Mozart and of a Mozartian melody, as tenderness is also a quality of the soul and countenance of the mother who smiles at her baby. Therefore, the creator appears immanent in the work only because there is a primary state of expression, in which there is not yet either work or creator, or in which something is revealed that can be related equally well to the work or to the creator. It is for this reason that we have been led to say that the affective is in the work itself, as well as in the spectator with whom the work resonates. Feeling is as deeply embedded in the object as it is in the subject, and the spectator experiences feeling because affective quality belongs to the object.

It is evident that our reflection has now taken an ontological turn. The logical sense of the *a priori* slides into the ontological. What was before a condition of possibility becomes a property of being. To be at once a determination of subject and object, the *a priori* must be a characteristic of being, which is anterior to

18. Is it not a contradiction to say that quality is an *a priori* if it is revealed by expression? Is not the *a priori* defined as that which cannot be given in an experience? But we should notice that, first, the *a priori* can be manifested only as dwelling in the *a posteriori*, thus as related to an experience. Second, expression is not an experience like perception and the deciphering of appearance, though it is, at least, an original experience.

subject and object and makes their affinity possible. Failing to acknowledge this anteriority lands one either in idealism, which subordinates the object to the subject and gives a purely logical sense to the *a priori*, or in realism, which, in subordinating the subject to the object, loses the very sense of the *a priori*. We shall have occasion to follow the direction indicated here, for the object which has just been invoked to show its solidarity with the subject is, in fact, only the world of the aesthetic object. In its fullest meaning, it is the real itself. Aesthetic experience can thus become the basis for reflection on the accord between man and the real.[19] In other words, when we speak of the identity between the existential and the cosmological, we should accord the richest meaning possible to the cosmological and thus to the cosmological aspect of the *a priori* as constitutive. Affective quality not only constitutes the world of the work—which is the world of the creator—it also bears on the real. As a result, the identity between the cosmological and existential does not merely designate the status of the aesthetic world. It poses, with regard to aesthetic experience, the problem of being, that is, the problem of the possibility of an affective meaning which the artist or spectator discovers, expresses, and yet does not found. But such a problem may be pursued only when the cosmological dimension of the world of the aesthetic object is extended to the real, that is, when we consider the truth of art.

Nevertheless, we should like to sketch briefly the ontological implications of a theory of the *a priori* with regard to the specific *a priori* which we have distinguished.

[III] THE MEANING OF THE A PRIORI OF PRESENCE AND REPRESENTATION

THE INVESTIGATION of the *a priori* of presence and of representation allows us to view the *a priori* itself in its broadest dimensions. This is especially true if we are willing to examine the consubstantiality of the existential and the cosmological— the subjective and the objective—for, in this instance, the cosmological designates the real and not simply the world immanent in the aesthetic object. Unquestionably, aesthetic experience again enjoys a privileged position, because the aesthetic

19. This would be even more the case if we were to consider the natural aesthetic object, which arises directly from the real.

object, which is made by man for man, lends itself naturally, through the qualities that constitute it as a known and lived object, to the demands of knowledge and of vital use. But let us for a moment go beyond the privileged case of the aesthetic and give the problem its full scope.[20] Can we, then, still speak of the *a priori* as anterior to its two aspects?

It seems that we can answer affirmatively with regard to the *a priori* of representation, for representation involves the possibility of subsumption. Now, Kant was concerned with subsumption to the exact extent to which he wished to escape idealism. For to say that understanding imposes its laws on nature is still to subordinate the object to the subject.[21] Thus, "all possible appearances, as representations, belong to the totality of a possible self-consciousness."[22] It is in this way that appearances are associated and that there can be an "affinity of the manifold." But does it suffice to say that the empirical affinity is "a necessary consequence of a synthesis in imagination"?[23] How does it happen that the given is associable, reproducible, and linked together in knowledge? Kant poses the question in a decisive way.

> If cinnabar were sometimes red, sometimes black, sometimes light, sometimes heavy, if a man changed sometimes into this and sometimes into that animal form, if the country on the longest day were sometimes covered with fruit, sometimes with ice and snow, my empirical imagination would never find opportunity when representing red color to bring to mind heavy cinnabar. Nor could there be an empirical synthesis of reproduction.[24]

Certainly, the empirical synthesis can be recognized only by the reproductive synthesis of imagination, which "belongs to the transcendental acts of the mind" and which Heidegger has justifiably stressed.[25] But it is also necessary that the transcendental

20. It is obvious that we can initiate here only the beginnings of a project which would require considerable enlargement. Thus we limit ourselves to indicating the context of an analysis of aesthetic experience. [See Dufrenne, *The Notion of the A Priori,* trans. Edward S. Casey (Evanston, Ill.: Northwestern University Press, 1967), *passim.*—Trans.]

21. "Thus the order and regularity in the appearances, which we entitle *nature,* we ourselves introduce. We could never find them in appearances, had not we ourselves, or the nature of our mind, originally set them there" (*Critique of Pure Reason,* A 125, p. 147). This assertion leads Bertrand Russell to say, somewhat hastily, that Kant's Copernican revolution is a "Ptolemaic counter-revolution" (*Human Knowledge: Its Scope and Limits* [London: Allen & Unwin, 1948], p. xi).

22. *Critique of Pure Reason,* A 113, p. 139.

23. *Ibid.,* A 122, p. 145.

24. *Ibid.,* A 100–101, p. 132.

25. See Heidegger, *Kant and the Problem of Metaphysics,* § 3.—Trans.

faculty of imagination, which operates on the basis of a sensible and nonintellectual intuition and to which the object is given, enter into complicity with the given of intuition. To think the identity of cinnabar throughout its diverse appearances, my thought must agree with itself; but cinnabar must also be faithful to itself, and the given must not be wholly disconcerting (in the sense in which Poincaré said that there would be no chemistry if there were only a million simple bodies). In other words, it is necessary that the transcendental object, which is "the formal unity of consciousness in the synthesis of the manifold of representations," [26] find a way to be incarnated in an empirical object which lends itself to unification. This way is found in the principle of finality. In the last paragraph of the Transcendental Deduction, Kant rejects the idea of a sort of preestablished harmony between thought and object. But he later allows such a harmony in the *Critique of Judgement:*

> [The] understanding is no doubt *a priori* in possession of universal laws of nature, apart from which nature would be incapable of being an object of experience at all. But over and above this it needs a certain order of nature in its particular rules.[27]

Undoubtedly, the principle of finality is only regulative—a "subjective principle of judgment"—but it is also an *"a priori* principle of the possibility of nature." [28] Hence the first *Critique* must be balanced by the third. After having shown that "all empirical laws are only special determinations of the pure laws of understanding, under which, and according to the norm of which,

26. *Critique of Pure Reason,* A 105, p. 135.
27. Kant, *Critique of Judgement,* trans. J. C. Meredith (Oxford: Oxford University Press, 1952), p. 24.
28. Moreover, the first *Critique* rejects the idea of finality because of its link with the notion that the *a priori* is in us "only a subjective disposition to think," a "subjective necessity which is arbitrary and innate in us." Kant is anxious to avoid subjectivism. Thus he locates the necessity of the *a priori* in the object. "The effect is linked with the cause in the object." Yet he also says that "all appearances, as possible experiences, thus lie *a priori* in the understanding" (*Critique of Pure Reason,* A 127, p. 148). Therefore, the subject, who is not synonymous with the subjective, is given a privileged position. Though manifested in the object, the necessity of the *a priori* is logical, not ontological. Hence Kant does not put himself in the position of saying that the subject and object are two aspects of the same being, or that the object exists through the concept while the concept exists in the object. The *Critique of Judgement* tends in this latter direction, but only Hegel will go the whole way and posit an identity between the logical and the ontological. We shall attempt to do the same, in our own fashion.

they first become possible," [29] Kant, to resolve the problem of subsumption, must establish conversely that phenomena lend themselves to the reception of this norm and that the accord of nature with our faculty of knowing is "presupposed *a priori* . . . by judgement." [30] It is not surprising that the case of art is then invoked to attest to the affinity of the object as known with the subject as knowing.

Yet this line of reflection can be pursued even further by pointing not only to the reciprocity of knower and known but also to the fact that what is, in us, a demand for intelligibility is, in the object, a structure of being. It is in this sense that we have spoken of a temporality belonging to the aesthetic object itself. The existence of this temporality shows that time belongs not merely to a temporalizing subjectivity but also to things. We may also speak of a knowledge inherent in the object, invoking Bergson's attempt in *Matter and Memory* to "pass from perception to matter, from subject to object." [31] Bergson posits the image both as a spectacle and as the being of things. The image is posited as spectacle, since "no philosopher can approach the problem of perception without assuming the possibility . . . of the virtual perception of all things." It is posited as being, because "in the case of images there is a simple difference in degree, and not in kind, between *being* and *being consciously perceived.*" [32] As a result, knowledge would exist in being as well as in the subject. But we make this suggestion only in the conditional tense.

Let us turn now to the *a priori* of presence. We can say that they constitute a certain quality of lived experience which is prior to the distinction between the living organism and its environment (or any object located within this environment) and which is common to both. This signifies, above all, that organism and environment are at one, and that the organism does not constitute, in idealist fashion, the environment according to its own norms. Instead, there is a reciprocity of the sort which we observe between work and artist or between work and public. Thus, if the organism "has" its environment, the environment also has its organisms—an idea formerly expressed by the notion of spontaneous generation. The organism expresses the environ-

29. *Critique of Pure Reason*, A 128, p. 148.
30. *Critique of Judgement*, p. 38.
31. Henri Bergson, *Matter and Memory*, trans. N. M. Paul and W. S. Palmer (Garden City, N.Y.: Doubleday, Finchor Books, 1959), p. 57.
32. *Ibid.*, pp. 24, 23. [The English translation has been somewhat modified.—Trans.]

ment and vice versa. A certain kind of wolf exists "for" the Siberian forest as the forest does for the wolf. The various biological *a priori* which constitute the wolf as wolf, e.g., a certain aggressiveness or style of life for which behavioral equivalents of what we have called the existential dimension could be discovered, correspond to the cosmological *a priori* that constitute the forest as forest, for which environmental equivalents of the artist's world could be discerned. Is this to reintroduce finality? If so, why not? An explanatory science would translate the relation of reciprocity into causal terms. Yet science itself is implicitly founded on this relation and (to adopt Kantian language) presupposes *a priori* an accord between environment and the capacity to live. We are not concerned here with the internal finality which is manifested by individual rule-bound behavior and which has been rehabilitated by contemporary science, but with the external finality exemplified in a reciprocal relation of adaptation. In terms of adaptation, the organism preforms the environment within itself and adjusts itself to the environment. The environment arranges itself for the sake of the organism and calls to it. As Raymond Ruyer says, "the fact that there are edible fruits for men and animals as well as reserves for the reproduction of plants is not so extraordinary when one considers the reciprocal adaptation of flowers and insects, of mimetic butterflies and their surroundings." [33] But perhaps we must also say that this accord is possible only because the vital overflows the living organism, as the human outstrips man, or knowledge extends beyond the knower. The organic and the inorganic both exist for the sake of the vital, within which the presence and activity of the living become possible. This reality of the vital may already have been sensed and sedimented in mythical knowledge. The animism of primitive myths can be seen as an attempt to express the forms of the vital as felt in the cosmos, just as the forms of the human as felt by the artist are fixed by art into types of affective qualities.

Aesthetic experience, considered on the level of presence where the object is still only an element of the environment and a stimulant for behavior, is once again enlightening. This is because the aesthetic object is made for the body and calls for the use which the body makes of it. The same phenomenon is present in fabricated objects, especially in those tools which have been shown by André Leroi-Gourhan to be subordinated, in

33. Raymond Ruyer, *Le Monde des valeurs* (Paris: Aubier-Montaigne, 1948), p. 144.

their most primitive forms, to an organic manipulation.[34] The technological environment is one which exists for the sake of a specific behavior and corresponds to the *a priori* of seeing, taking, raising, and moving. But we see something similar in aesthetic objects, which call for a certain attitude and use on the part of the body—witness again the cathedral that regulates the step and gait, the painting that guides the eye, the poem that disciplines the voice. The relation of the work to the performer— and to the spectator, insofar as he is also a performer—most clearly manifests the affinity of the aesthetic object with the vital *a priori*. Furthermore, aesthetic experience suggests that there may be, within the aesthetic object, a certain complicity with the performer or spectator as well as a response to the life which supports us, since the object is itself a product of this life, which permeates both the artist and the universe.

But we cannot dwell upon this now.[35] In evoking the *a priori* of presence and representation, we have sought only to attest to the idea of an ontological meaning of the *a priori*, which is common to subject and object only as founding both and as belonging principally to being. In fact, all philosophy is obliged to effect this movement from the *a priori* to the ontological, as soon as it becomes dissatisfied with a facile idealism and is unwilling simply to contrast the plane of the object with that of being or

34. See André Leroi-Gourhan, *Le Geste et la parole:* I, *Technique et langage* (Paris: Albin-Michel, 1964), *passim*. We find a similar idea in Alain: "The staircase outlines the form of man" (*Les Dieux* [Paris: Gallimard, 1947]). Commenting on Friedmann, *Les Problèmes humains du machinisme industriel,* Georges Canguilhem shows that it is presently a problem to reintroduce the organic into the technical and to institute a technique for adapting machines to man. "Moreover, this technique appears to Friedmann to be the knowing rediscovery of wholly empirical procedures by which primitive peoples tend to adapt their rudimentary instruments to the organic norms of an activity which is both efficacious and biologically satisfying. In such a technique, the positive and growing value of technical norms is sought in the attitudes of the organism at work struggling spontaneously against any exclusive subordination of the biological to the mechanical" (*Cahiers internationaux de sociologie,* III [1947], 129).

35. We reserve for a future work the study of how the vital, noetic, and affective *a priori* are related to each other. It is on the basis of reflecting on aesthetic experience that we have introduced them here. In this move, we have again implicitly favored the subject. But in following the direction which we have just indicated, we must subordinate both the subject's attitudes and the object's aspects to a primary being which contains and produces them both. It is within this being that we must seek the basis for the distinction between, and articulation among, the three modes of the vital, noetic, and affective—in each of which the dialectic of subject and object is operative. [See Dufrenne, *The Notion of the A Priori,* Introduction and pt. 3.—Trans.]

to reduce the *a priori* to a wholly subjective condition for apprehending the object. Only if there is a kinship between man and the real can there be anything like man's being in the world. For man can enter into relations with the real—relations which are established by presence, representation, and feeling—only on the condition that the real's otherness is not radical and that the various *a priori* are common to man and world and thereby gain an ontological dignity.

To demonstrate all this in terms of aesthetic experience, we must examine the *truth* of the aesthetic object, that is, the relationship between the cosmological and the existential, when the cosmological no longer designates the world of the aesthetic object but the real world. Thus we shall have to ask whether the affective *a priori* is still an *a priori* for the real world. Before this, however, we must consider another—the third—aspect of the *a priori,* according to which it is itself known *a priori*. This will pose an entirely different problem, that of the possibility of a pure aesthetics.

17 / *A Priori* Knowledge of the Affective *A Priori* and the Possibility of a Pure Aesthetics

[I] AFFECTIVE CATEGORIES

AFFECTIVE QUALITIES POSSESS another aspect which should be considered at this point. They constitute not only the *a priori* that we *are* but also the *a priori* that we *know*. For we always already know what the corporeal, intellectual, and affective *a priori* are and we live by this science, which precedes any specific scientific investigation. We know these *a priori* in advance of all experience, and, although such knowledge can remain implicit even when it is in operation, it may become explicit in the form of propositions which demand our assent. Indeed, these *a priori* are known even when they are undefinable, as in the case of affective qualities, and our knowledge of them is never mistaken. In much the same way, the *a priori* of presence appear at first to be ungraspable. It seems impossible to specify how a particular organism, with its own peculiar constitution, is related to its environment, that is, how it settles in a particular place, adjusts itself to its surroundings, and lives and dies there. And yet we immediately recognize a living being and understand how it operates. It is on the basis of such *a priori* knowledge, furthermore, that a comprehensive biology and psychology, such as that outlined by Goldstein, can found a

[463]

science of behavior.[1] They can found a science of behavior by showing how a living organism uses its body according to the way it utilizes the world and by enunciating the corporeal *a priori,* such as those of eating, attacking, and sleeping, which compose the schemata of such usage. Similarly, the *a priori* of representation are not yet knowable at the level of their existential roots. We cannot grasp pure intuition because it is only the possibility of intuition, that is, the manner in which the subject opens itself up to a particular being. Hence space and time possess such characteristics as being prior to every given, not being additive in nature, and not being perceptible as something in our field of vision.[2] Even the *a priori* of understanding, which are the foundation of the possibility of judgment, merely determine the objectivity of the object. This object is nothing more than its objectivity, that is, a sort of preobject whose only property is a unity prior to all diversity. Nor is the fundamental act to which the *a priori* of understanding correspond and by which the subject opens itself (the act which constitutes the "horizon of unity" necessary for all knowledge) capable of being grasped in itself. And yet, at least in their constitutive aspect, these *a priori* provide the basis for a pure science composed of apodictic propositions. This is also true of the various affective *a priori.* They elude our grasp and as such fall under the jurisdiction of feeling. Nevertheless, just as we know of space before it is articulated in geometry, we must have some acquaintance [*une connaissance*] with the affective *a priori* before they are revealed to us by feeling. We are able to feel the tragic in Racine, the pathetic in Beethoven, or the serene in Bach only because we possess an idea prior to the concrete feeling of the tragic, pathetic, or serene. This means that we must have ideas of what will henceforth be entitled affective categories, which are related to affective qualities as the general is to the singular, or as knowledge of the *a priori* is to the *a priori* itself.

1. See Kurt Goldstein, *The Organism,* trans. K. S. Lashley (Boston: Beacon Press, 1963).—Trans.

2. Kant points out with regard to points and moments (see *Metaphysical Foundations of Natural Science,* trans. Paul Carus [Chicago: Open Court, 1929]), every form of space and time always functions as a determination or limitation of an original space and time which are unique, homogeneous, and completely contained in each of their parts.

Admittedly, such categories probably cannot become the object of a pure aesthetics which would be as rigorous as geometry or pure physics. But the same is true for a pure biology. We are just as incapable of gaining a perfectly clear insight into such corporeal *a priori* as aggression, habitation, or nourishment as we are into affective *a priori* such as the comic, the gay, or the trivial. But this is not disastrous: even if I do not understand anything about geometry, my lack of understanding does not undermine geometry's *a priori* status. This would be true even if I were completely ignorant of geometry. For men have lived without geometry, yet their summary knowledge of space and time—that natural geometry which forms, as it were, a midway point between lived and reflected experience—was nonetheless already necessary and universal. Necessity and universality are not necessarily the characteristics of a science which has been established and perfected. They also belong to an implicit knowledge [*un savoir implicite*] which is present as soon as we escape from the immediacy of lived experience and begin to speak in such a way that thinking underlies our words. Moreover, today we are more Kantian than Kant, because we know that this pure science is never complete and that our initial knowledge is never exhausted. It is for this reason that we are justified in thinking that there is a pure aesthetics to which we refer implicitly whenever an affective quality is revealed to us by art—even if such a pure aesthetics, which is present within us, may never be definitively actualized.

Nevertheless, a pure aesthetics has often been a goal for aestheticians. In fact, even though its table of affective categories has never been interpreted in the manner we are attempting here, these categories have been determined and catalogued under other names. Let us briefly recall such efforts. They concern what have been called aesthetic categories, essences, or values, and they use such terms as the beautiful, the sublime, the pretty, the gracious, etc. (This constantly present "etc." should indicate sufficiently the limits of reflection, which is usually content to compare aesthetic values, instead of working out an exact inventory.) These terms denote what we mean by "affective categories," a phrase which seems the most precise for them. Why, in fact, should we speak of "values" in the manner of those axiologies which attempt to swallow up aesthetics unscrupulously? The beautiful alone can be called a value—and only on the conditions that it be considered separately from affective categories and that it denote the distinction possessed by certain aesthetic objects of being successful—that is, of fully expressing a given affective category, of undeniably manifesting the truth of a world. The beautiful is the aesthetically true. This is why the beautiful is a value. However, those categories whose truth the beautiful expresses are not themselves values. An affective category is simply an affirmation—the affirmation and the foundation of the world revealed by the work. Perhaps there is a value lying behind the affirmation, since this world is the world of a subject and has value by and for that subject, being for him the best of all possible worlds or, rather, the only true world. But this simply means that value is at the basis of being, to the extent that being is reciprocally related to a valorizing subject. In any case, we cannot define being *by* value. And we cannot define the categories which underlie the worlds expressed by art as values. The grotesque, the pretty, and the precious are realities—attitudes on the part of a subject, and characteristics of a world. They are not values.[3]

We would also reject the term "reflective essence" as understood by Souriau, who writes: "These reflective essences of the ethos *follow* the accomplishment of the instaurative progression, they do not direct it. They exist according to love and they come out of a reflective and contemplative return toward the work. . . . They are experiences, i.e., *a posteriori* controls, and not direct regulations or laws of the act."[4] We disagree with Souriau's claims, because these essences do not seem to be merely *a posteriori* controls or, rather, would be so only insofar as they need reflective elaboration and emerge from an examina-

---

3. It is a different problem when such qualities are subject to judgments of value in accordance with a taste that institutes a hierarchy of preferences, as in, for example, Victor Hugo's revival of the grotesque or Beethoven's exaltation of pathos. Fruits are not values, even though we may prefer pears to grapes. At most, they can be regarded as goods, as Scheler demonstrates, since values remain independent of their bearer even when they are incarnated in an object. The quality of the pleasing is within the fruit and even functions as an intrinsic property, but it is not the fruit itself. In the same way, the work of art and the *a priori* which is its ordering principle can be judged more or less beautiful, since beauty is an aesthetic value and an important factor for the work of art. But the work is something different from the beautiful, and the work can be said to be beautiful only in being what it itself is. On this point, we refer the reader back to the Introduction.

4. Etienne Souriau, "Art et vérité," *Revue philosophique de la France et de l'étranger,* CXV (March, 1933), 190.

tion of the work. Considered in terms of their original status, however, they lose that reflective character. If we think of them as bearing a double aspect which is simultaneously cosmological and human—like the affective quality of which they are the *a priori* "idea"—these essences lose their *a posteriori* character as well. They designate what is immanent in the work and contemporaneous with its creation, that is, that existential *a priori* which inspires the artist precisely because he is an artist. As Souriau points out, it would undoubtedly be absurd to believe that the artist envisions a category which he then strives to actualize in his work.[5] The artist thinks in an entirely different way, focusing his attention on the object to be created and judging only according to his taste. He does not imagine some intellectual norm such as the affective category would be if he were to take it as his goal. But it is due to the very fact that the artist does not think of anything like an affective category (and certainly not of himself as the bearer of this *a priori*) that he expresses himself just as he is. He is himself what is intended, the "meaning" [*sens*] of the category. The artist, furthermore, is incapable of executing a different kind of work. When the work is authentic, it bears witness to the artist. But a work is authentic only when the relation between it and its creator is one of consubstantiality and not simply one of fabrication—as between the artisan and his artifact. Briefly stated, affective categories, like affective qualities, are not only characteristics of a world but characteristics of a world *and* a subject together. Hence, whenever an artist expresses himself by expressing his world, the affective category becomes truly "a direct regulation and a law of the act."[6]

5. See Etienne Souriau, *L'Avenir de l'esthétique* (Paris: Alcan, 1929), p. 109.
6. Whatever name and function may be assigned to these reflective essences, the table given by Etienne Souriau remains the most precise and coherent. It is all the more valuable because Souriau was aware from the beginning that it could never be complete. He too must make use of the word "etc." when, in *L'Avenir de l'esthétique*, he writes of "the different values or aesthetic categories (such as the sublime, the tragic, the comic, etc.; we can no more construct a complete list of these categories than we could make a complete list of colors)" (p. 106). The principal merit of his table for our purposes is that it goes well beyond the traditional classifications of the beautiful, the pretty, the sublime, the ugly—in which every term seems precisely to gravitate around and carry the nuances of the beautiful. Souriau, on the contrary, gives a place to terms—such as the pathetic, the heroic, the fantastic—which cannot be called indications of

Because the affective category is a law of the act, it is a law of the work as well. Moreover, it is due to his examination of the work that Raymond Bayer (who, with Souriau, opposes the theories of Victor Basch in this respect) can specify what he calls "aesthetic categories," by which the aesthetic object acquires the maximum of objectivity and autonomy.[7] This doctrine is all the more important because it forces us to confront the most extreme difficulties of our own analysis by focusing on the very heart of the object. In this way, we must discern within the object, which is a law unto itself, the types of equilibrium which make the categories possible. It should not surprise us, moreover, that aesthetic reflection would in this case abandon the existential aspect of the categories in favor of their cosmological aspect and turn toward the world of the work rather than toward the subject who expresses himself in this world. Just as we would

a value, because they clearly designate qualities of the world which are tied to existential attitudes. But the reader can judge for himself. Below is the table.

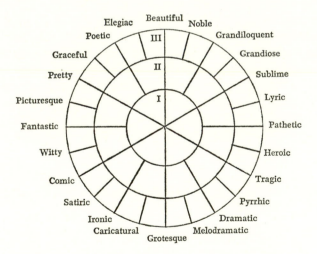

I, Classical; II, Romantic; III, Other Categories

7. Valentin Feldmann makes a practice of contrasting Souriau and Raymond Bayer with Victor Basch in his *Esthétique française contemporaine* (Paris: Alcan, 1936). We ourselves are unable to subscribe to Basch's theory. According to it, aesthetic categories are really subjective and express not the being of the object but the effect produced on the spectator by the object. Basch has retained the idea of the subjectivity of feeling, which was borrowed from Kant and became the basis of one of Scheler's principal criticisms of Kantian ethics.

attempt to understand a man by means of his gestures rather than by his intentions, so here we direct our attention to a world rather than to the *a priori* by which that world is constituted. The noema is more accessible than the noesis. Is it not the case that our language names the world more easily than it names the human categories which acquire names only as a function of the world? We have a word for the tragic as a characteristic of the world. We have no word for the sense of the tragic as a characteristic of the subject. What Bayer in fact defines, however, is *not* the world of the work but its objective structure. Such an undertaking is indispensable, for, as we have shown, the world of the work has unmistakable roots in the objective structure of the work. Yet we must make a definite distinction between that structure, which is elucidated by means of critical reflection, and the immediate experience by which feeling comes to know the work. Immediate experience calls for an affective category. That is why we need to distinguish affective categories from structural categories. This distinction is of crucial importance, since a consideration of structure alone may not account for the diversity of the categories. (For this reason, Bayer remains with the traditional classification, even though he points out important nuances, as in his analysis of the graceful.)

The *a priori* which interests us here, however, is not the *a priori* which is immanent in the artist and constitutive of the world of his work. It is, rather, the sort of *a priori* which serves as the object of an art of knowledge, that is, an affective category under which is subsumed an affective quality. Thus it must first be disclosed in the spectator of the aesthetic object. In fact, our coming to know [*la connaissance*] the affective quality delivered by feeling is always a sort of recognition [*une reconnaissance*]. Before the world revealed by feeling, I am not like a stranger whom nothing helps to orient in an unknown land. I seem to know beforehand what I read in expression. A sign is immediately meaningful, because its signification is known before having been learned. Any process of orientation I may undergo is simply the confirmation of some preliminary knowledge [*savoir préalable*]. The very fact that we can make feeling explicit and find names for the affective qualities feeling communicates attests to the presence of such preexisting knowledge. Nevertheless, this claim does not contradict the phenomenology of feeling that we outlined above. We argued that our feeling had to possess depth in order to reveal the depth of a work and that, accordingly, we ourselves had to possess depth. Now we are concerned with uncovering the transcendental aspect of the same depth whose ontological dimension we have already shown. To be equipped with our own experience is not enough to enable us to be sensitive and responsive to a work of art. We must also be equipped with the kind of knowledge which allows us to recognize what we feel before we can understand what we have felt. How could I express a particular affective quality without resorting to an affective category of which I have some sort of preliminary knowledge? How can I be sensitive to the expression of the aesthetic object which is present before me unless I previously had some secret kinship with it and unless I were somehow qualified to comprehend it? How could feeling be intelligent if I were not already in communication with [*d'intelligence avec*] expression? As Kant says, how could I know that every object is spatiotemporal unless space and time were *a priori* givens? In the same way, how could I read an expression and be assured that expression is possible unless I had some preliminary knowledge of what is expressed which does not result from reflection and which is thus *a priori*?

We can easily cite two things which would favor this *a priori* status. First, such knowledge is immediately immanent in feeling. Second, it is not the result of an empirical generalization. The fact that such *a priori* knowledge should be the soul of feeling takes nothing away from feeling's power of revelation. Feeling alone can open us up to the aesthetic object as to a unique sort of being, and only feeling can put us into contact with the object in such a way as to avoid all the problems which are brought about by reflection and which alter or at least retard the experience of communication. But it is still the case that feeling cannot be completely intelligent, or the aesthetic object fully recognized (we do not say "reflected upon"), except in the light of such *a priori* knowledge. Knowledge does not mask feeling or dull what is unique in the aesthetic object—that singular nuance which, though it is never completely explicit, I experience when I realize that the bitter fervor of El Greco is not the same as the serene fervor of Raphael, or that the shimmering purity of Fauré's quartets differs from the violent and magnificent purity of Franck's F Minor Quintet. But before I can experience the singularity of such a nuance, I must know fervor and purity as affective categories. Hence knowledge does not follow feeling. This sort of knowledge does not derive from reflecting on feeling in such a way that feeling would pass from a state of blindness to a state of intelligence, that is, from a state of participation to one of comprehension. Feeling is immediately intelligent. In the tragic qualities of *Phèdre* we immediately recognize the tragic as such and understand that the word or idea "the tragic" does not begin to exhaust the unique atmosphere of that work. Similarly, in Kant's view, sensations are not given first and then made meaningful by the addition of the forms of sensibility. Rather, we perceive objects as spatiotemporal immediately and consider them to be objects of an intelligible nature. The *a priori* is contemporaneous with the *a posteriori,* and affective categories are present to feeling. The knowledge [*le savoir*] constituted by these categories forms part of the equipment of that deep self which is capable of feeling. Feeling revives this knowledge, which in turn renders feeling intelligent. What I experience as expressed by the aesthetic object possesses a meaning and can be identified because of the echo it awakens within me—which we should recognize as the echo of an *a priori,* because it is not the work of an act of reflection. For the knowledge in question does not present itself as the result of reflecting on feeling from the outside. Instead of being reflection or the source of reflection, this knowledge is itself in need of reflection. It exists within us as a fundamental virtuality, having the character of acquaintance and not of action—a virtuality which our encounter with the aesthetic object and the feeling thus awakened serve to actualize. Such knowledge can also be conceived as a kind of "sense" that one has, as when we say that some people have a sense of mathematics or of painting, but with an important difference—one's sense of the affective *a priori* is something other than a matter of aptitude or taste. It is, rather, a sort of prior comprehension which is responsible for the fact that feeling is a knowing by acquaintance [*connaissance*]. But such a prior comprehension also needs reflection in order to be explicated, and even then it may never be explicated definitively. This comprehension is the raw material [*matière*] of reflection and not reflection itself. Furthermore, the knowledge constituted by affective categories cannot dispense with reflection on feeling. On the one hand, this knowledge is immanent in feeling and hence adds nothing to feeling. On the other hand, such knowledge is general and not entirely adequate to feeling, which receives a singular expression from a singular object. The category of the tragic never quite coincides with the singular nuance of the tragic revealed in *Phèdre,* or Rembrandt's *Ecce homo,* or Mozart's *Masonic Funeral Music.* The affective category clarifies the feeling I experience before the work and renders that feeling intelligible, but there is more to the feeling than is contained in the category.

The reason for this is that the affective category is something general and can be applied to a number of singular affective qualities, striking the fundamental note of their similarity without being able to capture their peculiar nuances. But the fact that the affective category is limited to the general is simply another indication of its *a priori* character, and the category is not a generalization resulting from comparing different affective qualities which characterize various works of art. Rather, the affective category *precedes* the revelation of these qualities through feeling. By invoking the tragic in the case of *Phèdre*, we are not searching for a common denominator between *Phèdre* and numerous other works which can also be said to express the tragic. Our procedure is, rather, to understand the world of *Phèdre* by means of a certain notion which is already present, a sort of light for the illumination of diverse works. Affective qualities also define a human world which can be understood and can enter into dialogue with other worlds. However, the human world can never be classified in terms of genus and specific difference, as a plant is classified in a particular flora or as early sociologists attempted to classify different societies, because such a classification would simply weaken this world's singularity. The relationship between the joy [*allégresse*] in a work by Mozart and joy as such is not a relationship of species and genus, any more than is the relationship between Don Quixote's courage and courage in general, or between the humility of a Franciscan friar and humility in general. Thus, as we shall see, the relationship between man and humanity is instituted within man himself as a delegate of humanity. Whoever attempts to understand this relationship finds that it involves the discovery of the human in man. Thus the generality contained in the notion of humanity does not resemble the generality which relates to things. The latter generality originates as an imitation of the way we would act on things, since they are, in effect, offered for us to act upon. The generality of the human always involves an idea of the totality of men and a feeling for the kinship between them and myself. This is above all the case if this generality is *a priori*, that is, if the idea of man is present before any schematic construction as the guarantee within me of my humanity.

Before taking a closer look at the relation between the singular and the general, however, we should emphasize that the generality of the affective category is not something abstract, in the sense that it does not substitute a schema deprived of humanity for the existential aspect of affective qualities. The concrete subject qualified by affective qualities becomes an impersonal subject in terms of the category, but he remains concrete and capable of possessing depth. The general does not destroy what is essential in the singular. It is, in fact, just as true for affective categories as for affective qualities that they are related to the subject and his world and that they institute between the two, over and above a simple relationship of subordination, an undeniable solidarity. Affective categories always presuppose a twofold reference to world *and* subject, that is, to a concrete world and a concrete subject. Affective categories differ from affective qualities only in that, in the case of categories, the concrete is not yet incarnated and remains a possible concreteness. The idea of the horrible which is inspired in me by a Bosch painting, a Romanesque capital, or a Baudelaire poem is both a characteristic of the world (however difficult it may be to define that characteristic: "It was a dark and stormy night") and an experience which must be lived through by becoming equal to its horrors, submitting to them, or defying them. The corpse described by Baudelaire in "La Charogne" is not something horrible for flies or maggots, but it is horrible for men, who are conscious of being alive and terrified by death. It is also horrifying that a man must live through the horrible. The paintings of hell produced by the Flemish primitives, for example, contain scenes of men delivered over to demons. These men are not merely elements or victims of the horrible or horrible in themselves, they are also witnesses to the horrible. The horrible is realized in them as it is in Oedipus when he tears out his eyes in order to destroy his vision. Greek tragedy, moreover, always includes a specific element—namely, the chorus—that bears the affective category in which the world of the work finds its correlate. In the same way, the donors depicted in medieval paintings possess a serenity which attests to the serenity of the *Annunciation* which they have just commissioned.[8] Hence

8. Both these examples make the spectator part of the work itself and an element of the spectacle. They show us how the public always, in a sense, belongs to the structure of the work. A spectator in a theater is not represented by a playwright, but he is still a necessary part of the work. A certain role is given to him which he must play in the fulfillment of aesthetic creation. His task is not only to be present with the proper solemnity but to be the guarantor of the world elicited by the work. He must not live this world as if it were a real situation but, rather, conceive someone who is capable of living it.

affective categories are, in the first place, aspects of the world—a world of things and of men, since men can be as grotesque, innocent, or tragic as things, and can serve just as well to concretize a world. The world designated by categories is not yet populated. It is a world which exists before things and men, before the distinction between figurative and literal sense—just as the world of Rameau is a world of elegance and grace which can be further specified by French gardens, courtesans dancing minuets, or beribboned shepherdesses dancing rounds. Thus we can call preciosity to mind whether we think of a svelte and sumptuous orchid, the subtle lines of the Erechtheum, or the conversations at the Hôtel de Rambouillet. Similarly, we can envision innocence with equal ease in the face of a child not yet burdened with the cares of life, in the frolicking deer of a terrestial paradise described by Charles Péguy, or in a scene such as the harvesting of the grapes in Rousseau's *La Nouvelle Héloïse*. In such instances, man is an element of the world expressed by the category and not the consciousness of this world—just as the characters of a novel and the whole of the world represented therein are the elements of the novel's expressed world. As long as man remains within the limits of the world expressed by a category, I can regard him with the most varied feelings. I can, for example, admire the person who holds fast in a tragic world or sympathize with the one who succumbs in a cruel world. But then I am not yet acquainted with a consciousness capable of inventing or being that world, in the sense that Mozart *is* the joy of the Mozartean world.

But, in the second place, affective categories constitute a dimension of consciousness which is strictly correlated with the dimension of a world. Though general, an affective category is also existential. Just as the world of a work implies its creator, so the world qualified by a category calls for a consciousness of which it is the correlate. This consciousness is like an impersonal creator who, from having been a particular person who creates, transforms himself into an absolute spectator, assuming and bearing within himself the meaning of the spectacle. Hence the idea of the world as tragic presupposes a consciousness which feels the tragic as a spectacle in the manner of a tragic chorus—and *not* a consciousness which lives the tragic as its destiny, in the sense of a hero whom the tragic draws into a concrete situation. An affective category expresses a certain way of opening oneself up to a world, that is, a certain "sense" of a world. We have a sense of the tragic or the grotesque, just as we have a sense of smell or touch. This sense is, furthermore, constitutive. The world of the tragic disappears the moment it is no longer seen in a certain way, just as the world of innocence disappears under Richard Lovelace's glare, or the world of preciosity at the approach of a Danube peasant. Conversely, such worlds appear with undeniable truth when there is a consciousness in accord with them. Thus the world of the artist possesses truth if the artist himself possesses truth. But the consciousness with which we are concerned here is impersonal. In other words, it is the consciousness of a possible artist conceived in the image of a real artist. We could also conceive of this consciousness as a possible structure of a subject who can be known implicitly outside of any reference to a real subject. Such a consciousness is like the direction of a pure look or, rather, the pure act which is responsible for the emergence of a certain world. It is like one human possibility among others. And if psychology, in Sartre's words, "is obliged to make use, without saying so, of the *a priori* essence of the human being," [9] it is perhaps because this essence naturally divides itself into several essential possibilities which can be assigned *a priori*. Emotion, in contrast, cannot be known *a priori*, because emotion is a concrete reaction on the part of a concrete subject, and, most important, because emotion is a secondary attitude resulting from, and not identical with, a certain basic prejudice on the part of the person who is already sensitive to a particular affective quality. [10] While emotions occur as mere accidents, the feelings expressed by affective categories can, on the contrary, legitimately be called human categories. Insofar as these categories are themselves known *a priori*, they are existential *a priori*. They designate the fundamental attitudes of a person in his relationship with a world to which he is sensitive.

Therefore, just as the affective *a priori* of the aesthetic object are at the same time existential in character, so affective categories are also human categories. *A priori* knowledge of the different countenances which the world may assume is also an *a priori* knowledge of the different attitudes that can be adopted by man. We know both man and his world in the same way

9. Jean-Paul Sartre, *Sketch for a Theory of the Emotions,* trans. Philip Mairet (London: Methuen, 1962), p. 22.

10. This does not deny that there is an essence of emotion or that eidetic knowledge of this essence is possible. But the articulation of this essence presupposes a reflection on the self or on others. Sartre argues that "the facticity of human existence renders a regular recourse to the empirical necessary" (*ibid.,* p. 52).

that we know both the work and its creator—as indissolubly bound together.

[II] THE VALIDITY OF AFFECTIVE CATEGORIES

HOWEVER, a category remains something general. A category is the idea of an *impersonal* world and subject, whereas feeling arises in the presence of a singular world and subject. How is it possible, then, for the general to be applied to the singular or for the singular to evoke within us the general by which it is clarified? How can we possibly recognize a singular work by means of a category and know a concrete fact through the agency of an idea? There is no difficulty here so long as we remain on the level of fact and consider ideas as instruments for grasping facts. The doctrine of intellectualism, for example, provides an understanding of the hold on facts which ideas afford and of the characteristic way in which facts are always the converse of ideas. We would also have no difficulty if we were to adhere to conceptualism, according to which an idea is a generality obtained by generalizing from individual cases. But neither of these solutions is satisfactory in the present instance. Aesthetic singularity is neither a fact that is subordinate to an idea nor an individual subsumable under a genre or type. We are tempted by these mistaken models only when we remain at a distance from the aesthetic object, restricting ourselves to reflecting on it in an objectifying manner. In this sort of reflection, we never come close to the object as it is in itself, either because we take it to be an object trapped in a historical situation and subject to certain laws, or because we concentrate too closely on its technical composition and classify it in an artistic genre on that basis. What is truly characteristic of the aesthetic object is that it is essentially singular—like the subjectivity of which it is the product and the reflection. The drive to innovate which we find in all artists provides our argument with indirect evidence. As Victor Hugo writes in his *Shakespeare,* one does not recreate a masterpiece, one creates something entirely different. An artist's admiration for the old masters or his fidelity to a given tradition does not absolve him from the obligation to innovate. The urge to innovate on the part of the artist, however, does not imply that he is surrendering to an obsession with nonconformity or that he wishes to be original at any price. He wishes simply to be himself, and his familiarity with the old masters compels him to surrender to his own genius.[11] It is because a work partakes of its creator that it—like his personality —is irreducible to a thing or a fact. The work is a unique individual, or, as Jaspers says about *Existenz,* an exception. But how then can the work be subject to a category, which surpasses the singular? How can the human be general? This ontological problem is also raised in philosophy, especially the philosophy of the subject, which takes the individual outside the spatio-temporal continuum and considers him as individuated not by matter but by his freedom. In terms of a philosophy of the subject, the problem becomes one of how there can be a similarity between freedoms which would allow the philosopher to say "we."[12] The solution, which must be the same for aesthetics as for philosophy, may be investigated in two ways. First, we can turn to what is known. In this case, we need to show that the singular harbors the general within itself, in order to justify the employment of categories with a general scope. The analogy of structure which may eventually be discerned within a certain group of works (in the same way that the human sciences discern common structures among men) would be only one consequence of the ontological affinity by which the work or the individual participates in a category and hence in the human universal. Second, if we turn to the knower, we must show that these categories are valid only because they are *a priori* (i.e., because individual men bear within themselves originally the idea of man) and because, by the same token, they also constitute a preconceptual and virtual knowledge of a special type. In this way, the categories' very indeterminacy makes them applicable to the singular. And, whenever reflection attempts to make the categories explicit, it runs the risk of losing something of their peculiar virtue. We shall consider these two points in turn. First, how does the singular work assume generality?

Initially, we may be tempted to claim that the work is general because it belongs to a genre which is determined by the matter

11. For this reason, as J. G. Hamann argued in his *Aesthetica in nuce,* the artist loves his work as he would a person, that is, for what it is and not for some ideal it may realize. The Pygmalion complex is at the root of narcissism. (See Hans-Martin Lumpp, *Philologica Crucis; zu Johann Georg Hamanns Auffassung von der Dichtkunst. Mit einem Kommentar zur Aesthetica in nuce* (1762) [Tubingen: Niemeyer, 1962.]

12. "Dieses Seiende, das wir selbst je sind" ("This entity which each of us is himself"), as Heidegger says. [See Martin Heidegger, *Being and Time,* trans. J. Macquarrie and E. Robinson (New York: Harper, 1962), p. 27.—Trans.]

[*la matière*] used in making the work and by the method of making [*le faire*]. For creation must be subject to rules, even the secondary creation which is involved in theatrical presentation or musical performance. These rules, furthermore, are general. They elaborate the indispensable, objective material [*matériau*] of the work which has been consecrated by a long tradition. They define the possible uses of this material. All technique is general, and there is no art without technique, even though technique is continually surpassed by the genius who puts it to use. We are well aware that the genuine artist despises rules, but even the rules he invents for his personal use bear the mark of generality. If he were to devise a new artistic genre, it would still be a genre—not only because it would be imitated and made the source of a tradition but also because the operation of fabrication itself is capable of being consciously determined and imitated as a result of the formulae it may involve, of what it presupposes and excludes (e.g., accidents, distractions, improvisations), and, in sum, of everything within it that pertains to craft. Similarly, the object produced in this operation can be subsumed under a concept or included in a class and is itself quite open to imitation. It is for this reason that we have a culture and a history of art.

Such generality is not, however, the generality peculiar to affective categories. Besides, the character of generality which results from the act of creation is not what appears when we contemplate the aesthetic object in itself. What we discover in this contemplation is the singularity of the object's expression. We no longer regard the artist as the fabricator of the object but as the individual who expresses himself in the object and who invites us into his world. When the fabrication of the work is concerted, such expression is natural and the work expresses its creator spontaneously—or at least that aspect of the creator which we identify with the work, that *a priori* which is both existential and constitutive and which is revealed beyond what is general in the work.[13] Can we still speak of expression on the

---

13. A psychology of creation would definitely confirm that a concern for technique and a respect for rules—care in general—does not exclude the authenticity and the expression of the self in a world which we bear and want to present to others. On the contrary, one finds oneself by losing oneself in the work. The best means of self-presentation is not necessarily through speaking about oneself. When the artist's attention is concentrated on his creation, expression is given as something extra. Consider, for example, the polytonal chord at the beginning of Stravinsky's *Petrouchka*. It introduces us with considerable force into a strange world of burlesque

level of the generality of the genre? The genre or type has, of course, its own character. The epic is heroic, the fresco majestic, and the elegy elegaic. Our very language invites us to characterize an artistic genre by an affective quality, or an affective quality by a genre. But it is not the total expression of the work, its genuinely singular quality, which distinguishes a Mozart allegro from a Beethoven allegro, or a comedy by Molière from one by Musset. The general quality is simply that aspect of the work which we expect, which orients our choice, and which allows us to prepare ourselves for the work and to follow it. The general quality enables us to locate ourselves in the work by means of something determinate to which we can refer. In view of the attention required by the aesthetic object and of the ease with which we may lose our bearings before a new object, such a premonitory and orienting factor, which guides anticipation, seems truly required. In the end, however, the general quality is not what surprises and possesses us, for it is not the revelation of a singular universe as epitomized in a singular quality.

The general knowledge of which we speak will be found only in the vicinity of such a revelation. In fact, something general resides at the heart of the singular—just as there is a general dimension of human existence and its creations through which humanity and also the truth of humanity become possible. We mean that each man possesses a certain way of being himself which makes him similar to other men. What distinguishes men are their disfigurements—all the vicissitudes which determine their lives and wrinkle their faces and souls. Men are different from one another to the extent that they are the products of different circumstances and histories. They differ according to their superficialities. Quite often, when they wish to distinguish between themselves, they accentuate these very superficialities and accordingly ratify the necessities which weigh on them. It is true that there is another, deeper element of men's personalities which makes each of them irreplaceable. We could, without disqualifying it, call this element a destiny. Or, we can account

---

and sadness. It is the solution to a technical problem as well as the result of honest labor. "F-sharp, no pity!" said the same Stravinsky when he was writing *Le Sacre du printemps*. Should we believe that the original intention of the most personal artists was to express themselves? The explosive experience they carried within them must be translated into artistic terms, but that can be done only unconsciously and because the artist is primarily a conscientious craftsman. Even when the artist has become self-conscious, he nevertheless experiences himself as an artist only in contact with technique. We have already shown how this is so.

for it in terms of freedom, whether we are representing it in mythical terms, as in the choice of lots in Plato's myth of Er, or in quasi-mythical terms, e.g., the existential project or the choice of an intelligible character.[14] This part of ourselves which constitutes our deepest nature is, in truth, both destiny and freedom. It is, moreover, this deep self,[15] expressing itself in the work of art, which is epitomized by the work's affective quality. Affective quality makes the deep self manifest by exhibiting the world of which this self is the soul and correlate.

Now, we may be closest to others precisely when we are most profoundly ourselves. This means not only that we are given means of communicating with the other and of being his confidant or model but also that we are consubstantial with and similar to the other. We rediscover humanity in our own innermost depths. The idea of humanity has a meaning primarily in comprehension, for each man carries this idea within him and experiences it whenever he assumes his singularity.[16] Similarity lies at the heart of the exceptional, not in the sense of being a structure—since similarity would disappear if every man did not rediscover and re-create it within himself—but in the sense of being a privileged pathway, an ideal limit, for every instance of singularity. Humanity is only a possibility within us, yet it is this possibility which founds our reality. Insofar as we accentuate our differences by creating and accepting ourselves, that is, insofar as we develop our reality, we attest to this possibility. Consequently, the solitude which Rilke recommended for poets and which great artists have often practiced (many times against their will) could, to the extent that it becomes an occasion for the deepening of the self, be considered as a means for rediscovering the human and for preparing to communicate with others from our innermost depths by becoming similar to all. This idea, moreover, has been implicit in all our analysis. By speaking of a nature of man, we allow the theme of the humanity within us to appear. Freedom is what individualizes men, but freedom also involves similarity. It is not just that we possess an

14. See *The Republic of Plato*, trans. F. M. Cornford (Oxford: Oxford University Press, 1960), pp. 321 ff.—Trans.

15. We feel justified in using Bergson's phrase here. In a sense, Bergson performed a psychological analysis of the self, while Jaspers attempted to establish its ontological status, and Scheler and personalism its phenomenology. Every philosophy of the subject deals with this problem in its own way.

16. In this way, humanity is not a species but a vocation and a brotherhood. We shall return to this point.

essential nature inextricably mingled with freedom but that freedom itself is like such a nature. In other words, to exist is an essence for man—a singular essence, of course, insofar as existence signifies freedom, but an essence nonetheless. And this is why Callicles (in Plato's *Gorgias*) possesses something of man within himself—not only for the sake of a logical definition of Callicles but for his very being as well. Yet precisely because we *are* freedom, this essence is not an invulnerable structure. It is, rather, a possibility and a task. Just as communication is something we always have to establish, humanity remains something always still to be attained.

Furthermore, it is in the great works of man, as embodied in philosophy and art, that we come across the active creation of humanity. We could show that, under the impulse of reason, philosophy tends toward the establishment of rational communication and the claim of a universal validity—which is best demonstrated in philosophy's language and its systematic character. We could also show that all philosophers tend to say the same thing beyond all the differences in language and doctrine (differences which are correctly emphasized by historians of philosophy and which should not be overlooked here). Yet this "same thing" is ultimately never said. The decision to practice philosophy is always unique, and so is every philosopher's chosen itinerary. Nevertheless, there may be a common but undeterminable center for all these perspectives, since all philosophers have their humanity in common. The same is true of art. As with every act of reflection, every creation could be said to envision a single and equally undeterminable end.[17] Even if all artists do not have the same intention, at least they all possess a common inquietude and will. A secret kinship exists among works that surpasses the differences occasioned by technique, temperament, or even the multiplicity of the arts themselves. In the last analysis, this kinship accounts for the possibility of analogies, correspondences, and transcriptions between works. Works of art communicate at their most profound level.

On this basis, we can begin to understand the legitimacy of a

17. It is on this point that we disagree with Hegel and any messianic theory that posits an end to history or an absolute knowledge which corresponds to a complete realization of humanity and, perhaps, to the definitive identification of God with man. Humanity is only a possibility, that is, a hope and a task. It is not surprising that Hegel announces the death of art. If everything can be said rationally and consciousness equals self-consciousness, then the language of art ends by being useless.

general knowledge of the work whose possibility is established by a critique of affectivity. I can employ the word "joy" as an admittedly imperfect name for the Mozartian world, and thus rediscover the general beneath the singular, because Mozart is more than Mozart and recaptures humanity within himself. The work expresses a singular experience which, however, harbors within itself—and eminently so—a human essence. In contrast, my recognition of the human in Callicles could be the result of the fact that Callicles presents merely external signs of humanity and that he is thus identified as an object would be, that is, without my sensing him to be a brother. But my recognition of human joy in Mozart's *Jupiter* Symphony involves an identification through participation. Feeling means participation, and we participate in the symphony because it presents more than just external signs. It presents a way in which the human may be assumed. A work's singular essence, therefore, is not a means of dressing, adorning, or camouflaging a human essence. The work's essence does not weave variations on a given theme or add specific differences to a preexistent genus. A work's singular essence is, rather, a means of realizing a human essence by assuming the human condition precisely in its singularity. The only way to be man is to be oneself. The work of art bears witness to the universal because it accepts this condition, that is, because it is itself. It is possible to argue that the work is capable of serving as a model not only for those who imitate it but also for those who recognize themselves within it—and for the reason that it itself has not followed a model. The work bears the general within it because the general does not act as something outside the work which must be reproduced but rather as something within the work. In other words, the truth of the work, that which subjects it to conceptual language, is internal to the work and implies the very singularity which causes the work to rebel against conceptual language. The work of art is, then, that singular essence which attains the universal because it takes singularity as far as it can go. Hence the work is permeated with a universal without ever losing its uniqueness. The work is capable of awakening within us a general *a priori* knowledge which lies at the heart of feeling, much as the universal is found at the heart of the singular.

There is, however, another reason why categories can be applied to singular affective qualities. As we have just seen, the singular may harbor the general. But, conversely, the general may harbor the singular. This latter relation results less from the general's logical character than from its psychological status. A category is within me as something which is myself or, at least, as a standard that I bear within myself in order to measure the import of the aesthetic message. The clarification of feeling by means of categories is not so much a matter of subsuming an act of perception under a concept which is possessed *a priori* as of confronting the aesthetic object with myself. My function, in this respect, is to bear knowledge [*un savoir*], but I am so impregnated with it that it becomes indistinguishable from myself. Such knowledge is not a general idea obtained through induction and bearing the aspect of the abstract (as, for example, those characterological concepts by which we attempt to grasp the mobile and singular reality of the individual). Nor is it a mere instrument—or at least its instrumentality has the character of an animal's organs, through which the animal comes into contact with and preforms an object from its own depths. For the *a priori* is, indeed, a means of preforming the object within ourselves. When the *a priori* is applied to the singular, the human aspect of myself encounters the human elements in the object. Thus we meet, once again, that reciprocity of two depths by which we have defined feeling.

The category, therefore, can be applied to the singular because it is itself both general and singular. As knowledge [*savoir*], it is general; and as knowledge which I *am*, it is singular. Thus, although such knowledge helps in making feeling explicit (even if feeling can never be totally formulated), it cannot itself be easily clarified. This knowledge is both precise and indeterminate —precise because it is a type of knowledge, and indeterminate because this type of knowledge is within me as if it were myself. We know what the tragic is. We have no trouble recognizing the tragic in any particular work and distinguishing it from those elements which have become intermingled with it to compose the unique quality of the particular work. And yet are we capable of saying exactly what the tragic is? Our knowledge of it is certain, illuminating, and yet also undefinable. Our knowledge is like a sort of prescience which needs to be continually converted into science but is the basis without which science is impossible. For this reason, it would be tempting to argue that this type of knowledge is also a type of feeling, with the result that what makes feeling possible would also be of the nature of feeling. And we can very well claim that we have a feeling of what the tragic is. But, by stressing what is hidden and indeterminate about such knowledge, the view that it is of the nature of feeling fails to accentuate its *a priori* character and the fact that it constitutes a system of references for aesthetic experience. What is unique about feeling is that it is awakened only in the presence of the object. Furthermore, if feeling is an intimate knowledge [*connaissance*], it is because we already possess an implicit knowledge [*savoir*], that is, a system of affective categories by means of which we are able to recognize the human countenance of the world. Therefore such implicit knowledge cannot be confused with feeling, for which it is the transcendental condition. It is like feeling in its implicit and undefinable nature, but it is, above all, a means of gaining an intimate knowledge of the object. It is the *a priori* idea of man and of the human world, just as the pure concepts of the understanding constitute the *a priori* idea of nature.

This preconceptual knowledge of the human is fundamentally the mark of our humanity within us. It represents the possibility of putting ourselves into harmony with other men. We are men not only because we assume the being of man through the existential *a priori* which we are but also because we bear within ourselves an implicit knowledge of man through the cognitive *a priori* which are activated in aesthetic perception. There is nothing human which is foreign to us. The form of the human lies within us and is known intimately by us. Every sign of the human revives within us an intimate knowledge which precedes all experience and by which experience is clarified.[18] But this is not a completely finished and elaborated sort of knowledge. It is, rather, a sort of familiarity in the sense of a way of being. Because it belongs to the being of the subject, we can say that this

18. We should say about all living beings what we have just said about the human. We are not only alive but also have an intimate knowledge of life. We are originally in harmony with life. For this reason, we grasp life's processes at first sight. There is a sort of affinity between consciousness and life, not only in that consciousness emerges from life and that duration is a result of life, but also in that consciousness has the power of knowing life. Consciousness does not face life as it would sheer matter, that is, equipped only with a few very general categories which simply outline a hollow form of nature. Consciousness faces life, rather, as it does the human, with a presentiment of its concrete determinations. Therefore consciousness is not only borne along by life but is in collaboration with life and capable of understanding life from within, as Bergson has shown. Even the case of simple physical matter can be understood anew in these terms. The metaphors we use in speaking of matter evince a certain familiarity with matter, almost a kinship with it. Nothing cosmic is foreign to one, either. [Implicitly in the last sentence, and explicitly in the text above, Dufrenne alludes to the epigram of Terence: "Homo sum: humani nihil me alienum puto."—Trans.]

cognitive *a priori,* which clarifies for us the existential *a priori* manifested by the aesthetic object, is itself existential. But suffice it to say that we are speaking here of a primordial knowing [*savoir primitif*] which exists within us as a *habitus* controlling and orienting our articulated knowledge [*savoir formulé*]. We are not, in this way, taking anything away from articulated knowledge but, rather, furnishing articulated knowledge with a sure foundation and guarantee. We can come to know man intimately—we can become familiar with him—because we bear within ourselves a tacit knowledge of the human through which humanity is possible.

[III] THE POSSIBILITY OF A PURE AESTHETICS

A BASIC QUESTION, however, has been left unanswered. We have just spoken of affective categories, discovered their presence at the heart of feeling, and, for better or worse, defined their status. But we have not yet said what they are. Is it possible to construct a table of these categories? What we have said so far would seem to call for a negative response to this question. This is so for two reasons. One pertains to the object of these categories, and the other to the subject which bears them. These same reasons guarantee the categories' applicability to the experience of singular objects while denying their ultimate determinability. Of course, the example of Kant's *Critique of Pure Reason* may be invoked. Was that work not successful in enumerating the *a priori* of representation? Was not the foremost project of the first *Critique*—over and above the effort to establish their *a priori* status—to construct a table of these categories? However, it is on this very point that Heidegger reproaches Kant and argues that, as a result of Kant's concern with setting up such a table, he was led to consider the categories in the articulated form they assume as elements of a pure science rather than in their original form, before being explicated as synthetic principles. (Still, Heidegger admits that Kant initiated a theory of schematism which would not only explain the subsumption of the perceived object under the concept but also permit a glimpse of the schema as the root of the concept). In view of the original aspect of *a priori* knowledge, that is, its status in man, we seem to have little hope of constructing a definitive chart of *a priori* categories. This is a point to which we shall return. But we are also discouraged for another reason, which has to do with the object of *a priori* knowledge. It was a legitimate enterprise, arising from the nature of his subject matter, for Kant to submit the representational *a priori* to an act of rationalization. They are the *a priori* of a knowledge of nature, and, because they define the conditions for objectivity, they are themselves easily objectified. It would, in fact, be difficult to define a state prior to these categories during which they would be prescience and not yet science. Because the affective categories are concerned with the human, however, they retain in their generality something of that singularity which they connote, as well as acquiring a certain indeterminacy from their proper object. With this we touch on the converse of the proposition which we have just examined, namely, that the singular takes on something of the general. There is something general in man, but this quality of generality is (1) tied to the singular, and (2) not generalizable. If there is a human nature, it is not in the sense of a determinate nature [*une nature naturée*],[19] but rather of a destiny for a freedom. The affective categories are not so objectifiable, because they themselves have a lesser claim to objective validity in regard to their subject matter. The subject is incapable of being certain about himself in the same way that he can be certain concerning nature. He is incapable of knowing whether there is a zero degree of passion in himself, while he does know of a zero degree of a particular quality. The subject is also incapable of knowing the composition of antagonistic motives in the way that we can know the composition of physical forces. The error of most attempts at philosophical anthropology has been their effort to apply the *a priori* of nature to man.

As human categories, the affective categories are, in fact, more concrete than the categories of nature and, at the same time, indefinite in number. One may wonder why Kant's pure science of nature does not involve more precise *a priori* which could deal with gravitation, velocity, or force. But we know that Kant took care precisely to limit the empire of his *a priori* and that he distinguished the transcendental not only from the empirical but also from the metaphysical. In Kantian terms, the reason for this limitation is clear. The *a priori* of representation appear in reference to a pure intuition which does no more than

19. An allusion to Spinoza's notion of *natura naturata,* as set forth in his *Ethics.*—Trans.

give form to phenomena. As soon as content is added by means of empirical intuition, the *a priori* vanishes into that for which it serves as a foundation. The affective categories, however, are limited by no such condition. The mode of the given to which they refer has the character of feeling rather than of intuition, for the human cannot be given by intuition—unless it is understood as an object of nature, in which case it is not truly human. Feeling, moreover, is already concrete. Even if we take the affective categories in their cosmological rather than their existential aspect (i.e., in terms of how they determine features of the world), they do not refer to an intuitable nature. What they determine precedes any distinction between the physical and the mental. Understood as an atmosphere, the world is no more nature than it is a represented world. For this reason, as well, affective categories cannot be determined in terms of a pure intuition which they would be in charge of ordering, as causality orders succession. If affective categories are founded on sensibility, it is on a sensibility entirely different from that set forth in the Transcendental Aesthetic. It is, rather, a sensibility—or, better, a sensitivity—to a world whose soul is constituted by these affective categories. They are, furthermore, always related reciprocally to human categories. Hence an *a priori* of man cannot be abstract and determined in the same way as an *a priori* of nature, because man is a being who is not determined according to different elementary dimensions. Rather, man determines himself in relation to many differing situations which he recognizes as such, and he can make multiple decisions concerning himself and assume various guises.

In addition, men—or, as Jaspers calls them, *Existenzen*—are not numerable entities subject to a system. The same is true for works of art, which can be classified according to genre, material, or technique, but which cannot be classified from the point of view of their existential truth. The relationships of opposition and similarity which are instituted by means of affective categories defy all objective classification and overturn the order of space and time. Nevertheless, these relationships are real, even if they are no longer subject to objective systematization. They exist on the level of communication. It is true that two men or two works, as well as the worlds expressed by the works, can be discovered or shown to be similar. This does not mean that, from our perspective, there is a truth which is external to these men or to these worlds—a truth which illuminates their similarities and oppositions—or even an external schema into which they can be integrated.[20] Men and worlds alike are a truth unto themselves. But this truth which men are, although unique insofar as it derives from them alone, is not beyond comparison, because men do allow themselves to become similar to one another and because, even in their singularity, they are delegates of humanity. Thus, although Jaspers insists on the unique character of truth and asserts that "an *Existenz* . . . will understand its choice of truth as the leap to the true originality,"[21] he nevertheless attempts a *Psychologie der Weltanschauungen,* that is, an inventory of the attitudes a subject may take, the corresponding "world images," and "a systematic construction of types of spirit."[22] His project is not so different from that of Hegel's *Phenomenology of Mind,* which also contains an inventory of the "forms of consciousness." Although the latter are spread out in history, through their successive appearance consciousness is made equal with itself and humanity realizes itself. A theory of human attitudes, however, is possible only if it denies itself as theory, that is, on condition of being assured that it cannot know and classify the human as an object and that it can speak of the human only with caution and only because the human lends itself to such a treatment. Throughout all this, furthermore, it must not alienate what is unconditional and incomparable within the human. Like human attitudes, affective categories (which allow us to apprehend these attitudes) are known implicitly without being capable of definition or enumeration. This all takes place as if our knowledge must always be incomplete, and yet we bear this knowledge within us as a potentiality without which we would know man only as an object and the world only as nature.

The second reason that knowledge of affective categories cannot lead to an objective science has to do, not with the object

20. This is true, even though we can reveal objective causes of an intimate relationship among diverse works by means of an analysis of the structures of these works, because these causes never function as the ultimate motif in which the aesthetic experience is realized. They appear only in the light of aesthetic experience.

21. Karl Jaspers, *Philosophy,* trans. E. B. Ashton (Chicago: University of Chicago Press, 1967), I, 363.

22. Jaspers' project is all the more legitimate because it has to do with spiritual types and not with existence, whose notion had not yet been elaborated by Jaspers at the time of the publication of *Psychologie der Weltanschauungen* (Berlin: Springer, 1922). While man is unique as existence, he takes on an impersonal dimension as spirit, since as spirit he is capable of reason and rational communication. Jaspers will argue that there is no existence without a subtending spirit, just as there is no man without a participation in humanity.

of such knowledge, but rather with its status in the subject, that is, with its subjective being. Kant approached the idea of this subjective being in terms of his theory of the imagination. However, he did not stress subjective being because of his overriding concern with the function of the *a priori*. As we have shown, the affective category is like an instrument which we use without being fully aware of how it works and in such a way that it is never completely exhausted by reflection. Consequently, the *a priori* is not inside me like an essence which has been deposited in my understanding and can be extracted as from a pigeonhole. Rather, the *a priori* is within me like a *habitus,* that is, like a sort of *a priori* sense of taste. Like an affective category, taste possesses the character of a confused and yet evident knowledge [*connaissance*] which anticipates and prepares the way for experience. Taste is a way of reacting with all one's being, as we see when we react negatively in disgust. It also manifests a power of anticipation, in the sense that it is, as Pradines calls it, an "outpost" in the experience of contact. The possession of taste presupposes discernment in the apprehension of certain values. This discernment presupposes, in turn, that a certain sense for these values and their hierarchy is present within us in virtue of certain fundamental tendencies, such as those analyzed by Sartre. Therefore, just as taste appreciates, chooses, and gains an intimate knowledge of its object without ever knowing itself, so do the affective categories. There can, furthermore, be an essence of affective categories, although such an essence cannot be formulated except by reflection.

In speaking of the table of artistic values mentioned earlier, Souriau indicates that these essences come from reflection and that they possess a "reflective role which necessarily follows on the real accomplishment of the creative process." [23] We would add to this, however, that they also follow upon the prereflective and yet certain consciousness which we bear within us. It is such certitude that is, in our opinion, the sign of the *a priori.* If we were to follow Scheler's example and try to define the essence of the tragic, we would have difficulty in enunciating that essence clearly.[24] We would hesitate, fumble, return to the empirical, and invoke singular works each of which expresses a certain aspect of the tragic. We would thus give the impression

23. Souriau, "Art et vérité," p. 185.
24. See Max Scheler, "On the Tragic," in *Tragedy: Modern Essays in Criticism,* ed. L. Michel and R. B. Sewell (Englewood Cliffs, N.J.: Prentice-Hall, 1963).—Trans.

of arriving at our definition by means of induction and generalization. Yet our very choice of examples and the definitions we propose are inspired and guided by a preliminary knowledge. We would not even be able to attempt such a definition unless we had already found and were in possession of the very essence which we are incapable of formulating. Just as there are essences of affective categories, there is also, no doubt, a table of such essences which would inspire the distinctions and classifications I attempt to formulate. But this table is also hidden in preconceptual knowledge in such a way that I can never master it totally. My very awareness that all articulated systems are only approximations attests to an active knowledge (which, however, is not explicit) of a system which acts as a norm for our attempts. This is not the same awareness that I have of the approximate nature of empirical systems—like Mendeleev's periodic table or a botanical classification, that is, systems which apply to a given domain of nature. In these cases, I know that the system is postulated as a necessary aid to intelligibility and that it can always be put in doubt by subsequent discoveries in such a way that this sort of research can proceed indefinitely. In the case of affective categories, in contrast, we are dealing with a plurality of possible worlds which correspond to a certain range of human possibilities. We are men only because we bear within ourselves possibilities by which we recognize those similar to us. The system is given within us. However, the system is given as a virtuality which is never completely realized. Thus it is not the research which proceeds indefinitely—as when the object of investigation is nature, which is an "other" and which is established as other by being separated from the researcher in order to be considered in terms of objectivity—but the effort at formalization, the becoming aware of the immediate consciousness that we have of the human. Reflection is indefinite because it attempts to become equal to the unreflective life of consciousness.

Therefore we cannot devise a definition or exhaustive inventory of affective categories, even though they form an *a priori* for aesthetic feeling. A pure aesthetics cannot be constituted definitively.[25] This is true even though reflection can always at-

25. This leads to the paradoxical result that the critique of affectivity which we have outlined ends by confessing that the articulation of the *a priori* can never be fully accomplished. Perhaps Kant would have arrived at the same conclusion concerning the *a priori* of reflection, if he had not been so concerned to construct a table of these *a priori*—that is, if he had taken into account history (which puts every static system into question),

tempt to force a translation into conceptual language of that aptitude within us which is the affective category and to map the scope of the knowledge [*savoir*] it constitutes in us. As we indicated at the beginning of this chapter, such an effort on the part of reflection has a legitimacy and a utility which we would not dispute. The limits encountered by reflection, moreover, in no sense invalidate the objectivity of the affective categories. The knowledge which the affective categories constitute in us inspires and orients us—without our ever being clearly conscious of it, since, in a sense, it *is* ourselves, just as the artist is his work. There is not enough distance between ourselves and such knowledge to enable us to gain a single panoramic view of it. Subjectivity never allows itself to be known completely, because it knows itself only through its acts. In other words, the *a priori* is known only through [*sur*] the *a posteriori.* Considered in its constitutive aspect, the *a priori* is known only through the object which it constitutes. Considered in its existential aspect, the *a priori* is known only in our concrete operations and in the actual use we make of it. Similarly, the table of affective categories, which we bear within ourselves as our essential ability to know the human and which we grasp only by means of a reflective and always provisional knowledge [*connaissance*], is known only through our experience with the aesthetic object.

There is even a further reason for the frailty of such knowledge—a reason which can be contrasted with Kantian dogmatism. Simply stated, it is a matter of the historicity of aesthetic experience, that is, both the historicity of art and the historicity of subjectivity. We shall consider the two separately.

If it is true that, although the affective categories are present to aesthetic experience, they are known only through reflection on that experience, then a system of aesthetic objects must be given before the system of categories can be completely known. Yet there does not appear to be any such system of aesthetic objects, and the history of art reads like a history of unforeseeable innovations. All that we can foresee is that no innovation will take us entirely unaware. This is certainly a strong claim, but how can we escape it? If we really do possess an ability to understand man, then we should not be surprised at his future.

---

and, on the other hand, if he had paid greater attention to the status of these *a priori,* a factor on which Heidegger lays great stress. Considering that the *a priori* is rooted in subjectivity, clearly it cannot be grasped in its original state. We realize today that even pure mathematics and pure physics are never completely realized.

Our acquaintance with his past should lead to a like acquaintance with his future. This is why new works tend to encounter indifference, surprise, or sarcasm. Only a few are able to recognize and accept new works, and they are those in whom the works arouse a knowledge which prepares the way for their acceptance. Here a category has been "ready" for such works, a category which their presence revived and which reflection can elaborate. Thus we see how the unity of the human is possible and how men can call each other forth. The voice made eloquent by art can be heard only if it arouses a latent knowledge of the human within us. Conversely, the voice is necessary if the knowledge is to be aroused, since the *a priori* is revealed only in [*dans*] the *a posteriori*. Now, this voice represents what is unforeseeable in history—a history that could be purely contingent. The appearance of a new work which illustrates a category to which we have as yet paid no attention may not be ordered by logical development. Even when the artistic innovation situates itself within a tradition and a historical context, it remains an unexpected revelation. Any logic in the movement of the aesthetic through history probably arises from a retrospective illusion.

In any event, we can be assured that the history of art has not come to an end. Not only will new nuances appear as a result of the uniqueness of every work, but so will new affective categories for which no former work, style, or genre can account. It has been said that love is an invention of the twelfth century. This means that Provençal poetry revealed a world of courtliness which would otherwise have remained buried in the entrails of the *a priori*. Similarly, a world of virile passion may never have been revealed without Corneille, or a world of spiritual dance without Bach. There is even a certain tone to the contemporary novel—a sense of distress, cruelty, and dereliction through which passes the Stoic *commendatus sibi,* but in this case against the setting of a dark and irrational world—which is difficult to name precisely but is still unmistakable.[26] Can we not claim that it has alerted the public to a certain zone of the affective *a priori* on which former art had not touched? One might object that in this way the idea of the *a priori* is undermined. As soon as we invoke history, do we not come to the conclusion that art imposes on us a form of sensibility which did not exist before art, and, moreover, that such a form of sensibility was not in-

26. Jean Cayrol has spoken of a "leprous literature." It is significant that such a world appeared at moments in the work of Malraux, Céline, and Sartre at the same time as the era of Fascist violence.

vented by art itself but, rather, imposed on the artist by the time in which he lived (with the result that artist and public understand one another precisely because they are both formed by their times)? Céline is not an inventor of a world of despair who inculcates his readers with a notion of this world. It is, rather, the despair of the real world which invents Céline and, at the same time, his public. Such a point of view cannot be ignored. Everything does, indeed, look as if artist and public express the historical moment in which they are living, in the precise sense that an art of preciosity could not be conceived and experienced in an age in which preciosity does not flourish, or a cruel art in a noncruel society. Now, to convert such historical influence into determinism is the procedure of an unrestrained dogmatism. But the influence itself, that is, the reality implied in this term, cannot be disputed. It needs only to be observed that, if the artist does express his time, then the very intention which he occasionally states explicitly—as during periods in which committed literature [*littérature engagée*] flourishes—of becoming conscious of his time and expressing it, provides evidence that he is not purely and simply determined. If he were, why should he wish, even out of presumption, to be a determining force? Belonging to one's time does not mean being determined by this time. We cannot doubt that the public too belongs to a particular historical period, a period in which appear the forms of art and art objects that will propose themselves to this public. Thus we must now consider the historicity of the subject, in order to realize that we are not surreptitiously undercutting the very notion of affective categories.

If, in principle, we are able to open ourselves up to any work of art, feel its affective qualities, and then recognize what it expresses, in fact and in good faith we are more or less sensitive to certain works and more or less indisposed toward others. It is thus that we belong to our time—by being open to certain expressions and closed to others. We should remember here what Scheler has said of values, namely, that they constitute an absolute which escapes the relativity of history and the subjectivity of consciousness. Not even the freedom of consciousness, which Comte had already subjected to scrutiny, can be invoked to introduce relativity into the absoluteness of values. Yet our consciousness of this absolute can vary. The magic lantern of history changes position in different epochs, in such a way that certain values appear completely illuminated while others are hidden in shadow. There exists, therefore, an essential historicity of what

Scheler calls "the ethos," that is, a historicity of the feeling of values and of their hierarchy. Furthermore, we cannot separate "their history from the history of [our] knowledge of them." [27] We can reasonably make a similar case for the ethos of affective categories, provided that we resolve the difficulties raised by Scheler. For it is perhaps inconsistent to claim that a system of values can be definitively brought to closure, while asserting that our perspective on these values varies according to history. This argument does not give enough credit to history. We need to admit that the philosopher is himself in a historical situation, in order to avoid granting him exorbitant privileges and situating him at the end, or outside, of history. The philosopher is capable of propounding systematically only what is given to him to apprehend by virtue of his situation. It is true that he must strive to transcend his situation, but such an effort itself attests to the reality of this situation.

This inconsistency on Scheler's part stems from an ambiguity in his very notion of the *a priori*. On the one hand, he distinguishes between the *a priori* and the innate.[28] Instead of being immanent to consciousness (as if every consciousness were a creator, or at least a bearer, of values), values are said to be given in a pure experience, without any material content (i.e., without being represented in a *Bilderfahrung*) and also independently of acts of evaluation. The *a priori* quality of values signifies the objectivity of an essence which owes nothing to the subject. Thus the phenomenological experience which delivers the *a priori* is an "essential intuiting" or *Wesensschau*.[29] One either has this experience or not, and when the *a priori* is possessed, the very possession of such an absolute is itself an absolute.[30] On the other hand, Scheler subordinates this possession of the *a priori* to the being of the subject and, more precisely, to the "person" within him. For a person is not only tied to his own

27. Max Scheler, *Formalism in Ethics and Non-Formal Ethics of Values*, trans. Manfred S. Frings and Roger L. Funk (Evanston, Ill.: Northwestern University Press, 1973), p. 296; cf. pp. 80, 215. Is it necessary, however, to privilege the spiritual life of a civilization over its material life? Perhaps it is sufficient to say that the ethos is the most revealing element in a society, the thread that guides the historian in the analysis of the society's character. But an understanding of a society means an understanding of it as a totality from the functionalist perspective, without attempting to explicate some predominant factor.

28. *Ibid.*, pp. 78 f.

29. Dufrenne refers here to Husserl's and Scheler's notion of *Wesensschau*: "intuition of essence" or "essential insight."—Trans.

30. See Scheler, *Formalism in Ethics*, p. 48.

values (there are values of a person, as well as of life and of spirit) but is also capable of grasping the highest values and hence the possibility of their hierarchy. The person, therefore, is the indispensable receiver of values. This holds even more for the collective person than for the singular person, since the collective person is a "community of persons" which remains an individual and possesses an autonomous consciousness capable of an original outlook. In this way, and with echoes of Hegel and of Durkheim, the idea of a historicity of values is revived—a historicity which is essential. But it does not seem, then, that the absolute and the relative aspects of the *a priori* have been reconciled. We could say that it is characteristic of values, to the extent that they are *a priori,* to appear as absolute and yet to do so historically. But, given the historicity of the appearance of values, how can we be sure that this historicity does not bear on their very being (as is claimed by relativists) and that we are not thus prevented from establishing a table of values?

If we are to take seriously the historicity of affective categories, it seems that we can avoid this impasse only on two conditions. First, we must give up the idea of establishing a definitive table. Second, we must give the *a priori* a physiognomy which is different from Scheler's, by accepting the fact that, as we have tried to show, the *a priori* is virtual and immanent and consubstantial with the subject.[31] Most important, by admitting that the *a priori* belongs to the virtual, we can finally understand how it is compatible with historicity. For the *a priori* must be *actualized*—and in the history either of an individual or of a civilization. In other words, an occasion must be given to the *a priori*—an occasion in which (in the case of the affective *a priori*) it is in contact with the aesthetic object—to become active and to manifest itself to the reflection which will make it explicit. Its appearing is therefore historical. Yet its being escapes historicity, since it lies at the origin of history, which has no meaning without it. Hence the various systems of geometry have no meaning independent of their relationship to a natural geometry of which they are the extraordinary and unforeseeable development. This example has implications for the historicity of the aesthetic object. Without a constantly contingent encounter with the work of art, that is, without a history of art,

31. It is thus that we would like to revive Scheler's theory of values. If values are given to feeling, it is because they are not given as objective essences but as the feeling of a possible evaluation which allows us to understand the meaning of a moral choice or judgment.

there would be no history of affective categories, since they would remain within us as unawakened. They would not be absent but, instead, implicit and unused. The *a priori* is actualized only through the *a posteriori*. However, this presupposes, once again, that the *a priori* belongs to the virtual, that it is my possibility of invoking a category rather than the category itself, which only appears after the fact and in history.

Yet the claim that the *a priori* belongs to the virtual implies the further claim that the *a priori* functions as a power at the disposal of subjectivity. We have mentioned the existential aspect of the affective quality which is an *a priori* for the work. Now we are led to argue that the implicit knowledge of this *a priori* is itself an existential *a priori*. Just as the world of the work expresses the absolute position of creative subjectivity, the recognition of this world by means of affective categories expresses the absolute position of a receptive subjectivity and the coefficient of humanity which is actively assumed by this subjectivity. The *a priori* is a characteristic of knowledge only because it is first and foremost the mode of being of a subject. I am conscious of the *a priori* in the same way that I am conscious of myself, because affective categories *are* myself as the bearer of virtualities. But consciousness is not knowledge. Thus affective categories can become the object only of a tedious reflection and not of a *Wesensschau*. Furthermore, since this virtual knowledge is immanent to subjectivity, we can also argue that it is historical. For subjectivity comes stamped with historicity, if we understand historicity not in a technical but in an existential sense. What I am is historical. This is so not only because I have a personal history and am inscribed in a general history in which I am actualized but also because I am the ordering principle of all history through the initial affirmation which constitutes me and which transcends considerations of temporality. Historicity designates the union of nature and freedom which defines a concrete subject. Historicity therefore expresses the limitation which dictates that an involvement in history means a submission to the constraints imposed on the subject who, nevertheless, realizes himself through these constraints. As the ordering principle of history, the subject consents to this limitation not merely to be subject to the limitation which is attached to every actualization of the virtual (with all the contingency involved in such actualization) but also to be constantly limited even in his virtualities. It may be true that each of us dies as a singular being, since we enter into history by a continual sacrifice of the possible to the real. Still, it is not entirely true that we are born in the plural—or at least not in an indefinitely numerous plural. Being born means to expose oneself to finitude and (let us leave to metaphysics the debate over the precise role of freedom) to choose or accept oneself as finite. For this reason, the actualization of the virtual encounters a double limitation: on one side, from history and its contingencies; and, on the other, from the historicity of the subject (who, because of what he is, can recognize only certain categories and must remain blind to others). Thus, on the one hand, the subject may have to encounter an actual work by Mozart before he can know himself to be capable of recognizing tenderness, just as there may have to be a war before he can know himself to be capable of courage or cowardice. Like a historical event, the presence of the aesthetic object provides the subject with opportunities to know the *a priori* of which he is the bearer. On the other hand, he must admit that understanding Mozart involves the risk of failing to understand other affective qualities. In short, the subject can understand only on the basis of his finitude. And the finitude of subjectivity is revealed in what it excludes, in its choices, and in its inabilities—particularly the inability to understand everything or to take on all the characteristics of the human.

It is, in fact, common for certain affective categories to remain foreign to certain individuals. The relativity of aesthetic tastes derives from this lack of comprehension. Aesthetic objects leave those who do not understand their expression indifferent, an indifference which manifests itself in various forms, such as ignorance or disdain. A particular epoch can also be blind to certain categories. The categories illustrated by the Gothic cathedral were not current in the seventeenth century, just as those illustrated by Molière found no audience in Rousseau, or those of Rousseau himself no acceptance by Jacques Maritain. It is possible, moreover, that the reasons for Rousseau's condemnation of Molière or Maritain's of Rousseau may have nothing to do with art, stemming instead from ethical or political reflection. Thus one can condemn a work of art without being insensitive to it. Indeed, one may condemn a work precisely to combat a strong attraction to it. In any event, a particular human dimension can remain foreign to us in the same way that the world of religion can remain closed to an atheist, or the world of a particular primitive tribe to an ethnologist. It is difficult to dispute the fact that our understanding of the human—which determines the range of affective categories to which we are sensitive—remains limited.

Still, an uncertainty remains for which we have not accounted by our recourse to experience. Must those limits imposed by lack of comprehension be attributed to the finitude of the virtual within us, or must they be attributed to the historicity of actualization as well? In other words, does the finitude of the subject entail the finitude of the virtual or merely the finitude of its actualization? Must we say that the *a priori* knowledge of affective categories, beyond being incapable of total actualization, cannot in itself be total? Strictly speaking, this would be the case only if such knowledge were within us as something as independent of our being as contents are of their container, that is, if it were a matter of a virtuality which we possess rather than one which we *are*. But this virtuality *is* ourselves. We are defined by this power by whose means we rediscover ourselves in the midst of others and their world. If it is not the fruit, it is at least the style, of our freedom. It is manifested in our projects, our relationships with other human beings, the world, and, especially, with aesthetic objects. But even though this power is ourselves, we must recognize that it is finite. And such a recognition may force us to modify our own previous claims. Can we any longer say that the subject is truly coextensive with humanity, and that there is nothing human in the past or the future to which he remains foreign?

However, a different and perhaps preferable interpretation is also possible, one which does not stamp the virtual with this sort of incapacity. In our comparison of the receptive *a priori* with the creative *a priori*—wherein we attributed to the receptive the character of existentiality we had at first given to the creative—we did not mean to confound the two. We must maintain, between them, the distance from the lived to the cognitive and from the work to its public. In a wider sense, since every man bears a unique world within himself which he does not convert into an aesthetic object in the way an artist does, the distance in question is that between a certain style of life which we adopt and a certain knowledge which we have of the human. In other words, it is the distance between the possibility of a concrete action and the possibility of an act of understanding. In spite of what we have said about the consubstantiality of the subject and the *a priori,* we may also call it the distance between being and having. Even though we are both what we can do and what we can know, we are not the two in the same manner. The existential *a priori* is what we are immediately and through all our experience, just as Mozart remains Mozart throughout all of his works. In Spinoza's terms, the existential *a priori* is the idea which we are as represented eternally in the divine understanding. The cognitive *a priori* is also what we are. But in this case it is the result of a power we possess, and it depends on the use we make of this power. Furthermore, though these two types of *a priori* are both singular, insofar as they are both finally existential, they do not have the same scope or possess the same logical status. The existential *a priori* retains the character of the person for whom it is the index. It is unique and inexpressible. The cognitive *a priori* retains the character of the knowledge of which it is the instrument. It is general and, instead of being man's specific difference, is that factor in man which makes him man. Hence a double relationship is instituted between these two kinds of *a priori,* a relationship which accentuates their differences. The existential *a priori* can become the object of the cognitive *a priori,* since the latter permits the former to be known in the same way as the aesthetic object. Conversely, the cognitive *a priori* is subordinate to the existential *a priori,* insofar as the singularity of our being is what orients the actualization of the virtual knowledge at our disposal.

In terms of this distinction, therefore, it is possible to comprehend that such virtual knowledge is not itself limited within us and that only its actualization in history is limited. The fact that we find ourselves closed to certain aesthetic expressions does not mean that our basic capacity is at fault but that there is something wrong with the use we make of that capacity. And this utilization is directed by what we are. The finitude or, better, the historicity of the existential *a priori* is what is responsible for the fragmentation of our knowledge and the singularity of our taste. It is the same finitude we find strikingly present in the unique and finite works of a given artist. These works also cannot express everything. On the contrary, they tend to say the same thing over and over again. Can we even conceive of the grotesque in Mozart, the noble in Daumier, or the precious in Faulkner? The aesthetic object expresses a world, not the cosmos of affective categories. By the same token, our sensibility to certain of these categories expresses the singularity of our being.

In any event, whether finitude is attached to the actualization of the virtual or to the virtual itself, it is impossible to deny the historicity of aesthetic comprehension. This fact alone should be sufficient to show the presumptuousness of any theory of affective categories which claims to be definitive. And such a theory is the work of reflection, and reflection comes only after the fact. Thus reflection occurs only after history has exhibited the objects which solicit the actualization of affective categories, and after the person—the concrete subject and also the collective person to which he is united—has, in accordance with his existential *a priori*, decided which categories will be actualized, that is, to which aesthetic objects he will be sensitive. Reflection can grasp the categories only provisionally and only to the extent that they become actualized in the flow of history, in accordance with how aesthetic objects appear and become known. There is no separate cosmos of these objects, just as there is no cosmos of the human. The claim that affective categories are never totally actualized rests on the further claim that man never brings a total comprehension of the human into play. Humanity is never totally transparent to itself or reconciled with itself. Men are continually blind to some aspect of man. History is the history of the dramas which arise from this ignorance. As a result, history is like a reproachful presence. Finitude is our lot and yet also our responsibility. Although there is always something left for us to understand, it seems that we also always possess the means to do so. Consequently, affective categories are still within us, even when we make no use of them. Thus if we are blind to the aesthetic object or if our taste is relative, this is no one's fault but our own.

But now we must ask if that human dimension which is within us as virtual and is also in the aesthetic object—through which the virtual is actualized—is not also to be found in the real? Does not this human dimension need to exist in the real if the aesthetic object is to be designated as "true"? And does not the *a priori*, by which the aesthetic object is constituted and which is itself known in an *a priori* manner, that is, an *a priori* that is both existential and constitutive, have to be constitutive not only of the world of the aesthetic object but of the real as well? Such are the questions which we must next attempt to answer.

18 / The Truth of the Aesthetic Object

THUS WE TAKE UP AGAIN the problem of the identity of the cosmological and the existential in the affective *a priori,* and precisely at the point where we left it in order to consider both the characteristic which the *a priori* has of being known in an *a priori* way through an affective category and the possibility that this characteristic opens the way to a pure aesthetics. Now we wish to discern the relationship between the world of the aesthetic object, of which the *a priori* is the affective quality, and the real world. In other words, we shall query whether the affective quality, which is an *a priori* for the world of the aesthetic object, is also an *a priori* for the real world. It is on this condition that the identity of the cosmological and the existential gains its full meaning and finally orients reflection, that is, reflection on the relationship between subject and object at the heart of being. Insofar as one restricts consideration to the aesthetic object in itself, this identity can have only an empirical meaning (which is, however, not negligible). It certifies that the creator expresses himself in the work and that the work delivers the world of the creator, as we have observed. But this anthropological exegesis appears insufficient as soon as one considers the natural aesthetic object. In the latter case, it is the real world which the affective quality governs. It is the real which speaks to us, without any particular someone's speaking through it. But how is nature capable of being aestheticized? The relationship which is established is no longer that of the object with its creator but of the object with us. But how does it happen that nature manifests this affinity with us? Now, we shall not attack this problem as such, since we have decided to limit ourselves to the aesthetic object and the work of art. Nevertheless, we are led to a problem which is just as important. Does the identity of the cosmological with the existential extend to the real world, not insofar as this world has been aestheticized, but to the degree that the aesthetic object is a witness to it? What can be the relation between the world of the aesthetic object—which is a unique world, since it is the world of its creator and not a real world and is bound to the represented object—and the real world.[1]

The problem which we thus encounter leads to the same problem as that posed by the examination of the natural aesthetic object, for we are still trying to discover whether and how nature elicits art, and whether there is not a being which grounds both nature and art and assures their affinity. For the moment, the problem which concerns us is that of the truth of the aesthetic object. Is the affective *a priori* which has been manifested through this object and constitutes it also constitutive with regard to the real, as are the *a priori* of presence and of representation at other levels?

One can easily see what is at stake anthropologically in this problem. By closing in on the nuanced aspects of aesthetic experience, do we not risk attenuating aesthetic experience under the pretext of preserving its purity? Above all, do we not suggest that aesthetic experience, culminating in the contemplation of the sensuous and the perusal of its expression, is pure diversion, since we have also separated it from both praxis and reflection? When we take pleasure in entering the world of the aesthetic object and thereby losing ourselves in it, it appears that we gain nothing more than the enjoyment of "an hour of oblivion." Then, as after enjoying a self-indulgent luxury, return to reality brings vague remorse at having sacrificed something. Such contemplation may also appear to be an alibi for action. At the moment when history presses in on us from all sides, we are no longer able to believe that salvation can reside in contemplation, whatever object contemplation may furnish to us. This is why an ethics of action and generosity like Sartre's must end

1. We have already pointed to this problem in the chapter on "Aesthetic Object and World." There, however, we were limited to justifying the recourse to the notion of world in order to designate that which the aesthetic object expresses.

by challenging art qua diversion, while making an exception for the arts of prose, which are placed in the service of the most urgent moral enterprise, that is, revolutionary praxis. Must we not be persuaded by our preceding analysis that art is only a game? Must not the autonomy of art lead us to justify dilettantism? Yet such a consequence appears to us to be ruinous. To avoid it, we must show how the artist is so profoundly engaged by his work that one cannot question the serious nature of his activity. The tragic character of so many artists' lives serves to confirm this seriousness. But it is not the testimony of the artist which we wish to collect. Now, one may also attempt, through a sociological analysis, to establish the reverberation and efficacy of art in the human world. Nothing would prevent us from tightening the bond that we have loosened, and, after having shown that art has a claim to its own history, locating it in its proper place in universal history in order to discern art's influence there. But we do not wish to invoke the testimony of history either. On the contrary, we must show that art is serious and can bear on history because art is *true*. And art is true for two reasons: because the signification of the aesthetic object transcends the subjectivity of the individual who expresses himself in it; and because this signification bears finally on a real world which is the locus of our judgments and decisions. The first of these two reasons has already been considered. We have seen that the singular is pregnant with the universal and that the artist, since we are able to understand him, acts as the delegate of humanity. We must now show that the human world is an aspect of the real world—in other words, that art has a cosmological function. This claim can be justified only if, on the one hand, art renders itself worthy of such a function, and if, on the other hand, the real lends itself to this function. Thus we must interrogate art and the real successively. And, in considering art, we shall make use of what the phenomenology of the aesthetic object has already suggested to us.

[I] THE AESTHETIC OBJECT AS TRUE

IN WHAT SENSE can one speak of a truth of the aesthetic object? Above all in two important senses, whose discussion will defer the solution to our problem.

(a) Two principal senses of aesthetic truth

We can say, in the first place, that the work is true with respect to itself. The work is true in that it is finished, discourages every idea of erasure or correction, and asserts itself sovereignly. One additional mark in the orchestral score, one more stroke on the canvas, and the balance would be destroyed, the form impaired. The true work is one which provides answers to every question. But such answers are not addressed to the understanding. It is in the sensuous and through the acquiescence of our body that we should test the fullness and the necessity of a "good form." Usually we do not dream of questioning this form. We are captivated by it, and it is difficult to resist the resulting impression of ease and security. If reflection exerts control over this impression, it is only when we are already familiar with the work. Thus the aesthetic object is true because nothing in it rings false, since it fully satisfies perception, answering at each instant or in each of its parts to the expectation which it awakens in our sensibility. It is to perception that the work reveals its coherence. It is the perceptible or sensuous which orders itself under our gaze with a rigor which owes nothing to logic. But it is not possible for us to be only a pure gaze which is animated and fulfilled by the object. Some other interest must be awakened in us, and the rigor of the object must be more than sensuous. Sensuous rigor must be the sign of some other rigor. Otherwise, we would be captivated without being seduced, and the perfect forms would soon appear to us as quite empty.

There is, in fact, a second kind of truth of the aesthetic object, a truth with respect to the artist. The work which is authentic and true corresponds to a necessity in the one who has created it. The authentic artist is the one who decides that his work is finished when a certain precipitation has taken place brusquely, a certain harmony has been realized in the very matter of the work—a work which prohibits all retouching. At the same time, he feels that he is himself inside the work and that the work is what he *had* to do and what was expected of him. He has the same response to a technical as to an intellectual demand, to realizing his work and to expressing himself. The *a priori* which animates him appears in the form of the work, because he has committed himself in his act of creation. For him, doing and being are the same thing. Like man, who, according to Marx, creates himself in making history, the artist creates himself in making his work—not because he merely dreams of doing it, but because he actually engages in creation. The work manifests not only a formal necessity but also an internal one, namely, the necessity at the heart of the artist who creates in terms of what he is.

For this reason, a given artist will always say the same thing. Through his techniques and choice of subjects, we recognize his peculiar mark—what we call his "style." Style is not a procedure offered to the artist as a mere means. Style is his inimitable posture, present in all the adventures which he pursues. Of course, it cannot be denied that the style of an artist is subject to change. There are sinuous careers, and all are sinuous to some degree. There are always those who search before they find. Balzac wrote serials, Rimbaud imitated Théodore de Banville. And many become lost after finding themselves, many exhaust themselves, and still others renew themselves through impulsive acts. In short, the artist is not always faithful to himself. But that can mean two quite different things—either he in fact changes his style, or he stops having one at all and thus stops being an artist. Let us consider the first case for a moment. To one who is not informed, it is quite difficult to attribute to the same Michelangelo the *Moses* and the Rondini *Pietà,* to the same Picasso *The Ironing Woman* and *Guernica,* or to the same Mozart the *Turkish March* and the *Funeral March.* But is it really the style which has changed? More often, from a blue period to a pink period, from one affiliation to another, it is the craft which has changed—the means rather than the content of the expression. One can say that our incapacity to recognize the same author, and thus the same style, because of different techniques, is due to our being accustomed to identifying the work with exterior signs and not with its more profound significations. If we were less concerned about being experts, especially when we do not have the required competence, if we would open ourselves more fully to aesthetic objects, we could discover the same meaning and the same existential necessity in apparently different works. However, it is possible for the artist to change his style and not merely his technique. A metamorphosis of the existential *a priori* is not unthinkable if one bears in mind, as we have done for the spectator, the paradox posed by the historicity of the *a priori*. At any rate, it suffices that, in order for a work to be authentic, the artist express himself as he is in the present and not as he is *sub specie aeternitatis*.

To what extent the personality of the artist commands the choice of his technique is a problem for existential psychoanalysis which we do not have to discuss. Yet it is clear that, even if we consider only the work as given in a performance, the expression of the artist's personality is inseparable from the choice of his technique. As people are judged by their looks, the artist is judged by his style. There are not two truths, one of the work and the other of the artist. The artist is indistinguishable from that which he does and from the way in which he does it.

This solidarity can be confirmed by a counterproof. An authentic work is not a true work unless it is physically completed. Many works animated by the most incontestable veracity and answering to the most urgent need to say something vital are still lacking, for want of genius—for not having realized a perfect form comparable to their inspiration. Authenticity is not by itself a guarantee of quality. Moreover, it is important to distinguish authenticity from sincerity. It is here that Hersch's warning concerning the sin of expressiveness is useful to us. To be authentic is not to be ostentatiously sincere or to achieve a good conscience cheaply by making a virtue of sincerity. To be authentic is to be beyond sincerity, to be sincere without seeking to be, by a kind of natural felicity. To express oneself is not to "tell all" and to make visible that which is merely showy in oneself. The stirring of moods and the crises of passion are, finally, masks. Expressing oneself, on the contrary, is achieved by repressing these indiscretions and by allowing what is most secret and most discreet to manifest its presence. Musset is more authentic in his *Comédies* than in *Les Nuits,* Gide in *La Porte étroite* than in *Les Nourritures terrestres,* Liszt in the *Legend of St. Francis of Paola* than in the Rhapsodies. Conversely, however, formal perfection alone does not suffice to consecrate a work. Whole garrets are filled with works by *epigoni* who fully possess the craft which they have taken from someone else but have nothing to say themselves. Such works are easily identified by the boredom which they exude, and we dismiss the artist who is only a good talker in the salons of Molière or Proust. Here one may invoke those artists who, lacking a prominent personality, are the workers within a certain aesthetic tradition and appear to carry on their craft for pleasure without having anything personal to say, similar to the way artisans create their masterpieces. These figures include anonymous Romanesque sculptors, French portrait painters of the sixteenth century, and the admirable group of French musicians from Lully to Rameau. Certainly in such cases one can speak of a collective style. But what does it matter? The essential thing is that, in looking more closely, one would see that these artists, if they recount nothing individual, nevertheless uncover something human in us and reveal a singular nuance of the human, even if it is repeated from one artist to the next. In this, they are authentic. They are so thoroughly identified with their art that, even if they are not conscious of having had something to say, they still have said something. In each school, they have opened for us a unique and irreplaceable world to which they hold the key. Musicians and architects never speak of themselves, painters are not always willing to paint their own portrait, poets do not always write in the first person. But they are nonetheless there, in the world to which their work gives us access, and they are there so completely that this world can be said to *be* their very presence.

Thus the aesthetic object is doubly true because it is doubly necessary. But it is still amenable to a third truth, which answers to the most common meaning of the word. The aesthetic object can be true in relation to the real. It is at this price that aesthetic experience absolves itself from the suspicion of being nothing but a game. Indeed, would the artist work so hard if it were only in order to play? Does he not feel himself to be vested with a greater burden? Would the spectator take as much interest in the work if it were only capricious and particular? It is already a remarkable fact that this work is comprehensible. The subjectivity of the aesthetic world is not a defect, because the singular (insofar as it is the human) is here universal. The nightmares of Bosch or the dreams of Cocteau lie in wait for us at night. The impiety of Lautréamont and the piety of Franck are dormant powers in us. Thus we can momentarily assume the identities of many people, when art allows us to test our possibilities. But do our possibilities correspond to aspects [*visages*] of the world?

(b) The truth of content

It is against the real that we must finally measure the truth of the aesthetic object. In this regard, it is the content of the work that must be considered and no longer its relationship to the subject, its existential truth. What relationship is there between the real world and the world of the aesthetic object, if one considers the latter's world simply as world and not as the world of the artist? Does it bear witness to the real world as it does to the artist's subjectivity? Finally, is not the world of the aesthetic object demanded by the real world as much as by the artist?

The examination of the content of the work brings us back to the problem of aesthetic representation. However, we must consider the expressed world as well as the represented world. We already know that representation is not the goal of art, since the work represents only in order to express. In relation to the expressed, the represented is both a means and an effect. We are here primarily interested in the represented as an effect. Expression gives birth to representation because expression needs representation. The grave and mysterious world of Rembrandt needs to picture those vague people who recede into the background. The sensual and wonderful world of Debussy needs the marvels of nature, of *La Terrase au clair de lune* or of *La Fille aux cheveux de lin*. However, it is in terms of representation that one is first tempted to ask about the truth of the aesthetic object.

A theory of artistic truth risks making a false start by establishing itself on an observation which is nevertheless correct, namely, that art cannot be true in the way science is, because science demonstrates and art only displays. One then asks of art what he does not ask of science—that it reproduce the real to the point of competing with the real. One does not ask that a physics book portray thunder but that it explain thunder. One will be tempted, however, to ask that thunder be portrayed by the painter as well as by the writer and even by the musician. One thus supposes that the real is already given, present to perception, and intelligible to science. One expects that art will repeat the real without asking, first, whether the real is given other than as real, that is, as brute presence, and second, whether art is able to reproduce the real at all. In this fashion, one takes the path of realism. One is especially tempted to do so in the case of the literary arts, in which the word carries its own signification. We seek psychology in drama, and sometimes sociology in the novel, just as we seek anatomy in sculpture, or geography in landscape painting. Undoubtedly, it is less the scientific explanation than the subject matter of the explanation that we expect from art. We do not forget, however, that, since the idea of a science of man is not self-guaranteeing, art, on some occasions, has tried to assume a didactic and moralistic function.

Many literary works have taken on this function and our age has reinforced the tendency by describing the mechanism of passions or disclosing the bases of social life. The remarkable thing is that what has saved the best of these enterprises is their very failure. Take Balzac, for example. In him, creative power was stronger than the will to observation, and his prejudices sometimes beclouded his vision, making him blind to what the Saint-Simonians recorded at the same moment. Yet he created a marvelous quasi world, in which his century is expressed rather than rationally accounted for. (One cannot question that there is, all the same, a subjective truth of this world, and it is precisely this which we shall try to understand.) The same thing happens to those writers who have not even dreamed of making a work of art and who have nevertheless done so unwittingly and at the expense of their other projects. I think of Cardinal Retz, who, under the cover of a noble casualness, endeavored to become a historian and moralist. With a few exceptions, it would appear that he understands nothing of history, and the maxims of morality or psychology which he utters with a superb dogmatism can easily be challenged.[2] But he is magnificent when he speaks of himself, when he describes what he sees, plans, and attempts—and when we penetrate into a world which is not true from the standpoint of the historian, but which is nevertheless Retz's own world. This world is not even the world which he recounts, but, through his story, the world which radiates from him, a world of cunning, nobility, and greed, a kingdom of beautiful individualities who are out of work because there are no more laws to promulgate or cities to build. In short, didactic art is art only in spite of itself. We can see this most clearly when such art invents, instead of the rational which it covets, something marvelous and new—when the overflow of subjectivity transforms the prose of the world, a world whose laws art dreams of discerning. But realism remains a permanent temptation which exists both for the artist, who attains genuine expression only on the condition of not seeking it, and for the spectator, who prides himself on understanding rather than feeling, since feeling requires a rigor for which he is not always prepared.

If we give priority to representation, what truth must we expect from art? None other than resemblance. To be true here is to imitate, and the summit of art is the artifice of still-life

2. Cardinal Retz (Paul de Gondi) was a seventeenth-century politician who wrote his *Mémoires*, to which Dufrenne refers in this passage.—Trans.

deception, which is an achievement of craft and not of style. In this case, painting becomes a matter of increasing mastery and, as such, tends to dominate the other arts: literature also seeks to paint and competes with drawing through words. Music also wishes to depict—not only to be descriptive by imitating the sounds of the forest or barnyard animals, but to be instructive by detailing human passions. (At the opera, for example, this is effected with sobs, swoons, and entreaties.) It is true that the painter, in turn, borrows from literature and from music. The personages whom the painter represents have eloquence, and sometimes even a theatrical grandiloquence. They are written into a composition which is a setting for them. They are given a role and play it with ostentation. They are, for example, the Holy Family, the hermit meditating in the desert, or the resolute martyr in anguish. The depth of interiority becomes eloquence— we are a long way from Byzantine or Roman art. It appears that painting has obtained what one calls expression only in order to prostitute it and lose it through an excess of zeal. The more painting "speaks"—and it is to understanding that painting speaks—the less it says. The same is true when painting attempts to express movement and overdoes it, as one also sees in baroque sculpture and architecture. Movement is no longer a vital force in which interiority is affirmed but a gesticulation with which interiority proclaims itself. Thus the pleats of draperies are no longer arranged as in a room but in the fake space of an opera stage. What saves great works is that they close in on themselves and thus attest to the sufficiency and necessity proper to the aesthetic object. They are successful to the extent that they are not content to externalize movement but, rather, seek a principle internal to themselves. They are then inspired with their own music, whose movement is not a flight beyond itself but the unfolding of a temporality. Hence in the gyratory compositions of Rubens everything is reassembled, everything converges toward that "generative harmonic center" of which Rameau speaks in connection with the resolution of chords. The baroque, here, rediscovers in its own fashion the principle of Romanesque stylization found in the draperies of the sculpted Christ at Vézelay, in which geometric immobility is the principle of movement. Movement, in such a case, is no longer imitation. Movement is reinvented by means proper to the plastic medium—which invites us to feel rather than to imagine it, to contemplate rather than to participate in it. It is thus that a higher truth is discovered, namely, that movement is not the mere negation of the motionless and attests to an essential immobility. But in order to achieve this insight, one must renounce the conception according to which truth is measured in terms of resemblance and the ideal of art is a portrait (the portrait being the most elementary form of the *adequatio*).

In fact, if art is imitation, what must it imitate? The real. But what is the real? To compel art to imitate is to presume that the real is already given and known as a model to be reproduced. The world is seen as simply *there* and has nothing to do with our gaze and our action. The world is cut and dried, and the Creation is an assurance of it. There is no uncertainty in knowledge. Everything is in place, absolutely determined. Things are distinguished according to the hierarchy of forms and are obedient to the laws of nature, and the good are separated from the wicked. The intellect and the heart present no problems, and art encounters no obstacles. The demand for truth, which is at the heart of the most humble perception, is presumed to be easily satisfied. Thus one presupposes a universe in which intentions are always already carried out and which is known before being perceived. If the artist attempts to give us something to see, he is only ratifying and exercising our conceptual powers. The aesthetics of truth is that nothing is beautiful except what is true. It is not a question of art inviting the artist or the spectator progressively to discover a truth made to his measure. Art exists only in terms of a preexisting and clearly conceivable truth. In this view, the marvelous must be tamed and reduced to the status of a transparent and entertaining allegory. (For it is remarkable that the kind of art which devotes itself to the service of truth aims at the same time to please and ordains "the pleasures of the enchanted island." It is as if it were aware that it has no other resource, once it is in the presence of a truth already constituted, and that it does not have to seek the deeper truth which is to be found in the living experience of a subjectivity who discovers and establishes a world.) In this way, art aspires to objectivity. Well-ordered and without mystery, the real is offered to a spectator who is delighted to receive it and who demands resemblance as the proof of truth. Versailles is recognizable in the mythologies of the opera, just as in the pomp of its palace. The king relives his victories in the works of poets or in the canvases of the painters, just as the lover follows his adventures on a map of love. In this official and valid world, there must also be a valid spectator who is able to recognize it and see himself in it. And it is here that the marriage of painting with theater appears to its best advantage. If painting represents [*répresente*], theater gives a presentation [*répresentation*]. Drama subjects the spectator to immobility—the very spectator whom painting had left standing and mobile. It is to this ideally placed spectator that the theatre refers (and one knows with what indifference theaters have been constructed which deliberately sacrifice all those spectators who are not in the orchestra or directly facing the stage). All arts are for the privileged and sovereign spectator who judges from an immobile position and is not a committed participant in the process of art. The stage illusion is that of a spectator who is not compromised by what he sees, as the reflexive *cogito* is not compromised by things. The real is thus deprived of mystery and ambiguity, and reflection is exercised without peril.

But is it, in fact, the real which is thus represented? And, to play on words, does not the theatrical and pictorial "representation" impair the noetic representation? Is not the real which one claims to depict for us simply the conventional? There certainly is a place for convention in the fictitious aspect of art. This is evident and cannot be put forward as an objection to figurative art. Art is unable to transpose the real into the unreal. But here convention would appear not only as the means but as the content of the representation. If one wishes the represented to be intelligible without affecting or engaging the spectator but only by amusing him, is it not necessary that the real be sweetened and conceptualized at the same time? To conceptualize is precisely to order the real, to eliminate from it that which is unique, unusual, or rebellious. Thus distance is controlled by perspective and ceases to be the multifarious and voracious space where I lose my way. Similarly, time is objectified and dominated by musical tempo. In these ways, the things and men of the represented world are made reasonable. The real is refined by the image of virtuous man, and a sense of measure as the norm of the work is introduced as the norm for the real. The unintelligible and the dissonant are both excluded from the represented object, which is as clear and as carefully designed as a Le Nôtre formal garden. The horrible has deserted gargoyles and the capitals of columns and is transferred to the monsters evoked in opera; passions are kept at a distance and denounced as errors. The theatrical here takes on its full meaning. It is both grandiloquence and pomp, the representation of a real which is eloquent and polished, and which is suited to please us without surprising or moving us emotionally. Undoubtedly all is not vain in these artifices. But such art cannot achieve the impossible task of being true and pleasing at the same time. That which it eliminates from the real is, in a way, the most real, that is, the surprising, the unforseeable, everything which disconcerts to the point of urging a radical change of attitude. Magic is replaced by allegory, which tames imagination and puts it in the service of knowing. Also abolished is the depth of time—as one sees in theater, where the heroes do not belong to an epoch but are from nowhere (in the fashion of objects to which mathematical reasoning is applied or of the mechanisms which Cartesian physics describes). Thus art is never fully representative. What art represents is a reality which is itself conventional.

Nevertheless, realism can invent other ways in which to be true, in order to protect the reality of the real and to transmit something of its inhumanity through the work. Realism can renounce the prohibitions of classical art and seek other means to express the real. It may content itself with the first move, the denial of prohibitions—as when Claudel added swear words to *Partage de Midi,* and Voltaire used a scaffold, which frightened the actress "La Clairon," in the production of a pseudo-Racinian drama. But it is not sufficient to reintroduce certain aspects of the real or certain real objects, which always risk taking on an incongruous appearance when they are integrated into the representation.[3] It is also necessary to force the spectator's adherence by giving to this copy of the real an air of reality, and thus inventing new techniques of representation to diminish the distance from the spectacle to the real as well as from spectacle to the spectator. Art strives to drive the spectator away from his comfortable position by obliging him to participate in some way in the spectacle. Thus painting renounces the single-centered perspective which is found in the theater, just as it modifies what one calls in film the medium shot (which film itself borrows from the theater). The eye of the painter is no longer identified with the eye of the ideal spectator. It is free to choose the same angles which the camera will adopt when it becomes mobile, to seek special effects through the tilt or oblique shot,

---

3. One sees this clearly in so-called "naïve" and primitive painting, which is only realistic in appearance. The meticulous realism of detail, e.g., in a bouquet of lilies, in Annunciations, or in the breastplate of Saint George, by no means gives an impression of reality. Instead, we are transported into an absolute, as in myth. The literal truth of represented objects is transfigured by an air of solemnity and fervor which Henri Rousseau has attempted to recover. In the experience of such painting, we come before the sacred, the nontemporal event which grounds time.

and to modify shots by approaching or moving back. This freedom of gaze, which the cinema will sanction, is invented by the plastic arts on their own in the diverse epochs of realism. For it is a matter of imitating what is inimitable in the real, that is, the aggressive and the refractory, as if to reveal the real in its intimacy instead of reproducing it in its official and formal aspect. But this is only on the condition that the spectator participate in this exploration, lose his impassivity, be astonished, and become a party to the movements which the work suggests. Thus the represented object may retain the power which the real object has of arousing our activity or of resisting it, and the spectator submits to this power. The hand which, in a portrait by Franz Hals, emerges from a sham skeleton, reaches out to seize us. An action which develops in depth (rather than on a transverse plane) in a painting by Caravaggio, Georges de La Tour, or Rembrandt calls upon us to mingle with it. We are summoned to the table along with the *Pilgrims at Emmaus,* or behind the tapestries and doors in Dutch interiors. Represented space is no longer the geometric space of linear perspective but the lived space where the distance interests and moves the whole body. It is not the space which one measures with the gaze, but the space in which one is engaged and where one is sometimes lost. Such space is comparable to the time of Wagnerian music—a time which is no longer punctuated and ordered but insidious, fascinating, and exciting. In literature, we see the same effort to restore the density of the real, to guide the spectator—or even to lead him astray, as Balzac does in a maze of objects and a multitude of characters—and yet without eliminating the unexpected, the multifarious, or the strange. In the same way, dance emancipates itself as much as it can within the confines of theater, but dance ceases being theatrical when classical forms, directly governed by music, are replaced by forms which are more free and more disquieting, and when the dancer's body attests to its reality by its inventions, risks, and extraordinary postures. Perhaps the novel even goes beyond theater, at least insofar as it demands less pomp and suggests more disorder and brutality.[4]

4. As for film, we only note a special problem. To the extent that film keeps the promises of painting and finds what painting seeks, must painting give up? Not at all. This is no more warranted than speaking of the death of art. One cannot simply announce the death of one art and its replacement by another. It is quite true that the painting of Caravaggio or of the impressionists—of Degas, above all—invents new perspectives or new schemes of composition. The same is true of the baroque artists when they seek to suggest movement by plastic and nonmusical means,

But realism cannot entirely deny to the spectator the status which classical art recognized so clearly, that is, the impassivity [*impassibilité*] which is the privilege of contemplation. The spectator experiences the work only with his gaze, and he withdraws before a closeup or penetrates into the depths of the field only metaphorically. In the case of film, it is not the spectator who moves, but the camera. This order of priorities is a necessity for art. To the extent that it has been aware of its own problems, painting has recognized that it must not make holes in the canvas, just as the screen cannot be punctured in films. The painting must be entirely enclosed within itself. The works that were invoked above, which employ all the resources of perspective in order to present represented objects in depth rather than make them march past us at the theater, manifest the two dimensions of the canvas and are not ashamed of being flat. Similarly, music, when it makes its form infinitely flexible, nevertheless retains in the measurement of time a character of proportion and objectivity which is imposed on the listener. The listener is *before* the melody and not inside it, whereas the dancer is *in* the fox trot, or the regiment *in* the military music. In short, realism can insist on the participation which the spectator accords to the represented object, but only on the condition of remembering that this participation is attached more to the expressed feeling than to the work. And, in any case, the represented cannot compete with the real. Significantly, it is its concern for perfection which informs art of this fact. The aesthetic object cannot be a completed whole unless it resides within itself, and unless the represented object itself does not pretend to be real by referring us to an external world and proposing action in that world. It is a properly aesthetic demand which forbids making holes in the canvas, burning the pages, or transforming music into movement. Art can be itself only by refusing to imitate the reality of the real. Moreover, could art ever fully succeed in this mimetic effort? Hersch has shown clearly that, with respect to the real, the represented must always possess the character of the *less*:

---

foreshadowing the cinema and seeming to call for it. Conversely, moreover, film, aware of its resources, imitates painting and even imitates that in painting which least resembles film. But when one art resolves problems posed by another, that does not signify the impoverishment of the latter. On the contrary, the latter can return to its own problems, deepening its own genius, and thus continuing its career by claiming a more rigorous division of labor. Contemporary painting is a painting liberated from film.

If a painted basket of plums were only the public object without its volume, its flavor, and its practical interest, it would exist less than the public basket of plums. If imitative music were only its sonorous model minus its spatial and practical efficacy, it would exist less than the sounds of nature or of technique. If performed drama were only the drama of practical life without its urgency for those whom it reaches, it would exist less than the lived drama. On every occasion, creation would amount to a diminution of the being of the created object. This would be to make an object descend several degrees lower on the existential modal scale of being.[5]

The aesthetic object is thus an eminently real object, but it does not pretend to produce the real within itself or even to copy the real. The aesthetic object *says* the real and thus discovers it. Between the real and the represented there is no more an equivalence than between ordinary perception and aesthetic perception, and the truth of art cannot consist in realizing such an equivalence. That which art says is not the reality of the real but a meaning of the real which art expresses. This meaning is true because it is the affective dimension through which the real may appear and not the reality of the real which a physical formula could capture.

(c) What is true in expression

The aesthetic object is a point of departure not so much for objective knowledge as for a reading of the expressiveness of the real. For this reason, the artist's subjectivity is eminently required. The world of the aesthetic object is the world of an affective category and, through this category, a world of real objects. The work leads us to the real through the affective. In the nonfigurative arts, what the work suggests of the real is not crystallized into representations—the space which the affective quality opens up remains empty. Consequently, it is on the basis of music that one must understand the realism of the representational arts, not vice versa.

Music does not intend the real directly. To be sure, there is a realistic music, in the first place the most naïve music, which attempts to imitate what it can of the real—noises. Realistic effects have been sought in every epoch, as demonstrated by

5. Jeanne Hersch, *L'Etre et la forme* (Neuchâtel: La Baconnière, 1946), p. 180.

The Battle of Marignan, The Cuckoo, the *Pastoral* Symphony, and *Pacific 231.*[6] But clearly, the work is musical only if the noises are converted into tones and integrated into a sonorous system where they gain their efficacy from their function in the system rather than from their resemblance to the real (resemblance is apperceived only if the author indicates it to us). The same must be said of works which, without being confined to the imitation of noises, pretend to annotate the real *in us* by giving a musical equivalent—for example, the Rameau's *Concerts,* Schumann's *Carnival,* Debussy's *Préludes,* and Moussorgsky's *Pictures at an Exhibition.* What assures us that Debussy's Prelude no. 1 represents a submerged cathedral? Only the popular title—"La Cathédrale engloutie." Without this title, would we evoke the object which it indicates? Probably not; instead, we would listen to the music. Moreover, is it suitable that we evoke this submerged cathedral, that we raise images of some fabulous city, of submarine ruins in transparent and perfidious water, and of bells whose spirit survives the disaster by some miracle? Such representations only obstruct the listening. We are not in a theater of shadows. We are at a concert to yield ourselves up to the enchantment of sensuous sounds, and this enchantment does not arouse images of the real in us unless we stop adhering to the universe of sounds. Finally, the same is true of works which join music and words (recited, sung, or declaimed), like a title which would accompany the music in its entirety. One cannot say simply that music indirectly intends the real through the verbal representation which the text offers it. Musicians who assure us that they follow the text and reduce the music to a mere commentary imitate the text as others directly imitate the real; thus one cannot take them at their word. Perhaps they are yielding to the history of creation, but their work refuses to be enslaved to the text. We know de Schloezer's theory. To the extent that the words have a rational sense and designate the real, they are musically indifferent. For de Schloezer, the music would no more be a commentary on the text than the text would be a commentary on the music. Between the verbal system ruled by considerations of intelligibility and the musical system ruled by a sensuous demand, there is neither com-

6. Dufrenne has selected examples of program music from various eras. *The Battle of Marignan* was composed by the sixteenth-century musician Clement Jannequin. *The Cuckoo* probably refers to *Capriccio on the Cuckoo's Call,* by the seventeenth-century composer Girolamo Frescobaldi. The *Pastoral* Symphony is by Beethoven. *Pacific 231* is by the twentieth-century composer, Arthur Honegger.—Trans.

mon measure nor reciprocity. However, only if the work unites the music with the word is it truly *one*. The work must be "uniquely a musical system in which the word finds itself totally assimilated by the music."[7] The unity of the work can be realized only by the sacrifice of one of the elements of the original duality. All that remains of language are the articulated sounds which become material for the vocal work, just as the instrumental sounds are incorporated into a sonorous system. The semantic character of the word loses its importance. Thus it matters little that one does not understand German when one listens to the melodies of Schubert, or Latin when one listens to a *Missa solemnis*. Music, by stripping the words of their meaning, rejects the grasp of the real that the words offer. There is in the end, only one kind of music, pure music which bears its whole meaning in itself and is heard for itself, without reference to a rational meaning or evocation of the real—a kind of music for which the sonata or the fugue serves as a model.

No doubt, it is tempting to adopt this approach and to challenge from the beginning everything which could alter the purity of the sensuous by introducing into it, like a strange body, an allusion to the real. And yet it is precisely with respect to pure music that we are able to rediscover a truth of the work which will justify vocal music or program music. This pure music, in fact, preserves a meaning which is not conceptual, since it does not recount, describe, or demonstrate. Nor is this meaning something sheerly spiritual which would constitute the sensuous as an autonomous totality. Pure music also has what de Schloezer calls a psychological meaning—which is what we have called expression. It is in expression, which is rigorously immanent in the sensuous and which is the opposite and not the poor relation of intellectual meaning, that the relation to the real is effected independent of all imitative representation. The affective quality thus expressed is the quality of a world. When we say that the joy expressed by a fugue opens Bach's world to us, the word "world" indicates a relation to the real. There are neither images to populate this world nor concepts to catalogue it, yet it remains a true world. In experiencing the affective quality which is communicated to me by the music, and as a result of its ineluctable rigor, I feel that it expresses no commonplace or skin-deep sentiment, as when I feel happy or sad in my moods or my encounters. What is expressed is something more profound and more

7. See Boris de Schloezer, *Introduction à J. S. Bach* (Paris: Gallimard, 1947).—Trans.

necessary—a revelation. And, although nothing is revealed to me except a light, I know that the real can appear through it. Nothing is given to me except a key, but I know that it can open doors. I know that the real can be seen in this way and even that it calls for such seeing. It is indeed Bach that I hear, and I fancy that I could never fail to recognize his music; but *through* [*à travers*] Bach it is the real which is expressed. There is no need for the real to be represented. The real is already present, not as a reservoir of identifiable objects or determined events which it is necessary to evoke and name, but as a being. This is why I do not need to verify that this world of joy bears on the real. I can do that later, when some other kind of expression introduces me to a world where I can rediscover the world of Bach, for example, in the innocent games of a child, the sparkling grace of a dancer or of the early spring, or the smiling face of a man who has quelled his passions through happiness and not through the law of conscience alone. In the presence of these examples, I know that Bach's world is true, since the real confirms it. Yet I already know this without having to anticipate these experiences —I know that "it is so." Further, it is even possible that I will never verify this knowledge. Suppose that a captive in his prison, delivered to hatred and seeing the sky only "beyond the roof-top," [8] hears a Bach fugue. He knows clearly that the music is not meant for him. Someone has banned him from the world of Bach, or he may have banned himself. Perhaps he could still appreciate it if he had the power of being happy in adversity. In any case, he cannot doubt that this world of Bach exists, even if it is reserved for enjoyment by others. There is joy, and it is of little importance which particular objects manifest it. For joy's reality is not contained in these objects. Rather, they draw their supreme reality from joy through rejoining its world. The privileged character of pure music is to reveal what is essential in the real without my having to anticipate the objects which give it a body. Pure music brings me the signification in advance of the signs, the world in advance of things. Here the sensuous represents nothing and has no other meaning than the quality which is fastened to its form or, rather, *is* the form itself. Consequently, the rational meaning and the psychological meaning are one. The affective quality bears on the real, even if it does not evoke the real. The affective *a priori* is cosmological in character.

8. Dufrenne is quoting the first line of Paul Verlaine, "Le ciel est, par-dessus le toit," from *Sagesse.*—Trans.

Nevertheless, some musical works do permit a role for representation and allow for the evocation of the real, whose affective essence they express. This group includes all musical works which bear a title or accompany a text in which the meaning orients us toward the real and no longer allows the world of the aesthetic object to be undetermined. What kind of determination is involved here? The function of music is always to make us hear certain sonorous systems and not to suggest images or to imitate the real. As a patient said to Charles Baudouin, when he was asked to "associate" to Ravel's *Pavane pour une infante défunte,* "manifested here are the impressions not when I play the *Pavane,* but when I think it." [9] When I hear the *Pavane,* I no longer think about it. I do not need to know that it is a dance of the Spanish court with a noble and slow rhythm, or to remind myself of the sumptuous and sad infants of Vélasquez, or to evoke a funeral procession and all the images which can be aroused by bringing together youth, passion, and aristocratic solemnity. There is no need to reconstitute a historical reality or the circumstances of creation which the title may evoke. The title only serves to induce or strengthen the affective quality which the music presents through its own affective quality. It does this through the poetic weight of the word "pavane," whose two *a*'s linger on, and to which the nasal sound of "défunte" corresponds because of the felicitous alliteration of the *f,* like a muffled, prolonged, and dying echo. Similarly, when I listen to Debussy's *La Mer,* the simple word itself (not to mention the proper titles of each movement) is also poetically charged. It orients me toward a certain affective quality. But I do not have to develop the images of glaucous water, waves, foam on the reefs, or noon at sea with its diamantine reflections. It is a symphony which I hear, and not a real landscape which I contemplate. If I have the impression of recognizing the sea, if the promises of the title appear to me to be kept, this is precisely because I hear the symphony. Something like the essence of the sea is revealed to me, with respect to which every image is gross and vain. We are concerned with what I experience when I am before the sea, of what there is of the truly "marine" in it—with its affective essence, which is more certain and more communicable than all empirical signals. It is the sea-as-world, just as the fugue by Bach was joy-as-world. And we must note that the object and the feeling are equally principles of a world, because feeling is

9. Charles Baudouin, *Psychanalyse de l'art* (Paris: Alcan, 1929), p. 191.

valid qua object and an object is valid qua feeling. Or, more exactly, the object is not valid for itself alone; it elicits and embodies a feeling which simultaneously grounds the object and surpasses it. This feeling is the feeling of the sea. Conversely, feeling is pregnant with objects which it does not expressly evoke but which are potential in feeling and which we can find again in the real. What the work proffers is not the object as an object in the world but the object as the principle of a world. The connection of the real with the affective essence is not the logical connection of individual and concept but the connection between the given and its expression, the thing and its world.

We are now in a position to distinguish between pure music and program music. Both awaken a feeling through which aspects of the real are disclosed. But in pure music, the feeling is self-sufficient and bears the actual name of a feeling. Joy and melancholy are subsumed spontaneously under the proper affective category. In program music, feeling is determined specifically by an object in the world to which it gives access, without losing, on that account, its quality of feeling. That is why, in program music, an affective category can only be applied to feeling with the approximateness which we have seen to be inevitable. And the determining object is present here only through its expressive value, that is, as the power of awakening the feeling which the music takes over but for which the music needs an auxiliary in order to be precise. But the relation to the real remains the same. The real is always intended by the feeling which delivers its affective essence.[10] It is the same for the text of a vocal work. If we insist on the importance of expression, we do not (as in the case of de Schloezer) have to absorb the text totally into the music. The text may, as with a language we

10. This is true even when the real, as indeterminate as it is, has a historical flavor. How can we separate seventeenth-century French music from Versailles? How can we separate Gregorian chant from medieval abbies? How can we separate the Wagnerian opera from Germanism? One can say that Lully opens the world of Versailles as Debussy opens the world of the sea, for an epoch can be the source of a world as well as of an object. More precisely: (1) the expression of the epoch is no more the goal of the work than is the description of the object; and (2) it is always an affective essence which is revealed by the aesthetic object. Consequently, all the explicit images and all the knowledge that I have of this epoch must remain in the background during the listening. Of course, this knowledge is not a matter of indifference. However, it only prepares for listening and by no means accompanies it. Of the "idea" into which such knowledge may be condensed, the music offers an equivalent in the form of feeling. Conversely, moreover, this equivalent will aid us afterward in elaborating the idea of the epoch, and thus in manifesting the truth of art.

do not understand, collaborate with the music, just as in poetry rational signification is surpassed in poetic signification. The text is valid through its expression, and this expression coincides with that of the music. This is the principle of all aesthetic transpositions. It is because we expect an equality and a convergence of the two elements of the work that we deplore their inequality. The melodies of Chausson lose nothing in being inspired by texts of minor poets, but we lament having to forget the text as we neglect the librettos of Mozart. At any rate, we do not have to elaborate the meaning of the text in order to rejoin the real through its mediation, as if the music had to represent, if not the real, at least its successor, namely, the text considered as prose. All that need be done is to furnish a musical equivalent of the poetic expression. Finally, the same may be said of the musical theater. It is perceived as a total work only if all the arts which it employs converge in an expression that is common to all. If it rejoins the real, it can be only through such expression, as in the case of pure music. But we shall understand this collaboration of arts better if we show that the plastic arts and the literary arts are true precisely as music is true, that is, without representation's bending this truth toward imitation.

The literary arts, and prose in particular, exist at the antipodes of music. Here it does appear that the words are selected primarily for their meaning and that their function is to translate the real. Do we not say that a novel is bad if, for example, its psychology is false or the characters that it represents do not "ring true"? Conversely, do we not employ literature to nourish a psychology which we expect to be true? But does the truth of the work consist in reproducing the real or in expressing the truth of the real in terms of affective quality? Let us look more closely. We were just speaking of psychological truth. Is this to say that the truth of the other sectors of the real, namely, the historical, geographical, and physical, is then merely optional? In fact, one readily admits that a novel can unfold in a universe of convention. We can see this in *L'Astrée, Suzanne et le Pacifique,* or *Les Rivages des Syrtes,* none of which obliges its author to a full-fledged integral realism.[11] The theater always makes use of this openness more or less liberally. One does not reproach Claudel's *L'Annonce faite à Marie* for being deficient because the action unfolds "in the Middle Ages of strict conventions," or *Phèdre* because a sea monster intervenes. Are not Prometheus

11. These novels are by Honoré D'Urfé, Jean Giraudoux, and Julien Gracq, respectively.—Trans.

and Faust true in the same manner as the canvases of Bosch or the heads of Vézelay? In these cases, we are warned that, even in the classical style, truth is not measured by imitation. The supernatural can be as true as the everyday. Sometimes, of course, art is concerned with precision and pursues the real down to its most insignificant details. Is it in this respect that art is true? Is a tragedy by Voltaire more true than a tragedy by Racine, just because the actors are clothed in togas and not in doublets? And are the Goncourts more true than Stendhal, because they used a card index in writing? What does this concern for realism signify for works which are not dupes or victims of it? For the artist, in the first place, realism is undoubtedly a means of arousing or maintaining inspiration. Just as it is possible that a voyage inspired Debussy's *La Mer,* so it may be that familiarity with history inspired Victor Hugo's *Notre-Dame de Paris,* and the spectacle of the world of the Restoration Balzac's *Comédie humaine.* For us as spectators, realism is not, insofar as we keep the aesthetic attitude, a means of instruction. Realism is, rather, a way of giving us a feeling of security, insofar as we are concerned not with truth but with verisimilitude. The anachronisms of which certain works have made a systematic employment (which extends to technique itself) remind us that the goal of art is not the exactitude of historical reconstruction. Nevertheless, certain works introduce us headfirst into the world of history, aspiring to historical truth of the present or the past. But they attain this truth (a truth that music sometimes attains without any express intention) only by doing what the historian does not succeed in doing so long as he is caught in the net of objective detail. They extricate a style proper to an epoch—just as there is a style proper to the behavior of an individual or a physiognomy proper to a landscape. What is aesthetically valuable in Zola's work is not the theory of heredity or that of social determinism, but the unanimist sentiment of *Germinal* or the evocation of the enchanted garden where Abbot Mouret succumbs.

If literature is not indifferent to the truth of the object or of history, still less is it indifferent to the truth of man. But how does literature render human truth? Works which pride themselves upon subtle psychology are tedious, like family portraits and *trompe-l'oeil* effects. They are even more ridiculous when they pretend to be informative. But if we refrain from explaining and judging, what is there to describe, and how? Behavior, in the fashion of the naturalist? The interior life, through monologue? One knows how these problems have troubled the contemporary novel. Perhaps they have done so in vain, if there is no method in art which guarantees success, and if something of man—that through which he is free—remains ungraspable. But they are not in vain, if research into techniques of the novel is combined with the acquisition of a style, and if it is through this style that a novel is true.

In fact, when is a novel true? When it has a certain manner of gripping us, so as to reveal something in us which is associated with a certain feeling. Then the novel transports us into a world which is proper to it. The magic carpet is no longer the melody, it is a certain treatment of language, involving syntax, the density of the paragraphs, the arrangement of the chapters, and even the choice of words. To be sure, the words are chosen for their meaning, but they are also chosen for their poetic power of shock and incantation, like the words which designate colors in Colette's work, the nuances of warmth in Mauriac's work, or the force or failure of the will in Malraux's work. Similarly, the scenes of the narrative or the characters are chosen for what they represent, but the representation is subordinate to the expression. The elements of the representation cooperate in reproducing a certain affective quality. Sido is an element in the world of Colette, and it is through this world that we seize Sido. But can one imagine Sido in the world of Mauriac?[12] No more than we can imagine the chords of the Ninth Symphony in the *Jupiter* Symphony, or a judge depicted by Rouault in a canvas by Matisse. Consequently, it is not the represented itself which gives access to the real, but the feeling, from which the representational element is now inseparable. Once more, we must say that the truth of the work is found not in what it recounts but in the fashion in which it recounts. The real which the work illuminates is not exactly that which it represents. I can certainly utilize Stendhal's *The Red and the Black* to develop a theory of ambition (although this use of the work, even if it presupposes aesthetic experience, remains foreign to it), but this does not imply that the portrait of Julien Sorel which the novel presents to me reproduces a real individual and his real story. It matters little that Stendhal was inspired by some miscellaneous fact. In any case, he did not copy the real. He created a work of art by choosing certain scenes, by contrasting certain characters, and by imposing a certain rhythm on the reader. Because of these factors,

12. Colette, *Sido* (Paris: Ferenczi, 1930).—Trans.

I can plunge into the lively and buoyant atmosphere of Stendhal's world, and it is through its illumination that I can understand certain aspects of ambition or of love as men live them. Julien Sorel does not exist in the real, but there *is* a Stendhalian sense of existence, just as there is a Mozartian sense. Similarly, being plunged into the world of Proust, I can discover the Proustian in the real, the sense of existence possessed by Norpois or Swann. I do so not so much because Proust has represented these characters but because the feeling awakened by his work allows me to recognize in the real the same type of individuals who populate his world. It is not a catalogue of characters or a psychological treatise which is given to me by *Remembrance of Things Past*. It is, rather, a light which illuminates certain aspects of the real, a real which (in Proust's vision) is finally desolate and sterile, where action is swallowed up. From this engulfing world there can emerge, as in the "petite phrase" of Vinteuil, only the purity of the moment—a moment which, in Mallarmé's words, "destroys the futility and inanity of sound." Thus we may say the same thing of representation that we said of music with titles (a kind of music for which representation is a potentiality). Representation specifies feeling, orients and nourishes feeling conjointly with the sensuous, from which representation is inseparable. It is through feeling that one rejoins the real—a real which is not necessarily the equivalent of what is represented—because feeling delivers an affective essence which the real readily accepts.[13]

However, the realist will ask whether the work cannot directly rejoin the real and refuse to be fiction. Do not Balzac, Jules Romains, and Sartre seek to make us conscious of and experience more resolutely the determinate world where their readers must live at the same moment as they? It is not an inner world which they express. It is Paris in 1906 or 1950, the German victory in 1940, or the present condition of blacks in the United States. But if their sole ambition is to present the real world to which they belong, why do they not become historians

13. The difference between program music and literature is somewhat like that between pure music and program music, a difference of degree. Representation contributes to the creation of the world of the aesthetic object, and thus this world has something determinate in it. The representational element, treated by art and transfigured by expression, in becoming a component of such a world, indicates more precisely than music what can be rediscovered in the real—in Proust's case, types like Saint Loup or Charlus, certain kinds of beaches or salons, and lives which possess the fear of living and which surround themselves with reminiscences.

—or even politicians, if they wish to be active in this world?[14] The reason is that they aim at something else, above all to express themselves, and perhaps even to lose themselves in what they express. However, this is beyond our concern. But, in addition, they know or have a presentiment that the real does not truly have a meaning, insofar as it is not oriented by a world. Thus it is incumbent on them to uncover such a world, outside of which there is only the blinding dust of facts. There are properly aesthetic means which constitute this world by awakening the feeling which it expresses. Only then is the real recaptured and the representation true. But this is only because representation has become expression through the genius of art, and not because representation is a faithful reproduction. That is why this truth has a vaster field of application than the real qua represented and surpasses the intentions of the writer (it is in this way that he becomes immortal). Homer remains true when the cannon replaces the lance and the Fifth Column replaces the Trojan Horse. Homer is true precisely through what is conventional in the epic and not because there is exact description of the equipment of the Achaean infantryman. Similarly, Benjy's monologue in *The Sound and the Fury* introduces me into the world of an idiot, because it invents a language which is in no way the shorthand report of remarks uttered by a precocious madman in a psychiatric hospital. One can see, moreover, that the novelist is tempted to imitate the real precisely in order to compensate for the multiplicity of conventions to which he is forced to resort. But in any case the truth of his work lies elsewhere, and his work can be just as true by turning aside from history or psychology. It suffices for the work to inaugurate history or psychology, and not to take orders from them.

In short, the literary work, like the fable, is true through its second meaning and not through the immediate meaning of that which it represents. The function of the representation is not so much to imitate the real as to serve the expression which allows the real to be grasped. This conclusion can be applied equally to the plastic arts. A painting is no less true when it allows for deformations demanded by a certain aesthetic treatment of the sensuous, for it is through such a treatment that the sensuous becomes expressive. We have already indicated sufficiently that the authentic painter cannot be entirely realistic. We must now

14. Sometimes they are politically active, but that does not prevent them from continuing to be novelists. This is undoubtedly due to the fact that the novel may be used as a weapon in the service of political ends.

demonstrate that it is not through its realism that the painting is true, for representation is here again in the service of expression.[15] Representation is a means of organizing the sensuous and of permitting the sensuous to be expressive. Even realistic painting is not true because of what it permits us to identify. A Crucifixion is not true because it demonstrates anatomy, a Dutch interior is not true because of the information it gives about the costume or the furniture of the epoch, a landscape is not true on geographical grounds. Rather, they are true because of the world they open, a world for which the subject is only a pretext. It is not necessarily into a Christian world that the Crucifixion introduces us; and, in any case, the specific religion may vary from one aesthetic object to another. Similarly, Vermeer does not introduce us into a Dutch world but into a world of tenderness and gentleness. Conversely, a painting which eliminates a subject altogether does not thereby cease to be true. It is significant that "abstract" painters frequently desire a title for their works. They are sanctioned to do so in the same way as musicians, and their paintings often involve us in the same way. We do not have to seek an object in symphonies of colors, nor do we look for the daughter of Corinth in the temple of Eupalinos. But we need to allow the feeling that the aesthetic object awakens to be deposited in us—a feeling which in turn illuminates the world where such an object can appear. It is on the basis of this experience that one must conceive, as well, the truth of realistic painting.

The aesthetic object is true before being verified, for two reasons. In the first place, it is true in relation to the real because it is true in relation to itself. We experience its truth in its perfection, since a high degree of rigor cannot deceive us. In contrast, the superficial *says* nothing. At the very most, the superficial narrates, and representation suffices for that. To make of the sensuous an authentic language which returns to the original function of expression is the miracle which art performs. Art performs this miracle by giving to the sensuous a fullness and a necessity which owe nothing to logic but are, rather, the mark of a style. Thus it is through its intrinsic quality and

15. The exactness of the drawing or design is to the painting what the semantic value of the word is to the literary arts—to design is to designate. One could even say that the two arts offer the same duality of the prosaic and the poetic. The design can, like the word, be absorbed into a utilitarian signification without having value by itself, or it can become a formally valid language which, through its own virtue, presents to vision what ordinary perception does not notice.

from within itself that the aesthetic object relates to the real and displays its truth there. The beautiful is the sign of the true; nothing is true but the beautiful. In the second place, the aesthetic object takes on the original function of truth, which is to precede the real in order to illuminate it, not to repeat it. But just because the object is in a position to illuminate does not imply that its truth loses its subjective import. It is also the case that there is truth only for a subjectivity. To be sure, the world which the aesthetic object reveals is a singular world into which one enters only by the narrow gate of the existential *a priori*. However, this world is not an arbitrary one. We know that the real will come to confirm it and not leave it empty, and we know that its light will clarify something, just as the mathematician knows the same concerning his algorithms.

But how do we know these things for sure? How is the world revealed through the aesthetic object able to instruct us concerning the real world? How can that world illuminate the real world? Does the real lend itself to such illumination? Does the real have need of this light? For an answer, we must inquire into the idea of the real. Then we shall be able to see how the affective *a priori* can possess a cosmological significance. We shall also see how this *a priori*, which is constitutive with regard to the world of the aesthetic object, can also be constitutive with respect to the real world.

[II] The Real as Illuminated by the Aesthetic

AT FIRST SIGHT, there seems to be no common measure between the world of the aesthetic object and the real world—that is, if one identifies "real" with "objective." The aesthetic object reveals a world which is subjective—indeed, less a world than an atmosphere of a world—and which represented objects illustrate but do not determine. This world is singular, insofar as it is internal to the work, and it is through this world that the aesthetic object finds the fullness and autonomy of its form. In short, the world of the aesthetic object is subjective, in that its unity is the unity of a personal *Weltanschauung*. The objective world, in contrast, is a totality, with an open horizon in which all things—all identifiable objects as dominated by consciousness—can find a place to the extent that knowledge [*le savoir*] discovers and articulates them. The objective world is infinite, in that it multiplies the finite and there is no end to the succession of appearances. Moreover, there is no principle of unity internal to the objective world. It has only the formal unity of the Kantian "I think," a unity of the understanding alone. However, the world of the aesthetic object, infinite in extensional terms, is finite in terms of the affective *a priori* which animates it. In the world of the aesthetic object, the unconditioned is not (as it is for Kant) the inaccessible totality of the series of conditions. The unconditioned is, rather, the unity of a singular feeling which may be undefinable but is, in any case, present to us. Confronted with such a contrast, must one say that aesthetic experience involves only a dyadic relationship between the work and the spectator (a spectator who penetrates into the world of the work by excluding any reference to the objective world)?

It is not with the objective world as conceived by science that one should compare the aesthetic object. Instead, the aesthetic object should be compared with the real, which we must intercept at the point where it does not yet have a determinate signification and can accept the signification which the aesthetic object confers on it. It is therefore necessary to distinguish between the real and the objective. The critique of aesthetic realism has already suggested this, since it teaches us that, even if art confronts the real or is inspired by it, art does not copy an objective world already given—since, in the end, there is no pre-existent objective world. What we consider to be the objective world becomes a world only through the *a priori* of representation, just as the aesthetic world becomes a world through the affective *a priori*. This parallelism prevents the two worlds from collapsing into each other. The objective world is the result of a projection onto the real. This act of projection is instituted by a *cogito* which makes itself impersonal, and it is constantly being renewed because of the fact that knowing has no end. The objective world is thus a compromise—between a purely rational demand of the kind which Kant analyzed that requires a dehumanization of the real, and the lived experience of singular totalities which have an immediate meaning, whether for action or for feeling (the immediate, as we have seen, has two different aspects, both opposed to the mediation of knowing). When I try to think the world, to give a determinate content to what is primarily the horizon for an unlimited search for rational connections, I refer implicitly to the immediate knowledge of a world which is present and near and given to unreflective consciousness. To think of the world as one, as total, is, in the first place, to give greater extension to the singular world by annexing to it the antipodes, the galaxies, prehistory. It is through this world that one hopes to rejoin the idea of a unity of phenomena given to an absolute knowledge. In fact, however, one only increases in extension a world which derives its meaning and its quality from the very notion of world. Moreover, for science itself, the world is a fibrous structure. The diverse scales of distinction which science brings into play—micro- or macrophysics, the rapid time of physiology, or the slow time of the displacement of the continents or the erosion of mountains—define worlds which are distinct in practice and are initially worlds for a concrete subject. For an archivist, the history of a medieval monastery may enjoy greater proximity than some contemporary event. For a nuclear physicist, the atom is closer than the trees which surround his laboratory. The world of science is first of all the world of the scientist. Thus an objective world cannot be conceived strictly for itself, except as a limit and an infinite task. And an objective world cannot be contrasted with subjective worlds in an effort to disqualify the latter under the pretext that they are several in number. To the extent that it is thought as a world, the objective world is rooted in subjective worlds. This is why, in turn, subjective worlds cannot be considered as elements detached from an objective world which would contain and encompass all of them. Further, each subjective world aspires to encompass the others. The real problem, especially for aesthetics, is that of knowing to what extent these worlds clarify or illuminate [*éclairent*] the real.

For the real does need to be illuminated, and this can occur through the agency of art as well as through science. The real is the preobjective. It is manifested in the bruteness of fact, the constraining character of being-there, the opacity of the in-itself. The reality of the real is a presence which I encounter and to which I submit. One can oppose a resistant and harsh reality to dreams, or work to leisure activity, just as one opposes perception to imagination. In the same vein, the only people who brag of being in the real are those at grips with an obstacle which it is necessary to conquer and which sometimes crushes them, those who struggle and suffer. And all the rest is only mystification . . . and literature, and deserves the blow of the staff which Molière's philosopher receives. The real is not a situation, a place where one settles oneself, or a "good" which one possesses. The real appears only in "boundary-situations," like those which Jaspers describes—suffering, illness, or death. And one cannot refuse to acknowledge all those who feel the weight of things and events as their unfortunate fate. But, even if this presence of brute being guarantees reality, it still does not provide a place for truth. There is truth only through the discovery of a meaning which illuminates and transfigures the real and through the ability of a subjectivity to seize this meaning. As soon as one characterizes the real—e.g., in saying what is inhuman, formidable, or sordid about it, in feeling nauseated by it, or in having pity for it—one surpasses naked reality in order to illuminate it. The most inhuman reality is inhuman only for a human subject. Consequently, just as the objective world presupposes the *a priori* of representation, the real itself is never present except in terms of the various *a priori* of presence which structure it and confer a meaning on it by structuring it in accordance with a vital subjectivity. The animated body is already intelligent in its own fashion, and it, too, judges the real. It cannot be denied that the real is always already there, both opaque and overflowing. But it is the body which experiences the real and instructs us, and it is for the body that the real has sovereign and unlimited presence. Even the nonsensical aspects of the real make sense at the level of lived experience. However, the real as such does not yet have the shape of a world. The overflowing character which it assumes is not yet a characteristic of a world, and we cannot enumerate or unify singular worlds within it. This overflowing character is like an inexhaustible reservoir of the given, but only because it holds nothing in reserve. It is an inexhaustible matrix of significations, but only because it has no signification of its own. Everything is united in it—flowers were blooming at the gates of the death camps, and the ascetic rubs shoulders in a crowd with the debauched. But such an indifferent unity of incongruities does not truly constitute a world, except for the person who cries out against this kind of injustice and considers the unity of this universe to be scandalous and inhuman. There is a world only for the person who discovers within and selects from the real a certain signification, even if it be the absence of signification. The unity of the world does not arise from the unity of the real but from the unity of the look which settles on the real (or, in the case of the objective world, from the unity of knowledge).

This objective world is at least thought—one may even say willed—as one. Must we then say that the world of Kafka and the world of Giraudoux, the world of Wagner and the world of Debussy, are different aspects or sectors of it? When I say that next to André Malraux's *Temps du mépris* there is Jules Romain's *Douceur de vivre*, or that next to the Apollonian there is the Dionysian, I do not merely juxtapose or add together two things, for then the whole would be an absence of world. The worlds regulated by the affective *a priori* do not have a common denominator in an objective world, any more than do the worlds structured by the vital *a priori*. In merging with the objective world, such worlds lose their essential character and refer to a look which is no longer that of a concrete subject, but an anonymous gaze which grounds objectivity. One cannot say that aesthetic worlds are parts of the objective world or even perspectives on it. Aesthetic worlds simply refuse to be measured against it. It is in relation to brute reality that they must be understood, since it is for this real that they are a light. The light of something possible? Yes, in the sense that the possible illuminates through an action of anticipation, as we have seen in our analysis of perception. One can also evoke the role played by possibilities which are inscribed both in our body (in the form of habits) and in the world (in the form of tools and trails). The real is lived as the field of possibilities. Furthermore, the real appears precisely through the mediation of the *a priori* taken as the purely possible. One reaches the real only as armed with possibilities.[16] But these possibilities, which are not compossible in relation to an objective world which would encompass them, are not to be considered unreal with respect to the real. They are not the poor relations of the real or something uncertain which the real determines and dominates. They are the meaning which illuminates the real and outlines a world within it.

Thus the real does not disavow aesthetic worlds, in spite of their peculiarity and diversity. On the one hand, the real does not transform their subjectivity into a motif of unreality. The real needs aesthetic worlds. The aesthetic object takes up the real in order to give meaning to the real. The aesthetic object founds and unifies the real in the light of the existential *a priori*. By giving form to the real, the aesthetic worlds deserve to be real. On the other hand, the real does not repudiate the plurality of aesthetic worlds, for it is through their very plurality that it is the real, that is, the overflowing. In fact, we must stress at this point the remarkable diversity of aesthetic objects, precisely be-

16. Even the type of explanation which tries to make the real into an objective world has recourse to the possible. Consider, for example, what Max Weber says of causality in history.

cause this diversity is often used as the principal objection to their truth. We shall thus be able to see that, even outside aesthetic experience, the diversity of worlds is already predelineated and initiated by the real—with the result that, even if these worlds are already structured by an existential project, they can also be suggested and called forth by the real which they illuminate.

Now, we have already observed that, strictly speaking, there are as many worlds as there are aesthetic objects and, in any case, as many as there are artists. The affective *a priori* which reveals and constitutes these worlds is a singular *a priori* which the affective category subsumes only imperfectly. Moreover, one can speak of worlds in a wider sense without their being determined by an aesthetic object which expresses them. Is it necessary to give aesthetic worlds a special fate and to reserve for them the privilege of being true? We should make a distinction here. There are, first, worlds which one is tempted to call illusory, e.g., the world of the hallucinated or of the mythomaniac. There can be, because of art, a truth concerning *Don Quixote* or *Madame Bovary,* just as there is, because of science, a certain explanation of paranoia. However, the world of Don Quixote, of Madame Bovary, or of a paranoiac is still not a true world. But to say that they have no world at all is to say too much. Psychiatrists who strive to understand paranoia and sympathize with it are not content to deny the patient's world or to dissolve it in the objective world; instead, they try to enter into it. Yet the goal is still to seize and tear out, within this world, the roots of paranoiac delusion—in short, to destroy such a world. They establish the subjectivity of the paranoiac's world in order to denounce its delusional character and to oppose it victoriously with the objective world. But why does the subjectivity of this world disqualify it, and why is it hoped that this subjectivity will disqualify it in the eyes of the very person who lives it? Because the patient is not truly himself. He is living in a state of blindness, frailty, or bad faith, and he is not actively and normatively at grips with the real. His world has become exhausted and dislocated—a world in which nothing is done. The artist, in contrast, has created his work, which speaks on his behalf and demands recognition from us. The distance from the true to the false is measured by the distance between the accounts of hallucinated people and Novalis' *Hymnen an die Nacht* or Rimbaud's *Illuminations.* The aesthetic world is true because the aesthetic object is true in the two principal senses which we have invoked. The aesthetic world finds in this object both an irrefutable expression and an authentic testimony. The dreams of Jean-Paul and of Novalis, the demons of Bosch and the angels of Giotto, Chinese dragons and the Hindu Shiva do not constitute the real, but they say something and bear a light which illuminates the real. There is something in the real which can be said through monsters, through metaphors, or simply through melody. To relate this world to the artist is not to explain it away in an effort to denounce and dissipate its imaginary character, but to understand that the subject alone can reveal such a world. And the real does not resist this revelation.

Indeed, the real seems to solicit disclosure. There is, in fact, another class of worlds which appear to be brought forth by the real itself rather than organized in terms of subjectivity. In this respect, the real seems to be articulated by configurations capable of expanding and expressing a world which proposes itself to the subject instead of the subject's appearing to take the initiative. Thus one speaks of a world of spring or winter, a world of health or illness, a world of the city or the country. Are we not lost in an endless pluralism? When we take a walk from one quarter of a city to another, we change worlds, just as we do from one hour to another as the light changes. Similarly, we change worlds by changing social roles, by leaving an office and going to a drawing room or leaving a grocery store and going to a playing field. There is the world of Debussy's *Le Jardin sous la pluie* along with the world of almond trees in flower beneath the sun. There is the world of war in addition to the world of peace, the world of prisons next to the world of free space and of conquerors, and the world of the sea beside the world of forests. There are innumerable worlds. We have no definite clue or *a priori* for dividing or classifying them, since they are opened to us only by the accidents of nature and history. In this regard, we are always squarely in the middle of the empirical: the sun this morning unveils a springlike world; a war has plunged this city into the world of devastation; the police attempt to break up a procession and thus provoke the world of violence. But must we speak here of worlds as in the case of the aesthetic object? What we must say is that these worlds are not supported by an object which is complete and richly meaningful, an object which compels us to disengage ourselves from the plane of lived experience so that we may read an expression and discover a depth which serves as a reservoir for possible objects. In short, such worlds are only suggestions which something trifling can awaken. The song of a cicada can evoke an entire wasteland, an osseous and blazing world where the passions themselves have the flaming intensity of fire. The call of a blackbird evokes the forest—a royal forest with the high trees and great ferns of the Ile-de-France and its surrounding meadows, where life springs up and murmurs with happiness, expressing the vegetable innocence and tenderness of Rousseau. Is there a world here? There are our emotions, the affluence of memories, and our willingness to inflate the moment. And yet there is also something real which gives rise to the emotions and images which magnify the real. The memories which invade us also bear on the real. It is not a case of the imagination's getting carried away and playing tricks on us by seeking to negate the real. On the contrary, we feel at one with the real, and it seems as if the real seeks to find in us all its amplitude and its resonance, acquiring a profundity which it perhaps does not have by itself. The real needs us and itself solicits the aesthetic attitude. It is at this point that the problems of the natural aesthetic object would be posed. In order that the real truly suggest a world, the real must become aestheticized, and we must make ourselves poets of the real. Once again, we see that there is no world which is not taken in and opened up by a subjectivity.

The worlds which we have just considered must be enveloped in an experience which is aesthetic or quasi-aesthetic. But certain other worlds seem to merit their name without calling forth the aesthetic attitude. This is the case, for example, when a historian speaks of a world of the Renaissance, a geographer of a world of forests or mountains, or a sociologist of a world of the church or of the military. But are these worlds not already objective worlds, instituted by a certain selection from the real world along lines proposed by the real itself? Can one not classify them, define them, and formulate them according to certain laws? Certainly, for these worlds do not have the fleeting and hazy character of worlds which a trifle suggests and which are inflated by an emotion. Instead, they proceed from intellectual operations and are the object of methodical explorations. They are isolated and catalogued with precision. For knowledge tends to reduce them to the objective world of which they constitute spatially and temporally circumscribed provinces. As a result, the world of the sea and that of the mountain, the Greek world and the Roman world, can be juxtaposed or can succeed one another, whereas the world of Valéry's *Cimetière marin* and the world of Cézanne's *Sainte Victoire,* Homer's world and that of

Virgil, are irreducibly diverse, although they are all true. To be sure, the examples in the first group are still worlds for someone. How does one come to define them, except by placing them in relationship to a concrete subject—just as one defines the heart by putting it in relationship with an organism? To define the world of the sea is to define it from the perspective of the sailor. Similarly, the world of the city is defined from the perspective of the city-dweller. The geographer or the ecologist should become a sailor or a city-dweller—at least for a while—in order to seize the phenomenon of the sea or the phenomenon of the city in its radical originality. In the same way, the ethnologist becomes primitive, the psychiatrist neurotic, while reserving the right to reflect on the condition which they have had to assume in the interest of comprehension. Thus, even when we circumscribe a world in order to objectify it, we must first feel it as subjective. There will always be an implicit reference to this feeling. But the geographer or the ecologist will try to overcome such reference through the objectivity of inquiry—to the point of showing how, in the end, the sailor and the city-dweller are produced by the sea or the city, that is, by a reality which is foreign to them and determines them. Finally, between what we call the world of the city or the world of the child and the world of Debussy or of Van Gogh, there is the difference that we attempt to objectify the one with the aid of the *a priori* of representation, and to feel the other in the light of the affective *a priori*. To be sure, we can objectify the aesthetic worlds just as well as the others, by unfolding the contents of the feeling which delivers them to us and by transposing this content into the historically real. And we may even attempt to explain the creator through reference to the objective world. We can pass, from the world of Debussy understood as a world expressed through the work of Debussy, to the world of Debussy understood as his immediate environment (in the latter sense, we speak of a world of the child or a world of the forest).[17] But it is still true that aesthetic worlds do not have to be objectified. They do not wait for someone to construct a truth for them, for they are already true by themselves.

It is in this respect that aesthetic worlds are incomparable to

17. The same transposition is possible when we speak of the world of the child, for that signifies simultaneously the world lived by the child (in which, for example, his parents are gods) and the world in which the child is placed. We readily realize that these two worlds are reciprocal. We know that the child is for adults a center of interest and that, conversely, the world experienced by the child is the projection of the environment which adults arrange for him.

others and particularly merit being called "worlds." Their plurality should not surprise us, since it attests to the unimpeachable fact of a plurality of subjectivities or of existential *a priori*. Of course, there is communication between consciousnesses, and in this respect the real is their common property. But the real, in its turn, needs these subjective worlds in order to appear and to manifest what is inexhaustible in the given. The real appeals to all possibilities, because it needs them in order to take on form, just as historical events have no importance except through the possibilities with which they are pregnant, and a city, a landscape, or an individual appears only through multifarious aspects. The sea can be the sea of Debussy's *Voiles*, the glossy and scintillating sea of Turner's seascapes, the arrogant and yet subjugated sea of Liszt's *Legend of St. Francis of Paola*, the voracious and somber sea of Victor Hugo's *Océano Nox*, and within the same poem a "tranquil roof" and an "absolute hydra." [18] Like the destiny of man, the real can be seen as the spiritual adventure of Franck's *Chorals*, the brief and finally bitter joy of Debussy's *Fêtes* or of Jean Renoir's *Partie de campagne*, the sordid existence of G. W. Pabst's *La Rue sans joie*, or the holiday celebrations of Versailles and of the opera. The real is the fact that all of this is possible. But, as in the case of Kant's kingdom of ends, the idea of a unity of the real remains only an idea. Every effort at objectification (including perception itself, as soon as representation is substituted for presence) attempts to realize this unity, without ever reaching it. Another unity—which is exclusive and not inclusive, and which is presented in depth and not on the surface—is immediately given as soon as the real dons an expressive visage and speaks to us. The world of objectivity is constituted at the expense of the worlds which are born of expression. Plurality is thus primary, and we acclimate ourselves to it easily. We have no more difficulty in passing from the world of Mozart to the world of Wagner than in passing from the world of winter to the world of summer or from the city to the country. In each case, we are plunged into a world without becoming conscious of its exclusive and singular character. It is only on reflection that we realize that there are other worlds, those of others (as well as other worlds for ourselves, to the extent that, with time, we will enjoy diverse experiences). Only after reflection does such plurality become a problem and a task, for we must both neutralize and respect this

18. The last two phrases are from Paul Valéry's *Cimetière marin*.—Trans.

diversity that we have come to understand. Thus, on the scientific plane, we elaborate a science of the universe, while also bearing in mind the heterogeneity of phenomena or the degrees of being. Similarly, on the moral plane, we recognize the rights of others, and we aim at a harmonious unity which would not undermine individual differences. But it is on the plane of art that we must respect these differences most fully and recognize the plurality of the human.

In sum, there are plural worlds only because a world (even an objective world) exists only as assumed and defined by a consciousness which is, first of all, a singular consciousness. The real is not initially given as an in-itself which is subsequently divided into particular worlds or into monadic perspectives. On the contrary, the unity of the real, understood as an objective world, can be felt and affirmed only on the basis of the experience of singular worlds. It is not as one that the real is real, but as perceived and given. Consequently, the plurality of aesthetic worlds does not mean that they are unreal (as they would be if the real were one). But it remains for us to show how affective signification—which, in spite of its indefinite and nonnumerical character, is nevertheless a meaning—can appear in the real. And if this meaning is the meaning of the real, must one not confer an ontological status on it? Finally, is it not the case that man, who reads and proclaims this meaning, and the real, which bears it, are both subordinate to it—in other words, that the anthropological and the ontic are in the end subordinate to the ontological?

19 / The Ontological Signification of Aesthetic Experience

By assigning an ontological signification to aesthetic experience, we are admitting that the cosmological and existential aspects of the affective *a priori* are grounded in being, that is, that being is the bearer of a meaning or sense which it stamps on reality and which it also forces man to utter.[1] Aesthetic experience illuminates the real because reality is like the obverse side of being—a being of which man is the witness. Consequently, art bespeaks the real because both art and reality are subordinate to being. We must therefore deny that man initiates aesthetic experience and instead credit it to being. But how is this possible? Is man not responsible for the meaning of things? Can we speak of a being of meaning—by identifying meaning with being—of which man is the servant and reality the manifestation? Until this point, in any event, we have not been in a position to find, for the truth of aesthetic experience, anything other than an anthropological or human justification.

[I] Anthropological Justification of Aesthetic Truth

As an answer to the question of how the aesthetic object can teach us about the real insofar as it reveals a world, we

1. This does not imply that the real is identical with meaning. As in the Hegelian dialectic, the real is meaning's essential other. And it is thus that it is the inexhaustible nonmeaning which exceeds meaning. What is nonmeaning, however, in relation to man remains meaning in relation to being. It is meaning which has become nature.

[539]

have been espousing an *ad hominem* argument which shows that reality is not the absolute basis of judging the aesthetic world, because reality needs the aesthetic world in order to appear as real. We have also said that the aesthetic object does not need to copy an already constituted reality but only to offer a light which can be projected onto the given. Thus the aesthetic object is true because it induces us to complete the constitutive movement of a truth. This is not a factual truth which would consist in establishing the aesthetic object as fact by relating it to still other facts until the network of an objective world were traced out. Art is useless in any such elaboration of an already given reality—an elaboration for which perception orients itself and surpasses itself toward science. But there is also a more fundamental truth, according to which a world is possible before any objectification. It is in terms of this truth that aesthetic experience prefigures the processes of consciousness as a whole. Aesthetic experience puts into play the various *a priori* which are presupposed by our apprehension of the real as a world. These *a priori* may not take chronological precedence over experience. But they are its condition and also constitute the subject as a subject who experiences the real. We could argue, further, that the subject anticipates the representation of the real because he is already bound to reality by his bodily presence. Even the body needs to anticipate and illuminate. The *a priori* is both an *a priori* in relation to the real and an *a priori* which we are. Without it, there would be no subject and no world.

In fact, at the origin of all consciousness, there is a process of self-withdrawal which Sartre has called "nihilation" [*néantisation*]. This is not merely a methodological doubt which puts truth in question but a sort of ontological doubt by which a for-itself is affirmed. Thus a distance opens up which intentionality will eventually traverse. For, although intentionality binds consciousness to its object, intentionality also defines consciousness as what is *not* the object and as the "not" [*ne pas*] from which the object emerges. This distance is what allows us to see. It is light. As Levinas writes, "Light is thus the occurrence of a suspension [of belief], an *epochē* . . . which defines the self in its power of infinite self-withdrawal." [2] But this light is not enough. It is only responsible for the possibility of a world in its most abstract and naked form, as the pure externality of space which

2. Emmanuel Levinas, *De l'existence à l'existant* (Paris: Vrin, 1947), p. 79.

corresponds to the pure interiority of time. This is a world for a consciousness which is itself abstract, an impersonal self which defines itself only by an abstract power of negation. Nevertheless, on the transcendental foundation of this absolute act of positing, the contours of a world begin to emerge and its unity tightens when we consider a personal subject, that is, a concrete for-itself which is neither a pure negation nor a pure project but the project of a particular world. The world becomes the world of a for-itself. The light in this world becomes more luminous— as the light of day takes on color—and it becomes a cosmological *a priori*. Such light is the meaning which orients our apprehension of the real and renders brute givens meaningful. In this way, reality becomes expressive. But expression can be read only by a being who has a self and who embodies an existential *a priori* which is also a cosmological *a priori*. That is, expression is read by the subject who *is* that expression. Expression is present to this subject before being taken in from the real. Expression is the truth which is given before the real. In sum, expression is the world as meaning—a world which is given before the objects in it.

The function of art is to put this truth to work. This function can be interpreted in an empirical sense, which we should discuss first. Art teaches us to perceive according to the *a priori* activated in every perception, and art facilitates the use of these *a priori*. The aesthetic object adjusts itself to the body by means of schemata by which the object is ordered. The aesthetic object rigorously outlines space and time and has the docile and convincing presence of a model object. Above all, it teaches us to grasp the affective *a priori* which constitutes it and which reveals an aspect of the world. In contrast, ordinary perception places us before objects which continually pose problems calling for understanding and will, reflection and action. These objects do not afford us the leisure to take in their expression. Of course, ordinary perception also reveals a world—a world which always lies at the horizon of the object which the subject utilizes and explores. All consciousness is consciousness of a world from the instant it is consciousness of an object. In other words, there is no relation to an object which is not also a relation to a world. This is why all perception is simultaneously imagination. But this world is outlined on the basis of the perceived object and has that object for its center. In fact, this world is no more than the indeterminate prolongation of the perceived object. When we take a train, the train is perceived as what takes us toward our destination. Its world is the space it must cross—a space which we are invited to anticipate by the presence of the train. Thus arises what is called the "atmosphere" of railroad stations, where consciousnesses with different projects jostle one another. People are headed for different parts of the world, a world which changes aspect depending on the station from which we are going. Perception proceeds from object to world, because the world is external to the object. It is an extended world which spreads itself before us in proportion to our care or impatience, for in ordinary perception we are concerned with seeking, beyond the object itself, the possibilities the object offers us and the ever closer relationships it sustains with other objects. Aesthetic perception, on the other hand, is never rushed and never hurries outside of its object. It examines its object thoroughly in order to discover, by means of feeling, an internal world which must therefore be a different world—a world which is not nourished by imagination or taken up by understanding but instead exists potentially in feeling. This is a world which can bear witness to the real, not by propounding what it is in positive fact but by presenting its countenance to us. Thus we can now see what the proper function of art is. By allowing us to perceive an exemplary object whose whole reality consists in being sensuous, art invites us and trains us to read expression and to discover the atmosphere which is revealed only to feeling. Art makes us undergo the absolute experience of the affective.[3] We can read expressions of the real because we are trained to do so in terms of the surreal or prereal object which is the aesthetic object. Thus art has, first of all, a propaedeutic function.

This is similar to what we learned from the critique of realism. By inventing new modes of representation, art teaches us to see. It is as if art invents the real at the very moment it believes it is reproducing the real—whether this be an established and conventional reality, as in classical art, or something more intractable, as in realistic art. The reality to which theories of imitation would like art to refer (in order to copy it) is not even, strictly speaking, seen. At least, seeing is mixed together with acting and being acted upon. Art is what allows us to rediscover

3. Similarly, is there not an absolute experience of spatiality and of materiality? We experience space, time, and matter in the natural geometry which is immanent to practical perception and in such a manner that all pure science finds its foundation in this primordial experience. There may also exist, within the immediate feeling possessed by the living creature in its vitality, an absolute experience of life which grounds biological knowledge.

the freshness and power of persuasion which are intrinsic to seeing. Art leads us back to beginnings. We believe that art repeats what we have already seen, because we can identify what art represents, follow a story, and understand characters. But in fact, we had not seen any of these things before. We had not yet seen the writhing power of the human torso before seeing Michelangelo's slaves, or the tortured form of the iris before seeing Van Gogh's bouquet, or the ancient streets of Paris before reading Balzac's *La Maison du chat qui pelote*, or the face of defeat before reading Sartre's *La Mort dans l'âme*. Art does not copy, because there is no reality given in a previous perception which aesthetic perception must simulate. We could almost say that perception begins with art.

The fact remains, however, that art is true because it helps us to know the real. Art expresses what the real, and not illusion or imagination, will express. But then, we shall constantly encounter the following questions. How can art anticipate the real? How is its truth possible—a truth which precedes the real rather than resulting from it? How can reality allow itself to be illuminated by this light? We could again try to make an empirical response, remaining within an anthropological perspective, by developing the idea of art's propaedeutic function in two ways. Now, whatever is paradoxical about the notion of the truth of the work results from the work's being the product of a subjective creation. The relation between the work and the real leads us, accordingly, to the relation between the subject who creates this work and the object which is the real as attested by the work. The aesthetic object can be true in a third sense because, as we have said, it is true in the first sense. All that remains for us to do is to bring the second sense of truth—that the work is true when it is authentic—into a more precise focus. This reciprocity between the work and the real must be examined, from the point of view of both the object and the subject, in terms of an insight on which we have already touched, namely, that to the authenticity of the artist who strives to bespeak the real must correspond an authenticity in the real itself which seeks to be spoken in art. Once again, we can consider this proximity of art and the real empirically.

If we consider the genesis of a given work, it will be easy to show that it is the work of someone involved in the real and to measure its authenticity by the seriousness of his involvement. The first concern of the artist is, of course, to create his work, but he knows that in creating the work he continues to be himself and to assume his unique situation in the midst of historical reality. This is so much the case that some aspect of this encompassing reality is inevitably reflected in his work. Thus the work gives evidence not only of the personality of its author but also of the nature of the real world in which he has lived. Mallarmé, Debussy, and Monet bear the stamp of an epoch just as much as Molière, Lully, Mansard, and Le Nôtre. For this reason, as well, the world of the aesthetic object tends to harden into historical images. The world of Lully becomes concretized in the world of Versailles, the world of El Greco in the world of a victorious and mystical Spain. Even when the work does not propose to represent the reality which is contemporaneous with its creation, it bears witness to this reality. What the work expresses is found to be the expression of the real as well. The important thing is that the artist has been authentic. By expressing himself and being true to his existential *a priori,* he cannot help but express his surrounding reality—a reality which bears him along and touches him on every side and to which all his activity is a constant response. Being oneself does not mean taking refuge in an invulnerable solitude but, rather, accepting one's being in the world and not attempting to escape, even under the pretext of artistic creation. Such creation has no substance if it is the work of a man who flees his destiny. Such an analysis as this has often been made, but it needs to be further specified in two ways. First, although the artist must actively involve himself in his work in order to be authentic, he need not involve his work in activist projects, as has sometimes been argued. The artist can express the real almost unconsciously and without claiming to represent it or act upon it with his work. But is this not dilettantism and therefore inauthenticity? Not if an exclusive concern for the creative act and an indifference to its immediate effectiveness are not the last word. Aesthetic disinterest must not be an alibi for the impotence of the "beautiful soul," and authenticity must be a response to a deeper need. Yet we should observe that the reality with which art thus reunites is only the historical reality which is contemporaneous with the work, a reality which is culturally limited in space and time. Perhaps the world revealed by the work is wider and capable of harboring a more diverse reality.

But we must recognize, still remaining on the empirical level, the obverse side of this sort of validity in art. This is found in the adaptation of the real to art. If art can reunite with the real, the real must be open to this union. Just as the real impregnates the artist, we can say that art impregnates the real. The reality which is illuminated by the work and in which we live constantly is, in fact, a cultural world in which objects of use rub shoulders with aesthetic objects. It is thus a world which is occupied by hovels as well as castles, fields as well as gardens, street sounds as well as concerts. The banalities of everyday life itself are so marked by the enterprise of art that the boundary between the aesthetic and the nonaesthetic cannot be easily determined. Hence it is not surprising that the world of the aesthetic object allows of application to the real. Surely art orients and refines our perception of reality. Nerval and the impressionists teach us how to see the Île-de-France, just as Retz and Corneille influence our view of the events of the Fronde, or portraits our sense of the human face. Our apprehension of the real is nourished by aesthetic experience. It both imitates this experience and is inspired by it. This is because, conversely, the real imitates art. The real thereby becomes aestheticized at the same time that it is humanized. As soon as the natural has been surpassed—and what is natural about our cultural world?—there is no great distance from the artificial to the aesthetic. The women we encounter on the street imitate, through their make-up or their carriage, film stars who themselves may imitate a famous portrait or a legendary ballerina. Our passions are not so spontaneous that they do not occasionally take on a theatrical air or adopt the language of some personal hero. In much the same way, things borrow their personalities from aesthetic models. Gardens imitate parks and fields imitate gardens. We could almost say that, after submitting to contemplation, even the most refractory things end up assuming the imprint of the human look. Thus the sky sometimes seems to imitate landscape painters, and the sea the poets who write about it. Inasmuch as the real lends itself to the human look, it lends itself to art. This is all the more the case when the action by which the real is stamped with the seal of man is inspired by aesthetic norms—or mimics the norms set forth by aesthetics. Therefore art can give us keys to the real, or at least to the real's affective aspects, because on its part art contributes to the elaboration of this reality. Art can be applied to the real because reality is, in a sense, its handiwork. Their affinity derives from a more fundamental relation of affiliation. Even as nature, the real is still a work of man and almost a work of art. With the same right as the aesthetic object, it is the

Sache selbst which Hegel constrasts with the *Ding*. It is the tamed object which reflects back to man his own image and in which is realized, at one and the same time, the affinity of art and the real and the unity of the cosmological and the existential.

This interpretation has the merit of bringing together the aesthetic and the human. We know by now that it is the peculiar virtue of the aesthetic to reveal the human. But the aesthetic depends uniquely on the initiative of man, who in the end finds the real to be human only because he has already humanized it by his action or at least by his look. Hence the aesthetic can never account for what is expressive in an inhuman nature, except by bold extrapolation. And is the aesthetic even capable of accounting for the natural aesthetic object? In any event, the aesthetic does not tell us why there is art, that is, why a meaning wishes to express itself. Is the artist not moved by a force and set to work at a task which surpasses him? Is it not the case that this meaning, which finally appears as a meaning of the real, is called forth by the real itself, instead of being imposed on it by a human project? And is it not being itself which summons man to bespeak [*dire*] this meaning and to read [*lire*] it in the real?

[II] METAPHYSICAL PERSPECTIVES

IF WE CANNOT SAY that man is the exclusive bearer of meaning or that he himself puts into the real the affective meaning disclosed in aesthetic experience, then two consequences follow: (1) the real does not acquire its affective meaning from man; and (2) being calls on man to be the witness and not the initiator of affective meaning. Let us outline these two points and thus venture an ontological view of art.

We must try to understand what is insufficient about anthropological exegesis, for which the meaning incarnated in the *a priori* is invented by the subject and transferred by him onto things. According to this doctrine, the real exists in the image of man, particularly in the image of art, because he perceives or makes the real in this image. If we deny to man the privilege of founding the true and instead found man himself on the true, then we transfer the initiative to being and being becomes meaning itself or, as we would suggest, that *a priori* which precedes its existential and cosmological determinations and seems to ground both subject and object, man and world.[4] In short, we must try to determine whether meaning—as it is found, or rather lost, in the real (insofar as the real is something other than meaning), and as it is reflected in man, who expresses it in art and discovers it in nature—is, in fact, the ordering principle for nature and man, instead of being projected by man onto nature, with the result that man's mission would be to bespeak meaning rather than invent it. Undoubtedly, this is what Heidegger has in mind when he cites Hölderlin's phrase, "that which lasts is instituted by poets," and adds that the gods are what force the poet, who has the courage to "situate himself in the intermediary realm between gods and men," to speak.[5]

We should point out in passing that we are dealing here, in a different form, with the same problem which haunted our earlier attempt to define the aesthetic object as an in-itself for-us, thus implying that the aesthetic perception to which the aesthetic object appeals authenticates the object but does not constitute it.[6] We have admitted that the aesthetic object possesses a being and a truth independent of perception, even though the object needs to be recognized by perception. Yet an ontological perspective invites us to ascend a step higher. We must admit that meaning has a being—that meaning *is* being—which precedes both the object in which it is manifested and the subject to whom it is manifested and which appeals to the solidarity of subject and object in order to be actualized. The problem posed by aesthetic perception would then be seen as, in a sense, willed by being itself. It would arise from the dialectic of being rather than reducing this dialectic to its own dimensions. We shall soon have to determine whether such a dialectic can be properly conceived.

In any event, we must admit that man is an episode in this dialectic and not the creator of meaning. However, the fact that reality does not acquire its meaning from man does not imply that the human is to be dismissed as of no consequence. Man, who is formed and made alert by aesthetic experience, is capable of recognizing this meaning and subsuming it under an affective category. We cannot question the accord which exists between man and the real. We must only credit the accord to being instead of to man. Man and the real both belong to being. Being

4. We cannot take up here the question of whether ontology excludes or presupposes theology.
5. "Hölderlin and the Essence of Poetry," trans. D. Scott, in *Existence and Being,* ed. W. Brock (Chicago: Regnery, 1950), p. 281.
6. See above, chap. 10, § III.

is precisely the identity of meaning and of the real—of meaning as it can be read by man and of the real as it is marked by meaning. But the human is not for this reason disqualified. Even if meaning is not constituted by man, it passes through him. The *a priori* continues to be shared by both object and subject. It remains both existential and constitutive, although constitution is not the activity of man but, rather, of being *through* man. As a result of aesthetic experience, something human is revealed in the real, a certain quality by which things are consubstantial with man, not because they can be known, but because they offer to the man capable of contemplating them a familiar face in which he can recognize himself without having himself composed the being of this face. Thus man can recognize his own passions in an ocean storm, his own nostalgia in an autumn sky, and his ardent purity in fire. We should take the human qualities in the real seriously—qualities in even better evidence in the natural aesthetic object—and not consider them to be a mere play of reflections or anthropomorphic imagery.

Minkowski has taken up this idea in his book *Vers une cosmologie*, where he seeks to define the "structural solidarity of the psychic and the cosmic" or "the cosmic bearing of psychical phenomena." [7]

> We know that man forms a *unit* with nature, not only because he takes part in nature and is its product, but also—and above all— because every movement of his soul finds a deep and therefore natural underpinning in the world and for this reason reveals to us a primordial quality of the structure of the universe. [8]

Thus Minkowski proclaims the kinship between the human and the real, as well as the presence of the human in what he calls ambience, "that vast and living totality . . . which is becoming," which must not be identified with the external world, and from which "the human personality detaches itself in order to affirm itself in relation to it." [9] For "the human vastly exceeds man, mingling with the universe and thus remaining the measure of all things." [10] Is not Minkowski speaking here of that kingdom of affective qualities which are constitutive of the aesthetic object and which include, within themselves, both a subject and

7. Eugène Minkowski, *Vers une cosmologie* (Paris: Aubier-Montaigne, 1967), pp. 169, 97.
8. *Ibid.*, p. 169.
9. *Ibid.*, p. 191.
10. *Ibid.*, p. 150.

a world? And to the question he raises and does not really answer —"Where can we find the human and how can we recognize it?" —we respond: in expression and, especially, in the expression of the aesthetic object, insofar as it discloses affective quality to us.[11] Minkowski himself cites poetry: "This structural solidarity [of the psychic and the cosmic] is one of the guarantees of the objectivity of the poetic side of life."[12] We would point out, however, that the life referred to here is not biological life but the life of meaning—the dialectical identity of meaning, such as man lives it or reads it, and of the real. This is an identity which defines being. The life of meaning requires man not so much to constitute meaning as to be its witness. Man is a moment in being, the moment in which meaning gathers itself together. The upsurge of the for-itself cannot be an absurd adventure if man is required by meaning instead of founding meaning.

There are two implications of this subordination of man to being that concern aesthetics. In the first place, the relation between art and the real is not what an aesthetic realism would suggest, namely, that art arbitrarily chooses to imitate the real because the real expects nothing from it. On the contrary, the real does expect something from art (we say "from art," and not "from the artist," advisedly). The real expects its meaning to be spoken. Since art's mission is to express this meaning—insofar as it is an affective meaning—we must say that the real or nature wills art. Art is, properly speaking, that element "without which things would be only what they are." Neither science nor praxis recognizes human qualities in things. Only art does, and art does

11. We can find, in Minkowski's own book, the answer to this question. Are the primordial qualities which phenomenology—understood here as a description of lived experience, with emphasis on the immediacy of this experience in a sense close to Merleau-Ponty's—resurrects, such as the three-dimensionality of space, not determinations of the human? Is this not, more generally, true for everything which is implied in metaphors and which thus involves a primitive meaning that precedes the division between the literal and the figurative, the sensory and the intellectual? The only difference between these fundamental qualities and affective qualities is that the fundamental qualities are oriented around representation rather than affectivity. Fundamental qualities thus designate a reality previous to the distinction between knower and known rather than to the distinction between "feeler" and felt. But we can say that they are also genuinely *a priori* and that perhaps "primitive space," as described in *Vers une cosmologie*, and "primitive time," as described in *Le Temps vécu*, are phenomenological forms, that is, Kantian *a priori* of sensibility as grasped in their original status before any objectivization. [See Eugène Minkowski, *Lived Time*, trans. Nancy Metzel (Evanston, Ill.: Northwestern University Press, 1970).—Trans.]

12. Minkowski, *Vers une cosmologie*, p. 169.

so even when it expresses the inhuman—as has been said about Cézanne's landscapes and may also be said about many works in which expression is solidified and excludes any sense of pathos. The aesthetic object is an object which does justice to and thus authenticates the human dimension of the real. The artist is the chosen locus where the real attains to consciousness in terms of what is most secret and yet most visible in it—its humanity. But it may not be enough to say that nature is expressed by the artist. Perhaps we should rather say that it is by means of the artist that nature seeks to express itself. Art thus becomes a ruse, and the artist a mere tool, for a nature in search of expression. All our suspicions of aesthetic subjectivism would then be removed. By expressing his world, the artist would fulfill a plan which would surpass that world and deliver nature of its most deeply hidden meaning. Would not this state of affairs represent the supreme guarantee of the truth of art? Art would become an instrument in the dialectic of being, that is, in the future of meaning which becomes alienated in nature and is reflected in man.

Is this not, however, to propound a metaphysical assertion that cannot be justified with certainty? Yet it is possible to give it some plausibility by relating it to other assertions which are at least partially justifiable or by seeking empirical antecedents or echoes within it. First, and in general, the thesis that man is necessary to nature (in order that nature's meaning can blossom out) is an idea that the Kantian critical philosophy has already justified in proclaiming the Copernican revolution. That nature wills man for its own fulfillment is an idea which can be approached from a different angle by considering that the history of matter may culminate in life and the history of life in man. This thesis, moreover, has always secretly drawn on teleological conceptions in which it appears that if man is nature's masterpiece, conversely, nature needs man in order to be both governed and justified.[13] But, if we allow ourselves to believe that the vital force [élan vital] culminates in man, we should not be prevented

13. This teleology could be a legacy, seasoned with rationality, of those ancient myths which tell of the passage from chaos to cosmos and describe, in their own way, how reality is ordered in becoming a world through the operation of consciousness. In any event, even if we cannot be sure that the in-itself needs the for-itself, we can at least conceive that the in-itself may engender the for-itself. This notion can find a certain basis in two of Bergson's doctrines: (1) in the essential continuity between the vital and the psychic (and perhaps between matter itself and mind, since matter is the reverse side, and in effect the relaxation, of tension); and (2) conjointly, in the expansion of the forms of life in man.

from thinking that man in turn contributes something to the nature from which he originated. And what does he contribute if not the consciousness of meaning? Second, more precisely, we can find in the Hegelian dialectic of life and of the becoming conscious of life an analogue to the assertion that the real calls on the artist in an effort to express itself in the work. Does it not seem that life experiences the need to be reflected in man, who is capable both of risking his life and of contemplating death? Becoming conscious of life constitutes the truth of life, a truth which is realized only in human experience. Life's aptitude—which is almost an act of will—to reflect itself, to become reflected, can be extended to all the real. As a consequence, we can presume that, if the vital tends to realize itself in consciousness, then the affective, the human dimension of the real, is realized in art. The result is that art becomes something essential to nature.[14] It appears at the dawn of history as soon as man has surpassed the animal stage. It is as if the human in nature were impatient to express itself, urging man to open up the world in which it will be capable of expansion.[15]

We may recall here our earlier analysis of affective qualities as *a priori*. We saw that the *a priori* tends to realize itself both in the subject, where it is existential, and in the object, where it is cosmological. Thus we said that the Racinian affective category gives rise to both Racine and his work. Admittedly, the *a priori* has a fundamentally logical significance. Its constitutive power appears in a critical analysis and cannot be confused with productive efficacy. When we constitute a world, we do not produce the real but, rather, disengage its meaning. Yet, inasmuch as our disengagement of meaning is itself an event, we can legitimately divert logic and constitution in the direction of

14. If art is in this way a cosmological phenomenon, we may wonder whether or not nature attempts to realize art before the appearance of man. A consideration of the natural aesthetic object would have to treat this problem.

15. Primitive art is, of course, tied less to the exercise of aesthetic contemplation than to magical activity and, later, to religious thought. But does not the fact that magic and religion invent art, and that the object of use arises at the same time as the aesthetic object, indicate an effort to promote art and show that art appears at the very horizon of history? As Marcel Mauss has shown, the rhythmic formulae recited endlessly by the Arunta like a sort of barbarian chant, on the occasion of the rites of "Intichiuma," are a nascent form of prayer, however distant the two may be. But they also contain the germs of poetry, from which prayer is at first inseparable. An aspect of the world is already being expressed in the Arunta's elementary cosmology, which invokes totemic ancestors and is joined to a naïve and brutal desire for nourishment.

actualization. Philosophies of history in which the ontological represents the conjunction of the logical and the chronological would be examples of this diversion. If it is admitted that the *a priori* really has the ontological meaning which we have given it, then we cannot say that it preexists history (since history begins with it) but, rather, that it is realized in history. Thus history is elevated to the level of the absolute, and something is genuinely produced at this level. But what is brought forth is not simply a reality which extends other realities or is added to them. Brute nature has no history, but it becomes history as soon as its meaning is made manifest. This is what the real expects and requires. The real bears the various *a priori*—just as man bears within himself the virtual knowledge of these *a priori* —insofar as it is prone to receive all the meanings which these *a priori* will disclose. The real is nothing other than this indefinite possibility of meaning. However, a subject must arise out of nature before the *a priori* can become what it is, a determination of being and a meaning which is reflected in nature and comes to be reflected in man. Such a history, which is absolute for the real, is also absolute for man. The virtual is realized for the sake of the real, something in the real proclaims itself, and at the same time that the real becomes a world it becomes human. Man is bound to this future of meaning, because he is himself real and as such becomes himself by making the real emerge and by participating in the adventure of being. Once again, as the meaning of the *a priori* of the world, affective quality is also the *a priori* of a subject. Just as art is the way in which this affective quality appears in order to constitute both the world and man, so nature and man possess a similar need of art. Through art, man gains his being, while at the same time nature acquires its meaning.

However, we are speaking of art and not of the artist. The subordination of man to being implied in an ontology of meaning does not allow us—and this is the second conclusion we must draw—to grant the artist any initiative through which he could invent the meaning he expresses. To place art before the artist is to imply that being engages itself, as it were, in art, and thus that art is important to being. Is this not what Maurice Blanchot means when he asserts that "the work is its own absence," that "all masterpieces tend to be no more than brilliant traces of an anonymous and impersonal movement which is that of art as a totality," and that "art exists no longer in the depth of a work; it is *nowhere*"?[16] But we cannot subscribe to these ideas. Can we really believe that the aesthetic object negates itself? If we did, we would be placing the aesthetic object in the service of a negative ontology where negation is no longer simply the opposite of affirmation. What animates an art which persists in negating all its works is not a will *to* nothingness but the will *of* nothingness. Here, non-sense becomes the only sense. Rather, art is primary only in relation to the artist and not in relation to the work. This means that we cannot attribute to man as an individual the meaning by which he is constituted existentially and which he discovers in the real. Meaning, even that of the human, precedes man. Thus the idea that art is willed by nature continues to carry conviction. The artist is not the willing agent. Instead, the artist himself is willed by art. The idea of the authenticity of the creator thus reappears —an idea to which we were led by the phenomenology of the aesthetic object.

The authenticity of the artist is not simply his fidelity to himself but also his fidelity to his work. He feels the need to create —to the point of sacrificing everything to his creation and even immolating himself—because he feels that he has been entrusted with a mission. Inspiration is primarily the feeling that there is something to say which only he can say and that his work, however unworthy it may be, is necessary in this task. But necessary to whom? To the artist himself, because he expresses himself in the work? This is true, but he does not express himself for the simple personal pleasure of expressing himself but because he is constrained to do so by the sense of mission which is imposed on him. He does not express himself like a Pharisee who struts in public in order to be admired, or even like a sinner who confesses in order to be forgiven. The artist was *chosen* to express himself, and expressing himself is the means through which he can fulfill a task that surpasses him. Is the work then necessary to the artist's peers? Yes, since the work furnishes them with an exemplary object which will regulate their perception and also procure for them an incomparable pleasure. Moreover, this pleasure, however disinterested it may be, may secretly answer to the satisfaction of a special need which surpasses all man's vital interests, just as creation is a demand arising in the artist which nevertheless surpasses the artist. Nevertheless, art is above

16. These passages are from Maurice Blanchot, "Le Musée, l'art et le temps," *Critique*, Vol. VI (December, 1950–January, 1951).—Trans.

all necessary to nature. Art is a form of service which nature expects from man. In this connection, authenticity and inspiration acquire their full meaning. The artist feels himself called by being and responsible before being. But let us not be misinterpreted here. Being, as we understand it, is not a tribunal which impassively renders judgment. Being is the very becoming of meaning. To the extent that man cooperates with this becoming through reflecting and bespeaking the meaning proposed to him by the real, he is not pleading his case before being but participating in being. This is why he creates himself in his act. In his obedience to art, he is also obedient to himself. In other words, he is willed as willing himself. There is no more of a contradiction between the voluntary and involuntary aspects of the artist's vocation than there is between subjectivity and the truth of the world revealed by the artist. The artist is authentic without disavowing himself.

As authentic, the artist is also innocent. For him, there is no separation between being and doing—no more than there is between his creative act and the real. His act precedes the subject-object distinction. Instead of opposing man to the real, this act, in which the human is realized, fulfills both man and the real and also manifests their affinity. Innocence is not lost until the appearance of law. And there is no law for the artist, since he is a law unto himself. Law has two primary aspects. On the one hand, it is characterized by a universality which represses anarchical singularity. But the artist does not need to renounce his singularity, because it is through this singularity that a world is expressed. On the other hand, law presupposes passion, the rupture of man both with himself and with others. Art, in contrast, presupposes and realizes intersubjectivity, inviting the other to be himself.

Such authenticity is a prerogative which extends to the spectator as well as to the artist. The aesthetic object needs the spectator in order to be recognized and completed, just as nature needs art. But while the spectator is thus solicited by the aesthetic object, he is also summoned by nature to promote the cause of art in general. Nature calls for this act of promotion on the part of man. It is in this way that man also participates in that absolute history in which all the *a priori* are realized. This participation may provide a clue as to why aesthetic perception is a task and why reflection on such perception cannot prevent itself from being normative. If art is true, it is to be taken seriously. There is a serious quality about art which also affects its public.

But, at the same time, the spectator shares in the dignity of the artist with whom he collaborates. The spectator also alienates himself in the aesthetic object, as if to sacrifice himself for the sake of its advent and as if this were a duty which he must fulfill. Still, losing himself in this way, the spectator finds himself. He must contribute something to the aesthetic object. This does not mean that he should add to the object a commentary consisting of images or representations which will eventually lead him away from aesthetic experience. Rather, he must be himself fully by gathering himself together as a whole, without forcing the silent plenitude of the work to become explicit or extracting any representations from this treasure trove. Thus the spectator's alienation is simply the culmination of the process of attention by which he discovers that the world of the aesthetic object into which he is plunged is also *his* world. He is at home in this world. He understands the affective quality revealed by the work because he *is* that quality, just as the artist is his work. Therefore, at the same time that the aesthetic object invites the spectator to be himself, it teaches him what he is. The spectator discovers himself by discovering a world which is his own world. He learns that the existential (which he *is*) and the cosmological are one, that the human is common to both him and the real, and that the real and he himself belong to the same race to the extent that one and the same *a priori* is realized in both and illuminates them with a single light. For a brief moment, the spectator, sensing his own innocence, feels reconciled with the real.

Thus an ontology of aesthetic experience is explicable in terms of the essential themes treated by its phenomenology. This ontology rediscovers the idea that the aesthetic object needs a spectator and yet imposes itself on the spectator to such an extent that intentionality in aesthetic perception becomes a form of alienation. In turn, this idea illustrates the idea of a structural solidarity between subject and object. Such solidarity, which is borne out in an analysis of form, is also manifested in the affinity of nature with art. This solidarity is finally manifested in man's aptitude for reflecting on the meaning which is enveloped and, as it were, lost in the real and thus for participating in being. But can such an ontology be accepted without reservation? Does not this return to the human—a return to the artist and spectator as preconditions which seems to illustrate and justify this ontology—at the same time place it in question? For as soon as we invoke man again, we must attempt to do justice to him.

In sum, does not the ontological lead us back once more to the anthropological and hence to the empirical? Should we not be satisfied with the modest empirical justification which we proposed in the beginning?

Let us return for a moment to the plurality of affective *a priori* (leaving aside the vital and noetic *a priori*). Whatever status we give to meaning, it is in the end immeasurable. Should we, as a consequence, pay homage to being as Spinoza does, by speaking of the infinite number of its attributes? Or must we say, rather, that this infinite belongs to an undeterminable becoming which is bound to man and to his history, to the history of art and of aesthetic experience insofar as this history involves affective significations? To speak of being would thus be to transpose arbitrarily the relative to the absolute. To claim that the absolute is dialectical in nature would not in any way remove the arbitrariness of this transposition. The only genuine dialectic remains that of human history, the infinite discovery of significations which bear on the real throughout the succession of aesthetic experiences that are true. Reflection on aesthetic experience thus conducts us to the threshold of the following problems. Such reflection invites us to admit an accord between man and the real—an accord which is primarily manifested in the status of the aesthetic object as an in-itself for-us, and secondarily in the signification of this object, which does not express its creator alone but also reveals an aspect of the real. But this reflection will not allow us to say whether this accord exists ultimately for the benefit of a being who governs it and realizes himself in it. Nor does it allow us to say whether becoming is a becoming of meaning or a becoming of man, or whether art preexists both work and artist. An anthropological exegesis of aesthetic experience is always possible, and a critique of this experience need not turn to ontology. Perhaps absolute knowledge lies in the realization that there is no absoluteness in knowledge, but that there is, rather, a will to the absolute in man—a will attested precisely in the deep concern for the aesthetic which we find in the spectator as well as in the artist. Perhaps the last word is that there is no last word.

Selective Bibliography

WE ARE NOT presenting here an exhaustive or systematic bibliography bearing on the problem of aesthetic experience. The "dogmatic" character of this work makes doing so unnecessary, in any case. But it is only honest to cite one's primary sources. Unfortunately we cannot name our friends—philosophers, novelists, painters, and musicians—with whom we have had discussions as clarifying and stimulating as anything that we have read. It is to these friends that we dedicate the present book. Yet we can at least mention the principal works which have inspired us. The majority of these (though not all) are cited somewhere in the text.

[I] REFLECTION ON THE OBJECT IN GENERAL AND ON THE RELATION OF THE SUBJECT TO THE OBJECT

Hegel, Georg Wilhelm Friedrich. *The Phenomenology of Mind.* Translated by J. B. Baillie. New York: Humanities Press, 1964.

Heidegger, Martin. *Kant and the Problem of Metaphysics.* Translated by James S. Churchill. Bloomington: Indiana University Press, 1962.

Husserl, Edmund. *Ideas: General Introduction to Pure Phenomenology.* Translated by W. R. Boyce Gibson. New York: Humanities Press, 1931.

[557]

Kant, Immanuel. *Critique of Pure Reason*. Translated by Norman Kemp Smith. New York: St. Martin's Press, 1929.

Levinas, Emmanuel. *De l'existence à l'existant*. Paris: Vrin, 1947.

Lewin, Kurt. *Principles of Topological Psychology*. Translated by Fritz Heider and Grace Heider. New York: McGraw-Hill, 1936.

Marcel, Gabriel. *Metaphysical Journal*. Translated by Bernard Wall. Chicago: Regnery, 1952.

Merleau-Ponty, Maurice. *Phenomenology of Perception*. Translated by Colin Smith. New York: Humanities Press, 1962.

Ricoeur, Paul. "Husserl's *Ideas II:* Analyses and Problems." In *Husserl: An Analysis of His Phenomenology,* translated by Edward G. Ballard and Lester E. Embree, pp. 35–81. Evanston, Ill: Northwestern University Press, 1967.

Sartre, Jean-Paul. *Being and Nothingness*. Translated by Barnes. New York: Philosophical Library, 1956.

———. *The Psychology of Imagination*. Translated by Bernard Frechtman. New York: Washington Square Press, 1966.

Souriau, Etienne. *L'Instauration philosophique*. Paris: Alcan, 1939.

———. *Les Différents Modes d'existence*. Paris: Presses Universitaires de France, 1943.

[II] ANALYSIS OF AESTHETIC EXPERIENCE

Alain [Emile Chartier]. *Système des beaux-arts*. Paris: Gallimard, 1926.

———. *Vingt Leçons sur les beaux-arts*. Paris: Gallimard, 1931.

Bachelard, Gaston. *L'Air et les songes*. Paris: Corti, 1943.

———. *L'Eau et les rêves*. Paris: Corti, 1942.

———. *The Psychoanalysis of Fire*. Translated by Alan C. M. Ross. Boston: Beacon Press, 1964.

———. *La Terre et les rêveries du repos*. Paris: Corti, 1948.

———. *La Terre et les rêveries de la volonté*. Paris: Corti, 1948.

Basch, Victor. *Essais d'esthétique, de philosophie et de littérature*. Paris: Alcan, 1934.

Bayer, Raymond. *L'Esthétique de la grace*. 2 vols. Paris: Alcan, 1934.

Conrad, Waldemar. "Das ästhetische Objekt." *Zeitschrift für Ästhetik und allgemeine Kunstwissenschaft* III–IV (1904–5).

Croce, Benedetto. *The Essence of Aesthetic*. Translated by Douglas Ainslie. London: Heinemann, 1921.

———. *La Poésie*. Translated by D. Dreyfus. Paris: Presses Universitaires de France, 1950.

Hegel, George Wilhelm Friedrich. *The Philosophy of Fine Art*. Translated by F. P. B. Osmaston. London: G. Bell & Sons, 1920.

Heidegger, Martin. "Hölderlin and the Essence of Poetry." Translated by D. Scott. In *Existence and Being*, edited by Werner Brock. Chicago: Regnery, 1950.

———. "The Origin of the Work of Art." Translated by Albert Hofstadter. In *Poetry, Language, and Thought*. New York: Harper & Row, 1971.

Jaspers, Karl. *Strindberg und Van Gogh*. Berlin: Springer, 1926.

Malraux, André. *The Voices of Silence*. Translated by Stuart Gilbert. Garden City, N.Y.: Doubleday, 1953.

Sartre, Jean-Paul. *What Is Literature?* Translated by Bernard Frechtman. New York: Harper & Row, 1965.

Souriau, Etienne. *L'Avenir de l'esthétique*. Paris: Alcan, 1929.

[III] ANALYSIS OF THE WORK OF ART

Brelet, Gisèle. *Esthétique et création musicale*. Paris: Presses Universitaires de France, 1947.

Ghyka, Matila. *L'Esthétique des proportions dans la nature et dans les arts*. Paris: Gallimard, 1938.

Gouhier, Henri. *L'Essence du théâtre*. Paris: Plon, 1943.

Ingarden, Roman. *The Literary Work of Art*. Translated by George G. Grabowicz. Evanston, Ill.: Northwestern University Press, 1973.

Lhote, Andrè. *De la palette à l'écritoire*. Paris: Corrêa, 1946.

Munro, Thomas. *The Arts and Their Interrelations*. New York: Liberal Arts Press, 1949.

Pouillon, Jean. *Temps et roman*. Paris: Gallimard, 1946.

Schloezer, Boris de. *Introduction à J. S. Bach*. Paris: Gallimard, 1947.

Souriau, Etienne. *La Correspondance des arts*. Paris: Flammarion, 1947.

Venturi, Lionello. *Painting and Painters: How to Look at a Picture*. New York: Scribners, 1945.

Wölfflin, Heinrich. *Principles of Art History*. Translated by M. D. Hottinger. New York: Dover, 1956.

[IV] STUDY OF THE AFFECTIVE A PRIORI

Bergson, Henri. *Matter and Memory*. Translated by N. M. Paul and W. S. Palmer. New York: Doubleday, Anchor Books, 1959.

Goldstein, Kurt. *The Organism*. Translated by K. S. Lashley. Boston: Beacon Press, 1963.

Kant, Immanuel. *Critique of Judgement*. Translated by James Creed Meredith. Oxford: Oxford University Press, 1952.

Merleau-Ponty, Maurice. *The Structure of Behavior*. Translated by Alden L. Fisher. Boston: Beacon Press, 1963.

Minkowski, Eugène. *Vers une cosmologie*. Paris: Aubier-Montaigne, 1967.

Scheler, Max. *Formalism in Ethics and Non-Formal Ethics of Values*. Translated by Manfred S. Frings and Roger L. Funk. Evanston, Ill.: Northwestern University Press, 1973.

Souriau, Etienne. "Art et vérité." *Revue philosophique de la France et de l'étranger*, Vol. CXV (March, 1933).

[V] STUDIES OF THE PRESENT WORK

Barilli, R. *Per un' estetica mondana*, pp. 271–98, 323–28. Bologna: Mulino, 1964.

Beardsley, Monroe C. *Aesthetics from Classical Greece to the Present*, pp. 271–72, 395–96. New York: Macmillan, 1966.

Coleman, Francis J. "A Phenomenology of Aesthetic Reasoning." *Journal of Aesthetics and Art Criticism*, Vol. XXV (Winter, 1966).

Gilson, E., Langan, T., and Maurer, A. *Recent Philosophy: Hegel to the Present*, pp. 396–401. New York: Random House, 1966.

Kaelin, Eugene. *An Existentialist Aesthetic*, pp. 359–95. Madison: University of Wisconsin Press, 1962.

Morpurgo-Tagliabue, Guido. *L'Esthétique contemporaine*, pp. 460–68. Milan: Marzorati, 1960.

Piguet, Claude. "Esthétique et phénoménologie." *Kant-Studien*, XLVII (1955–56), 192–208.

Spiegelberg, Herbert. *The Phenomenological Movement: A His-

torical Introduction. 2d ed., 2 vols., II, 579–85. The Hague: Nijhoff, 1965.

Taminiaux, Jacques. "Notes sur une phénoménologie de l'expérience esthétique." *Revue philosophique de Louvain,* LV (1957), 93–110.

Index of Names

Alain (Emile Chartier), xlv, 32, 48,
49, 50, 61, 63, 85, 94, 95, 96, 97,
152, 284, 292n, 308, 320, 321,
340, 355, 356, 363, 366, 399, 427,
451
Aristotle, lvii, 21, 144, 230, 409, 420

Bach, Johann Sebastian, lxiv, 23,
167, 316, 389, 391, 409, 444, 445,
464, 492, 518–19
Bachelard, Gaston, 120n, 192n, 288,
320n, 355, 379n, 437–38
Balzac, Honoré de, lx, 7, 46n, 100,
167, 171, 173, 178, 190, 364, 405,
452, 505, 509, 514, 523, 525, 543
Basch, Victor, 426, 468
Baudelaire, Charles, 473
Bayer, Raymond, lix, 78, 96, 223,
468–69
Beethoven, Ludwig van, 26, 111,
124, 181, 204, 254, 261, 267, 268,
449, 452, 464, 479
Bergson, Henri, 34n, 37, 57, 82,
261, 262, 265, 270, 271, 277, 321,
327, 338n, 343, 355, 356, 397,
459, 550n
Blanchot, Maurice, 159–60, 552–53
Boileau, Nicolas, lix, lxiv, 126
Bosch, Hieronymus, 197, 369, 392,
395, 442, 473, 507, 523, 534
Braque, Georges, 141
Brelet, Gisèle, 253 ff., 270
Breton, André, 424
Breughel, Pieter, 175

Caravaggio, 106, 291, 514
Céline, Louis-Ferdinand, 493

Cézanne, Paul, 28, 55, 59, 105–6,
121, 190, 284, 285, 287, 289, 297,
317, 324, 325, 341, 367, 535, 550
Chagall, Marc, 106, 186
Chopin, Frédéric, 167, 260
Claudel, Paul, 20n, 27, 49, 167,
368, 390, 513
Cocteau, Jean, 507
Colette, 524
Comte, Auguste, 68, 69n, 74, 112,
125, 170, 394, 493
Conrad, Waldemar, 56, 140n, 205,
215–18, 224
Constable, John, 290
Corneille, Pierre, 306, 382, 492, 545
Croce, Benedetto, 53–54, 63n, 180n

Daumier, Honoré, 378, 499
Da Vinci, Leonardo, 277
Debussy, Claude, 23, 24, 86, 129,
141, 156, 268, 272, 327, 328, 361,
430, 452, 508, 517, 520, 523, 531,
536, 537, 544
Delacroix, Eugène, 141n, 142, 156,
289, 290, 298, 315
Descartes, René, 86, 118
De Schloezer, Boris, 113, 212–15,
249 ff., 255n, 256, 270, 283, 327,
517–18, 521
D'Indy, Vincent, 254–55, 266n,
267, 268
Dos Passos, John, 170, 178
Dufy, Raoul, 367
Durkheim, Emile, 495

El Greco, 186, 544
Eliade, Mircea, 120

Subject Index

This Index and the Index of Names have been newly prepared for the present translation and thus differ from the index for the original French editions. Passages of special importance are indicated by the use of italics.—Trans.

Absolute, the, 556. *See also* Knowledge, absolute
Accord: with aesthetic object, 340; between man and the real, 556; between man and world, 456. *See also* Affinity
Action, 83, 114, 127, 147, 218, 335, 343, 352, 359, 373, 377, 378, 381n, 405, 441, 471, 502, 529, 541, 549
Actor, 21–22, 28–29, 49, 50n; spectator as, 152
Aesthetic, the, xlvi–vii, lxi, 84, 182n, 546, 556; of creation, xlvii, lviii
—experience, xlv–vi, l–li, liv, lxvi, 16 ff., 199, 237, 339, 372, 379, 386, 429–30, 434, 437, 502, 535, 555–56; and the *a priori*, 540; of artist, xlv–vi; and consciousness, 540; and the real, 545–46, 548; of spectator, xlvi ff., lxvi. *See also* Aesthetic object; Aesthetic perception; Truth
—object, xlvii ff., lxii ff., lxv ff., 3 ff., *10 ff.*, 48, 75–76, 98, 138–39, 264, 388–89, 413, 417 ff., 547–56; attitudes before, 426–34; and consciousness, 414; its epiphany, 48; and form, 222–32; its identity, 69; as inexhaustible,

43, 396–98; as language, 79; and living being, 73–79, 164n; and natural object, 79–92, 164; as nature, 85, 88, 91, 230, 329; 342, 412; and object of use, 79–83, 92–114; as perceived, 218–22; and the real, 516, 539–40; and signifying object, *114–38. See also* Work of art, in relation to aesthetic object
—perception, xlviii ff., lxi ff., 5 ff., 12 ff., 16–17, 20, 30–31, 39, 44, 46 ff., 85–86, 92, 121, 123, 143, 151, 198, 199, 215, 216–18, 287, 298, 314, 329, 333–34, 345, 358–69, 370, 375, 395, 410, 415, *418–25*, 542–46, 554–56; and aesthetic object, lxvi; of music, 258, 261, 265, 267; vs. ordinary perception, 516; of painting, 275. *See also* Perception; Presence; Representation
Aesthetician, 197
Aestheticization, lxi, 72, 84, 93, 95, 152 ff., 179, 180, 290, 305, 501, 535, 545
Aesthetics, lxiii, 477, 549; classical, 117; pure, 442, 446, 462, 465, 485–500
Affective, the, 542, 551. *See also* A *Priori;* Category; Quality

[567]

DATE DUE

DEC 0 8 2002			

JOSTEN'S NO. 30-505